LITERATURE
Reading to Write

Elizabeth Howells
Armstrong Atlantic State University

Longman

Boston   Columbus   Indianapolis   New York   San Francisco   Upper Saddle River
Amsterdam   Cape Town   Dubai   London   Madrid   Milan   Munich   Paris   Montréal   Toronto
Delhi   Mexico City   São Paulo   Sydney   Hong Kong   Seoul   Singapore   Taipei   Tokyo

To David, and my girls, Elsie and Kit, for all of the love, inspiration, and joy
they give me. And in loving memory of Dorothy Bryce Howells for inspiring
me with her passion for reading and writing.

Senior Acquisitions Editor: Vivian Garcia
Executive Marketing Manager: Joyce Nilsen
Production Manager: Bob Ginsberg
Project Coordination, Text Design, and Electronic Page Makeup: Elm Street
 Publishing Services, Integra Software Services Pvt. Ltd.
Cover Design Manager/Cover Designer: John Callahan
Cover photos *(left to right):* Jhughes/Dreamstime.com; Pete Bax/
 iStockphoto; Cheryl Casey/Shutterstock.com
Photo Researcher: Julie Tesser
Senior Manufacturing Buyer: Roy L. Pickering, Jr.
Printer and Binder/Cover Printer: RR Donnelley & Sons Company/Harrisonburg

For permission to use copyrighted material, grateful acknowledgment is made to the
copyright holders on pp. 568–571, which are hereby made part of this copyright page.

Library of Congress Cataloging-in-Publication Data
Howells, Elizabeth.
 Literature: reading to write/Elizabeth Howells.
  p. cm.
 Includes bibliographical references and index.
 ISBN 978-0-205-83430-3
 1. College readers. 2. Literature—History and criticism. 3. Literature—Study
and teaching. 4. Reading comprehension. 5. Report writing. I. Title.
 PE1417.H685 2011
 808'.0427—dc22

2010023218

1 2 3 4 5 6 7 8 9 10—DOH—13 12 11 10

Longman
is an imprint of

www.pearsonhighered.com

ISBN-13: 978-0-205-83430-3
ISBN-10: 0-205-83430-2

CONTENTS

PART **TWO**   WRITING IN RESPONSE TO LITERATURE   53

3   LOVE AND SYMBOLISM
Interpreting Themes   54

4   A STUDY IN STYLE
Analyzing Patterns   101

PART THREE EXPERIENCING CONTEMPORARY LITERATURE 359

16 INTEGRATING PRIMARY AND SECONDARY SOURCES   530

17 USING THE MLA STYLE OF DOCUMENTATION   549

E-ANTHOLOGY TABLE OF CONTENTS

Two hundred additional selections, many of them with multimedia support, are available in the eAnthology featured in MyLiteratureLab. MyLiteratureLab may be packaged at no additional cost with this book. To order, use the following ISBN: 0-205-83551-1

DRAMA

PEARSON
myliteraturelab™

MEDIA RESOURCES FEATURED IN MYLITERATURELAB.COM

DRAMA

SELECTIONS BY GENRE

SELECTIONS BY GENRE

xviii

FOREWORD

Composing is the way we make sense of the world: it's our way of learning.
—Ann Berthoff

We speak of composing often in writing classes. Gathering ideas, developing them, shaping and revising them, we practice the "composing process" to produce texts—essays, stories, reports—that we have crafted to make effective. But, as Ann Berthoff's remark implies, the composing process is about more than just writing. It's how we make sense of the world around us, how we read that world. Reading texts and writing them are both acts of composing, ways of learning. And so readers compose, too. They use what they know to form ideas about what they read and to revise those ideas as they read more. Like writers, they employ a composing process. They *form*—that is, create—just as writers do.

Literature: Reading to Write demonstrates that reading and writing are much more than similar acts. They explain and reinforce one another. As the great reading theorist Louise Rosenblatt says, "Both writer and reader transact with texts, both compose meanings." When we read, in other words, we are writing the text we are reading. When we write, we are reading the text we're writing. *Literature: Reading to Write* helps students recognize and practice that essential connection, shows students how they compose meaning in writing and reading. This important and useful book demonstrates how writing strengthens reading pleasure and skill and how reading deepens and broadens writing effectiveness, how together reading and writing aid students in developing as people who make sense of and act on the world around them.

If teachers believe that reading and writing go together, and we do, we sometimes find it difficult to put into practice. We sometimes make reading primary and writing secondary or reduce both reading and writing to competence in a narrow set of competency skills. Too often in textbooks, writing exercises become only the proof that reading has happened, and reading becomes the comprehension questions at the end of the chapter. A contribution of *Literature: Reading to Write* lies in the practical strategies it employs to make its readers conscious of how deeply intertwined reading and writing are. Students who use this book build confidence in their own interpretations moving from reading to writing and vice versa, when they read *The Glass Menagerie* and write about families, or when they write about what they remember from high school and read "We Real Cool." Students are taught methods to deepen their critical acumen, ways of understanding language, character and context that help them shape their responses to the texts they read and those they write.

This textbook puts to the test of practice the theories of some of the most creative thinkers about reading and writing, writing theorists, reading specialists and teachers, whose ideas about interpretation, rhetoric, language and literary study find a place in early sections of the book where critical terms and contexts are introduced to students. The brief biographies and Context Boxes, the analysis of critical approaches and the discussion of terms, all build students' *repertoires*, the wealth of experiences and information readers draw on in order to read effectively. Activities that accompany these background discussions help students use the repertoire they are developing. As students write before they read, they begin to write the texts they will read; as they accomplish freewriting and journal keeping, they conduct the "continual audit of meaning" that leads to engagement with what they read and confidence in their own writing. The book allows students to practice writing before and during their reading, to use writing to stimulate reading as well as the other way around.

As Professor Howells indicates in her Preface, the book emphasizes literature and the importance of engaging students in the reading experience. The core of the book explores literary reading through creative assignments that use students' growing understandings and literary genres, terms and methods. One especially appealing facet of *Literature: Reading to Write* is its selection of texts from a broad range of time periods and cultures, as well as genres. The book's arrangement and array of texts invite teachers to juxtapose current and classic writers, new and standard genres, literary works and analyses of them. To link Shakespeare with Sharon Olds provokes keen awareness of timeless themes and new forms. To juxtapose Shakespeare to seventeenth-century poet Anne Bradstreet fosters new understandings of the importance of context, of culture, and of gender in producing forms and exploring themes. A section on contemporary literature bridges forms familiar to students—horror stories, cartoons, graphic novels—and less familiar texts and forms. It's clear that all the readings have been carefully chosen to stimulate the imagination, in both student and teacher.

Underlying this book is the clear sense that composing in both writing and reading is imagining. Imagination is not at all the opposite of close reading; it is the condition for it. The student who reads closely reads with her whole experience—remembering, comparing, responding. As the book implies through its careful sequence of readings and tasks, the imagination allows students to create the world of the texts they enter as readers and the ones they build as writers. For to imagine is not to create a fairy castle; it is simply to create. Reading and writing, like being in the world, are acts of creation. We need to compose to make sense of the world; we need books like this one that help us imagine how we do it.

HEPHZIBAH ROSKELLY
University of North Carolina, Greensboro

PREFACE

Reading to Write: Connecting Composition and Literature

"'Tis the good reader that makes the good book... One must be an inventor to read well... There is then creative reading as well as creative writing. When the mind is braced by labor and invention, the page of whatever book we read becomes luminous with manifold allusion. Every sentence is doubly significant, and the sense of our author is as broad as the world."
—Ralph Waldo Emerson

Think of our lives and tell us your particularized world. Make up a story. Narrative is radical, creating us at the very moment it is being created.
—Toni Morrison

When I teach composition studies to future teachers or even introduction to composition to first-year students, one of my favorite assignments to give is a literacy history. I ask students to tell the story of their becoming literate through certain representative artifacts and their reflections on those examples—what inspired them in their journeys to literacy and what challenged them, what opened their eyes and what might have closed the door. The stories they tell in these histories are of people, places, books, and ideas that moved them, compelled them to action, and ultimately shaped their identities. Students often testify to the works that got them excited about reading, that surprised them, intrigued them, confused them, and stuck with them. A variety of texts compete for our students' attention and multiple literacies are required to remain competitive and fluent today. But literature and narrative still have a place in our students' lives, whether *Harry Potter* or *Hamlet*, Stephen King or "Story of an Hour," Facebook or Faulkner. This textbook can be read as a literacy history for today's students. It includes works that already resonate with students and works that can speak to them with a little guidance. *Literature: Reading to Write* illustrates how engaged reading can be fostered through thoughtful writing and demonstrates how literature can be made "luminous" through the connections we make.

Not unlike Morrison's Nobel Prize speech, quoted above, the power of narrative is explored in this text using works ranging from classic literary texts in Part II to very contemporary genres such as songs and graphic novel excerpts in Part III. Reading is made meaningful by helping students forge connections between their own experiences and the literature, through Pre-Reading prompts and postreading Focused Free Write suggestions. Reading and writing instruction is given in stages to help students assimilate what they are learning and understand the different aspects of the processes in which they are engaged.

Woven into both reading and writing are the acts of critical thinking that underlie critical reading and engaged writing. Critical thinking is also put in particular contexts, and students are shown how meaning might be made in different ways, in the Context Boxes that follow selected texts. While this textbook includes all the features that composition and literature instructors have come to expect from such books, it should provide some unexpected pleasures and additional help for perennial writing challenges students face as they write about literature.

Organization

- The two chapters of **Part I: Reading and Writing About Literature** introduce the idea of literature, the writing process, critical thinking acts, and the general terminology of the genres. With shorter selections, instructors can use these mini-chapters during the first days of class to acclimate students.

- The core of the book is the next five chapters, **Part II: Writing in Response to Literature**. While selections are organized by genres within individual chapters, each chapter focuses on a particular stylistic element, a corresponding theme, and the appropriate critical thinking act to provide a scaffold for students as they develop as readers and writers. For example, in Chapter 3, the theme of love is intertwined with study of the literary element symbol and the critical thinking act of interpretation. Students examine how the theme of love is talked about through symbol and learn to interpret symbols and themes through writing. Chapter 4 consists of selections that address style as a theme, and students are challenged to use the interpretive critical thinking act from the previous chapter to analyze style. Chapter 5 brings together works that highlight voice and narration in content and form, calling on students to use interpretation and analysis to engage in argument. Chapter 6 highlights the characters that make up families so that students can develop their comparison skills. Finally, in Chapter 7, students incorporate these critical thinking acts developed previously to examine themes of oppression in their analytical arguments. One recent reviewer described the book as "[a] rhetorical approach to writing about reading grounded on a postmodernist approach to literary genres."

- **Part III: Experiencing Contemporary Literature** offers mini-chapters that allow instructors to make connections between genres students already know and like and their less familiar literary counterparts. Perhaps one way to make literature relevant to students is remind them of the literature of their contemporary lives in the forms of comedies, music, graphic novels, horror stories, and experimental literature. These short chapters could be assigned for one day as an interlude between the longer chapters or could be assigned to separate groups in a class for group presentations. Students may thus be encouraged to make connections between the reading work that excites them personally and the work that is assigned to them and defined as "literary." These chapters maintain a fairly standard structure, establishing a kind of literary family tree which defines the genre at hand, includes potentially familiar examples, introduces new texts, and identifies the roots of the genre of focus.

- In **Part IV: Research for Writing**, the research process is thoroughly outlined and modeled. Entire chapters are broken down into the detailed steps necessary for developing a topic and stating a thesis, finding and evaluating sources, understanding critical perspectives, integrating primary and secondary sources, and using the MLA style of documentation. A sample student project is illustrated through these chapters to demonstrate the assigned tasks such as developing a proposal, an annotated bibliography, the research paper, and the works cited list. Students are introduced to a step-by-step process for producing either a literary or historical research project. Three critical casebooks offer excerpts from literary criticism to showcase the acts of synthesizing and incorporating criticism. With detailed attention to everything from brainstorming on a topic to the syntax of integrating sources to the logistics of citing sources, this textbook provides guidance for every step of the research project and will be the only resource your students will need.

Key Features

Literature: Reading to Write offers instructors the following features to organize and focus this challenging class.

Integrated writing instruction.   The chapters in Part II provide concrete, detailed instructions for reading and writing about the literary selections. Rather than addressing writing primarily in the first three chapters or in an appendix, these five chapters at the heart of the book also break the writing process down into building blocks outlining *how* to produce better writing, including such lessons as developing topics, writing focused theses, incorporating detailed support, integrating textual evidence, and editing and proofreading. A recent reviewer said she would adopt the text "because of two points: the practical writing style involving stair-step process writing and the wise blend of the canonical and contemporary readings." Examples of writing instruction throughout include:

- **Writing to Read Prompts: Pre-Reading prompts and postreading Focused Free Write and discussion prompts.** These pedagogical features demonstrate how writing should be an integrated part of the reading process. These informal writing prompts throughout the chapters will elicit creative, critical, and thoughtful responses from students, and they will demonstrate how writing can be an integral part of reading. While useful as journal or homework assignments, these prompts also provide an excellent opportunity for minute papers at the beginning of class to help students prepare a concrete contribution to the day's discussion or prewriting work to develop future formal projects.
- **Formal Writing Prompts in the form of intensive sections of writing instruction focused at the end of each chapter.** While writing is incorporated throughout the chapter through Pre-Reading and Focused Free Write prompts and discussions of the critical thinking acts, the end of the chapter charges students with a particular formal writing assignment showcasing interpretation, analysis, argument, or comparison. These sections offer detailed attention to

specific writing issues, exercises to address writing concerns, and models for writing about literature.

- **Student Samples.** The writing instruction at the end of each chapter includes student reflections and student samples from real students. These examples will be useful classroom tools for critiquing and modeling.

Critical thinking as the basis for writing about literature. While the first two chapters introduce students to writing tools such as summary, explication, and making connections, the five chapters at the center of the book establish interpretation, analysis, argument, and comparison as critical-thinking acts that build one on the other in formal writing projects. A critical-thinking act is introduced and modeled early in the chapter. It is assigned as a formal writing task at the end of each chapter and students are guided through a series of steps from brainstorming to developing their own formal projects. This critical-thinking act is thus employed organically as a means to better understand the theme and stylistic element of focus in each chapter.

Select examples of fiction, poetry, and drama balancing expected texts and diverse selections. The literary selections included here are the result of three years of extensive manuscript reviewing with instructors who teach literature and composition courses, as well as a survey of 99 instructors who commented solely on selections. As one recent reviewer describes the range of works: "There is a sensible, even daring balance between the traditional works and the more contemporary works. It's Sophocles meets Spielberg in the classroom." Although the range is wide, the text is selective: the selections allow for a less overwhelming and more particular format. In this economy, and at institutions like mine, we must be conscious and attentive to what students need and what they can afford. This book is focused and respectful when it comes to student learning. Unique organization and creative juxtapositions of classical and contemporary texts encourage focus on compelling themes. Each chapter groups the works by genre; however, the order of the genres varies from chapter to chapter so neither fiction, poetry, nor drama is prioritized as the first example or rushed through as the last selections in every chapter. The focused drama selections allow instructors a chance to work with their Pearson reps to select additional dramas of their choosing, thus customizing their curricula.

Context Discussions in the form of Biographical Sketches and Historical, Literary, and Critical Context Boxes. Throughout Parts I and II, biographical Context Boxes introduce works and context boxes following select texts to illustrate how historical, literary, or critical contexts might open up a text and make it meaningful in a distinct way. These context boxes then illustrate the act of reading as subjective, demonstrating how a particular perspective might shed new light and introduce new ways of thinking. These boxes are located after students have examined their own understandings and thus allow them to revise or rethink the text they have just read, perhaps encouraging them to challenge their initial interpretation or negotiate this new approach with their own. Instructors may use these context boxes to launch discussions or as an illustration of just one alternative reading before introducing others. As the book progresses, the context boxes decrease and less apparatus encourages students to use what they have been learning about meaning making in previous chapters to open up the new texts they are encountering. Finally, these context boxes may also inspire formal research projects.

Interactive approach creates common ground and community. The interactive approach of this textbook requires, encourages, and teaches students to produce their own writings as samples in their own classrooms. In other words, this text is student driven and challenges students to respond to bring the literary works to life in their classrooms through **Pre-Reading** prompts, **Focused Free Write** questions, and ideas for developing contexts in **Context Boxes** in each chapter of Part I. It is a dynamic text that calls for engagement of prior knowledge and the contribution of new and diverse knowledge; therefore, teachers and students should be expected to contribute their own responses, contexts, and approaches. Part III uses texts with which students are familiar to introduce them to genres they might like to study in innovative ways.

Detailed research instruction. This textbook actually teaches writing, thinking, and reading as well as research in a detailed and focused way. The process is broken down and instruction attends to every step through examples and exercises.

Ultimately, this textbook offers a conscientious choice when it comes to composition and literature instruction—it is selective and thus recognizes the value in a thorough and thoughtful, careful and creative discussion of reading and writing.

Acknowledgments

Many voices were sources of inspiration, direction, and motivation here. I would like to express sincere thanks to the reviewers who helped shape the many drafts of this book:

Leslie Angel-Cann, Collin County Community College; Cathy Allen, University of Memphis; Booker T. Anthony, Fayetteville State University; Consuella Bennett, Morehouse College; Melanie R. Benson, University of Hartford; Bethany Blankenship, University of Montana Western; Dawn Brickey, Charleston Southern University; Lisa Carl, North Carolina Central University; Thad Cockrill, Southwest Tennessee Community College; Jeana DelRosso, College of Notre Dame of Maryland; Christy Desmet, University of Georgia; Dr. Deborah De Vries, Oxnard College; Bonnie Dowd, Montclair State University; Mary Dutterer, Howard Community College; Marie G. Eckstrom, Rio Hondo College; Margaret Ellington, Georgia Southwestern State University; Kimberly Fangman, Southeast Community College; Daniel Fitzstephens, University of Colorado at Boulder; Dawn Gallo, Montclair State University; Gayle Gaskill, St. Catherine University; Sally Jayne Gilpin, Collin County Community College; Dwonna N. Goldstone, Austin Peay State University; William H. Harris, University of Texas at Brownsville;

Debra G. Harroun, Baker College of Clinton Township; David A. James, Houston Community College Northwest; JoAnne James, Pitt Community College; Catherine Keohane, Montclair State University; James Knippling, University of Cincinnati; Julie Kratt, Cowley County Community College; Anne M. Kuhta; Northern Virginia Community College; Kelly Martin, Collin County Community College David G. McGuirk, Miami Dade College; Deborah Miller, University of Georgia; Teresa Purvis, Lansing Community College; Robert Randolph, Texas State University; Chivas Sandage, Westfield State College; Linda E. Smith, Fort Hays State University; Frederick Smock, Bellarmine University; Michael D. Sollars, Texas Southern University; Ronald J. Tulley, The University of Findlay; Susan Vervaet, Montclair State University; Bente Videbaek, Stony Brook University; Stephanie Vie, University of Arizona; and Jessica Walker, University of Georgia.

I would like to offer thanks to the Pearson staff who walked me through the process over the years with special thanks to Vivian Garcia, for her professional and positive support and encouragement on things book and baby related; to Heather Vomero, for her courteous and prompt handling of all matters from the large to the small; to Leslie Taggart, who pushed me even when I didn't want to be pushed and who taught me how to revise and elaborate like no one has; to Joe Terry, whose direction, guidance, and thoughtful conversation about publishing and football made the process a pleasure. Thanks to Debbie Meyer of Elm Street for attending to details.

And moments like this give one pause to think of those over the years who impacted this project directly and indirectly. While there is not space or enough time, I would like to thank a few: to Hepsie and Elizabeth who helped me rethink reading and writing. To Katie Ryan, Cynthia Nearman, Jackie Grutsch-McKinney, Chris Bachelder, and Jenn Habel, who were rich resources and generous supporters on this project as well as dear friends. I am also grateful for the support of my academic home, Armstrong Atlantic State University. Over the years, Ed Wheeler, Laura Barrett, Mark Finlay, Richard Nordquist, and Judy Dubus were generous with their advice, wisdom and support as needed. The members of the department of Languages, Literature, and Philosophy were always encouraging with special appreciation for David Wheeler, Nancy Remler, and Christy Mroczek, for their ever sage and always timely advice. An enthusiastic shout-out to the students who helped me over the years, those in the comp classrooms I have taught and those outside of class time like Ricardo Lyons, Kim Davies, Ashley Walden, Stephanie Roberts, Erin Christian, and James Lewis.

My love and gratitude also needs to be extended to my family and friends. I am so grateful that my family always believed anyone anywhere was "lucky to have me." I also owe thanks to my friends, here in Savannah and elsewhere, who remind me constantly that they have "the greatest faith in me." To our Nonie, Elaine Hughes, who manages our house and loves us as her own. Finally, I would like to thank the people who lived with this project besides me: to the girls, Elsie and Kit, for their unconditional approval and for making me play, and to David Thompson, my husband, whose belief in me runs so deep that thanks are not enough.

ELIZABETH HOWELLS
Armstrong Atlantic State University

PART ONE

READING AND WRITING ABOUT LITERATURE

These two initial chapters introduce the idea of literature, the writing process, critical thinking acts, and the general terminology of the genres. With shorter selections, these mini-chapters are an ideal introduction to reading, thinking, and writing about literature.

1
WHAT IS LITERATURE?

Interpreting Fairy Tales. Here we have one interpretation of the classic fairy tale heroine Sleeping Beauty from nineteenth-century painter Edward Burne-Jones' *Briar Rose* series. What part of the story does it tell? What aspects of the fairy tale story does this painting emphasize? What does it leave out? What other fairy tales are you familiar with? What other examples of revisions of fairy tales or interpretations of fairy tales have you encountered? How do they endorse conventional ideas and themes common in fairy tales and how do they challenge them?

What is literature?

This question may hardly seem worth asking. The answer may seem obvious, and perhaps not entirely relevant. You are reading this right now for a required course, so who cares what literature is. It is just required. But why? Ultimately, as Oscar Wilde suggests in his preface to *Dorian Gray*, "All art is quite useless." You don't use it in the real world to get a job, pay your bills, or drive your car. You will not be tested on literature in the future or have to write in MLA style to get a raise. Knowing about *Moby Dick* won't help you in your marriage, and *Pride and Prejudice* doesn't necessarily offer child rearing advice. So why read it? What does it do for you? What is its purpose? What can it get you? In order to determine the purpose of literature or its usefulness, we might begin by defining what it is.

FOCUSED FREE WRITE

Think about the literature you have studied so far. What makes a piece of writing literature?

What do these texts have in common? Take a few moments to write down your thoughts.

You may have answered the question as my students have:

- Literature is telling stories.
- Literature is a way to record what happened.
- Literature is a poem, play, or story.
- Literature is a way to express oneself.
- Literature is a way to communicate.
- Literature is a way for readers to connect to their own experiences.
- Literature is a beautiful work of art.
- Literature is whatever you decide.

These are good places to start, but they still might be a bit vague. Does a *People* magazine article fit one of these definitions of literature? A news article fits the second definition—does that make it literature? And does it matter in what style a piece is written? And what does it mean that it is written down? The Oxford English Dictionary (OED) defines literature as "writing which has claim to consideration on the ground of beauty of form or emotional effect." This definition seems to focus on something that is written and carefully crafted by the author. Literature must be artful. Poets like Wordsworth, Shelley, and Keats chose every word with care to convey the power of poetry and the possibilities of the new form of the lyric poem. News stories intended to convey information may not meditate on form in a literary way.

The second part of this OED definition addresses the role of the reader in determining the nature of literature. The "emotional effect" is derived from the impact of the work on the reader. In her essay, "Careful What You Let in the

Door," Barbara Kingsolver writes that "Art is entertainment but it's also celebration, condolence, exploration, duty, and communion. The artistic consummation of a novel is created by the author and reader together, in an act of joint imagination, and that's not to be taken lightly" (253). Aristotle emphasized the dynamic relationship among a rhetor (speaker or writer), an audience (listeners or readers), and a text in a similar way in describing the rhetorical triangle:

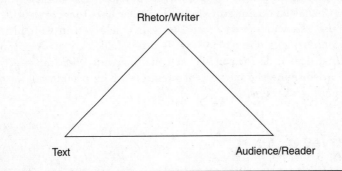

FIGURE 1.1 Aristotle's Rhetorical Triangle

Meaning is created through the interactions among reader, writer, and text. Each brings something to bear on achieving understanding. For instance, when I was in the audience watching Helen Mirren in the film *The Queen*, I remembered my own reaction to news of Princess Diana's death, and I reflected on what I had been doing at that time. While watching the movie, I found myself critical of Queen Elizabeth II and sympathizing with the British people as they mourned the death of the "people's princess." When I was reading Shakespeare's *The Tempest*, the history of English exploration under Queen Elizabeth I came to mind. I wondered if Shakespeare was offering a commentary on the costs of imperialism. In both of these cases, my work as a reader expanded the meaning and scope of the text.

In any given case of interpretation, one or another angle of the rhetorical triangle may be emphasized. One reading of a piece of literature might emphasize the author's intention; another might focus on the style of the text; a third might be related to the reader's personal experiences. Schools of literary criticism have become established that may emphasize one angle of the triangle over another. In future chapters you will learn about formalist criticism, historical criticism, gender criticism, and biographical criticism, among others, and you will see how this understanding of meaning making can be expanded and made more complex. In fact, each of those schools can be understood as emphasizing one angle of the rhetorical triangle.

There is a third component to the OED definition of literature. This third part is veiled and indirect, yet it is the first part of the definition: "writing **which has claim to consideration on** the ground of beauty of form or emotional effect." A question arises about this first clause: Who does the considering? Who makes the decision about what is literature? This question points to a much larger debate about the **canon**, that is, the works considered literature, a topic explored at greater length later in this chapter and this book. Two and three hundred years ago, literary study was undertaken by male students in elite universities where they read ancient classics in Greek and Latin. Today, however, the study of literature is much broader and more subject to debate. More students are eligible to study literature, and more people are literate and are able to read. More writers are being published, and books and stories and poems are more widely available. Discussions about which works deserve to be "canonized," and why, are lively open debates. Certainly, this textbook represents this author's consideration of what works are "literature." But as you read, you too can identify your own standards and create your own definition of literature and of the canon.

LITERARY Contexts

Authors Define Literature

Following are comments that various famous writers have made about the value of literature.

In a real sense, people who have read good literature have lived more than people who cannot or will not read. It is not true that we have only one life to live; if we can read, we can live as many more lives and as many kinds of lives as we wish.
—S. I. Hayakawa

Literature is the last banquet between minds.
—Edna O'Brien

The test of literature is, I suppose, whether we ourselves live more intensely for the reading of it.
—Elizabeth Drew

Literature is the record of our discontent.
—Virginia Woolf

We tell ourselves stories in order to live.
—Joan Didion

Books are the carriers of civilization. Without books, history is silent, literature dumb, science crippled, thought and speculation at a standstill. I think that there is nothing, not even crime, more opposed to poetry, to philosophy, ay, to life itself than this incessant business.
—Henry David Thoreau

Literature is my Utopia. Here I am not disenfranchised. No barrier of the senses shuts me out from the sweet, gracious discourse of my book-friends. They talk to me without embarrassment or awkwardness.
—Helen Keller

Literature adds to reality, it does not simply describe it. It enriches the necessary competencies that daily life requires and provides; and in this respect, it irrigates the deserts that our lives have already become.
—C. S. Lewis

(continued)

(continued)
Our American professors like their literature clear, cold, pure and very dead.

— Sinclair Lewis

Is one of these ideas more true for you than the others? How? Why? React in writing.

Which one might you challenge? What makes you disagree? Explain.

What surprises you, intrigues you, or confuses you in these statements? Discuss.

HISTORICAL Contexts

Forms of Literature Through Time

Today, anthologies categorize and define literature in terms of the genres of **poetry**, **drama**, and **fiction** (which includes **short stories** and **novels**), and, increasingly, **nonfiction**. These terms originated in the nineteenth century, and they have come to identify literature as imaginative.

The earliest forms of writing, however, can be traced back to Sumeria, Egypt, and China. These texts are evidence of early record-keeping or nonfiction historical accounts. The earliest literature, though, is often identified today as primarily religious: the myths and legends that examined human interaction with God or gods and the natural world. You may have encountered some early Greek examples of this literature: Homer's *Iliad* and *Odyssey* transcribed the epic oral **poetry** chronicling human struggles with god and nature. There is also a rich history of ancient poetry recounting religious and heroic tales from Chinese, Indian, and Middle Eastern cultures.

The birth of **drama** as we know it can be traced back to the Greek plays of Aeschylus, Sophocles, Euripedes, and Aristophanes. These early forms of the genre, again, address the human struggle with god and nature through human interaction and poetic dialogue. Almost two thousand years later, Shakespeare would make his contributions to the genre with plays addressing similar themes. What we see in this early history is that literature was born out of the human desire to make meaning of human existence, purpose, identity, and autonomy. Like literature today, these early forms of literature express human conflict with self, other, and environment.

In some ways, **fiction** as we know it can be identified as the newest form of literature. Many attribute the first **novel**, or example of prose fiction, to Cervantes in his 1547 *Don Quixote*. Another early example of the novel you may have encountered is Jonathan Swift's *Gulliver's Travels*. Fiction and nonfiction became increasingly popular with the advent of the printing press in 1450 and the increase in the number of people who were literate; both developments were products of the rise of industrialization. Periodicals, serial novels, circulating libraries, and cheaper printed material made all forms of literature more available to a broader public throughout the eighteenth and nineteenth centuries. With certain changes in the university population and curricula around the same time, there was a shift in education from a classical influence to a vernacular emphasis. In England and America, students read "modern literature" in their contemporary language as opposed to texts in the original Greek or Latin.

Literature was defined as imaginative until the mid-1900s when the **canon**, the body of works accepted as "literature," began to expand to include **nonfiction** with all its imaginative possibilities. We also see the canon expanding to recognize other contributions to literature. This revaluation takes into account texts once suppressed because of form or subject matter or authors once oppressed because of race, gender, class, or other status. This expansion of the canon can also be seen in the consideration of alternative forms of literature including film and other popular culture mediums. Some of these are introduced in Part III of this textbook.

List literary works that you imagine were once excluded from the canon and are now included. Identify why you think they may have been overlooked.

What do you notice about who is included in the canon of literature? What about other kinds of canons, such as the canon of history?

Examine the table of contents of this textbook. Characterize this book as a canon. What does it represent? What does it exclude?

STORIES

The short short stories that follow can offer an introduction to early literature in the form of a fairy tale as well as its revision in a modern counterpart. The first story is likely one of the earliest kinds of stories you were exposed to in reading fairy tales or watching Disney movies. It establishes some of the conventions of storytelling. The story that follows it then challenges those conventions in explicit ways, thereby redefining storytelling, or literature:

PRE-READING   Which fairy tales have you read? What were they about?

Charles Perrault (1628–1703). *Born in Paris to well-established parents, Charles Perrault was trained to be a lawyer. However, early success in poetry and verse inspired him to launch a literary life. He became a leading member of the Academie Francaise, through which he championed the moderns over the ancients in current literary debates. Perrault was known best for his fairy tales, which were revisions of popular folk tales. His tales then inspired countless other revisions, including operas, ballets, and Disney films.*

Charles Perrault

THE SLEEPING BEAUTY IN THE WOOD

There were formerly a king and a queen, who were so sorry that they had no children; so sorry that it cannot be expressed. They went to all the waters in the world; vows, pilgrimages, all ways were tried, and all to no purpose.

At last, however, the Queen had a daughter. There was a very fine christening; and the Princess had for her godmothers all the fairies they could find in the whole kingdom (they found seven), that every one of them might give her a gift, as was the custom of fairies in those days. By this means the Princess had all the perfections imaginable.

After the ceremonies of the christening were over, all the company returned to the King's palace, where was prepared a great feast for the fairies. There was placed before every one of them a magnificent cover with a case of massive gold, wherein were a spoon, knife, and fork, all of pure gold set with diamonds and rubies. But as they were all sitting down at table they saw come into the hall a very old fairy, whom they had not invited, because it was above fifty years since she had been out of a certain tower, and she was believed to be either dead or enchanted.

The King ordered her a cover, but could not furnish her with a case of gold as the others, because they had seven only made for the seven fairies. The old Fairy fancied she was slighted, and muttered some threats between her teeth. One of the young fairies who sat by her overheard how she grumbled; and, judging that she might give the little Princess some unlucky gift, went, as soon as they rose from table, and hid herself behind the hangings, that she might speak last, and repair, as much as she could, the evil which the old Fairy might intend.

In the meanwhile all the fairies began to give their gifts to the Princess. The youngest gave her for gift that she should be the most beautiful person in the world; the next, that she should have the wit of an angel; the third, that she should have a wonderful grace in everything she did; the fourth, that she should dance perfectly well; the fifth, that she should sing like a nightingale; and the sixth, that she should play all kinds of music to the utmost perfection.

The old Fairy's turn coming next, with a head shaking more with spite than age, she said that the Princess should have her hand pierced with a spindle and die of the wound. This terrible gift made the whole company tremble, and everybody fell a-crying.

At this very instant the young Fairy came out from behind the hangings, and spake these words aloud:

"Assure yourselves, O King and Queen, that your daughter shall not die of this disaster. It is true, I have no power to undo entirely what my elder has done. The Princess shall indeed pierce her hand with a spindle; but, instead of dying, she shall only fall into a profound sleep, which shall last a hundred years, at the expiration of which a king's son shall come and awake her."

The King, to avoid the misfortune foretold by the old Fairy, caused immediately proclamation to be made, whereby everybody was forbidden, on pain of death, to spin with a distaff and spindle, or to have so much as any spindle in their houses. About fifteen or sixteen years after, the King and Queen being gone to one of their houses of pleasure, the young Princess happened one day to divert herself in running up and down the palace; when going up from one apartment to another, she came into a little room on the top of the tower, where a good old woman, alone, was spinning with her spindle. This good woman had never heard of the King's proclamation against spindles.

"What are you doing there, goody?" said the Princess.

"I am spinning, my pretty child," said the old woman, who did not know who she was.

"Ha!" said the Princess, "this is very pretty; how do you do it? Give it to me, that I may see if I can do so."

She had no sooner taken it into her hand than, whether being very hasty at it, somewhat unhandy, or that the decree of the Fairy had so ordained it, it ran into her hand, and she fell down in a swoon.

The good old woman, not knowing very well what to do in this affair, cried out for help. People came in from every quarter in great numbers; they threw water upon the Princess's face, unlaced her, struck her on the palms of her hands, and rubbed her temples with Hungary-water; but nothing would bring her to herself.

And now the King, who came up at the noise, bethought himself of the prediction of the fairies, and, judging very well that this must necessarily come to pass, since the fairies had said it, caused the Princess to be carried into the finest apartment in his palace, and to be laid upon a bed all embroidered with gold and silver.

One would have taken her for a little angel, she was so very beautiful; for her swooning away had not diminshed one bit of her complexion: her cheeks were carnation, and her lips were coral; indeed her eyes were shut, but she was heard to breathe softly, which satisfied those about her that she was not dead. The King commanded that they should not disturb her, but let her sleep quietly till her hour of awaking was come.

The good Fairy who had saved her life by condemning her to sleep a hundred years was in the kingdom of Matakin, twelve thousand leagues off, when this accident befell the Princess; but she was instantly informed of it by a little dwarf, who had boots of seven leagues, that is, boots with which he could tread over seven leagues of ground in one stride. The Fairy came away immediately, and she arrived, about an hour after, in a fiery chariot drawn by dragons.

The King handed her out of the chariot, and she approved everything he had done; but as she had very great foresight, she thought when the Princess should awake she might not know what to do with herself, being all alone in this old palace; and this was what she did: she touched with her wand everything in the palace (except the King and the Queen)—governess, maids of honor, ladies of the bedchamber, gentlemen, officers, stewards, cooks, undercooks, scullions, guards, with their beefeaters, pages, footmen; she likewise touched all the horses which were in the stables, as well pads as others, the great dogs in the outward court and pretty little Mopsey too, the Princess's littel spaniel, which lay by her on the bed.

Immediately upon her touching them they all fell asleep, that they might not awake before their mistress, and that they might be ready to wait upon her when she wanted them. The very spits at the fire, as full as they could hold of partridges and pheasants, did fall asleep also. All this was done in a moment. Fairies are not long in doing their business.

And now the King and the Queen, having kissed their dear child without waking her, went out of the palace and put forth a proclamation that nobody should dare to come near it.

This, however, was not necessary, for in a quarter of an hour's time there grew up all round about the park such a vast number of trees, great and small, bushes and brambles, twining one within another, that neither man nor beast could pass through; so that nothing could be seen but the very top of the towers of the palace; and that, too, not unless it was a good way off. Nobody doubted but the Fairy gave herein a very extraordinary sample of her art, that the Princess, while she continued sleeping, might have nothing to fear from any curious people.

When a hundred years were gone and passed the son of the King then reigning, and who was of another family from that of the sleeping Princess, being gone a-hunting on that side of the country, asked:

"What those towers were which he saw in the middle of a great thick wood?"

Everyone answered according as they had heard. Some said:

"That it was a ruinous old castle, haunted by spirits;"

Others, "That all the sorcerers and witches of the country kept there their sabbath or night's meeting."

The common opinion was that an ogre lived there, and that he carried thither all the little children he could catch, that he might eat them up at his leisure, without anybody being able to follow him, as having himself only the power to pass through the wood.

The Prince was at a stand, not knowing what to believe, when a very aged countryman spake to him thus:

"May it please your royal highness, it is now about fifty years since I heard from my father, who heard my grandfather say, that there was then in this castle a princess, the most beautiful was ever seen; that she must sleep there a hundred years, and should be waked by a king's son, for whom she was reserved."

The young Prince was all on fire at these words, believing, without weighing the matter, that he could put an end to this rare adventure; and, pushed on by love and honor, resolved that moment to look into it.

Scarce had he advanced towards the wood when all the great trees, the bushes, and brambles gave way of themselves to let him pass through; he walked up to the castle which he saw at the end of a large avenue which he went into; and what a little surprised him was that he saw none of his people could follow him, because the trees closed again as soon as he had passed through them. However, he did not cease from continuing his way; a young and amorous prince is always valiant.

He came into a spacious outward court, where everything he saw might have frozen up the most fearless person with horror. There reigned over all a most frightful silence; the image of death everywhere showed itself, and there was nothing to be seen but stretched-out bodies of men and animals, all seeming to be dead. He, however, very well knew, by the ruby faces and pimpled noses of the beefeaters, that they were only asleep; and their goblets, wherein still remained some drops of wine, showed plainly that they fell asleep in their cups.

He then crossed a court paved with marble, went up the stairs and came into the guard chamber, where guards were standing in their ranks, with their muskets upon their shoulders, and snoring as loud as they could. After that he went through several rooms full of gentlemen and ladies, all asleep, some stand-ing, others sitting. At last he came into a chamber all gilded with gold, where he saw upon a bed, the curtains of which were all open, the finest sight was ever beheld—a princess, who appeared to be about fifteen or sixteen years of age, and whose bright and, in a manner, resplendent beauty, had somewhat in it divine. He approached with trembling and admiration, and fell down before her upon his knees.

And now, as the enchantment was at an end, the Princess awaked, and looking on him with eyes more tender than the first view might seem to admit of:

"Is it you, my Prince?" said she to him. "You have waited a long while."

The Prince, charmed with these words, and much more with the manner in which they were spoken, knew not how to show his joy and gratitude; he assured her that he loved her better than he did himself; their discourse was not well connected, they did weep more than talk—little eloquence, a great deal of love. He was more at a loss than she, and we need not wonder at it: she had time to think on what to say to him; for it is very probable (though history mentions nothing of it) that the good Fairy, during so long a sleep, had given her very agreeable dreams. In short, they talked four hours together, and yet they said not half what they had to say.

In the meanwhile all the palace awaked; everyone thought upon their partic-ular business, and as all of them were not in love they were ready to die for hunger. The chief lady of honor, being as sharp set as other folks, grew very impatient, and told the Princess aloud that supper was served up. The Prince helped the Princess to rise; she was entirely dressed, and very magnificently, but his royal highness took care not to tell her that she was dressed like his great-grandmother, and had a point band peeping over a high collar; she looked not a bit the less charming and beautiful for all that.

They went into the great hall of looking-glasses, where they supped, and were served by the Princess's officers; the violins and hautboys[1] played old tunes, but very excellent, though it was now above a hundred years since they had played; and after supper, without losing any time, the lord almoner married them in the chapel of the castle, and the chief lady of honor drew the curtains. They had but very little sleep—the Princess had no occasion; and the Prince left her next morning to return into the city, where his father must needs have been in pain for him. The Prince told him:

That he lost his way in the forest as he was hunting, and that he had lain in the cottage of a charcoal-burner, who gave him cheese and brown bread.

The King, his father, who was a good man, believed him; but his mother could not be persuaded it was true; and seeing that he went almost every day a-hunting, and that he always had some excuse ready for so doing, though he had lain out three or four nights together, she began to suspect that he was married, for he lived with the Princess above two whole years, and had by her two children, the eldest of which, who was a daughter, was named *Morning*, and the youngest, who was a son, they called *Day*, because he was a great deal handsomer and more beautiful than his sister.

The Queen spoke several times to her son, to inform herself after what manner he did pass his time, and that in this he ought in duty to satisfy her. But he never dared to trust her with his secret; he feared her, though he loved her, for she was of the race of the Ogres, and the King would never have married her had it not been for her vast riches; it was even whispered about the Court that she had Ogreish inclinations, and that, whenever she saw little children passing by, she had all the difficulty in the world to avoid falling upon them. And so the Prince would never tell her one word.

But when the King was dead, which happened about two years afterwards, and he saw himself lord and master, he openly declared his marriage; and he went in great ceremony to conduct his Queen to the palace. They made a magnificent entry into the capital city, she riding between her two children.

Soon after the King went to make war with the Emperor Contalabutte, his neighbor. He left the government of the kingdom to the Queen his mother, and earnestly recommended to her care his wife and children. He was obliged to continue his expedition all the summer, and as soon as he departed the Queen-mother sent her daughter-in-law to a country house among the woods, that she might with the more ease gratify her horrible longing.

Some few days afterwards she went thither herself, and to her clerk of the kitchen:

"I have a mind to eat little Morning for my dinner tomorrow."

"Ah! madam," cried the clerk of the kitchen.

"I will have it so," replied the Queen (and this she spoke the tone of an Ogress who had a strong desire to eat fresh meat), "and will eat her with a *sauce Robert*."

The poor man, knowing very well that he must not play tricks with Ogresses, took his great knife and went up into little Morning's chamber. She was then four

---

[1] **hautboys**: oboes.

years old, and came up to him jumping and laughing, to take him about the neck, and ask him for some sugar-candy. Upon which he began to weep, the great knife fell out of his hand, and he went into the back yard, and killed a little lamb, and dressed with such good sauce that his mistress assured him she had never eaten anything so good in her life. He had at the same time taken up little Morning, and carried her to his wife, to conceal her in the lodging he had at the bottom of the courtyard.

About eight days afterwards the wicked Queen said to the clerk of the kitchen, "I will sup upon little Day."

He answered not a word, being resolved to cheat her as he had done before. He went to find out little Day, and saw with a little foil in his hand, with which he was fencing with a great monkey, the child being then only three years of age. He took him up in his arms and carried him to his wife, that she might conceal him in her chamber along with his sister, and in the room of little Day cooked up a young lamb very tender, which the Ogress found to be wonderfully good.

This was hitherto all mighty well; but one evening this wicked Queen said to her clerk of the kitchen:

"I will eat the Queen with the same sauce I had with her children."

It was now that the poor clerk of the kitchen despaired of being able to deceive her. The young Queen was turned of twenty, not reckoning the hundred years she had been asleep; and how to find in the yard a beast so firm was what puzzled him. He took then a resolution, that he might save his own life, to cut the Queen's throat; and going up into her chamber, with intent to do it at once, he put himself into as great fury as he could possibly, and came into the young Queen's room with his dagger in his hand. He would not, however, surprise her, but told her, with a great deal of respect, the orders he had received from the Queen-mother.

"Do it; do it," said she, stretching out her neck. "Execute your orders, and then I shall go and see my children, my poor children, whom I so much and so tenderly loved."

For she thought them dead ever since they had been taken away without her knowledge.

"No, no madam," cried the poor clerk of the kitchen, all in tears; "you shall not die, and yet you shall see your children again; but then you must go home with me to my lodgings, where I have concealed them, and I shall deceive the Queen once more, by giving her in your stead a young hind."

Upon this he forthwith conducted her to his chamber, where, leaving her to embrace her children, and cry along with them, he went and dressed a young hind, which the Queen had for her supper, and devoured it with the same appetite as if it had been the young Queen. Exceedingly was she delighted with her cruelty, and she had invented a story to tell the King, at his return, how the mad wolves had eaten up the Queen his wife and her two children.

One evening, as she was, according to her custom, rambling round about the courts and yards of the palace to see if she could smell any fresh meat, she heard, in a ground room, little Day crying, for his mamma was going to whip him, because he had been naughty; and she heard, at the same time, little Morning begging pardon for her brother.

The Ogress presently knew the voice of the Queen and her children, and being quite mad that she had been thus deceived, she commanded next morning, by break of day (with a most horrible voice, which made everybody tremble), that they should bring into the middle of the great court a large tub, which she caused to be filled with toads, vipers, snakes, and all sorts of serpents, in order to have thrown into it the Queen and her children, the clerk of the kitchen, his wife and maid; all whom she had given orders should be brought thither with their hands tied behind them.

They were brought out accordingly, and the executioners were just going to throw them into the tub, when the King (who was not so soon expected) entered the court on horse-back (for he came post) and asked, with the utmost astonishment, what was the meaning of that horrible spectacle.

No one dared to tell him, when the Ogress, all enraged to see what had happened, threw herself head foremost into the tub, and was instantly devoured by the ugly creatures she had ordered to be thrown into it for others. The King could not but be very sorry, for she was his mother; but he soon comforted himself with his beautiful wife and his pretty children.

THE MORAL   [1697]

Many a girl has waited long
For a husband brave or strong;
But I'm sure I never met
Any sort of woman yet
Who could wait a hundred years,
Free from fretting, free from fears.

Now, our story seems to show
That a century or so,
Late or early, matters not;
True love comes by fairy-lot.
Some old folk will even say
It grows better by delay.

Yet this good advice, I fear,
Helps us neither there nor here.
Though philosophers may prate
How much wiser 'tis to wait,
Maids will be a sighing still—
Young blood must when young blood will!

FOCUSED FREE WRITES

1. How is this fairy tale like those you remember? How is it different?
2. What do you think of the moral that appears at the end of this story? Did you come to this same conclusion as to the purpose of the story? What other "morals" may apply? How can stories be effective or ineffective in teaching lessons?

LITERARY Contexts

Defining Plot

Most simply, the **plot** is the arrangement of the action of the story. The plots of fairy tales and classic myths are fairly conventional, that is, they follow an accepted, established pattern. Sometimes these narratives can be imagined in the triangular form of **Freytag's pyramid**, adapted from Gustav Freytag's *Technik des Dramas* of 1863. One example of a conventional narrative structure is the **hero's journey**, identified by comparative mythologist Joseph Campbell, who traced the basic pattern common in world mythologies and religions.

Conventionally, narratives have an **introduction** or an **exposition** to introduce characters.

- Often, the hero's journey begins with a **call to adventure** in the introduction in which the main character, aided by a **guide** or **supernatural helper,** is called to a quest.

Narratives center on a **conflict** or some problem that needs resolution.

- Often, the hero refuses the call to adventure, but then must succumb because of a conflict.

The **rising action** is the portion of the narrative in which the conflict must be overcome.

- The **rising action** can be illustrated in the various **thresholds** and **trials** the hero must undertake on his or her journey. Often, a significant moment in this rising action is an episode in which the hero must hibernate and look within for strength, called the **belly of the whale** episode. The hero is transformed by this event and made ready to achieve the task of the quest.

The **climax** is the point of highest tension in the hero's journey.

- In a hero's journey, the **climax** comes when the hero must battle for good, often against authority or patriarchy, even against his or her own parents.

The **conclusion** of the story is the **resolution** or **denouement** (literally, the unraveling) of all of the conflicts.

- In the hero's journey, this ending is marked by a **return** in which the hero comes back to where he began somehow improved or enlightened, ready to lead and serve his or her community.

Not all narratives are organized with a conventional plot structure. Many writers defy convention in restructuring this basic plot movement.

(continued)

(continued)

Furthermore, some plots involve **flashbacks** and other shifts in time which serve to complicate a straightforward structure. Stories can also have **subplots**, which allow for parallels and complexities. Readers can also look for elements of **foreshadowing**, which allude to future action.

Map out the plot of this fairy tale. In what ways is it a hero's journey? In what ways is it not?

Discuss an example of a plot that you know with a conventional narrative structure, perhaps a hero's journey.

PRE-READING

A few years back, "Politically Correct Fairy Tales" were very popular. What modern versions of fairy tales are you aware of?

Margaret Atwood (1939–). *Margaret Atwood has come to be one of Canada's most heralded writers over the last half century. Dedicating herself to the writing life at 16, her career in literature was launched at the University of Toronto where she earned a BA and honors in English literature. Her studies continued at Radcliffe and Harvard. Atwood worked odd jobs until the breakout success of her award-winning collection of poetry, The Circle Game in 1966. Her long and productive career in fiction, poetry, and criticism has addressed various themes from meditations on language, myth, isolation, and identity to political commentary on human rights, women's issues, and nationalism.*

Margaret Atwood
_____

THERE WAS ONCE   [1992]

—There was once a poor girl, as beautiful as she was good, who lived with her wicked stepmother in a house in the forest.

—Forest? *Forest* is passé, I mean, I've had it with all this wilderness stuff. It's not a right image of our society, today. Let's have some *urban* for a change.

—There was once a poor girl, as beautiful as she was good, who lived with her wicked stepmother in a house in the suburbs.

—That's better. But I have to seriously query this word *poor.*

5 —But she *was* poor!

—Poor is relative. She lived in a house, didn't she?

—Yes.

—Then socioeconomically speaking, she was not poor.

—But none of the money was *hers!* The whole point of the story is that the wicked stepmother makes her wear old clothes and sleep in the fireplace—

10 —Aha! They had a *fireplace!* With *poor*, let me tell you, there's no fireplace. Come down to the park, come to the subway stations after dark, come down to where they sleep in cardboard boxes, and I'll show you *poor!*

—There was once a middle-class girl, as beautiful as she was good—

—Stop right there. I think we can cut the *beautiful*, don't you? Women these days have to deal with too many intimidating physical role models as it is, what with those bimbos in the ads. Can't you make her, well, more average?

—There was once a girl who was a little overweight and whose front teeth stuck out, who—

—I don't think it's nice to make fun of people's appearances. Plus you're encouraging anorexia.

15 —I wasn't making fun! I was just describing—

—Skip the description. Description oppresses. But you can say what color she was.

—What color?

—You know. Black, white, red, brown, yellow. Those are the choices. And I"m telling you right now, I've enough of white. Dominant culture this, dominant culture that—

—I don't know what color.

20 —Well, it would probably be *your* color, wouldn't it?

—But this isn't *about* me! It's about this girl—

—Everything is about you.

—Sounds to me like you don't want to hear this story at all.

—Oh well, go on. You could make her ethnic. That might help.

25 —There was once a girl of indeterminate descent, as average-looking as she was good, who lived with her wicked—

—Another thing. *Good* and *wicked.* Don't you think you should transcend those puritanical judgmental moralistic epithets? I mean, so much of that is conditioning, isn't it?

—There was once a girl, as average-looking as she was well-adjusted, who lived with her stepmother, who was not a very open and loving person because she herself had been abused in childhood.

—Better. But I am so *tired* of negative female images! And stepmothers— they always get it in the neck! Change it to step*father*, why don't you? That would make more sense anyway, considering the bad behavior you're about to describe. And throw in some whips and chains. We all know what those twisted, repressed, middle-aged men are like—

—*Hey, just a minute! I'm a middle-aged*—

30 —Stuff it, Mister Nosy Parker. Nobody asked you to stick in your oar, or whatever you want to call that thing. This is between the two of us. Go on.

—There was once a girl—

—How old was she?

—I don't know. She was young.

—This ends with a marriage, right?

35 —Well, not to blow the plot, but—yes.

—Then you can scratch the condescending paternalistic terminology. It's *woman*, pal. *Woman.*

—There was once—

—What's this *was, once?* Enough of the dead past. Tell me about *now.*

—There—

40 —So?

—So what?

—So, why not *here?*

FOCUSED FREE WRITES

1. How are these two stories similar? How are they different? How does Atwood revise the conventional fairy tale? What is Atwood saying about fairy tales?
2. While Perrault's tale explicitly states the moral at story's end, what might the moral of Atwood's tale be?
3. According to this story, what is literature?
4. How would you characterize the plot of this story? Is there a plot? Is the story structured conventionally?

POEMS

These two poems address large questions: What is poetry? What is literature? What is art? They offer an introduction to the genre and to the themes of this chapter.

PRE-READING

Some say that good art withstands the test of time. Should it? Does it? Is an "old" piece of art more or less valuable than a new one? What is the point of museums?

Percy Bysshe Shelley (1792–1822). *Percy Bysshe Shelley was born the eldest son of an established family. Raised and educated at Eton and Oxford, Shelley disappointed his conservative family by becoming a radical and atheist poet. Forced to live off others and in debt, Shelley found himself at odds with the revered William Godwin after he eloped with his daughter Mary*

Wollstonecraft Godwin. While their marriage was plagued by tragedy on many levels, Shelley produced much poetry and prose, all cut short by Shelley's drowning in 1822.

Percy Bysshe Shelley
_____

OZYMANDIAS [1817]

I met a traveler from an antique land
Who said: Two vast and trunkless legs of stone
Stand in the desert...Near them, on the sand,
Half sunk, a shattered visage lies, whose frown,
5 And wrinkled lip, and sneer of cold command,
Tell that its sculptor well those passions read
Which yet survive, stamped on these lifeless things,
The hand that mocked them, and the heart that fed:
And on the pedestal these words appear:
10 "My name is Ozymandias, King of Kings:
Look on my works, ye Mighty, and despair!"
Nothing beside remains. Round the decay
Of that colossal wreck, boundless and bare
The lone and level sands stretch far away.

FOCUSED FREE WRITES

1. Break this poem into its basic elements: What is the poem about? What happens? What is described? Who is speaking?
2. According to this poem, what is the value of art?

COMPARING THEMES

In order to highlight a particular theme or stylistic element, it can be useful to compare two distinctly different poems. In the pairing that follows, poems by different authors writing from distinct perspectives are compared in order to allow us to interpret similar meanings achieved through different means. These pairings throughout the book then allow us to practice the skill we will be developing more fully in Chapter 6, "Families and Their Characters: Comparing Works of Literature."

PRE-READING

A **metaphor** can be understood as one thing pictured as if it were something else, thereby suggesting a likeness or an analogy between them. Can you think of a metaphor to describe what an artist is like?

Adrienne Rich (1929–).   *Adrienne Rich's most recent books of poetry are* Telephone Ringing in the Labyrinth: Poems 2004–2006 *and* The School Among the Ruins: 2000–2004. *A selection of her essays,* Arts of the Possible: Essays and Conversations, *appeared in 2001. She edited Muriel Rukeyser's Selected Poems for the Library of America.* A Human Eye: Essays on Art in Society, *appeared in April 2009. She is a recipient of the National Book Foundation's 2006 Medal for Distinguished Contribution to American Letters, among other honors. She lives in California.*

Adrienne Rich

DIVING INTO THE WRECK [1973]

First having read the book of myths,
and loaded the camera,
and checked the edge of the knife-blade,
I put on
5   the body armor of black rubber
the absurd flippers
the grave and awkward mask.
I am having to do this
not like Cousteau with his
10   assiduous team[1]
aboard the sun-flooded schooner
but here alone.

There is a ladder.
The ladder is always there
15   hanging innocently
close to the side of the schooner.
We know what it is for,
we who have used it.
Otherwise
20   it's a piece of maritime floss
some sundry equipment.

I go down.
Rung after rung and still
the oxygen immerses me
25   the blue light
the clear atoms
of our human air.
I go down.
My flippers cripple me,
30   I crawl like an insect down the ladder
and there is no one

---

[1] **assiduous:** perservering; diligent; industrious.

to tell me when the ocean
will begin.

First the air is blue and then
35 it is bluer and then green and then
black I am blacking out and yet
my mask is powerful
it pumps my blood with power
the sea is another story
40 the sea is not a question of power
I have to learn alone
to turn my body without force
in the deep element.

And now: it is easy to forget
45 what I came for
among so many who have always
lived here
swaying their crenellated fans[2]
between the reefs
50 and besides
you breathe differently down here.

I came to explore the wreck.
The words are purposes.
The words are maps.
55 I came to see the damage that was done
and the treasures that prevail.
I stroke the beam of my lamp
slowly along the flank
of something more permanent
60 than fish or weed

the thing I came for:
the wreck and not the story of the wreck
the thing itself and not the myth
the drowned face always staring
65 toward the sun
the evidence of damage
worn by salt and sway into this threadbare beauty
the ribs of the disaster
curving their assertion
70 among the tentative haunters.

This is the place.
And I am here, the mermaid whose dark hair

---

[2] **crenellated:** indented; notched.

streams black, the merman in his armored body
We circle silently
75 about the wreck
we dive into the hold.
I am she: I am he

whose drowned face sleeps with open eyes
whose breasts still bear the stress
80 whose silver, copper, vermeil cargo lies[3]
obscurely inside barrels
half-wedged and left to rot
we are the half-destroyed instruments
that once held to a course
85 the water-eaten log
the fouled compass

We are, I am, you are
by cowardice or courage
the one who find our way
90 back to this scene
carrying a knife, a camera
a book of myths
in which
our names do not appear.

_____
[3] **vermeil:** metal that has been gilded.

Lawrence Ferlinghetti (1919–). *Ferlinghetti's father, an Italian immigrant and professor of languages, died suddenly, resulting in his wife's collapse and death by the time Ferlinghetti was two. His early years were characterized by transition until he was adopted by the Bisland family (founders of Sarah Lawrence). Ferlinghetti nurtured his interest in writing and journalism at Chapel Hill as an undergraduate. After a brief stint in the Navy, he continued his education at Columbia and in Paris before assuming ownership of the City Lights press and bookstore in San Francisco. City Lights became the heart of the Beat literary renaissance and Ferlinghetti became its leader.*

Lawrence Ferlinghetti

CONSTANTLY RISKING ABSURDITY [1958]

Constantly risking absurdity
                                and death
                    whenever he performs
                            above the heads
5   of his audience
            the poet like an acrobat
                        climbs on rime

```
                                    to a high wire of his own making
             and balancing on eyebeams
10                                        above a sea of faces

                 paces his way
                              to the other side of the day
             performing entrechats
                              and sleight-of-foot tricks
15           and other high theatrics
                          and all without mistaking
                 any thing
                          for what it may not be
                 For he's the super realist
20                                    who must perforce perceive

                 taut truth
                          before the taking of each stance or step
             in his supposed advance
                              toward that still higher perch
25           where Beauty stands and waits
                              with gravity
                                  to start her death-defying leap
             And he
                     a little charleychaplin man
30                               who may or may not catch

                 her fair eternal form
                          spreadeagled in the empty air
                 of existence
```

FOCUSED FREE WRITES

1. What stories does each of these poems tell?
2. What is the meaning of each of theses poems? What are they trying to say about literature?
3. Are there any similarities in these poems? How do these poems address similar themes in different ways?
4. What comparison, analogy, or metaphor is used in each poem?

Reflecting on the Writing Process

Think back to your experience in high school or in your first-semester composition course. What do you remember about the writing process? Chances are, you learned about certain processes and even structures for your writing. We will review some of these here.

Prewriting

Writing is not just about recording a thought you already had; it is a tool for figuring out what you are thinking.

The first part of figuring out what you are thinking is prewriting, so called because it is everything you do before you begin an actual draft of an essay or other writing project. In some ways, just thinking about the assignment as you're driving in your car, walking to class, and exercising is prewriting. In fact, today's writers often dispense with creating separate files for prewriting and drafts because it's so easy to revise text when using a word processor. But in whatever form it takes, brainstorming and free writing are ways to get your thinking on paper, which in turn helps you discover more about your ideas.

- When you **brainstorm**, you list all your ideas freely. Some people call this form of prewriting a "jot list." Later, you can go back through them to see what makes the most sense, but while you are brainstorming, don't censor any ideas.
- **Free writing** is similar to brainstorming, except that you write your ideas as running text instead of in a list. The questions in the **Focused Free Write** features throughout this book may help you find things to write about. Again, later, when you are ready to move from prewriting to drafting, you can decide whether to elaborate on any of the ideas that came up during free writing.
- If you would rather use a more visual method, you can **map** to create a picture of your ideas, or **web** or **cluster** to show the connections between your ideas. These methods work by dividing a blank piece of paper into sections or quadrants that allow you to group or represent similar ideas through proximity. Many students prefer this looser and visual form of outlining.

It doesn't matter exactly how you prewrite, only that you use a method you feel comfortable with. Prewriting doesn't have to be pretty and often it isn't graded, but it does make the writing process less stressful. When you prewrite, remember that you are just writing to learn what you know, not to prove what you think.

Since in this course you'll be writing in response to literature, see if your prewriting leads you to ideas about what is important about a work—its theme, or its most important scene or line or bit of dialog. How do the other parts of the work seem to coalesce around this one? Go back to the work you are reading as needed to investigate your ideas further.

You might prewrite your way through several rounds of writing and rereading. When you have an idea you think is worth pursuing, jot it down as a general statement, and then see if you can list all the reasons you believe this to be true about the work you are considering. List references to specific parts of the work, and note how each one supports your general statement.

Drafting

Depending in part on how much prewriting you did, drafting your essay will be more or less messy, but the main idea is to write out your ideas in sentences and paragraphs. You might want to make a formal outline with Roman numerals

(I, II, III, IV, and so on) or even just an informal outline, a sketchy list, before you draft. Or you might want to just start writing a paragraph that explains your main assertion. When you are drafting, be sure to include details from the work that illustrate the point you are making. Identify which parts of the text help prove your idea to be true.

Just like prewriting, drafting may provoke new discoveries. Be open to them. Just be sure to stay close to the literary text itself, since you will have to share with readers those details that support your "reading" of the text.

Some writers are able to keep both content and organization under control when they draft, but many others choose to leave organization for the revising stage. Either way is fine, as long as you eventually organize your ideas in a way that is logical and that makes your essay easy to understand.

Revising

Revising an essay often includes making decisions about how best to present your ideas to readers. In prewriting and drafting, you were probably mostly writing to figure things out for yourself. In revising, you turn your attention to your readers. In what order should you present your ideas so readers will understand and even agree with you? The traditional organization of an essay into a beginning, middle, and end or an **introduction**, **body paragraphs**, and **conclusion**, will help you here. While this chapter offers a general overview of **the writing process**, the subsequent chapters will address aspects of the process in greater detail.

Your introduction should assert your **thesis** or the point you are making about the text's theme. You will want to work throughout your essay to prove this point.

Body paragraphs focus on the support for your thesis. These paragraphs will include your own ideas predominantly. You will also need to include moments from the text to support your argument; often, the terminology of the elements of literature (plot, character, theme, setting, and so on) is used to discuss the support. You may briefly refer to the text using **summary,** or reword specific parts of the text as **paraphrase**. When the language of the text is essential to your discussion, you may also **quote** words, lines, or longer passages. Because quotations can be tricky to punctuate and cite properly, pay careful attention to the information given in later chapters when you edit your revised essay.

Throughout the body paragraphs, use **transitions** between paragraphs to remind the reader of your purpose and inform the reader of how that purpose is connected to the point at hand.

Finally, your **conclusion** should emphasize the significance of your purpose rather than simply restating it.

Assignment: Reading to Write

Practice your writing process in responding to the following prompt:
What is literature? Using examples from this chapter, define the nature, function, and value of literature.

2
READING AND WRITING
Contexts for Thinking

Attending Readings. Here we have a photograph of former Poet Laureate Billy Collins at a public reading of his poetry. What sorts of preconceptions of poets and poetry do you have? What is your experience with literary readings? Do you prefer to hear poetry read or read poetry on your own? Are there some poems that lend themselves to being read aloud and some to being read? Which ones? What should one keep in mind when attending a reading?

Have you ever gotten lost when reading?

Have you ever had a reading experience in which you became so engaged, so engrossed in the book in your lap that you forgot where you were, what day it was, or what time it was? Perhaps you were so involved in Stephen King's thriller or Danielle Steele's romance or J.R.R. Tolkien's remote world that you got lost in a faraway time or place. You had to come to—as if from a deep sleep—to find yourself again on the beach, in a hammock, or on an airplane. You must blink your eyes in the bright light of day, as if exiting a movie theater, to remember who you are and what you are about and where you parked your car. This displacement represents a powerful reading moment and demonstrates the ultimate in active reading.

We have all had reading experiences in which we got lost in a bad way. We turned page after page of a book or article only to realize ten pages later that we have not retained a single idea. Our eyes have glanced at the marks on the page, but we have not actively engaged with the text. We cannot say what was written, or how it was written, because we were passive in the reading experience. This class will encourage you to become actively engaged in reading and to develop personal strategies for active reading that can be applied anytime you need to understand complex material.

One of the most important things to learn in this class is how to read—how to really read for meaning and significance. You'll investigate the meanings of stories, poems, and plays, thinking not only about what is written, but also why something is written in the precise way that it is. That's because in literature, form matters as much as content. Among all types of writing, perhaps literature best illustrates our attempts as humans to connect with one another using the subtle powers of language.

In her book, *The Reader, the Text, the Poem: The Transactional Theory of the Literary Work,* Louise Rosenblatt gives us terminology that can help us understand how to become actively engaged in texts. She describes the reading process in terms of a **transaction**. Our goal when reading is to engage with a text in a dynamic relationship involving a back-and-forth interaction, rather than a passive or static mode of mindlessly turning pages. Rosenblatt defines two kinds of reading:

Efferent Reading: *Efferent* means "to take away." In this kind of reading, you must take away information from a text to use elsewhere. Often, when you read the owner's manual to your car or DVD player, you are practicing efferent reading. You are gleaning information you can use elsewhere, perhaps under the hood or when you program your remote control. This is an important kind of reading and something that may be necessary in some classes or settings.

Aesthetic Reading: The second kind of reading is *aesthetic* reading. In this process, readers bring their own experiences and contexts to a text, and these individual histories mold their experiences of the work of literature. Literature can have an "emotional effect" on the reader and the text then comes to light based on an individual reader's interaction with it. In other words, the reader must make contributions for the text to come alive. For example, when you read a menu, you bring your predilections, your likes, dislikes, allergies, ethical beliefs, and health concerns to make your decision about what to order. If you are a vegetarian, you probably won't spend much time examining the surf and turf section of your menu. Likewise, if you are reading the stories of Huck Finn or Holden Caufield, you might contribute your own disillusionment with people, experiences growing up, or desire to be free of society's obligations in order to understand Huck or Holden. As you've doubtless realized, we'll be concentrating on developing aesthetic reading in this course.

Rosenblatt suggests that we can recognize reading as subjective and located within a given **context**, while always using the text as a starting point and a basis for making meaning. The context of a work can be understood as the circumstances in which the event of reading occurs, a setting, in a way. The project of this textbook is to solicit your prior experiences to provide part of the context for reading. We also encourage you to approach texts from alternative perspectives with other contexts in mind, first by suggesting a few ourselves, and then by hoping your instructor and class will discuss others to help you open up the text. Chapter 3 outlines the kinds of contexts introduced in this book: **biographical**, **historical**, **literary**, and **critical**.

Active Reading

To become active when reading, write something: move your pen to reflect your mind's activity. Your former teachers may have recommended that you outline, take notes, write lists, draw maps, use sticky notes, or make notecards about your reading. These are all things you can do to stay active. You can also mark up the text right on the page as you are reading (supposing, of course, that you own the book; otherwise, make a copy to mark up). The idea is to develop a personal reading process that works for you. For example, you can:

- **Pay attention** to your reactions as you read, and where you feel a shift in your emotions or thoughts, mark that place in the text with a line or symbol of your own devising.
- **Be curious.** What happens next? Why? How? In places where the text stimulates your curiosity, mark that with an exclamation point or question mark. Write your question in the margin.
- **Prioritize.** Underline, star, or highlight important moments or lines. Come back and assess which parts of the story, poem, or play are most significant.
- **Stay alert** for words that seem oddly placed or used in a sense that seems different from what you might expect, or that could have several meanings; mark these, perhaps with a squiggly line.
- **Try to imagine the scene** an author is describing, and take quick notes on anything that strikes you as very typical or atypical. Write "Yes!" or "Hmmmm" in the margin at these moments.
- **Write your responses freely,** whether you want to reply "You've got to be kidding me!" or "Ha!" or "Woohoo!" or "Huh?"

- **Ask questions.** Why is the author doing this or that to a character? How can this event lead to that event? and so on. Write down your questions and come back to them later.
- **Think** about how your past affects your reading of this particular work. Where did you grow up—in a place similar to or different from the setting in this work? What was your family like? Your friends? Your school? Your neighborhood? You may find that certain aspects of your history seem more relevant than others in relation to a particular story, poem, or play. Make a note in the margin when you believe you need to explore these connections after reading.
- **Make connections** to other literary texts or other things you have read. If a line, a character, or an image reminds you of something you read elsewhere, mark that moment.

Begin by considering the ideas introduced in the **prereading questions** printed in this book preceding the literary texts. They will introduce ideas and themes that will prime you for your reading experience. Use them to get situated in the right frame of mind. Then read. Read and write. After you read a text for the first time, take a few minutes to absorb its impact. Take ten minutes to write down your thoughts and feelings. Give yourself time to develop reactions. Then read again. The second time you read a text, you will almost surely notice new things about it. You might want to use a second color of ink to record your responses this time through the text. You may even want to answer some of the questions you asked the first time you read it, or add a new comment about an old comment. The more you engage in this back-and-forth dialog with the text and with your previous readings of a text, the richer and more complex your response will become—and the better any paper you write about it will be.

Writing About Your Reading Experience

Often, you must write to communicate with others, for instance, in an email to a friend or a letter to a potential employer. However, writing about reading is different—it is a way to work out your thinking. In other words, this writing is about the process ("What thoughts can I develop?"), not the product ("How can I best communicate my thoughts?"). The act of writing about reading facilitates your thinking and produces your understanding. It should underscore what you know or have come to learn about the text. This is **informal writing**.

The Focused Free Writes are available throughout the book to guide your informal writing. They will direct you to examine various aspects of a piece of literature to make meaning. These quick writes or minute papers represent just a few of the possible responses to the text, and so you may want to expand your response beyond these questions.

This kind of writing to read and think can give rise to **formal writing**. In other words, the revelations you have when thinking about your reading through your writing might be a starting point for a formal writing product such as an essay or a research paper—writing designed to communicate with your peers, other readers, and your teacher. At the end of each chapter in Part II, you will be guided to construct a formal writing product.

Thinking Critically About the Text

This book will guide you in thinking and writing about your reading. In order to identify the kinds of **critical thinking** you will perform, we will distinguish them through distinct kinds of formal writing. The following questions will introduce us to these acts:

- **Interpretation:** What does this mean?
- **Analysis:** How does the author suggest that meaning? How do I as the reader pick up on that?
- **Argument:** Why should my reader believe this interpretation and this analysis? How can I present my reasons persuasively?
- **Comparison and Contrast:** How is this the same as or different from other texts I've read?
- **Using Critical Perspectives:** What specific approaches might be useful in making meaning of this text?

The following story will introduce us to these critical thinking acts.

STORY

Read the following story actively, using your own personal shorthand to mark the text.

PRE-READING   What ideas does the title bring to mind? Have you read any other works by Kate Chopin? If so, what do you remember about them?

Kate Chopin (1851–1904). *Kate Chopin was born and raised by a well-established Irish/Creole family in St. Louis as Katherine O'Flaherty. After marrying a Louisiana cotton broker from the bayou, Chopin served as a society matron and mother of six. The loss of her husband, however, led to her assuming responsibilities in business and then as a writer. Eventually devoting herself entirely to writing, Chopin achieved success in short stories and then in her once forgotten and condemned but now classic and celebrated The Awakening (1899), infamous then famous for its story of female self-discovery.*

Kate Chopin

THE STORY OF AN HOUR   [1891]

Knowing that Mrs. Mallard was afflicted with a heart trouble, great care was taken to break to her as gently as possible the news of her husband's death.

It was her sister Josephine who told her, in broken sentences, veiled hints that revealed in half concealing. Her husband's friend Richards was there, too, near her. It was he who had been in the newspaper office when intelligence of the railroad disaster was received, with Brently Mallard's name leading the list of "killed." He had only taken the time to assure himself of its truth by a second telegram, and had hastened to forestall any less careful, less tender friend in bearing the sad message.

She did not hear the story as many women have heard the same, with a paralyzed inability to accept its significance. She wept at once, with sudden, wild abandonment, in her sister's arms. When the storm of grief had spent itself she went away to her room alone. She would have no one follow her.

There stood, facing the open window, a comfortable, roomy armchair. Into this she sank, pressed down by a physical exhaustion that haunted her body and seemed to reach into her soul.

5   She could see in the open square before her house the tops of trees that were all aquiver with the new spring life. The delicious breath of rain was in the air. In the street below a peddler was crying his wares. The notes of a distant song which some one was singing reached her faintly, and countless sparrows were twittering in the eaves.

There were patches of blue sky showing here and there through the clouds that had met and piled above the other in the west facing her window.

She sat with her head thrown back upon the cushion of the chair quite motionless, except when a sob came up into her throat and shook her, as a child who has cried itself to sleep continues to sob in its dreams.

She was young, with a fair, calm face, whose lines bespoke repression and even a certain strength. But now there was a dull stare in her eyes, whose gaze was fixed away off yonder on one of those patches of blue sky. It was not a glance of reflection, but rather indicated a suspension of intelligent thought.

There was something coming to her and she was waiting for it, fearfully. What was it? She did not know; it was too subtle and elusive to name. But she felt it, creeping out of the sky, reaching toward her through the sounds, the scents, the color that filled the air.

10   Now her bosom rose and fell tumultuously. She was beginning to recognize this thing that was approaching to possess her, and she was striving to beat it back with her will—as powerless as her two white slender hands would have been.

When she abandoned herself a little whispered word escaped her slightly parted lips. She said it over and over under her breath: "Free, free, free!" The vacant stare and the look of terror that had followed it went from her eyes. They stayed keen and bright. Her pulses beat fast, and the coursing blood warmed and relaxed every inch of her body.

She did not stop to ask if it were or were not a monstrous joy that held her. A clear and exalted perception enabled her to dismiss the suggestion as trivial.

She knew that she would weep again when she saw the kind, tender hands folded in death; the face that had never looked save with love upon her, fixed and gray and dead. But she saw beyond that bitter moment a long procession of years to come that would belong to her absolutely. And she opened and spread her arms out to them in welcome.

There would be no one to live for during those coming years; she would live for herself. There would be no powerful will bending hers in that blind persistence with which men and women believe they have a right to impose a private will upon a fellow creature. A kind intention or a cruel intention made the act seem no less a crime as she looked upon it in that brief moment of illumination.

15   And yet she had loved him—sometimes. Often she had not. What did it matter! What could love, the unsolved mystery, count for in face of this possession of self-assertion which she suddenly recognized as the strongest impulse of her being.

"Free! Body and soul free!" she kept whispering.

Josephine was kneeling before the closed door with her lips to the keyhole, imploring for admission. "Louise, open the door! I beg; open the door—you will make yourself ill. What are you doing, Louise? For heaven's sake open the door."

"Go away. I am not making myself ill." No; she was drinking in a very elixir of life through that open window.

Her fancy was running riot along those days ahead of her. Spring days, and summer days, and all sorts of days that would be her own. She breathed a quick prayer that life might be long. It was only yesterday she had thought with a shudder that life might be long.

20   She arose at length and opened the door to her sister's importunities. There was a feverish triumph in her eyes, and she carried herself unwittingly like a goddess of Victory. She clasped her sister's waist, and together they descended the stairs. Richards stood waiting for them at the bottom.

Some one was opening the front door with a latchkey. It was Brently Mallard who entered, a little travel-stained, composedly carrying his grip-sack and umbrella. He had been far from the scene of accident, and did not even know there had been one. He stood amazed at Josephine's piercing cry; at Richards' quick motion to screen him from the view of his wife.

But Richards was too late.

When the doctors came they said she had died of heart disease—of joy that kills.

FOCUSED FREE WRITES

1. Looking back at this short short story and what you have marked, what are the most significant moments?
2. What may be the most important line?
3. What may be the most important word? Why? What words did your peers choose? How would you argue for your own choice?
4. What did you think of the story's ending? What led you to expect it? At what point were you surprised?

Critical Thinking Acts

In the Focused Free Writes, we made personal connections with the language of the text. The next step, however, is to determine how the different parts of a piece of literature work together to create certain effects on readers in order to figure out *why* we reacted the way we did. Critical thinking functions as a starting point for exploring the significance of the content and craft of a piece of literature. And these acts serve as building blocks for formal writing projects. Using Chopin's "The Story of an Hour" as an example, we can see how personal reactions can be transformed through critical thinking. By chapter's end and throughout the subsequent chapters, we will see how formal writing projects can develop out of these acts.

Interpretation

An **interpretation** is an explanation of a text's meaning, presented in understandable terms. For some types of literary works, such as **allegories**, the meaning of a work may be readily apparent; the message is delivered in explicit terms. (One famous allegory, *Pilgrim's Progress,* is about a Christian pilgrim's progress toward the "Celestial City.") However, for most literary texts, the meaning may be veiled, diffused, or identifiable, but not summarized in a single neat sentence. In fact, Flannery O'Connor, a Southern writer, once wrote,

> When you can state the theme of a story, when you can separate it from the story itself, then you can be sure the story is not a very good one. The meaning of a story has to be embodied in it, has to be made concrete in it. A story is a way to say something that can't be said any other way, and it takes every word in the story to say what the meaning is. ("Writing Short Stories," *Mystery and Manners,* 96)

What the poem, play, or story means is often subject to debate, and what the text means works on multiple levels in multiple ways. The work may be **ironic**, in fact, and so the intended meaning may be implied and not overt at all.

In an interpretation, we will be engaged in asserting the meaning of a piece of literature. For example, in "The Story of an Hour," though the story is short, the meaning is not necessarily "short." In fact, while it is straightforward to summarize what happens in the story, that is distinct from what it means. We might interpret the story to be about a particular theme such as freedom, identity, or discovery. Our interpretation would then explain what the story says about one of these things or how the meaning of the story can be understood in terms of that idea. The thesis of our interpretation would be an assertion about what the story means. For example, we might state that "The Story of an Hour" is about a woman's imprisonment in and then freedom from marriage at the turn of the nineteenth century. Chapter 3 will offer an in-depth focus on the act of interpretation.

Analysis

Analysis is a separation of the component parts of something (a substance, a process, a situation) in order to discover its true nature or inner relationships. Once we have established the meaning of a work, we must work to determine *how* it means, not just *what* it means. We move from the broader work of interpretation to the more focused work of analysis, focusing the lens on the individual elements, not the big picture. In analysis, we separate a story, play, or poem into its component parts and identify a few for close study. The elements that make up the text contribute to its meaning in a particular way.

In an analysis, we generally study a few elements in relation to the whole story or the meaning of the story. If we were to analyze "The Story of an Hour," we might demonstrate how the process of discovery works on multiple levels not only for the character Mrs. Mallard but also for the reader. Both the main character and the reader make surprising discoveries, in fact, in seeing the "truth." Our analysis might break down the process of discovery for the reader through the construction of the plot: the foreshadowing, the climax, and the denouement. We could then analyze the symbols that represent Mrs. Mallard's discoveries about herself. Chapter 4 examines the act of analysis.

Argument

Argument is a verbal address or composition intended to convince others of a point of view through persuasive discourse. Whenever we write essays, we should construct persuasive arguments with coherent, concise, and arguable thesis statements. And, in many ways, interpretation and analysis are themselves tasks in arguing; however, we can think of those tasks as more descriptive and the argument as more assertive. In this case, the reader's argument works to identify an understanding or meaning that may not be inherent to the text or intentional by the author, but might be a viable reading nonetheless. The reader then marshals support from the text for this assertion by identifying evidence or support through close reading. The reader stakes a claim or makes a case that needs developed details for proof.

In other words, the thesis of an argument must be in the form of an assertion that needs proof to be true. For example, for an argument, we would need a thesis such as, "Irony operates on a number of levels in Kate Chopin's 'The Story of an Hour': verbally, situationally, and even dramatically." To make such an argument would require interpretation and analysis. In Chapter 5, we will focus on argument.

Comparison/Contrast

Comparison/contrast is an examination of the character or qualities of a text to discover resemblances and differences. When we compare two texts, we identify similarities; when we contrast two texts, we identify differences. We still may be interpreting or analyzing, and we are always arguing. The difference is that we are using one text to shed light on another. Therefore, when we choose two texts to focus on, we should choose them based on their similarities or differences. A text that is decidedly different from another should be acknowledged as different and, therefore, contrasted; however, the bulk of the project should work to distinguish subtle similarities between them. Calling attention to obviously similar texts does not make for a strong project; rather, we should confirm the similarity of these works by comparison in order to tease out their differences.

So, if we were to compare "The Story of an Hour" to Toni Cade Bambara's "The Lesson" (a story that appears later in this book), we might acknowledge the differences between the main characters, one an adult woman and the other a young girl, but we might suggest that the gender imprisonment of Mrs. Mallard bears some resemblance to the class imprisonment of Bambara's characters, especially in terms of the authors' use of the landscapes as symbols. Or, we might look at two similar works by Chopin, "The Story of an Hour" and *The Awakening*, perhaps, and examine how the deaths of the main characters represent different responses to the same question about gender. Each chapter provides opportunities to compare works, which is a useful strategy for making meaning. Chapter 6 focuses on comparison and contrast as a formal writing project.

In some ways, dividing these critical thinking acts is artificial or really just a matter of semantics, but it may be useful for us to think of these acts as building blocks and as steps in a process. Therefore, a discussion of each of these steps is developed throughout the next five chapters. Your Focused Free Writes will prompt you to read actively; however, they will also encourage you to engage in these critical thinking acts as preliminary work for your formal writing projects.

LITERARY Contexts

Making Meaning of Fiction

A quick review of some of the significant terms used to describe the elements of literature may be useful at this point. These terms will be explored in greater depth in each of the chapters that follow.

Theme: The central meaning or dominant idea of a literary work is the theme. This meaning unifies the story and gives it purpose. All other elements are organized around a story's theme and should work in support of the central theme. (See Chapter 3 for an expanded discussion.)

What is a central theme of Chopin's "The Story of an Hour"?

Plot: Most simply, the plot is the arrangement of the action of the story. (See Chapter 1 for a full discussion.)

Describe the plot of Chopin's story.

Symbols: People, objects, actions, situations, or images that come to characterize main ideas in the story or some larger idea, or which are charged with meaning in some way, are symbols. (See Chapter 3 for a full discussion.)

What symbols can you identify in the story? What might be the importance of Mrs. Mallard's views from the window?

Style: The author's style is the individual and distinctive manner of expression evident in the work, or the way the writer arranges words. (See Chapter 4 for a full discussion.)

Characterize the story's style. What sorts of patterns do you notice in the language of the story? Why is the story told the way it is?

Narration/Point of View: Who tells (narrates) the story can dramatically impact our understanding of what is being said. (See Chapter 5 for a full discussion.)

(continued)

(continued)

What can you tell about the narrator of this story?

Character: Characters people the story. They bring the story to life and make it real to the reader. (See Chapter 6 for a full discussion.)

List the characters in "The Story of an Hour." Do any of these characters change in the course of the story?

Setting: The location and time of a story is its setting. We must be aware of the setting to understand the context of a work. (See Chapter 7 for a full discussion.)

Where and when does "The Story of an Hour" take place? Why is that significant?

Questions like these can be useful when reading and thinking about any short story. Try them out as you examine the stories in this book. These elements will also be explored in depth in the chapters that follow.

PLAY

Let's shift genres now from fiction to drama. While fiction may seem like the genre you are most familiar with, you see screenplays or scripts visualized in films and on TV every day. When *reading* drama, though, you have the opportunity to perform the screenplay in your mind's eye—all the casting and staging decisions are up to you. In the short play that follows, closely read to imagine how you might best convey this text's meaning on film.

| PRE-READING | If you had three wishes, what would they be? |

Jane Martin. *Jane Martin, apparently from Kentucky, is the pseudonym of a mysterious playwright. After earning early praise for Talking With..., a series of monologs first performed at the 1981 Humana Festival of New American Plays at the Actors' Theatre of Louisville and various nominations and awards for full-length plays like Keely and Du, Criminal Hearts, Audition, and Anton in Show Business, she continues to refuse to provide interviews, biographies, and photographs. Jon Jory, retired artistic director of the Actors' Theatre of Louisville, is the spokesperson for the playwright and, some believe, the writer behind the pen name. He denies this allegation, stating that Jane Martin prefers the plays to stand on their own.*

BEAUTY

CHARACTERS

CARLA

BETHANY

SCENE: *An apartment. Minimalist set. A young woman, Carla, on the phone.*

CARLA: In love with me? You're in love with me? Could you describe yourself again? Uh-huh. Uh-huh. And you spoke to me? (*A knock at the door.*) Listen, I always hate to interrupt a marriage proposal, but... could you possibly hold that thought? (*Puts phone down and goes to door. Bethany, the same age as Carla and a friend, is there. She carries the sort of mid-eastern lamp we know of from Aladdin.*)

BETHANY: Thank God you were home. I mean, you're not going to believe me.

CARLA: Somebody on the phone. (*Goes back to it.*)

BETHANY: I mean, I just had a beach urge, so I told them at work my uncle was dying...

CARLA (*Motions to Bethany for quiet.*): And you were the one in the leather jacket with the tattoo? What was the tattoo? (*Carla again asks Bethany, who is gesturing wildly that she should hang up, to cool it.*) Look, a screaming eagle from shoulder to shoulder, maybe. There were a lot of people in the bar.

BETHANY (*Gesturing and mouthing.*): I have to get back to work.

CARLA (*On phone.*): See, the thing is, I'm probably not going to marry someone I can't remember... particularly when I don't drink. Sorry. Sorry. Sorry. (*She hangs up.*) Madness.

BETHANY: So I ran out to the beach...

CARLA: This was some guy I never met who apparently offered me a beer...

BETHANY:... low tide and this... (*The lamp.*)... was just sitting there, lying there...

CARLA:... and he tracks me down...

BETHANY:... on the beach, and I lift this lid thing...

CARLA:... and seriously proposes marriage.

BETHANY:... and a genie comes out.

CARLA: I mean, that's twice in a... what?

BETHANY: A genie comes out of this thing.

CARLA: A genie?

BETHANY: I'm not kidding, the whole Disney kind of thing, swirling smoke, and then this twenty-foot-high, see-through guy in like an Arabian outfit.

CARLA: Very funny.

BETHANY: Yes, funny, but twenty feet high! I look up and down the beach, I'm alone. I don't have my pepper spray or my hand alarm. You know me, when I'm petrified I joke. I say his voice is too high for Robin Williams, and he says he's a castrati. Naturally. Who else would I meet?

CARLA: What's a castrati?

BETHANY: You know...

(*The appropriate gesture.*)

CARLA: Bethany, dear one, I have three modeling calls. I am meeting Ralph Lauren!

BETHANY: Okay, good. Ralph Lauren. Look, I am not kidding!

CARLA: You're not kidding what?!

BETHANY: There is a genie in this thingamajig.

CARLA: Uh-huh. I'll be back around eight.

BETHANY: And he offered me *wishes*!

CARLA: Is this some elaborate practical joke because it's my birthday?

BETHANY: No, happy birthday, but I'm like crazed because I'm on this deserted beach with a twenty-foot-high, see-through genie, so like sarcastically...you know how I need a new car...I said fine, gimme 25,000 dollars...

CARLA: On the beach with the genie?

BETHANY: Yeah, right, exactly, and it rains down out of the sky.

CARLA: Oh sure.

BETHANY: (*pulling a wad out of her purse.*): Count it, those are thousands. I lost one in the surf.

(*Carla sees the top bill. Looks at Bethany, who nods encouragement. Carla thumbs through them.*)

CARLA: These look real.

BETHANY: Yeah.

CARLA: And they rained down out of the sky?

BETHANY: Yeah.

CARLA: You've been really strange lately, are you dealing?

BETHANY: Dealing what, I've even given up chocolate.

CARLA: Let me see the genie.

BETHANY: Wait, wait.

CARLA: Bethany, I don't have time to screw around. Let me see the genie or let me go on my appointments.

BETANY: Wait! So I pick up the money...see, there's sand on the money...and I'm like nuts so I say, you know, "Okay, look, ummm, big guy, my uncle is in the hospital"...because as you know when I said to the people at work my uncle was dying, I was on one level telling the truth although it had nothing to do with the beach, but he was in Intensive Care after the accident, and that's on my mind, so I say, okay, Genie, heal my uncle...which is like impossible given he was hit by two trucks, and the genie says, "Yes, Master"...like they're supposed to say, and he goes into this like kind of whirlwind, kicking up sand and stuff, and I'm like, "Oh my God!" and the air clears, and he bows, you know, and says, "It is done, Master," and I say, "Okay, whatever-you-are, I'm calling on my cell phone," and I get it out and I get this doctor who is like dumbstruck who says my uncle came to, walked out of Intensive Care and left the hospital! I'm not kidding, Carla.

CARLA: On your mother's grave?

BETHANY: On my mother's grave.

(*They look at each other.*)

CARLA: Let me see the genie.

BETHANY: No, no, look, that's the whole thing…I was just, like, reacting, you know, responding, and that's already two wishes…although I'm really pleased about my uncle, the $25,000 thing, I could have asked for $10 million, and there is only one wish left.

CARLA: So ask for $10 million.

BETHANY: I don't think so. I don't think so. I mean, I gotta focus in here. Do you have a sparkling water?

CARLA: No. Bethany, I'm missing Ralph Lauren now. Very possibly my one chance to go from catalogue model to the very, very big time, so, if you are joking, stop joking.

BETHANY: Not joking. See, see, the thing is, I know what I want. In my guts. Yes. Underneath my entire bitch of a life is this unspoken, ferocious, all-consuming urge…

CARLA (*Trying to get her to move this along.*): Ferocious, all-consuming urge…

BETHANY: I want to be like you.

CARLA: Me?

BETHANY: Yes.

CARLA: Half the time you don't even like me.

BETHANY: Jealous. The ogre of jealousy.

CARLA: You're the one with the $40,000 job straight out of school. You're the one who has published short stories. I'm the one hanging on by her finger-nails in modeling. The one who has creeps calling her on the phone. The one who had to have a nose job.

BETHANY: I want to be beautiful.

CARLA: You are beautiful.

BETHANY: Carla, I'm not beautiful.

CARLA: You have charm. You have personality. You know perfectly well you're pretty.

BETHANY: "Pretty," see, that's it. Pretty is the minor leagues of beautiful. Pretty is what people discover about you after they know you. Beautiful is what knocks them out across the room. Pretty, you get called a couple of times a year; *beautiful* is 24 hours a day.

CARLA: Yeah? So?

BETHANY: So?! We're talking *beauty* here. Don't say "So?" Beauty is the real deal. You are the center of any moment of your life. People stare. Men flock. I've seen you get offered discounts on makeup for no reason. Parents treat beautiful children better. Studies show your income goes up. You can have sex anytime you want it. Men have to know me. That takes up to a year. I'm continually horny.

CARLA: Bethany, I don't even like sex. I can't have a conversation without men coming on to me. I have no privacy. I get hassled on the street. They start pressuring me from the beginning. Half the time, it never occurs to them to start with a conversation. Smart guys like you. You've had three long-term relationships, and you're only twenty-three. I haven't had one. The good guys, the smart guys are scared to death of me. I'm surrounded by male bimbos who think a preposition is when you go to school away from home. I have no woman friends except you. I don't even want to talk about this!

BETHANY: I knew you'd say something like this. See, you're "in the club" so you can say this. It's the way beauty functions as an elite. You're trying to keep it all for yourself.

CARLA: I'm trying to tell you it's no picnic.

BETHANY: But it's what everybody wants. It's the nasty secret at large in the world. It's the unspoken tidal desire in every room and on every street. It's the unspoken, the soundless whisper . . . millions upon millions of people longing hopelessly and forever to stop being whatever they are and be beautiful, but the difference between those ardent multitudes and me is that I have a goddamn genie and one more wish!

CARLA: Well, it's not what I want. This is me, Carla. I have never read a whole book. Page 6, I can't remember page 4. The last thing I read was "The Complete Idiot's Guide to WordPerfect". I leave dinner parties right after the dessert because I'm out of conversation. You know the dumb blond joke about the application where it says, "Sign here," she put Sagittarius? I've done that. Only beautiful guys approach me, and that's because they want to borrow my eye shadow. I barely exist outside a mirror! You don't want to *be me*.

BETHANY: None of you tell the truth. That's why you have no friends. We can all see you're just trying to make us feel better because we aren't in your league. This only proves to me it should be my third wish. Money can only buy things. Beauty makes you the center of the universe.

(Bethany picks up the lamp.)

CARLA: Don't do it. Bethany, don't wish it! I am telling you you'll regret it. *(Bethany lifts the lid. There is a tremendous crash, and the lights go out. Then they flicker and come back up, revealing Bethany and Carla on the floor where they have been thrown by the explosion. We don't realize it at first, but they have exchanged places.)*

CARLA/BETHANY: Oh God.

BETHANY/CARLA: Oh God.

CARLA/BETHANY: Am I bleeding? Am I dying?

BETHANY/CARLA: I'm so dizzy. You're not bleeding.

CARLA/BETHANY: Neither are you.

BETHANY/CARLA: I feel so weird.

CARLA/BETHANY: Me too. I feel . . . *(Looking at her hands.)* Oh, my God, I'm wearing your jewelry. I'm wearing your nail polish.

BETHANY/CARLA: I know I'm over here, but I can see myself over there.

CARLA/BETHANY: I'm wearing your dress. I have your legs!!

BETHANY/CARLA: These aren't my shoes. I can't meet Ralph Lauren wearing these shoes!

CARLA/BETHANY: I wanted to be beautiful, but I didn't want to be you.

BETHANY/CARLA: Thanks a lot!!

CARLA/BETHANY: I've got to go. I want to pick someone out and get laid.

BETHANY/CARLA: You can't just walk out of here in my body!

CARLA/BETHANY: Wait a minute. Wait a minute. What's eleven eighteenths of 1,726

BETHANY/CARLA: Why?

CARLA/BETHANY: I'm a public accountant. I want to know if you have my brain.

BETHANY/CARLA: One hundred thirty-two and a half.

CARLA/BETHANY: You have my brain.

BETHANY/CARLA: What shade of Rubenstein lipstick does Cindy Crawford wear with teal blue?

CARLA/BETHANY: Raging Storm.

BETHANY/CARLA: You have my brain. You poor bastard.

CARLA/BETHANY: I don't care. Don't you see?

BETHANY/CARLA: See what?

CARLA/BETHANY: We both have the one thing, the one and only thing everybody wants.

BETHANY/CARLA: What is that?

CARLA/BETHANY: It's better than beauty for me; it's better than brains for you.

BETHANY/CARLA: What? What?!

CARLA/BETHANY: Different problems.

(Blackout.)

FOCUSED FREE WRITES

1. What is this play about? What is its theme or message?
2. Describe the differences between the characters.
3. How would you stage this production? Which actresses would you cast in these roles? What would the setting look like? What "special effects" would you use?
4. What is the difference between reading a play and reading fiction? What is involved in reading a play carefully?

LITERARY Contexts

Making Meaning of Drama

In a play, the text is created to be performed; thus, along with the other elements we've discussed, such as **plot, character, narration, setting, symbol,** and **theme,** other elements to be considered are specific to this genre.

Dialog: The narration in a play is in the form of **dialog** in which the language, voice, and tone of the characters (and, when performed, the actors) create the action. Dialog involves two or more speakers, while a **monolog** refers to the speech of one. A soliloquy is a monolog that is spoken by a character as if alone, thereby expressing his or her state of mind. An aside is a much briefer comment made by a character directly to the audience.

(continued)

(continued)

Identify any important speeches in the play. Why is this speech significant to plot, character, or theme?

Staging: Another literary element important in plays is the aspect of the setting known as **staging,** to which the set, light, sound, backdrop, costumes, and scenery, as well as the movements and gestures of the actors, all contribute.

Identify significant elements of the staging of Beauty.

The **stage directions,** sometimes stated by the playwright in the script of the play, can inform how the director stages the play, and in many cases, the stage directions can be found embedded in the dialog of the text itself. This is true of Shakespeare's plays; we must infer many of the stage directions from the dialog.

Which stage directions are of note in the play?

These questions are useful when reading any play, from the short, comic *Beauty* to longer and more serious works, and these elements will be explored in depth in the chapters that follow.

LITERARY Contexts

Making Meaning of Poetry

Poetry may seem difficult, but if you start reading it just as you would a story or play, you should be able to find your way. Begin by answering some of the questions below. You can apply them to the poems that follow and consider them whenever you approach poetry.

■ Address **plot:** What is happening?

Can you paraphrase the action of the poem?

■ Determine the **narrator** and **characters** of the poem: Who is speaking to whom?

Who is the speaker? Do other characters appear in the poems?

■ Get a sense of the **tone** or the speaker's attitude toward the topic. Try to read for **irony,** an implied meaning that is distinct from what is actually stated.

How does the narrator feel about the topic? What is the general feeling or atmosphere of the poem? Is the poem ironic?

■ Establish where and when the poem is set. Describe the **setting.**

Is there an occasion for the poem? What is the setting?

- Consider the author's **diction**, or word choice.

Which words stand out as used in a distinctive way? Which words are emphasized or repeated? Which words are new to you, and which do you need to look up?

- Look for **figures of speech**, expressions or comparisons that do not rely on literal or denotative meanings, but rather on suggestive or connotative meanings. A few kinds of figurative language are **similes** (comparisons using *like* or *as*), **metaphors** (comparisons that do not use *like* or *as*), and **personification** (endowing non-human things, animals, or abstractions with human characteristics).

What figures of speech are present in the poem?

- Look for any **imagery**, words or series of words that refer to sensory experience. Try to get a feel for what **images** these words create in your head.

Which images are significant? What senses are evoked?

- Identify any **symbols**—persons, places, or things—that suggest meaning beyond the literal sense.

What symbols do you see?

- Listen to the **sound** of the poem. Listen for repetitions of sounds such as **rhyme** (two or more words containing an identical or similar sound) or **alliteration** (repetition of consonant sounds).

What is distinctive about the way the poem sounds?

- The pattern of stresses and pauses in a poem is the **rhythm**, and any fixed or recurring rhythm is the **meter**. Look at the consistency of each of the lines and which words are stressed. Which words do you emphasize when you read the poem aloud, and which words do you skim over quickly?

How does the poem feel when you read it? What is the rhythm like? Is there a particular meter? Is there a particular line, word, or moment that is emphasized?

- Look at the **syntax** of the poem.

Is each line the same length? When and why do lines break? How does the poem look?

Understanding these elements can help you figure out the meaning of the poem or its theme. Your goal is to determine why the action, conversation, or situation is happening or what the words mean. Summarize the poem's **theme**.

What is the theme or central idea of the poem? Can you restate it in a single sentence?

POEMS

These questions can be useful when reading any poem and these elements will be explored in depth in the chapters that follow. Try them out as you examine the poems in this book.

COMPARING THEMES

In order to highlight a particular theme or stylistic element, it can be useful to compare two distinctly different poems. In the pairings that follow, poems by different authors writing from distinct perspectives are set side by side to allow us to compare and contrast them. The poems also allow us to practice the skill we will be developing more fully in Chapter 6, "Families and Their Characters: Comparing Works of Literature."

> **PRE-READING**   Have your words ever been misinterpreted? Can indirect language like poetry ever be necessary or useful in conveying meaning? When? How?

Sylvia Plath (1932–1963).   *The daughter of German immigrants who were both academics, Plath was traumatized at age eight by the death of her father. The young poet achieved early success in the publishing world and at Smith and Cambridge, where she met and married poet Ted Hughes in 1956. Later, estranged from her husband, Plath committed suicide in London in 1963, leaving two children and a manuscript of highly acclaimed poetry.*

Sylvia Plath

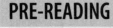 **METAPHORS**   [1959]

I'm a riddle in nine syllables,
An elephant, a ponderous house,
A melon strolling on two tendrils.
O red fruit, ivory, fine timbers!
This loaf's big with its yeasty rising.
Money's new-minted in this fat purse.
I'm a means, a stage, a cow in calf.
I've eaten a bag of green apples,
Boarded the train there's no getting off.

Billy Collins (1941–).   *Born in New York City, Collins earned his PhD in Romantic poetry from the University of California at Riverside in 1971. After receiving numerous prestigious fellowships and awards, Collins was appointed Poet*

Laureate of the United States in 2001. He currently teaches and writes in New York.

Billy Collins

INTRODUCTION TO POETRY [1988]

I ask them to take a poem
and hold it up to the light
like a color slide

or press an ear against its hive.

5 I say drop a mouse into a poem
and watch him probe his way out,

or walk inside the poem's room
and feel the walls for a light switch.

I want them to waterski
10 across the surface of a poem
waving at the author's name on the shore.

But all they want to do
is tie the poem to a chair with rope
and torture a confession out of it.

15 They begin beating it with a hose
to find out what it really means.

FOCUSED FREE WRITES

1. What is Plath's poem trying to say? What about Collins's poem? How do these poems speak to each other? How are they different approaches to similar ideas? How are they at odds?
2. Do these poems have plots, settings, or characters?
3. What images or symbols stand out?
4. Do these poets use rhyme or meter? What makes them poems?
5. Examine the words themselves. Which ones are distinctive? What figurative language is used? Do you see any metaphors or similes?
6. How do these poets use the idea of metaphor? How does the idea of metaphor relate to the general function of poetry? How does the idea of metaphor illustrate a general function of language?
7. How do these poems contribute to or address the difficulty of understanding poetry?
8. What other contexts are necessary to understand these poems?

Assignments: Reading to Write

The following prompts will give you an opportunity to practice close reading and to develop your writing process. They will also give you a chance to practice preliminary types of writing that will be useful in your formal writing in subsequent chapters. These forms of writing involve skills you will need later; they will be components of your formal projects that will interpret, analyze, argue, compare/contrast, and use critical perspectives.

- A **reaction** is simply a response to a text. Readers often first respond to a reading experience with an emotional reaction. They may respond favorably, or not; they may think a text is successful, or not. They might have been bored, or thrilled. While a reaction should not be the topic of a formal paper, your reactions might well influence which texts you choose to examine and which ones you don't.

- In a **summary**, a reader covers the main points succinctly. Often, in the course of supporting a formal interpretation, analysis, or argument, the writer needs to summarize an action or character in the story, poem, or play. While your project should not consist only of summary, it alone may provide useful evidence. For example, you might summarize the differences between the characters in Jane Martin's "Beauty."

- In an **explication**, a reader gives a detailed explanation of a part of a play, poem, or short story. Explications can offer evidence in an interpretation, analysis, or argument. For example, in order to argue that Plath's poem "Metaphors" is about pregnancy, the reader might need to explicate, or carefully explain, each line of the poem.

- When **evaluating**, readers determine the significance, worth, or condition of an aspect of a literary text, usually through careful appraisal and study. For example, in constructing an analysis of Collins's "Introduction to Poetry," a reader might evaluate the use of the metaphors listed in the poem.

- One of the most exciting aspects of reading literature is the potential for **making connections**. In making connections, readers find common ground between ideas, experiences, or people. You might connect some event in a story to an event you experienced. Or you might notice that a character in one play is like a character in another play, or story, or poem. While this book offers sections on "Comparing Themes" to help you make connections between poems, and Part III even suggests other comparisons, you are strongly encouraged to do your own aesthetic reading and discover—or create—your own connections.

Begin your writing process by going back to your reading notes and Focused Free Writes. Identify a text that interested you—one that engaged you as you read, one that stimulated a lot of writing, or one that provoked a good class discussion. Then choose one of the following writing prompts and respond to it.

1. **React to a text.** What surprised you, intrigued you, or confused you in this text? How did you come to make meaning of it? Use examples from your reading to demonstrate your thinking and reading process.
2. **Summarize and explicate a text.** Demonstrate how the text goes about making its case or expressing its main idea. Show us the work that it does. Give a detailed explanation of what happens.
3. **Evaluate a text.** Discuss why you liked or disliked a particular piece of literature. What about it made it successful or unsuccessful, in your estimation? Find moments in the text that best illustrate your opinions.
4. **Make a personal connection to a piece of literature.** What was your experience with a similar topic or character? What is the piece of literature saying about this topic or character? How does the literature say it?

STUDENT WRITER In Ashley's Words...

I tackled Question #4. When reading Chopin's "Story of an Hour," I identified with Louise Mallard's need for personal freedom and it reminded me of some ideas I had learned about the Victorian era in a few of my other classes. Although there are undeniable differences between Mrs. Mallard's Victorian world and the era I live in, I share Mrs. Mallard's need to have an identity I have created, rather than one that is based on stereotypical gender roles or socially accepted actions. I think Chopin emphasizes that Mrs. Mallard is first and foremost looking for the ability to live as she pleases and be an individual— she wants freedom that is primarily personal, not political. Even though society has evolved since the era from Chopin's story, readers can still connect with the desire for individuality.

Sample Student Paper

Ashley Walden's biography may be found on page 567.

Ashley Walden

Dr. Howells

English 102

12 September 2009

Breaking Boundaries in Chopin's

"The Story of an Hour"

As I child, I rebelled against my parents. As a high school student, I wanted to be free of the cliques and silly social drama of my surroundings. Now, as a college student, I find myself challenging fashion convention and struggling against current political figures. Everyone craves some form of freedom. Whether one desires to break away from large social restraints or smaller local issues, freedom is an undeniable part of past and present struggles. Often personal freedom struggles are not isolated cases, but involve larger global issues. Kate Chopin's "The Story of an Hour" illustrates both Louise Mallard's struggle to gain freedom from the duties of her marriage and the restraints which society put on women. Chopin uses important yet subtle symbols and other elements to depict this struggle for freedom. Chopin's "The Story of an Hour" illustrates the struggle for freedom which is both a personal struggle for Mrs. Mallard and a larger universal struggle for society.

Mrs. Mallard's feelings of repression drive her inner fight for personal freedom. As Chopin reveals the death of Mrs. Mallard's husband, she also exposes Mrs. Mallard's feelings of repression. These feelings become the basis of the short story. Chopin points out suppression using both corporal and emotional characteristics. As Mrs. Mallard retreats to her room alone, Chopin writes that she displays "a physical exhaustion that haunted her body and seemed to reach into her soul" (31). While her sudden wave of grief undoubtedly contributes to the exhaustion, the fatigue is akin to the repression which the duties of Victorian-era marriage and domesticity produced. Although Louise's reactions of grief at the initial news clearly indicates that she does care for her husband and thereby honors the duties society demands from her, it's just as clear that she feels the oppression of her marriage. Chopin subtly reveals this, describing Louise Mallard as "young, with a fair, calm face, whose lines bespoke repression and even a certain strength" (31). This paints a picture of a woman whose years of submission to her husband and her social sphere are manifested in both her physical body and her soul. Chopin furthers acknowledges this notion of a physical and mental burden as she notes Mrs. Mallard's heart condition: "Mrs. Mallard was afflicted with a heart trouble" (30). Although Mrs. Mallard lives in a presumably safe, protected environment with all the necessities that make life comfortable, she wants the ability to live life as she wishes and experience things outside the confines of the home. This idea is the essence of the personal struggle, a battle where even those in the best of environments desire to step outside boundaries, break free from what they know, and taste new ideas.

Chopin relays these desires for freedom from the suffocating world in which Mrs. Mallard endures through subtle yet powerful, vital symbols. After learning of her husband's alleged death, Louise Mallard seeks solace in her room. Chopin describes this key setting: "[t]here stood, facing the open window, a comfortable, roomy armchair" (31). The setting is the epitome of the freedom which Mrs. Mallard searches for. The open window is her gate to the outside world, a place that offers her freedom from the duties of her marriage. The expansive, comfortable chair contrasts with Mrs. Mallard's restricted, rigid world to offer her a new unrestricted place. The view outside the confines of Mrs. Mallard's room also contains symbols of freedom. Chopin describes this scene: "[s]he could see in the open square [window] before her house the tops of trees that were all aquiver with new spring life. The delicious breath of rain was in the air...The notes of a distant song which someone was singing reached her faintly..." (31). As Mrs. Mallard looks upon this scene, she breathes in a new life of independence, not unlike the newness of the spring scene. The incoming rain shower also reinforces this idea. As the rain washes away the remnants of past days, freedom sweeps away the boundaries that bind Mrs. Mallard. Similarly, the songbird that calls from the outside world beckons Mrs. Mallard to experience her new freedom. Such personal freedom allows those who posses it to fly above their restraints. Chopin's symbols reinforce the struggle for freedom.

Chopin also uses elements of contrast to emphasize Mrs. Mallard's oppression. The two contrasting surroundings around her create a distinct conflict. This provides an ideal foundation upon which to build the clashing worlds that those who struggle for freedom inhabit. Chopin notes that although Mrs. Mallard's face is young and fair, it contains lines that reveal repression. These contrasting images offer physical evidence of her two worlds, with lines of struggle delineating the smooth skin that society expected of Victorians wives. Mrs. Mallard lives torn between the world she wants and the world she is in, a crucial part of the struggle. Chopin contrasts grief and joy to further enhance this duality:

> She knew that she would weep again when she saw the kind, tender hands folded in death; the face that has never looked save with love upon her, fixed gray and dead. But she saw beyond that bitter moment a

long procession of years to come that would belong
to her absolutely. And she opened and spread her
arms out to them in welcome. (31)

Although Louise knows that she will grieve again over her
husband, she also feels the lightness of a life without the burden
of duty. Chopin furthers this idea with Mrs. Mallard's reflection,
explaining "[s]he breathed a quick prayer that life might be long. It
was only yesterday she had thought with a shudder that life might
be long" (32). These radically different wishes illustrate the transition between the suppression of past and the promise of the future.
The world which freedom promises is a drastic change from the
current environs, regardless of what one seeks freedom for or from.
Thus, coexisting contrasts in appearance, emotion, and thought
provide a vehicle for understanding the freedom fight.

Mrs. Mallard's desire to be free is not an isolated personal
want. Chopin connects her character's struggle to the universal
struggle of Victorian women. Mrs. Mallard's marriage is typical of
how society expected women to live confined to their own sphere
inside the home. Chopin makes reference to these separate spheres
as she notes the peddler outside Louise Mallard's bedroom window.
Mrs. Mallard views the peddler's world, a place foreign to her, from
the confines of her own inner circle. Women, as the "angels of the
house," simply could not travel outside their circle. Part of Mrs.
Mallard's struggle is not only to break free from her own marriage,
but to challenge the boundaries that suppressed women of the time
period. Chopin later explains this point as she reflects on Mrs.
Mallard's release from her marriage: "[t]here would be no powerful
will bending her in that blind persistence with which men and
women believe they have a right to impose a private will upon a
fellow-creature" (31–32). Mrs. Mallard's marriage is more than her
personal desire to escape duty, repression, and confinement; it is

symbolic of all women who only desire to shatter the binding ties of social ideals and experience life for themselves.

Through striking contrasts and symbols, Chopin connects the personal struggle of one woman to the universal struggle of all. Chopin's story transcends Mrs. Mallard's personal struggle and raises awareness of the double lives which Victorian-era women led as they maintained a household and marriage, all while yearning to experience the outside world. This struggle, both personal and global, is the core of every fight for freedom.

Work Cited

Chopin, Kate. "Story of an Hour." *Literature: Reading to Write.*
Ed. Elizabeth Howells. New York: Pearson, *2010*. 30–32.
Print.

PART TWO

WRITING IN RESPONSE TO LITERATURE

Each of these five chapters focuses on a particular stylistic element, a corresponding theme, and the appropriate critical thinking act to provide a scaffold that helps develop readers and writers. In Chapter 3, the theme of love is intertwined with study of the literary element symbol and the critical thinking act of interpretation. The chapter examines how the theme of love is talked about through symbol and shows how to interpret symbols and themes through writing. Chapter 4 consists of selections that address style as a theme and uses the interpretive critical thinking act from the previous chapter to analyze style. Chapter 5 brings together works that highlight voice and narration in content and form. This same chapter uses interpretation and analysis to engage in argument. Chapter 6 emphasizes the characters that make up families and encourages the development of comparison skills. Finally, in Chapter 7, all the critical thinking acts developed previously are incorporated to examine themes of oppression in analytical arguments. All selections are organized by genres within individual chapters.

3

LOVE AND SYMBOLISM
Interpreting Themes

Literary Portraits. Much like the poems that open this chapter, this painting (John Singer Sargent's "Madame X") represents a woman as an object of beauty. Are such portraits tributes or celebrations of women? How so? What do they celebrate? What do they leave out? What sorts of portraits of men do we commonly see? How do such representations of the genders differ?

What is love?

The question, "What is love?" helps illustrate the need for literature. Words simply aren't precise enough to capture the emotion. Even in our everyday lives, we often find that the names the rest of the world uses to address our loved ones are inadequate to express our feelings, so we use figurative language to indicate their sweetness or value to us: "honey" or "sugar," "dear" or "precious."

In her poem of the same title, Emily Dickinson writes "tell all the truth but tell it slant." This first line and title has been used to describe the goal of storytelling or literature. In telling it "slant," writers craft new ways to use the power of language to tell certain "truths." For example, often in movies it is the dialog that says it "slant" that most appeals to us. We cling to the romance of "you had me at hello" more than any explicit love scene. We are more intrigued by the pithy "Reader, I married him" than by any romance novel. The unspoken or the restrained often is the most stimulating. Sometimes the best way of saying "I love you" proves to be not saying it at all.

Symbols work in the same way. **Symbols** are concrete objects that represent abstract ideas. Often, good literature touches us by leaving clichés unsaid and focusing instead on the power of specific symbols. Symbols can be shared within a particular culture: flags for patriotism, a baby for innocence, crosses for Christianity, or water for purity or baptism. Other times, symbols are based on the particular development within a story, poem, or play. For instance, the toys in Bambara's story "The Lesson" in Chapter 4 reflect the wealthy and the inequity of the world. In Chapter 7, the yellow wallpaper in Gilman's short story comes to represent the main character Jane's imprisonment by societal expectations.

Imagery is another tool writers use to make other abstractions such as love more concrete. Imagery refers to sensory experience: what we see, hear, smell, feel, and taste. Imagery can make a scene come to life. Li Ho's poem "A Beautiful Girl Combs Her Hair" early in this chapter is particularly rich in imagery, with references to the fragrance of the girl's hair, the cool silk of the curtains, and the sounds outside her window.

Sometimes imagery becomes a motif when it recurs in a story. **Motifs** are images, words, or ideas that are repeated to emphasize particular themes. In fact, any recurring element that has symbolic significance can be considered a motif. For example, in "Shiloh," reprinted toward the end of the chapter, the image of the log cabin may become a motif to be reexamined by story's end.

Symbols, imagery, and motifs, then, can help writers "tell it slant"—talk about love while not talking about it. Because of its potential to make readers feel strong emotion and its elusive quality in telling it "slant," literature must be interpreted to determine its meaning.

PRE-READING	Do you remember a particular attempt to capture and express your emotions, specifically love, in writing to a family member or to a significant other? What challenges did you face?

POEMS

The following four poems can be read together as examples of writers trying to use poetry to capture passion, or literature to transcend language.

Li Ho

A BEAUTIFUL GIRL COMBS HER HAIR [date unknown]

Translated by David Young

Awake at dawn
she's dreaming
by cool silk curtains

fragrance of spilling hair
5   half sandalwood, half aloes

windlass creaking at the well
singing jade

the lotus blossom wakes, refreshed

her mirror
10   two phoenixes
a pool of autumn light

standing on the ivory bed
loosening her hair
watching the mirror

15   one long coil, aromatic silk
a cloud down to the floor

drop the jade comb—no sound

delicate fingers
pushing the coils into place
20   color of raven feathers

shining blue-black stuff
the jeweled comb will hardly hold it

spring wind makes me restless
her slovenly beauty upsets me

25   eighteen and her hair's so thick
she wears herself out fixing it!

she's finished now
the whole arrangement in place

in a cloud-patterned skirt
30 she walks with even steps
a wild goose on the sand

turns away without a word
where is she off to?

down the steps to break a spray of
35   cherry blossoms

FOCUSED FREE WRITES

1. Good poetry should not only tell us, but show us. The poem's title tells us that the subject of the poem is beautiful. What images are used to show us how she is beautiful?
2. What does the poem tell us about the relationship between the speaker and the object of affection?

Sir Thomas Wyatt

I FIND NO PEACE, AND ALL MY WAR IS DONE

(translated Sonnet 134 by Francesco Petrarch)

I find no peace, and all my war is done,
I fear and hope, I burn and freeze like ice,
I fly above the wind, yet can I not arise,
And nought I have, and all the world I season.
5   That looseth nor locketh, holdeth me in prison,
And holdeth me not, yet can I 'scape nowise,
Nor letteth me live, nor die at my device,
And yet of death it giveth me occasion.
Without eyen I see, and without tongue I plain,
10   I desire to perish, and yet I ask health,
I love another, and thus I hate myself,
I feed me in sorrow, and laugh in all my pain,
Likewise displeaseth me both death and life:
And my delight is causer of this strife.

FOCUSED FREE WRITES

1. This sonnet was written to Petrarch's "Laura," the woman he loved hopelessly from afar. However, the poem seems full of contradictions. Identify those contradictions.
2. What does the use of such paradoxical terms mean? Why are they used here?

UPON JULIA'S CLOTHES [1648]

Whenas in silks my Julia goes,
Then, then (methinks) how sweetly flows
That liquefaction of her clothes.

Next, when I cast mine eyes and see
5   That brave[1] vibration, each way free
O, how that glittering taketh me.

---
[1] **brave:** splendid.

FOCUSED FREE WRITES

1. As you read this poem, what symbols or imagery did you notice?
2. How is love expressed specifically rather than generally in this poem?

THE INDIAN GIRL'S SONG [1822]

I arise from dreams of thee
In the first sleep of night—
The winds are breathing low
And the stars are burning bright.
5   I arise from dreams of thee—
And a spirit in my feet
Has borne me—Who knows how?
To thy chamber window, sweet!—

The wandering airs they faint
10 On the dark silent stream—
The champak[1] odours fail
Like sweet thoughts in a dream;
The nightingale's complaint—
It dies upon her heart—
15 As I must die on thine
O beloved as thou art!

O lift me from the grass!
I die, I faint, I fail!
Let thy love in kisses rain
20 On my lips and eyelids pale.

---
[1] **champak**: a southern Asian tree similar to a magnolia with fragrant blossoms.

My cheek is cold and white, alas!
My heart beats loud and fast.
Oh press it close to thine again
Where it will break at last.

FOCUSED FREE WRITES

1. Does this poem qualify as good love poetry? If so, how?
2. What emotions are used to describe love?

The Act of Interpretation

An interpretation is an attempt to explain the meaning or theme of a work. When we interpret a symbol in a piece of literature, we determine the meaning of a symbol. And when we interpret a poem, short story, or play, we determine the meaning of the work as a whole. For example, we might interpret the preceding poems included above as being about the nature of one person's love for or infatuation with another. However, we might interpret Li Ho's poem to be about the power of beauty more generally or about beauty as inspiration for poetry. Thus, the poem might have multiple interpretations. The reader will determine the meaning of the poem; the reader makes meaning of the work. Much like an interpreter might translate a foreign language to an audience, the interpreter of a poem translates the text and creates its meaning. When interpreting a piece of literature, we ask *what* it means.

It may seem natural to react first to a text in terms of pleasure or displeasure: "I liked this poem," "I hated that story," or "This play was boring." However, none of these are interpretative statements. They are evaluative. While **evaluation** may be a natural reaction, critical thinking demands deeper understanding. We must look beyond a general reaction to understand the purpose of a text and how it works to connect with an audience more generally. For example, while you might not like a particular food, piece of clothing, or movie, it might appeal to others. The same goes for literature. Your responsibility as a reader extends further than determining whether you like it; rather, you should determine what it means and how it means. A personal opinion then should give way to interpretation.

Another natural inclination may be to describe what happened in a poem, short story, or play. This inclination is not interpretation, but **summary**. Telling what happened is not the same as interpreting the meaning of these events. As the writing task in Chapter 1 illustrated, summary is helpful when writing about plot. Interpretation is necessary for understanding theme—our current task.

Many times, making meaning is one of the first steps we take when approaching a piece of literature. We read what the text says and then try to determine what it means. When reading literature, this may mean determining a theme. Chapter 1 introduced the idea of **theme** as central meaning or dominant idea of a literary work. This meaning unifies the work and gives it purpose.

All the other elements of the work—its characters and how they develop, the events that occur, the situation that characters find themselves in—could be argued to be organized around a work's theme and support this central idea. For example, I might interpret Herrick's poem "Upon Julia's Clothes" to be about the theme of infatuation and how it can possess someone. Interpretation can be understood as the big-picture approach to making meaning. It focuses on the general idea of the text.

How would you make meaning of any of the poems in this section above? How would you interpret each of them?

Accounting for Key Symbols and Other Elements

In order to be plausible, an interpretation must account for key elements of the work. In other words, "anything goes" isn't good enough. A piece of literature does not mean *whatever* the reader wants it to mean. An interpretation is bound by the details provided by the text. So, when interpreting a piece of literature, the elements of the text will determine *how* it means. The act of **analysis** in the next chapter will narrow the focus of interpretation from general meaning-making to the breaking down of details that add up to an interpretation.

In other words, an interpretation needs to be consistent with the work's details. While a text may, in fact, mean something beyond what the author intended it is impossible to interpret the meaning of a text to be about something if the text itself does not suggest that something as a possibility. There must be something in the work to direct us to a possible interpretation. For example, I cannot interpret "Upon Julia's Clothes" to be about the plague, baseball, or even how sad the speaker would be if he married Julia and got divorced. The words and images and ideas in the poem do not provide support for these interpretations.

While a reader makes meaning, an interpretation then is also determined by the following two guidelines:

- An interpretation is consistent with the elements in the text: characters, description, word choice, symbols, imagery, dialogue, etc.
- An interpretation can't be obviously contradicted by evidence in the text.

What are some elements that support your interpretations of the poems in the previous section?

For the sake of illustration, what are some interpretations that cannot be supported by the texts?

Taking Contexts into Account

To be relevant, an interpretation must take into account the context of the work. For example, Herrick's poem "Upon Julia's Clothes" cannot be about the speaker watching Julia model on Lifetime's *Project Runway*. The poem was written in the seventeenth century and this context would make such a reading anachronistic.

The contexts of any given work include those you will encounter throughout this textbook:

Biographical context—A reader might consider the background of the author when engaging in interpretation. For example, readers of Li Ho's poetry might use the facts of the author's early death and the theme of transience evident throughout his poetry as elements necessary in an interpretation.

- **Historical context**—A reader might consider the time period and location of a text when determining a work's meaning. For example, some readers might examine Robert Herrick's work in the style of the Cavalier poets, that is, poets who supported King Charles I during the English Civil War.

- **Literary context**—A reader might consider the genre of a text, its literary allusions, or its relationship to similar works. In comparing works, we establish a literary context. For example, many readers of the poet Percy Shelley might consider his poetry in light of the Romantic Era and his fellow poets, such as Wordsworth and Coleridge, who were also at work writing dramatic lyrics.

- **Critical context**—A reader might consider literary criticism or engage in research to make meaning of a text. For example, a reader could take a formalist or deconstructive approach to examine the use of metaphor or metonymy in Petrarch's "Sonnet 134." Or a reader might consult Sandra Bermann's 1988 book on the sonnet.

While an interpretation is grounded in the text itself, these extra-textual factors may contribute to making meaning. These elements may be detailed, like those discussed in the four poem examples. However, such contexts may also be more general; for example, readers who know generally about Hemingway's life and that he killed himself might identify evidence of depression in his works. Or readers of Anne Bradstreet's poetry might search out Puritan themes in light of the time period and setting of her life.

What are some contexts you might consider in interpreting the poems earlier in this chapter?

This chapter offers examples of each of the contexts listed. Throughout Part II of this textbook, you will find multiple context boxes in each chapter that offer suggestions for contexts to consider in interpretations. However, it is important to remember that these are not the only contexts necessary or available for interpreting texts. As a reader, you should be actively engaged in making meaning and should use any available resources—textual and contextual—to construct informed, unique, viable interpretations.

POEMS

Each of the following poems address various perspectives on the theme of love. Some are conventional representations of love: the older poems are more traditional and might be considered along with "classic love poetry" like the sonnets of William Shakespeare or Elizabeth Barrett Browning. However, the poems span three centuries and move from examples of early poetry to examples of very contemporary poetry that challenge classic or clichéd descriptions of this universal theme.

People often complain about poetry. Why is poetry hard to read? What strategies do you use to make reading poetry easier?

William Shakespeare (1564–1616). *For someone who represents one of the major forces of Western culture, surprisingly little is known of William Shakespeare. We know he was born around April 23, 1564 at Stratford-on-Avon in England. We know he received limited education before making his way in the theater. When he was eighteen, he married Anne Hathaway, and they produced three children. After traveling to London around 1585, Shakespeare established himself in the theater and as a poet. He produced as many as thirty-five plays and 154 sonnets in twenty-five years before dying at the age of fifty-two on or around his birthdate. Famously, he left his wife his second-best bed.*

William Shakespeare

SHALL I COMPARE THEE TO A SUMMER'S DAY? (Sonnet No. 18) [1609]

Shall I compare thee to a summer's day?
Thou art more lovely and more temperate:
Rough winds do shake the darling buds of May,
And summer's lease hath all too short a date:
5   Sometime too hot the eye of heaven shines,
And often is his gold complexion dimm'd;
And every fair from fair sometime declines,
By chance or nature's changing course untrimm'd;
But thy eternal summer shall not fade
10 Nor lose possession of that fair thou ow'st;
Nor shall Death brag thou wand'rest in his shade,
When in eternal lines to time thou grow'st;
So long as men can breathe or eyes can see,
So long lives this and this gives life to thee.

William Shakespeare

MY MISTRESS' EYES ARE NOTHING LIKE THE SUN (Sonnet No. 130) [1609]

My mistress' eyes are nothing like the sun;
Coral is far more red than her lips' red;
If snow be white, why then her breasts are dun;
If hairs be wires, black wires grow on her head.
5   I have seen roses damasked, red and white,
But no such roses see I in her cheeks;
And in some perfumes is there more delight
Than in the breath that from my mistress reeks.
I love to hear her speak, yet well I know
10 That music hath a far more pleasing sound;

I grant I never saw a goddess go;
My mistress, when she walks, treads on the ground.
And yet, by heaven, I think my love as rare
As any she belied with false compare.

FOCUSED FREE WRITES

1. Who is speaking about whom? Who are the characters in these poems?
2. What are they speaking about, and why? What is the plot?
3. And the themes of the poems? What are they trying to say? How are these love poems? How are they not?
4. What images or symbols stand out?

PRE-READING
If you were to make a pro and con list, what are some of the wonders of love? What are some of the problems?

Edna St. Vincent Millay (1892–1950). *After surviving a challenging childhood in Rockland, Maine, Millay's early interest in literature won her a scholarship to Vassar where she made a name for herself both socially and literarily. Her love of poetry and charisma inspired many admirers of both sexes and soon Millay was reading to full houses across the country. Millay became a kind of icon of the Jazz Age and was the first woman to win the Pulitzer Prize for poetry.*

Edna St. Vincent Millay

LOVE IS NOT ALL
[1931]

Love is not all: it is not meat nor drink
Nor slumber nor a roof against the rain;
Nor yet a floating spar to men that sink
And rise and sink and rise and sink again;
5 Love cannot fill the thickened lung with breath,
Nor clean the blood, nor set the fractured bone;
Yet many a man is making friends with death
Even as I speak, for lack of love alone.
It well may be that in a difficult hour,
10 Pinned down by pain and moaning for release,
Or nagged by want past resolution's power,
I might be driven to sell your love for peace,
Or trade the memory of this night for food.
It well may be. I do not think I would

Wislawa Szymborska (1923–). *Born in Poland, Wislawa Szymborska has lived and worked in Krakow for most of her life. After studying literature at Jagiellonian University, she began working as a poetry editor for a literary* journal while publishing her own poetry. Poems from her sixteen collections have been widely translated and much acclaimed, earning her the 1996 Nobel Prize for literature.

Wislawa Szymborska

TRUE LOVE

[1972]

True love. Is it normal
is it serious, is it practical?
What does the world get from two people
who exist in a world of their own?

5   Placed on the same pedestal for no good reason,
drawn randomly from millions, but convinced
it had to happen this way—in reward for what?
     For nothing.
The light descends from nowhere.
10 Why on these two and not on others?
Doesn't this outrage justice? Yes it does.
Doesn't it disrupt our painstakingly erected principles,
and cast the moral from the peak? Yes on both accounts.

Look at the happy couple.
15 Couldn't they at least try to hide it,
fake a little depression for their friends' sake?
Listen to them laughing—it's an insult.
The language they use—deceptively clear.
And their little celebrations, rituals,
20 the elaborate mutual routines—
it's obviously a plot behind the human race's back!

It's hard even to guess how far things might go
if people start to follow their example.
What could religion and poetry count on?
25 What would be remembered? What renounced?
Who'd want to stay within bounds?

True love. Is it really necessary?
Tact and common sense tell us to pass over it in silence,
like a scandal in Life's highest circles.
30 Perfectly good children are born without its help.
It couldn't populate the planet in a million years,
it comes along so rarely.

Let the people who never find true love
keep saying that there's no such thing.

35 Their faith will make it easier for them to live and die.

FOCUSED FREE WRITES

1. How would you interpret the meaning of these poems? What elements support this interpretation?
2. Are the poems in favor of love or not? How so?
3. What are the disadvantages of love, according to these poems?
4. What are the advantages of love, according to the logic of the poems? Is love a necessity?
5. How are these love poems similar? How are they different?
6. What symbols, images, or motifs are used? How are they used?
7. What other contexts might be useful in opening up these poems?

PRE-READING

When you talk about love, do you have to talk about sex? What happens when sex enters the equation? Does it help or hinder relationships?

Sharon Olds (1942–).   *Born in San Francisco, Olds was educated at Stanford and Columbia. Known as a confessional poet, her poetry is characterized by emotional directness, tight craftsmanship, and attention to domestic subjects and themes as well as a sense of humor. Much acclaimed and awarded, Olds's poetry has been published in eight volumes, numerous collections, journals, and magazines. From 1998–2000, she was poet laureate of New York state. She currently serves on the faculty of the creative writing program at NYU.*

Sharon Olds

SEX WITHOUT LOVE [1984]

How do they do it, the ones who make love
without love? Beautiful as dancers,
Gliding over each other like ice-skaters
over the ice, fingers hooked
5 inside each other's bodies, faces
red as steak, wine, wet as the
children at birth, whose mothers are going to
give them away. How do they come to the
come to the come to the God come to the
10 still waters, and not love
the one who came there with them, light
rising slowly as steam off their joined
skin? These are the true religious,
the purists, the pros, the ones who will not
15 accept a false Messiah, love the
priest instead of the God. They do not
mistake the lover for their own pleasure,

they are like great runners: they know they are alone
with the road surface, the cold, the wind,
20   the fit of their shoes, their over-all cardio-
vascular health—just factors, like the partner
in the bed, and not the truth, which is the
single body alone in the universe
against its own best time.

Beth Ann Fennelly (1971–).   *Born in New Jersey, Fennelly grew up in Lake Forest, Illinois. After graduating from the University of Notre Dame, she taught English overseas before earning an MFA from the University of Arkansas. She taught at Knox College before joining the faculty at the University of Mississippi. Her three volumes of poetry have been lauded, and Fennelly received a National Endowment of the Arts Award to work on her third book* Tender Hooks, *which takes up new motherhood as one of its themes.*

Beth Ann Fennelly

WHY I CAN'T COOK FOR YOUR SELF-CENTERED ARCHITECT COUSIN

Because to me a dinner table's like a bed—
without love, it's all appetite and stains. Let's buy
take-out for your cousin, or order pizza—his toppings—

but I can't lift a spatula to serve him what I am.
Instead, invite our favorite misfits over: I'll feed
shaggy Otis who, after filet mignon, raised his plate

and sipped merlot sauce with such pleasure
my ego pardoned his manners. Or I'll call Mimi,
the chubby librarian, who paused over tiramisu—

"I haven't felt so satisfied since..." then cried
into its curls of chocolate. Or Randolph might stop by,
who once, celebrating his breakup with the vegetarian,

so packed the purse seine of his wiry body with shrimp
he unbuttoned his jeans and spent the evening
couched, "waiting for the swelling to go down."

Or maybe I'll just cook for us. I'll crush pine nuts
unhinged from the cones' prickly shingles.
I'll whittle the parmesan, and if I grate a knuckle

it's just more of me in my cooking. I'll disrobe
garlic cloves of rosy sheaths, thresh the basil
till moist, and liberate the oil. Then I'll dance

that green joy through the fettuccine, a tumbling,
leggy dish we'll imitate, after dessert.
If my embrace detects the five pounds you win

each year, you will merely seem a generous
portion. And if you bring my hand to your lips
and smell the garlic that lingers, that scents

the sweat you lick from the hollows of my clavicles,
you're tasting the reason that I can't cook
for your cousin—my saucy, my strongly seasoned love.

FOCUSED FREE WRITES

1. What do these poems mean? What are they saying? What elements support this meaning?
2. What do the poets say about the relationship between sex and love? How do they talk about sex?
3. How are these love poems similar? How are they different?
4. Each poet uses distinctive symbols, images, or motifs. What are they, and how are they used?
5. What other contexts would be useful in opening up these poems?

STORIES

The following stories are variations on the theme of love. While the first examines love other than romantic love, the other story offers contemporary perspectives on the theme of romantic love. In each story, certain symbols, images, motifs, or stylistic methods allow the author to talk about love without talking about love.

PRE-READING

Sometimes people come to love passionately a thing or things, rather than another person. Can you think of any examples of such a case?

Guy de Maupassant (1850–1893).   *Henry-Rene-Albert-Guy de Maupassant was born into nobility. After growing up in Normandy, he studied law for a time in Paris before volunteering to serve in the army. While working as a civil servant, he began publishing his own verse, then fiction. In the 1880s, he wrote 300 short stories, six novels, three travel books, and one book of verse. The syphilis he contracted in his 20s led to increasing mental disorders and seemed to inspire a number of horror stories. After attempting suicide, de Maupassant was placed in an asylum and died the following year.*

THE NECKLACE [1885]

She was one of those pretty and charming girls who are sometimes, as if by a mistake of destiny, born in a family of clerks. She had no dowry, no expectations, no means of being known, understood, loved, wedded by any rich and distinguished man; and she let herself be married to a little clerk at the Ministry of Public Instruction.

She dressed plainly because she could not dress well, but she was as unhappy as though she had really fallen from her proper station, since with women there is neither caste nor rank: and beauty, grace, and charm act instead of family and birth. Natural fineness, instinct for what is elegant, suppleness of wit, are the sole hierarchy, and make from women of the people the equals of the very greatest ladies.

She suffered ceaselessly, feeling herself born for all the delicacies and all the luxuries. She suffered from the poverty of her dwelling, from the wretched look of the walls, from the worn-out chairs, from the ugliness of the curtains. All those things, of which another woman of her rank would never even have been conscious, tortured her and made her angry. The sight of the little Breton peasant, who did her humble housework aroused in her regrets which were despairing, and distracted dreams She thought of the silent antechambers hung with Oriental tapestry, lit by tall bronze candelabra, and of the great footmen in knee breeches who sleep in the big armchairs, made drowsy by the heavy warmth of the hot-air stove. She thought of the long *salons*[1] fitted up with ancient silk, of the delicate furniture carrying priceless curiosities, and of the coquettish perfumed boudoirs made for talks at five o'clock with intimate friends, with men famous and sought after, whom all women envy and whose attention they all desire.

When she sat down to dinner, before the round table covered with a tablecloth three days old, opposite her husband, who uncovered the soup tureen and declared with an enchanted air, "Ah, the good *pot-au-feu*![2] I don't know anything better than that," she thought of dainty dinners, of shining silverware, of tapestry which peopled the walls with ancient personages and with strange birds flying in the midst of a fairy forest; and she thought of delicious dishes served on marvelous plates, and of the whispered gallantries which you listen to with a sphinxlike smile, while you are eating the pink flesh of a trout or the wings of a quail.

5 She had no dresses, no jewels, nothing. And she loved nothing but that; she felt made for that. She would so have liked to please, to be envied, to be charming, to be sought after.

She had a friend, a former schoolmate at the convent, who was rich, and whom she did not like to go and see any more, because she suffered so much when she came back.

But one evening, her husband returned home with a triumphant air, and holding a large envelope in his hand.

"There," said he. "Here is something for you."

---

[1] *salons*: drawing-rooms.

[2] *pot-au-feu*: stew.

She tore the paper sharply, and drew out a printed card which bore these words:

10   "The Minister of Public Instruction and Mme. Georges Ramponneau request the honor of M. and Mme. Loisel's company at the palace of the Ministry on Monday evening, January eighteenth."

Instead of being delighted, as her husband hoped, she threw the invitation on the table with disdain, murmuring:

"What do you want me to do with that?"

"But, my dear, I thought you would be glad. You never go out, and this is such a fine opportunity. I had awful trouble to get it. Everyone wants to go; it is very select, and they are not giving many invitations to clerks. The whole official world will be there."

She looked at him with an irritated glance, and said, impatiently:

15   "And what do you want me to put on my back?"

He had not thought of that; he stammered:

"Why, the dress you go to the theater in. It looks very well, to me."

He stopped, distracted, seeing his wife was crying. Two great tears descended slowly from the corners of her eyes toward the corners of her mouth. He stuttered:

"What's the matter? What's the matter?"

20   But, by violent effort, she had conquered her grief, and she replied, with a calm voice, while she wiped her wet cheeks:

"Nothing. Only I have no dress and therefore I can't go to this ball. Give your card to some colleague whose wife is better equipped than I."

He was in despair. He resumed:

"Come, let us see, Mathilde. How much would it cost, a suitable dress, which you could use on other occasions. Something very simple?"

She reflected several seconds, making her calculations and wondering also what sum she could ask without drawing on herself an immediate refusal and a frightened exclamation from the economical clerk.

25   Finally, she replied, hesitatingly:

"I don't know exactly, but I think I could manage it with four hundred francs."

He had grown a little pale, because he was laying aside just that amount to buy a gun and treat himself to a little shooting next summer on the plain on Nanterre, with several friends who went to shoot larks down there, of a Sunday.

But he said:

"All right. I will give you four hundred francs. And try to have a pretty dress."

30   The day of the ball drew near, and Mme. Loisel seemed said, uneasy, anxious. Her dress was ready, however. Her husband said to her one evening:

"What is the matter? Come, you've been so queer these last three days."

And she answered:

"It annoys me not to have a single jewel, not a single stone, nothing to put on. I shall look like distress. I should almost rather not go at all."

He resumed:

35   "You might wear natural flowers. It's very stylish at this time of the year. For ten francs you can get two or three magnificent roses."

She was not convinced.

"No; there's nothing more humiliating than to look poor among other women who are rich."

But her husband cried:

"How stupid you are! Go look up your friend Mme. Forestier, and ask her to lend you some jewels. You're quite thick enough with her to do that."

She uttered a cry of joy:

"It's true. I never thought of it."

The next day she went to her friend and told of her distress.

Mme. Forestier went to a wardrobe with a glass door, took out a large jewel-box, brought it back, opened it, and said to Mme. Loisel:

"Choose, choose, my dear."

She saw first of all some bracelets, then a pearl necklace, then a Venetian cross, gold and precious stones of admirable workmanship. She tried on the ornaments before the glass, hesitated, could not make up her mind to part with them, to give them back. She kept asking:

"Haven't you any more?"

"Why, yes. Look. I don't know what you like."

All of a sudden she discovered, in a black satin box, a superb necklace of diamonds, and her heart began to beat with an immoderate desire. Her hands trembled as she took it. She fastened it around her throat, outside her high-necked dress, and remained lost in ecstasy at the sight of herself.

Then she asked, hesitating, filled with anguish:

"Can you lend me that, only that?"

"Why, yes, certainly."

She sprang upon the neck of her friend, kissed her passionately, then fled with her treasure.

The day of the ball arrived. Mme. Loisel made a great success. She was prettier than them all, elegant, gracious, smiling, and crazy with joy. All the men looked at her, asked her name, endeavored to be introduced. All the attachés of the Cabinet wanted to waltz with her. She was remarked by the minister himself.

She danced with intoxication, with passion, made drunk by pleasure, forgetting all, in the triumph of her beauty, in the glory of her success, in a sort of cloud of happiness composed of all this homage, of all this admiration, of all these awakened desires, and of that sense of complete victory which is so sweet to a women's heart.

She went away about four o'clock in the morning. Her husband had been sleeping since midnight, in a little deserted anteroom, with three other gentlemen whose wives were having a good time. He threw over her shoulders the wraps which he had brought, modest wraps of common life, whose poverty contrasted with the elegance of the ball dress. She felt this, and wanted to escape so as not to be remarked by the other women, who were enveloping themselves in costly furs.

Loisel held her back.

"Wait a bit. You will catch cold outside. I will go and call a cab."

But she did not listen to him, and rapidly descended the stairs. When they were in the street they did not find a carriage; and they began to look for one, shouting after the cabmen whom they saw passing by at a distance.

They went down toward the Seine, in despair, shivering with cold. At last they found on the quay one of those ancient noctambulant coupés which, exactly as if they were ashamed to show their misery during the day, are never seen round Paris until after nightfall.

60 It took them to their door in the Rue des Martyrs, and once more, sadly, they climbed up homeward. All was ended, for her. And as to him, he reflected that he must be at the Ministry at ten o'clock.

She removed the wraps which covered her shoulders, before the glass, so as once more to see herself in all her glory. But suddenly she uttered a cry. She no longer had the necklace around her neck!

Her husband, already half undressed, demanded:

"What is the matter with you?"

She turned madly toward him:

65 "I have—I have—I've lost Mme. Forestier's necklace."

He stood up, distracted.

"What!—how?—impossible!"

And they looked in the folds of her dress, in the folds of her cloak, in her pockets, everywhere. They did not find it.

He asked:

70 "You're sure you had it on when you left the ball?"

"Yes, I felt it in the vestibule of the palace."

"But if you had lost it in the street we should have heard it fall. It must be in the cab."

"Yes. Probably. Did you take his number?"

"No. And you, didn't you notice it?"

75 "No."

They looked, thunderstruck, at one another. At last Loisel put on his clothes.

"I shall go back on foot," said he, "over the whole route which we have taken to see if I can find it."

And he went out. She sat waiting on a chair in her ball dress, without strength to go to bed, overwhelmed, without fire, without a thought.

Her husband came back about seven o'clock. He had found nothing.

80 He went to Police Headquarters, to the newspaper offices, to offer a reward; he went to the cab companies—everywhere, in fact, whither he was urged by the least suspicion of hope.

She waited all day, in the same condition of mad fear before this terrible calamity.

Loisel returned at night with a hollow, pale face; he had discovered nothing.

"You must write to your friend," said he, "that you have broken the clasp of her necklace and that you are having it mended. That will give us time to turn round."

She wrote at his dictation.

85 At the end of a week they had lost all hope.

And Loisel, who had aged five years, declared:

"We must consider how to replace that ornament."

The next day they took the box which had contained it, and they went to the jeweler whose name was found within. He consulted his books.

"It was not I, madame, who sold that necklace; I must simply have furnished the case."

90 Then they went from jeweler to jeweler, searching for a necklace like the other, consulting their memories, sick both of them with chagrin and anguish.

They found, in a shop at the Palais Royal, a string of diamonds which seemed to them exactly like the one they looked for. It was worth forty thousand francs. They could have it for thirty-six.

So they begged the jeweler not to sell it for three days yet. And they made a bargain that he should buy it back for thirty-four thousand francs, in case they found the other one before the end of February.

Loisel possessed eighteen thousand francs which his father had left him. He would borrow the rest.

He did borrow, asking a thousand francs of one, five hundred of another, five louis here, three louis[3] there. He gave notes, took up ruinous obligations, dealt with usurers and all the race of lenders. He compromised all the rest of his life, risked his signature without even knowing if he could meet it; and, frightened by the pains yet to come, by the black misery which was about to fall upon him, by the prospect of all the physical privation and of all the moral tortures which he was to suffer, he went to get the new necklace, putting down upon the merchant's counter thirty-six thousand francs.

95 When Mme. Loisel took back the necklace, Mme. Forestier said to her, with a chilly manner:

"You should have returned it sooner; I might have needed it."

She did not open the case, as her friend had so much feared. If she had detected the substitution, what would she have thought, what would she have said? Would she not have taken Mme. Loisel for a thief?

Mme. Loisel now knew the horrible existence of the needy. She took her part, moreover, all of a sudden, with heroism. That dreadful debt must be paid. She would pay it. They dismissed their servant; they changed their lodgings; they rented a garret under the roof.

She came to know what heavy housework meant and the odious cares of the kitchen. She washed the dishes, using her rosy nails on the greasy pots and pans. She washed the dirty linen, the shirts, and the dishcloths, which she dried upon a line; she carried the slops down to the street every morning, and carried up the water, stopping for breath at every landing. And, dressed like a woman of the people, she went to the fruiterer, the grocer, the butcher, her basket on her arm, bargaining, insulted, defending her miserable money sou by sou.

100 Each month they had to meet some notes, renew others, obtain more time.

Her husband worked in the evening making a fair copy of some tradesman's accounts, and late at night he often copied manuscript for five sous a page.

And this life lasted for ten years.

At the end of ten years, they had paid everything, everything, with the rates of usury, and the accumulations of the compound interest.

Mme. Loisel looked old now. She had become the woman of impoverished households—strong and hard and rough. With frowsy hair, skirts askew, and red hands, she talked loud while washing the floor with great swishes of water.

---

[3] **louis**: a gold coin worth 20 francs.

But sometimes, when her husband was at the office, she sat down near the window, and she thought of that gay evening of long ago, of that ball where she had been so beautiful and so fêted.

105 What would have happened if she had not lost that necklace? Who knows? Who knows? How life is strange and changeful! How little a thing is needed for us to be lost or to be saved!

But one Sunday, having gone to take a walk in the Champs Elysées to refresh herself from the labor of the week, she suddenly perceived a woman who was leading a child. It was Mme. Forestier, still young, still beautiful, still charming.

Mme. Loisel felt moved. Was she going to speak to her? Yes, certainly. And now that she had paid, she was going to tell her all about it. Why not?

She went up.

"Good-day, Jeanne."

110 The other, astonished to be familiarly addressed by this plain goodwife, did not recognize her at all, and stammered:

"But—madam!—I do not know—you must be mistaken."

"No. I am Mathilde Loisel."

Her friend uttered a cry.

"Oh, my poor Mathilde! How you are changed!"

115 "Yes, I have had days hard enough, since I have seen you, days wretched enough—and that because of you!"

"Of me! How so?"

"Do you remember that diamond necklace which you lent me to wear at the ministerial ball?"

"Yes. Well?"

"Well, I lost it."

120 "What do you mean? You brought it back."

"I brought you back another just like it. And for this we have been ten years paying. You can understand that it was not easy for us, who had nothing. At last it is ended, and I am very glad."

Mme. Forestier had stopped.

"You say that you bought a necklace of diamonds to replace mine?"

"Yes. You never noticed it, then! They were very like."

125 And she smiled with a joy which was proud and naïve at once.

Mme. Forestier, strongly moved, took her two hands.

"Oh, my poor Mathilde! Why, my necklace was paste. It was worth at most five hundred francs!"

FOCUSED FREE WRITES

1. How would you interpret the meaning of this story? What is the theme?
2. What does Mathilde come to learn by the end of the story? What has she lost? What has she gained?
3. What is this necklace a symbol of?
4. How is this a story about love?

Bobbie Ann Mason (1940–). *Bobbie Ann Mason was born the first of four children on a dairy farm in Kentucky. After graduating from the University of Kentucky, she moved to New York to write for fan magazines. She then earned a master's degree at SUNY Binghampton and a PhD at the University of Connecticut. Mason, however, maintained both her academic and pop culture interests publishing on both Nabokov and Nancy Drew. While an assistant professor at Mansfield State in Pennsylvania, she began writing short stories and novels characterized by "ordinary" characters and a minimalist style to positive critical responses. She now resides and writes in Kentucky.*

Bobbie Ann Mason
_____

SHILOH

[1982]

Leroy Moffit's wife, Norma Jean, is working on her pectorals. She lifts three-pound dumbbells to warm up, then progresses to a twenty-pound barbell. Standing with her legs apart, she reminds Leroy of Wonder Woman.

"I'd give anything if I could get these muscles to where they're real hard," says Norma Jean. "Feel this arm. It's not as hard as the other one."

"That's 'cause you're right-handed," says Leroy, dodging as she swings the barbell in an arc.

"Do you think so?"

5   "Sure."

Leroy is a truckdriver. He injured his leg in a highway accident four months ago, and his physical therapy which involves weights and a pulley, promoted Norma Jean to try building herself up. Now she is attending a body-building class. Leroy has been collecting temporary disability since his tractor-trailer jackknifed in Missouri, badly twisting his left leg in its socket. He has a steel pin in his hip. He will probably not be able to drive his rig again. It sits in his backyard, like a gigantic bird that has flown home to roost. Leroy has been home in Kentucky for three months, and his leg is almost healed, but the accident frightened him and he does not want to drive any more long hauls. He is not sure what to do next. In the meantime, he makes things from craft kits. He started by building a miniature log cabin from notched Popsicle sticks. He varnished it and placed it on the TV set, where it remains. It reminds him of a rustic Nativity scene. Then he tried string art (sailing ships on black velvet), a macramé owl kit, a snap-together B-17 Flying Fortress, and a lamp made out of a model truck, with a light fixture screwed in the top of the cab. At first the kits were diversions, something to kill time, but now he is thinking about building a full-scale log house from a kit. It would be considerably cheaper than building a regular house, and besides, Leroy has grown to appreciate how things are put together. He has begun to realize that in all the years he was on the road he never took time to examine anything. He was always flying past scenery.

"They won't let you build a log cabin in any of the new subdivisions," Norma Jean tells him.

"They will if I tell them it's for you," he says, teasing her. Ever since they were married, he has promised Norma Jean he would build her a new home one day. They have always rented, and the house they live in is small and nondescript. It does not even feel like a real home, Leroy realizes now.

Norma Jean works at the Rexall drugstore, and she has acquired an amazing amount of information about cosmetics. When she explains to Leroy the three stages of complexion care, involving creams, toners, and moisturizers, he thinks happily of other petroleum products—axle grease, diesel fuel. This is a connection between him and Norma Jean. Since he has been home, he has felt unusually tender about his wife and guilty over his long absences. But he can't tell what she feels about him. Norma Jean has never complained about his traveling; she has never made hurt remarks, like calling his truck a "widow-maker." He is reasonably certain she has been faithful to him, but he wishes she would celebrate his permanent homecoming more happily. Norma Jean is often startled to find Leroy at home, and he thinks she seems a little disappointed about it. Perhaps he reminds her too much of the early days of their marriage, before he went on the road. They had a child who died as an infant, years ago. They never speak about their memories of Randy, which have almost faded, but now that Leroy is home all the time, they sometimes feel awkward around each other, and Leroy wonders if one of them should mention the child. He has the feeling that they are waking up out of a dream together—that they must create a new marriage, start afresh. They are lucky they are still married. Leroy has read that for most people losing a child destroys the marriage—or else he heard this on *Donahue*. He can't always remember where he learns things anymore.

10   At Christmas, Leroy bought an electric organ for Norma Jean. She used to play the piano when she was in high school. "It don't leave you," she told him once. "It's like riding a bicycle."

The new instrument had so many keys and buttons that she was bewildered by it at first. She touched the keys tentatively, pushed some buttons, then pecked out "Chopsticks." It came out in an amplified fox-trot rhythm, with marimba sounds.

"It's an orchestra!" she cried.

The organ had a pecan-look finish and eighteen preset chords, with optional flute, violin, trumpet, clarinet, and banjo accompaniments. Norma Jean mastered the organ almost immediately. At first she played Christmas songs. Then she bought *The Sixties Songbook* and learned every tune in it, adding variations to each with the rows of brightly colored buttons.

"I didn't like these old songs back then," she said. "But I have this crazy feeling I missed something."

15   "You didn't miss a thing," said Leroy.

Leroy likes to lie on the couch and smoke a joint and listen to Norma Jean play "Can't Take My Eyes Off You" and "I'll Be Back." He is back again. After fifteen years on the road, he is finally settling down with the woman he loves. She is still pretty. Her skin is flawless. Her frosted curls resemble pencil trimmings.

Now that Leroy has come home to stay, he notices how much the town has changed. Subdivisions are spreading across western Kentucky like an oil slick. The sign at the edge of town says "Pop: 11,500"—only seven hundred more than it said twenty years before. Leroy can't figure out who is living in all the new houses. The farmers who used to gather around the courthouse square on Saturday afternoons to play checkers and spit tobacco juice have gone. It has been years since Leroy has thought about the farmers, and they have disappeared without his noticing.

Leroy meets a kid named Stevie Hamilton in the parking lot at the new shopping center. While they pretend to be strangers meeting over a stalled car, Stevie tosses an ounce of marijuana under the front seat of Leroy's car. Stevie is wearing orange jogging shoes and a T-shirt that says CHATTAHOOCHEE SUPER-RAT. His father is a prominent doctor who lives in one of the expensive subdivisions in a new white-columned brick house that looks like a funeral parlor. In the phone book under his name there is a separate number, with the listing "Teenagers."

"Where do you get this stuff?" asks Leroy. "From your pappy?"

20 "That's for me to know and you to find out," Stevie says. He is slit-eyed and skinny.

"What else you got?"

"What you interested in?"

"Nothing special. Just wondered."

Leroy used to take speed on the road. Now he has to go slowly. He needs to be mellow. He leans back against the car and says, "I'm aiming to build me a log house, soon as I get time. My wife, though, I don't think she likes the idea."

"Well, let me know when you want me again," Stevie says. He has a cigarette in his cupped palm, as though sheltering it from the wind. He takes a long drag,

25 then stomps it on the asphalt and slouches away.

Stevie's father was two years ahead of Leroy in high school. Leroy is thirty-four. He married Norma Jean when they were both eighteen, and their child Randy was born a few months later, but he died at the age of four months and three days. He would be about Stevie's age now. Norma Jean and Leroy were at the drive-in, watching a double feature (*Dr. Strangelove* and *Lover Come Back*), and the baby was sleeping in the back seat. When the first movie ended, the baby was dead. It was sudden infant death syndrome. Leroy remembers handing Randy to a nurse at the emergency room, as though he were offering her a large doll as a present. A dead baby feels like a sack of flour. "It just happens sometimes," said the doctor, in what Leroy always recalls as a nonchalant tone. Leroy can hardly remember the child anymore, but he still sees vividly a scene from *Dr. Strangelove* in which the President of the United States was talking in a folksy voice on the hot line which to the Soviet premier about the bomber accidentally headed toward Russia. He was in the War Room, and the world map was lit up. Leroy remembers Norma Jean standing catatonically beside him in the hospital and himself thinking: Who is this strange girl? He had forgotten who she was. Now scientists are saying that crib death is caused by a virus. Nobody knows anything, Leroy thinks. The answers are always changing.

When Leroy gets home from the shopping center, Norma Jean's mother, Mabel Beasley, is there. Until this year, Leroy has not realized how much time she spends with Norma Jean. When she visits, she inspects the closets and then the plants, informing Norma Jean when a plant is droopy or yellow. Mabel calls the plants "flowers," although there are never any blooms. She also notices if Norma Jean's laundry is piling up. Mabel is a short, overweight woman whose tight, brown-dyed curls look more like a wig than the actual wig she sometimes wears. Today she has brought Norma Jean an off-white dust ruffle she made for the bed; Mabel works in a custom upholstery shop.

"This is the tenth one I made this year," Mabel says. "I got started and couldn't stop."

"It's real pretty," says Norma Jean.

30   "Now we can hide things under the bed," says Leroy, who gets along with his mother-in-law primarily by joking with her. Mabel has never really forgiven him for disgracing her by getting Norma Jean pregnant. When the baby died, she said that was mocking her.

"What's that thing?" Mabel says to Leroy in a loud voice, pointing to a tangle of yarn on a piece of canvas.

Leroy holds it up for Mabel to see. "It's my needlepoint," he explains. "This is a *Star Trek* pillow cover."

"That's what a woman would do," says Mabel. "Great day in the morning!"

"All the big football players on TV do it," he says.

35   "Why, Leroy, you're always trying to fool me. I don't believe you for one minute. You don't know what to do with yourself—that's the whole trouble. Sewing!"

"I'm aiming to build us a log house," says Leroy. "Soon as my plans come."

"Like *heck* you are," says Norma Jean. She takes Leroy's needlepoint and shoves it into a drawer. "You have to find a job first. Nobody can afford to build now anyway."

Mabel straightens her girdle and says, "I still think before you get tied down y'all ought to take a little run to Shiloh."

"One of these days, Mama," Norma Jean says impatiently.

40   Mabel is talking about Shiloh, Tennessee. For the past few years, she has been urging Leroy and Norma Jean to visit the Civil War battleground there. Mabel went there on her honeymoon—the only real trip she ever took. Her husband died of a perforated ulcer when Norma Jean was ten, but Mabel, who was accepted into the United Daughters of the Confederacy in 1975, is still preoccupied with going back to Shiloh.

"I've been to kingdom come and back in that truck out yonder," Leroy says to Mabel, "but we never yet set foot in that battleground. Ain't that something? How did I miss it?"

"It's not even that far," Mabel says.

After Mabel leaves, Norma Jean reads to Leroy from a list she has made. "Things you could do," she announces. "You could get a job as a guard at Union Carbide, where they'd let you sit on a stool. You could get on at a lumberyard. You could do a little carpenter work, if you want to build so bad. You could—"

"I can't do something where'd I'd have to stand up all day."

45   "You ought to try standing up all day behind a cosmetics counter. It's amazing that I have strong feet, coming from two parents that never had strong feet at all." At the moment Norma Jean is holding on to the kitchen counter, raising her knees one at a time as she talks. She is wearing two-pound ankle weights.

"Don't worry," says Leroy. "I'll do something."

"You could truck calves to slaughter for somebody. You wouldn't have to drive any big old truck for that."

"I'm going to build you this house," says Leroy. "I want to make you a real home."

"I don't want to live in any log cabin."

"It's not a cabin. It's a house."

"I don't care. It looks like a cabin."

"You and me together could lift those logs. It's just like lifting weights."

Norma Jean doesn't answer. Under her breath, she is counting. Now she is marching through the kitchen. She is doing goose steps.

Before his accident, when Leroy came home he used to stay in the house with Norma Jean, watching TV in bed and playing cards. She would cook fried chicken, picnic ham, chocolate pie—all his favorites. Now he is home alone much of the time. In the mornings, Norma Jean disappears, leaving a cooling place in the bed. She eats a cereal called Body Buddies, and she leaves the bowl on the table, with the soggy tan balls floating in a milk puddle. He sees things about Norma Jean that he never realized before. When she chops onions, she stares off into a corner, as if she can't bear to look. She puts on her house slippers almost precisely at nine o'clock every evening and nudges her jogging shoes under the couch. She saves bread heels for the birds. Leroy watches the birds at the feeder. He notices the peculiar way goldfinches fly past the window. They close their wings, then fall, then spread their wings to catch and lift themselves. He wonders if they close their eyes when they fall. Norma Jean closes her eyes when they are in bed. She wants the lights turned out. Even then, he is sure she closes her eyes.

He goes for long drives around town. He tends to drive a car rather carelessly. Power steering and an automatic shift make a car feel so small and inconsequential that his body is hardly involved in the driving process. His injured leg stretches out comfortably. Once or twice he has almost hit something, but even the prospect of an accident seems minor in a car. He cruises the new subdivisions, feeling like a criminal rehearsing a robbery. Norma Jean is probably right about a log house being inappropriate here in the new subdivision. All the houses look grand and complicated. They depress him.

One day when Leroy comes home from a drive he finds Norma Jean in tears. She is in the kitchen making a potato and mushroom-soup casserole, with grated cheese topping. She is crying because her mother caught her smoking.

"I didn't hear her coming. I was standing here puffing away pretty as you please," Norma Jean says, wiping her eyes.

"I knew it would happen sooner or later," says Leroy, putting his arm around her.

"She don't know the meaning of the word 'knock,'" says Norma Jean. "It's a wonder she hadn't caught me years ago."

"Think of it this way," Leroy says. "What if she caught me with a joint?"

"You better not let her!" Norma Jean shrieks. "I'm warning you, Leroy Moffitt!"

"I'm just kidding. Here, play me a tune. That'll help you relax."

Norma Jean puts the casserole in the oven and sets the timer. Then she plays a ragtime tune, with horns and banjo, as Leroy lights up a joint and lies on the couch, laughing to himself about Mabel's catching him at it. He thinks of Stevie Hamilton—a doctor's son pushing grass. Everything is funny. The whole town seems crazy and small. He is reminded of Virgil Mathis, a boastful policeman Leroy used to shoot pool with. Virgil recently led a drug bust in a back room at a bowling alley, where he seized ten thousand dollars worth of marijuana. The newspaper had a picture of him holding up the bags of grass and grinning widely. Right now, Leroy can imagine Virgil breaking down the door and arresting him with a lungful of smoke. Virgil would probably have been alerted to the scene because of all the racket Norma Jean is making. Now she sounds like a hard-rock band. Norma Jean is terrific. When she switches to a Latin-rhythm version of "Sunshine Superman," Leroy hums along. Norma Jean's foot goes up and down, up and down.

"Well, what do you think?" Leroy says, when Norma Jean pauses to search through her music.

65 "What do I think about what?"

His mind has gone blank. Then he says, "I'll sell my rig and build us a house." That wasn't what he wanted to say. He wanted to know what she thought— what she *really* thought—about them.

"Don't start in on that again," says Norma Jean. She begins playing "Who'll Be the Next in Line?"

Leroy used to tell hitchhikers his whole life story—about his travels, his hometown, the baby. He would end with a question: "Well, what do you think?" It was just a rhetorical question. In time, he had the feeling that he'd been telling the same story over and over to the same hitchhikers. He quit talking to hitchhikers when he realized how his voice sounded—whining and self-pitying, like some teenage-tragedy song. Now Leroy has the sudden impulse to tell Norma Jean about himself, as if he had just met her. They have known each other so long they have forgotten a lot about each other. They could become reacquainted. But when the oven timer goes off and she runs to the kitchen, he forgets why he wants to do this.

The next day, Mabel drops by. It is Saturday and Norma Jean is cleaning. Leroy is studying the plans of his log house, which have finally come in the mail. He has them spread out on the table—big sheets of stiff blue paper, with diagrams and numbers printed in white. While Norma Jean runs the vacuum, Mabel drinks coffee. She sets her coffee cup on a blueprint.

70 "I'm just waiting for time to pass," she says to Leroy, drumming her fingers on the table.

As soon as Norma Jean switches off the vacuum, Mabel says in a loud voice, "Did you hear about the datsun dog that killed the baby?"

Norma Jean says, "The word is 'dachshund.' "

"They put the dog on trial. It chewed the baby's legs off. The mother was in the next room all the time." She raises her voice. "They thought it was neglect."

Norma Jean is holding her ears. Leroy manages to open the refrigerator and get some Diet Pepsi to offer Mabel. Mabel still has some coffee and she waves away the Pepsi.

75 "Datsuns are like that," Mabel says. "They're jealous dogs. They'll tear a place to pieces if you don't keep an eye on them."

"You better watch out what you're saying, Mabel," says Leroy.

"Well, facts is facts."

Leroy looks out the window at his rig. It is like a huge piece of furniture gathering dust in the backyard. Pretty soon it will be an antique. He hears the vacuum cleaner. Norma Jean seems to be cleaning the living room rug again.

Later, she says to Leroy, "She just said that about the baby because she caught me smoking. She's trying to pay me back."

80 "What are you talking about?" Leroy says, nervously shuffling blueprints.

"You know good and well," Norma Jean says. She is sitting in a kitchen chair with her feet up and her arms wrapped around her knees. She looks small and helpless. She says, "The very idea, her bringing up a subject like that! Saying it was neglect."

"She didn't mean that," Leroy says.

"She might not have *thought* she meant it. She always says things like that. You don't know how she goes on."

"But she didn't really mean it. She was just talking."

85 Leroy opens a king-sized bottle of beer and pours it into two glasses, dividing it carefully. He hands a glass to Norma Jean and she takes it from him mechanically. For a long time, they sit by the kitchen window watching the birds at the feeder.

Something is happening. Norma Jean is going to night school. She has graduated from her six-week body-building course and now she is taking an adult-education course in composition at Paducah Community College. She spends her evenings outlining paragraphs.

"First you have a topic sentence," she explains to Leroy. "Then you divide it up. Your secondary topic has to be connected to your primary topic."

To Leroy, this sounds intimidating. "I never was any good in English," he says.

"It makes a lot of sense."

90 "What are you doing this for, anyhow?"

She shrugs. "It's something to do." She stands up and lifts her dumbbells a few times.

"Driving a rig, nobody cared about my English."

"I'm not criticizing your English."

Norma Jean used to say, "If I lose ten minutes' sleep, I just drag all day." Now she stays up late, writing compositions. She got a B on her first paper—a how-to theme on soup-based casseroles. Recently Norma Jean has been cooking unusual foods—tacos, lasagna, Bombay chicken. She doesn't play the organ anymore, though her second paper was called "Why Music Is Important to Me." She sits at the kitchen table, concentrating on her outlines, while Leroy plays with his log house plans, practicing with a set of Lincoln Logs. The thought of getting a truckload of notched, numbered logs scares him, and he wants to be prepared. As he and Norma Jean work together at the kitchen table, Leroy has the hopeful thought that they are sharing something, but he knows he is a fool to think this. Norma Jean is miles away. He knows he is going to lose her. Like Mabel, he is just waiting for time to pass.

95 One day, Mabel is there before Norma Jean gets home from work, and Leroy finds himself confiding in her. Mabel, he realizes, must know Norma Jean better than he does.

"I don't know what's got into that girl," Mabel says. "She used to go to bed with the chickens. Now you say she's up all hours. Plus her a-smoking. I like to died."

"I want to make her this beautiful home," Leroy says, indicating the Lincoln Logs. "I don't think she even wants it. Maybe she was happier with me gone."

"She don't know what to make of you, coming home like this."

"Is that it?"

100 Mabel takes the roof off his Lincoln Log cabin. "You couldn't get me in a log cabin," she says. "I was raised in one. It's no picnic, let me tell you."

"They're different now," says Leroy.

"I tell you what," Mabel says, smiling oddly at Leroy.

"What?"

"Take her on down to Shiloh. Y'all need to get out together, stir a little. Her brain's all balled up over them books."

105 Leroy can see traces of Norma Jean's features in her mother's face. Mabel's worn face has the texture of crinkled cotton, but suddenly she looks pretty. It occurs to Leroy that Mabel has been hinting all along that she wants them to take her with them to Shiloh.

"Let's all go to Shiloh," he says. "You and me and her. Come Sunday."

Mabel throws up her hands in protest. "Oh, no, not me. Young folks want to be by theirselves."

When Norma Jean comes in with groceries, Leroy says excitedly, "Your mama here's been dying to go to Shiloh for thirty-five years. It's about time we went, don't you think?"

"I'm not going to butt in on anybody's second honeymoon," Mabel says.

110 "Who's going on a honeymoon, for Christ's sake?" Norma Jean says loudly.

"I never raised no daughter of mine to talk that-a-way," Mabel says.

"You ain't seen nothing yet," says Norma Jean. She starts putting away boxes and cans, slamming cabinet doors.

"There's a log cabin at Shiloh," Mabel says. "It was there during the battle. There's bullet holes in it."

"When are you going to *shut up* about Shiloh, Mama?" asks Norma Jean.

115 "I always thought Shiloh was the prettiest place, so full of history," Mabel goes on. "I just hoped y'all could see it once before I die, so you could tell me about it." Later, she whispers to Leroy, "You do what I said. A little change is what she needs."

"Your name means 'the king,' " Norma Jean says to Leroy that evening. He is trying to get her to go to Shiloh, and she is reading a book about another century.

"Well, I reckon I ought to be right proud."

"I guess so."

"Am I still king around here?"

120 Norma Jean flexes her biceps and feels them for hardness. "I'm not fooling around with anybody, if that's what you mean," she says.

"Would you tell me if you were?"

"I don't know."

"What does your name mean?"

"It was Marilyn Monroe's real name."

125 "No kidding!"

"Norma comes from the Normans. They were invaders," she says. She closes her book and looks hard at Leroy. "I'll go to Shiloh with you if you'll stop staring at me."

On Sunday, Norma Jean packs a picnic and they go to Shiloh. To Leroy's relief, Mabel says she does not want to come with them. Norma Jean drives, and Leroy, sitting beside her, feels like some boring hitchhiker she has picked up. He tries some conversation, but she answers him in monosyllables. At Shiloh, she drives aimlessly through the park, past bluffs and trails and steep ravines. Shiloh is an immense place, and Leroy cannot see it as a battleground. It is not what he expected. He thought it would look like a golf course. Monuments are everywhere, showing through the thick clusters of trees. Norma Jean passes the log cabin Mabel mentioned. It is surrounded by tourists looking for bullet holes.

"That's not the kind of log house I've got in mind," says Leroy apologetically.

"I know *that*."

130   "This is a pretty place. Your mama was right."

"It's O.K.," says Norma Jean. "Well, we've seen it. I hope she's satisfied."

They burst out laughing together.

At the park museum, a movie on Shiloh is shown every half hour, but they decide that they don't want to see it. They buy a souvenir Confederate flag for Mabel, and then they find a picnic spot near the cemetery. Norma Jean has brought a picnic cooler, with pimiento sandwiches, soft drinks, and Yodels. Leroy eats a sandwich and then smokes a joint, hiding it behind the picnic cooler. Norma Jean has quit smoking altogether. She is picking cake crumbs from the cellophane wrapper, like a fussy bird.

Leroy says, "So the boys in gray ended up in Corinth. The Union soldiers zapped 'em finally. April 7, 1862."

135   They both know that he doesn't know any history. He is just talking about some of the historical plaques they have read. He feels awkward, like a boy on a date with an older girl. They are still just making conversation.

"Corinth is where Mama eloped to," says Norma Jean.

They sit in silence and stare at the cemetery for the Union dead and, beyond, at a tall cluster of trees. Campers are parked nearby, bumper to bumper, and small children in bright clothing are cavorting and squealing. Norma Jean wads up the cake wrapper and squeezes it tightly in her hand. Without looking at Leroy, she says, "I want to leave you."

Leroy takes a bottle of Coke out of the cooler and flips off the cap. He holds the bottle poised near his mouth but cannot remember to take a drink. Finally he says, "No, you don't."

"Yes, I do."

140   "I won't let you."

"You can't stop me."

"Don't do me that way."

Leroy knows Norma Jean will have her own way. "Didn't I promise to be home from now on?" he says.

"In some ways, a woman prefers a man who wanders," says Norma Jean. "That sounds crazy, I know."

"You're not crazy."

Leroy remembers to drink from his Coke. Then he says, "Yes, you *are* crazy. You and me could start all over again. Right back at the beginning."

"We *have* started all over again," says Norma Jean. "And this is how it turned out."

"What did I do wrong?"

"Nothing."

150 "Is this one of those women's lib things?" Leroy asks.

"Don't be funny."

The cemetery, a green slope dotted with white markers, looks like a subdivision site. Leroy is trying to comprehend that his marriage is breaking up, but for some reason he is wondering about white slabs in a graveyard.

"Everything was fine till Mama caught me smoking," says Norma Jean, standing up. "That set something off."

"What are you talking about?"

155 "She won't leave me alone—*you* won't leave me alone." Norma Jean seems to be crying, but she is looking away from him. "I feel eighteen again. I can't face that all over again." She starts walking away. "No, it *wasn't* fine. I don't know what I'm saying. Forget it."

Leroy takes a lungful of smoke and closes his eyes as Norma Jean's words sink in. He tries to focus on the fact that thirty-five hundred soldiers died on the grounds around him. He can only think of that war as a board game with plastic soldiers. Leroy almost smiles, as he compares the Confederates' daring attack on the Union camps and Virgil Mathis's raid on the bowling alley. General Grant, drunk and furious, shoved the Southerners back to Corinth, where Mabel and Jet Beasley were married years later, when Mabel was still thin and good-looking. The next day, Mabel and Jet visited the battleground, and then Norma Jean was born, and then she married Leroy and they had a baby, which they lost, and now Leroy and Norma Jean are here at the same battleground. Leroy knows he is leaving out a lot. He is leaving out the insides of history. History was always just names and dates to him. It occurs to him that building a house out of logs is similarly empty—too simple. And the real inner workings of a marriage, like most of history, have escaped him. Now he sees that building a log house is the dumbest idea he could have had. It was clumsy of him to think Norma Jean would want a log house. It was a crazy idea. He'll have to think of something else, quickly. He will wad the blueprints into tight balls and fling them into the lake. Then he'll get moving again. He opens his eyes. Norma Jean has moved away and is walking through the cemetery, following a serpentine brick path.

Leroy gets up to follow his wife, but his good leg is asleep and his bad leg still hurts him. Norma Jean is far away, walking rapidly toward the bluff by the river, and he tries to hobble toward her. Some children run past him, screaming noisily. Norma Jean has reached the bluff, and she is looking out over the Tennessee River. Now she turns toward Leroy and waves her arms. Is she beckoning to him? She seems to be doing an exercise for her chest muscles. The sky is unusually pale—the color of the dust ruffle Mabel made for their bed.

FOCUSED FREE WRITES

1. As Leroy says in the story, "Well, what do you think?" What is the meaning or theme of this story? What evidence can you identify to support this theme?
2. How have these characters changed? How has their marriage changed?
3. A number of objects in the story seem to have symbolic value. They might even qualify as motifs. What are they? What do they mean?
4. In this story, Leroy says, "Nobody knows anything ... The answers are always changing." What is he referring to? Does this line have larger significance in the story?
5. What is the role of history in this story?

Writing an Interpretation: Reading for Meaning in Literature

Earlier in this chapter, interpretation was introduced as a strategy for reading. When you interpret a text, you read to determine the meaning of that story, play, or poem. You ask what that work of literature means. Interpretation is not evaluation, and it is not plot summary—although those may seem like natural initial reactions. Instead, interpretation asks you to go one step deeper, not to figure out what you personally think about a work or what happens in a work, but rather what meaning all of the story's elements convey. When we interpret, we determine a work's larger theme or themes.

Interpretations are grounded in what is said in the text itself and any information we may have about its context. Evidence in the text should not contradict an interpretation, and an interpretation must take into account any relevant context.

Prewriting: Identifying a Topic

Throughout this chapter, the first Focused Free Write prompts after each work asked you to begin to imagine an interpretation of the text. The subsequent Focused Free Writes then called for you to examine evidence that could support an interpretation. We will use these instances of informal writing as starting points for developing more formal interpretations.

Look back at your responses to any of the prompts in this chapter. Identify a response in which you think you really identified the meaning of a story, poem, or play. Circle or highlight this moment in your writing. This idea will be your starting point. For example, a reader might reflect on her responses to Mason's story "Shiloh" and realize that she was interested in the symbolism of Leroy's log cabin.

We will follow along James's process in developing an interpretation of Guy de Maupassant's story "The Necklace."

The following writing is James's in-class response to a focused free write prompt after reading the story:

> In Guy de Maupassant's story, I found that the necklace came to symbolize both Mathilde's desire for a better life and the unhappiness that that obsessive striving eventually brings upon her. Mathilde and her husband could be quite happy in their life together, but her assumption that a better, richer life is somehow her right drives her to seek happiness in mere things. By the end of the story, after ten years of hard work to pay off her debts, she discovers that the necklace that had for so long represented her acceptance into the upper classes was nothing but glass. It was a fake. This ending underlines de Maupassant's point that love of objects should never dominate one's life. Human relationships are more important, more real, than what one owns.

In returning to this free write, James was interested in the idea that desire for objects should never dominate one's life. Human relationships are more important, more real, than what one owns. He wants to use this as his starting point. This is his topic.

Forming an Interpretation: Offering a Big Idea

Once you have settled on a topic, you can begin your interpretation. The reader who is interpreting "Shiloh" might think that in this story, the log cabin works as a symbol of Leroy's misunderstanding of his wife and his marriage, even after all this time. Perhaps she thinks that this symbol illustrates a realization that Leroy has about his own lack of vision. Here she has an interpretation. She is not summarizing what happens in the story, and she is not saying whether or not she likes the story. Instead, she is stating what the story means. In this example, the symbol of the log cabin can be understood as one illustration of the larger theme of his lack of connection with his wife.

James expanded his topic into an interpretation of the de Maupaussant story:

> In this story, the necklace represents how a life dedicated to material objects instead of human relationships is ultimately empty and meaningless.

Bringing in Evidence: Close-Reading for Textual Support

The next step is tracking down evidence. Read and reread the text. Mark it up, take notes, and map out all the moments that connect to your idea. Now look back at these moments as well as your Focused Free Writes; if necessary, modify your interpretation based on any other evidence you've found. What evidence supports your idea about the meaning of the story? For example, while the student interpreting "Shiloh" started with one example (the log cabin) that illustrates the meaning of the story, she needs to find more support. She might look back at "Shiloh" and mark some useful quotations, like the following one:

> At first the kits were diversions, something to kill time, but now he is thinking about building a full-scale log house from a kit. It would be considerably cheaper than building a regular house, and besides, Leroy has grown to appreciate how things are put together. He has begun to realize that in all the years he was on the road he never took time to examine anything. He was always flying past scenery.

Passages like this one illustrate Leroy's growing realization that he and his wife have become distant. He is not "flying past" anymore; instead, he is learning to slow down and "examine" things like his marriage, for the first time. To demonstrate this recognition in other ways, the reader might also mark Leroy's comments about his truck and his crafts as well as those on Norma's work, school, and interests. Finally, she might use not only the log cabin but also Shiloh as symbols that illustrate this interpretation of the story. So, now she has a rough outline:

1. Leroy's interests: crafts, his truck, the log cabin
2. Norma's interests: work, school, weights
3. Log cabin: Leroy's dream for their future
4. Shiloh: the honeymoon they never had
5. The baby's death: the tragedy they never discussed

Leroy's recognition of the meaning of all these items inspires his new vision of their marriage.

The interpreter now has a list of topics she wants to cover to support her interpretation, and this list will help her organize her essay.

STUDENT WRITER In James's Words...

James read and reread to find evidence for his interpretation. He then identified the following list of topics:

1. Mathilde constantly desires things she cannot afford.
2. The necklace: Mathilde's passport to the life of which she dreams.
3. The necklace is lost: it now serves as a punishment for Mathilde's envy.
4. The "real" necklace: it was a fake and never had any real power.

Shaping a Thesis: Constructing a Statement

Until now, your work has been thinking work more than writing work. In some ways, of course, that is the hardest work. Without a good topic and smart evidence, you would have nothing intelligent to write about. The importance of this preliminary work, then, cannot be overestimated.

Your topic became your interpretation, and now your interpretation can become your thesis. Your thesis statement must be phrased as an assertion, a claim you want to stake. You will use evidence from your close-reading to demonstrate to readers that your assertion is plausible.

For example, the "Shiloh" reader might offer the following as a preliminary thesis:

> Even though Leroy, the main character of Bobbie Ann Mason's story "Shiloh," is physically injured, he comes to see what he must do to heal his marriage.

Be sure you identify the author's name and the work's title in your first paragraph, if not in your thesis statement.

Remember that your paper will not summarize what happens in the story; instead, your task is to make meaning. So this next sentence is not a successful thesis statement:

> Norma Jean and Leroy have been married for a long time.

This is a fact; there is nothing to prove. A more successful thesis would be this sentence:

> The story is about Leroy facing and deciding to do something about the demise of his marriage.

Such a statement requires support to explain your reasons for saying so.

STUDENT WRITER In James's Words...

James is using the following thesis statement as a starting point:

> In Guy de Maupassant's story, "The Necklace," Mathilde's sins of greed, envy, and pride drive her desire for the jewelry of the title. In the end, her desires are shown to be as unreal as the necklace.

This assertion gives James a guide for writing the rest of his paper. Every single sentence that follows should be constructed to support this thesis.

Writing to Advance the Thesis: The Formal Essay

Plan to start with an introduction that establishes your interpretation, topic, and thesis. In the body of the essay, each supporting detail should be discussed in its own paragraph with a topic sentence that offers a direct connection to the thesis statement. Finally, you should plan to conclude your formal essay by returning to your thesis and topic.

The Introduction

You may find it useful to think of the introduction as consisting of four important elements.

1. The lead: The lead, or first sentence, is important, yet it can be hard to write, so many writers choose to draft it after they have already warmed up on other parts of their paper. The lead is your first chance to draw the reader in. Sometimes, writers start with one of these common strategies for the lead:

- generalizations about the topic that will help readers make connections
- illustrative examples or anecdotes
- surprising statements
- statistics of some sort—perhaps rare in a literary analysis, but still a possibility

Avoid beginning too generally: "Since the beginning of time, humans have entered into relationships…" You might also want to avoid rhetorical questions such as "Do you believe in marriage?" or dictionary definitions ("According to the Merriam Webster Dictionary online, the definition of marriage is…"). These kinds of leads have become clichéd. Instead, try to draw your reader into your topic in a more specific way. You may well need more than one sentence to entice your audience to care about the topic.

The "Shiloh" reader might begin her paper by reminding readers of commonly held beliefs about marriage:

> When talking of marriage, some people claim "opposites attract" while others will argue that "birds of a feather flock together"; however, marriage is not as simple as forming an initial attraction. Instead, marriage is an ongoing dynamic process.

STUDENT WRITER In James's Words . . .

James's lead uses a number of sentences to establish some common ground with readers:

> In today's overly commercialized culture, one often finds oneself in a state of constant desire. From the television shows and the motion pictures we watch to the billboards lining the roads we travel, every aspect of our lives seems designed to drive our desire for objects that we think will somehow make us more beautiful, more stylish, or more intelligent. However, once these objects are acquired, what happens more often than not is that either our excitement for them fades quickly or, worse, we discover that what we thought were diamonds and gold are merely glass and cheap metal. All our yearnings are thwarted by this ruse—until our attentions are captured and our desires are stoked by another seemingly unattainable object claiming to have the power to make us truly happy.

2. A statement of the topic: After your lead, state your topic. Your statement of topic should introduce the author's name, the work's title, and the subject of your paper generally. It may be as simple as "In her story 'Shiloh,' Bobbie Ann Mason addresses the problem of marriage." Avoid useless space wasters like "Bobbie Ann Mason wrote the story 'Shiloh.'" Instead, get to the point. Remember, too, that plot summary is unnecessary; you can assume your reader has read the text. Unless the author's biographical context is directly linked to your specific interpretation, leave out details about the author's life.

STUDENT WRITER In James's Words...

The above is not just a scene played out in the countless shopping malls of modern America. It also appeared some one hundred and twenty years previously in Guy de Maupassant's short story, "The Necklace." In this story, the author places some of humanity's worst sins on display—greed, envy, and pride.

3. The thesis statement: Your topic statement and thesis statement may be stated separately or as a single sentence. But be sure to state your thesis explicitly; the reader shouldn't have to guess your point. For instance, the writer's point about "Shiloh," stated as a thesis, might look like this:

> Bobbie Ann Mason's story "Shiloh" is about the main character Leroy's realization that he must act to remedy the growing distance in his marriage.

STUDENT WRITER In James's Words...

By linking these emotions with the jewelry of the story's title, de Maupassant is able to demonstrate just how destructive these emotions can be and (due to the revelation at the story's end), ultimately, how empty the things we desire really are.

4. A navigating statement: You may want to conclude your introduction with a navigating sentence. The navigating sentence sets out the direction of your paper for your reader. It summarizes the topics, and the order of the topics, that you will be addressing in your interpretation. The student writing about "Shiloh" might say:

> Leroy describes the difference between his new interests and Norma Jean's in order to recognize his transformed understanding of important symbols in his life like the log cabin, Shiloh, and the death of their baby.

James combined his thesis statement with his navigating statement. His thesis statement maps out the paper's direction, moving from the trouble with these emotions to the lesson learned by story's end:

> *By linking these emotions with the jewelry of the story's title, de Maupassant is able to demonstrate just how destructive these emotions can be and (due to the revelation at the story's end), ultimately, how empty the things we desire really are.*

The Body

At the beginning of each paragraph, state the connection between the topic at hand and the thesis guiding the paper. In other words, each body paragraph should begin with a topic sentence. These sentences can help ensure you are not falling into the trap of plot summary and are staying on track in your interpretation. They help you take control of the argument. For example, toward the end of the "Shiloh" paper, the writer might use the following as a topic sentence:

> Leroy finally realizes that the death of their child may have created a chasm in their marriage that must be bridged.

Here the writer has set out the topic of this particular paragraph yet alludes to the "realization" theme that is part of her larger thesis. In each paragraph, you are making meaning by explaining the interpretation you developed during your close reading of the work. You may interpret the plot or characters' actions. You may close-read a word or a series of words or a line that is of particular importance and explain why and how it is important. When the language in the work is essential to the discussion, quote it directly. Otherwise, paraphrase or summarize the information.

Quoting must always be done for a purpose. You should discuss each quotation and explain how it connects to your thesis. The writer might say this, for example, about Leroy:

> Earlier in the story Leroy remembers looking at Norma Jean and asking "Who is this strange girl?" when they were at the hospital after the baby's death. However, he comes to have a new vision of Norma Jean:
>
>> Leroy is home all the time, they sometimes feel awkward around each other, and Leroy wonders if one of them should mention the child. He has the feeling that they are waking up out of a dream together—that they must create a new marriage, start afresh. They are lucky they are still married. (75)
>
> Leroy has awakened from the catatonic state that followed the child's death and wants to claim a new marriage and a new life. He wants to fix what ails them. He recognizes that they must communicate about this empty history to have a full life together.

Quotations must be introduced and their relevance to your thesis explained. Introduce the quotation to connect it to what came before in your essay, and after the quotation, discuss its significance in detail. When you discuss the quotation, refer directly to its language or ideas.

STUDENT WRITER In James's Words...

See this example of James's integration of quotations:

> Within the first few paragraphs, de Maupassant establishes the character of Mathilde Loisel as someone who is obsessed with her place in society, with material wealth and her lack of it. She is described as someone "as if by a mistake of destiny, born in a family of clerks" (68). De Maupassant writes that "[s]he had no dresses, no jewels, nothing. And she loved nothing but that; she felt made for that" (68). She is further described as a young woman out of her class. Mathilde constantly fixates on what she does not have. She always thinks "of the long salons fitted up with ancient silk, of the delicate furniture carrying priceless curiosities" (68). Her husband, "a little clerk at the Ministry of Public Instructions" (68), on the other hand, seems to be happy with what he has. While he is excited about being served a good potpie on a "covered with a tablecloth three days old," Mathilde cannot help but imagine herself being invited to "dainty dinners...of delicious dishes served on marvelous plates" (68). In these passages, Mathilde is shown to be a person to whom material possessions mean everything. To live without them is seemingly not to be alive.

The Conclusion

In the conclusion, you'll want to return to your interpretation and restate it in a new way. Consider these strategies to make your conclusion interesting:

Widen the Lens

You might examine the larger significance of your topic. You might address its implications by making connections between this topic and ideas in other literary works or in the world generally. If, in your introduction, you began with a general statement before focusing in on your specific argument, you might widen the lens back out again in the conclusion. For example, in the writer's conclusion, she might connect "Shiloh" to the prevalence of divorce rates in America today, or suggest that while romance stories and "happily ever after" stories are popular, the hard work of marriage is rarely depicted.

Come Full Circle

While you return to the idea of your thesis and restate it in a new way in your conclusion, you might also return to the language of your lead and resurrect that opening image to provide closure at paper's end. For example, the writer might harken back to those clichés that opened the paper on "Shiloh" and suggest that clichés are too simplistic and don't address the real work of marriage.

In James's conclusion, he comes full circle:

> Guy de Maupassant's story, "The Necklace," superbly illustrates the consequences of a life spent trying to acquire possessions in the hopes that these mere objects will give one's life meaning, an "immoderate desire" or love of material objects. At the end of the story, it is not for the loss of her friend's necklace that Mathilde and her husband are punished, but for what drove her to borrow the jewelry in the first place: greed, envy, and pride. These emotions are shown to be the true source of Mathilde's unhappiness and inadequacy, not her inability to acquire riches and live the life that she thinks she truly deserves.

Integrating and Citing Source Material

Any source materials you use in your essay, including quotations from the story, play, or poem you are interpreting, should be cited. The material quoted should typically be placed inside a pair of quotation marks. (But see page 536 for block quotations.) The citation usually includes the author's last name and then the line number (for poems), page number (for stories), or the act, scene, and line numbers (for plays). This information is placed inside a pair of parentheses before the period in a sentence in which a quotation is integrated. If the quotation ends the sentence, then the final quotation mark comes before the opening parenthesis of the citation.

For a more complete discussion of integrating and citing source material, see pages 533–538.

Here is the first of many examples from James's paper:

> Within the first few paragraphs, de Maupassant establishes the character of Mathilde Loisel as someone who is obsessed with her place in society, with material wealth and her lack of it. She is described as someone "as if by a mistake of destiny, born in a family of clerks" (68). De Maupassant writes that "[s]he had no dresses, no jewels, nothing. And she loved nothing but that; she felt made for that" (68). She is further described as a young woman out of her class.

Revising, Editing, and Proofreading

Once you have a reasonable draft of your essay, it's time to rewrite. When you get to the rewriting stage, you may find it helpful to consider the process in terms of the three kinds of activities that follow.

Revising

When you revise your writing, you address global issues: purpose, structure, organization, support, and transitions. In this first step of the rewriting process, you might address the following questions:

■ Is your thesis really your thesis? Does the rest of the paper support the assertion you set out? If not, revise the thesis or alter the rest of the paper so they correspond.

■ Have you used the best examples? Go back to the work. Are there other examples or quotations that could further bolster your interpretation or provide stronger support?

■ Is your essay structured in a logical way? Here are a few smart structural strategies.

1. Arrange topics in the order they appear in the work.
2. Move from relatively simple or minor examples to increasingly more complex or major examples.
3. Introduce a relatively important example first, give a couple of less important examples in the middle, and end with the most important example.

Be prepared to move paragraphs around as needed to ensure your essay has a logical flow.

■ Within each paragraph, are ideas presented in a logical order? Should the sentences within a paragraph be reorganized? Are new ideas introduced by linking them to known ideas?

■ Do topic sentences between paragraphs directly address the topic of the paragraph that follows? Do these transitions remind the reader of the thesis? It is always a good idea to strengthen transitions during revision.

STUDENT WRITER In James's Words...

When I came to this point in the rewriting process, I sought to make it clearer to the reader the reasons for the quotations I chose to use. This entailed adding explication at the beginning and end of paragraphs in order to place the quotations in their proper context. Working on transitions are something I always try to address when revising.

Editing

After you make changes to the larger structures of the essay, in editing you can turn your attention to sentences and words. You can reorganize sentences so they will sound better, change how they flow from one to the next, and choose words carefully to convey the meaning you want. In editing, you might address the following questions:

■ Is your sentence structure varied? Do you use all one kind of sentence or all another? Vary your sentence openings so that they don't sound too choppy or dull.

- Sometimes it is useful to consider what kind of sentence you want to use where. Here are a few ideas.
  1. You might use a simple sentence to clearly explain a complicated idea.
  2. In a transitional sentence that begins a new paragraph, you might refer to the topic of the previous paragraph in a first, subordinate clause and then move to the topic of the new paragraph in the second, independent clause. For example, the next sentence comes after a paragraph about the log cabin and at the beginning of a paragraph about Leroy understanding his losses: "While the log cabin is an important symbol in the story, Shiloh also helps Leroy see the losses his marriage has sustained."
  3. Use that same technique to keep readers moving easily from one sentence to the next; that is, refer back to an idea in the previous sentence in an opening phrase or subordinate clause and then introduce new information in the following independent clause.
- Finally, writing is about precision and words are slippery. Do you use the most precise words possible? The best words to express your meaning? Can you include some of the language from the text itself? Can you use active, vivid words? Can you avoid tired language like "to be" verbs?

Proofreading

Proofreading is the act of making sure that no word errors, spelling errors, punctuation errors, or typos remain. These kinds of errors can be embarrassing to the writer and distracting for the reader. Poor proofreading might also suggest that you don't care how readers will react to your project. To proofread, focus on sentence-level and word-choice issues one at a time:

- Reread your paper once looking only at the spelling of each and every word. Realize that the spellcheck function on your computer is not able to find homonym errors like *there* for *their* or distinguish between *too*, *two*, and *to*. Be certain to spell the name of the author and the title of the work correctly. Check the spelling of your professor's name in the heading of your paper.
- Read your essay aloud to notice any missing words or extra words that get in the way of your meaning.
- Check your verbs. Are they consistently in the proper tense? When writing about literature, you should use the present tense (**the literary present**) to discuss actions in the story, poem, or play, or when describing the author's writing of the work: "Mason writes about a husband and wife," not "Mason wrote..." or "Leroy thinks about his wife," not "Leroy thought about his wife."
- Do the subject and verb in each sentence agree? Do pronouns agree with their antecedents?
- Watch for punctuation errors. Did you use commas correctly? What about other punctuation marks? Did you forget any punctuation marks?
- Examine quotations. Are they punctuated correctly? Do quotation marks enclose each quotation? Are parenthetical citations handled correctly? (See pages 90 and 533–538.)

- Double check your quotations. Did you quote the work word for word, exactly? Did you forget any words? Do you need to adjust any quotations with brackets for agreement reasons? (See page 536.) Did you write down the correct page number(s) on which the quotation appeared in the original source?

Craft your writing so how something is said reflects what is said. When this happens, you have created art!

Sample Student Paper

James Lewis's biography may be found on page 567.

James Lewis

English 102

Dr. Howells

9 March 2010

Immoderate Desire in Guy de Maupassant's

"The Necklace"

In today's overly commercialized culture, one often finds oneself in a state of constant desire. From the television shows and the motion pictures we watch to the billboards lining the roads we travel, every aspect of our lives seems designed to drive our desire for objects that we think will somehow make us more beautiful, more stylish, or more intelligent. However, once these objects are acquired, what happens more often than not is that either our excitement for them fades quickly or, worse, we discover that what we thought were diamonds and gold are merely glass and cheap metal. All our yearnings are thwarted by this ruse—until our attentions are captured and our desires are stoked by another seemingly unattainable object claiming to have the power to make us truly happy.

The above is not just a scene played out in the countless shopping malls of modern America. It also appeared some one hundred and twenty years previously in Guy de Maupassant's short story, "The Necklace." In this story, the author places some of humanity's worst sins on display—greed, envy, and pride. By linking these emotions with the jewelry of the story's title, de Maupassant is able to demonstrate just how destructive these emotions can be and (due to the revelation at the story's end), ultimately, how empty the things we desire really are.

Within the first few paragraphs, de Maupassant establishes the character of Mathilde Loisel as someone who is obsessed with her place in society, with material wealth and her lack of it. She is described as someone "as if by a mistake of destiny, born in a family of clerks" (68). De Maupassant writes that "[s]he had no dresses, no jewels, nothing. And she loved nothing but that; she felt made for that" (68). She is further described as a young woman out of her class. Mathilde constantly fixates on what she does not have. She always thinks "of the long *salons* fitted up with ancient silk, of the delicate furniture carrying priceless curiosities" (68). Her husband, "a little clerk at the Ministry of Public Instructions" (68), on the other hand, seems to be happy with what he has. While he is excited about being served a good potpie on a "covered with a tablecloth three days old," Mathilde cannot help but imagine herself being invited to "dainty dinners...of delicious dishes served on marvelous plates" (68). In these passages, Mathilde is shown to be a person to whom material possessions mean everything. To live without them is seemingly not to be alive.

Mathilde's feelings of greed and envy are seemingly solved by her husband's procurement of an invitation to an exclusive party. Instead of being happy for her good fortune, however, she is "irritated" and filled with "disdain" (69). She seems to love objects more than her husband, in fact. She claims to "have no dress" (69) to wear to the gathering. Even when her husband agrees to forego purchasing "a gun" with which he might "treat himself to a little shooting next summer" and buys her a new dress, she is still "sad, uneasy, anxious" (69). The reason for this is that she is "annoy[ed] not to have a single jewel, not a single stone, nothing to put on" (69). In a manner similar to what one sees on reality television shows, like MTV's "My Super Sweet 16,"

Mathilde is concerned with nothing more than acquiring objects that will give a good impression to others. She is filled with the anxiety of not being accepted by those she thinks are superior to her. She can think of "nothing more humiliating than to look poor among other women who are rich" (70). Her pride will not allow her to follow her husband's advice to "wear natural flowers" (69). She must give the impression to these other women that she herself is one of them, that she is rich; she must have a jewel at any cost.

At Mrs. Forestier's house, Mathilde finds "a superb necklace of diamonds" that makes "her heart...beat with an immoderate desire" (70). It is this necklace and her "immoderate desire" for it that precipitates her downfall. At the party, Mathilde is "a great success" and "danced with intoxication, with passion, made drunk by pleasure" (70). However, when the time comes for her and her husband to leave the party and return home, the pride of her newly "awakened desires" (70) will not allow her to be viewed in her unseemly "modest wraps of common life, whose poverty contrasted with the elegance of the ball dress" (70). She leaves the party hastily and discovers upon arriving at home that she "no longer had the necklace around her neck!" (71). The very thing with which she identified all her desires is gone and must be replaced. Finding an exact replica, Mathilde's husband "gave notes, took up ruinous promises, dealt with usurers and all the race of lenders" (72). In the end, he paid "thirty-six thousand francs" (72) for the replacement necklace, after which he and Mathilde set about the task of paying off their debts.

The necklace, which originally symbolized all Mathilde's dreams come true, is now a symbol of the failure of those dreams. What was a representation of a life of luxury and leisure becomes a symbol of "the horrible existence of the needy" and "odious" work (72). That this simple piece of jewelry can be a symbol of all these emotional states is the main strength of this short work. De Maupassant sets a carrot in front of Mathilde's nose, and the reader watches her follow it blindly. The necklace is invested with meaning by Mathilde in the same way that the people of today seek meaning in SUVs, designer clothing, and big-screen television sets. For too many—in de Maupassant's day as well as today—the objects of desire insidiously take on a power of their own, becoming symbols of their owner's lack of power. In other words, instead of imbuing my possessions—my clothes, for instance—with my own meaning, I allow them to define and, in time, to replace me. This gives the saying "the clothes make the man" an especially sinister tinge. It is just this process in which Mathilde engages, and it gives the ending of the story a particularly tragic and ironic twist.

Mathilde's life of toil lasted for ten years. She and her husband had paid off the debt, and now she feels that she can come clean with her friend, Mrs. Forestier, who is unaware that the original necklace had ever been lost. While her friend is "still young, still beautiful, still charming" (73), Mathilde "had become the woman of impoverished households—strong and hard and rough" (73). When told that it has taken the past ten years to pay for the necklace's replacement, Mrs. Forestier replies: "Oh, my poor Mathilde! Why, my necklace was paste. It was worth at most five hundred francs" (73). In the end, the necklace not only symbolizes Mathilde's desire for a better life and the price to be paid for that life, it represents the meaninglessness of that life, as well. The necklace for which she and her husband have slaved to repay "with the rates of usury, and the accumulations of the compound interest" (72) is shown to be nothing more than, well, a necklace. It is not happiness incarnate; it is not the answer to Mathilde's dreams of an upper-class life. The necklace was without any special meaning; it was merely glass and metal.

Guy de Maupassant's story, "The Necklace," superbly illustrates the consequences of a life spent trying to acquire possessions in the hopes that these mere objects will give one's life meaning, an "immoderate desire" or love of material objects. At the end of the story, it is not for the loss of her friend's necklace that Mathilde and her husband are punished, but for what drove her to borrow the jewelry in the first place: greed, envy, and pride. These emotions are shown to be the true source of Mathilde's unhappiness and inadequacy, not her inability to acquire riches and live the life that she thinks she truly deserves.

Work Cited

De Maupassant, Guy. "The Necklace." *Literature: Reading to Write.* Ed. Elizabeth Howells. New York: Pearson, 2010. 68–73. Print.

4

A STUDY IN STYLE
Analyzing Patterns

Reading Plays. John Malkovich and Karen Allen star in the filmed version of a stage production of Tennessee Williams' *The Glass Menagerie*. Are plays meant to be seen or read? What are the benefits of encountering a play as a written text? As a performed production? How should one approach a play in text form differently from reading works in other genres? What are some plays you have seen?

What does it mean when you say a person has style?

When magazine editors report on celebrities, they often take note of their style in columns such as "Style Watch." Katherine Hepburn was a great movie actress of the last century and what people commented on was her style. She was both strong and feminine, individual and personable, and her identity was reflected in what movies she did—romantic comedies like *Bringing Up Baby*; in how she talked—in rapid-fire accented dialog like in *Philadelphia Story*; in whom she loved—her unconventional relationship with Spencer Tracy; and in what she wore—wide-legged pants and blousy cinched tops. In other words, she had a distinctive style that was conveyed in these varied and distinct elements of her persona.

Celebrities today who are known for their style include actresses like Penelope Cruz, Halle Berry, and Jennifer Aniston, and actors such as Will Smith, Johnny Depp, and George Clooney. Heidi Klum has become a style icon. She can go from Armani on the red carpet to designer jeans and baby sling at her husband's concerts. She is known for her fashion savvy and her business smarts, choosing the right outfits and the right work. She knows what she is about and conveys that image through her style. On the other hand, some celebrities find themselves on the "Don't" list more often than not for ripped fishnet stockings, bad hair, and a sloppy lifestyle. You may be able to think of some examples. The elements of a person's style often work together to convey a focused message or coherent identity, even as that style might transform over time and be translated in particular contexts.

Authors also have distinctive styles. The way an author chooses words (**diction**); arranges them in sentences, dialog, or verse (**syntax**); and conveys emotion (**tone**) all work together to convey an individual style. By studying how a writer develops ideas, characters, and actions with description, imagery, and other literary techniques, readers can characterize a writer's style. While we might identify some aspects of an author's style through theme, plot, character, narration, and setting, we need to examine how these are created through language—that is, how the author precisely arranges the most basic elements of style: words.

For example, William Faulkner (1897–1962) and Ernest Hemingway (1899–1961) often are compared because of their contrasting styles. Both were American writers working at the same time, and both won Pulitzer Prizes and Nobel Prizes for literature. Yet each writer had a distinct style. In examining the opening paragraphs of two of their famous short stories, the difference becomes obvious.

The first passage is from the beginning of Faulkner's story "Barn Burning":

The store in which the justice of the Peace's court was sitting smelled of cheese. The boy, crouched on his nail keg at the back of the crowded room, knew he smelled cheese, and more: from where he sat he could see the ranked shelves close-packed with the solid, squat, dynamic shapes of tin cans whose labels his stomach read, not from the lettering which meant nothing to his mind but from the scarlet devils and the silver curve of fish—this, the cheese which he knew he smelled and the hermetic meat which his intestines believed he smelled coming in intermittent gusts momentary and brief between the other constant one, the smell and sense just a little of fear because mostly of despair and grief, the old fierce pull of blood. He could not see the table where the Justice sat and before which his father and his father's enemy (*our enemy* he thought in that despair; *ourn! mine and hisn both! He's my father!*) stood, but he could hear them, the two of them that is, because his father had said no word yet:

"But what proof have you, Mr. Harris?"

This next passage is from the first paragraph of Hemingway's "A Clean Well-Lighted Place," which appears later in this chapter:

It was very late and everyone had left the cafe except an old man who sat in the shadow the leaves of the tree made against the electric light. In the day time the street was dusty, but at night the dew settled the dust and the old man liked to sit late because he was deaf and now at night it was quiet and he felt the difference. The two waiters inside the cafe knew that the old man was a little drunk, and while he was a good client they knew that if he became too drunk he would leave without paying, so they kept watch on him.

Clearly, Faulkner's paragraph has more words than Hemingway's. In fact, the second sentence alone has more than the total number of words in Hemingway's introduction. The kinds of sentences are also representative of the two writers' diverse styles—notice the layering of clauses in Faulkner's complex sentences, in stark contrast to the direct compound constructions found in Hemingway's prose. (Compound constructions are grammatical elements joined with coordinating conjunctions—*and, but, or,* and so on.) Faulkner once criticized Hemingway for never challenging his readers to use a dictionary; he was drawing attention to Hemingway's spare prose. And many readers have held up Faulkner's 35-page sentence in the short story "The Bear" as the epitome of his verbose ways.

The nature of the words and sentences themselves reflects the conflicting approaches to narrative by these writers. These contrary styles reflect each writer's divergent thematic concerns in these texts. In other words, Faulkner delves into the psychology of the boy's character, moving from the surface image of the smell to the deeply embedded "fierce pull of blood." However, Hemingway takes a more journalistic approach, introducing us to setting and multiple perspectives before moving in to observe the waiters in particular.

To examine the style of these writers, we analyze their prose. We separate the component parts of the text to determine the meaning of that text. We look for patterns in these separate elements to distinguish not only *what* a text means, as the last chapter did, but *how* it means. In other words, the meaning of the work—its identity or theme—is constructed through particular stylistic choices.

Ideally, what the best literature can do is reflect the theme in the style itself. The highest form of art in literature is when the form reflects the matter. What great literature aspires to is what great music achieves. The nineteenth-century writer Walter Pater makes this case when he compares literature to music. In music, we usually cannot distinguish the subject matter from the formal composition itself. Great music makes its case when the notes convey emotion that can't exactly be translated into language—it's a translation of emotion itself. However, in literature, the elements of style (the words, sentences, and tone) are the elements that express emotion, imagery, description, character, plot, or theme. Those elements should be singled out to understand the inner workings of style.

We can look at the style of any writer or any given piece of literature, but in this chapter we will examine how certain authors have made some very self-conscious decisions to foreground stylistic choices or perhaps even to address style as a theme. These distinctive examples of style will help us look at more subtle choices in other chapters.

How would you characterize your own personal style? Who would you characterize as having a noticeably distinct identity? How does that style convey this person's identity?

POEMS

The following two poems address style overtly, both as a theme and through a form. They will help us learn how to construct analyses.

William Wordsworth

NUNS FRET NOT AT THEIR CONVENT'S NARROW ROOM   [1807]

Nuns fret not at their convent's narrow room;
And hermits are contented with their cells;
And students with their pensive citadels;
Maids at the wheel, the weaver at his loom,
5 Sit blithe and happy; bees that soar for bloom,
High as the highest Peak of Furness-fells,[1]
Will murmur by the hour in foxglove bells:
In truth the prison, unto which we doom
Ourselves, no prison is: and hence for me,
10 In sundry moods, 'twas pastime to be bound
Within the Sonnet's scanty plot of ground;
Pleased if some Souls (for such there needs must be)
Who have felt the weight of too much liberty,
Should find brief solace there, as I have found.

---

[1] **Furness Fells:** hills and mountains in England's Lake District, where Wordsworth lived.

FOCUSED FREE WRITES

1. What does this poem mean? What is its theme, and what story does it tell?
2. What problem is presented? What solution is suggested? In which lines?

LITERARY Contexts

Stanza Lengths and Sonnets

One way to begin to look at poems is to identify their parts. A poem can be made up of paragraphs known as **stanzas**. Often, the stanzas illustrate a **rhyme scheme** that can be broken into segments based on particular repetitions of sound patterns. In these **fixed-form** poems (also called "closed form poems), you may find the following.

Couplets—pairs of lines that rhyme
Tercets—three-line stanzas
Triplets—three rhyming lines
Quatrain—four-line stanzas with a rhyme scheme
Quintet—five-line stanzas
Sestet—six-line stanzas
Septet—seven-line stanzas
Octave—eight-line stanzas

A **sonnet** is a fixed form of lyric poem made up of fourteen lines. It can be constructed based on the **Italian Petrarchan** model of an **octave** (an 8-line stanza with end rhymes such as *abbaabba*) and a **sestet** (a 6-line stanza with end rhymes such as *cdecde*). Or a sonnet can be constructed as an **English Shakespearean** sonnet consisting of three quatrains and a couplet with end rhymes such as *abab, cdcd, efef, gg*.

Sonnets are brief, compact, and demanding. The subject matter usually takes advantage of the brevity and rigidity of the form to express intense, concentrated feeling. Often, sonnets present an argument, proposition, or generalization that takes a turn before a final application or reversal in the concluding lines.

What kind of sonnet has Wordsworth written above: an Italian Petrarchan or an English Shakespearean sonnet?

How does this poem talk about the sonnet form? What does Wordsworth say about it? Does he tell us about the form or demonstrate the form?

What sonnet forms did you encounter in Chapter 3?

PRE-READING   Which people or things have you lost in your life? Which loss has affected you the most?

Elizabeth Bishop (1911–1979). *Born in Worcester, Massachusetts, Bishop endured a tragic childhood, losing a father who died young and a mother to a mental ward. Raised by her father's family in Nova Scotia and Cape Cod and suffering from* fragile health, she turned to reading and writing as a kind of alternate universe. Bishop began publishing poetry at Vassar; after graduating, she traveled extensively as a working poet, publishing many acclaimed volumes. After living for a time in Brazil, Bishop returned the United States to teach at Harvard. She received high praise, honorary degrees, prizes, grants, and posts as one of the most significant post–war poets of the century.

Elizabeth Bishop

ONE ART [1976]

The art of losing isn't hard to master;
so many things seem filled with the intent
to be lost that their loss is no disaster.

Lose something every day. Accept the fluster
5 of lost door keys, the hour badly spent.
The art of losing isn't hard to master.

Then practice losing farther, losing faster:
places, and names, and where it was you meant
to travel. None of these will bring disaster.

10 I lost my mother's watch. And look! my last, or
next-to-last, of three loved houses went.
The art of losing isn't hard to master.

I lost two cities, lovely ones. And, vaster,
some realms I owned, two rivers, a continent.
15 I miss them, but it wasn't a disaster.

—Even losing you (the joking voice, a gesture
I love) I shan't have lied. It's evident
the art of losing's not too hard to master
though it may look like (_Write it!_) like disaster.

FOCUSED FREE WRITES

1. What is this poem's purpose? How and where does the poem articulate its purpose?
2. Trace the progress of the poem's story. How do the differences between the lost objects develop as the poem progresses?
3. What is significant about the break in the repetition in the last few lines? Why does Bishop insert this parenthetical phrase?

LITERARY Contexts

Poetic Forms—The Villanelle

A **villanelle**, like the sonnet, is a closed form, also known as a **fixed form**. It consists of nineteen lines organized into six **stanzas**—five **tercets** and a concluding **quatrain**. The rhyme scheme is quite rigid with an *aba* rhyme repeated in each tercet and then repeated in the final two lines of the quatrain. Line one is repeated as lines 6, 12, and 18, while line 3 is repeated as lines 9, 15, and 19.

How does this form reflect or reinforce the meaning or theme of "One Art"? How does it contribute to the ironic message of the work?

The Act of Analysis

An analysis is a separating or distinguishing of the component parts of something so as to discover its true nature or the inner relationships among its parts. Asking questions such as *why* the author did something and *how* the author created certain effects are analytic questions. While we might interpret *what* the meaning of a work is, we then must go one step further to determine *how* it means. We move from the big picture approach of an interpretation to focus the lens on the individual elements in an analysis.

In fact, we engage in the act of analysis everyday. We analyze what clothes to wear, what movies to see, and why others act the way they do. In order to determine if my crush likes me, I would analyze if he laughs at what I say, if he makes eye contact, and if his body language is somehow suggestive. I would look at all of these aspects of his behavior and try to determine what they mean. Or, predicated on the belief that he does like me, I might look for signs in his text messages, gestures, or verbal cues that prove my hunch true.

Analyzing a text works much the same way. We close-read a text and try to distinguish the gestures of the writer and how those gestures convey a certain meaning. When analyzing literature, we want to determine which elements or parts of the work reinforce a particular theme. Those parts of a poem, short story, or play might include any of the following:

What, where, and *when* elements	*Who* elements	*How* elements
title	character	imagery
setting	narration	symbols
plot	point of view	syntax
structure	tone	diction
		figurative language

When determining what a piece of literature means, we need to determine *how* that meaning is conveyed and which elements are significant in that communication of meaning. Is the meaning found in what the text is about, what happens, where it happens, or when it happens? Or is it found in the characters, in the identity of the speaker, or in the author's attitude toward this topic? Finally, is the meaning of the text found not in what is said or who is saying it, but *how* it is said—through imagery, symbols, syntax, diction, allusion, or figurative language? Of course, the meaning of a successful piece of literature will be found in all these things, but when you analyze it, you decide which elements are most significant and most specifically emphasized.

Often, then, when we undertake analysis, we analyze the author's style. We look at the choices a writer makes in terms of language, syntax, or tone—the parts that make up the whole. We could examine the manner of expression of a particular writer and how this manner is produced by word choices, grammatical structures, use of literary devices, and all the other possible elements of language use. For example, in both "One Art" and "Nuns Fret Not," the authors use closed forms to convey their themes. Wordsworth demonstrates the freedom of limits in his celebration of the sonnet form. Bishop comments that losing the rhythm of the villanelle is hard to do, but even its repetition will not assuage the pain of losing. In other words, in distinguishing the style of the poems, in breaking the texts into their component elements to identify the forms, we can understand how the theme is conveyed.

Using the chart on page 107, which elements in "Nuns Fret Not" and "One Art" are significant in creating the poems' meanings?

Supporting Theme Through Analysis

There are two ways to begin a textual analysis: Identify a theme and then find support for it, or discover patterns in the work and then identify their theme. In the first, once the reader understands the meaning of a work, he or she attempts to identify how that meaning is made. Much like a mechanic opens up an engine to determine its inner workings, a reader close-reads a text to determine what makes it tick.

For example, if Wordsworth's poem is about the freedom of limits, a reader would think of the elements in the chart on page 107, and then identify the ways this theme was supported:

1. images of other people who find freedom in confined spaces: nuns, hermits, students, maids, and weavers
2. the symbol of the bee who rejects the horizon for "home" in the foxglove bells
3. the sonnet form used to illustrate this theme
4. the diction used to demonstrate that opposite ideas like freedom and limits are alike, by use of words that sound alike or are set up to be alike even though they don't seem alike: *bloom* and *doom*, *bound* and *ground* and *found*, *weight* and *liberty*

Through analysis, the reader can dissect the poem to witness its internal operations. All of these composite parts combine to convey the poem's general message about the possibilities in imprisonment. At some point, these parts could serve as topics for supporting paragraphs.

How does Bishop's poem address the pain of loss? What stylistic elements compose this theme?

Finding Patterns Through Analysis

Unlike the first example, the second way to engage in analysis works inductively rather than deductively. Perhaps you notice a certain pattern in the prose, which then leads you to a certain conclusion about meaning. For example, when I listen to a person giving a speech, I might notice that he or she uses a number of "filler" words such as *um*, *like*, or *you know*. In fact, I remember one colleague who used the phrase *nevertheless* repeatedly when speaking to groups. Once I observed this pattern, I concluded that these stylistic quirks indicate that she is a bit nervous speaking publicly in this formal way. In other words, my analysis of her speaking style allowed me to come to a conclusion about a meaning she did not even intend to convey.

When analyzing a text and keeping in mind the elements listed in the chart on page 107, we might also be able to distinguish certain patterns or repetitions. For example, in Elizabeth Bishop's poem, we can find several types of patterns:

1. *In form.* Line 1 is repeated as lines 6, 12, and 18 while line 3 is repeated as lines 9, 15, and 19. We keep hearing that "The art of losing isn't hard to master" and that "losing is no disaster."
2. *In imagery.* The items lost seem to progress in importance from concrete objects like keys and time to figurative and priceless places and people like heirlooms, houses, "realms," and ultimately "you."
3. *In tone.* The poem seems to be ironic in tone; it seems to mean the opposite of what it says.

While the poem seems to say that "losing is no disaster," the imagery and ultimately the interruption of the form in the last line suggest otherwise. The poem seems to conclude that losing is hard to talk about—the speaker is forced to "*Write it!*"—and hard to bear. Through analysis, the reader must draw conclusions about the meaning of these stylistic elements or composite parts. The word choice, syntax, imagery, and symbolism that make up the style of the poem determine its theme. Analysis, then, is a tool that engages interpretation to demonstrate *how* the theme is constructed.

What patterns arise in Wordsworth's "Nuns Fret Not"? What is the meaning of the repetition of these elements?

POEMS

The following poems are classics and contemporaries, by men and women, in the 19th century and the 20th century, in America and in England; however, they all demonstrate distinctive and overt stylistic moves, making them ripe for analysis.

PRE-READING What do you expect a poem to look like? Does it have to look that way?

E.E. Cummings (1894–1962).   *Edward Estlin Cummings, born in Cambridge, Massachusetts, was the son of a Unitarian minister. He began writing conventional poetry at the age of eight before becoming more experimental during his years at Harvard. He served for a time in the military and was imprisoned during World War I. After living in New York and Paris after the war, studying art and writing poetry, Cummings settled in New York's Greenwich Village in 1923 until the end of his life. He achieved success in producing, poetry, plays, travel writing, drawing, and choreographing a ballet.*

E.E. Cummings

 # L(A)   [1958]

l(a

le
af
fa

ll

s)
one
l

iness

FOCUSED FREE WRITES

1. What surprises you, intrigues you, or confuses you about this poem?
2. What elements of the poem are most significant? Which lines or images stand out?
3. What is the poem about? Which words or lines articulate the poem's meaning?
4. What stories does the poem tell?
5. How would you talk about the structure or style of this poem?

LITERARY Contexts

Open Form Poems

Poetry can be in a **fixed form** (or **closed form**) that includes a speci-fied pattern of repeated lines, rhymes, and rhythms. **Sonnets, villanelles, epigrams, haikus, elegies,** and **odes** are all fixed form poems. Poems can also be in **free verse form** or **open form,** characterized by freedom from consistency in such elements as rhyme, line length, metrical pattern, and overall structure. Open form poems can be equally as deliberate as closed form poems, yet not be able to be scanned for a predominant meter or rhyme. Free verse poetry can have other rhythmic qualities, however, achieved through repetition of words, images, phrases, or structures; arrangement of words on the page or spaces between the words or lines, or some other means.

How would you describe the form of E.E. Cummings' poems? Are they fixed or open forms?

How do they achieve meaning in alternative ways from fixed form?

How do the poems' forms reflect their meanings? Or, how are the poems meaningful in what they say and how they say it?

COMPARING THEMES

In order to highlight a particular theme or stylistic element, it can be useful to compare two distinctly different poems. In the pairings that follow, poems by different writers with distinct perspectives allow us to interpret similar meanings achieved through different means. These two pairings then allow us to practice the skill we will be developing more fully in Chapter 6, "Families and Their Characters: Comparing Works of Literature."

PRE-READING   Beyond worship services, where and when can a higher power be acknowledged?

Emily Dickinson (1830–1886).   *Born to strong-willed and well-educated parents in Amherst, Massachusetts, Dickinson learned from them a respect for religion and education. Pursuing a non-conformist perspective on the Puritan religion and after receiving a rather progressive education, Dickinson turned to poetry. While her twenties were characterized by a rather involved social life in the college town of Amherst, Dickinson retreated to her poetry, books, and correspondence thereafter publishing few poems but circulating many in her prolific letters.*

Emily Dickinson

SOME KEEP THE SABBATH GOING TO CHURCH   [1862]

Some keep the Sabbath going to Church –
I keep it, staying at Home –
With a Bobolink for a Chorister –
And an Orchard, for a Dome –

5 Some keep the Sabbath in Surplice [1]–
  I just wear my Wings –
  And instead of tolling the Bell, for Church,
  Our little Sexton[2] – sings.

10 God preaches, a noted Clergyman –
  And the sermon is never long,
  So instead of getting to Heaven, at least –
  I'm going, all along.

_____

[1] **surplice:** a loose-fitting, broad-sleeved, white ecclestastical vestment.

[2] **sexton:** a church official charged with taking care of the edifice of the church and duties like tolling the bell, burying the dead, etc.

Gerard Manley Hopkins (1844–1889).   *Born to an artistic family and having received an education in classics at Oxford, Hopkins showed an early interest in poetry and religion. However, when he turned from the Anglicanism of his upbringing to Jesuit training, he gave up poetry for devotional writing to return to it later at the age of thirty-one. Hopkins' poetry demonstrates the competing Victorian influences of religion and beauty, the late Romanticism of proof of God in nature, and the classical training in formal poetry with his interest in the sonnet and internal rhythms.*

Gerard Manley Hopkins

GOD'S GRANDEUR [1877]

The world is charged with the grandeur of God.
  It will flame out, like shining from shook foil;
  It gathers to a greatness, like the ooze of oil
Crushed. Why do men then now not reck his rod?[1]
5 Generations have trod, have trod, have trod;
  And all is seared with trade; bleared, smeared with toil;
  And wears man's smudge and shares man's smell: the soil
Is bare now, nor can foot feel, being shod.
And for all this, nature is never spent;
10   There lives the dearest freshness deep down things;
And though the last lights off the black West went
  Oh, morning, at the brown brink eastward, springs—
Because the Holy Ghost over the bent
  World broods with warm breast and with ah! bright wings.

_____

[1] **reck his rod:** God as king holds a scepter, making official laws through scriptures which people ("men") disobey.

FOCUSED FREE WRITES

1. What stories do these poems tell?
2. What themes do the poems address? Provide specific examples from the texts.

3. How are similar purposes achieved through different means? How would you characterize the differences between these poems?
4. Which of the *what*, *where*, and *when* elements—title, setting, plot, or structure (listed in the chart on page 107)—are important to the meaning of these poems? How would you describe the form of these poems?
5. What about the *who* elements—character, narration, point of view, and tone? What would you say about the speaker's attitude toward this topic—the tone? What kind of god or religion is being described? Are they similar or different?
6. How about the *how* elements (imagery, symbols, syntax, diction, figurative language)? What can you say about the style or words used and how they are arranged?
7. What patterns do you notice, particularly repetitions of imagery or symbols in each poem? What do they mean?

CRITICAL Contexts

Formalist Criticism

Formalist critics examine texts in isolation, without consideration of biographical or historical information. Defined after World War I by a group of American **New Critics**, this form of criticism demands a close reading of the text itself, particularly poetry, in order to examine language, structure, and tone. Formalist critics examine how meaning is achieved through formal arrangement and may study in detail diction, irony, paradox, metaphor, and symbol. One of the early New Critics, Allan Tate, wrote a famous article in 1932 in which he examined Dickinson's poetry from a New Critical perspective. He examined the patterns in diction and sound, the allusions and connotations of the imagery, and the structure of lines and stanzas.

Examine the formal elements of Dickinson's poem in this way. In focusing on the words on the page, what do you notice about the form, structure, syntax, diction, imagery, or symbols used? Are any ideas emphasized through particular stylistic choices or distinctive patterns?

Hopkins's poetry has always been fruitful for formalist critics. "God's Grandeur" is an excellent example of a poem that can be read for its many allusions to Biblical images such as the *light*, the *flame*, the *olives*, the *rod*, the *soil*, the *bird*, and the *shod feet*. We hear of both God's condescension to *ooze* and *grandeur in flame*. We hear of how the bruised can be transformed and resurrected. Hopkins uses the form of a Petrarchan sonnet (an octave and a sestet) to trace a message about God's power in spite of human frailty.

(continued)

> Act as a formalist critic and examine the three parts of the poem: lines 1–4, lines 5–8, and lines 9–14. What story do these lines tell? What is the poem's theme?
>
> How is this story or theme reflected in how the lines sound? their rhythm? the rhyme? What patterns or repetitions do you notice?

PRE-READING

Benjamin Franklin once quipped "Certainty? In this world nothing is certain but death and taxes." One thing that is also certain is that writers since time immemorial have addressed death, wrestling with its mystery and inevitability. What are some examples of artists trying to come to grips with the universal theme of death?

Robert Frost (1874–1963).   *While considered a New England poet by most, Robert Frost was actually born in San Francisco, the son of a New England father and Scottish mother. Following his father's death, young Frost moved east where he began writing poetry in high school and then during his short time at Dartmouth. Upon marrying his high school sweetheart, Frost worked at odd jobs, teaching and farming, to support his growing family, while publishing poetry. His reputation and livelihood as a poet were established during three years in England. Afterward, he was able to assume the writer's life as a celebrated, award-winning poet and teacher in rural New England where he lived the rest of his life.*

Robert Frost

STOPPING BY WOODS ON A SNOWY EVENING

[1923]

Whose woods these are I think I know.
His house is in the village though;
He will not see me stopping here
To watch his woods fill up with snow.

5 My little horse must think it queer
To stop without a farmhouse near
Between the woods and frozen lake
The darkest evening of the year.

He gives his harness bells a shake
10 To ask if there is some mistake.
The only other sound's the sweep
Of easy wind and downy flake.

The woods are lovely, dark and deep.
But I have promises to keep,
15 And miles to go before I sleep,
And miles to go before I sleep.

Gwendolyn Brooks (1917–2000). *Gwendolyn Brooks's mother was a schoolteacher and her father was a janitor who had aspired to be a doctor. Brooks was encouraged in her writing by her parents and read and wrote extensively at a young age, publishing her first poetry as a teenager. She attended junior college and worked as a cleaning lady and secretary before marrying and becoming a mother. Her experimental poetry was met with praise and publication. After early offerings with mainstream publishers, Brooks shifted to African American small presses and began focusing her poetry on her political interests. She lectured, wrote, and occasionally taught until the end of her life.*

Gwendolyn Brooks

WE REAL COOL

[1959]

The Pool Players.
Seven at the Golden Shovel.

We real cool. We
Left school. We

Lurk late. We
Strike straight. We

5 Sing sin. We
Thin gin. We

Jazz June. We
Die soon.

FOCUSED FREE WRITES

1. These poems are quite different. Explain the differences in terms of theme, plot, setting, narrator, voice, tone, symbol, or style.
2. Are there any similarities of note? Identify particular themes or lines.
3. What stories are these poems telling?
4. What details make each poem distinctive? Provide specific examples.
5. What about the *how* elements of imagery, symbols, syntax, diction, and figurative language? What can you say about the style or words used and how they are arranged? How are they important to the meaning of the poem?
6. What patterns do you notice, particularly repetitions of imagery or symbols, rhythms or sounds? What do they mean?

LITERARY Contexts

Scanning Lines of Poetry

Scansion is the analysis of a line of poetry for **rhythm** and **meter**. To express the rhythm in music, we tap our feet or clap our hands or move our bodies to the beat of a song, and we could do the same when listening to a poem. To analyze the rhythm of a poem, we listen for the **stressed** (hard) and **unstressed** (soft) syllables in words. When you scan a line of poetry, you mark the stressed syllables with a ′ above the hard syllables and a ˘ above the soft syllables. Add marks above syllables to the following:

Jack and Jill went up the hill to fetch a pail of water.

Often, lines of poetry develop a rhythmic pattern in which stressed and unstressed syllables recur. These units of repeated patterns are called **feet**. The basic unit of a **foot** has either two or three syllables in it. There are four basic feet:

> **iambic:** unstressed syllable, then a stressed syllable
> > the bird   a crow
>
> **trochaic:** stressed syllable, then an unstressed syllable
> > swallow   parrot
>
> **anapestic:** two unstressed syllables, then a stressed syllable
> > turtledove   yellow duck
>
> **dactylic:** one stressed syllable, then two unstressed syllables
> > cardinal   kingfisher

Two auxillary feet include:

> **spondaic:** two stressed syllables
> > seagull   penguin
>
> **pyrrhic:** two unstressed syllables
> > in the   as she

The number of feet in a line determine a poem's meter:

> **monometer:** one foot
> **dimeter:** two feet
> **trimeter:** three feet
> **tetrameter:** four feet
> **pentameter:** five feet
> **hexameter:** six feet
> **heptameter:** seven feet
> **octameter:** eight feet

For example, we could look at Shakespeare's sonnet from Chapter 3:

My mis/tress' eyes/ are no/thing like/ the sun

This line is written in the most common pattern for poetry in English, **iambic pentameter** (five feet of unstressed then stressed syllables).

Finally, a caesura, or a pause, in a line may be represented by a double slash (//).

Scan the poems by Frost and Brooks, or any other poems in this chapter. How does the rhythm and meter of these poems contribute to the meaning of the words? In other words, how does the sound contribute to the theme?

PLAY

The following play is rich in its thematic focus on the presence of the past and in the development of these complex family members as characters. It can also be fruitful for stylistic analysis. As you read, determine in what ways the form of the play embodies its meaning.

PRE-READING

What are some classic conflicts between parents and children? How can the past be an obstacle to the future?

Tennessee Williams (1911–1983). *Born Thomas Lanier Williams, Tennessee Williams once wrote that he assumed the pseudonym to cover up a brief but poor career as a poet. Grandson of an Episcopal clergyman and son of a traveling salesman, Williams also described his early affinity for the South and his distress at being uprooted from it at an early age. Unable to afford college, Williams survived by working odd jobs until a few fellowships and a script writing opportunity for MGM allowed him time and money to produce* The Glass Menagerie, *the play that established his career. Many successes and awards followed for plays that often tackled controversial and taboo topics.*

Tennessee Williams

THE GLASS MENAGERIE   [1945]

THE CHARACTERS

AMANDA WINGFIELD (*the mother*)

A little woman of great but confused vitality clinging frantically to another time and place. Her characterization must be carefully created, not copied from type. She is not paranoiac, but her life is paranoia. There is much to admire in Amanda, and as much to love and pity as there is to laugh at. Certainly she has endurance and a kind of heroism, and though her foolishness makes her unwittingly cruel at times, there is tenderness in her slight person.

LAURA WINGFIELD (*her daughter*)

Amanda, having failed to establish contact with reality, continues to live vitally in her illusions, but Laura's situation is even graver. A childhood illness has left her crippled, one leg slightly shorter than the other, and held in a brace. This defect need not be more than suggested on the stage. Stemming from this, Laura's separation increases till she is like a piece of her own glass collection, too exquisitely fragile to move from the shelf.

TOM WINGFIELD (*her son*)

And the narrator of the play. A poet with a job in a warehouse. His nature is not remorseless, but to escape from a trap he has to act without pity.

JIM O'CONNOR (*the gentleman caller*)

A nice, ordinary, young man.

PRODUCTION NOTES[1]

Being a "memory play," *The Glass Menagerie* can be presented with unusual freedom of convention. Because of its considerably delicate or tenuous material, atmospheric touches and subtleties of direction play a particularly important part. Expressionism and all other unconventional techniques in drama have only one valid aim, and that is a closer approach to truth. When a play employs unconventional techniques, it is not, or certainly shouldn't be, trying to escape its responsibility of dealing with reality, or interpreting experience, but is actually or should be attempting to find a closer approach, a more penetrating and vivid expression of things as they are. The straight realistic play with its genuine Frigidaire and authentic ice-cubes, its characters who speak exactly as its audience speaks, corresponds to the academic landscape and has the same virtue of a photographic likeness. Everyone should know nowadays the unimportance of the photographic in art: that truth, life, or reality is an organic thing which the poetic imagination can represent or suggest, in essence, only through transformation, through changing into other forms than those which were merely present in appearance.

These remarks are not meant as a preface only to this particular play. They have to do with a conception of a new, plastic theatre which must take the place of the exhausted theatre of realistic conventions if the theatre is to resume vitality as a part of our culture.

THE SCREEN DEVICE: There is *only one important difference between the original and the acting version of the play* and that is the *omission* in the latter of the device that I tentatively included in my *original* script. This device was the use of a screen on which were projected magic-lantern slides bearing images or titles. I do not regret the omission of this device from the original Broadway production. The extraordinary power of Miss Taylor's° performance made it suitable to have the utmost simplicity in the physical production. But I think it may be interesting to some readers to see how this device was conceived. So I am putting it into the published manuscript. These images and legends, projected

---

[1] The production notes are by Williams and are part of the play. °**Miss Taylor's:** The role of Amanda was first played by the American actress Laurette Taylor (1884–1946).

from behind, were cast on a section of wall between the front-room and dining-room areas, which should be indistinguishable from the rest when not in use.

The purpose of this will probably be apparent. It is to give accent to certain values in each scene. Each scene contains a particular point (or several) which is structurally the most important. In an episodic play, such as this, the basic structure or narrative line may be obscured from the audience; the effect may seem fragmentary rather than architectural. This may not be the fault of the play so much as a lack of attention in the audience. The legend or image upon the screen will strengthen the effect of what is merely allusion in the writing and allow the primary point to be made more simply and lightly than if the entire responsibility were on the spoken lines. Aside from this structural value, I think the screen will have a definite emotional appeal, less definable but just as important. An imaginative producer or director may invent many other uses for this device than those indicated in the present script. In fact the possibilities of the device seem much larger to me than the instance of this play can possibly utilize.

5 The Music: Another extra-literary accent in this play is provided by the use of music. A single recurring tune, "The Glass Menagerie,"° is used to give emotional emphasis to suitable passages. This tune is like circus music, not when you are on the grounds or in the immediate vicinity of the parade, but when you are at some distance and very likely thinking of something else. It seems under those circumstances to continue almost interminably and it weaves in and out of your preoccupied consciousness; then it is the lightest, most delicate music in the world and perhaps the saddest. It expresses the surface vivacity of life with the underlying strain of immutable and inexpressible sorrow. When you look at a piece of delicately spun glass you think of two things: how beautiful it is and how easily it can be broken. Both of those ideas should be woven into the recurring tune, which dips in and out of the play as if it were carried on a wind that changes. It serves as a thread of connection and allusion between the narrator with his separate point in time and space and the subject of his story. Between each episode it returns as reference to the emotion, nostalgia, which is the first condition of the play. It is primarily Laura's music and therefore comes out most clearly when the play focuses upon her and the lovely fragility of glass which is her image.

THE LIGHTING: The lighting in the play is not realistic. In keeping with the atmosphere of memory, the stage is dim. Shafts of light are focused on selected areas or actors, sometimes in contradistinction to what is the apparent center. For instance, in the quarrel scene between Tom and Amanda, in which Laura has no active part, the clearest pool of light is on her figure. This is also true of the supper scene, when her silent figure on the sofa should remain the visual center. The light upon Laura should be distinct from the others, having a peculiar pristine clarity such as light used in early religious portraits of female saints or madonnas. A certain correspondence to light in religious paintings, such as El Greco's,° where the figures are radiant in atmosphere that is relatively dusky,

---

° 5 **"The Glass Menagerie"**: Original music, including this recurrent theme, was composed for the play by Paul Bowles. 6 **El Greco**: Greek painter (c. 1548–1614) who lived in Spain; typical paintings have elongated and distorted figures and extremely vivid foreground lighting set against a murky background.

could be effectively used throughout the play. (It will also permit a more effective use of the screen.) A free, imaginative use of light can be of enormous value in giving a mobile, plastic quality to plays of a more or less static nature.

Tennessee Williams

SCENE 1

0.1   *The Wingfield apartment is in the rear of the building, one of those vast hive-like conglomerations of cellular living-units that flower as warty growths in overcrowded urban centers of lower middle-class population and are symptomatic of the impulse of this largest and fundamentally enslaved section of American society to avoid fluidity and differentiation and to exist and function as one interfused mass of automatism.*

0.2   *The apartment faces an alley and is entered by a fire escape, a structure whose name is a touch of accidental poetic truth, for all of these huge buildings are always burning with the slow and implacable fires of human desperation. The fire escape is part of what we see—that is, the landing of it and steps descending from it.*

0.3   *The scene is memory and is therefore nonrealistic. Memory takes a lot of poetic license. It omits some details; others are exaggerated, according to the emotional value of the articles it touches, for memory is seated predominantly in the heart. The interior is therefore rather dim and poetic.*

0.4   *At the rise of the curtain, the audience is faced with the dark, grim rear wall of the Wingfield tenement. This building is flanked on both sides by dark, narrow alleys which run into murky canyons of tangled clotheslines, garbage cans, and the sinister latticework of neighboring fire escapes. It is up and down these side alleys that exterior entrances and exits are made during the play. At the end of Tom's opening commentary, the dark tenement wall slowly becomes transparent° and reveals the interior of the ground-floor Wingfield apartment.*

0.5   *Nearest the audience is the living room, which also serves as a sleeping room for* LAURA, *the sofa unfolding to make her bed. Just beyond, separated from the living room by a wide arch or second proscenium with transparent faded portieres° (or second curtain), is the dining room. In an old-fashioned whatnot° in the living room are seen scores of transparent glass animals. A blown-up photograph of the father hangs on the wall of the living room, to the left of the archway. It is the face of a very handsome young man in a doughboy's° First World War cap. He is gallantly smiling, ineluctably smiling, as if to say "I will be smiling forever."*

0.6   *Also hanging on the wall, near the photograph, are a typewriter keyboard chart and a Gregg shorthand diagram. An upright typewriter on a small table stands beneath the charts.*

0.7   *The audience hears and sees the opening scene in the dining room through both the transparent fourth wall of the building and the transparent gauze portieres of the dining-room arch. It is during this revealing scene that the fourth wall slowly ascends, out of sight. This transparent exterior wall is not brought down again until the very end of the play, during Tom's final speech.*

°0.4 **transparent:** The wall is painted on a scrim, a transparent curtain that is opaque when lit from the front and transparent when lit from behind. 0.5 **portieres:** curtains hung in a doorway; in production, these may also be painted on a scrim. **whatnot:** a small set of shelves for ornaments. **doughboy:** popular name for an American infantryman during World War I.

0.8   *The narrator is an undisguised convention of the play. He takes whatever license with dramatic convention is convenient to his purposes.*

0.9   *Tom enters, dressed as a merchant sailor, and strolls across to the fire escape. There he stops and lights a cigarette. He addresses the audience.*

TOM: Yes, I have tricks in my pocket, I have things up my sleeve. But I am the opposite of a stage magician. He gives you illusion that has the appearance of truth. I give you truth in the pleasant disguise of illusion.

To begin with, I turn back time. I reverse it to that quaint period, the thirties, when the huge middle class of America was matriculating in a school for the blind. Their eyes had failed them, or they had failed their eyes, and so they were having their fingers pressed forcibly down on the fiery Braille alphabet of a dissolving economy.

In Spain there was revolution. Here there was only shouting and confusion.
1.3   In Spain there was Guernica.° Here there were disturbances of labor, sometimes pretty violent, in otherwise peaceful cities such as Chicago, Cleveland, Saint Louis....This is the social background of the play.

[*Music begins to play.*]

The play is memory. Being a memory play, it is dimly lighted, it is sentimental, it is not realistic. In memory everything seems to happen to music. That explains the fiddle in the wings.

I am the narrator of the play, and also a character in it. The other characters are my mother, Amanda, my sister, Laura, and a gentleman caller who appears in the final scenes. He is the most realistic character in the play, being an emissary from a world of reality that we were somehow set apart from. But since I have a poet's weakness for symbols, I am using this character also as a symbol; he is the long-delayed but always expected something that we live for.

There is a fifth character in the play who doesn't appear except in this larger-than-life-size photograph over the mantel. This is our father who left us a long time ago. He was a telephone man who fell in love with long distances; he gave up his job with the telephone company and skipped the light fantastic out of town....

The last we heard of him was a picture postcard from Mazatlan, on the Pacific coast of Mexico, containing a message of two words: "Hello—Goodbye!" and no address.

I think the rest of the play will explain itself....

[*AMANDA's voice becomes audible through the portieres.*]

[*Legend on screen: "Où sont les neiges."°*]

[*TOM divides the portieres and enters the dining room. AMANDA and LAURA are seated at a drop-leaf table. Eating is indicated by gestures without food or utensils. AMANDA*

°1.3 **Guernica:** a Basque town that was destroyed in 1937 by German planes fighting on General Franco's side during the Spanish Civil War. The huge moral *Guernica*, painted by Pablo Picasso, depicts the horror of that bombardment.

°1.8 S.D.: **"Où sont les neiges":** "Where are the snows (of yesteryear)," refrain from "The Ballade of Dead Ladies" by the French poet François Villon (c. 1431–1463).

faces the audience. TOM and LAURA are seated profile. The interior has lit up softly and through the scrim we see AMANDA and LAURA seated at the table.]

AMANDA: [*calling*] Tom?
TOM: Yes, Mother.
AMANDA: We can't say grace until you come to the table!
5 TOM: Coming, Mother. [*He bows slightly and withdraws, reappearing a few moments later in his place at the table.*]
AMANDA: [*to her son*] Honey, don't *push* with your *fingers*. If you have to push with something, the thing to push with is a crust of bread. And chew—chew! Animals have secretions in their stomachs which enable them to digest food without mastication, but human beings are supposed to chew their food before they swallow it down. Eat food leisurely, son, and really enjoy it. A well-cooked meal has lots of delicate flavors that have to be held in the mouth for appreciation. So chew your food and give your salivary glands a chance to function!

[*TOM deliberately lays his imaginary fork down and pushes his chair back from the table.*]

TOM: I haven't enjoyed one bite of this dinner because of your constant directions on how to eat it. It's you that make me rush through meals with your hawk-like attention to every bite I take. Sickening—spoils my appetite—all this discussion of—animals' secretion—salivary glands—mastication!
AMANDA: [*lightly*] Temperament like a Metropolitan star.°

[*TOM rises and walks toward the living room.*]

You're not excused from the table.
10 TOM: I'm getting a cigarette.
AMANDA: You smoke too much.

[*LAURA rises.*]

LAURA: I'll bring in the blanc mange.°

[*TOM remains standing with his cigarette by the portieres.*]

AMANDA: [*rising*] No, sister, no, sister°—you be the lady this time and I'll be the darky.
LAURA: I'm already up.
AMANDA: Resume your seat, little sister—I want you to stay fresh and pretty— for gentlemen callers!
15 LAURA: [*sitting down*] I'm not expecting any gentlemen callers.
AMANDA: [*crossing out to the kitchenette, airily*] Sometimes they come when they are least expected! Why, I remember one Sunday afternoon in Blue Mountain°—

°8 **Metropolitan star:** the Metropolitan Opera in New York City; opera stars are traditionally considered to be highly temperamental.

°11 **blanc mange:** a bland molded pudding or custard. 12 **sister:** In the South of Amanda's youth, the oldest daughter in a family was frequently called "sister" by her parents and siblings. 16 **Blue Mountain:** an imaginary town in northwest Mississippi modeled after Clarksville, where Williams spent much of his youth. Blue Mountain (Clarksville) is at the northern edge of the Mississippi Delta, a large fertile plain that supports numerous plantations. This is the recollected world of Amanda's youth—plantations, wealth, black servants, and gentlemen callers who were the sons of cotton planters.

[*She enters the kitchenette.*]

TOM: I know what's coming!

LAURA: Yes. But let her tell it.

TOM: Again?

20 LAURA: She loves to tell it.

[*AMANDA returns with a bowl of dessert.*]

AMANDA: One Sunday afternoon in Blue Mountain—your mother received— seventeen!—gentlemen callers! Why, sometimes there weren't chairs enough to accommodate them all. We had to send the nigger over to bring in folding chairs from the parish house.

TOM: [*remaining at the portieres*] How did you entertain those gentlemen callers?

AMANDA: I understood the art of conversation!

TOM: I bet you could talk.

25 AMANDA: Girls in those days *knew* how to talk, I can tell you.

TOM: Yes?

[*Image on screen: AMANDA as a girl on a porch, greeting callers.*]

AMANDA: They knew how to entertain their gentlemen callers. It wasn't enough for a girl to be possessed of a pretty face and a graceful figure—although I wasn't slighted in either respect. She also needed to have a nimble wit and a tongue to meet all occasions.

TOM: What did you talk about?

AMANDA: Things of importance going on in the world! Never anything coarse or common or vulgar.

[*She addresses TOM as though he were seated in the vacant chair at the table though he remains by the portieres. He plays this scene as though reading from a script.°*]

My callers were gentleman—all! Among my callers were some of the most prominent young planters of the Mississippi Delta—planters and sons of planters!

[*TOM motions for music and a spot of light on AMANDA. Her eyes lift, her face glows, her voice becomes rich and elegiac.*]

[*Screen legend: "Où sont les neiges d'antan?"°*]

There was young Champ Laughlin who later became vice-president of the Delta Planters Bank. Hadley Stevenson who was drowned in Moon Lake and left his widow one hundred and fifty thousand in Government bonds. There were the Cutrere brothers, Wesley and Bates. Bates was one of my bright particular beaux! He got in a quarrel with that wild Wainwright boy. They shot it out on the floor of Moon Lake Casino. Bates was shot through the stomach. Died in the ambulance on his way to Memphis. His widow was also well provided-for, came into eight or ten thousand acres, that's all. She married

---

° 29.1 S.D. **script:** Here Tom becomes both a character in the play and the stage manager.

° 29.2 S.D. *"Où sont les neiges d'antan?":* Where are the snows of yesteryear?

him on the rebound—never loved her—carried my picture on him the night he died! And there was that boy that every girl in the Delta had set her cap for! That beautiful, brilliant young Fitzhugh boy from Greene County!

30   TOM: What did he leave his widow?

AMANDA: He never married! Gracious, you talk as though all of my old admirers had turned up their toes to the daisies!

TOM: Isn't this the first you've mentioned that still survives?

AMANDA: That Fitzhugh boy went North and made a fortune—came to be known as the Wolf of Wall Street! He had the Midas touch,° whatever he touched turned to gold! And I could have been Mrs. Duncan J. Fitzhugh, mind you! But—I picked your *father!*

LAURA: [*rising*] Mother, let me clear the table.

35   AMANDA: No, dear, you go in front and study your typewriter chart. Or practice your shorthand a little. Stay fresh and pretty!—It's almost time for our gentlemen callers to start arriving. [*She flounces girlishly toward the kitchenette.*] How many do you suppose we're going to entertain this afternoon?

[*TOM throws down the paper and jumps up with a groan.*]

LAURA: [*alone in the dining room*] I don't believe we're going to receive any, Mother.

AMANDA: [*reappearing airily*] What? No one?—not one? You must be joking!

[*LAURA nervously echoes her laugh. She slips in a fugitive manner through the half-open portieres and draws them gently behind her. A shaft of very clear light is thrown on her face against the faded tapestry of the curtains. Faintly the music of "The Glass Menagerie" is heard as she continues lightly:*]

> Not one gentleman caller? It can't be true! There must be a flood, there must have been a tornado!

LAURA: It isn't a flood, it's not a tornado, Mother. I'm just not popular like you were in Blue Mountain....

[*TOM utters another groan. LAURA glances at him with a faint, apologetic smile. Her voice catches a little:*]

> Mother's afraid I'm going to be an old maid.

[*The scene dims out with the "Glass Menagerie" music.*]

SCENE 2

On the dark stage the screen is lighted with the image of blue roses. Gradually LAURA's figure becomes apparent and the screen goes out. The music subsides.

LAURA is seated in the delicate ivory chair at the small clawfoot table. She wears a dress of soft violet material for a kimono—her hair is tied back from her forehead with a ribbon. She is washing and polishing her collection of glass. AMANDA appears on the fire escape steps. At the sound of her ascent, LAURA catches her breath, thrusts the bowl of ornaments away, and seats herself stiffly before the diagram of the typewriter keyboard as though it held her spellbound. Something has happened to AMANDA. It is

---

° 33 **Midas touch:** In Greek mythology, King Midas was given the power to turn everything he touched into gold.

written in her face as she climbs to the landing: a look that is grim and hopeless and a little absurd. She has on one of those cheap or imitation velvety-looking cloth coats with imitation fur collar. Her hat is five or six years old, one of those dreadful cloche hats that were worn in the late Twenties, and she is clutching an enormous black patent-leather pocketbook with nickel clasps and initials. This is her full-dress outfit, the one she usually wears to the D.A.R.° Before entering she looks through the door. She purses her lips, opens her eyes very wide, rolls them upward and shakes her head. Then she slowly lets herself in the door. Seeing her mother's expression, LAURA touches her lips with a nervous gesture.

LAURA: Hello, Mother, I was—[*She makes a nervous gesture toward the chart on the wall. AMANDA leans against the shut door and stares at LAURA with a martyred look.*]

AMANDA: Deception? Deception? [*She slowly removes her hat and gloves, continuing the sweet suffering stare. She lets the hat and gloves fall on the floor—a bit of acting.*]

LAURA: [*shakily*] How was the D.A.R. meeting?

[*AMANDA slowly opens her purse and removes a dainty white handkerchief which she shakes out delicately and delicately touches to her lips and nostrils.*]

Didn't you go to the D.A.R. meeting, Mother?

AMANDA: [*faintly, almost inaudibly*]—No.—No. [*then more forcibly:*] I did not have the strength—to go to the D.A.R. In fact, I did not have the courage! I wanted to find a hole in the ground and hide myself in it forever! [*She crosses slowly to the wall and removes the diagram of the typewriter keyboard. She holds it in front of her for a second, staring at it sweetly and sorrowfully— then bites her lips and tears it in two pieces.*]

5   LAURA: [*faintly*] Why did you do that, Mother?

[*AMANDA repeats the same procedure with the chart of the Gregg Alphabet.*]

Why are you—

AMANDA: Why? Why? How old are you, Laura?

LAURA: Mother, you know my age.

AMANDA: I thought you were an adult; it seems that I was mistaken. [*She crosses slowly to the sofa and sinks down and stares at LAURA.*]

LAURA: Please don't stare at me, Mother.

[*AMANDA closes her eyes and lowers her head. There is a ten-second pause.*]

10   AMANDA: What are we going to do, what is going to become of us, what is the future?

[*There is another pause.*]

LAURA: Has something happened, Mother?

[*AMANDA draws a long breath, takes out the handkerchief again, goes through the dabbing process.*]

Mother, has—something happened?

AMANDA: I'll be all right in a minute, I'm just bewildered—[*She hesitates.*]— by life. . . .

° 0.2 **D.A.R.**: Daughters of the American Revolution, a patriotic women's organization (founded in 1890) open only to women whose ancestors aided the American Revolution.

LAURA: Mother, I wish that you would tell me what's happened!

AMANDA: As you know, I was supposed to be inducted into my office at the D.A.R. this afternoon.

[*Screen image: A swarm of typewriters.*]

But I stopped off at Rubicam's Business College to speak to your teachers about your having a cold and ask them what progress they thought you were making down there.

15 LAURA: Oh....

AMANDA: I went to the typing instructor and introduced myself as your mother. She didn't know who you were.

"Wingfield," she said, "We don't have any such student enrolled at the school!"

I assured her she did, that you had been going to classes since early in January.

"I wonder," she said, "if you could be talking about that terribly shy little girl who dropped out of school after only a few days' attendance?"

"No," I said, "Laura, my daughter, has been going to school every day for the past six weeks!"

"Excuse me," she said. She took the attendance book out and there was your name, unmistakably printed, and all the dates you were absent until they decided that you had dropped out of school.

I still said, "No, there must have been some mistake! There must have been some mix-up in the records!"

And she said, "No—I remember her perfectly now. Her hands shook so that she couldn't hit the right keys! The first time we gave a speed test, she broke down completely—was sick at the stomach and almost had to be carried into the wash room! After that morning she never showed up any more. We phoned the house but never got any answer"—While I was working at Famous-Barr,° I suppose, demonstrating those—

[*She indicates a brassiere with her hands.*]

Oh! I felt so weak I could barely keep on my feet! I had to sit down while they got me a glass of water! Fifty dollars' tuition, all of our plans—my hopes and ambitions for you—just gone up the spout, just gone up the spout like that.

[LAURA *draws a long breath and gets awkwardly to her feet. She crosses to the Victrola and winds it up.*°]

What are you doing?

LAURA: Oh! [*She releases the handle and returns to her seat.*]

AMANDA: Laura, where have you been going when you've gone out pretending that you were going to business college?

LAURA: I've just been going out walking.

20 AMANDA: That's not true.

°16.8 **Famous-Barr:** a department store in St. Louis. 16.11 S. D. *winds it up*: Laura is using a spring-powered (rather than electric) phonograph that has to be rewound frequently.

LAURA: It is. I just went walking.

AMANDA: Walking? Walking? In winter? Deliberately courting pneumonia in that light coat? Where did you walk to, Laura?

LAURA: All sorts of places—mostly in the park.

AMANDA: Even after you'd started catching that cold?

25 LAURA: It was the lesser of two evils, Mother.

[Screen image: Winter scene in a park.]

I couldn't go back there. I—threw up—on the floor!

AMANDA: From half past seven till after five every day you mean to tell me you walked around the park, because you wanted to make me think that you were still going to Rubicam's Business College?

LAURA: It wasn't as bad as it sounds. I went inside places to get warmed up.

AMANDA: Inside where?

LAURA: I went in the art museum and the bird houses at the Zoo. I visited the penguins every day! Sometimes I did without lunch and went to the movies. Lately I've been spending most of my afternoons in the Jewel Box, that big glass house where they raise the tropical flowers.

30 AMANDA: You did all this to deceive me, just for deception? [LAURA looks down.] Why?

LAURA: Mother, when you're disappointed, you get that awful suffering look on your face, like the picture of Jesus' mother in the museum!

AMANDA: Hush!

LAURA: I couldn't face it.

[There is a pause. A whisper of strings is heard. Legend on screen: "The Crust of Humility."]

AMANDA: [hopelessly fingering the huge pocketbook] So what are we going to do the rest of our lives? Stay home and watch the parades go by? Amuse ourselves with the glass menagerie, darling? Eternally play those worn-out phonograph records your father left as a painful reminder of him? We won't have a business career—we've given that up because it gave us nervous indigestion! [She laughs wearily.] What is there left but dependency all our lives? I know so well what becomes of unmarried women who aren't prepared to occupy a position. I've seen such pitiful cases in the South—barely tolerated spinsters living upon the grudging patronage of sister's husband or brother's wife!—stuck away in some little mousetrap of a room—encouraged by one in-law to visit another—little birdlike women without any nest—eating the crust of humility all their life!

Is that the future that we've mapped out for ourselves? I swear it's the only alternative I can think of! [She pauses.] It isn't a very pleasant alternative, is it? [She pauses again.] Of course—some girls do marry.

[LAURA twists her hands nervously.]

Haven't you ever liked some boy?

35 LAURA: Yes. I liked one once. [She rises.] I came across his picture a while ago.

AMANDA: [with some interest] He gave you his picture?

LAURA: No, it's in the yearbook.

AMANDA: [disappointed] Oh—a high school boy.

[Screen image: JIM as the high school hero bearing a silver cup.]

LAURA: Yes. His name was Jim. [*She lifts the heavy annual from the claw-foot table.*] Here he is in *The Pirates of Penzance.*°

40 AMANDA: [*absently*] The what?

LAURA: The operetta the senior class put on. He had a wonderful voice and we sat across the aisle from each other Mondays, Wednesdays and Fridays in the Aud. Here he is with the silver cup for debating! See his grin?

AMANDA: [*absently*] He must have had a jolly disposition.

LAURA: He used to call me—Blue Roses.

[Screen image: Blue roses.]

AMANDA: Why did he call you such a name as that?

45 LAURA: When I had that attack of pleurosis—he asked me what was the matter when I came back. I said pleurosis—he thought that I said Blue Roses! So that's what he always called me after that. Whenever he saw me, he'd holler, "Hello, Blue Roses!" I didn't care for the girl that he went out with. Emily Meisenbach. Emily was the best-dressed girl at Soldan. She never struck me, though, as being sincere....It says in the Personal Section—they're engaged. That's—six years ago! They must be married by now.

AMANDA: Girls that aren't cut out for business careers usually wind up married to some nice man. [*She gets up with a spark of revival.*] Sister, that's what you'll do!

[LAURA utters a startled, doubtful laugh. She reaches quickly for a piece of glass.]

LAURA: But, Mother—

AMANDA: Yes? [*She goes over to the photograph.*]

LAURA: [*in a tone of frightened apology*] I'm—crippled!

50 AMANDA: Nonsense! Laura, I've told you never, never to use that word. Why, you're not crippled, you just have a little defect—hardly noticeable, even! When people have some slight disadvantage like that, they cultivate other things to make up for it—develop charm—and vivacity—and— *charm*! That's all you have to do! [*She turns again to the photograph.*] One thing your father had *plenty of*—was *charm*!

[The scene fades out with music.]

SCENE 3

[Legend on screen: "After the fiasco—"

TOM speaks from the fire escape landing.]

TOM: After the fiasco at Rubicam's Business College, the idea of getting a gentleman caller for Laura began to play a more and more important part in Mother's calculations. It became an obsession. Like some archetype of the universal unconscious, the image of the gentleman caller haunted our small apartment....

° 39 *The Pirates of Penzance:* a comic light opera (1879) by W. S. Gilbert and Arthur Sullivan.

[Screen image: A young man at the door of a house with flowers.]

An evening at home rarely passed without some allusion to this image, this specter, this hope....Even when he wasn't mentioned, his presence hung in Mother's preoccupied look and in my sister's frightened, apologetic manner—hung like a sentence passed upon the Wingfields!

Mother was a woman of action as well as words. She began to take logical steps in the planned direction. Late that winter and in the early spring—realizing that extra money would be needed to properly feather the nest and plume the bird—she conducted a vigorous campaign on the telephone, roping in subscribers to one of those magazines for matrons called The Homemaker's Companion, the type of journal that features the serialized sublimations of ladies of letters who think in terms of delicate cuplike breasts, slim, tapering waists, rich, creamy thighs, eyes like wood smoke in autumn, fingers that soothe and caress like strains of music, bodies as powerful as Etruscan sculpture.

[Screen image: The cover of a glamor magazine.]

Amanda enters with the telephone on a long extension cord. She is spotlighted in the dim stage.]

AMANDA: Ida Scott? This is Amanda Wingfield! We missed you at the D.A.R. last Monday! I said to myself: She's probably suffering with that sinus condition! How is that sinus condition?

Horrors! Heaven have mercy!—You're a Christian martyr, yes, that's what you are, a Christian martyr!

Well, I just now happened to notice that your subscription to the *Companion's* about to expire! Yes, it expires with the next issue, honey!—just when that wonderful new serial by Bessie Mae Hopper is getting off to such an exciting start. Oh, honey, it's something that you can't miss! You remember how *Gone with the Wind*° took everybody by storm? You simply couldn't go out if you hadn't read it. All everybody *talked* was Scarlett O'Hara. Well, this is a book that critics already compare to *Gone with the Wind*. It's the *Gone with the Wind* of the post-World-War generation!—What?—Burning?—Oh, honey, don't let them burn, go take a look in the oven and I'll hold the wire! Heavens—I think she's hung up!

[The scene dims out.]

[Legend on screen: "You think I'm in love with Continental Shoemakers?"]

[Before the lights come up again, the violent voices of TOM *and* AMANDA *are heard. They are quarreling behind the portieres. In front of them stands* LAURA *with clenched hands and panicky expression. A clear pool of light is on her figure throughout this scene.]*

TOM: What in Christ's name am I—
AMANDA: *[shrilly]* Don't you use that—

° 2.3 *Gone with the Wind*: popular novel (1936) by Margaret Mitchell (1900–1949), set in the South before, during, and after the Civil War. Scarlett O'Hara was the heroine.

5   TOM: —supposed to do!

AMANDA: —expression! Not in my—

TOM: Ohhh!

AMANDA: —presence! Have you gone out of your senses?

TOM: I have, that's true, *driven* out!

10   AMANDA: What is the matter with you, you—big—big—IDIOT!

TOM: Look!—I've got *no thing*, no single thing—

AMANDA: Lower your voice!

TOM: —in my life here that I can call my OWN! Everything is—

AMANDA: Stop that shouting!

15   TOM: Yesterday you confiscated my books! You had the nerve to—

AMANDA: I took that horrible novel back to the library—yes! That hideous book
    by that insane Mr. Lawrence.°

[*TOM laughs wildly.*]

    I cannot control the output of diseased minds or people who cater to them—

[*TOM laughs still more wildly.*]

BUT I WON'T ALLOW SUCH FILTH BROUGHT INTO MY HOUSE! No, no, no, no, no!

TOM: House, house! Who pays rent on it, who makes a slave of himself to—

AMANDA: [*fairly screeching*] Don't you DARE to—

TOM: No, no, I mustn't say things! *I've* got to just—

20   AMANDA: Let me tell you—

TOM: I don't want to hear any more!

[*He tears the portieres open. The dining-room area is lit with turgid smoky red glow.
Now we see AMANDA; her hair is in metal curlers and she is wearing a very old
bathrobe, much too large for her slight figure, a relic of the faithless Mr. Wingfield.
The upright typewriter now stands on the drop-leaf table, along with a wild disarray
of manuscripts. The quarrel was probably precipitated by AMANDA's interruption of
TOM's creative labor. A chair lies overthrown on the floor. Their gesticulating shadows
are cast on the ceiling by the fiery glow.*]

AMANDA: You *will* hear more, you—

TOM: No, I won't hear more, I'm going out!

AMANDA: You come right back in—

25   TOM: Out, out, out! Because I'm—

AMANDA: Come back here, Tom Wingfield! I'm not through talking to you!

TOM: Oh, go—

LAURA: [*desperately*]—Tom!

AMANDA: You're going to listen, and no more insolence from you! I'm at the end
    of my patience!

[*He comes back toward her.*]

30   TOM: What do you think I'm at? Aren't I supposed to have any patience to reach
    the end of, Mother? I know, I know. It seems unimportant to you, what I'm
    doing—what I *want* to do—having a little *difference* between them! You
    don't think that—

°16 **Lawrence**: D. H. Lawrence (1885–1930), English poet and fiction writer, popularly known as an
advocate of passion and sexuality.

AMANDA: I think you've been doing things that you're ashamed of. That's why you act like this. I don't believe that you go every night to the movies. Nobody goes to the movies night after night. Nobody in their right minds goes to the movies as often as you pretend to. People don't go to the movies at nearly midnight, and movies don't let out at two A.M. Come in stumbling. Muttering to yourself like a maniac! You get three hours' sleep and then go to work. Oh, I can picture the way you're doing down there. Moping, doping, because you're in no condition.

TOM: [*wildly*] No, I'm in no condition!

AMANDA: What right have you got to jeopardize your job? Jeopardize the security of us all? How do you think we'd manage if you were—

TOM: Listen! You think I'm crazy about the *warehouse*? [*He bends fiercely toward her slight figure.*] You think I'm in love with the Continental Shoemakers? You think I want to spend fifty-five *years* down there in that—*celotex interior!* with—*fluorescent—tubes!* Look! I'd rather somebody picked up a crowbar and battered out my brains—than go back mornings! I *go!* Every time you come in yelling that God damn "*Rise and Shine!*" "*Rise and Shine!*" I say to myself, "How *lucky dead* people are!" But I get up. I *go!* For sixty-five dollars a month I give up all that I dream of doing and being *ever!* And you say self—*self's* all I ever think of. Why, listen, if self is what I thought of, Mother, I'd be where he is— GONE! [*He points to his father's picture.*] As far as the system of transportation reaches! [*He starts past her. She grabs his arm.*] Don't grab at me, Mother!

35 AMANDA: Where are you going?

TOM: I'm going to the *movies!*

AMANDA: I don't believe that lie!

[*TOM crouches toward her, overtowering her tiny figure. She backs away, gasping.*]

TOM: I'm going to opium dens! Yes, opium dens, dens of vice and criminals' hangouts, Mother. I've joined the Hogan Gang,° I'm a hired assassin, I carry a tommy gun in a violin case! I run a string of cat houses in the Valley! They call me Killer, Killer Wingfield, I'm leading a double life, a simple, honest warehouse worker by day, by night a dynamic *czar* of the *underworld, Mother.* I go to gambling casinos, I spin away fortunes on the roulette table! I wear a patch over one eye and a false mustache, sometimes I put on green whiskers. On those occasions they call me—*El Diablo!*° Oh, I could tell you many things to make you sleepless! My enemies plan to dynamite this place. They're going to blow us all sky-high some night! I'll be glad, very happy, and so will you! You'll go up, up on a broomstick, over Blue Mountain with seventeen gentlemen callers! You ugly—babbling old—*witch....*

[*He goes through a series of violent, clumsy movements, seizing his overcoat, lunging to the door, pulling it fiercely open. The women watch him, aghast. His arm catches in the sleeve of the coat as he struggles to pull it on. For a moment he is pinioned by the bulky garment. With an outraged groan he tears the coat off again, splitting the shoulder of it, and hurls it across the room. It strikes against the shelf of LAURA's glass collection, and there is a tinkle of shattering glass. LAURA cries out as if wounded.*]

° 38 **Hogan Gang:** one of the major criminal organizations in St. Louis in the 1920s and 1930s.
° 38 *El Diablo:* the devil.

Music.

Screen legend: "The Glass Menagerie."]

LAURA: [*shrilly*] My glass!—menagerie.... [*She covers her face and turns away.*]

[*But* AMANDA *is still stunned and stupefied by the "ugly witch" so that she barely notices this occurrence. Now she recovers her speech.*]

40 AMANDA: [*in an awful voice*] I won't speak to you—until you apologize!

[*She crosses through the portieres and draws them together behind her.* TOM *is left with* LAURA. LAURA *clings weakly to the mantel with her face averted.* TOM *stares at her stupidly for a moment. Then he crosses to the shelf. He drops awkwardly on his knees to collect the fallen glass, glancing at* LAURA *as if he would speak but couldn't.*]

"The Glass Menagerie" music steals in as the scene dims out.]

SCENE 4

The interior of the apartment is dark. There is a faint light in the alley. A deep-voiced bell in a church is tolling the hour of five.

    TOM *appears at the top of the alley. After each solemn boom of the bell in the tower, he shakes a little noisemaker or rattle as if to express the tiny spasm of man in contrast to the sustained power and dignity of the Almighty. This and the unsteadiness of his advance make it evident that he has been drinking. As he climbs the few steps to the fire escape landing light steals up inside.* LAURA *appears in the front room in a nightdress. She notices that* TOM's *bed is empty.* TOM *fishes in his pockets for his door key, removing a motley assortment of articles in the search, including a shower of movie ticket stubs and an empty bottle. At last he finds the key, but just as he is about to insert it, it slips from his fingers. He strikes a match and crouches below the door.*

TOM: [*bitterly*] One crack—and it falls through!

[LAURA *opens the door.*]

LAURA: Tom! Tom, what are you doing?

TOM: Looking for a door key.

LAURA: Where have you been all this time?

5 TOM: I have been to the movies.

LAURA: All this time at the movies?

TOM: There was a very long program. There was a Garbo° picture and a Mickey Mouse and a travelogue and a newsreel and a preview of coming attractions. And there was an organ solo and a collection for the Milk Fund—simultaneously—which ended up in a terrible fight between a fat lady and an usher!

LAURA: [*innocently*] Did you have to stay through everything?

TOM: Of course! And, oh I forgot! There was a big stage show! The headliner on this stage show was Malvolio° the Magician. He performed wonderful tricks, many of them, such as pouring water back and forth between pitchers. First

---

°7 **Garbo:** Greta Garbo (1905–1990), Swedish star of American silent and early sound films.
9 **Malvolio:** the name, borrowed from a puritanical character in Shakespeare's *Twelfth Night*, means "malevolence" or "ill-will."

it turned to wine and then it turned to beer and then it turned to whisky. I know it was whisky it finally turned into because he needed somebody to come up out of the audience to help him, and I came up—both shows! It was Kentucky Straight Bourbon. A very generous fellow, he gave souvenirs. [*He pulls from his back pocket a shimmering rainbow-colored scarf.*] He gave me this. This is his magic scarf. You can have it, Laura. You wave it over a canary cage and you get a bowl of goldfish. You wave it over the goldfish bowl and they fly away canaries.... But the wonderfullest trick of all was the coffin trick. We nailed him into a coffin and he got out of the coffin without removing one nail. [*He has come inside.*] There is a trick that would come in handy for me—get me out of this two-by-four situation! [*He flops onto the bed and starts removing his shoes.*]

10 LAURA: Tom—shhh!

TOM: What're you shushing me for?

LAURA: You'll wake up Mother.

TOM: Goody, goody! Pay 'er back for all those "Rise an' Shines." [*He lies down, groaning.*] You know it don't take much intelligence to get yourself into a nailed-up coffin, Laura. But who in hell ever got himself out of one without removing one nail?

[*As if in answer, the father's grinning photograph lights up. The scene dims out.*]

[*Immediately following, the church bell is heard striking six. At the sixth stroke the alarm clock goes off in AMANDA's room, and after a few moments we hear her calling: "Rise and Shine! Rise and Shine! Laura, go tell your brother to rise and shine!"*]

TOM: [*sitting up slowly*] I'll rise—but I won't shine.

[*The light increases.*]

15 AMANDA: Laura, tell your brother his coffee is ready.

[*LAURA slips into the front room.*]

LAURA: Tom!—It's nearly seven. Don't make Mother nervous.

[*He stares at her stupidly.*]

[*Beseechingly.*] Tom, speak to Mother this morning. Make up with her, apologize, speak to her!

TOM: She won't to me. It's her that started not speaking.

LAURA: If you just say you're sorry she'll start speaking.

TOM: Her not speaking—is that such a tragedy?

20 LAURA: Please—please!

AMANDA: [*calling from the kitchenette*] Laura, are you going to do what I asked you to do, or do I have to get dressed and go out myself?

LAURA: Going, going—soon as I get on my coat!

[*She pulls on a shapeless felt hat with a nervous, jerky movement, pleadingly glancing at TOM. She rushes awkwardly for her coat. The coat is one of AMANDA's, inaccurately made-over, the sleeves too short for LAURA.*]

Butter and what else?

AMANDA: [*entering from the kitchenette*] Just butter. Tell them to charge it.

LAURA: Mother, they make such faces when I do that.

25 AMANDA: Sticks and stones can break our bones, but the expression on Mr. Garfinkel's face won't harm us! Tell your brother his coffee is getting cold.

LAURA: [*at the door*] Do what I asked you, will you, will you, Tom?

[*He looks sullenly away.*]

AMANDA: Laura, go now or just don't go at all!

LAURA: [*rushing out*] Going—going!

[*A second later she cries out. TOM springs up and crosses to the door. TOM opens the door.*]

TOM: Laura?

30 LAURA: I'm all right. I slipped, but I'm all right.

AMANDA: [*peering anxiously after her*] If anyone breaks a leg on those fire-escape steps, the landlord ought to be sued for every cent he possesses! [*She shuts the door. Now she remembers she isn't speaking to TOM and returns to the other room.*]

[*As TOM comes listlessly for his coffee, she turns her back to him and stands rigidly facing the window on the gloomy gray vault of the areaway. Its light on her face with its aged but childish features is cruelly sharp, satirical as a Daumier print.*°]

The music of "Ave Maria"° *is heard softly.*

TOM *glances sheepishly but sullenly at her averted figure and slumps at the table. The coffee is scalding hot; he sips it and gasps and spits it back in the cup. At his gasp,* AMANDA *catches her breath and half turns. Then she catches herself and turns back to the window.* TOM *blows on his coffee, glancing sidewise at his mother. She clears her throat.* TOM *clears his. He starts to rise, sinks back down again, scratches his head, clears his throat again.* AMANDA *coughs.* TOM *raises his cup in both hands to blow on it, his eyes staring over the rim of it at his mother for several moments. Then he slowly sets the cup down and awkwardly and hesitantly rises from the chair.*]

TOM: [*hoarsely*] Mother. I—I apologize, Mother.

[AMANDA *draws a quick, shuddering breath. Her face works grotesquely. She breaks into childlike tears.*]

I'm sorry for what I said, for everything that I said, I didn't mean it.

AMANDA: [*sobbingly*] My devotion has made me a witch and so I make myself hateful to my children!

TOM: *No, you* don't.

35 AMANDA: I worry so much, don't sleep, it makes me nervous!

TOM: [*gently*] I understand that.

AMANDA: I've had to put up a solitary battle all these years. But you're my right-hand bower!° Don't fall down, don't fail!

TOM: [*gently*] I try, Mother.

AMANDA: [*with great enthusiasm*] Try and you will *succeed!* [*The notion makes her breathless.*] Why, you—you're just *full* of natural endowments! Both of my children—they're *unusual* children! Don't you think I know it? I'm so—*proud!*

°31.2 S. D. **Daumier print:** Honoré Daumier (1808–1879), French painter and engraver whose prints frequently satirized his society. 31.2 S. D. *"Ave Maria":* a Roman Catholic prayer to the Virgin Mary; the musical setting called for here is by Franz Schubert (1797–1828).

°37 **right-hand bower** or **rightbower:** the Jack of trump in the card game *500,* the second-highest card (below the joker).

Happy and—feel I've—so much to be thankful for but—promise me one thing, son!

40 TOM: What, Mother?

AMANDA: Promise, son, you'll—never be a drunkard!

TOM: [*turns to her grinning*] I will never be a drunkard, Mother.

AMANDA: That's what frightened me so, that you'd be drinking! Eat a bowl of Purina!

TOM: Just coffee, Mother.

45 AMANDA: Shredded wheat biscuit?

TOM: No. No, Mother, just coffee.

AMANDA: You can't put in a day's work on an empty stomach. You've got ten minutes—don't gulp! Drinking too-hot liquids makes cancer of the stomach.... Put cream in.

TOM: No, thank you.

AMANDA: To cool it.

50 TOM: No! No, thank you, I want it black.

AMANDA: I know, but it's not good for you. We have to do all that we can to build ourselves up. In these trying times we live in, all that we have to cling to is— each other.... That's why it's so important to—Tom, I—I sent out your sister so I could discuss something with you. If you hadn't spoken I would have spoken to you. [*She sits down.*]

TOM: [*gently*] What is it, Mother, that you want to discuss?

AMANDA: *Laura!*

[*TOM puts his cup down slowly.*]

[*Legend on screen "Laura." Music: "The Glass Menagerie."*]

TOM: —Oh.—Laura...

55 AMANDA: [*touching his sleeve*] You know how Laura is. So quiet but—still water runs deep! She notices things and I think she—broods about them.

[*TOM looks up.*]

A few days ago I came in and she was crying.

TOM: What about?

AMANDA: You.

TOM: Me?

AMANDA: She has an idea that you're not happy here.

60 TOM: What gave her that idea?

AMANDA: What gives her any idea? However, you do act strangely.—I'm not criticizing, understand *that!* I know your ambitions do not lie in the ware- house, that like everybody in the whole wide world—you've had to—make sacrifices, but—Tom—Tom—life's not easy, it calls for—Spartan endurance! There's so many things in my heart that I cannot describe to you! I've never told you but I—*loved* your father....

TOM: [*gently*] I know that, Mother.

AMANDA: And you—when I see you taking after his ways! Staying out late— and—well, you *had* been drinking the night you were in that—terrifying condition! Laura says that you hate the apartment and that you go out nights to get away from it! Is that true, Tom?

TOM: No. You say there's so much in your heart that you can't describe to me. That's true of me, too. There's so much in my heart that I can't describe to *you!* So let's respect each other's—

65 AMANDA: But, why—*why*, Tom—are you always so restless? Where do you go to, nights?

TOM: I—go to the movies.

AMANDA: Why do you go to the movies so much, Tom?

TOM: I go to the movies because—I like adventure. Adventure is something I don't have much of at work, so I go to the movies.

AMANDA: But, Tom, you go to the movies *entirely* too *much!*

70 TOM: I like a lot of adventure.

[AMANDA *looks baffled, then hurt. As the familiar inquisition resumes,* TOM *becomes hard and impatient again. Amanda slips back into her querulous attitude toward him.*

Image on screen: A sailing vessel with Jolly Roger.°]

AMANDA: Most young men find adventure in their careers.

TOM: Then most young men are not employed in a warehouse.

AMANDA: The world is full of young men employed in warehouses and offices and factories.

TOM: Do all of them find adventure in their careers?

75 AMANDA: They do or they do without it! Not everybody has a craze for adventure.

TOM: Man is by instinct a lover, a hunter, a fighter, and none of those instincts are given much play at the warehouse!

AMANDA: Man is by instinct! Don't quote instinct to me! Instinct is something that people have got away from! It belongs to animals! Christian adults don't want it!

TOM: What do Christian adults want, then, Mother?

AMANDA: Superior things! Things of the mind and the spirit! Only animals have to satisfy instincts! Surely your aims are somewhat higher than theirs! Than monkeys—pigs—

80 TOM: I reckon they're not.

AMANDA: You're joking. However, that isn't what I wanted to discuss.

TOM: [*rising*] I haven't much time.

AMANDA: [*pushing his shoulders*] Sit down.

TOM: You want me to punch in red° at the warehouse, Mother?

85 AMANDA: You have five minutes. I want to talk about Laura.

[*Screen legend: "Plans and Provisions."*]

TOM: All right! What about Laura?

AMANDA: We have to be making some plans and provisions for her. She's older than you, two years, and nothing has happened. She just drifts along doing nothing. It frightens me terribly how she just drifts along.

TOM: I guess she's the type that people call home girls.

°70.2 S. D. **Jolly Roger:** the traditional flag of a pirate ship—a skull and crossbones on a field of black. 84 **punch in red:** arrive late for work; the time clock stamps late arrival times in red on the time card.

AMANDA: There's no such type, and if there is, it's a pity! That is unless the home is hers, with a husband!

90 TOM: What?

AMANDA: Oh, I can see the handwriting on the wall as plain as I see the nose in front of my face! It's terrifying! More and more you remind me of your father! He was out all hours without explanation!—Then *left! Goodbye!* And me with the bag to hold. I saw that letter you got from the Merchant Marine. I know what you're dreaming of. I'm not standing here blindfolded. [*She pauses.*] Very well, then. Then *do* it! But not till there's somebody to take your place.

TOM: What do you mean?

AMANDA: I mean that as soon as Laura has got somebody to take care of her, married, a home of her own, independent—why, then you'll be free to go wherever you please, on land, on sea, whichever way the wind blows you! But until that time you've got to look out for your sister. I don't say me because I'm old and don't matter! I say for your sister because she's young and dependent.

I put her in business college—a dismal failure! Frightened her so it made her sick at the stomach. I took her over to the Young People's League at the church. Another fiasco. She spoke to nobody, nobody spoke to her. Now all she does is fool with those pieces of glass and play those worn-out records. What kind of a life is that for a girl to lead?

TOM: What can I do about it?

95 AMANDA: Overcome selfishness! Self, self, self is all that you ever think of!

[*TOM springs up and crosses to get his coat. It is ugly and bulky. He pulls on a cap with earmuffs.*]

Where is your muffler? Put your wool muffler on!

[*He snatches it angrily from the closet, tosses it around his neck and pulls both ends tight.*]

Tom! I haven't said what I had in mind to ask you.

TOM: I'm too late to—

AMANDA: [*catching his arm—very importunately; then shyly*] Down at the warehouse, aren't there some—nice young men?

TOM: No!

AMANDA: There *must* be—*some* . . .

100 TOM: Mother—[*He gestures.*]

AMANDA: Find out one that's clean-living—doesn't drink and ask him out for sister!

TOM: What?

AMANDA: For *sister!* To *meet!* Get *acquainted!*

TOM: [*stamping to the door*] Oh, my *go-osh!*

105 AMANDA: Will you? [*He opens the door. She says, imploringly:*] Will you?

[*He starts down the fire escape.*]

Will you? *Will* you, dear?

TOM: [*calling back*] Yes!

[*AMANDA closes the door hesitantly and with a troubled but faintly hopeful expression.*

Screen image: The cover of a glamor magazine.

The spotlight picks up AMANDA on the phone.]

AMANDA: Ella Cartwright? This is Amanda Wingfield! How are you honey? How is that kidney condition? [*There is a five-second pause.*] Horrors! [*There is another pause.*]

You're a Christian martyr, yes, honey, that's what you are, a Christian martyr! Well, I just now happened to notice in my little red book that your subscription to the *Companion* has just run out! I knew that you wouldn't want to miss out on the wonderful serial starting in this new issue. It's by Bessie Mae Hopper, the first thing she's written since *Honeymoon for Three*. Wasn't that a strange and interesting story? Well, this one is even lovelier, I believe. It has a sophisticated, society background. It's all about the horsey set on Long Island!

[*The light fades out.*]

SCENE 5

[*Legend on the screen: "Annunciation."*

Music is heard as the light slowly comes on.

It is early dusk of a spring evening. Supper has just been finished in the Wingfield apartment. AMANDA and LAURA, in light-colored dresses, are removing dishes from the table in the dining room, which is shadowy, their movements formalized almost as a dance or ritual, their moving forms as pale and silent as moths. TOM, in white shirt and trousers, rises from the table and crosses toward the fire escape.]

AMANDA: [*as he passes her*] Son, will you do me a favor?
TOM: What?
AMANDA: Comb your hair! You look so pretty when your hair is combed!

[*Tom slouches on the sofa with the evening paper. Its enormous headline reads: "Franco Triumphs."°*]

There is only one respect in which I would like you to emulate your father.
5   TOM: What respect is that?
AMANDA: The care he always took of his appearance. He never allowed himself to look untidy.

[*He throws down the paper and crosses to the fire escape.*]

Where are you going?
TOM: I'm going out to smoke.
AMANDA: You smoke too much. A pack a day at fifteen cents a pack. How much would that amount to in a month? Thirty times fifteen is how much, Tom? Figure it out and you will be astounded at what you could save. Enough to give you a night-school course in accounting at Washington U.°! Just think what a wonderful thing that would be for you, son!

[*TOM is unmoved by the thought.*]

° 3.1 S. D. **"Franco Triumphs"**: Francisco Franco (1892–1975), dictator of Spain from 1939 until his death, was the general of the victorious Falangist armies in the Spanish Civil War (1936–1939).
7 **Washington U**: Washington University, a highly competitive liberal arts school in St. Louis.

TOM: I'd rather smoke. [*He steps out on the landing, letting the screen door slam.*]

AMANDA: [*sharply*] I know! That's the tragedy of it.... [*Alone, she turns to look at her husband's picture.*]

[*Dance music: "The World Is Waiting for the Sunrise!"°*]

10 TOM: [*to the audience*] Across the alley from us was the Paradise Dance Hall. On evenings in spring the windows and doors were open and the music came outdoors. Sometimes the lights were turned out except for a large glass sphere that hung from the ceiling. It would turn slowly about and filter the dusk with delicate rainbow colors. Then the orchestra played a waltz or a tango, something that had a slow and sensuous rhythm. Couples would come outside, to the relative privacy of the alley. You could see them kissing behind ash pits and telephone poles. This was the compensation for lives that passed like mine, without any change or adventure. Adventure and change were imminent in this year. They were waiting around the corner for all these kids. Suspended in the mist over Berchtesgaden,° caught in the folds of Chamberlain's umbrella. In Spain there was Guernica! But here there was only hot swing music and liquor, dance halls, bars, and movies, and sex that hung in the gloom like a chandelier and flooded the world with brief, deceptive rainbows....All the world was waiting for bombardments!

[*AMANDA turns from the picture and comes outside.*]

AMANDA: [*sighing*] A fire escape landing's a poor excuse for a porch. [*She spreads a newspaper on a step and sits down, gracefully and demurely as if she were settling into a swing on a Mississippi veranda.*] What are you looking at?

TOM: The moon.

AMANDA: Is there a moon this evening?

TOM: It's rising over Garfinkel's Delicatessen.

15 AMANDA: So it is! A little silver slipper of a moon. Have you made a wish on it yet?

TOM: Um-hum.

AMANDA: What did you wish for?

TOM: That's a secret.

AMANDA: A secret, huh? Well, I won't tell mine either. I will be just as mysterious as you.

20 TOM: I bet I can guess what yours is.

AMANDA: Is my head so transparent?

TOM: You're not a sphinx.°

AMANDA: No, I don't have secrets. I'll tell you what I wished for on the moon. Success and happiness for my precious children! I wish for that whenever there's a moon, and when there isn't a moon, I wish for it, too.

TOM: I thought perhaps you wished for a gentleman caller.

°9.1 S. D. **"The World...Sunrise"**: popular song, copyright 1919, written by Eugene Lockhart and Ernest Seitz.

°10 **Berchtesgaden...Guernica:** The three names mentioned are all foreshadowings of World War II. Berchtesgaden, a resort in the Bavarian Alps, was Adolf Hitler's favorite residence. Neville Chamberlain was the British prime minister who signed the Munich Pact with Hitler in 1938, allowing Nazi Germany to occupy parts of Czechoslovakia. Chamberlain, who always carried an umbrella, declared that he had ensured "peace in our time." The bombardment of Guernica during the Spanish Civil War made the name of the town synonymous with the horrors of war, and especially the killing of civilian women and children. 22 **sphinx:** a mythological monster with the head of a woman and body of a lion, famous for her riddles.

25 AMANDA: Why do you say that?

TOM: Don't you remember asking me to fetch one?

AMANDA: I remember suggesting that it would be nice for your sister if you brought home some nice young man from the warehouse. I think that I've made that suggestion more than once.

TOM: Yes, you have made it repeatedly.

AMANDA: Well?

30 TOM: We are going to have one.

AMANDA: *What?*

TOM: A gentleman caller!

[*The annunciation is celebrated with music.*

AMANDA *rises.*

Image on screen: A caller with a bouquet.]

AMANDA: You mean you have asked some nice young man to come over?

TOM: Yep. I've asked him to dinner.

35 AMANDA: You really did?

TOM: I did!

AMANDA: You did, and did he—*accept?*

TOM: He did!

AMANDA: Well, well—well, well! That's—lovely!

40 TOM: I thought that you would be pleased.

AMANDA: It's definite then?

TOM: Very definite.

AMANDA: Soon?

TOM: Very soon.

45 AMANDA: For heaven's sake, stop putting on and tell me some things, will you?

TOM: What things do you want me to tell you?

AMANDA: *Naturally* I would like to know when he's *coming!*

TOM: He's coming tomorrow.

50 AMANDA: *Tomorrow?*

TOM: Yep. Tomorrow.

AMANDA: But, Tom!

TOM: Yes, Mother?

AMANDA: Tomorrow gives me no time!

TOM: Time for what?

55 AMANDA: Preparations! Why didn't you phone me at once, as soon as you asked him, the minute that he accepted? Then, don't you see, I could have been getting ready!

TOM: You don't have to make any fuss.

AMANDA: Oh, Tom, Tom, Tom, of course I have to make a fuss! I want things nice, not sloppy! Not thrown together. I'll certainly have to do some fast thinking, won't I?

TOM: I don't see why you have to think at all.

AMANDA: You just don't know. We can't have a gentleman caller in a pigsty! All my wedding silver has to be polished, the monogrammed table linen ought to be laundered! The windows have to be washed and fresh curtains put up. And how about clothes? We have to *wear* something, don't we?

60 TOM: Mother, this boy is no one to make a fuss over!

AMANDA: Do you realize he's the first young man we've introduced to your sister? It's terrible, disgraceful that poor little sister has never received a single gentleman caller! Tom, come inside! [*She opens the screen door.*]

TOM: What for?

AMANDA: I want to ask you some things.

TOM: If you're going to make such a fuss, I'll call it off, I'll tell him not to come!

65 AMANDA: You certainly won't do anything of the kind. Nothing offends people worse than broken engagements. It simply means I'll have to work like a Turk! We won't be brilliant, but we will pass inspection. Come on inside.

[TOM *follows her inside, groaning.*]

Sit down.

TOM: Any particular place you would like me to sit?

AMANDA: Thank heavens I've got that new sofa! I'm also making payments on a floor lamp I'll have sent out! And put the chintz covers on, they'll brighten things up! Of course I'd hoped to have these walls re-papered.... What is the young man's name?

TOM: His name is O'Connor.

AMANDA: That, of course, means fish°—tomorrow is Friday! I'll have that salmon loaf—with Durkee's dressing! What does he do? He works at the warehouse?

70 TOM: Of course! How else would I—

AMANDA: Tom, he—doesn't drink?

TOM: Why do you ask me that?

AMANDA: Your father *did!*

TOM: Don't get started on that!

75 AMANDA: He *does* drink, then?

TOM: Not that I know of!

AMANDA: Make sure, be certain! The last thing I want for my daughter's a boy who drinks!

TOM: Aren't you being a little bit premature? Mr. O'Connor has not yet appeared on the scene!

AMANDA: But will tomorrow. To meet your sister, and what do I know about his character? Nothing! Old maids are better off than wives of drunkards!

80 TOM: Oh, my God!

AMANDA: Be still!

TOM: [*leaning forward to whisper*] Lots of fellows meet girls whom they don't marry!

AMANDA: Oh, talk sensibly, Tom—and don't be sarcastic! [*She has gotten a hairbrush.*]

TOM: What are you doing?

85 AMANDA: I'm brushing that cowlick down! [*She attacks his hair with the brush.*] What is this young man's position at the warehouse?

TOM: [*submitting grimly to the brush and the interrogation*] This young man's position is that of a shipping clerk, Mother.

AMANDA: Sounds to me like a fairly responsible job, the sort of job *you* would be in if you just had more *get-up.* What is his salary? Have you any idea?

° 69 **fish**: Amanda assumes that O'Connor is Catholic. Until the 1960s, Roman Catholics were required by the church to abstain from meat on Fridays.

TOM: I would judge it to be approximately eighty-five dollars a month.

AMANDA: Well—not princely, but—

90 TOM: Twenty more than I make.

AMANDA: Yes, how well I know! But for a family man, eighty-five dollars a month is not much more than you can just get by on. . . .

TOM: Yes, but Mr. O'Connor is not a family man.

AMANDA: He might be, mightn't he? Some time in the future?

TOM: I see. Plans and provisions.

95 AMANDA: You are the only young man that I know of who ignores the fact that the future becomes the present, the present the past, and the past turns into everlasting regret if you don't plan for it!

TOM: I will think that over and see what I can make of it.

AMANDA: Don't be supercilious with your mother! Tell me some more about this—what do you call him?

TOM: James D. O'Connor. The D. is for Delaney.

AMANDA: Irish on *both* sides! *Gracious!* And he doesn't drink?

100 TOM: Shall I call him up and ask him right this minute?

AMANDA: The only way to find out about those things is to make discreet inquiries at the proper moment. When I was a girl in Blue Mountain and it was suspected that a young man drank, the girl whose attentions he had been receiving, if any girl *was*, would sometimes speak to the minister of his church, or rather her father would if her father was living, and sort of feel him out on the young man's character. That is the way such things are discreetly handled to keep a young woman from making a tragic mistake!

TOM: Then how did you happen to make a tragic mistake?

AMANDA: That innocent look of your father's had everyone fooled! He *smiled*—the world was *enchanted!* No girl can do worse than put herself at the mercy of a handsome appearance! I hope that Mr. O'Connor is not too good-looking.

TOM: No, he's not too good-looking. He's covered with freckles and hasn't too much of a nose.

105 AMANDA: He's not right-down homely, though?

TOM: Not right-down homely. Just medium homely, I'd say.

AMANDA: Character's what to look for in a man.

TOM: That's what I've always said, Mother.

AMANDA: You've never said anything of the kind and I suspect you would never give it a thought.

110 TOM: Don't be so suspicious of me.

AMANDA: At least I hope he's the type that's up and coming.

TOM: I think he really goes in for self-improvement.

AMANDA: What reason have you to think so?

TOM: He goes to night school.

115 AMANDA: [*beaming*] Splendid! What does he do, I mean study?

TOM: Radio engineering and public speaking!

AMANDA: Then he has visions of being advanced in the world! Any young man who studies public speaking is aiming to have an executive job some day! And radio engineering? A thing for the future! Both of these facts are very illuminating. Those are the sort of things that a mother should know concerning any young man who comes to call on her daughter. Seriously or—not.

TOM: One little warning. He doesn't know about Laura. I didn't let on that we had dark ulterior motives. I just said, why don't you come and have dinner with us? He said okay and that was the whole conversation.

AMANDA: I bet it was! You're eloquent as an oyster. However, he'll know about Laura when he gets here. When he sees how lovely and sweet and pretty she is, he'll thank his lucky stars he was asked to dinner.

120 TOM: Mother, you mustn't expect too much of Laura.

AMANDA: What do you mean?

TOM: Laura seems all those things to you and me because she's ours and we love her. We don't even notice she's crippled any more.

AMANDA: Don't say crippled! You know that I never allow that word to be used!

TOM: But face facts, Mother. She is and—that's not all—

125 AMANDA: What do you mean "not all"?

TOM: Laura is very different from other girls.

AMANDA: I think the difference is all to her advantage.

TOM: Not quite all—in the eyes of others—strangers—she's terribly shy and lives in a world of her own and those things make her seem a little peculiar to people outside the house.

AMANDA: Don't say peculiar.

130 TOM: Face the facts. She is.

[*The dance hall music changes to a tango that has a minor and somewhat ominous tone.*]

AMANDA: In what way is she peculiar—may I ask?

TOM: [*gently*] She lives in a world of her own—a world of little glass ornaments, Mother....

[*He gets up.* AMANDA *remains holding the brush, looking at him, troubled.*]

She plays old phonograph records and—that's about all—[*He glances at himself in the mirror and crosses to the door.*]

AMANDA: [*sharply*] Where are you going?

TOM: I'm going to the movies. [*He goes out the screen door.*]

135 AMANDA: Not to the movies, every night to the movies! [*She follows quickly to the screen door.*] I don't believe you always go to the movies!

[*He is gone.* AMANDA *looks worriedly after him for a moment. Then vitality and optimism return and she turns from the door, crossing to the portieres.*]

Laura! Laura!

[LAURA *answers from the kitchenette.*]

LAURA: Yes, Mother.

AMANDA: Let those dishes go and come in front!

[LAURA *appears with a dish towel.* AMANDA *speaks to her gaily.*]

Laura, come here and make a wish on the moon!

[*Screen image: The Moon.*]

LAURA: [*entering*] Moon—moon?

AMANDA: A little silver slipper of a moon. Look over your left shoulder, Laura, and make a wish!

[LAURA *looks faintly puzzled as if called out of sleep.* AMANDA *seizes her shoulders and turns her at an angle by the door.*]

Now! Now, darling, *wish!*

140   LAURA: What shall I wish for, Mother?

AMANDA: [*her voice trembling and her eyes suddenly filling with tears*] Happiness! Good fortune!

[*The sound of the violin rises and the stage dims out.*]

SCENE 6

[*The light comes up on the fire escape landing. Tom is leaning against the grill, smoking. Screen image: The high school hero.*]

TOM: And so the following evening I brought Jim home to dinner. I had known Jim slightly in high school. In high school Jim was a hero. He had tremendous Irish good nature and vitality with the scrubbed and polished look of white chinaware. He seemed to move in a continual spotlight. He was a star in basketball, captain of the debating club, president of the senior class and the glee club and he sang the male lead in the annual light operas. He was always running or bounding, never just walking. He seemed always at the point of defeating the law of gravity. He was shooting with such velocity through his adolescence that you would logically expect him to arrive at nothing short of the White House by the time he was thirty. But Jim apparently ran into more interference after his graduation from Soldan. His speed had definitely slowed. Six years after he left high school he was holding a job that wasn't much better than mine.

[*Screen image: The Clerk.*]

He was the only one at the warehouse with whom I was on friendly terms. I was valuable to him as someone who could remember his former glory, who had seen him win basketball games and the silver cup in debating. He knew of my secret practice of retiring to a cabinet of the washroom to work on poems when business was slack in the warehouse. He called me Shakespeare. And while the other boys in the warehouse regarded me with suspicious hostility, Jim took a humorous attitude toward me. Gradually his attitude affected the others, their hostility wore off and they also began to smile at me as people smile at an oddly fashioned dog who trots across their path at some distance.

I knew that Jim and Laura had known each other at Soldan, and I had heard Laura speak admiringly of his voice. I didn't know if Jim remembered her or not. In high school Laura had been as unobtrusive as Jim had been astonishing. If he did remember Laura, it was not as my sister, for when I asked him to dinner, he grinned and said, "You know, Shakespeare, I never thought of you as having folks!"

He was about to discover that I did....

[*Legend on screen: "The accent of a coming foot."*]

[*The light dims out on Tom and comes up in the Wingfield living room—a delicate lemony light. It is about five on a Friday evening of late spring which comes "scattering poems in the sky."*]

AMANDA *has worked like a Turk in preparation for the gentleman caller. The results are astonishing. The new floor lamp with its rose silk shade is in place, a colored paper* lantern conceals the broken light fixture in the ceiling, new billowing white curtains are at the windows, chintz covers are on the chairs and sofa, a pair of new sofa pillows make their initial appearance. Open boxes and tissue paper are scattered on the floor.

LAURA *stands in the middle of the room with lifted arms while* AMANDA *crouches before her, adjusting the hem of a new dress, devout and ritualistic. The dress is colored and designed by memory. The arrangement of* LAURA's *hair is changed; it is softer and more becoming. A fragile, unearthly prettiness has come out in* LAURA: *she is like a piece of translucent glass touched by light, given a momentary radiance, not actual, not lasting.*]

AMANDA: [*impatiently*] Why are you trembling?

LAURA: Mother, you've made me so nervous!

AMANDA: How have I made you nervous?

5 LAURA: By all this fuss! You make it seem so important!

AMANDA: I don't understand you, Laura. You couldn't be satisfied with just sitting home, and yet whenever I try to arrange something for you, you seem to resist it. [*She gets up.*] Now take a look at yourself. No, wait! Wait just a moment—I have an idea!

LAURA: What is it now?

[AMANDA *produces two powder puffs which she wraps in handkerchiefs and stuffs in* LAURA's *bosom.*]

LAURA: Mother, what are you doing?

AMANDA: They call them "Gay Deceivers"!

10 LAURA: I won't wear them!

AMANDA: You will!

LAURA: Why should I?

AMANDA: Because, to be painfully honest, your chest is flat.

LAURA: You make it seem like we were setting a trap.

15 AMANDA: All pretty girls are a trap, a pretty trap, and men expect them to be.

[*Legend on screen: "A pretty trap."*]

Now look at yourself, young lady. This is the prettiest you will ever be! [*She stands back to admire* LAURA.] I've got to fix myself now! You're going to be surprised by your mother's appearance!

[AMANDA *crosses through the portieres, humming gaily.* LAURA *moves slowly to the long mirror and stares solemnly at herself. A wind blows the white curtains inward in a slow, graceful motion and with a faint, sorrowful sighing.*]

AMANDA: [*from somewhere behind the portieres*] It isn't dark enough yet.

[LAURA *turns slowly before the mirror with a troubled look.*

Legend on screen: "This is my sister: Celebrate her with strings!" Music plays.]

AMANDA: [*laughing, still not visible*] I'm going to show you something. I'm going to make a spectacular appearance!

LAURA: What is it, Mother?

AMANDA: Possess your soul in patience—you will see! Something I've resurrected from that old trunk! Styles haven't changed so terribly much after all.... [*She parts the portieres.*] Now just look at your mother! [*She wears a girlish frock of yellowed voile with a blue silk sash. She carries a bunch of jonquils—the legend of her youth is nearly revived. Now she speaks feverishly:*] This is the dress in which

I led the cotillion. Won the cakewalk twice at Sunset Hill, wore one Spring to the Governor's Ball in Jackson!° See how I sashayed around the ballroom, Laura? [*She raises her skirt and does a mincing step around the room.*] I wore it on Sundays for my gentlemen callers! I had it on the day I met your father....I had malaria fever all that Spring. The change of climate from East Tennessee to the Delta—weakened resistance. I had a little temperature all the time—not enough to be serious—just enough to make me restless and giddy! Invitations poured in—parties all over the Delta! "Stay in bed," said Mother, "you have a fever!"—but I just wouldn't. I took quinine° but kept on going, going! Evenings, dances! Afternoons, long, long rides! Picnics—lovely! So lovely, that country in May—all lacy with dogwood, literally flooded with jonquils! That was the spring I had the craze for jonquils. Jonquils became an absolute obsession. Mother said, "Honey, there's no more room for jonquils." And still I kept on bringing in more jonquils. Whenever, wherever I saw them, I'd say, "Stop! Stop! I see jonquils!" I made the young men help me gather the jonquils! It was a joke, Amanda and her jonquils. Finally there were no more vases to hold them, every available space was filled with jonquils. No vases to hold them? All right, I'll hold them myself! And then I— [*She stops in front of the picture. Music plays.*] met your father! Malaria fever and jonquils and then—this—boy. ... [*She switches on the rose-colored lamp.*] I hope they get here before it starts to rain. [*She crosses the room and places the jonquils in a bowl on the table.*] I gave your brother a little extra change so he and Mr. O'Connor could take the service car home.

20 LAURA: [*with an altered look*] What did you say his name was?

AMANDA: O'Connor.

LAURA: What is his first name?

AMANDA: I don't remember. Oh, yes, I do. It was—Jim.

[*LAURA sways slightly and catches hold of a chair.*

Legend on screen: "Not Jim!"]

LAURA: [*faintly*] Not—Jim!

25 AMANDA: Yes, that was it, it was Jim! I've never known a Jim that wasn't nice!

[*The music becomes ominous.*]

LAURA: Are you sure his name is Jim O'Connor?

AMANDA: Yes. Why?

LAURA: Is he the one that Tom used to know in high school?

AMANDA: He didn't say so. I think he just got to know him at the warehouse.

30 LAURA: There was a Jim O'Connor we both knew in high school—[*Then, with effort.*] If that is the one that Tom is bringing to dinner—you'll have to excuse me, I won't come to the table.

AMANDA: What sort of nonsense is this?

LAURA: You asked me once if I'd ever liked a boy. Don't you remember I showed you this boy's picture?

AMANDA: You mean the boy you showed me in the yearbook?

° 19 **Jackson:** capital of Mississippi. Amanda refers to the social events of her youth. A cotillion is a formal ball, often given for debutantes. The cakewalk is a strutting dance step. **quinine:** long used as a standard drug to control malaria.

LAURA: Yes, that boy.

35 AMANDA: Laura, Laura, were you in love with that boy?

LAURA: I don't know, Mother. All I know is I couldn't sit at the table if it was him!

AMANDA: It won't be him! It isn't the least bit likely. But whether it is or not, you will come to the table. You will not be excused.

LAURA: I'll have to be, Mother.

AMANDA: I don't intend to humor your silliness, Laura. I've had too much from you and your brother, both! So just sit down and compose yourself till they come. Tom has forgotten his key so you'll have to let them in, when they arrive.

40 LAURA: [*panicky*] Oh, Mother—*you* answer the door!

AMANDA: [*lightly*] I'll be in the kitchen—busy!

LAURA: Oh, Mother, please answer the door, don't make me do it!

AMANDA: [*crossing into the kitchenette*] I've got to fix the dressing for the salmon. Fuss, fuss—silliness!—over a gentleman caller!

[*The door swings shut, LAURA is left alone.*

Legend on screen: "Terror!"

She utters a low moan and turns off the lamp—sits stiffly on the edge of the sofa, knotting her fingers together.

Legend on screen: "The Opening of a Door!"

TOM and JIM appear on the fire escape steps and climb to the landing. Hearing their approach, LAURA rises with a panicky gesture. She retreats to the portieres. The doorbell rings. LAURA catches her breath and touches her throat. Low drums sound.]

AMANDA: [*calling*] Laura, sweetheart! The door!

[*LAURA stares at it without moving.*]

JIM: I think we just beat the rain.

45 TOM: Uh-huh. [*He rings again, nervously. JIM whistles and fishes for a cigarette.*]

AMANDA: [*very, very gaily*] Laura, that is your brother and Mr. O'Connor! Will you let them in, darling?

[*LAURA crosses toward the kitchenette door.*]

LAURA: [*breathlessly*] Mother—you go to the door!

[*AMANDA steps out of the kitchenette and stares furiously at LAURA. She points imperiously at the door.*]

LAURA: Please, please!

50 AMANDA: [*in a fierce whisper*] What is the matter with you, you silly thing?

LAURA: [*desperately*] Please, you answer it, *please!*

AMANDA: I told you I wasn't going to humor you, Laura. Why have you chosen this moment to lose your mind?

LAURA: Please, please, please, you go!

AMANDA: You'll have to go to the door because I can't.

55 LAURA: [*despairingly*] I can't either!

AMANDA: *Why?*

LAURA: I'm *sick!*

AMANDA: I'm sick, too—of your nonsense! Why can't you and your brother be normal people? Fantastic whims and behavior!

[*TOM gives a long ring.*]

Preposterous goings on! Can you give me one reason—[*She calls out lyrically.*] Coming! Just one second!—why you should be afraid to open a door? Now you answer it, Laura!

LAURA: Oh, oh, oh . . . [*She returns through the portieres, darts to the Victrola, winds it frantically and turns it on.*]

60 AMANDA: Laura Wingfield, you march right to that door!

LAURA: *Yes—yes, Mother!*

[*A faraway, scratchy rendition of "Dardanella"° softens the air and gives her strength to move through it. She slips to the door and draws it cautiously open. TOM enters with the caller, JIM O'CONNOR.*]

TOM: Laura, this is Jim. Jim, this is my sister, Laura.

JIM: [*stepping inside*] I didn't know that Shakespeare had a sister!

LAURA: [*retreating, stiff and trembling, from the door*] How—how do you do?

65 JIM: [*heartily, extending his hand*] Okay!

[*LAURA touches it hesitantly with hers.*]

JIM: Your hand's *cold*, Laura!

LAURA: Yes, well—I've been playing the Victrola. . . .

JIM: Must have been playing classical music on it! You ought to play a little hot swing music to warm you up!

LAURA: Excuse me—I haven't finished playing the Victrola. . . . [*She turns awkwardly and hurries into the front room. She pauses a second by the Victrola. Then she catches her breath and darts through the portieres like a frightened deer.*]

70 JIM: [*grinning*] What was the matter?

TOM: Oh—with Laura? Laura is—terribly shy.

JIM: Shy, huh? It's unusual to meet a shy girl nowadays. I don't believe you ever mentioned you had a sister.

TOM: Well, now you know. I have one. Here is the *Post Dispatch.*° You want a piece of it?

JIM: Uh-huh.

TOM: What piece? The comics?

JIM: Sports! [*He glances at it.*] Ole Dizzy Dean° is on his bad behavior.

TOM: [*uninterested*] Yeah? [*He lights a cigarette and goes over to the fire-escape door.*]

JIM: Where are *you* going?

TOM: I'm going out on the terrace.

80 JIM: [*going after him*] You know, Shakespeare—I'm going to sell you a bill of goods!

TOM: What goods?

JIM: A course I'm taking.

TOM: Huh?

JIM: In public speaking! You and me, we're not the warehouse type.

85 TOM: Thanks—that's good news. But what has public speaking got to do with it?

JIM: It fits you for—executive positions!

°61 S. D. **"Dardanella"**: a popular song and dance tune, copyright 1914, by Fred Fisher, Felix Bernard, and Johnny S. Black. 73 **Post Dispatch:** the *St. Louis Post Dispatch*, a newspaper.

°76 **Dizzy Dean:** Jerome Herman (or Jay Hanna) Dean (1911–1974), outstanding pitcher with the St. Louis Cardinals during the 1930s.

Tom: Awww.

Jim: I tell you it's done a helluva lot for me.

[*Image on screen: Executive at his desk.*]

Tom: In what respect?

90 Jim: In every! Ask yourself what is the difference between you an' me and men in the office down front? Brains?—No!—Ability?—No! Then what? Just one little thing—

Tom: What is that one little thing?

Jim: Primarily it amounts to—social poise! Being able to square up to people and hold your own on any social level!

Amanda: [*from the kitchenette*] Tom?

Tom: Yes, Mother?

95 Amanda: Is that you and Mr. O'Connor?

Tom: Yes, Mother.

Amanda: Well, you just make yourselves comfortable in there.

Tom: Yes, Mother.

Amanda: Ask Mr. O'Connor if he would like to wash his hands.

100 Jim: Aw, no—no—thank you—I took care of that at the warehouse. Tom—

Tom: Yes?

Jim: Mr. Mendoza was speaking to me about you.

Tom: Favorably?

Jim: What do you think?

105 Tom: Well—

Jim: You're going to be out of a job if you don't wake up.

Tom: I am waking up—

Jim: You show no signs.

Tom: The signs are interior.

[*Image on screen: The sailing vessel with the Jolly Roger again.*]

110 Tom: I'm planning to change. [*He leans over the fire escape rail, speaking with quiet exhilaration. The incandescent marquees and signs of the first-run movie houses light his face from across the alley. He looks like a voyager.*] I'm right at the point of committing myself to a future that doesn't include the warehouse and Mr. Mendoza or even a night-school course in public speaking.

Jim: What are you gassing about?

Tom: I'm tired of the movies.

Jim: Movies!

Tom: Yes, movies! Look at them—[*a wave toward the marvels of Grand Avenue*] All of those glamorous people—having adventures—hogging it all, gobbling the whole thing up! You know what happens? People go to the *movies* instead of *moving!* Hollywood characters are supposed to have all the adventures for everybody in America, while everybody in America sits in a dark room and watches them have them! Yes, until there's a war. That's when adventure becomes available to the masses! *Everyone's* dish, not only Gable's!° Then the

---

°114 **Gable:** Clark Gable (1901–1960), popular American screen actor and matinee idol from the 1930s to his death.

people in the dark room come out of the dark room to have some adventures themselves—goody, goody! It's our turn now, to go to the South Sea Island—to make a safari—to be exotic, far-off! But I'm not patient. I don't want to wait till then. I'm tired of the *movies* and I am *about* to *move!*

115 JIM: [*incredulously*] Move?

TOM: Yes.

JIM: When?

TOM: Soon!

JIM: Where? Where?

[*The music seems to answer the question, while* TOM *thinks it over. He searches in his pockets.*]

120 TOM: I'm starting to boil inside. I know I seem dreamy, but inside—well, I'm boiling! Whenever I pick up a shoe, I shudder a little thinking how short life is and what I am doing! Whatever that means, I know it doesn't mean shoes—except as something to wear on a traveler's feet! [*He finds what he has been searching for in his pockets and holds out a paper to* JIM.] Look—

JIM: What?

TOM: I'm a member.

JIM: [*reading*] The Union of Merchant Seamen.

TOM: I paid my dues this month, instead of the light bill.

125 JIM: You will regret it when they turn off the lights.

TOM: I won't be here.

JIM: How about your mother?

TOM: I'm like my father. The bastard son of a bastard! Did you notice how he's grinning in his picture in there? And he's been absent going on sixteen years!

JIM: You're just talking, you drip. How does your mother feel about it?

130 TOM: Shhh! Here comes Mother! Mother is not acquainted with my plans!

AMANDA: [*coming through the portieres*] Where are you all?

TOM: On the terrace, Mother.

[*They start inside. She advances to them.* TOM *is distinctly shocked at her appearance. Even* JIM *blinks a little. He is making his first contact with the girlish Southern vivacity and in spite of the night-school course in public speaking is somewhat thrown off the beam by the unexpected outlay of social charm. Certain responses are attempted by* JIM *but are swept aside by* AMANDA's *gay laughter and chatter.* TOM *is embarrassed but after the first shock* JIM *reacts very warmly. He grins and chuckles, is altogether won over.*

Image on screen: AMANDA *as a girl.*]

AMANDA: [*coyly smiling, shaking her girlish ringlets*] Well, well, well, so this is Mr. O'Connor. Introductions entirely unnecessary. I've heard so much about you from my boy. I finally said to him, Tom—good gracious!—why don't you bring this paragon to supper? I'd like to meet this nice young man at the warehouse!—instead of just hearing him sing your praises so much! I don't know why my son is so stand-offish—that's not Southern behavior!

Let's sit down and—I think we could stand a little more air in here! Tom, leave the door open. I felt a nice fresh breeze a moment ago. Where has it gone to? Mmm, so warm already! And not quite summer, even. We're going to burn up when summer really gets started. However, we're having—we're having a very light supper. I think light things are better fo' this time of year. The same as light clothes are. Light clothes an' light food are what warm weather calls fo'. You know our blood gets so thick during th' winter—it takes a while fo' us to *adjust* ourselves!—when the season changes....It's come so quick this year. I wasn't prepared. All of sudden—heavens! Already summer! I ran to the trunk an' pulled out this light dress—terribly old! Historical almost! But feels so good—so good an' co-ol, y'know....

TOM: Mother—

135 AMANDA: Yes, honey?

TOM: How about—supper?

AMANDA: Honey, you go ask Sister if supper is ready! You know that Sister is in full charge of supper! Tell her you hungry boys are waiting for it. [*To* JIM.] Have you met Laura?

JIM: She—

AMANDA: Let you in? Oh, good, you've met already! It's rare for a girl as sweet an' pretty as Laura to be domestic! But Laura is, thank heavens, not only pretty but also very domestic. I'm not at all. I never was a bit. I never could make a thing but angel-food cake. Well, in the South we had so many servants. Gone, gone, gone. All vestige of gracious living! Gone completely! I wasn't prepared for what the future brought me. All of my gentlemen callers were sons of planters and so of course I assumed that I would be married to one and raise my family on a large piece of land with plenty of servants. But man proposes—and woman accepts the proposal! to vary that old, old saying a little but—I married no planter! I married a man who worked for the telephone company! That gallantly smiling gentleman over there! [*She points to the picture.*] A telephone man who—fell in love with long-distance! Now he travels and I don't even know where! But what am I going on for about my—tribulations? Tell me yours—I hope you don't have any! Tom?

140 TOM: [*returning*] Yes, Mother?

AMANDA: Is supper nearly ready?

TOM: It looks to me like supper is on the table.

AMANDA: Let me look—[*She rises prettily and looks through the portieres.*] Oh lovely! But where is Sister?

TOM: Laura is not feeling well and she says that she thinks she'd better not come to the table.

145 AMANDA: What? Nonsense! Laura? Oh, Laura!

LAURA: [*from the kitchenette, faintly*] Yes, Mother.

AMANDA: You really must come to the table. We won't be seated until you come to the table! Come in, Mr. O'Connor. You sit over there and I'll....Laura? Laura Wingfield! You're keeping us waiting, honey! We can't say grace until you come to the table!

[*The kitchenette door is pushed weakly open and* LAURA *comes in. She is obviously quite faint, her lips trembling, her eyes wide and staring. She moves unsteadily toward the table.*

Screen legend: "Terror!"

Outside a summer storm is coming on abruptly. The white curtains billow inward at the windows and there is a sorrowful murmur from the deep blue dusk.

LAURA *suddenly stumbles; she catches at a chair with a faint moan.*]

TOM: Laura!

AMANDA: Laura!

[*There is a clap of thunder.*

Screen legend: "Ah!"]

     [*despairingly*] Why, Laura, you are ill, darling! Tom, help your sister into the living room, dear! Sit in the living room, Laura—rest on the sofa. Well! [*To* JIM *as* TOM *helps his sister to the sofa in the living room.*] Standing over the hot stove made her ill! I told her that it was just too warm this evening, but—

[TOM *comes back to the table.*]

     Is Laura all right now?

150 TOM: Yes.

AMANDA: What is that? Rain? A nice cool rain has come up! [*She gives* JIM *a frightened look.*] I think we may—have grace—now . . . [TOM *looks at her stupidly.*] Tom, honey—you say grace!

TOM: Oh . . . "For these and all thy mercies—"

[*They bow their heads,* AMANDA *stealing a nervous glance at* JIM. *In the living room* LAURA, *stretched on the sofa, clenches her hand to her lips, to hold back a shuddering sob.*]

     God's Holy Name be praised—

[*The scene dims out.*]

SCENE 7

[*It is half an hour later. Dinner is just being finished in the dining room,* LAURA *is still huddled upon the sofa, her feet drawn under her, her head resting on a pale blue pillow, her eyes wide and mysteriously watchful. The new floor lamp with its shade of rose-colored silk gives a soft, becoming light to her face, bringing out the fragile, unearthly prettiness which usually escapes attention. From outside there is a steady murmur of rain, but it is slackening and soon stops; the air outside becomes pale and luminous as the moon breaks through the clouds. A moment after the curtain rises, the lights in both rooms flicker and go out.*]

JIM: Hey, there, Mr. Light Bulb!

[AMANDA *laughs nervously.*

Legend on screen: "Suspension of a public service."]

AMANDA: Where was Moses when the lights went out? Ha-ha. Do you know the answer to that one, Mr. O'Connor?

JIM: No, Ma'am, what's the answer?

AMANDA: In the dark!

[JIM *laughs appreciatively.*]

     Everybody sit still. I'll light the candles. Isn't it lucky we have them on the table? Where's a match? Which of you gentlemen can provide a match?

5 JIM: Here.

AMANDA: Thank you, Sir.

JIM: Not at all, Ma'am!

AMANDA: [*as she lights the candles*] I guess the fuse has burnt out. Mr. O'Connor, can you tell a burnt-out fuse? I know I can't and Tom is a total loss when it comes to mechanics. [*They rise from the table and go into the kitchenette, from where their voices are heard.*] Oh, be careful you don't bump into something. We don't want our gentleman caller to break his neck. Now wouldn't that be a fine howdy-do?

JIM: Ha-ha! Where is the fuse-box?

10 AMANDA: Right here next to the stove. Can you see anything?

JIM: Just a minute.

AMANDA: Isn't electricity a mysterious thing? Wasn't it Benjamin Franklin who tied a key to a kite? We live in such a mysterious universe, don't we? Some people say that science clears up all the mysteries for us. In my opinion it only creates more! Have you found it yet?

JIM: No, Ma'am. All these fuses look okay to me.

AMANDA: Tom!

15 TOM: Yes, Mother?

AMANDA: That light bill I gave you several days ago. That one I told you we got the notices about?

[*Legend on screen: "Ha!"*]

TOM: Oh—yeah.

AMANDA: You didn't neglect to pay it by any chance?

TOM: Why, I—

20 AMANDA: Didn't! I might have known it!

JIM: Shakespeare probably wrote a poem on that light bill, Mrs. Wingfield.

AMANDA: I might have known better than to trust him with it! There's such a high price for negligence in this world!

JIM: Maybe the poem will win a ten-dollar prize.

AMANDA: We'll just have to spend the remainder of the evening in the nineteenth century, before Mr. Edison made the Mazda lamp!°

25 JIM: Candlelight is my favorite kind of light.

AMANDA: That shows you're romantic! But that's no excuse for Tom. Well, we got through dinner. Very considerate of them to let us get through dinner before they plunged us into everlasting darkness, wasn't it, Mr. O'Connor?

JIM: Ha-ha!

AMANDA: Tom, as a penalty for your carelessness you can help me with the dishes.

JIM: Let me give you a hand.

30 AMANDA: Indeed you will not!

JIM: I ought to be good for something.

AMANDA: Good for something? [*Her tone is rhapsodic.*] *You?* Why, Mr. O'Connor, nobody, *nobody's* given me this much entertainment in years—as you have!

JIM: Aw, now, Mrs. Wingfield!

° 24 **Mazda lamp:** Thomas A. Edison (1847–1931) developed the first practical incandescent lamp in 1879.

AMANDA: I'm not exaggerating, not one bit! But Sister is all by her lonesome. You
go keep her company in the parlor! I'll give you this lovely old candelabrum
that used to be on the altar at the Church of the Heavenly Rest. It was
melted a little out of shape when the church burnt down. Lightning struck it
one spring. Gypsy Jones was holding a revival at the time and he intimated
that the church was destroyed because the Episcopalians gave card parties.

35 JIM: Ha-ha.

AMANDA: And how about you coaxing Sister to drink a little wine? I think it
would be good for her! Can you carry both at once?

JIM: Sure. I'm Superman!

AMANDA: Now, Thomas, get into this apron!

[*JIM comes into the dining room, carrying the candelabrum, its candles lighted, in one
hand and a glass of wine in the other. The door of the kitchenette swings closed on
AMANDA's gay laughter; the flickering light approaches the portieres. LAURA sits up
nervously as JIM enters. She can hardly speak from the almost intolerable strain of
being alone with a stranger.*]

Screen legend: "I don't suppose you remember me at all!"

*At first, before JIM's warmth overcomes her paralyzing shyness, LAURA's voice is thin
and breathless, as though she had just run up a steep flight of stairs. JIM's attitude is
gently humorous. While the incident is apparently unimportant, it is to LAURA the
climax of her secret life.*]

JIM: Hello there, Laura.

40 LAURA: [*faintly*] Hello.

[*She clears her throat.*]

JIM: How are you feeling now? Better?

LAURA: Yes. Yes, thank you.

JIM: This is for you. A little dandelion wine. [*He extends the glass toward her with
extravagant gallantry.*]

45 LAURA: Thank you.

JIM: Drink it—but don't get drunk!

[*He laughs heartily. LAURA takes the glass uncertainly; she laughs shyly.*]

Where shall I set the candles?

LAURA: Oh—oh, anywhere . . .

JIM: How about here on the floor? Any objections?

LAURA: No.

JIM: I'll spread a newspaper under to catch the drippings. I like to sit on the
floor. Mind if I do?

50 LAURA: Oh, no.

JIM: Give me a pillow?

LAURA: What?

JIM: A pillow!

LAURA: Oh . . . [*She hands him one quickly.*]

55 JIM: How about you? Don't you like to sit on the floor?

LAURA: Oh—yes.

JIM: Why don't you, then?

LAURA: I—will.

JIM: Take a pillow!

[*Laura does. She sits on the floor on the other side of the candelabrum. JIM crosses his legs and smiles engagingly at her.*]

I can't hardly see you sitting way over there.

60 LAURA: I can—see you.
JIM: I know, but that's not fair, I'm in the limelight.

[*LAURA moves her pillow closer.*]

Good! Now I can see you! Comfortable?
LAURA: Yes.
JIM: So am I. Comfortable as a cow! Will you have some gum?
LAURA: No, thank you.
65 JIM: I think that I will indulge, with your permission. [*He musingly unwraps a stick of gum and holds it up.*] Think of the fortune made by the guy that invented the first piece of chewing gum. Amazing, huh? The Wrigley Building° is one of the sights of Chicago—I saw it when I went up to the Century of Progress.° Did you take in the Century of Progress?
LAURA: No, I didn't.
JIM: Well, it was quite a wonderful exposition. What impressed me most was the Hall of Science. Gives you an idea of what the future will be in America, even more wonderful than the present time is! [*There is a pause. JIM smiles at her.*] Your brother tells me you're shy. Is that right—Laura?
LAURA: I—don't know.
JIM: I judge you to be an old-fashioned type of girl. Well, I think that's a pretty good type to be. Hope you don't think I'm being too personal—do you?
70 LAURA: [*Hastily, out of embarrassment*] I believe I *will* take a piece of gum, if you—don't mind. [*clearing her throat*] Mr. O'Connor, have you—kept up with your singing?
JIM: Singing? Me?
LAURA: Yes. I remember what a beautiful voice you had.
JIM: When did you hear me sing?

[*LAURA does not answer, and in the long pause which follows a man's voice is heard singing offstage.*]

VOICE:

> O blow, ye winds, heigh-ho,
> A-roving I will go!
>   I'm off to my love
>   With a boxing glove—
> Ten thousand miles away!°

75 JIM: You say you've heard me sing?
LAURA: Oh, Yes! Yes, very often . . . I—don't suppose—you remember me—at all?

° 65 **Wrigley Building:** Finished in 1924, this was one of the first skyscrapers in the United States. **Century of Progress:** a world's fair held in Chicago (1933–1934) to celebrate the city's centennial.

° 74 **O blow . . . :** This is a simplified version of the refrain of "A Capital Ship" (1885), a song that Charles E. Carryl (1841–1920) wrote for the music of the early-nineteenth-century Irish sea shanty "Ten Thousand Miles Away."

JIM: [*smiling doubtfully*] You know I have an idea I've seen you before. I had that idea soon as you opened the door. It seemed almost like I was about to remember your name. But the name that I started to call you—wasn't a name! And so I stopped myself before I said it.

LAURA: Wasn't it—Blue Roses?

JIM: [*springing up, grinning*] Blue Roses! My gosh, yes—Blue Roses! That's what I had on my tongue when you opened the door! Isn't it funny what tricks your memory plays? I didn't connect you with high school somehow or other. But that's where it was; it was high school. I didn't even know you were Shakespeare's sister! Gosh, I'm sorry.

80 LAURA: I didn't expect you to. You—barely knew me!

JIM: But we did have a speaking acquaintance, huh?

LAURA: Yes, we—spoke to each other.

JIM: When did you recognize me?

LAURA: Oh, right away!

85 JIM: Soon as I came in the door?

LAURA: When I heard your name I thought it was probably you. I knew that Tom used to know you a little in high school. So when you came in the door— well, then I was—sure.

JIM: Why didn't you *say* something, then?

LAURA: [*breathlessly*] I didn't know what to say, I was—too surprised!

JIM: For goodness' sakes! You know, this sure is funny!

90 LAURA: Yes! Yes, isn't it, though...

JIM: Didn't we have a class in something together?

LAURA: Yes, we did.

JIM: What class was that?

LAURA: It was—singing—chorus!

95 JIM: Aw!

LAURA: I sat across the aisle from you in the Aud.

JIM: Aw!

LAURA: Mondays, Wednesdays, and Fridays.

JIM: Now I remember—you always came in late.

100 LAURA: Yes, it was so hard for me, getting upstairs. I had that brace on my leg— it clumped so loud!

JIM: I never heard any clumping.

LAURA: [*wincing at the recollection*] To me it sounded like—thunder!

JIM: Well, well, well, I never even noticed.

LAURA: And everybody was seated before I came in. I had to walk in front of all those people. My seat was in the back row. I had to go clumping all the way up the aisle with everyone watching!

105 JIM: You shouldn't have been self-conscious.

LAURA: I know, but I was. It was always such a relief when the singing started.

JIM: Aw, yes, I've placed you now! I used to call you Blue Roses. How was it that I got started calling you that?

LAURA: I was out of school a little while with pleurosis. When I came back you asked me what was the matter. I said I had pleurosis—you thought that I said *Blue Roses*. That's what you always called me after that!

JIM: I hope you didn't mind.

110 LAURA: Oh, no—I liked it. You see, I wasn't acquainted with many—people....
JIM: As I remember you sort of stuck by yourself.
LAURA: I—I—never had much luck at—making friends.
JIM: I don't see why you wouldn't.
LAURA: Well, I—started out badly.
115 JIM: You mean being—
LAURA: Yes, it sort of—stood between me—
JIM: You shouldn't have let it!
LAURA: I know, but it did, and—
JIM: You were shy with people!
120 LAURA: I tried not to be but never could—
JIM: Overcome it?
LAURA: No, I—I never could!
JIM: I guess being shy is something you have to work out of kind of gradually.
LAURA: [sorrowfully] Yes—I guess it—
125 JIM: Takes time!
LAURA: Yes—
JIM: People are not so dreadful when you know them. That's what you have to remember! And everybody has problems, not just you, but practically everybody has got some problems. You think of yourself as having the only problems, as being the only one who is disappointed. But just look around you and you will see lots of people as disappointed as you are. For instance, I hoped when I was going to high school that I would be further along at this time, six years later, than I am now. You remember that wonderful write-up I had in *The Torch*?

LAURA: Yes! [*She rises and crosses to the table.*]
JIM: It said I was bound to succeed in anything I went into!

[LAURA *returns with the high school yearbook.*]

Holy Jeez! *The Torch!*

[*He accepts it reverently. They smile across the book with mutual wonder.* LAURA *crouches beside him and they begin to turn the pages.* LAURA's *shyness is dissolving in his warmth.*]

130 LAURA: Here you are in *The Pirates of Penzance!*
JIM: [*wistfully*] I sang the baritone lead in that operetta.
LAURA: [*raptly*] So—*beautifully!*
JIM: [*protesting*] Aw—
LAURA: Yes, yes—beautifully—beautifully!
135 JIM: You heard me?
LAURA: All three times!
JIM: No!
LAURA: Yes!
JIM: All three performances?
140 LAURA: [*looking down*] Yes.
JIM: Why?
LAURA: I—wanted to ask you to—autograph my program. [*She takes the program from the back of the yearbook and shows it to him.*]
JIM: Why didn't you ask me to?

LAURA: You were always surrounded by your own friends so much that I never had a chance to.

145 JIM: You should have just—

LAURA: Well, I—thought you might think I was—

JIM: Thought I might think you was—what?

LAURA: Oh—

JIM: [*with reflective relish*] I was beleaguered by females in those days.

150 LAURA: You were terribly popular!

JIM: Yeah—

LAURA: You had such a—friendly way—

JIM: I was spoiled in high school.

LAURA: Everybody—liked you!

155 JIM: Including you?

LAURA: I—yes, I—did, too—[*She gently closes the book in her lap.*]

JIM: Well, well, well! Give me that program, Laura.

[*She hands it to him. He signs it with a flourish.*]

There you are—better late than never!

LAURA: Oh, I—what a—surprise!

JIM: My signature isn't worth very much right now. But some day—maybe—it will increase in value! Being disappointed is one thing and being discouraged is something else. I am disappointed but I am not discouraged. I'm twenty-three years old. How old are you?

160 LAURA: I'll be twenty-four in June.

JIM: That's not old age!

LAURA: No, but—

JIM: You finished high school?

LAURA: [*with difficulty*] I didn't go back.

165 JIM: You mean you dropped out?

LAURA: I made bad grades in my final examinations. [*She rises and replaces the book and the program on the table. Her voice is strained.*] How is—Emily Meisenbach getting along?

JIM: Oh, that kraut-head!

LAURA: Why do you call her that?

JIM: That's what she was.

170 LAURA: You're not still—going with her?

JIM: I never see her.

LAURA: It was in the "Personal" section that you were—engaged!

JIM: I know, but I wasn't impressed by that—propaganda!

LAURA: It wasn't—the truth?

175 JIM: Only in Emily's optimistic opinion!

LAURA: Oh—

[*Legend: "What have you done since high school?"*]

JIM lights a cigarette and leans indolently back on his elbows smiling at LAURA with a warmth and charm which lights her inwardly with altar candles. She remains by the table, picks up a piece from the glass menagerie collection, and turns it in her hands to cover her tumult.]

JIM: [*after several reflective puffs on his cigarette*] What have you done since high
school?

[*She seems not to hear him.*]

Huh?

[*LAURA looks up.*]

I said what have you done since high school, Laura?

LAURA: Nothing much.

JIM: You must have been doing something these six long years.

180 LAURA: Yes.

JIM: Well, then, such as what?

LAURA: I took a business course at business college—

JIM: How did that work out?

LAURA: Well, not very—well—I had to drop out, it gave me—indigestion—

[*JIM laughs gently.*]

185 JIM: What are you doing now?

LAURA: I don't do anything—much. Oh, please don't think I sit around doing
nothing! My glass collection takes up a good deal of time. Glass is something
you have to take good care of.

JIM: What did you say—about glass?

LAURA: Collection I said—I have one—[*She clears her throat and turns away again,
acutely shy.*]

JIM: [*abruptly*] You know what I judge to be the trouble with you? Inferiority
complex! Know what that is? That's what they call it when someone low-
rates himself! I understand it because I had it too. Although my case was not
so aggravated as yours seems to be. I had it until I took up public speaking,
developed my voice, and learned that I had an aptitude for science. Before
that time I never thought of myself as being outstanding in any way what-
soever! Now I've never made a regular study of it, but I have a friend
who says I can analyze people better than doctors that make a profession of
it. I don't claim that to be necessarily true, but I can sure guess a person's
psychology. Laura! [*He takes out his gum.*] Excuse me, Laura. I always take it
out when the flavor is gone. I'll use this scrap of paper to wrap it in. I know
how it is to get it stuck on a shoe. [*He wraps the gum in paper and puts it in his
pocket.*] Yep—that's what I judge to be your principal trouble. A lack of confidence in yourself as a person. You don't have the proper amount of faith in
yourself. I'm basing that fact on a number of your remarks and also on certain observations I've made. For instance that clumping you thought was so
awful in high school. You say that you even dreaded to walk into class. You
see what you did? You dropped out of school, you gave up an education
because of a clump, which as far as I know was practically nonexistent! A
little physical defect is what you have. Hardly noticeable even! Magnified
thousands of times by imagination! You know what my strong advice to you
is? Think of yourself as *superior* in some way!

190 LAURA: In what way would I think?

JIM: Why, man alive, Laura! Just look about you a little. What do you see?
A world full of common people! All of 'em born and all of 'em going to die!

Which of them has one-tenth of your good points! Or mine! Or anyone else's, as far as that goes—gosh! Everybody excels in some one thing. Some in many! [*He unconsciously glances at himself in the mirror.*] All you've got to do is discover in *what!* Take me, for instance. [*He adjusts his tie at the mirror.*] My interest happens to lie in electro-dynamics. I'm taking a course in radio engineering at night school, Laura, on top of a fairly responsible job at the warehouse. I'm taking that course and studying public speaking.

LAURA: Ohhhh.

JIM: Because I believe in the future of television! [*turning his back to her*] I wish to be ready to go up right along with it. Therefore I'm planning to get in on the ground floor. In fact I've already made the right connections and all that remains is for the industry itself to get under way! Full steam—[*His eyes are starry.*] *Knowledge—*Zzzzzp! *Money—*Zzzzzp!—Power! That's the cycle democracy is built on!

[*His attitude is convincingly dynamic.* LAURA *stares at him, even her shyness eclipsed in her absolute wonder. He suddenly grins.*]

I guess you think I think a lot of myself!

LAURA: No—o-o-o, I—

195 JIM: Now how about you? Isn't there something you take more interest in than anything else?

LAURA: Well, I do—as I said—have my—glass collection—

[*A peal of girlish laughter rings from the kitchenette.*]

JIM: I'm not right sure I know what you're talking about. What kind of glass is it?

LAURA: Little articles of it, they're ornaments mostly! Most of them are little animals made out of glass, the tiniest little animals in the world. Mother calls them a glass menagerie! Here's an example of one, if you'd like to see it! This one is one of the oldest. It's nearly thirteen.

[*Music: "The Glass Menagerie." He stretches out his hand.*]

Oh, be careful—if you breathe, it breaks!

JIM: I'd better not take it. I'm pretty clumsy with things.

200 LAURA: Go, on, I trust you with him! [*She places the piece in his palm.*] There now—you're holding him gently! Hold him over the light, he loves the light! You see how the light shines through him?

JIM: It sure does shine!

LAURA: I shouldn't be partial, but he is my favorite one.

JIM: What kind of a thing is this one supposed to be?

LAURA: Haven't you noticed the single horn on his forehead?

205 JIM: A unicorn, huh?

LAURA: Mmmm-hmmm!

JIM: Unicorns—aren't they extinct in the modern world?

LAURA: I know!

JIM: Poor little fellow, he must feel sort of lonesome.

210 LAURA: [*smiling*] Well, if he does, he doesn't complain about it. He stays on a shelf with some horses that don't have horns and all of them seem to get along nicely together.

JIM: How do you know?

LAURA: [*lightly*] I haven't heard any arguments among them!

JIM: [*grinning*] No arguments, huh? Well, that's a pretty good sign! Where shall I set him?

LAURA: Put him on the table. They all like a change of scenery once in a while!

215 JIM: Well, well, well, well—[*He places the glass piece on the table, then raises his arms and stretches.*] Look how big my shadow is when I stretch!

LAURA: Oh, oh, yes—it stretches across the ceiling!

JIM: [*crossing to the door*] I think it's stopped raining. [*He opens the fire-escape door and the background music changes to a dance tune.*] Where does the music come from?

LAURA: From the Paradise Dance Hall across the alley.

JIM: How about cutting the rug a little, Miss Wingfield?

220 LAURA: Oh, I—

JIM: Or is your program filled up? Let me have a look at it. [*He grasps an imaginary card.*] Why, every dance is taken! I'll just have to scratch some out.

[*Waltz music: "La Golondrina"°*]

      Ahh, a waltz! [*He executes some sweeping turns by himself, then holds his arms toward LAURA.*]

LAURA: [*breathlessly*] I—can't dance.

JIM: There you go, that inferiority stuff!

LAURA: I've never danced in my life!

225 JIM: Come on, try!

LAURA: Oh, but I'd step on you!

JIM: I'm not made out of glass.

LAURA: How—how—how do we start?

JIM: Just leave it to me. You hold your arms out a little.

230 LAURA: Like this?

JIM: [*taking her in his arms*] A little bit higher. Right. Now don't tighten up, that's the main thing about it—relax.

LAURA: [*laughing breathlessly*] It's hard not to.

JIM: Okay.

LAURA: I'm afraid you can't budge me.

235 JIM: What do you bet I can't? [*He swings her into motion.*]

LAURA: Goodness, yes, you can!

JIM: Let yourself go, now, Laura, just let yourself go.

LAURA: I'm—

JIM: Come on!

240 LAURA: —trying!

JIM: Not so stiff—easy does it!

LAURA: I know but I'm—

JIM: Loosen th' backbone! There now, that's a lot better.

LAURA: Am I?

245 JIM: Lots, lots better! [*He moves her about the room in a clumsy waltz.*]

LAURA: Oh, my!

° 221 S. D. **"La Golondrina"**: a popular Mexican song (1883) written by Narciso Serradel Sevilla (1843–1910). It is not a waltz.

JIM: Ha-ha!

LAURA: Oh, my goodness!

JIM: Ha-ha-ha!

[*They suddenly bump into the table, and the glass piece on it falls to the floor. Jim stops the dance.*]

What did we hit?

250 LAURA: Table.

JIM: Did something fall off it? I think—

LAURA: Yes.

JIM: I hope that it wasn't the little glass horse with the horn!

LAURA: Yes. [*She stoops to pick it up.*]

255 JIM: Aw, aw, aw. Is it broken?

LAURA: Now it is just like all the other horses.

JIM: It's lost its—

LAURA: Horn! It doesn't matter. Maybe it's a blessing in disguise.

JIM: You'll never forgive me. I bet that that was your favorite piece of glass.

260 LAURA: I don't have favorites much. It's no tragedy, Freckles. Glass breaks so easily. No matter how careful you are. The traffic jars the shelves and things fall off them.

JIM: Still I'm awfully sorry that I was the cause.

LAURA: [*smiling*] I'll just imagine he had an operation. The horn was removed to make him feel less—freakish!

[*They both laugh.*]

Now he will feel more at home with the other horses, the ones that don't have horns....

JIM: Ha-ha, that's very funny! [*Suddenly he is serious.*] I'm glad to see that you have a sense of humor. You know—you're—well—very different! Surprisingly different from anyone else I know! [*His voice becomes soft and hesitant with a genuine feeling.*] Do you mind me telling you that?

[*LAURA is abashed beyond speech.*]

I mean it in a nice way—

[*LAURA nods shyly, looking away.*]

You make me feel sort of—I don't know how to put it! I'm usually pretty good at expressing things, but—this is something that I don't know how to say!

[*LAURA touches her throat and clears it—turns the broken unicorn in her hands. His voice becomes softer.*]

Has anyone ever told you that you were pretty?

[*There is a pause, and the music rises slightly. LAURA looks up slowly, with wonder, and shakes her head.*]

Well, you are! In a very different way from anyone else. And all the nicer because of the difference, too.

[*His voice becomes low and husky. LAURA turns away, nearly faint with the novelty of her emotions.*]

I wish that you were my sister. I'd teach you to have some confidence in yourself. The different people are not like other people, but being different is nothing to be ashamed of. Because other people are not such wonderful people. They're one hundred times one thousand. You're one times one! They walk all over the earth. You just stay here. They're common as—weeds, but—you—well, you're—*Blue Roses*!

[*Image on screen: Blue Roses. The music changes.*]

LAURA: But blue is wrong for—roses. . . .

265 JIM: It's right for you! You're—pretty!

LAURA: In what respect am I pretty?

JIM: In all respects—believe me! Your eyes—your hair—are pretty! Your hands are pretty! [*He catches hold of her hand.*] You think I'm making this up because I'm invited to dinner and have to be nice. Oh, I could do that! I could put on an act for you, Laura, and say lots of things without being very sincere. But this time I am. I'm talking to you sincerely. I happened to notice you had this inferiority complex that keeps you from feeling comfortable with people. Somebody needs to build your confidence up and make you proud instead of shy and turning away and—blushing. Somebody—ought to—*kiss* you, Laura!

[*His hand slips slowly up her arm to her shoulder as the music swells tumultuously. He suddenly turns about and kisses her on the lips. When he releases her, LAURA sinks on the sofa with a bright, dazed look. Jim backs away and fishes in his pocket for a cigarette.*

Legend on screen: "A souvenir."]

Stumblejohn!

[*He lights the cigarette, avoiding her look. There is a peal of girlish laughter from AMANDA in the kitchenette. LAURA slowly raises and opens her hand. It still contains the little broken glass animal. She looks at it with a tender, bewildered expression.*]

Stumblejohn! I shouldn't have done that—that was way off the beam. You don't smoke, do you?

[*She looks up, smiling, not hearing the question. He sits beside her rather gingerly. She looks at him speechlessly—waiting. He coughs decorously and moves a little further aside as he considers the situation and senses her feelings, dimly, with perturbation. He speaks gently.*]

Would you—care for a mint?

[*She doesn't seem to hear him but her look grows brighter even.*]

Peppermint? Life Saver? My pocket's a regular drugstore—wherever I go. . . . [*He pops a mint in his mouth. Then he gulps and decides to make a clean breast of it. He speaks slowly and gingerly.*] Laura, you know, if I had a sister like you, I'd do the same thing as Tom. I'd bring out fellows and—introduce her to them. The right type of boys—of a type to—appreciate her. Only—well—he made a mistake about me. Maybe I've got no call to be saying this. That may not have been the idea in having me over. But what if it was? There's nothing wrong about that. The only trouble is that in my case—I'm not in a situation to—do the right thing. I can't take down your number and say I'll phone. I can't call up next week and—ask for a date. I thought I had better explain the situation in case you—misunderstood it and—I hurt your feelings. . . .

[*There is a pause. Slowly, very slowly,* LAURA's *look changes, her eyes returning slowly from his to the glass figure in her palm.* AMANDA *utters another gay laugh in the kitchenette.*]

LAURA: [*faintly*] You—won't—call again?

JIM: No, Laura, I can't. [*He rises from the sofa.*] As I was just explaining, I've—got strings on me, Laura, I've—been going steady! I go out all the time with a girl named Betty. She's a home-girl like you, and Catholic, and Irish, and in a great many ways we—get along fine. I met her last summer on a moonlight boat trip up the river to Alton,° on the *Majestic.* Well—right away from the start it was—love!

[*Legend: Love!*

LAURA *sways slightly forward and grips the arm of the sofa. He fails to notice, now enrapt in his own comfortable being.*]

Being in love has made a new man of me!

[*Leaning stiffly forward, clutching the arm of the sofa,* LAURA *struggles visibly with her storm. But* JIM *is oblivious; she is a long way off.*]

The power of love is really pretty tremendous! Love is something that— changes the whole world, Laura!

[*The storm abates a little and* LAURA *leans back. He notices her again.*]

It happened that Betty's aunt took sick, she got a wire and had to go to Centralia.° So Tom—when he asked me to dinner—I naturally just accepted the invitation, not knowing that you—that he—that I—[*He stops awkwardly.*] Huh—I'm a stumblejohn!

[*He flops back on the sofa. The holy candles on the altar of* LAURA's *face have been snuffed out. There is a look of almost infinite desolation.* JIM *glances at her uneasily.*]

I wish that you would—say something.

[*She bites her lip which was trembling and then bravely smiles. She opens her hand again on the broken glass figure. Then she gently takes his hand and raises it level with her own. She carefully places the unicorn in the palm of his hand, then pushes his fingers closed upon it.*]

What are you—doing that for? You want me to have him? Laura?

[*She nods.*]

What for?

270 LAURA: A—souvenir. . . .

[*She rises unsteadily and crouches beside the Victrola to wind it up.*

° 269.1 **Alton:** a city in Illinois about twenty miles north of St. Louis on the Mississippi River.
° 269.8 **Centralia:** a city in Illinois about sixty miles east of St. Louis.

Legend on screen: "Things have a way of turning out so badly!" Or image: "Gentleman caller waving goodbye—gaily."

At this moment AMANDA *rushes brightly back into the living room. She bears a pitcher of fruit punch in an old-fashioned cut-glass pitcher, and a plate of macaroons. The plate has a gold border and poppies painted on it.*]

AMANDA: Well, well, well! Isn't the air delightful after the shower? I've made you children a little liquid refreshment. [*She turns gaily to* JIM.] Jim, do you know that song about lemonade?

> "Lemonade, lemonade
> Made in the shade and stirred with a spade—
> Good enough for any old maid!"

JIM: [*uneasily*] Ha-ha! No—I never heard it.

275 AMANDA: Why, Laura! You look so serious!

JIM: We were having a serious conversation.

AMANDA: Good! Now you're better acquainted!

JIM: [*uncertainly*] Ha-ha! Yes.

AMANDA: You modern young people are much more serious-minded than my generation. I was so gay as a girl!

JIM: You haven't changed, Mrs. Wingfield.

AMANDA: Tonight I'm rejuvenated! The gaiety of the occasion, Mr. O'Connor! [*She tosses her head with a peal of laughter, spilling some lemonade.*] Oooo! I'm baptizing myself!

280 JIM: Here—let me—

AMANDA: [*setting the pitcher down*] There now. I discovered we had some maraschino cherries. I dumped them in, juice and all!

JIM: You shouldn't have gone to that trouble, Mrs. Wingfield.

AMANDA: Trouble, trouble? Why, it was loads of fun! Didn't you hear me cutting up in the kitchen? I bet your ears were burning! I told Tom how outdone with him I was for keeping you to himself so long a time! He should have brought you over much, much sooner! Well, now that you've found your way, I want you to be a very frequent caller! Not just occasional but all the time. Oh, we're going to have a lot of gay times together! I see them coming! Mmm, just breathe that air! So fresh, and the moon's so pretty! I'll skip back out—I know where my place is when young folks are having a—serious conversation!

JIM: Oh, don't go out, Mrs. Wingfield. The fact of the matter is I've got to be going.

285 AMANDA: Going, now? You're joking! Why, it's only the shank of the evening,° Mr. O'Connor!

JIM: Well, you know how it is.

AMANDA: You mean you're a young workingman and have to keep workingmen's hours. We'll let you off early tonight. But only on the condition that next time you stay later. What's the best night for you? Isn't Saturday night the best night for you workingmen?

° 285 **shank of the evening**: still early, the best part of the evening.

JIM: I have a couple of time-clocks to punch, Mrs. Wingfield. One at morning, another one at night!

AMANDA: My, but you *are* ambitious! You work at night, too?

290 JIM: No, Ma'am, not work but—Betty!

[*He crosses deliberately to pick up his hat. The band at the Paradise Dance Hall goes into a tender waltz.*]

AMANDA: Betty? Betty? Who's—Betty!

[*There is an ominous cracking sound in the sky.*]

JIM: Oh, just a girl. The girl I go steady with!

[*He smiles charmingly. The sky falls.*

Legend: "The Sky Falls."]

AMANDA: [*a long-drawn exhalation*] Ohhh...Is it a serious romance, Mr. O'Connor?

JIM: We're going to be married the second Sunday in June.

295 AMANDA: Ohhh—how nice! Tom didn't mention that you were engaged to be married.

JIM: The cat's not out of the bag at the warehouse yet. You know how they are. They call you Romeo and stuff like that. [*He stops at the oval mirror to put on his hat. He carefully shapes the brim and the crown to give a discreetly dashing effect.*] It's been a wonderful evening, Mrs. Wingfield. I guess this is what they mean by Southern hospitality.

AMANDA: It really wasn't anything at all.

JIM: I hope it don't seem like I'm rushing off. But I promised Betty I'd pick her up at the Wabash depot, an' by the time I get my jalopy down there her train'll be in. Some women are pretty upset if you keep 'em waiting.

AMANDA: Yes, I know—the tyranny of women! [*She extends her hand.*] Goodbye, Mr. O'Connor. I wish you luck—and happiness—and success! All three of them, and so does Laura! Don't you, Laura?

300 LAURA: Yes!

JIM: [*taking LAURA's hand*] Goodbye, Laura. I'm certainly going to treasure that souvenir. And don't you forget the good advice I gave you. [*He raises his voice to a cheery shout.*] So long, Shakespeare! Thanks again, ladies. Good night!

[*He grins and ducks jauntily out. Still bravely grimacing, Amanda closes the door on the gentleman caller. Then she turns back to the room with a puzzled expression. She and LAURA don't dare to face each other. LAURA crouches beside the Victrola to wind it.*]

AMANDA: [*faintly*] Things have a way of turning out so badly. I don't believe that I would play the Victrola. Well, well—well! Our gentleman caller was engaged to be married? [*She raises her voice.*] Tom!

TOM: [*from the kitchenette*] Yes, Mother?

AMANDA: Come in here a minute. I want to tell you something awfully funny.

305 TOM: [*entering with a macaroon and a glass of the lemonade*] Has the gentleman caller gotten away already?

AMANDA: The gentleman caller has made an early departure. What a wonderful joke you played on us!

TOM: How do you mean?

AMANDA: You didn't mention that he was engaged to be married.

TOM: Jim? Engaged?

310 AMANDA: That's what he just informed us.

TOM: I'll be jiggered! I didn't know about that.

AMANDA: That seems very peculiar.

TOM: What's peculiar about it?

AMANDA: Didn't you call him your best friend down at the warehouse?

315 TOM: He is, but how did I know?

AMANDA: It seems extremely peculiar that you wouldn't know your best friend was going to be married!

TOM: The warehouse is where I work, not where I know things about people!

AMANDA: You don't know things anywhere! You live in a dream; you manufacture illusions!

[*He crosses to the door.*]

Where are you going?

TOM: I'm going to the movies.

320 AMANDA: That's right, now that you've had us make such fools of ourselves. The effort, the preparations, all the expense! The new floor lamp, the rug, the clothes for Laura! All for what? To entertain some other girl's fiancé! Go to the movies, go! Don't think about us, a mother deserted, an unmarried sister who's crippled and has no job! Don't let anything interfere with your selfish pleasure! Just go, go, go—to the movies!

TOM: All right, I will! The more you shout about my selfishness to me the quicker I'll go, and I won't go to the movies!

AMANDA: Go, then! Go to the moon—you selfish dreamer!

[*TOM smashes his glass on the floor. He plunges out on the fire escape, slamming the door. LAURA screams in fright. The dance-hall music becomes louder. Tom stands on the fire escape, gripping the rail. The moon breaks through the storm clouds, illuminating his face.*

Legend on screen: "And so goodbye ..."

TOM's closing speech is timed with what is happening inside the house. We see, as though through soundproof glass, that AMANDA appears to be making a comforting speech to LAURA, who is huddled upon the sofa. Now that we cannot hear the mother's speech, her silliness is gone and she has dignity and tragic beauty. LAURA's hair hides her face until, at the end of the speech, she lifts her head to smile at her mother. AMANDA's gestures are slow and graceful, almost dancelike, as she comforts her daughter. At the end of her speech she glances a moment at the father's picture—then withdraws through the portieres. At the close of TOM's speech, LAURA blows out the candles, ending the play.]

TOM: I didn't go to the moon, I went much further—for time is the longest distance between two places. Not long after that I was fired for writing a poem on the lid of a shoe box. I left Saint Louis. I descended the steps of this fire escape for a last time and followed, from then on, in my father's footsteps, attempting to find in motion what was lost in space. I traveled around a great deal. The cities swept about me like dead leaves, leaves that were brightly colored but torn away from the branches. I would have stopped, but I was pursued by something. It always came upon me unawares, taking me altogether by surprise. Perhaps it was a familiar bit of music. Perhaps it was only a piece of transparent glass. Perhaps I am walking along a street at night, in some strange city, before I have found companions. I pass the lighted window of a shop where perfume is sold. The window is filled with pieces of colored glass, tiny transparent bottles in delicate colors, like bits of a shattered rainbow. Then all at once my sister touches my shoulder. I turn around and look into her eyes. Oh, Laura, Laura, I tried to leave you behind me, but I am more faithful than I intended to be! I reach for a cigarette, I cross the street, I run into the movies or a bar, I buy a drink, I speak to the nearest stranger—anything that can blow your candles out!

[LAURA *bends over the candles.*]

For nowadays the world is lit by lightning! Blow out your candles, Laura—and so good bye....

[*She blows the candles out.*]

FOCUSED FREE WRITES

Part I: Scenes I–V

1. At the play's opening, the time is said to be "now and the past." What does that mean? How does that setting contribute to the theme of the play?
2. How would you describe these characters? What are they like? What are their flaws? What are their secrets?
3. So far, what is the theme of the play?
4. Which stage directions are significant in furthering the plot and theme of the play?

Part II: Scenes VI–VII

1. What is the significance of the title of the play? The epigram is by E.E. Cummings: "nobody, not even the rain, has such small hands." You read some other poems by Cummings earlier in this chapter. Why would Williams quote Cummings? Why this quotation?
2. What are some of the play's themes?
3. *The Glass Menagerie* is described as a "memory play." What does that mean? How is it a "memory play"?
4. Identify some of the symbols in this play. What objects bear extra meaning? How do they bear their abstract meaning beyond their concrete presence? Provide specific examples.
5. How do the stage directions, the props, and the setting contribute to the characters and their dialog and actions? What is the function of the screens? What else is significant in how the play is presented?

LITERARY Contexts

Realism

> The straight realistic play with its genuine frigidaire and authentic ice cubes, its characters that speak exactly as its audience speaks... has the same virtue of a photographic likeness. Everyone nowadays should know the unimportance of the photographic in art...

In these introductory notes to *The Glass Menagerie* (1944), Tennessee Williams critiques the naturalism and realistic conventions of contemporary theatre. Instead, he argues for a "plastic theatre" capable of expressing the "poetic imagination." Williams challenged contemporary realism by creating a play not true to life but true to theatre, art, film, and imaginative endeavors. *The Glass Menagerie* foregrounds its unrealistic elements and staging devices to create a "memory play" that illustrates the subjectivity of memory.

Which aspects of The Glass Menagerie *are realistic? Which aspects are the most un-realistic? What function do the nonrealistic elements serve?*

STORIES

The following stories all represent experiments with fictional styles—from Bambara's social commentary to DeLillo's postmodern meditation and O'Brien's Vietnam tour de force. Analysis will allow us to uncover the crafting of these powerful themes.

| **PRE-READING** | Children often complain: "That's not fair." What examples of life's unfairness can you cite? |

Toni Cade Bambara (1939–1995). *Bambara was born Miltona Mirkin Cade and took the nickname Toni as a young child and the family name Bambara as a young adult. She published her first story at the age of twenty, graduating from Queens College with a degree in English that same year. After a brief period doing social work, Bambara studied in Paris before earning a master's degree from the City College of New York, where she began teaching the following year. Bambara edited groundbreaking anthologies of African American literature at the outset of her literary career before publishing her own work. At the end of her life, while battling colon cancer, Bambara was achieving great success in producing documentary films.*

THE LESSON [1972]

Back in the days when everyone was old and stupid or young and foolish and me and Sugar were the only ones just right, this lady moved on our block with nappy hair and proper speech and no makeup. And quite naturally we laughed at her, laughed the way we did at the junk man who went about his business like he was some big-time president and his sorry-ass horse his secretary. And we kinda hated her too, hated the way we did the winos who cluttered up our parks and pissed on our handball walls and stank up our hallways and stairs so you couldn't halfway play hide-and-seek without a goddamn gas mask. Miss Moore was her name. The only woman on the block with no first name. And she was black as hell, cept for her feet, which were fish-white and spooky. And she was always planning these boring-ass things for us to do, us being my cousin, mostly, who lived on the block cause we all moved North the same time and to the same apartment then spread out gradual to breathe. And our parents would yank our heads into some kinda shape and crisp up our clothes so we'd be presentable for travel with Miss Moore, who always looked like she was going to church though she never did. Which is just one of the things the grownups talked about when they talked behind her back like a dog. But when she came calling with some sachet she'd sewed up or some gingerbread she'd made or some book, why then they'd all be too embarrassed to turn her down and we'd get handed over all spruced up. She'd been to college and said it was only right that she should take responsibility for the young ones' education, and she not even related by marriage or blood. So they'd go for it. Specially Aunt Gretchen. She was the main gofer in the family. You got some ole dumb shit foolishness you want somebody to go for, you send for Aunt Gretchen. She been screwed into the go-along for so long, it's a blood-deep natural thing with her. Which is how she got saddled with me and Sugar and Junior in the first place while our mothers were in a la-de-da apartment up the block having a good ole time.

So this one day Miss Moore rounds us all up at the mailbox and it's purdee° hot and she's knockin herself out about arithmetic. And school suppose to let up in summer I heard, but she don't never let up. And the starch in my pinafore scratching the shit outta me and I'm really hating this nappy-head bitch and her goddamn college degree. I'd much rather go to the pool or to the show where it's cool. So me and Sugar leaning on the mailbox being surly, which is a Miss Moore word. And Flyboy checking out what everybody brought for lunch. And Fat Butt already wasting his peanut-butter-and-jelly sandwich like the pig he is. And Junebug punchin on Q.T.'s arm for potato chips. And Rosie Giraffe shifting from one hip to the other waiting for somebody to step on her foot or ask her if she from Georgia so she can kick ass, preferably Mercedes'. And Miss Moore asking us do we know what money is like we a bunch of retards. I mean real money, she say, like it's only poker chips or monopoly papers we lay on the grocer. So right away I'm tired of this and say so. And would much rather snatch Sugar and go to the Sunset and terrorize the West Indian kids and take their

---

° *purdee:* pretty.

hair ribbons and their money too. And Miss Moore files that remark away for next week's lesson on brotherhood, I can tell. And finally I say we oughta get to the subway cause it's cooler an' besides we might meet some cute boys. Sugar done swiped her mama's lipstick, so we ready.

So we heading down the street and she's boring us silly about what things cost and what our parents make and how much goes for rent and how money ain't divided up right in this country. And then she gets to the part about we all poor and live in the slums which I don't feature. And I'm ready to speak on that, but she steps out in the street and hails two cabs just like that. Then she hustles half the crew in with her and hands me a five-dollar bill and tells me to calculate 10 percent tip for the driver. And we're off. Me and Sugar and Junebug and Flyboy hangin out the window and hollering to everybody, putting lipstick on each other cause Flyboy a faggot anyway, and making farts with our sweaty armpits. But I'm mostly trying to figure how to spend this money. But they are fascinated with the meter ticking and Junebug starts laying bets as to how much it'll read when Flyboy can't hold his breath no more. Then Sugar lays bets as to how much it'll be when we get there. So I'm stuck. Don't nobody want to go for my plan, which is to jump out at the next light and run off to the first bar-b-que we can find. Then the driver tells us to get the hell out cause we there already. And the meter reads eighty-five cents. And I'm stalling to figure out the tip and Sugar say give him a dime. And I decide he don't need it bad as I do, so later for him. But then he tries to take off with Junebug foot still in the door so we talk about his mama something ferocious. Then we check out that we on Fifth Avenue and everybody dressed up in stockings. One lady in a fur coat, hot as it is. White folks crazy.

"This is the place," Miss Moore say, presenting it to us in the voice she uses at the museum. "Let's look in the windows before we go in."

5   "Can we steal?" Sugar asks very serious like she's getting the ground rules squared away before she plays. "I beg your pardon," say Miss Moore, and we fall out. So she leads us around the windows of the toy store and me and Sugar screamin, "This is mine, that's mine, I gotta have that, that was made for me, I was born for that," till Big Butt drowns us out.

"Hey, I'm goin to buy that there."

"That there? You don't even know what it is, stupid."

"I do so," he say punchin on Rosie Giraffe. "It's a microscope."

"Whatcha gonna do with a microscope, fool?"

10   "Look at things."

"Like what, Ronald?" ask Miss Moore. And Big Butt ain't got the first notion. So here go Miss Moore gabbing about the thousands of bacteria in a drop of water and the somethinorother in a speck of blood and the million and one living things in the air around us is invisible to the naked eye. And what she say that for? Junebug go to town on that "naked" and we rolling. Then Miss Moore ask what it cost. So we all jam into the window smudgin it up and the price tag say $300. So then she ask how long'd take for Big Butt and Junebug to save up their allowances. "Too long," I say. "Yeh," adds Sugar, "outgrown it by that time." And Miss Moore say no, you never outgrow learning instruments. "Why, even medical students and interns and," blah, blah, blah. And we ready to choke Big Butt for bringing it up in the first damn place.

"This here costs four hundred eighty dollars," say Rosie Giraffe. So we pile up all over her to see what she pointin out. My eyes tell me it's a chunk of glass cracked with something heavy, and different-color inks dripped into the splits, then the whole thing put into a oven or something. But for $480 it don't make sense.

"That's a paperweight made of semi-precious stones fused together under tremendous pressure," she explains slowly, with her hands doing the mining and all the factory work.

"So what's a paperweight?" asks Rosie Giraffe.

15 "To weigh paper with, dumbbell," say Flyboy, the wise man from the East.

"Not exactly," say Miss Moore, which is what she say when you warm or way off too. "It's to weigh paper down so it won't scatter and make your desk untidy." So right away me and Sugar curtsy to each other and then to Mercedes who is more the tidy type.

"We don't keep paper on top of the desk in my class," say Junebug, figuring Miss Moore crazy or lyin one.

"At home, then," she say. "Don't you have a calendar and a pencil case and a blotter and a letter-opener on your desk at home where you do your home-work?" And she know damn well what our homes look like cause she nosys around in them every chance she gets.

"I don't even have a desk," say Junebug. "Do we?"

20 "No. And I don't get no homework neither," says Big Butt.

"And I don't even have a home," say Flyboy like he do at school to keep the white folks off his back and sorry for him. Send this poor kid to camp posters, is his specialty.

"I do," says Mercedes. "I have a box of stationery on my desk and a picture of my cat. My godmother bought the stationery and the desk. There's a big rose on each sheet and the envelopes smell like roses."

"Who wants to know about your smelly-ass stationery," say Rosie Giraffe fore I can get my two cents in.

"It's important to have a work area all your own so that..."

25 "Will you look at this sailboat, please," say Flyboy, cuttin her off and pointin to the thing like it was his. So once again we tumble all over each other to gaze at this magnificent thing in the toy store which is just big enough to maybe sail two kittens across the pond if you strap them to the posts tight. We all start reciting the price tag like we in assembly. "Hand-crafted sailboat of fiberglass at one thousand one hundred ninety-five dollars."

"Unbelievable," I hear myself say and am really stunned. I read it again for myself just in case the group recitation put me in a trance. Same thing. For some reason this pisses me off. We look at Miss Moore and she lookin at us, waiting for I dunno what.

"Who'd pay all that when you can buy a sailboat set for a quarter at Pop's, a tube of glue for a dime, and a ball of string for eight cents? It must have a motor and a whole lot else besides," I say. "My sailboat cost me about fifty cents."

"But will it take water?" say Mercedes with her smart ass.

"Took mine to Alley Pond Park once," say Flyboy. "String broke. Lost it. Pity."

30 "Sailed mine in Central Park and it keeled over and sank. Had to ask my father for another dollar."

"And you got the strap," laugh Big Butt. "The jerk didn't even have a string on it. My old man wailed on his behind."

Little Q.T. was staring hard at the sailboat and you could see he wanted it bad. But he too little and somebody'd just take it from him. So what the hell. "This boat for kids, Miss Moore?"

"Parents silly to buy something like that just to get all broke up," say Rosie Giraffe.

"That much money it should last forever," I figure.

35   "My father'd buy it for me if I wanted it."

"Your father, my ass," say Rosie Giraffe getting a chance to finally push Mercedes.

"Must be rich people shop here," say Q.T.

"You are a very bright boy," say Flyboy. "What was your first clue?" And he rap him on the head with the back of his knuckles, since Q.T. the only one he could get away with. Though Q.T. liable to come up behind you years later and get his licks in when you half expect it.

"What I want to know is," I says to Miss Moore though I never talk to her, I wouldn't give the bitch that satisfaction, "is how much a real boat costs? I figure a thousand'd get you a yacht any day."

40   "Why don't you check that out," she says, "and report back to the group?" Which really pains my ass. If you gonna mess up a perfectly good swim day least you could do is have some answers. "Let's go in," she say like she got something up her sleeve. Only she don't lead the way. So me and Sugar turn the corner to where the entrance is, but when we get there I kinda hang back. Not that I'm scared, what's there to be afraid of, just a toy store. But I feel funny, shame. But what I got to be shamed about? Got as much right to go in as anybody. But somehow I can't seem to get hold of the door, so I step away from Sugar to lead. But she hangs back too. And I look at her and she looks at me and this is ridiculous. I mean, damn, I have never ever been shy about doing nothing or going nowhere. But then Mercedes steps up and then Rosie Giraffe and Big Butt crowd in behind and shove, and next thing we all stuffed into the doorway with only Mercedes squeezing past us, smoothing out her jumper and walking right down the aisle. Then the rest of us tumble in like a glued-together jigsaw done all wrong. And people lookin at us. And it's like the time me and Sugar crashed into the Catholic church on a dare. But once we got in there and everything so hushed and holy and the candles and the bowin and the handkerchiefs on all the drooping heads, I just couldn't go through with the plan. Which was for me to run up to the altar and do a tap dance while Sugar played the nose flute and messed around in the holy water. And Sugar kept givin me the elbow. Then later teased me so bad I tied her up in the shower and turned it on and locked her in. And she'd be there till this day if Aunt Gretchen hadn't finally figured I was lyin about the boarder takin a shower.

Same thing in the store. We all walkin on tiptoe and hardly touchin the games and puzzles and things. And I watched Miss Moore who is steady watchin us like she waitin for a sign. Like Mama Drewery watches the sky and sniffs the air and takes note of just how much slant is in the bird formation. Then me and Sugar bump smack into each other, so busy gazing at the toys, 'specially the sailboat. But we don't laugh and go into our fat-lady bump-stomach routine. We just stare at that price tag. Then Sugar run a finger over the whole boat. And I'm jealous and want to hit her. Maybe not her, but I sure want to punch somebody in the mouth.

"Watcha bring us here for, Miss Moore?"

"You sound angry, Sylvia. Are you mad about something?" Givin me one of them grins like she tellin a grown-up joke that never turns out to be funny. And she's lookin very closely at me like maybe she plannin to do my portrait from memory. I'm mad, but I won't give her that satisfaction. So I slouch around the store bein very bored and say, "Let's go."

Me and Sugar at the back of the train watchin the tracks whizzin by large then small then gettin gobbled up in the dark. I'm thinkin about this tricky toy I saw in the store. A clown that somersaults on a bar then does chin-ups just cause you yank lightly at his leg. Cost $35. I could see me askin my mother for a $35 birthday clown. "You wanna who that costs what?" she'd say, cocking her head to the side to get a better view of the hole in my head. Thirty-five dollars could buy new bunk beds for Junior and Gretchen's boy. Thirty-five dollars and the whole household could go visit Grand-daddy Nelson in the country. Thirty-five dollars would pay for the rent and the piano bill too. Who are these people that spend that much for performing clowns and $1000 for toy sailboats? What kinda work they do and how they live and how come we ain't in on it? Where we are is who we are, Miss Moore always pointin out. But it don't necessarily have to be that way, she always adds then waits for somebody to say that poor people have to wake up and demand their share of the pie and don't none of us know what kind of pie she talking about in the first damn place. But she ain't so smart cause I still got her four dollars from the taxi and she sure ain't gettin it. Messin up my day with this shit. Sugar nudges me in my pocket and winks.

45   Miss Moore lines us up in front of the mailbox where we started from, seem like years ago, and I got a headache for thinkin so hard. And we lean all over each other so we can hold up under the draggy ass lecture she always finishes us off with at the end before we thank her for borin us to tears. But she just looks at us like she readin tea leaves. Finally she say, "Well, what did you think of F.A.O. Schwarz?"

Rosie Giraffe mumbles, "White folks crazy."

"I'd like to go there again when I get my birthday money," says Mercedes, and we shove her out the pack so she has to lean on the mailbox by herself.

"I'd like a shower. Tiring day," say Flyboy.

Then Sugar surprises me by sayin, "You know, Miss Moore, I don't think all of us here put together eat in a year what that sailboat costs." And Miss Moore lights up like somebody goosed her. "And?" she say, urging Sugar on. Only I'm standin on her foot so she don't continue.

50   "Imagine for a minute what kind of society it is in which some people can spend on a toy what it would cost to feed a family of six or seven. What do you think?"

"I think," say Sugar pushing me off her feet like she never done before cause I whip her ass in a minute, "that this is not much of a democracy if you ask me. Equal chance to pursue happiness means an equal crack at the dough, don't it?" Miss Moore is besides herself and I am disgusted with Sugar's treachery. So I stand on her foot one more time to see if she'll shove me. She shuts up, and Miss Moore looks at me, sorrowfully I'm thinkin. And somethin weird is goin on, I can feel it in my chest. "Anybody else learn anything today?" lookin dead at me. I walk away and Sugar has to run to catch up and don't even seem to notice when I shrug her arm off my shoulder.

55 "Well, we got four dollars anyway," she says.

"Uh hunh."

"We could go to Hascombs and get half a chocolate layer and then go to the Sunset and still have plenty money for potato chips and ice cream sodas."

"Uh hunh."

"Race you to Hascombs," she say.

We start down the block and she gets ahead which is O.K. by me cause I'm going to the West End and then over to the Drive to think this day through. She can run if she want to and even run faster. But ain't nobody gonna beat me at nuthin.

FOCUSED FREE WRITES

1. What is "the lesson" learned here?
2. Who are the different characters in this story? How are they characterized? How do we distinguish one from the other?
3. Summarize the story's plot.
4. How would you explain the story's theme?
5. Returning to the act of analysis discussed earlier, what is distinctive about this writer's style? How does it convey the meaning of the story? Which elements are significant?
   - What, where, when? Title, setting, plot, or structure?
   - Who? Character, narration, point of view, tone?
   - How? Imagery, symbols, syntax, diction, or figurative language?

LITERARY Contexts

Dialog

Dialog is a distinctive stylistic element that playwrights depend on since the majority of their content is in this form. Poets employ dialog when writing dramatic dialogs, and fiction writers use it strategically to develop voice. Dialog records the exchanges between characters, often without the supervising commentary of a narrator; it also reveals the attitudes, beliefs, and natures of characters directly to the reader. This story uses dialog as a stylistic element to show—and not tell—how lessons can be learned.

How are these characters in "The Lesson" characterized through their ways of speaking? What do we learn about them in how they talk and what they say?

| PRE-READING | What are some possible reasons our culture is so obsessed with reality television? |

Don DeLillo (1936–). *Born in the Bronx to Italian-American Catholic parents, DeLillo studied history, philosophy, and theology at Fordham University to earn a degree, but reportedly much preferred extracurricular writing, reading, and studying of such interests as French New Wave films and James Joyce. After a brief time working in advertising and getting a story published, he began writing full time and soon published his first of fourteen novels to date. Heralded as one of the best known and most respected of American writers today, DeLillo has bridged the commercial and critical markets successfully.*

Don DeLillo

VIDEOTAPE*

It shows a man driving a car. It is the simplest sort of family video. You see a man at the wheel of a medium Dodge.

It is just a kid aiming her camera through the rear window of the family car at the windshield of the car behind her.

You know about families and their video cameras. You know how kids get involved, how the camera shows them that every subject is potentially charged, a million things they never see with the unaided eye. They investigate the meaning of inert objects and dumb pets and they poke at family privacy. They learn to see things twice.

It is the kid's own privacy that is being protected here. She is twelve years old and her name is being withheld even though she is neither the victim nor the perpetrator of the crime but only the means of recording it.

It shows a man in a sport shirt at the wheel of his car. There is nothing else to see. The car approaches briefly, then falls back.

You know how children with cameras learn to work the exposed moments that define the family cluster. They break every trust, spy out the undefended space, catching Mom coming out of the bathroom in her cumbrous robe and turbaned towel, looking bloodless and plucked. It is not a joke. They will shoot you sitting on the pot if they can manage a suitable vantage.

The tape has the jostled sort of noneventness that marks the family product. Of course the man in this case is not a member of the family but a stranger in a car, a random figure, someone who has happened along in the slow lane.

It shows a man in his forties wearing a pale shirt open at the throat, the image washed by reflections and sunglint, with many jostled moments.

It is not just another video homicide. It is a homicide recorded by a child who thought she was doing something simple and maybe halfway clever, shooting some tape of a man in a car.

He sees the girl and waves briefly, wagging a hand without taking it off the wheel—an underplayed reaction that makes you like him.

It is unrelenting footage that rolls on and on. It has an aimless determination, a persistence that lives outside the subject matter. You are looking into the mind of home video. It is innocent, it is aimless, it is determined, it is real.

He is bald up the middle of his head, a nice guy in his forties whose whole life seems open to the handheld camera.

But there is also an element of suspense. You keep on looking not because you know something is going to happen—of course you do know something is going to happen and you do look for that reason but you might also keep on looking if you came across this footage for the first time without knowing the outcome. There is a crude power operating here. You keep on looking because things combine to hold you fast—a sense of the random, the amateurish, the accidental, the impending. You don't think of the tape as boring or interesting. It is crude, it is blunt, it is relentless. It is the jostled part of your mind, the film that runs through your hotel brain under all the thoughts you know you're thinking.

The world is lurking in the camera, already framed, waiting for the boy or girl who will come along and take up the device, learn the instrument, shooting old Granddad at breakfast, all stroked out so his nostrils gape, the cereal spoon baby-gripped in his pale fist.

It shows a man alone in a medium Dodge. It seems to go on forever.

There's something about the nature of the tape, the grain of the image, the sputtering black-and-white tones, the starkness—you think this is more real, truer to life than anything around you. The things around you have a rehearsed and layered and cosmetic look. The tape is superreal, or maybe underreal is the way you want to put it. It is what lies at the scraped bottom of all the layers you have added. And this is another reason why you keep on looking. The tape has a searing realness.

It shows him giving an abbreviated wave, stiff-palmed, like a signal flag at a siding.

You know how families make up games. This is just another game in which the child invents the rules as she goes along. She likes the idea of videotaping a man in his car. She has probably never done it before and she sees no reason to vary the format or terminate early or pan to another car. This is her game and she is learning it and playing it at the same time. She feels halfway clever and inventive and maybe slightly intrusive as well, a little bit of brazenness that spices any game.

And you keep on looking. You look because this is the nature of the footage, to make a channeled path through time, to give things a shape and a destiny.

Of course if she had panned to another car, the right car at the precise time, she would have caught the gunman as he fired.

The chance quality of the encounter. The victim, the killer, and the child with a camera. Random energies that approach a common point. There's something here that speaks to you directly, saying terrible things about forces beyond your control, lines of intersection that cut through history and logic and every reasonable layer of human expectation.

She wandered into it. The girl got lost and wandered clear-eyed into horror. This is a children's story about straying too far from home. But it isn't the family car that serves as the instrument of the child's curiosity, her inclination to explore. It is the camera that puts her in the tale.

You know about holidays and family celebrations and how somebody shows up with a camcorder and the relatives stand around and barely react because they're numbingly accustomed to the process of being taped and decked and shown on the VCR with the coffee and cake.

He is hit soon after. If you've seen the tape many times you know from the handwave exactly when he will be hit. It is something, naturally, that you wait for. You say to your wife, if you're at home and she is there, Now here is where he gets it. You say, Janet, hurry up, this is where it happens.

Now here is where he gets it. You see him jolted, sort of wireshocked—then he seizes up and falls toward the door or maybe leans or slides into the door is the proper way to put it. It is awful and unremarkable at the same time. The car stays in the slow lane. It approaches briefly, then falls back.

You don't usually call your wife over to the TV set. She has her programs, you have yours. But there's a certain urgency here. You want her to see how it looks. The tape has been running forever and now the thing is finally going to happen and you want her to be here when he's shot.

Here it comes, all right. He is shot, head-shot, and the camera reacts, the child reacts—there is a jolting movement but she keeps on taping, there is a sympathetic response, a nerve response, her heart is beating faster but she keeps the camera trained on the subject as he slides into the door and even as you see him die you're thinking of the girl. At some level the girl has to be present here, watching what you're watching, unprepared—the girl is seeing this cold and you have to marvel at the fact that she keeps the tape rolling.

It shows something awful and unaccompanied. You want your wife to see it because it is real this time, not fancy movie violence—the realness beneath the layers of cosmetic perception. Hurry up, Janet, here it comes. He dies so fast. There is no accompaniment of any kind. It is very stripped. You want to tell her it is realer than real but then she will ask what that means.

The way the camera reacts to the gunshot—a startle reaction that brings pity and terror into the frame, the girl's own shock, the girl's identification with the victim.

You don't see the blood, which is probably trickling behind his ear and down the back of his neck. The way his head is twisted away from the door, the twist of the head gives you only a partial profile and it's the wrong side, it's not the side where he was hit.

And maybe you're being a little aggressive here, practically forcing your wife to watch. Why? What are you telling her? Are you making a little statement? Like I'm going to ruin your day out of ordinary spite. Or a big statement? Like this is the risk of existing. Either way you're rubbing her face in this tape and you don't know why.

It shows the car drifting toward the guard-rail and then there's a jostling sense of two other lanes and part of another car, a split-second blur, and the tape ends here, either because the girl stopped shooting or because some central authority, the police or the district attorney or the TV station, decided there was nothing else you had to see.

This is either the tenth or eleventh homicide committed by the Texas Highway Killer. The number is uncertain because the police believe that one of the shootings may have been a copycat crime.

And there is something about videotape, isn't there, and this particular kind of serial crime? This is a crime designed for random taping and immediate playing. You sit there and wonder if this kind of crime became more possible when the means of taping and playing an events—playing it immediately after the taping—became part of the culture. The principal doesn't necessarily commit the sequence of crimes in order to see them taped and played. He commits the crimes as if they were a form of taped-and-played event. The crimes are inseparable from the idea of taping and playing. You sit there thinking that this is a crime that has found its medium, or vice versa—cheap mass production, the sequence of repeated images and victims, stark and glary and more or less unremarkable.

It shows very little in the end. It is a famous murder because it is on tape and because the murderer has done it many times and because the crime was recorded by a child. So the child is involved, the Video Kid as she is sometimes called because they have to call her something. The tape is famous and so is she. She is famous in the modern manner of people whose names are strategically withheld. They are famous without names or faces, spirits living apart from their bodies, the victims and witnesses, the underage criminals, out there somewhere at the edges of perception.

Seeing someone at the moment he dies, dying unexpectedly. This is reason alone to stay fixed to the screen. It is instructional, watching a man shot dead as he drives along on a sunny day. It demonstrates an elemental truth, that every breath you take has two possible endings. And that's another thing. There's a joke locked away here, a note of cruel slapstick that you are completely willing to appreciate. Maybe the victim's a chump, a dope, classically unlucky. He had it coming, in a way, like an innocent fool in a silent movie.

You don't want Janet to give you any crap about it's on all the time, they show it a thousand times a day. They show it because it exists, because they have to show it, because this is why they're out there. The horror freezes your soul but this doesn't mean that you want them to stop.

FOCUSED FREE WRITES

1. What surprised you, intrigued you, or confused you about this story?
2. What might this story be about? How would you interpret it?
3. Whose point of view is this story told from? Why and how is that significant in the story? Cite specific examples from the text.
4. How is the form of this story distinctive? Does its form reflect its meaning at all? What would you say about the style—the what, where when of the text? the who? the how? Which elements are significant?

Reality

The United States has become obsessed with reality programming. Now described as the first reality TV show, *An American Family* first appeared on PBS in 1973 and over the course of twelve hours of programming summarized the three hundred hours shot describing the demise of the Loud family to over 10 million viewers. Almost twenty years later, MTV got into the game with *The Real World* and its "seven strangers picked to live in a house..." Fox television began establishing itself as the leader in reality programming with *Cops* in 1989 and its explosion of reality shows around the year 2000. *Survivor, American Idol*, and their imitators and competitors flood the channels today.

How does this DeLillo story participate in and comment on the nature of reality and reality TV?

PRE-READING   What things do you always carry with you? Literally? Figuratively?

Tim O'Brien (1946–).   *Tim O'Brien spent much of his small-town Minnesota youth in the library, turning to reading as refuge and escape. After graduating summa cum laude in political science from Macalester College in St. Paul, O'Brien was drafted and seriously considered fleeing to Canada. Already opposed to the Vietnam War, O'Brien's year in battle confirmed his disillusionment. He earned a Purple Heart and returned to enter in Harvard's doctoral program in government, working summers as a reporter for the Washington Post. He wrote his first novel instead of a dissertation and left Harvard without a degree. Instead, O'Brien began to write novels, stories, and nonfiction full time while lecturing and teaching on occasion, which he continues to do today.*

Tim O'Brien

THE THINGS THEY CARRIED   [1990]

First Lieutenant Jimmy Cross carried letters from a girl named Martha, a junior at Mount Sebastian College in New Jersey. They were not love letters, but Lieutenant Cross was hoping, so he kept them folded in plastic at the bottom of his rucksack. In the late afternoon, after a day's march, he would dig his foxhole, wash his hands under a canteen, unwrap the letters, hold them with the tips of his fingers, and spend the last hour of light pretending. He would imagine romantic camping trips into the White Mountains in New Hampshire. He would sometimes taste the envelope flaps, knowing her tongue had been there. More than anything, he wanted Martha to love him as he loved her, but the letters were mostly chatty, elusive on the matter of love. She was a virgin, he was almost sure. She was an English major at Mount Sebastian, and she wrote beautifully about her professors and roommates and midterm exams, about her respect for Chaucer and her great affection for Virginia Woolf. She often quoted lines of poetry; she never mentioned the war, except to say, Jimmy, take care of yourself. The letters weighed 10 ounces. They were signed Love, Martha, but Lieutenant Cross understood that Love was only a way of signing and did not mean what he sometimes pretended it meant. At dusk, he would carefully return the letters to his rucksack. Slowly, a bit distracted, he would get up and move among his men, checking the perimeter, then at full dark he would return to his hole and watch the night and wonder if Martha was a virgin.

The things they carried were largely determined by necessity. Among the necessities or near-necessities were P-38 can openers, pocket knives, heat tabs, wristwatches, dog tags, mosquito repellent, chewing gum, candy, cigarettes, salt tablets, packets of Kool-Aid, lighters, matches, sewing kits, Military Payment Certificates, C rations, and two or three canteens of water. Together, these items weighed between 15 and 20 pounds, depending upon a man's habits or rate of metabolism. Henry Dobbins, who was a big man, carried extra rations; he was especially fond of canned peaches in heavy syrup over pound cake. Dave Jensen, who practiced field hygiene, carried a toothbrush, dental floss, and several hotel-sized bars of soap he'd stolen on R&R in Sydney, Australia. Ted Lavender, who was scared, carried tranquilizers until he was shot in the head outside the village of Than Khe in mid-April. By necessity, and because it was SOP,[1] they all carried steel helmets that weighed 5 pounds including the liner and camouflage cover. They carried the standard fatigue jackets and trousers. Very few carried underwear. On their feet they carried jungle boots—2.1 pounds—and Dave Jensen carried three pairs of socks and a can of Dr. Scholl's foot powder as a precaution against trench foot. Until he was shot, Ted Lavender carried six or seven ounces of premium dope, which for him was a necessity. Mitchell Sanders, the RTO,[2] carried condoms. Norman Bowker carried a diary. Rat Kiley carried comic books. Kiowa, a devout Baptist, carried an illustrated New Testament that had been presented to him by his father, who taught Sunday school in Oklahoma City, Oklahoma. As a hedge against bad times, however, Kiowa also carried his grandmother's distrust of the white man, his grandfather's old hunting hatchet. Necessity dictated. Because the land was mined and booby-trapped, it was SOP for each man to carry a steel-centered, nylon-covered flak jacket, which weighed 6.7 pounds, but which on hot days seemed much heavier. Because you could die so quickly, each man carried at least one large compress bandage, usually in the helmet band for easy access. Because the nights were cold, and because the monsoons were wet, each carried a green plastic poncho that could be used as a raincoat or groundsheet or makeshift tent. With its quilted liner, the poncho weighed almost two pounds, but it was worth every ounce. In April, for instance, when Ted Lavender was shot, they used his poncho to wrap him up, then to carry him across the paddy, then to lift him into the chopper that took him away.

---

[1] **SOP:** standard operating procedure.

[2] **RTO:** Radio Telephone Operator, or enlisted man responsible for the unit's communication device(s).

They were called legs or grunts.

To carry something was to hump it, as when Lieutenant Jimmy Cross humped his love for Martha up the hills and through the swamps. In its intransitive form, to hump meant to walk, or to march, but it implied burdens far beyond the intransitive.

5   Almost everyone humped photographs. In his wallet, Lieutenant Cross carried two photographs of Martha. The first was a Kodacolor snapshot signed Love, though he knew better. She stood against a brick wall. Her eyes were gray and neutral, her lips slightly open as she stared straight-on at the camera. At night, sometimes, Lieutenant Cross wondered who had taken the picture, because he knew she had boyfriends, because he loved her so much, and because he could see the shadow of the picture-taker spreading out against the brick wall. The second photograph had been clipped from the 1968 Mount Sebastian yearbook. It was an action shot—women's volleyball—and Martha was bent horizontal to the floor, reaching, the palms of her hands in sharp focus, the tongue taut, the expression frank and competitive. There was no visible sweat. She wore white gym shorts. Her legs, he thought, were almost certainly the legs of a virgin, dry and without hair, the left knee cocked and carrying her entire weight, which was just over one hundred pounds. Lieutenant Cross remembered touching that left knee. A dark theater, he remembered, and the movie was *Bonnie and Clyde*, and Martha wore a tweed skirt, and during the final scene, when he touched her knee, she turned and looked at him in a sad, sober way that made him pull his hand back, but he would always remember the feel of the tweed skirt and the knee beneath it and the sound of the gunfire that killed Bonnie and Clyde, how embarrassing it was, how slow and oppressive. He remembered kissing her good night at the dorm door. Right then, he thought, he should've done something brave. He should've carried her up the stairs to her room and tied her to the bed and touched that left knee all night long. He should've risked it. Whenever he looked at the photographs, he thought of new things he should've done.

What they carried was partly a function of rank, partly of field specialty.

As a first lieutenant and platoon leader, Jimmy Cross carried a compass, maps, code books, binoculars, and a .45-caliber pistol that weighed 2.9 pounds fully loaded. He carried a strobe light and the responsibility for the lives of his men.

As an RTO, Mitchell Sanders carried the PRC-25 radio, a killer, 26 pounds with its battery.

As a medic, Rat Kiley carried a canvas satchel filled with morphine and plasma and malaria tablets and surgical tape and comic books and all the things a medic must carry, including M&M's for especially bad wounds, for a total weight of nearly 20 pounds.

10   As a big man, therefore a machine gunner, Henry Dobbins carried the M-60, which weighed 23 pounds unloaded, but which was almost always loaded. In addition, Dobbins carried between 10 and 15 pounds of ammunition draped in belts across his chest and shoulders.

As PFCs or Spec 4s, most of them were common grunts and carried the standard M-16 gas-operated assault rifle. The weapon weighed 7.5 pounds unloaded, 8.2 pounds with its full 20-round magazine. Depending on numerous factors, such as topography and psychology, the riflemen carried anywhere from 12 to 20 magazines, usually in cloth bandoliers,[3] adding on another 8.4 pounds at minimum, 14 pounds at maximum. When it was available, they also carried M-16 maintenance gear—rods and steel brushes and swabs and tubes of LSA[4] oil—all of which weighed about a pound. Among the grunts, some carried the M-79 grenade launcher, 5.9 pounds unloaded, a reasonably light weapon except for the ammunition, which was heavy. A single round weighed 10 ounces. The typical load was 25 rounds. But Ted Lavender, who was scared, carried 34 rounds when he was shot and killed outside Than Khe, and he went down under an exceptional burden, more than 20 pounds of ammunition, plus the flak jacket and helmet and rations and water and toilet paper and tranquilizers and all the rest, plus the unweighed fear. He was dead weight. There was no twitching or flopping. Kiowa, who saw it happen, said it was like watching a rock fall, or a big sandbag or something—just boom, then down—not like the movies where the dead guy rolls around and does fancy spins and goes ass over teakettle—not like that, Kiowa said, the poor bastard just flat-fuck fell. Boom. Down. Nothing else. It was a bright morning in mid-April. Lieutenant Cross felt the pain. He blamed himself. They stripped off Lavender's canteens and ammo, all the heavy things, and Rat Kiley said the obvious, the guy's dead, and Mitchell Sanders used his radio to report one U.S. KIA and to request a chopper. Then they wrapped Lavender in his poncho. They carried him out to a dry paddy, established security, and sat smoking the dead man's dope until the chopper came. Lieutenant Cross kept to himself. He pictured Martha's smooth young face, thinking he loved her more than anything, more than his men, and now Ted Lavender was dead because he loved her so much and could not stop thinking about her. When the dustoff arrived, they carried Lavender aboard. Afterward they burned Than Khe. They marched until dusk, then dug their holes, and that night Kiowa kept explaining how you had to be there, how fast it was, how the poor guy just dropped like so much concrete. Boom-down, he said. Like cement.

In addition to the three standard weapons—the M-60, M-16, and M-79—they carried whatever presented itself, or whatever seemed appropriate as a means of killing or staying alive. They carried catch-as-catch-can. At various times, in various situations, they carried M-14s and CAR-15s and Swedish Ks and grease guns and captured AK-47s and Chi-Coms and RPGs and Simonov carbines and black market Uzis and .38-caliber Smith & Wesson handguns and 66 mm LAWs and shotguns and silencers and blackjacks and bayonets and C-4 plastic explosives. Lee Strunk carried a slingshot; a weapon of last resort, he called it. Mitchell Sanders carried brass knuckles. Kiowa carried his grandfather's feathered hatchet. Every third or fourth man carried a Claymore antipersonnel mine—3.5 pounds with its firing device. They all carried fragmentation grenades—14 ounces each. They all carried at least one M-18 colored smoke grenade—24 ounces. Some carried CS or tear gas grenades. Some carried white phosphorus grenades. They carried all they could bear, and then some, including a silent awe for the terrible power of the things they carried.

• • •

---

[3] **bandolier:** pocketed belt for holding ammunition.

[4] **LSA:** Lubricant Solution All-purpose, or Lubricant Small Arms.

In the first week of April, before Lavender died, Lieutenant Jimmy Cross received a good-luck charm from Martha. It was a simple pebble, an ounce at most. Smooth to the touch, it was a milky white color with flecks of orange and violet, oval-shaped, like a miniature egg. In the accompanying letter, Martha wrote that she had found the pebble on the Jersey shoreline, precisely where the land touched water at high tide, where things came together but also separated. It was this separate-but-together quality, she wrote, that had inspired her to pick up the pebble and to carry it in her breast pocket for several days, where it seemed weightless, and then to send it through the mail, by air, as a token of her truest feelings for him. Lieutenant Cross found this romantic. But he wondered what her truest feelings were, exactly, and what she meant by separate-but-together. He wondered how the tides and waves had come into play on that afternoon along the Jersey shoreline when Martha saw the pebble and bent down to rescue it from geology. He imagined bare feet. Martha was a poet, with the poet's sensibilities, and her feet would be brown and bare, the toenails unpainted, the eyes chilly and somber like the ocean in March, and though it was painful, he wondered who had been with her that afternoon. He imagined a pair of shadows moving along the strip of sand where things came together but also separated. It was phantom jealousy, he knew, but he couldn't help himself. He loved her so much. On the march, through the hot days of early April, he carried the pebble in his mouth, turning it with his tongue, tasting sea salt and moisture. His mind wandered. He had difficulty keeping his attention on the war. On occasion he would yell at his men to spread out the column, to keep their eyes open, but then he would slip away into daydreams, just pretending, walking barefoot along the Jersey shore, with Martha, carrying nothing. He would feel himself rising. Sun and waves and gentle winds, all love and lightness.

What they carried varied by mission.

15   When a mission took them to the mountains, they carried mosquito netting, machetes, canvas tarps, and extra bug juice.

If a mission seemed especially hazardous, or if it involved a place they knew to be bad, they carried everything they could. In certain heavily mined AOs, where the land was dense with Toe Poppers and Bouncing Betties, they took turns humping a 28-pound mine detector.[5] With its headphones and big sensing plate, the equipment was a stress on the lower back and shoulders, awkward to handle, often useless because of the shrapnel in the earth, but they carried it anyway, partly for safety, partly for the illusion of safety.

On ambush, or other night missions, they carried peculiar little odds and ends. Kiowa always took along his New Testament and a pair of moccasins for silence. Dave Jensen carried night-sight vitamins high in carotene. Lee Strunk carried his slingshot; ammo, he claimed, would never be a problem. Rat Kiley carried brandy and M&M's candy. Until he was shot, Ted Lavender carried the starlight scope, which weighed 6.3 pounds with its aluminum carrying case. Henry Dobbins carried his girlfriend's panty-hose wrapped around his neck as a comforter. They all carried ghosts. When dark came, they would move out single file across the meadows and paddies to their ambush coordinates, where they would quietly set up the Claymores and lie down and spend the night waiting.

---

[5] **AOs:** Areas of Operation.
Toe-Poppers and Bouncing Betties: land mines.

Other missions were more complicated and required special equipment. In mid-April, it was their mission to search out and destroy the elaborate tunnel complexes in the Than Khe area south of Chu Lai. To blow the tunnels, they carried one-pound blocks of pentrite high explosives, four blocks to a man, 68 pounds in all. They carried wiring, detonators, and battery-powered clackers. Dave Jensen carried earplugs. Most often, before blowing the tunnels, they were ordered by higher command to search them, which was considered bad news, but by and large they just shrugged and carried out orders. Because he was a big man, Henry Dobbins was excused from tunnel duty. The others would draw numbers. Before Lavender died there were 17 men in the platoon, and whoever drew the number 17 would strip off his gear and crawl in headfirst with a flashlight and Lieutenant Cross's .45-caliber pistol. The rest of them would fan out as security. They would sit down or kneel, not facing the hole, listening to the ground beneath them, imagining cobwebs and ghosts, whatever was down there—the tunnel walls squeezing in—how the flashlight seemed impossibly heavy in the hand and how it was tunnel vision in the very strictest sense, compression in all ways, even time, and how you had to wiggle in—ass and elbows—a swallowed-up feeling—and how you found yourself worrying about odd things: Will your flashlight go dead? Do rats carry rabies? If you screamed, how far would the sound carry? Would your buddies hear it? Would they have the courage to drag you out? In some respects, though not many, the waiting was worse than the tunnel itself. Imagination was a killer.

On April 16, when Lee Strunk drew the number 17, he laughed and muttered something and went down quickly. The morning was hot and very still. Not good, Kiowa said. He looked at the tunnel opening, then out across a dry paddy toward the village of Than Khe. Nothing moved. No clouds or birds or people. As they waited, the men smoked and drank Kool-Aid, not talking much, feeling sympathy for Lee Strunk but also feeling the luck of the draw. You win some, you lose some, said Mitchell Sanders, and sometimes you settle for a rain check. It was a tired line and no one laughed.

20   Henry Dobbins ate a tropical chocolate bar. Ted Lavender popped a tranquilizer and went off to pee.

After five minutes, Lieutenant Jimmy Cross moved to the tunnel, leaned down, and examined the darkness. Trouble, he thought—a cave-in maybe. And then suddenly, without willing it, he was thinking about Martha. The stresses and fractures, the quick collapse, the two of them buried alive under all that weight. Dense, crushing love. Kneeling, watching the hole, he tried to concentrate on Lee Strunk and the war, all the dangers, but his love was too much for him, he felt paralyzed, he wanted to sleep inside her lungs and breathe her blood and be smothered. He wanted her to be a virgin and not a virgin, all at once. He wanted to know her. Intimate secrets: Why poetry? Why so sad? Why that grayness in her eyes? Why so alone? Not lonely, just alone—riding her bike across campus or sitting off by herself in the cafeteria—even dancing, she danced alone—and it was the aloneness that filled him with love. He remembered telling her that one evening. How she nodded and looked away. And how, later, when he kissed her, she received the kiss without returning it, her eyes wide open, not afraid, not a virgin's eyes, just flat and uninvolved.

Lieutenant Cross gazed at the tunnel. But he was not there. He was buried with Martha under the white sand at the Jersey shore. They were pressed together, and the pebble in his mouth was her tongue. He was smiling. Vaguely, he was aware of how quiet the day was, the sullen paddies, yet he could not bring himself to worry about matters of security. He was beyond that. He was just a kid at war, in love. He was twenty-four years old. He couldn't help it.

A few moments later Lee Strunk crawled out of the tunnel. He came up grinning, filthy but alive. Lieutenant Cross nodded and closed his eyes while the others clapped Strunk on the back and made jokes about rising from the dead.

Worms, Rat Kiley said. Right out of the grave. Fuckin' zombie.

25 The men laughed. They all felt great relief.

Spook city, said Mitchell Sanders.

Lee Strunk made a funny ghost sound, a kind of moaning, yet very happy, and right then, when Strunk made that high happy moaning sound, when he went *Ahhooooo*, right then Ted Lavender was shot in the head on his way back from peeing. He lay with his mouth open. The teeth were broken. There was a swollen black bruise under his left eye. The cheekbone was gone. Oh shit, Rat Kiley said, the guy's dead. The guy's dead, he kept saying, which seemed profound—the guy's dead. I mean really.

. . .

The things they carried were determined to some extent by superstition. Lieutenant Cross carried his good-luck pebble. Dave Jensen carried a rabbit's foot. Norman Bowker, otherwise a very gentle person, carried a thumb that had been presented to him as a gift by Mitchell Sanders. The thumb was dark brown, rubbery to the touch, and weighed four ounces at most. It had been cut from a VC[6] corpse, a boy of fifteen or sixteen. They'd found him at the bottom of an irrigation ditch, badly burned, flies in his mouth and eyes. The boy wore black shorts and sandals. At the time of his death he had been carrying a pouch of rice, a rifle and three magazines of ammunition.

You want my opinion, Mitchell Sanders said, there's a definite moral here.

30 He put his hand on the dead boy's wrist. He was quiet for a time, as if counting a pulse, then he patted the stomach, almost affectionately, and used Kiowa's hunting hatchet to remove the thumb.

Henry Dobbins asked what the moral was.

Moral?

You know. *Moral.*

Sanders wrapped the thumb in toilet paper and handed it across to Norman Bowker. There was no blood. Smiling, he kicked the boy's head, watched the flies scatter, and said, It's like with that old TV show—Paladin. Have gun, will travel.

35 Henry Dobbins thought about it.

Yeah, well, he finally said. I don't see no moral.

There it *is*, man.

Fuck off.

They carried USO[7] stationery and pencils and pens. They carried Sterno, safety pins, trip flares, signal flares, spools of wire, razor blades, chewing tobacco,

---

[6] **VC**: abbreviation for Vietnamese Communist or Viet Cong.

[7] **USO**: United Service Organization, an interfaith movement to build morale of military service members.

liberated joss sticks[8] and statuettes of the smiling Buddha, candles, grease pencils, *The Stars and Stripes*, fingernail clippers, Psy Ops leaflets, bush hats, bolos, and much more. Twice a week, when the resupply choppers came in, they carried hot chow in green mermite[9] cans and large canvas bags filled with iced beer and soda pop. They carried plastic water containers, each with a two-gallon capacity. Mitchell Sanders carried a set of starched tiger fatigues for special occasions. Henry Dobbins carried Black Flag insecticide. Dave Jensen carried empty sandbags that could be filled at night for added protection. Lee Strunk carried tanning lotion. Some things they carried in common. Taking turns, they carried the big PRC-77 scrambler radio, which weighed 30 pounds with its battery. They shared the weight of memory. They took up what others could no longer bear. Often, they carried each other, the wounded or weak. They carried infections. They carried chess sets, basketballs, Vietnamese-English dictionaries, insignia of rank, Bronze Stars and Purple Hearts, plastic cards imprinted with the Code of Conduct. They carried diseases, among them malaria and dysentery. They carried lice and ringworm and leeches and paddy algae and various rots and molds. They carried the land itself—Vietnam, the place, the soil—a powdery orange-red dust that covered their boots and fatigues and faces. They carried the sky. The whole atmosphere, they carried it, the humidity, the monsoons, the stink of fungus and decay, all of it, they carried gravity. They moved like mules. By daylight they took sniper fire, at night they were mortared, but it was not battle, it was just the endless march, village to village, without purpose, nothing won or lost. They marched for the sake of the march. They plodded along slowly, dumbly, leaning forward against the heat, unthinking, all blood and bone, simple grunts, soldiering with their legs, toiling up the hills and down into the paddies and across the rivers and up again and down, just humping, one step and then the next and then another, but no volition, no will, because it was automatic, it was anatomy, and the war was entirely a matter of posture and carriage, the hump was everything, a kind of inertia, a kind of emptiness, a dullness of desire and intellect and conscience and hope and human sensibility. Their principles were in their feet. Their calculations were biological. They had no sense of strategy or mission. They searched the villages without knowing what to look for, not caring, kicking over jars of rice, frisking children and old men, blowing tunnels, sometimes setting fires and sometimes not, then forming up and moving on to the next village, then other villages, where it would always be the same. They carried their own lives. The pressures were enormous. In the heat of early afternoon, they would remove their helmets and flak jackets, walking bare, which was dangerous but which helped ease the strain. They would often discard things along the route of march. Purely for comfort, they would throw away rations, blow their Claymores[10] and grenades, no matter, because by nightfall the resupply choppers would arrive with more of the same, then a day or two later still more, fresh watermelons and crates of ammunition and sunglasses and woolen sweaters—the resources were stunning—sparklers for the Fourth of July, colored eggs for Easter—it was the

---

[8] **joss sticks:** incense.

[9] **Mermite cans:** insulated sturdy container, a kind of cooler.

[10] **Claymores:** land mines.

great American war chest—the fruits of science, the smokestacks, the canneries, the arsenals at Hartford, the Minnesota forests, the machine shops, the vast fields of corn and wheat—they carried like freight trains; they carried it on their backs and shoulders—and for all the ambiguities of Vietnam, all the mysteries and unknowns, there was at least the single abiding certainty that they would never be at a loss for things to carry.

40   After the chopper took Lavender away, Lieutenant Jimmy Cross led his men into the village of Than Khe. They burned everything. They shot chickens and dogs, they trashed the village well, they called in artillery and watched the wreckage, then they marched for several hours through the hot afternoon, and then at dusk, while Kiowa explained how Lavender died, Lieutenant Cross found himself trembling.

    He tried not to cry. With his entrenching tool, which weighed five pounds, he began digging a hole in the earth.

    He felt shame. He hated himself. He had loved Martha more than his men, and as a consequence Lavender was now dead, and this was something he would have to carry like a stone in his stomach for the rest of the war.

    All he could do was dig. He used his entrenching tool like an ax, slashing, feeling both love and hate, and then later, when it was full dark, he sat at the bottom of his foxhole and wept. It went on for a long while. In part, he was grieving for Ted Lavender, but mostly it was for Martha, and for himself, because she belonged to another world, which was not quite real, and because she was a junior at Mount Sebastian College in New Jersey, a poet and a virgin and uninvolved, and because he realized she did not love him and never would.

    Like cement, Kiowa whispered in the dark. I swear to God—boom, down. Not a word.

45   I've heard this, said Norman Bowker.

    A pisser, you know? Still zipping himself up. Zapped while zipping.

    All right, fine. That's enough.

    Yeah, but you had to see it, the guy just—

    I *heard*, man. Cement. So why not shut the fuck *up*?

50   Kiowa shook his head sadly and glanced over at the hole where Lieutenant Jimmy Cross sat watching the night. The air was thick and wet. A warm dense fog had settled over the paddies and there was the stillness that precedes rain.

    After a time Kiowa sighed.

    One thing for sure, he said. The lieutenant's in some deep hurt. I mean that crying jag—the way he was carrying on—it wasn't fake or anything, it was real heavy-duty hurt. The man cares.

    Sure, Norman Bowker said.

    Say what you want, the man does care.

55   We all got problems.

    Not Lavender.

    No, I guess not, Bowker said. Do me a favor, though.

Shut up?

That's a smart Indian. Shut up.

60   Shrugging, Kiowa pulled off his boots. He wanted to say more, just to lighten up his sleep, but instead he opened his New Testament and arranged it beneath his head as a pillow. The fog made things seem hollow and unattached. He tried not to think about Ted Lavender, but then he was thinking how fast it was, no drama, down and dead, and how it was hard to feel anything except surprise. It seemed unchristian. He wished he could find some great sadness, or even anger, but the emotion wasn't there and he couldn't make it happen. Mostly he felt pleased to be alive. He liked the smell of the New Testament under his cheek, the leather and ink and paper and glue, whatever the chemicals were. He liked hearing the sounds of night. Even his fatigue, it felt fine, the stiff muscles and the prickly awareness of his own body, a floating feeling. He enjoyed not being dead. Lying there, Kiowa admired Lieutenant Jimmy Cross's capacity for grief. He wanted to share the man's pain, he wanted to care as Jimmy Cross cared. And yet when he closed his eyes, all he could think was Boom-down, and all he could feel was the pleasure of having his boots off and the fog curling in around him and the damp soil and the Bible smells and the plush comfort of night.

    After a moment Norman Bowker sat up in the dark.

What the hell, he said. You want to talk, *talk*. Tell it to me.

Forget it.

No, man, go on. One thing I hate, it's a silent Indian.

65   For the most part they carried themselves with poise, a kind of dignity. Now and then, however, there were times of panic, when they squealed or wanted to squeal but couldn't, when they twitched and made moaning sounds and covered their heads and said Dear Jesus and flopped around on the earth and fired their weapons blindly and cringed and sobbed and begged for the noise to stop and went wild and made stupid promises to themselves and to God and to their mothers and fathers, hoping not to die. In different ways, it happened to all of them. Afterward, when the firing ended, they would blink and peek up. They would touch their bodies, feeling shame, then quickly hiding it. They would force themselves to stand. As if in slow motion, frame by frame, the world would take on the old logic—absolute silence, then the wind, then sunlight, then voices. It was the burden of being alive. Awkwardly, the men would reassemble themselves, first in private, then in groups, becoming soldiers again. They would repair the leaks in their eyes. They would check for casualties, call in dust-offs, light cigarettes, try to smile, clear their throats and spit and begin cleaning their weapons. After a time someone would shake his head and say, No lie. I almost shit my pants, and someone else would laugh, which meant it was bad, yes, but the guy had obviously not shit his pants, it wasn't that bad, and in any case nobody would ever do such a thing and then go ahead and talk about it. They would squint into the dense, oppressive sunlight. For a few moments, perhaps, they would fall silent, lighting a joint and tracking its passage from man to man, inhaling, holding in the humiliation. Scary stuff, one of them might say. But then someone else would grin or flick his eyebrows and say, Roger-dodger, almost cut me a new asshole, *almost*.

There were numerous such poses. Some carried themselves with a sort of wistful resignation, others with pride or stiff soldierly discipline or good humor or macho zeal. They were afraid of dying but they were even more afraid to show it.

They found jokes to tell.

They used a hard vocabulary to contain the terrible softness. *Greased* they'd say. *Offed, lit up, zapped while zipping.* It wasn't cruelty, just stage presence. They were actors. When someone died, it wasn't quite dying, because in a curious way it seemed scripted, and because they had their lines mostly memorized, irony mixed with tragedy, and because they called it by other names, as if to encyst and destroy the reality of death itself. They kicked corpses. They cut off thumbs. They talked grunt lingo. They told stories about Ted Lavender's supply of tranquilizers, how the poor guy didn't feel a thing, how incredibly tranquil he was.

There's a moral here, said Mitchell Sanders.

70   They were waiting for Lavender's chopper, smoking the dead man's dope.

The moral's pretty obvious, Sanders said, and winked. Stay away from drugs. No joke, they'll ruin your day every time.

Cute, said Henry Dobbins.

Mind blower, get it? Talk about wiggy. Nothing left, just blood and brains.

They made themselves laugh.

75   There it is, they'd say. Over and over—there it is, my friend, there it is—as if the repetition itself were an act of poise, a balance between crazy and almost crazy, knowing without going, there it is, which meant be cool, let it ride, because Oh yeah, man, you can't change what can't be changed, there it is, there it absolutely and positively and fucking well *is*.

They were tough.

They carried all the emotional baggage of men who might die. Grief, terror, love, longing—these were intangibles, but the intangibles had their own mass and specific gravity, they had tangible weight. They carried shameful memories. They carried the common secret of cowardice barely restrained, the instinct to run or freeze or hide, and in many respects this was the heaviest burden of all, for it could never be put down, it required perfect balance and perfect posture. They carried their reputations. They carried the soldier's greatest fear, which was the fear of blushing. Men killed, and died, because they were embarrassed not to. It was what had brought them to the war in the first place, nothing positive, no dreams of glory or honor, just to avoid the blush of dishonor. They died so as not to die of embarrassment. They crawled into tunnels and walked point and advanced under fire. Each morning, despite the unknowns, they made their legs move. They endured. They kept humping. They did not submit to the obvious alternative, which was simply to close the eyes and fall. So easy, really. Go limp and tumble to the ground and let the muscles unwind and not speak and not budge until your buddies picked you up and lifted you into the chopper that would roar and dip its nose and carry you off to the world. A mere matter of falling, yet no one ever fell. It was not courage, exactly; the object was not valor. Rather, they were too frightened to be cowards.

By and large they carried these things inside, maintaining the masks of composure. They sneered at sick call. They spoke bitterly about guys who had found release by shooting off their own toes or fingers. Pussies, they'd say. Candy-asses. It was fierce, mocking talk, with only a trace of envy or awe, but even so the image played itself out behind their eyes.

They imagined the muzzle against flesh. So easy: squeeze the trigger and blow away a toe. They imagined it. They imagined the quick, sweet pain, then the evacuation to Japan, then a hospital with warm beds and cute geisha nurses.

80   And they dreamed of freedom birds.

At night, on guard, staring into the dark, they were carried away by jumbo jets. They felt the rush of takeoff. *Gone!* they yelled. And then velocity—wings and engines—a smiling stewardess—but it was more than a plane, it was a real bird, a big sleek silver bird with feathers and talons and high screeching. They were flying. The weights fell off; there was nothing to bear. They laughed and held on tight, feeling the cold slap of wind and altitude, soaring, thinking *It's over, I'm gone!*—they were naked, they were light and free—it was all lightness, bright and fast and buoyant, light as light, a helium buzz in the brain, a giddy bubbling in the lungs as they were taken up over the clouds and the war, beyond duty, beyond gravity and mortification and global entanglements—*Sin loi!* they yelled. *I'm sorry, motherfuckers, but I'm out of it, I'm goofed, I'm on a space cruise, I'm gone!*—and it was a restful, unencumbered sensation, just riding the light waves, sailing that big silver freedom bird over the mountains and oceans, over America, over the farms and great sleeping cities and cemeteries and highways and the golden arches of McDonald's, it was flight, a kind of fleeing, a kind of falling, falling higher and higher, spinning off the edge of the earth and beyond the sun and through the vast, silent vacuum where there were no burdens and where everything weighed exactly nothing—*Gone!* they screamed. *I'm sorry but I'm gone!*—and so at night, not quite dreaming, they gave themselves over to lightness, they were carried, they were purely borne.

On the morning after Ted Lavender died, First Lieutenant Jimmy Cross crouched at the bottom of his foxhole and burned Martha's letters. Then he burned the two photographs. There was a steady rain falling, which made it difficult, but he used heat tabs and Sterno to build a small fire, screening it with his body, holding the photographs over the tight blue flame with the tips of his fingers.

He realized it was only a gesture. Stupid, he thought. Sentimental, too, but mostly just stupid.

Lavender was dead. You couldn't burn the blame.

85   Besides, the letters were in his head. And even now, without photographs, Lieutenant Cross could see Martha playing volleyball in her white gym shorts and yellow T-shirt. He could see her moving in the rain.

When the fire died out, Lieutenant Cross pulled his poncho over his shoulders and ate breakfast from a can.

There was no great mystery, he decided.

In those burned letters Martha had never mentioned the war, except to say, Jimmy, take care of yourself. She wasn't involved. She signed the letters Love, but it wasn't love, and all the fine lines and technicalities did not matter. Virginity was no longer an issue. He hated her. Yes, he did. He hated her. Love, too, but it was a hard, hating kind of love.

The morning came up wet and blurry. Everything seemed part of everything else, the fog and Martha and the deepening rain.

90   He was a soldier, after all.

Half smiling, Lieutenant Jimmy Cross took out his maps. He shook his head hard, as if to clear it, then bent forward and began planning the day's march. In ten minutes, or maybe twenty, he would rouse the men and they would pack up and head west, where the maps showed the country to be green and inviting. They would do what they had always done. The rain might add some weight, but otherwise it would be one more day layered upon all the other days.

He was realistic about it. There was that new hardness in his stomach. He loved her but he hated her.

No more fantasies, he told himself.

Henceforth, when he thought about Martha, it would be only to think that she belonged elsewhere. He would shut down the daydreams. This was not Mount Sebastian, it was another world, where there were no pretty poems or midterm exams, a place where men died because of carelessness and gross stupidity. Kiowa was right. Boom-down, and you were dead, never partly dead.

95   Briefly, in the rain, Lieutenant Cross saw Martha's gray eyes gazing back at him.

He understood.

It was very sad, he thought. The things men carried inside. The things men did or felt they had to do.

He almost nodded at her, but didn't.

Instead he went back to his maps. He was now determined to perform his duties firmly and without negligence. It wouldn't help Lavender, he knew that, but from this point on he would comport himself as an officer. He would dispose of his good-luck pebble. Swallow it, maybe, or use Lee Strunk's slingshot, or just drop it along the trail. On the march he would impose strict field discipline. He would be careful to send out flank security, to prevent straggling or bunching up, to keep his troops moving at the proper pace and at the proper interval. He would insist on clean weapons. He would confiscate the remainder of Lavender's dope. Later in the day, perhaps, he would call the men together and speak to them plainly. He would accept the blame for what had happened to Ted Lavender. He would be a man about it. He would look them in the eyes, keeping his chin level, and he would issue the new SOPs in a calm, impersonal tone of voice, a lieutenant's voice, leaving no room for argument or discussion. Commencing immediately, he'd tell them, they would no longer abandon equipment along the route of march. They would police up their acts. They would get their shit together, and keep it together, and maintain it neatly and in good working order.

100   He would not tolerate laxity. He would show strength, distancing himself.

Among the men there would be grumbling, of course, and maybe worse, because their days would seem longer and their loads heavier, but Lieutenant Jimmy Cross reminded himself that his obligation was not to be loved but to lead. He would dispense with love; it was not now a factor. And if anyone quarreled or complained, he would simply tighten his lips and arrange his shoulders in the correct command posture. He might give a curt little nod.

Or he might not. He might just shrug and say, Carry on, then they would saddle up and form into a column and move out toward the villages west of Than Khe.

FOCUSED FREE WRITES

1. What might the theme of this story be? Can you interpret its meaning?
2. What are "the things" they carried? Identify specific examples. How or in what ways are they significant?
3. This story is not organized like the conventional plots we have discussed. How is it ordered or structured? Or is it?
4. This story is written very lyrically. Rewrite a few paragraphs of this story as a poem in short imagistic lines. Read this found poem aloud. Does it work as a poem? How is it similar to a poem or different from one?

 # LITERARY Contexts

Imagery

Often, poetry is celebrated for its **imagery**—language that appeals to the senses. This story by O'Brien, however, illustrates how fiction, too, can use imagery in surprising and compelling ways by listing all the soldiers' literal and concrete baggage, from weapons to memories of Martha. Images put into language the physical world to be re-created by our imaginations. Images are concrete representations of senses, feelings, or ideas—specific details that stimulate our senses and trigger our memories. Even though the word "images" conjures sights, images may also be details of sound, smell, taste, or texture. Theme, plot, setting, character, and point of view create what a story is about; images and style are the means by which these are crafted.

How does O'Brien use imagery to convey the experience of war?

Writing an Analysis: The Elements of Style

While you have been engaged in the critical thinking act of analysis in the course of this chapter through your reading and informal writing, your thinking work must be translated into formal writing. So now you will build on your interpretive abilities to analyze the text. Your assignment is to write a textual analysis of one of the works in this chapter. Identify by what means the text accomplishes its purpose: *how* it does *what*. Break up the text into its component parts to determine how meaning is constructed. Examine the writer's style and the text's construction. For example, you might consider the following elements.

What, where, and *when* elements	*Who* elements	*How* elements
title	character	imagery
setting	narration	symbol
plot	point of view	syntax
structure	tone	diction
		figurative language

How do a few of these particular literary elements work together to create the theme of the work? For example, Cummings structures the line breaks in his poem "l(a" to visually illustrate loneliness. Dickinson uses natural imagery of the bird and the orchard to demonstrate an alternative way to worship. Hopkins uses the repetition of the diction "have trod, have trod, have trod" so readers can feel the weight of the world.

Moving from Free Writes to Ideas

Ideally, you will have begun the prewriting work of analysis through some of your informal writing—your Focused Free Writes—throughout the chapter. They will have prompted you to determine *what* a text means and to begin to figure out *how* it means. Look back at those Focused Free Writes to see where you are most engaged in the text or the writing. Once you have targeted one of these FFWs as a starting point, reread the story, poem, or play so it is fresh in your mind. Mark any moments that seem related to the initial idea from your reflection. What actions, people, objects, words, or lines seem connected?

For example, initially when a reader wrote about Don DeLillo's "Videotape," he wrote about how surprised he was when the writer addressed him, the reader, as "you." In going back to the story, he marked this passage:

> You keep on looking not because you know something is going to happen—of course you do know something is going to happen and you do look for that reason but you might also keep on looking if you came across this footage for the first time without knowing the outcome. There is a crude power operating here. You keep on looking because things combine to hold you fast—a sense of the random, the amateurish, the accidental, the impending. You don't think of the tape as boring or interesting. It is crude, it is blunt, it is relentless. It is the jostled part of your mind, the film that runs through your hotel brain under all the thoughts you know you're thinking. (177)

The writer seems to capture what happens when people see accidents or watch videos of things, like JFK's assassination. This seems related in some way to the reader's initial idea, but he is not sure how yet.

We will follow Ashley's process in developing an analysis of Tennessee Williams's *The Glass Menagerie*:

I begin generating ideas by freewriting about broad themes or issues that I notice in a text. When reflecting on Tennessee Williams's *The Glass Menagerie*, I freely wrote on the characters' fixation on remembering things that happened in the past. I noted that even though the ongoing search for a husband for Laura dominates the action in the play, the Wingfields spend just as much time, if not more, recalling the past as they do planning for the future. My free write particularly concentrated on how Laura Wingfield and her mother Amanda view the past. While Amanda fondly recalls happy past memories, Laura painfully recalls awkward social situations. When reflecting on the presence of recollection in the play, I noticed how Amanda and Laura magnify, glorify, and distort past events through memory.

Finding a Focus

At this point, you have something less than a topic, so here are two ways to start developing a topic:

- Identify the work's theme and then try to identify compelling ways this theme is made manifest; in other words, interpret the theme first and then identify the elements that make up this theme.
- Identify what you believe are some patterns in the text and try to figure out why those moments are repeated and how they are essential in terms of the theme's development; in other words, find the elements first and then interpret them.

For example, instead of focusing on his free write on the *you* in DeLillo (discussed in the previous section), the reader of "Videotape" might have begun with a free write connecting DeLillo's story to the "rubbernecking" phenomenon: people can't help but slow down to watch car accidents. Using this idea, he would analyze the text or break it up into parts to look for examples of rubbernecking in the text.

Or perhaps, in beginning with his earlier focus on *you* and that passage he marked, he can combine those examples with the last line: "The horror freezes your soul but this doesn't mean you want them to stop." These are all examples of how people can't help but act as voyeurs and watch things that are horrible or uninteresting. The reader's analysis helped him determine the importance of this theme.

In order to find a focus for a paper, I try to determine what I believe the text is saying about the broad theme I have explored in freewriting. After freewriting, I noticed that it seems Williams is not only just showing the audience that memory is important, but he is also stressing that an audience cannot always regard memory as truth. With the theme of distorted memory in mind, I returned to the play and looked for instances where Williams hints that the dialog and events of the play cannot be regarded as hard truth.

Shaping a Thesis

Your topic can be revised and specified to become a thesis. A good thesis statement should be a complete sentence. It should be an assertion, not a statement of fact, because it should be something that needs to be proven to your readers.

For example, a topic is distinct from a thesis statement. Topics for an essay on DeLillo might include voyeurism, rubbernecking, American culture, reality, and the media. However, all of these are topics. They are not complete sentences, and they do not assert anything.

Furthermore, your thesis should be focused and specific. A broad thesis like "DeLillo writes an interesting story" is difficult to prove. What interests some people may not interest others. And such a general statement would yield a superficial paper.

Instead, a thesis statement is like a hypothesis. It is a complete sentence that needs analysis and discussion of the mechanics of the text to support it. Examples of thesis statements might include these:

> DeLillo's story "Videotape" demonstrates the fine line between horror and fascination.

> In his story "Videotape," Don DeLillo demonstrates how technology and the media have transformed American culture.

> DeLillo's short story "Videotape" accuses all Americans of voyeurism.

> In "Videotape," DeLillo argues that new technology only serves to emphasize essential and ancient behaviors.

> DeLillo juxtaposes shooting video and shooting people in his short story "Videotape."

You could use analysis to elaborate on and develop each of these statements through identifying supporting evidence from the story. Also, notice the identifying information in the sample thesis statements. It is a good idea to identify the author and the title of the work in your thesis statement, or somewhere nearby in your introduction.

STUDENT WRITER In Ashley's Words...

When I begin to form a thesis for a paper, I look at my prewriting work and determine what sort of claim I want to make about the topic I've explored. After freewriting and finding a focus, I settled on the topic of memory—specifically, how past events become distorted through memory. After looking at places in the text where stage direction and setting add to the play's presentation of memory, I arrived at the thesis that "Williams's dialog and stage directions remind readers that as a memory play, the lives of Laura, Amanda, and Tom Wingfield are recreated and rearranged through the lens of memory."

Finding Significance in Small Moments and Specific Details

Constructing an analysis works dialogically, in cycles of looking, thinking and writing, and looking again at a text to find meaning. So now that the writer has a topic and thesis, he must go back to the text to develop a list of evidence that supports his main idea. Evidence can be found in the *who, what,* or *when* of the text in actions of the narrative, setting, characters, or speakers. It can also be found in the *how* of the text in the words, sentences, images, or symbols of a work.

For example, the writer could return to "Videotape" to look for examples of the idea about "rubbernecking" and "voyeurism" to prove this thesis statement: "DeLillo's short story accuses all Americans of voyeurism." For this thesis, the writer might mark the following as supporting evidence:

1. Point of view—the use of "you," which suggests everyone participates
2. Talk about what all families do with their video cameras
3. Maybe this quotation: "You know how families make up games. This is just another game in which the child invents the rules as she goes along. She likes the idea of videotaping a man in his car. She has probably never done it before and it she sees no reason to vary the format or terminate early or pan to another car. This is her game and she is learning it and playing it at the same time. She feels halfway clever and inventive and maybe slightly intrusive as well, a little bit of brazenness that spices any game."
4. The videocamera as a symbol of this paradoxical desire to watch and fear of seeing
5. The last line: "The horror freezes your soul but this doesn't mean you want them to stop."

Many other moments or lines could be marked as well. Or the writer might go back to the story to dig up more evidence. Since all parts of a text are eligible for analysis, this searching process could go on forever! It is important to avoid getting overwhelmed in the searching and to plan time for writing as well.

Avoid focusing on superficial or obvious moments—"The character of the girl makes the theme and without this character we would have no story." Well, obviously! But what if you focused on the fact that she was "the Video Kid"? For example, you could say the following: "In DeLillo's story, one of the main characters is known as the Video Kid. Her anonymity suggests she is famous in a modern way, as a phenomenon representative of our culture, not as an individual person." At this point you could quote from the text as support. In other words, be specific.

It may be useful to consider yourself a *creative reader*. Try to find a moment you might not have discussed in class, a line you did not see initially, or an example others have skipped over. Make significant a smaller moment or talk about a commonly discussed moment in a new way. Experiment with being a groundbreaker—who is grounded in the text, of course.

STUDENT WRITER *In Ashley's Words...*

When finding evidence for a paper, I closely read the text and look for specific sentences or thoughts which support my thesis. For my *Glass Menagerie* paper, I pulled my evidence for my thesis from moments in the play where I thought the characters' dialog and William's stage directions really worked to distinguish the division between remembered events and actual events. For example, I noted the stage directions which indicate how Laura's glass collection appears to inadvertently break in one scene and reappear as whole shortly thereafter. These directions emphasize that the play occurs in someone's memory and not in reality. Additionally, I also found that dialog, such as the conversation where Amanda Wingfield shares her experiences with a multitude of gentlemen callers, also reinforce the notion that the characters alter past events for the sake of memory. Through closely examining stage directions and dialogue, I pinpointed evidence of memory and distorted reality throughout the play.

Writing to Advance the Thesis
Making a Plan

Once you have a thesis to guide your paper, you can use your list of supporting ideas to begin to craft topic sentences that will advance it. And as you develop your thesis statement and topic sentences, you can determine what order is best for your supporting ideas.

Thesis: DeLillo exposes the perverse yet universal desire to be a voyeur through the point of view, characterization, symbolism, and theme of his short story "Videotape."

Topic Sentence #1 on point of view: Through the story's point of view and the invasive use of *you*, DeLillo accuses everyone of acting as voyeurs.

Evidence: examples of use of *you* throughout the story—how DeLillo implicates the audience

Topic Sentence #2 on characterization: The anonymity of the Video Kid and the generalizations about her behavior and the behavior of families suggest that all people, like these people, like to look and can't help but look.

Evidence: description of the Video Kid and generalizations about families

Topic Sentence #3 on symbolism: The videocamera acts as a tangible symbol of watching others.

Evidence: discussion of the videocamera

Topic Sentence #4 on theme: The last line of the story summarizes this theme of voyeurism: "The horror freezes your soul but this doesn't mean you want them to stop."

Evidence: the last line and other direct allusions to the theme throughout

STUDENT WRITER In Ashley's Words...

When making a plan for a paper, I return to my evidence and look at which elements in the text can be grouped together to form paragraph topics. For example, I noticed that while Amanda exaggerates stories (such as that of her sixteen gentlemen callers) to make the past grander, Laura magnifies small occurrences (such as the noise made during her daily walk into the chorus room) and makes the past possibly more painful than it actually was. Thus, I formed topic sentences which revolved around each character and his or her treatment of memory.

Developing and Supporting Your Thesis

You can plan a chronological approach like the one listed in the previous section. In discussing each of those elements of the story, the writer traced how the theme of voyeurism is present by moving through the story step by step, picking out the moments where this theme arises. I might have to decide if this is the best order for these paragraphs, however. Perhaps I might decide Topic Sentence #4 should be my first topic sentence, even though it appears last in the story, because it is the most significant. Often, planning and drafting a project involves repeated rearranging. Ultimately, a writer should make conscious choices though there may not be any one "right" answer.

However, let's say the writer wanted to analyze the story in light of this thesis: "DeLillo's story 'Videotape' demonstrates the fine line between horror and fascination." The essay might be organized based on an alternative logic. The writer might begin with smaller examples to build up to the thrust of the argument, and thus leave readers with the best idea most clearly in their mind at paper's end. So, the writer might begin by focusing on Janet, the Video Kid, the speaker, and then *you*. The plan is to begin with a minor example and then move to major examples.

In each of these body paragraphs, state the topic of the paragraph and how it connects to the thesis. If you were working with the thesis discussed above ("DeLillo exposes the perverse yet universal desire to be a voyeur through the point of view, characterization, symbolism, and theme of his short story 'Videotape.'"), you would want to have a paragraph about point of view. Take a look at the following first-draft paragraph about the point of view:

> In "Videotape," Don DeLillo uses *you* over and over again. He talks about what *you* see. He describes how *you* see the man, the girl, and the killing. He also talks about what *you* know, such as what *you* know about families. Throughout the story, DeLillo uses *you*.

This is a good start: the paragraph alludes to particular parts of the text the writer is thinking of when he considers DeLillo's use of *you*. Now, he needs to make each point specifically so that readers can understand his experience of reading the text. The paragraph is too vague. What is missing here?

Each body paragraph should begin with a specific topic sentence that addresses the connection between the thesis and the topic at hand. The sentences that follow should develop this topic with examples the writer summarizes or paraphrases of actions or characters from the story. Or these sentences might provide evidence in the form of the writer's analysis of the story's style and language through the use of direct quotation. If quotations provide support, they should be discussed thoroughly, integrated smoothly, and punctuated correctly (see Chapter 16).

Take a look at the second draft of this paragraph, which has been greatly expanded with a topic sentence and specific details to support it:

Topic sentence	DeLillo's use of the second person point of view, the *you*, accuses all people of being fascinated by horror. The third sen-
Writer's interpretation	tence of the story shocks us when it tells us what we see: "You see a man at the wheel of a medium Dodge" (176). All of the sudden, the reader becomes a part of the narrative, a part of the story, a
Summary and paraphrase	witness—a voyeur, in fact. In the next few paragraphs, DeLillo focuses not on what *you* see but what *you* know; the reader settles in and participates in the understanding of common knowledge about what families do and what kids do. The narrator offers exam- ples that the reader might connect to: have *your* kids videoed *you*? Have they invaded *your* privacy? Throughout the story, DeLillo returns to the idea that you have sympathy for and an understand-
Quotation	ing of this fascination with watching, spying, and being watched or spied on. In the middle of the story, the narrator talks about *your* anticipation of the shooting: "It is something, naturally, that

you wait for. You say to your wife, if you're home and she is there, Now here is where he gets it. You say, Janet, hurry up, this is where it happens" (178). Not only are *you* involved and drawn to the horror, but you draw in others who cannot escape it either.

STUDENT WRITER *In Ashley's Words...*

When developing body paragraphs for a paper, I first briefly introduce the topic that I will discuss in that paragraph, and how that topic relates to my thesis. Then I provide evidence from the play and explain how I am using that evidence to support my thesis. For example, in the third paragraph of my essay, I first include a topic sentence which introduces that I will discuss how the lack of props furthers my thesis that the play alters reality. I then include textual evidence where Williams references the lack of props, and finally provide my own claim that the absence of props helps to distinguish the memory play from reality.

Revising to Polishing

The previous chapter provided an overview of the revision process, and subsequent chapters will go into even more detail. The first step in revision involves rewriting:

- Clarify your thesis. Make certain it clearly states the focus of your analysis.
- Do you transition from one idea to the next clearly? Does it make sense to order the ideas in your essay the way they are organized? Within each paragraph, do the ideas flow well? Do sentences logically follow one other?
- Does the main idea of every paragraph relate directly to the thesis?
- Do you discuss your examples thoroughly and explain how they support your paragraphs' main ideas or paper's thesis? Could you elaborate?

Editing

- Focus on making your language precise and specific.
- Correct and vary your sentences.
- Be deliberate and strategic in your word choice.

A Lesson in Style

Professional writers have distinctive styles, and beginning writers should also pay attention to their own styles. Remember that you have the power to make conscious choices that will influence your readers' experiences of your ideas.

When you revise and edit your essay, pay attention to your syntax and diction. Take a look at the following examples and exercises:

First draft of Ashley's introduction

"Memory" has become an important part of American culture. One needs to look no further than a craft store. Society obsesses over memory. Memory doesn't last. People revise the past. Tennessee Williams explores memory in his play *The Glass Menagerie*. Williams uses dialog and stage directions to emphasize memory.

Notice all the simple sentences—they read more like a list than a paragraph. However, Ashley could revise these sentences to make the connections between the ideas more obvious through the use of a variety of sentence structures: simple, compound, and complex.

Revised for better sentence variety

"Memory" has become an important part of American culture. One needs to look no further than a craft store to see how society obsesses over memory and tries to preserve it. However, moments don't last and people revise the past through memory. Tennessee Williams explores this quality of memory in his play *The Glass Menagerie* through his dialog and stage directions.

Since the two ideas in the second and third sentences are closely related, she can rewrite them as one sentence. Since the idea in the following sentence contrasts with the previous one, she uses a transitional conjunctive adverb such as "however" to indicate that relationship. The subjects of the last two sentences are repeated, so Ashley rewrites them as one sentence.

In this paragraph, we could consider the word choice as well. Ashley should consider the connotations and the sounds of her selections.

Revised for better word choices

"Memory" has become a consumable part of American culture. One needs to look no further than a craft store to see how society attempts to purchase, adorn, and document memories. However, memory is not as tangible as these embellished photos make it appear. Rather, memory is an ephemeral and fleeting quality, and is always subject to the latent wishes, fickle emotions, and unconscious revisions of the 'rememberer.' Tennessee Williams explores the complicated and clouded world of memory in his play *The Glass Menagerie*. Specifically, Williams's dialog and stage directions remind readers that as a memory play, the lives of Laura, Amanda, and Tom Wingfield are re-created and rearranged through the lens of memory.

Ashley tried to be more specific with her word choice in her revision. She explained what she meant by "important" through the use of the word "consumable." She expanded on the idea of obsession by describing the scrapbooking phenomenon when people "purchase, adorn, and document memories." She looked for ways to restate the idea of something "not lasting" as "tangible," "ephemeral," and "fleeting." She tried to elaborate on why memories get changed as "subject to the latent wishes, fickle emotions, and unconscious revisions of the 'rememberer.'" She used adjectives to describe the vague "this quality" as "the complicated and clouded world of memory." Finally, Ashley was concerned that her thesis statement was not directive enough and broke it into two sentences to elaborate and explain the structure of the paper that followed.

Style Checklist
Sentence Structure:

Consider the syntax of your paper, the structure of your sentences and their relationships to each other.

Combine sentences to avoid repetition and to express relationships between ideas:
- Use a semicolon to join two complete sentences with closely related ideas.
- Reword sentences to use a compound subject or compound predicate.
- Use **coordinating conjunctions** and **coordinating adverbs** to express comparisons, contrasts, and causation:
    Addition: and, both ... and, also, besides, furthermore, moreover
    Choice: either ... or, not only ... but also, or
    Contrast: but, yet, either ... or, however, instead, neither ... nor
    Causation: accordingly, for, so, therefore
- Use **subordinating conjunctions** to clarify logical relationships or hierarchies between ideas:
    Comparison/Contrast: although, despite, even though
    Causation: as, because, in order that, so, so that, since
    Condition: even, if, unless
    Choice: than, rather than
    Time or space: after, as, before, since, until, when, whenever, where, wherever, while

Vary sentence structure to avoid monotony:

- **Simple sentences (independent clauses)** consist of the subject, verb, and any objects or modifiers.
- **Compound sentences** consist of two or more **simple sentences** or **independent clauses**.
- **Complex sentences** consist of a **simple sentence** (an **independent clause**) and a **dependent clause** that contains a subject and verb as well as a **subordinating conjunction** (such as those listed above) or a relative pronoun (such as *who, which, that*).
- **Compound complex sentences** include at least two **independent clauses** and one **dependent clause**.

Word Choice:

- Explain exactly what you mean. Don't just say something is *important*—say why and how or explain what you mean by *important*.
- Expand and elaborate on your point through examples. If you state that people are obsessed with memory, demonstrate what you mean by that.
- Restate your idea using vivid language that precisely captures your thinking.
  - Use concrete specific nouns. Avoid abstract and general nouns like "things"!
  - Use strong active verbs by replacing state-of-being verbs (such as "to be" verbs, *appear, become, seem,* and *exist*) and overused, weak verbs like *do, get, go, have,* and *make*.
  - Turn nouns into verbs. Instead of saying: "The video of the murder is a continuing fascination for the characters in "Videotape," state that the "The video of the murder fascinates the characters."
  - Use active voice, not passive voice. As opposed to "Memories were discussed by the family," try "The family discussed their memories."
- Use descriptive phrases to clarify and specify your understanding.
  - Use specific and concrete modifiers to replace abstract and vague ones. Watch overused terms like *good, bad, nice,* and *interesting*. Describe objects in a unique way.

EXERCISES

Using the lessons above and the Style Checklist, how could you rewrite the following paragraphs using more effective sentence structure and more precise language? Work individually and then compare your revisions with a partner or in a group.

1. The glass menagerie is a symbol for Laura. It is also a symbol for the other characters. Laura has a fragile existence. She is like the animals made of glass. Her ill health isolates her. It also makes her unique. She is like the unicorn. The other characters also exist outside reality. They are fragile too.

2. Tim O'Brien writes about all of the different things people carry to convey the weight of war. He focuses on soldiers at war. The soldiers carry actual objects like rations, guns, and ammunition. They also carried pictures, letters, and cigarettes. Then O'Brien says they also carry "grief, terror, love, longing" (190). The lists build to his description of a soldier's death.

3. Emily Dickinson writes a poem about going to church. She does not celebrate church in a building. She celebrates at home. She shows how everyday objects can be religious. She shows how she is just as religious, maybe more, at home.

You will want to apply these same revision skills to your own projects.

Proofreading

- Proofread and attend to all grammar issues, particularly those you have had trouble with in the past.
- Watch spelling, typos, verb use, and punctuation.

Sample Student Paper

Ashley Walden's biography can be found on page 567.

Ashley Walden

English 102 Analysis

Dr. Howells

25 Nov. 2010

Analyzing Stage Direction, Dialog, and Memory

in Williams's *The Glass Menagerie*

"Memory" has become a consumable part of American culture. One needs to look no further than a craft store in order to examine how society attempts to purchase, adorn, and document elements of memory. However, memory is not as tangible as these embellished photos make it appear. Rather, memory is an ephemeral and fleeting quality, and is always subject to the latent wishes and emotions of the 'rememberer.' Tennessee Williams explores the complicated and clouded world of memory in his play *The Glass Menagerie*. Specifically, Williams's dialog and stage directions remind readers that as a memory play, the lives of Laura, Amanda, and Tom Wingfield are re-created and rearranged through the lens of memory.

The play's style relies on setting and stage direction to advance the plot. As the first scene opens, Williams's stage directions note that "the scene is memory and therefore nonrealistic. Memory takes a lot of poetic license. It omits some details, others are exaggerated, according to the emotional value of the articles it touches"(120). At first glance, Williams appears to merely create instructions for the play's stage setup. However, the brief discussion of the scene as "memory" foreshadows the impending thoughts and conversations of the Wingfields. Typically, an audience views a play as a scripted re-creation of an important event, with the focus shifting to whatever character makes the scene memorable.

However, Williams's play is not merely a *re-creation* of events; it is a production of recollections which now exist in the mind of the Wingfields. The play is not completely lifelike, an aspect which the setting that includes a transparent barrier reflects:

> The audience hears and sees the opening scene in the dining room through both the transparent fourth wall of the building and the transparent gauze portieres of the dining-room arch. It is during this revealing scene that the fourth wall slowly ascends, out of sight. This transparent exterior wall is not brought down again until the very end of the play, during Tom's final speech (120–121).

This wall is more than a setting feature. The transparent wall becomes a membrane between reality and memory as it separates the audience, or reality, from the stage, or memory.

Similarly, the absence of material objects from the stage set further casts the play as a production of memory. Williams notes the absence of such props when he comments that "eating is indicated by gestures without food or utensils" (121). Scenery or props typically add realism to a play as they help create a more believable setting for the play's action. Props indicate a concreteness; they are a symbol that the play's events are happening right at the particular moment in which the audience is viewing them. However, a prop-free play suggests the possibility that reminiscence can alter or even eliminate both large and small details. Rather than create a believable world, complete with props, Williams leaves out such items in order to further create a hazy setting of memory.

The proof of memory through prop and stage directions continues in the matter of Laura Wingfield's glass collection. The menagerie becomes symbolic of Laura and her fragile nature, but it also serves as another example of the fleeting nature of memory. In Act 3,

Tom inadvertently flings his jacket during a fight with his mother and the garment "strikes against the shelf of Laura's glass collection, and there is a tinkle of shattering glass. Laura cries out as if wounded" (167). The action creates a union between setting and style. The glass props (with their physical stage presence debatable) shatter in order to emphasize how the Wingfields' fight affects Laura, as well as the brokenness of the Wingfield home. In contrast, in the final act, Laura returns to her now-intact menagerie during an interaction with Jim O'Conner, her "gentleman caller." In a reality-based play, such a self-repairing glass collection would appear as an error; in Williams's play, the menagerie is not only a symbol of Laura, but it also represents the fluid, ever-changing properties of memory.

The existence of *The Glass Menagerie* as a memory play continues with dialog. Because the performance is from the Wingfields' recollection, its events are undoubtedly subject to bias, which the dialog of characters such as Amanda later proves. The development of Amanda as a character devoted to memory begins in the character descriptions, as Williams notes that Amanda is "a little woman of great but confused vitality clinging frantically to another time and place" (117). This description casts Amanda as one of many characters who will live through the past, rather accept the present. Amanda not only clings to the past, but she also potentially rearranges her personal history in order to provide a more exciting memory. For example, Amanda eagerly recalls her own experiences with "gentlemen callers" to her children. In Scene 1, Amanda exclaims, "One Sunday afternoon in the Blue Mountain—your mother received—*seventeen!*—gentlemen callers!" and goes on to claim that one suitor "carried my picture on him the night he died!" (124). The audience accepts Amanda's story as accurate; however, the play's status as a memory production gently reminds readers that even these seemingly mild recollections are potentially colored by memory. Mrs. Wingfield draws great strength from her memories; recollections of past popularity sustain her. However, it is impossible for the audience to truly know if Mrs. Wingfield's lively descriptions of her past are accurate. Tom hints at Amanda's fluid, changing memory when he comments after one story in Scene 1 when he asks, "isn't this the first you've mentioned that still survives?" (124). Tom's dialog subtly reminds the audience that while Amanda lives on and through her memories, these recollections may not be accurate, as they are merely the vocal reminders of a woman fixated on memory.

Tom's dialog further expresses the connection between real and memory. Rather than retell his past, Tom (as narrator and character) directly speaks to the audience and informs them of the nonrealistic setting of the play: "The play is memory. Being a memory play, it is dimly lighted, it is sentimental, it is not realistic. In memory everything seems to happen to music" (121). Though Tom's dialog shows an awareness of the play's nonrealistic state, he embraces the memory play rather than skeptically rejecting it. For example, Tom proves this point when he speaks of Laura's gentleman caller, saying "since I have a poet's weakness for symbols, I am using this character also as a symbol; he is the long-delayed but always expected something that we live for" (121). Williams, via Tom, cautions the audience that the play's setting, which includes lighting and stage music, will not be perfectly realistic; Tom further makes this point when he states "I am the opposite of a stage magician. He gives you illusion that has the appearance of truth. I give you truth in the pleasant disguise of illusion" (121). Instead, the stage will echo the alterations and soundtracks which memory casts upon an incident. While some play narrators serve as a liaison between audience and cast, Tom delivers dialog without breaking the theme of memory.

Like her brother and mother, memory also consumes Laura's world. However, through dialog and stage direction, Laura emphasizes the painful element of memory. Williams's character notes describe Laura, observing that her "separation increases till she is like a piece of her own glass collection, too exquisitely fragile to move from the shelf" (156). Like Amanda, Laura also magnifies areas of the past, but does so in a way that amplifies painful rather than pleasurable memories. For example, in Scene 7, Laura describes her recollections of high-school chorus to Jim O'Conner, her caller. Laura explains, "it was so hard for me, getting upstairs. I had that brace on my leg—it clumped so loud!" and further proclaims "to me it sounded like—thunder!"(156). However, in the same scene, Jim refutes Laura's claim and perhaps places her recollections into perspective when he states, "you give up an education because of a clump, which as far as I know was practically non-existent!" (156). Though Laura describes the past pain from her experience, her description suggests that time has only magnified the pain. Furthermore, in Laura's "transformation" for the arrival of Jim O'Conner in Scene 6, memory controls the description: "the dress is colored and designed by memory. The arrangement of Laura's hair is changed; it is softer and more becoming. A fragile, unearthly prettiness has come out in Laura: she is like a piece of translucent glass touched by light, given a momentary radiance, not actual, not lasting" (145). At first glance, this appears as a detailed catalog of Laura's appearance. However, her appearance, which is "designed by memory" and "not actual, not lasting," results only from the recollection of her form and cannot be conjured in any other way. Laura's description is and will always be changing and dependent upon memory.

Tennessee Williams explores such worlds of memory through the lives of Laura Wingfield, Amanda Wingfield, and Tom Wingfield. However, Williams also pushes the family into reality as he shatters the prototypical, expected fairytale ending. Williams's reminder signals that the play is more than a re-creation of past events; rather, it is a production clouded with the dim and sometimes painful shadows of memory. Despite mass-marketed journals and photograph books, memory is not a consumable commodity. Though pictures and records produce an exact visual copy, the fleeting feelings and descriptions of past events will always be subject to the intangible quality of memory.

Work Cited

Williams, Tennessee. *The Glass Menagerie. Literature: Reading to Write:* Ed. Elizabeth Howells. New York: Pearson, 2010. 117–168. Print.

5

VOICE AND NARRATION
Arguing for an
Interpretation

Framing Women. This painting represents just one of the portraits Christina Rossetti described as inhabiting her brother's studio in her poem "In an Artist's Studio." Dante Gabriel Rossetti painted it to accompany his poem "The Blessed Damozel." What is she saying about her brother's representations in her poem? Like many nineteenth-century images, it depicts a woman at a window. Why would such an image be so popular at that time?

Who is speaking?

How would you respond if your teacher asked you what you did last weekend? What if it were your classmate? Your roommate? Your best friend? A colleague at work? Now consider how you would respond if your parent, your minister, or your boss asked you the same question. What would you include in your description for one listener, and what would you leave out for another? And how do you decide what to say? Most people would make choices about how to tell the story based on their audience. You might tell your teacher how hard you studied, your friend how hard you partied, or your parent how hard you slept. All those things might be true (or might not be), but you would choose what to emphasize based on what you think would most appeal to your audience. And in part, you would be basing your decisions on how you want them to view you—as a serious student, devout churchgoer, or some kind of party animal.

Furthermore, your best buddy's account of the weekend would be slightly different from yours, even if you had done the same things: you would both have different perspectives or different points of view and would have emphasized some moments or left out others in your accounts of the weekend. As you already know, paying attention to where information is coming from helps you decide whether or not you can trust it. The same holds true when you read works by professional storytellers—novelists, poets, playwrights, and even essayists. You can decide how trustworthy the speaker is or understand his or her point of view by noticing what kinds of events and what kinds of details are revealed, and which are held back.

Stories are conveyed by **narration**, or through a recital of events. In some texts, particularly in novels or short stories, an explicit **narrator** may tell the story, that is, the author creates a character to tell the story. In plays, the narrative is delivered through dialog among characters though sometimes an explicit narrator is present to speak directly to the audience about the play's happenings. In *The Glass Menagerie*, Tom acts as both a character and a narrator. In poems, the voice communicating the poem is called the **persona**. The persona cannot be assumed to be the poet herself but should be considered as a kind of mask representing the poet's point of view. No matter whom the narrator is, he or she will be telling a certain version of the story, just as you and your friend relayed different versions of the weekend.

The narration is characterized by the **point of view**, which is the **speaker, voice, narrator,** or **persona** of a work or the position from which the narrative is conveyed. If the narrator has a single, distinct voice, the point of view is **first person**, distinguished by the narrator's use of the pronoun "I." First person points of view are fairly common. Some famous examples are in the novels *Catcher in the Rye* by J. D. Salinger and *Lolita* by Vladimir Nabokov.

Second person points of view are more rare. These narrators speak directly to "you," the reader, telling you what to notice or think or remember. The "Dear Reader" convention of eighteenth-century novels reflects the **epistolary** form of the novel (the novels were written as exchanges of letters, also called "epistles") and sounds a bit old-fashioned today. On occasion, second person is used to connect with the reader in a particular way, such as to convey the universal obsession with voyeurism in Don DeLillo's "Videotape" in Chapter 4 or even at moments throughout the narration of this textbook. Movies like *Ferris Bueller's*

Day Off or television shows like *Malcolm in the Middle* are some instances of second person point of view.

A narrator speaking from the **third person** point of view reports what characters did or do, referring to them as "he," "she," or "it." The usage of this point of view is fairly common. Just like the first person, the third person point of view can be **omniscient**, seeing into all the characters' perspectives or **limited** to just one perspective

Can you think of other examples of each of these points of view?

Certainly, narration is an aspect of an author's style along with the other elements of style discussed in the previous chapter. **Tone** is another part of style. As in Faulkner's "A Rose for Emily," sometimes it can be complicated characterizing the author's **tone** or the author's attitude toward the subject. Tone is conveyed through the characters or narrator and the words they use or the diction or word choice employed to describe them and their actions.

Sometimes, however, the author's attitude may be beneath the surface and run contrary to what is said on the page. Authors use **irony** to complicate their telling of a tale. Sometimes they want to tell a story from a particular point of view that allows for a literal meaning of the events conveyed and an implied meaning for the reader to read between the lines and understand. You might notice how that is so in Faulkner before taking a look at Browning's dramatic monologues. There are specific kinds of irony; for example, **verbal irony** is the contrast between what is said and what is meant. I might say "that's just great" when I mean the opposite, or the duke might say something as simple as "Then all smiles stopped together" and mean something quite sinister. **Dramatic irony** is the contrast between what the audience knows and what is actually taking place. For example, the audience is aware that Oedipus is traveling down a dangerous path when he vows to punish the origin of the curse of Thebes; the audience knows he is dooming himself. Through irony then, the reader must detect meaning from verbal clues or through implication.

Can you think of an example of a work of literature with a particularly distinctive voice or point of view? What about a television show or film? How did the perspective of the narrative impact its meaning?

STORIES

The author of short fiction must choose a narrator to tell the story. The narrator is for the most part a single entity or person, but it isn't always. The narrator may be reliable, or not. Readers will always want to carefully consider how the narrative is mediated.

PRE-READING   In a review, Updike once wrote: "My purpose in reading has ever secretly been not to come and judge but to come and steal." What do you think he meant by that? What is your purpose in reading?

John Updike (1932–2009).   *The son of a schoolteacher father and a writer mother, John Updike was born in Pennsylvania, received a scholarship to and graduated from Harvard, and wrote for* The New Yorker *before joining the staff. Settled in Massachusetts for the past forty years, Updike has written award-winning novels such as the Rabbit trilogy and* The Witches of Eastwick, *the basis of the 1987 movie. He died in 2009 at age 76.*

John Updike
_____

A & P°   [1961]

In walks these three girls in nothing but bathing suits. I'm in the third checkout slot, with my back to the door, so I don't see them until they're over by the bread. The one that caught my eye first was the one in the plaid green two-piece. She was a chunky kid, with a good tan and a sweet broad soft-looking can with those two crescents of white just under it, where the sun never seems to hit, at the top of the backs of her legs. I stood there with my hand on a box of HiHo crackers trying to remember if I rang it up or not. I ring it up again and the customer starts giving me hell. She's one of these cash-register-watchers, a witch about fifty with rouge on her cheekbones and no eyebrows, and I know it made her day to trip me up. She'd been watching cash registers for fifty years and probably never seen a mistake before.

By the time I got her feathers smoothed and her goodies into a bag—she gives me a little snort in passing, if she'd been born at the right time they would have burned her over in Salem—by the time I got her on her way the girls had circled around the bread and were coming back, without a pushcart, back my way along the counters, in the aisle between the checkouts and the Special bins. They didn't even have shoes on. There was this chunky one, with the two-piece—it was bright green and the seams on the bra were still sharp and her belly was still pretty pale so I guessed she just got it (the suit)—there was this one, with one of those chubby berry-faces, the lips all bunched together under her nose, this one; and a tall one, with black hair that hadn't quite frizzed right, and one of these sunburns right across under the eyes, and a chin that was too long—you know, the kind of girl other girls think is very "striking" and "attractive" but never quite makes it, as they very well know, which is why they like her so much—and then the third one, that wasn't quite so tall. She was the queen. She kind of led them, the other two peeking around and making their shoulders round. She didn't look around, not this queen, she just walked straight on slowly, on these long white prima-donna legs. She came down a little hard on her heels, as if she didn't walk in her bare feet that much, putting down her heels and letting the weight move along to her toes as if she was testing the floor with every step, putting a little deliberate extra action into it. You never know for sure how girls' minds work (do you really think it's a mind in there or just a little buzz like a bee in a glass jar?) But you got the idea she had talked the other two into coming in here with her, and now she was showing them how to do it, walk slow and hold yourself straight.

She had on a kind of dirty-pink—beige maybe, I don't know—bathing suit with a little nubble all over it and, what got me, the straps were down. They

_____
° *A & P:* the Great Atlantic and Pacific Tea Company, a large grocery chain established in 1859 and still flourishing in 18 states, with more than 800 A & P stores in the United States and 200 in Canada.

were off her shoulders looped loose around the cool tops of her arms, and I guess as a result the suit had slipped a little on her, so all around the top of the cloth there was a shining rim. If it hadn't been there you wouldn't have known there could have been anything whiter than those shoulders. With the straps pushed off, there was nothing between the top of the suit and the top of her head except just *her*, this clean bare plane of the top of her chest down from the shoulder bones like a dented sheet of metal tilted in the light. I mean, it was more than pretty.

She had sort of oaky hair that the sun and salt had bleached, done up in a bun that was unraveling, and a kind of prim face. Walking into the A & P with your straps down, I suppose it's the only kind of face you *can* have. She held her head so high her neck, coming up out of those white shoulders, looked kind of stretched, but I didn't mind. The longer her neck was, the more of her there was.

5   She must have felt in the corner of her eye me and over my shoulder Stokesie in the second slot watching, but she didn't tip. Not this queen. She kept her eyes moving across the racks, and stopped, and turned so slow it made my stomach rub the inside of my apron, and buzzed to the other two, who kind of huddled against her for relief, and then they all three of them went up the cat-and-dog-food-breakfast-cereal-macaroni-rice-raisins-seasonings-spreads-spaghetti-soft-drinks-crackers-and-cookies aisle. From the third slot I look straight up this aisle to the meat counter, and I watched them all the way. The fat one with the tan sort of fumbled with the cookies, but on second thought she put the package back. The sheep pushing their carts down the aisle—the girls were walking against the usual traffic (not that we have one-way signs or anything)—were pretty hilarious. You could see them, when Queenie's white shoulders dawned on them, kind of jerk, or hop, or hiccup, but their eyes snapped back to their own baskets and on they pushed. I bet you could set off dynamite in an A & P and the people would by and large keep reaching and checking oatmeal off their lists and muttering "Let me see, there was a third thing, began with A, asparagus, no ah, yes, applesauce!" Or whatever it is they do mutter. But there was no doubt this jiggled them. A few house slaves in pin curlers even looked around after pushing their carts past to make sure what they had seen was correct.

You know, it's one thing to have a girl in a bathing suit down on the beach, where what with the glare nobody can look at each other much anyway, and another thing in the cool of the A & P, under the fluorescent lights, against all those stacked packages, with her feet paddling along naked over our checker-board green-and-cream rubber-tile floor.

"Oh Daddy," Stokesie said beside me. "I feel so faint."

"Darling," I said, "Hold me tight." Stokesie's married, with two babies chalked up on his fuselage already, but as far as I can tell that's the only difference. He's twenty-two, and I was nineteen this April.

"Is it done?" he asks, the responsible married man finding his voice. I forgot to say he thinks he's going to be manager some sunny day, maybe in 1990 when it's called the Great Alexandrov and Petrooshki° Tea Company or something.

° **Great Alexandrov and Petrooshki:** apparently a reference to the possibility that someday Russia might rule the United States.

What he meant was, our town is five miles from a beach, with a big summer colony out on the Point, but we're right in the middle of town, and the women generally put on a shirt or shorts or something before they get out of the car into the street. And anyway these are usually women with six children and varicose veins mapping their legs and nobody, including them, could care less. As I say, we're right in the middle of town, and if you stand at our front doors you can see two banks and the Congregational church and the newspaper store and three real-estate offices and about twenty-seven old freeloaders tearing up Central Street because the sewer broke again. It's not as if we're on the Cape,° we're north of Boston and there's people in this town haven't seen the ocean for twenty years.

The girls had reached the meat counter and were asking McMahon something. He pointed, they pointed, and they shuffled out of sight behind a pyramid of Diet Delight peaches. All that was left for us to see was old McMahon patting his mouth and looking after them sizing up their joints. Poor kids, I began to feel sorry for them, they couldn't help it.

Now here comes the sad part of the story, at least my family says it's sad, but I don't think it's so sad myself. The store's pretty empty, it being Thursday afternoon, so there was nothing much to do except lean on the register and wait for the girls to show up again. The whole store was like a pinball machine and I didn't know which tunnel they'd come out of. After a while they come around out of the far aisle, around the light bulbs, records at discount of the Caribbean Six or Tony Martin Sings or some such gunk you wonder they waste the wax on, six packs of candy bars, and plastic toys done up in cellophane that fall apart when a kid looks at them anyway. Around they come, Queenie still leading the way, and holding a little gray jar in her hand. Slots Three through Seven are unmanned and I could see her wondering between Stokes and me, but Stokesie with his usual luck draws an old party in baggy gray pants who stumbles up with four giant cans of pineapple juice (what do these bums *do* with all that pineapple juice? I've often asked myself) so the girls come to me. Queenie puts down the jar and I take it into my fingers icy cold. Kingfish Fancy Herring Snacks in Pure Sour Cream: 49¢ Now her hands are empty, not a ring or a bracelet, bare as God made them, and I wonder where the money's coming from. Still with that prim look she lifts a folded dollar bill out of the hollow at the center of her nubbled pink top. The jar went heavy in my hand. Really, I thought that was so cute.

Then everybody's luck begins to run out. Lengel comes in from haggling with a truck full of cabbages on the lot and is about to scuttle into the door marked MANAGER behind which he hides all day when the girls touch his eye. Lengel's pretty dreary, teaches Sunday school and the rest, but he doesn't miss that much. He comes over and says, "Girls, this isn't the beach."

Queenie blushed, though maybe it's just a brush of sunburn I was noticing for the first time, now that she was so close. "My mother asked me to pick up a jar of herring snacks." Her voice kind of startled me, the way voices do when you see the people first, coming out so flat and dumb yet kind of tony, too, the way it ticked over "pick up" and "snacks." All of a sudden I slid right down her

---

° *the Cape:* Cape Cod, the southeastern area of Massachusetts, a place of many resorts and beaches.

voice into her living room. Her father and the other men were standing around in ice-cream coats and bow ties and the women were in sandals picking up herring snacks on toothpicks off a big glass plate and they were all holding drinks the color of water with olives and sprigs of mint in them. When my parents have somebody over they get lemonade and if it's a real racy affair Schlitz in tall glasses with "They'll Do It Every Time"° cartoons stenciled on.

15   "That's all right," Lengel said. "But this isn't the beach." His repeating this struck me as funny, as if it had just occurred to him, and he had been thinking all these years the A & P was a great big dune and he was the head lifeguard. He didn't like my smiling—as I say he doesn't miss much—but he concentrates on giving the girls that sad Sunday-school-superintendent stare.

Queenie's blush is no sunburn now, and the plump one in plaid, that I liked better from the back—a really sweet can—pipes up, "We weren't doing any shopping. We just came in for the one thing."

"That makes no difference," Lengel tells her, and I could see from the way his eyes went that he hadn't noticed she was wearing a two-piece before. "We want you decently dressed when you come in here."

"We *are* decent," Queenie says suddenly, her lower lip pushing, getting sore now that she remembers her place, a place from which the crowd that runs the A & P must look pretty chummy. Fancy Herring Snacks flashed in her very blue eyes.

"Girls, I don't want to argue with you. After this come in here with your shoulders covered. It's our policy." He turns his back. That's policy for you. Policy is what the kingpins want. What the others want is juvenile delinquency.

20   All this while, the customers had been showing up with their carts but, you know, sheep, seeing a scene, they had all bunched up on Stokesie, who shook open a paper bag as gently as peeling a peach, not wanting to miss a word. I could feel in the silence everybody getting nervous, most of all Lengel, who asks me, "Sammy, have you rung up this purchase?"

I thought and said "No" but it wasn't about that I was thinking. I go through the punches, 4, 9, GROC, TOT—it's more complicated than you think, and after you do it often enough, it begins to make a little song, that you hear words to, in my case "Hello (*bing*) there, you (*gung*) hap-py *pee*-pul (*splat*)!"—the splat being the drawer flying out. I uncrease the bill, tenderly as you may imagine, it just having come from between the two smoothest scoops of vanilla I had ever known were there, and pass a half and a penny into her narrow pink palm, and nestle the herrings in a bag and twist its neck and hand it over, all the time thinking.

The girls, and who'd blame them, are in a hurry to get out, so I say "I quit" to Lengel quick enough for them to hear, hoping they'll stop and watch me, their unsuspected hero. They keep right on going, into the electric eye; the door flies open and they flicker across the lot to their car, Queenie and Plaid and Big Tall Goony-Goony (not that as raw material she was so bad), leaving me with Lengel and a kink in his eyebrow.

"Did you say something, Sammy?"

"I said I quit."

25   "I thought you did."

° **"They'll Do It Every Time"**: syndicated daily and Sunday cartoon created by Jimmy Harlo.

"You didn't have to embarrass them."

"It was they who were embarrassing us."

I started to say something that came out "Fiddle-de-doo." It's a saying of my grandmother's, and I know she would have been pleased.

"I don't think you know what you're saying," Lengel said.

30   "I know you don't," I said. "But I do." I pull the bow at the back of my apron and start shrugging it off my shoulders. A couple customers that had been heading for my slot begin to knock against each other, like scared pigs in a chute.

Lengel sighs and begins to look very patient and old and gray. He's been a friend of my parents for years. "Sammy, you don't want to do this to your Mom and Dad," he tells me. It's true, I don't. But it seems to me that once you begin a gesture it's fatal not to go through with it. I fold the apron, "Sammy" stitched in red on the pocket, and put it on the counter, and drop the bow tie on top of it. The bow tie is theirs, if you've ever wondered. "You'll feel this for the rest of your life," Lengel says, and I know that's true, too, but remembering how he made that pretty girl blush makes me so scrunchy inside I punch the No Sale tab and the machine whirs "pee-pul" and the drawer splats out. One advantage to this scene taking place in summer, I can follow this up with a clean exit, there's no fumbling around getting your coat and galoshes, I just saunter into the electric eye in my white shirt that my mother ironed the night before, and the door heaves itself open, and outside the sunshine is skating around on the asphalt.

I look around for my girls, but they're gone, of course. There wasn't anybody but some young married screaming with her children about some candy they didn't get by the door of a powder-blue Falcon° station wagon. Looking back in the big windows, over the bags of peat moss and aluminum lawn furniture stacked on the pavement, I could see Lengel in my place in the slot, checking the sheep through. His face was dark gray and his back stiff, as if he'd just had an injection of iron, and my stomach kind of fell as I felt how hard the world was going to be to me hereafter.

° **Falcon:** small car that had recently been introduced by the Ford Motor Company.

FOCUSED FREE WRITES

1. What do you think of Sammy? How would you characterize him? Is he young? Stupid? Misogynist? Old-fashioned? Go the text to find passages that support your opinion.

2. If you were to tell this story from another point of view, such as from Queenie's or Lengel's, what would it be like? What moments would be emphasized or altered, and in what ways?

3. What do you understand about the ending? Why does Sammy quit? What does his act of quitting mean?

4. How does Sammy's voice affect the story in significant ways? What diction or word choices are unique to Sammy? How would you characterize them?

CRITICAL Contexts

You Decide

Books don't usually provide readers with information on how best to read them, as this book has been providing in the various Contexts boxes. In fact, as we move through the chapters in this book, less context will accompany the text, and it will be up to you and your classmates to construct your own approaches to reading. Careful readers can use context clues within the text, prior knowledge, and other outside information to inform a reading.

Based on the different approaches or choices you have encountered so far in this book, what context do you believe is important to understanding Updike's story? What research would you do to understand it better from a historical perspective, a biographical perspective, a regional perspective? What kind of critical approach do you think would open this text up the most? What would the reader need to bring to this text to understand it fully?

PRE-READING Do you know of a time or a place where everyone seemed to be in everyone else's business? What was it like? How was this outside interest helpful? How was it not helpful?

William Faulkner (1897–1962). *Faulkner's writing reflects his own upbringing in a small Mississippi town by an old family who never quite recovered from the losses they suffered during the Civil War. His fiction is set in the imagined Yoknapatwpha County, which bears many similarities to the area around his hometown of Oxford. However, Faulkner's genius has been celebrated for far more than its regionalism. Faulkner's experimental style and his lyrical use of language, along with the tragic humor of his characters, won him the 1949 Nobel Prize for literature and success as a novelist and short story writer.*

William Faulkner

A ROSE FOR EMILY [1931]

I

When Miss Emily Grierson died, our whole town went to her funeral; the men through a sort of respectful affection for a fallen monument, the women mostly out of curiosity to see the inside of her house, which no one save an old manservant—a combined gardener and cook—had seen in at least ten years.

It was a big, squarish frame house that had once been white, decorated with cupolas and spires and scrolled balconies in the heavily lightsome style of the seventies, set on what had once been our most select street. But garages and cotton gins had encroached and obliterated even the august names of that neighborhood; only Miss Emily's house was left, lifting its stubborn and coquettish decay above the cotton wagons and the gasoline pumps—an eyesore among eyesores. And now Miss Emily had gone to join the representatives of those august names where they lay in the cedar-bemused cemetery among the ranked and anonymous graves of Union and Confederate soldiers who fell at the battle of Jefferson.

Alive, Miss Emily had been a tradition, a duty, and a care; a sort of hereditary obligation upon the town, dating from that day in 1894 when Colonel Sartoris, the mayor—he who fathered the edict that no Negro woman should appear on the streets without an apron—remitted her taxes, the dispensation dating from the death of her father on into perpetuity. Not that Miss Emily would have accepted charity. Colonel Sartoris invented an involved tale to the effect that Miss Emily's father had loaned money to the town, which the town, as a matter of business, preferred this way of repaying. Only a man of Colonel Sartoris' generation and thought could have invented it, and only a woman could have believed it.

When the next generation, with its more modern ideas, became mayors and aldermen, this arrangement created some little dissatisfaction. On the first of the year they mailed her a tax notice. February came, and there was no reply. They wrote her a formal letter, asking her to call at the sheriff's office at her convenience. A week later the mayor wrote her himself, offering to call or to send his car for her, and received in reply a note on paper of an archaic shape, in a thin, flowing calligraphy in faded ink, to the effect that she no longer went out at all. The tax notice was also enclosed, without comment.

5   They called a special meeting of the Board of Aldermen. A deputation waited upon her, knocked at the door through which no visitor had passed since she ceased giving china-painting lessons eight or ten years earlier. They were admitted by the old Negro into a dim hall from which a stairway mounted into still more shadow. It smelled of dust and disuse—a close, dank smell. The Negro led them into the parlor. It was furnished in heavy, leather-covered furniture. When the Negro opened the blinds of one window, they could see that the leather was cracked; and when they sat down, a faint dust rose sluggishly about their thighs, spinning with slow motes in the single sun-ray. On a tarnished gilt easel before the fireplace stood a crayon portrait of Miss Emily's father.

They rose when she entered—a small, fat woman in black, with a thin gold chain descending to her waist and vanishing into her belt, leaning on an ebony cane with a tarnished gold head. Her skeleton was small and spare; perhaps that was why what would have been merely plumpness in another was obesity in her. She looked bloated, like a body long submerged in motionless water, and of that pallid hue. Her eyes, lost in the fatty ridges of her face, looked like two small pieces of coal pressed into a lump of dough as they moved from one face to another while the visitors stated their errand.

She did not ask them to sit. She just stood in the door and listened quietly until the spokesman came to a stumbling halt. Then they could hear the invisible watch ticking at the end of the gold chain.

Her voice was dry and cold. "I have no taxes in Jefferson. Colonel Sartoris explained it to me. Perhaps one of you can gain access to the city records and satisfy yourselves."

"But we have. We are the city authorities, Miss Emily. Didn't you get a notice from the sheriff, signed by him?"

10 "I received a paper, yes," Miss Emily said. "Perhaps he considers himself the sheriff...I have no taxes in Jefferson."

"But there is nothing on the books to show that, you see. We must go by the—"

"See Colonel Sartoris. I have no taxes in Jefferson."

"But, Miss Emily—"

"See Colonel Sartoris." (Colonel Sartoris had been dead almost ten years.) "I have no taxes in Jefferson. Tobe!" The Negro appeared. "Show these gentlemen out."

II

15 So she vanquished them, horse and foot, just as she had vanquished their fathers thirty years before about the smell. That was two years after her father's death and a short time after her sweetheart—the one we believed would marry her— had deserted her. After her father's death she went out very little; after her sweetheart went away, people hardly saw her at all. A few of the ladies had the temerity to call, but were not received, and the only sign of life about the place was the Negro man—a young man then—going in and out with a market basket.

"Just as if a man—any man—could keep a kitchen properly," the ladies said; so they were not surprised when the smell developed. It was another link between the gross, teeming world and the high and mighty Griersons.

A neighbor, a woman, complained to the mayor, Judge Stevens, eighty years old.

"But what will you have me do about it, madam?" he said.

"Why, send her word to stop it," the woman said. "Isn't there a law?"

20 "I'm sure that won't be necessary," Judge Stevens said. "It's probably just a snake or a rat that nigger of hers killed in the yard. I'll speak to him about it."

The next day he received two more complaints, one from a man who came in diffident deprecation. "We really must do something about it, Judge. I'd be the last one in the world to bother Miss Emily, but we've got to do something." That night the Board of Aldermen met—three greybeards and one younger man, a member of the rising generation.

"It's simple enough," he said. "Send her word to have her place cleaned up. Give her a certain time to do it in, and if she don't..."

"Damn it, sir," Judge Stevens said, "will you accuse a lady to her face of smelling bad?"

So the next night, after midnight, four men crossed Miss Emily's lawn and slunk about the house like burglars, sniffing along the base of the brickwork and at the cellar openings while one of them performed a regular sowing motion with his hand out of a sack slung from his shoulder. They broke open the cellar door and sprinkled lime there, and in all the outbuildings. As they recrossed the lawn, a window that had been dark was lighted and Miss Emily sat in it, the light behind her, and her upright torso motionless as that of an idol. They crept quietly across the lawn and into the shadow of the locusts that lined the street. After a week or two the smell went away.

25 That was when people had begun to feel really sorry for her. People in our town, remembering how old lady Wyatt, her great-aunt, had gone completely

crazy at last, believed that the Griersons held themselves a little too high for what they really were. None of the young men were quite good enough to Miss Emily and such. We had long thought of them as a tableau; Miss Emily a slender figure in white in the background, her father a spraddled silhouette in the foreground, his back to her and clutching a horsewhip, the two of them framed by the backflung front door. So when she got to be thirty and was still single, we were not pleased exactly, but vindicated; even with insanity in the family she wouldn't have turned down all of her chances if they had really materialized.

When her father died, it got about that the house was all that was left to her; and in a way, people were glad. At last they could pity Miss Emily. Being left alone, and a pauper, she had become humanized. Now she too would know the old thrill and the old despair of a penny more or less.

The day after his death all the ladies prepared to call at the house and offer condolence and aid, as is our custom. Miss Emily met them at the door, dressed as usual and with no trace of grief on her face. She told them that her father was not dead. She did that for three days, with the ministers calling on her, and the doctors, trying to persuade her to let them dispose of the body. Just as they were about to resort to law and force, she broke down, and they buried her father quickly.

We did not say she was crazy then. We believed she had to do that. We remembered all the young men her father had driven away, and we knew that with nothing left, she would have to cling to that which had robbed her, as people will.

III

She was sick for a long time. When we saw her again, her hair was cut short, making her look like a girl, with a vague resemblance to those angels in colored church windows—sort of tragic and serene.

30 The town had just let the contracts for paving the sidewalks, and in the summer after her father's death they began the work. The construction company came with riggers and mules and machinery, and a foreman named Homer Barron, a Yankee—a big, dark, ready man, with a big voice and eyes lighter than his face. The little boys would follow in groups to hear him cuss the riggers, and the riggers singing in time to the rise and fall of picks. Pretty soon he knew everybody in town. Whenever you heard a lot of laughing anywhere about the square, Homer Barron would be in the center of the group. Presently we began to see him and Miss Emily on Sunday afternoons driving in the yellow-wheeled buggy and the matched team of bays from the livery stable.

At first we were glad that Miss Emily would have an interest, because the ladies all said, "Of course a Grierson would not think seriously of a Northerner, a day laborer." But there were still others, older people, who said that even grief could not cause a real lady to forget *noblesse oblige* without calling it *noblesse oblige*.[1] They just said, "Poor Emily. Her kinsfolk should come to her." She had some kin in Alabama; but years ago her father had fallen out with them over the estate of old lady Wyatt, the crazy woman, and there was no communication between the two families. They had not even been represented at the funeral.

---

[1] **nobless oblige:** The obligation, derived from upper-class birth, to be honorable and generous to those less fortunate.

And as soon as the old people said "Poor Emily," the whispering began. "Do you suppose it's really so?" they said to one another. "Of course it is. What else could...." This behind their hands; rustling of craned silk and satin behind jalousies[2] closed upon the sun of Sunday afternoon as the thin, swift clop-clop-clop of the matched team passed: "Poor Emily."

She carried her head high enough—even when we believed that she was fallen. It was as if she demanded more than ever the recognition of her dignity as the last Grierson; as if it had wanted that touch of earthiness to reaffirm her imperviousness. Like when she bought the rat poison, the arsenic. That was over a year after they had begun to say "Poor Emily," and while the two female cousins were visiting her.

"I want some poison," she said to the druggist. She was over thirty then, still a slight woman, though thinner than usual, with cold, haughty black eyes in a face the flesh of which was strained across the temples and about the eye sockets as you imagine a light-house-keeper's face ought to look. "I want some poison," she said.

35 "Yes, Miss Emily. What kind? For rats and such? I'd recom—"

"I want the best you have. I don't care what kind."

The druggist named several. "They'll kill anything up to an elephant. But what you want is—"

"Arsenic," Miss Emily said. "Is that a good one?"

"Is...arsenic? Yes, ma'am. But what you want—"

40 "I want arsenic."

The druggist looked down at her. She looked back at him, erect, her face like a strained flag. "Why, of course," the druggist said. "If that's what you want. But the law requires you to tell what you are going to use it for."

Miss Emily just stared at him, her head tilted back in order to look him eye for eye, until he looked away and went and got the arsenic and wrapped it up. The Negro delivery boy brought her the package; the druggist didn't come back. When she opened the package at home, there was written on the box, under the skull and bones: "For rats."

IV

So the next day we all said, "She will kill herself"; and we said it would be the best thing. When she had first begun to be seen with Homer Barron, we had said, "She will marry him." Then we said, "She will persuade him yet," because Homer himself had remarked—he liked men, and it was known that he drank with the younger men in the Elks Club—that he was not a marrying man. Later we said "Poor Emily" behind the jalousies as they passed on Sunday afternoon in the glittering buggy, Miss Emily with her head high and Homer Barron with his hat cocked and a cigar in his teeth, reins and whip in a yellow glove.

Then some of the ladies began to say that it was a disgrace to the town and a bad example to the young people. The men did not want to interfere, but at last the ladies forced the Baptist minister—Miss Emily's people were Episcopal—to call upon her. He would never divulge what happened during that interview, but he refused to go back again. The next Sunday they again drove about the

---

[2] **jalousies**: window blinds.

streets, and the following day the minister's wife wrote to Miss Emily's relations in Alabama.

45   So she had blood-kin under her roof again and we sat back to watch developments. At first nothing happened. Then we were sure that they were to be married. We learned that Miss Emily had been to the jeweler's and ordered a man's toilet set in silver, with the letters H.B. on each piece. Two days later we learned that she had bought a complete outfit of men's clothing, including a nightshirt, and we said, "They are married." We were really glad. We were glad because the two female cousins were even more Grierson than Miss Emily had ever been.

    So we were not surprised when Homer Barron—the streets had been finished some time since—was gone. We were a little disappointed that there was not a public blowing-off, but we believed that he had gone on to prepare for Miss Emily's coming, or to give her a chance to get rid of the cousins. (By that time it was a cabal, and we were all Miss Emily's allies to help circumvent the cousins.) Sure enough, after another week they departed. And, as we had expected all along, within three days Homer Barron was back in town. A neighbor saw the Negro man admit him at the kitchen door at dusk one evening.

    And that was the last we saw of Homer Barron. And of Miss Emily for some time. The Negro man went in and out with the market basket, but the front door remained closed. Now and then we would see her at a window for a moment, as the men did that night when they sprinkled the lime, but for almost six months she did not appear on the streets. Then we knew that this was to be expected too; as if that quality of her father which had thwarted her woman's life so many times had been too virulent and too furious to die.

    When we next saw Miss Emily, she had grown fat and her hair was turning gray. During the next few years it grew greyer and greyer until it attained an even pepper-and-salt iron gray, when it ceased turning. Up to the day of her death at seventy-four it was still that vigorous iron-gray, like the hair of an active man.

    From that time on her front door remained closed, save for a period of six or seven years, when she was about forty, during which she gave lessons in china painting. She fitted up a studio in one of the downstairs rooms, where the daughters and granddaughters of Colonel Sartoris' contemporaries were sent to her with the same regularity and in the same spirit that they were sent to church on Sundays with a twenty-five-cent piece for the collection plate. Meanwhile her taxes had been remitted.

50   Then the newer generation became the backbone and the spirit of the town, and the painting pupils grew up and fell away and did not send their children to her with boxes of color and tedious brushes and pictures cut from the ladies' magazines. The front door closed upon the last one and remained closed for good. When the town got free postal delivery, Miss Emily alone refused to let them fasten the metal numbers above her door and attach a mailbox to it. She would not listen to them.

    Daily, monthly, yearly we watched the Negro grow greyer and more stooped, going in and out with the market basket. Each December we sent her a tax notice, which would be returned by the post office a week later, unclaimed. Now and then we would see her in one of the downstairs windows—she had evidently shut up the top floor of the house—like the carven torso of an idol in a niche, looking or not looking at us, we could never tell which. Thus she passed from generation to generation—dear, inescapable, impervious, tranquil, and perverse.

And so she died. Fell ill in the house filled with dust and shadows, with only a doddering Negro man to wait on her. We did not even know she was sick; we had long since given up trying to get any information from the Negro. He talked to no one, probably not even to her, for his voice had grown harsh and rusty, as if from disuse.

She died in one of the downstairs rooms, in a heavy walnut bed with a curtain, her grey head propped on a pillow yellow and moldy with age and lack of sunlight.

V

The Negro met the first of the ladies at the front door and let them in, with their hushed, sibilant voices and their quick, curious glances, and then he disappeared. He walked right through the house and out the back and was not seen again.

The two female cousins came at once. They held the funeral on the second day, with the town coming to look at Miss Emily beneath a mass of bought flowers, with the crayon face of her father musing profoundly above the bier and the ladies sibilant and macabre; and the very old men—some in their brushed Confederate uniforms—on the porch and the lawn, talking of Miss Emily as if she had been a contemporary of theirs, believing that they had danced with her and courted her perhaps, confusing time with its mathematical progression, as the old do, to whom all the past is not a diminishing road but, instead, a huge meadow which no winter ever quite touches, divided from them now by the narrow bottle-neck of the most recent decade of years.

Already we knew that there was one room in that region above stairs which no one had seen in forty years, and which would have to be forced. They waited until Miss Emily was decently in the ground before they opened it.

The violence of breaking down the door seemed to fill this room with pervading dust. A thin, acrid pall as of the tomb seemed to lie everywhere upon this room decked and furnished as for a bridal: upon the valence curtains of faded rose color, upon the rose-shaded lights, upon the dressing table, upon the delicate array of crystal and the man's toilet things backed with tarnished silver, silver so tarnished that the monogram was obscured. Among them lay a collar and tie, as if they had just been removed, which, lifted, left upon the surface a pale crescent in the dust. Upon a chair hung the suit, carefully folded; beneath it the two mute shoes and the discarded socks.

The man himself lay in the bed.

For a long while we just stood there, looking down at the profound and fleshless grin. The body had apparently once lain in the attitude of an embrace, but now the long sleep that outlasts love, that conquers even the grimace of love, had cuckolded him. What was left of him, rotted beneath what was left of the nightshirt, had become inextricable from the bed in which he lay; and upon him and upon the pillow beside him lay that even coating of the patient and biding dust.

Then we noticed that in the second pillow was the indentation of a head. One of us lifted something from it, and leaning forward, that faint and invisible dust dry and acrid in the nostrils, we saw a long strand of iron-grey hair.

55

60

FOCUSED FREE WRITES

1. Who is telling this story? What parts of the text provide the evidence to support your conclusion as to the point of view?
2. Imagine how this story would be different if told from another point of view. Recast an event from the story from another perspective.
3. Examine how the story is constructed. How does Faulkner use foreshadowing or build suspense?
4. What is Faulkner's tone? What message is he communicating to the reader about the events that happen? What does he want the reader to understand? If his message is different from the narrator's, where is your evidence of that discrepancy?

CRITICAL Contexts

A Historical/Feminist Approach to Miss Emily

Faulkner has been the subject of prolific criticism and commentary. One approach taken by some critics is to situate Miss Emily in her contemporary context. For instance, we might try to understand the role of women in her time. In *Faulkner and Southern Womanhood*, critic Diane Roberts addresses the way Faulkner both produced and was produced by stereotypes of Southern femininity:

"[Miss Emily's] father does not lock her up physically..., but he does lock her into a rigid Old South concept of ladyhood, elevating her out of reach of the young men of Jefferson. Miss Emily's handicap, stemming from her being, the narrator reiterates, 'Grierson,' as if that were a synonym for *royal*, leads her finally to defy conventional community sexual standards for her gender and her rank...Miss Emily has been taught to repress 'gross' physicality, buying into her culture's insistence that white ladies be spirit not body, angel not whore." (158–159)

Some may call this way of reading a **historical approach** or a **feminist approach**.

Do you agree with this reading of the story? Why or why not?

The Act of Argument

Chapter 3 discussed the act of interpretation. Interpreting a literary text is the process of making meaning of its theme. Not only literary texts are interpreted, of course: people draw conclusions about the meanings of all kinds of things—movies, conversations, other people's behaviors. After talking with my friend about weekend plans, I might conclude that she was in a bad mood. She may not have come out and said that, but her words and tone might have conveyed the meaning I then gleaned through my interpretation.

Chapter 4 described the act of analysis. When you analyze a text, you ask questions such as why the author did something, or how the author created certain effects. When analyzing the conversation with my disgruntled friend, I might focus on her listless salutation, her uncharacteristic "I don't care, I don't care," and her abrupt good-bye as the elements that convey her "bad mood." I might find, though, that I want to call my friend back and talk to her about her mood. When I do, I would need to make an argument explaining the evidence I've gathered for why I think she's being a pill. In conversation, I would list those elements I analyzed in support of my interpretation. This is how I argue my case.

The focus of this chapter is making a good case for your interpretation and analysis so that readers can be persuaded that your stance toward the work is logical. While yours may not be the only interpretation of a given text, you must demonstrate that the meaning you are suggesting is plausible through argument. Your job is to be persuasive in gathering support for your stance on the text's meaning and perhaps to call into question alternative perspectives.

It may be useful to revisit the rhetorical triangle discussed in Chapter 1, which illustrates how meaning is made through the dynamic relationship among the writer, the text, and the readers. When crafting arguments as a writer, you must attend to those three things: your interpretation as the writer, the elements of the text, and the readers' perspectives.

Describe a time when you had to construct an argument. What did you do to make your case successful or unsuccessful?

The Writer: Evaluating Your Interpretation

In order to make a case for your argument, you must have something you are trying to prove—your interpretation or the meaning you have made of the text at hand. An interpretation must be guided by the following concerns:

- An interpretation is consistent with the elements in the text: characters, description, word choice, symbols, imagery, dialog, and so on.
- An interpretation can't be obviously contradicted by evidence in the text.

We might interpret the short story "A Rose for Emily" and decide it is about how the town bears some responsibility for Miss Emily's action. The emphasis here is on the writer drawing conclusions about the story's meaning. The interpretation may not encompass the meaning of the entire work, it may focus on the meaning of a character, a scene, or an object. The interpretation will emphasize *a* meaning, not *the* meaning.

How else might you interpret the story? How could you interpret a particular scene or character?

The Text: Evaluating Your Analysis

The second piece of making a case for your argument is marshalling your text as proof of this interpretation. You will want to determine what elements of the literary text serve as support for your argument. For example, in order to prove that the story chronicles the implication of the community, I would want to line up my evidence:

1. the role of gossip
2. the isolation of Miss Emily
3. the use of the first person plural point of view

I would need to focus just on information that supports my interpretation of this particular meaning, text, or character. Therefore, while certain speeches, characters, or scenes might be valuable or famous, they may not refer directly to the meaning on which I am focused. For example, while Southern history or Faulkner's biography may be interesting and important, it would not be essential for discussion of my interpretation or my meaning in this specific argument.

What evidence could you use to support your own interpretation of Faulkner's story?

The Readers: Evaluating Your Audience

The last aspect of the act of argument is evaluating your audience. When you craft this argument, you will want to consider how best to persuade your readers. Certainly, detailed support will make for a strong case; however, it may also be necessary to consider counterarguments or consider how you construct your argument.

In a class discussion of "A Rose for Emily," people may offer their own interpretations or perspectives. For example, someone might state that Miss Emily is just into necrophilia or is just plain crazy. When you discuss the chronology of Miss Emily's demise, you will want to react to this counterargument and illustrate how Miss Emily reacted to the world around her and her community.

To figure out how your readers might respond to your overall argument, you may want to evaluate the strength of your interpretation and then the strength of each of the various parts of your analysis. When you have a sense of which parts of your analysis are stronger or weaker, you can then decide how best to arrange your ideas to persuade your readers. The writing section at the end of this chapter will emphasize how to consider structuring your argument.

What are some counterarguments that might arise in reaction to your interpretation of Faulkner's short story? How would you argue against them? What would be the most persuasive way to make your case to your audience?

POEMS

Often readers assume the narrator of a poem is actually the poet. However, it is more accurate to think of the narrator as a **persona** or mask, the speaker of the work created by the poet. The following poems illustrate the range of possibilities and points of view for the poetic persona.

PRE-READING   Do you know anyone who is excessively possessive? How so? What do they do that is possessive?

PART II Writing in Response to Literature

Robert Browning (1812–1889). *Robert Browning, or "Mrs. Browning's husband" as he was known during the Victorian era in England, came to be known as one of the great poets of the age only in retrospect. His wife occupied the spotlight at the time, and their clandestine love affair and elopement to escape from her domineering father caused quite a stir in London society. Browning attended private school, received home tutoring, and studied Greek at the University of London for one year before venturing out on his own to write. While his own celebrity was initially eclipsed by his wife's renown, his collection of dramatic monologues* Dramatis Personae *(1864) and* The Ring and the Book *(1868–69) later received much acclaim.*

Robert Browning

MY LAST DUCHESS   [1842]

Ferrara

That's my last Duchess painted on the wall,
Looking as if she were alive. I call
That piece a wonder, now: Fra Pandolf's hands
Worked busily a day, and there she stands.
5   Will't please you sit and look at her? I said
"Frà Pandolf" by design, for never read
Strangers like you that pictured countenance,
The depth and passion of its earnest glance,
But to myself they turned (since none puts by
10 The curtain I have drawn for you, but I)
And seemed as they would ask me, if they durst,
How such a glance came there; so, not the first
Are you to turn and ask thus. Sir, 'twas not
Her husband's presence only, called that spot
15 Of joy into the Duchess' cheek: perhaps
Frà Pandolf chanced to say "Her mantle laps
Over my lady's wrist too much," or "Paint
Must never hope to reproduce the faint
Half-flush that dies along her throat": such stuff
20 Was courtesy, she thought, and cause enough
For calling up that spot of joy. She had
A heart—how shall I say?—too soon made glad,
Too easily impressed; she liked whate'er
She looked on, and her looks went everywhere.
25 Sir, 'twas all one! My favor at her breast,
The dropping of the daylight in the West,
The bough of cherries some officious fool
Broke in the orchard for her, the white mule
She rode with round the terrace—all and each
30 Would draw from her alike the approving speech,
Or blush, at least. She thanked men—good! but thanked
Somehow—I know not how—as if she ranked

My gift of a nine-hundred-years-old name
With anybody's gift. Who'd stoop to blame
35 This sort of trifling? Even had you skill
In speech—(which I have not)—to make your will
Quite clear to such an one, and say, "Just this
Or that in you disgusts me; here you miss,
Or there exceed the mark"—and if she let
40 Herself be lessoned so, nor plainly set
Her wits to yours, forsooth, and made excuse
—E'en then would be some stooping; and I choose
Never to stoop. Oh sir, she smiled, no doubt,
Whene'er I passed her; but who passed without
45 Much the same smile? This grew; I gave commands;
Then all smiles stopped together. There she stands
As if alive. Will't please you rise? We'll meet
The company below, then. I repeat,
The Count your master's known munificence
50 Is ample warrant that no just pretense
Of mine for dowry will be disallowed;
Though his fair daughter's self, as I avowed
At starting, is my object. Nay, we'll go
Together down, sir. Notice Neptune, though,
55 Taming a sea horse, thought a rarity,
Which Claus of Innsbruck cast in bronze for me!

FOCUSED FREE WRITES

1. This poem is a **dramatic monolog,** a form in which Browning was very adept. Dramatic monologs have certain elements that make them read like a play or a dialog, though we only hear one side speak:
   - an implied narrator
   - an implied setting and implied action
   - an implied interlocutor or listener
   Identify these elements in Browning's poem.
2. What are the most important lines in this Browning poem, and why? How is word choice significant?
3. How is the poem ironic, or how is the implied meaning different from the literal meaning? Is Browning trying to say something without just coming out and saying it?
4. How does knowing who is speaking impact our understanding of the poem?
5. Identify the uses of different kinds of irony: both verbal and dramatic.
6. What is the significance of the last few lines of "My Last Duchess"?

HISTORICAL Contexts

The Duke's Two Wives

Browning based this poem on an actual historical figure. Some versions publish the text with this historical background to help us understand the text in context.

EPIGRAPH Ferrara: In the sixteenth century, the duke of this Italian city arranged to marry a second time after the mysterious death of his very young first wife.

Some sources say the first wife or late wife was possibly as young as fourteen. Fra. Pandolf, however, is a fictitious artist.

How might knowing this information affect your understanding of the poem?

COMPARING THEMES

Read the next four poems in pairs to discuss how different styles may allow for different approaches to similar themes.

PRE-READING Both men and women struggle to find their own voices or identities as people. What specific struggles have women faced historically in this regard? What pressures do women face today to conform to the ideals of others?

Christina Rossetti (1830–1894).   *As the child of a Dante scholar and sister of two members of the Pre-Raphaelite Brotherhood, Rossetti grew up in a household that nurtured her interest in writing and the arts. Her mother's religious devotion was a significant influence and inspired her social work. It was perhaps this influence that encouraged her to turn down a wedding proposal and remain unmarried for her lifetime. Rossetti's poetry often reflects the tension between these influences.*

Christina Rossetti

IN AN ARTIST'S STUDIO   [1856]

One face looks out from all his canvases,
   One selfsame figure sits or walks or leans:
   We found her hidden just behind those screens,
4 That mirror gave back all her loveliness.
A queen in opal or in ruby dress,

A nameless girl in freshest summer-greens
A saint, an angel—every canvas means
8 That same one meaning, neither more nor less.
He feeds upon her face by day and night,
    And she with true kind eyes looks back on him,
Fair as the moon and joyful as the light:
12   Not wan with waiting, nor with sorrow dim;
Not as she is, but was when hope shone bright;
    Not as she is, but as she fills his dream.

Marge Piercy (1936–). *Born in Detriot, Michigan, Piercy's poetry has been characterized by its female subjects and interest in women's issues, a theme carried through in not only her poetry but also in her drama and her prose. Piercy was the first in her family to attend college. She worked various odd jobs as a young writer, and always remained dedicated to social activism in various forms before establishing herself as an amazingly prolific and diverse author.*

Marge Piercy

BARBIE DOLL

[1969]

This girlchild was born as usual
and presented dolls that did pee-pee
and miniature GE stoves and irons
and wee lipsticks the color of cherry candy.
5 Then in the magic of puberty, a classmate said:
You have a great big nose and fat legs.

She was healthy, tested intelligent,
possessed strong arms and back,
abundant sexual drive and manual dexterity.
10 She went to and fro apologizing.
Everyone saw a fat nose on thick legs.

She was advised to play coy,
exhorted to come on hearty,
exercise, diet, smile and wheedle.
15 Her good nature wore out
like a fan belt.
So she cut off her nose and her legs
and offered them up.
In the casket displayed on satin she lay
20 with the undertaker's cosmetics painted on,
a turned-up putty nose,
dressed in a pink and white nightie.
Doesn't she look pretty? everyone said.

Consummation at last.
25 To every woman a happy ending.

FOCUSED FREE WRITES

1. How do Browning's poems provide a good introduction to these poems?
2. What stories do these poems tell? How would you characterize their themes? What evidence can you identify as support for your interpretation?
3. Identify words you think are distinctive. Do these words have connotations that make them particularly powerful and suggestive beyond their denotations?
4. How can these poems be read from a feminist perspective or read to understand the particular struggles of fitting society's definition of "feminine"?

HISTORICAL Contexts

Comparing the Themes

Christina Rossetti's brother Dante Gabriel Rossetti was a very influential painter during the Victorian era. His paintings and those of his peers in the Pre-Raphaelite Brotherhood came to define a kind of female beauty fashionable for the era. His "stunners" were voluptuous, full-lipped, red-haired women, and they provided muses for his richly colorful portraits reflecting women in exotic romantic settings. Lizzie Siddal, one possible subject for the poem above, was a stunner discovered in a millinery shop who later became Rossetti's wife. A few short years after the poem was written, Lizzie, an artist, overdosed on laudanum when Rossetti went out to spend the evening with another "stunner."

There are some surprising similarities between Rossetti's poem and Piercy's, written 150 years later. We are very much aware today of the way media images represent and advertise a certain kind of female beauty. It has also come to light how such images can be dangerous.

How do these poems express similar concerns?

PRE-READING   What do you imagine the experience of war is like?

Thomas Hardy (1840–1928).   *Many details of Hardy's birthplace near Dorchester are recorded in his fictional accounts of Wessex county. Hardy began his career as an architect and sometimes poet before turning to fiction. After the age of thirty, he wrote sixteen novels, but abruptly stopped writing after Jude the Obscure was accused of immorality. He wrote nothing but poetry for the rest of his life. To this day, poets cite Hardy as a major influence.*

⬛ CHANNEL FIRING [1914]

That night your great guns, unawares,
Shook all our coffins as we lay,
And broke the chancel window squares,
We thought it was the Judgement-day

5 And sat upright. While drearisome
Arose the howl of wakened hounds:
The mouse let fall the altar-crumb,[1]
The worms drew back into their mounds,

The glebe cow[2] drooled. Till God called, "No;
10 It's gunnery practice out at sea
Just as before you went below;
The world is as it used to be:

"All nations striving strong to make
Red war yet redder. Mad as hatters
15 They do no more for Christés sake
Than you that are helpless in such matters.

"That this is not the judgement-hour
For some of them's a blessèd thing,
For if it were they'd have to scour
20 Hell's floor for so much threatening....

"Ha, ha. It will be warmer when
I blow the trumpet (if indeed
I ever do; for you are men,
And rest eternal sorely need)."

25 So down we lay again. "I wonder,
Will the world ever saner be,"
Said one, "than when He sent us under
In our indifferent century!"

And many a skeleton shook his head.
30 "Instead of preaching forty year,"
My neighbour Parson Thirdly said,
"I wish I had stuck to pipes and beer."

Again the guns disturbed the hour,
Roaring their readiness to avenge,
35 As far inland as Stourton tower
And Camelot, and starlit Stonehenge.[3]

---

[1] **altar-crumb:** crumbs from communion bread

[2] **glebe-cow:** cow kept in church pasture

[3] **Stourton Tower/ And Camelot, and starlit Stonehenge:** three landmarks in English history. Stourton Tower commemorates King Alfred's ninth-century defeat of the Danes. Camelot is the legendary site of King Arthur's Court, and Stonehenge is the circle of upright stones built as a ceremonial site before 1000 B.C.E.

Randall Jarrell (1914–1965). *Born in Nashville, Jarrell attended Vanderbilt and Kenyon before publishing his first book of poems and substantial criticism at the age of 28. After flying as a pilot during World War II, his poetry described the profound effects of war with unique insight and brought him much acclaim. In later years, he established himself as a poet, critic, teacher, editor, and even a children's writer.*

Randall Jarrell

DEATH OF A BALL TURRET GUNNER [1945]

From my mother's sleep I fell into the State
And I hunched in its belly till my wet fur froze.
Six miles from earth, loosed from its dream of life,
I woke to black flak and the nightmare fighters.
When I died they washed me out of the turret with a hose.

HISTORICAL and LITERARY
Contexts

The Literature of War

Artists have long sought to interpret war and to create moving tributes to the victims of war. The photographer Matthew Brady recorded on film the horrors of the Civil War. Picasso tried to interpret the Spanish Civil War in his renowned *Guernica*. Film versions of war, such as *Gallipoli* and *A Very Long Engagement*, have achieved critical and popular success. Tim O'Brien's fiction has attempted to make sense of the Vietnam War in novels and short stories like the one you read in Chapter 4, "The Things They Carried." Poets have written poems to record the ravages of war; in fact, a group of poets writing during World War I—Wilfred Owen, Rupert Brooke, Siegfried Sassoon, and Isaac Rosenberg, among others—have come to be known as the War Poets. Thomas Hardy also memorializes World War I. Thirty years later, Jarrell wrote poems about World War II.

Consider how artists might be inspired by war, or confounded by war. Explore some artists besides those you find here. What artists in your lifetime have been inspired by the experience of war? This may be a research project to pursue.

T. S. Eliot (1888–1965).   *Thomas Stearns Eliot was born to a New England family who had settled in St. Louis. After attending prep school in Boston and studying at Harvard, Eliot emigrated to London in 1915, where he worked in insurance at Lloyd's of London and later as an editor at Faber and Faber. After becoming a British citizen and member of the Church of England in 1927, Eliot served London as an air-raid warden. As a result of a career producing influential and iconic poetry, essays, and even verse plays that came to define Modernism, Eliot received the Nobel Prize in literature in 1948.*

T. S. Eliot
_____

THE LOVE SONG OF J. ALFRED PRUFROCK   [1915, 1911]

> *S'io credesse che mia risposta fosse*
> *A persona che mai tornasse al mondo,*
> *Questa fiamma staria senza piu scosse.*
> *Ma per ciò che giammai di questo fondo*
> *Non tornò vivo alcun, s'i'odo il vero,*
> *Senza tema d'infamia ti rispondo.*[1]

Let us go then, you and I,
When the evening is spread out against the sky
Like a patient etherized upon a table;
Let us go, through certain half-deserted streets,
5 The muttering retreats
Of restless nights in one-night cheap hotels
And sawdust restaurants with oyster shells;
Streets that follow like a tedious argument
Of insidious intent
10 To lead you to an overwhelming question...
Oh, do not ask, "What is it?"
Let us go and make our visit.

In the room the women come and go
Talking of Michelangelo.

15 The yellow fog that rubs its back upon the windowpanes,
The yellow smoke that rubs its muzzle on the windowpanes
Licked its tongue into the corners of the evening,
Lingered upon the pools that stand in drains,
Let fall upon its back the soot that falls from chimneys,
20 Slipped by the terrace, made a sudden leap,
And seeing that it was a soft October night,
Curled once about the house, and fell asleep.

And indeed there will be time[2]
For the yellow smoke that slides along the street,

_____

[1] **Epigraph:** In Dante's *Inferno* XXVII, the spirit, Guido da Montefeltro, responds to Dante's inquiry about his life's story as follows: "If I thought that my answer were to one who might ever return to this world, this flame would shake no more; but since from this depth none ever returned alive, if what I hear is true, I answer you without fear of infamy."

[2] **There will be time** refers to Ecclesiastes 3:1-8: "To everything there is a season, and a time to every purpose under heaven."

25 Rubbing its back upon the windowpanes;
There will be time, there will be time
To prepare a face to meet the faces that you meet;
There will be time to murder and create,
And time for all the works and days of hands
30 That lift and drop a question on your plate;
Time for you and time for me,
And time yet for a hundred indecisions,
And for a hundred visions and revisions,
Before the taking of a toast and tea.

35 In the room the women come and go
Talking of Michelangelo.

And indeed there will be time
To wonder, "Do I dare?" and, "Do I dare?"
Time to turn back and descend the stair,
40 With a bald spot in the middle of my hair—
(They will say: "How his hair is growing thin!")
My morning coat, my collar mounting firmly to the chin,
My necktie rich and modest, but asserted by a simple pin—
(They will say: "But how his arms and legs are thin!")
45 Do I dare
Disturb the universe?
In a minute there is time
For decisions and revisions which a minute will reverse.

For I have known them all already, known them all—
50 Have known the evenings, mornings, afternoons,
I have measured out my life with coffee spoons;
I know the voices dying with a dying fall
Beneath the music from a farther room.
      So how should I presume?

55 And I have known the eyes already, known them all—
The eyes that fix you in a formulated phrase,
And when I am formulated, sprawling on a pin,
When I am pinned and wriggling on the wall,
Then how should I begin
60 To spit out all the butt-ends of my days and ways?
And how should I presume?

And I have known the arms already, known them all—
Arms that are braceleted and white and bare
(But in the lamplight, downed with light brown hair!)
65 Is it perfume from a dress
That makes me so digress?
Arms that lie along a table, or wrap about a shawl.
      And should I then presume?
      And how should I begin?

* * * * *

70 Shall I say, I have gone at dusk through narrow streets
And watched the smoke that rises from the pipes
Of lonely men in shirt-sleeves, leaning out of windows?...
I should have been a pair of ragged claws
Scuttling across the floors of silent seas.

* * * * *

75 And the afternoon, the evening, sleeps so peacefully!
Smoothed by long fingers,
Asleep...tired...or it malingers,
Stretched on the floor, here beside you and me.
Should I, after tea and cakes and ices,
80 Have the strength to force the moment to its crisis?
But though I have wept and fasted, wept and prayed,
Though I have seen my head (grown slightly bald) brought in upon a platter,[3]
I am no prophet—and here's no great matter;
I have seen the moment of my greatness flicker,
85 And I have seen the eternal Footman hold my coat, and snicker,
And in short, I was afraid.

And would it have been worth it, after all,
After the cups, the marmalade, the tea,
Among the porcelain, among some talk of you and me,
90 Would it have been worth while,
To have bitten off the matter with a smile,
To have squeezed the universe into a ball[4]
To roll it toward some overwhelming question,
To say: "I am Lazarus, come from the dead,
Come back to tell you all, I shall tell you all"—
95 If one, settling a pillow by her head,
        Should say: "That is not what I meant at all.
        That is not it, at all."

And would it have been worth it, after all,
100 Would it have been worth while,
After the sunsets and the dooryards and the sprinkled streets,
After the novels, after the teacups, after the skirts that trail along the floor—
And this, and so much more?—
It is impossible to say just what I mean!
105 But as if a magic lantern threw the nerves in patterns on a screen:
Would it have been worth while
If one, settling a pillow or throwing off a shawl,
And turning toward the window, should say:
        "That is not it at all,
110   That is not what I meant, at all."

* * * * *

---

[3] **platter:** a reference to John the Baptist (Matthew 14:1-12).

[4] **squeezed the universe into a ball:** See lines 41–42 of Marvell's "To His Coy Mistress" (chapter six).

No! I am not Prince Hamlet, nor was meant to be;
Am an attendant lord, one that will do
To swell a progress, start a scene or two,
Advise the prince; no doubt, an easy tool,
115 Deferential, glad to be of use,
Politic, cautious, and meticulous;
Full of high sentence, but a bit obtuse;
At times, indeed, almost ridiculous—
Almost, at times, the Fool.

120 I grow old...I grow old...
I shall wear the bottoms of my trousers rolled.

Shall I part my hair behind? Do I dare to eat a peach?
I shall wear white flannel trousers, and walk upon the beach.
I have heard the mermaids singing, each to each.

125 I do not think that they will sing to me.

I have seen them riding seaward on the waves,
Combing the white hair of the waves blown back
When the wind blows the water white and black.

We have lingered in the chambers of the sea
130 By sea-girls wreathed with seaweed red and brown,
Till human voices wake us, and we drown.

FOCUSED FREE WRITES

1. Who is J. Alfred Prufrock? What is he doing during the course of the poem? What is he thinking about? Describe him as a character, and construct the plot of the poem.
2. What words, lines, and images are important in this poem? Why?
3. What is the meaning of the title? Prufrock's name?
4. What allusions can you identify based on the footnotes and based on your own reading experiences?
5. What elements of poetry can you identify in this poem? Plot? Character? Setting? Voice? Diction? Imagery? Symbolism?

LITERARY Contexts

Making Meaning of *Prufrock*

Prufrock illustrates both the frustration and joy of poetry, and in a way, of all literature. What can be frustrating is that a number of themes are at work. How can a reader sort them out? The joy, however, is that readers may arrive at multiple interpretations and can make a case for any given meaning based on their understandings. But the meaning of the poem must be guided by a careful reading of the text. The reader can't just make it up! In *Prufrock*, a number of themes seem to be at work:

Is Prufrock a seduction poem or a "seize the day" poem? Is it revising some of the themes we see in Marvell's "To His Coy Mistress" or Robert Herrick "To the Virgins, to Make Much of Time"? Does the poem narrate a man paralyzed by action or urging action?

Is *Prufrock* a poem about the modern dilemma or a kind of disillusionment with society and civilization? Is the poem lamenting a culture that metes out time by "coffee spoons" or a society too pedestrian for mermaids?

Is the poem about the universal fear of growing old or aging? Is the main character lamenting aging, balding, and their corresponding figurative impotence? Is he anxious about the passage of time?

Is the poem about finding one's place in the world, or knowing with certainty when and how to act? Do we hear echoes of Hamlet's "To be or not to be..." when the paralyzed Prufrock wonders if he dares to eat a peach or if he can "have the strength to force the moment to its crisis"?

Find evidence to support any of the above interpretations.

What other meanings could be found in this poem? How would you support that meaning?

Arguing for an Interpretation

In this chapter, you have been engaged in the critical thinking act of argument. Now it is time to translate this thinking work into a formal written project. You will need to use the skills of interpretation and analysis to construct an argument about one of the works in this chapter. You are going to prove your interpretation of the meaning of some aspect of this text through your analysis or close reading. You might determine a meaning of the work as a whole or the meaning of some aspect of the text like a character, a scene, or a particular symbol. Your job will be to prove how the text makes meaning in some way.

Using Visual Techniques to Discover Ideas

The first step will be to determine what you might want to write about. You can always return to Focused Free Writes or class notes developed as you were reading the works for the first time. These might indicate what ideas were of interest to you or moments you wanted to investigate further. You might employ some of the prewriting tools discussed in Chapter 1. However, some writers work visually and find that they need to map out ideas before engaging in writing:

Clustering

Clustering or **webbing** is a form of prewriting or brainstorming in which a stimulus text, word, character, scene, object, or idea is set out as a starting point for generating ideas. Associations with this word are made through connected bubbles. Patterns and connections can be mapped out. For example, secondary bubbles might be dedicated to elements of literature like "character," "plot," and so on.

For example, I might begin with the character of the Duchess from Browning's poem. In brainstorming about her, I might include bubbles about her portrait, her favorite things, and the footnote. In so doing, I might recognize that fondness for objects was different from her husband and this might direct me to a potential topic.

Jot Listing

Jot listing is a form of prewriting or brainstorming in which a blank piece of paper is used to arrange lists of related ideas. By listing ideas and identifying their relationships by proximity, writers can determine fruitful topics and possible support as well as hierarchies of ideas and relationships among them.

For example, I might begin with a blank piece of paper and no idea for a topic at all. I might know that I want to address women writers or women characters from some of the works in this chapter. I could construct various jot lists about these topics and look at those to figure out which I have the most to say about:

Emily
daughter
townswoman
south
rules of society

Duchess

young
easily pleased
like an object—an art object
most likely murdered

In an Artist's Studio

appears as different women
never like herself
artist consumes her
beauty fades

Shaping a Persuasive Thesis

When writing an argument, the thesis is the single most important component; the success of the paper rides on the viability of the thesis. A thesis is an assertion, a claim staked, a point made, something that needs proving to be true.

It is not a summary: "The Duchess is dead."

This summarizes part of the plot of the play and does not need to be proved. It is a fact.

This thesis could be improved and expanded to include some interpretative element explaining the meaning of this act to the play: "The Duchess' demise was because she had favorite things that weren't the same as her husband's favorite things."

This summary could be further improved by expanding it to include some analytical components demonstrating the how and why of this interpretation or by alluding to the evidence in support of this interpretation: "While the Duchess is made glad by objects in the world around her, the Duke wants to own and possess his favorite things."

Finally, in reflecting on this thesis—for instance, while clustering potential support for that tentative thesis statement—the writer might be able to connect it to other ideas in the play. Another way to improve it would be to focus it further to go into more detail about the argument to come.

- To discuss both the Duchess' death and the reason for it, the writer might expand the thesis like this: "The Duchess serves as an unlikely foil to the Duke in their reactions to enjoying beautiful things in the world around them."
- To focus the discussion, the writer might argue that "the final image of the poem of the sea horse is the key that unlocks the meaning and characters of the whole poem."

EXERCISES

Take the following topic or summary statements and develop them into persuasive thesis statements. Consider expanding them to include both interpretive and analytical elements like those illustrated previously.

1. In Faulkner's "A Rose for Emily," Emily Grierson dies alone.
2. In Browning's "My Last Duchess," the Duchess makes her husband mad.
3. In Rossetti's "In an Artist's Studio," the artist paints lots of pictures of a woman.

Now, return to these potential theses and cluster or list potential support. Rework your thesis statement based on this prewriting.

Writing to Advance the Thesis
Support Your Interpretation Through Analysis

After you have a thesis statement, brainstorm potential support. Each supporting idea (a character, a line, a speech, a scene, a symbol, a plot point, a stylistic element) might have its own paragraph. These paragraphs should be articulated as support for your thesis.

For example, you can see in Erin's essay at the end of the chapter that she outlined support for her thesis about Emily Grierson as a product of her social environment: her father, the townspeople, and her status in this southern town.

Consider writing each paragraph as a module. In other words, write each paragraph as a self-contained unit, without transitions to other paragraphs. This should make it easier to rearrange the paragraphs later. For this draft, begin each paragraph with a statement relating it to the thesis such as: "This paragraph demonstrates that..."

Support Your Argument by Addressing Counterarguments

As you draft, keep track of arguments against your case. Consider what other interpretations could be made. Take note of the arguments your classmates have come up with in class discussions or group work; they may be useful to you. You may want to suggest that certain other arguments are not as likely or accurate or provocative as your own, or you may need to allow for the possibility that aspects of others' arguments do have merit.

- Consider soliciting peer feedback.
- You might get other students in your class to rate your thesis statement on a scale of 1 to 10. Are people generally in favor of your interpretation or not? Will your audience be resistant to your argument?
- Next, have your peers rank each paragraph, evaluating the success of the supporting evidence for the thesis. Ask them to order the paragraphs with 1 being the strongest on down to 4 or 5 as the weakest, depending on the number of paragraphs.
- Finally, ask your peer reviewers to write responses to these paragraphs. Ask them to argue against you.

All of these responses can be useful for revising and strengthening your argument. You should plan to anticipate counterarguments in your own argument.

STUDENT WRITER In Erin's Words...

I wanted to craft my introduction keeping in mind my classmates' comments about Miss Emily's perversions and insanity. I wanted to address the idea that the town and society "enabled" her behavior. What she did was kind of their fault too!

Revising with Your Audience in Mind
Write the Introduction and Conclusion

Identify your audience for this paper. Your teacher will be one audience member, and your classmates will certainly constitute other readers. What if this essay were submitted to a departmental or university writing contest? What if it were submitted to the publisher for inclusion in this textbook? Imagine to whom you might appeal in this essay. Assume your readers have read the text. Imagine different introductions and conclusions in relation to these different audiences. What common knowledge might you share with your readers that might be used to craft a provocative introduction? What sorts of implications might indicate the significance of your project in your conclusion and connect with a particular audience?

Strengthen Weaker Paragraphs

Be certain every paragraph is as strong as it can be. Find textual evidence to support your interpretation: use paraphrase, summary, or direct quotations. Revise those paragraphs readers ranked as weak and include further support.

Arrange Your Paragraphs

Consider the order in which you will present your ideas. Chronological order based on the location where you evidence appears in the text is but one example. You can be strategic as you organize your support.

Emphatic order is the arrangement of ideas according to their importance. Do you want your strongest, most important point to hit the reader immediately, or do you want to build up to your strongest examples? Do you have simple support you could address briefly before developing a more involved example? Depending on your topic and your purpose, you should consider what effect these points may have on your readers. There are two arrangements of ideas well suited to persuading readers:

- Weakest piece of analysis
- Stronger piece of analysis
- Strongest piece of analysis

The other order, often the most persuasive, is this:

- Second strongest analysis
- Weakest analysis
- Strongest analysis

STUDENT WRITER In Erin's Words . . .

I wanted to be sure to build up to the murder, a moment where the environment had really allowed her to have this extraordinary sense of herself and, thus, "permitted" murder. Therefore, I arranged her essay to build to this strongest evidence.

Decide Where to Handle Other Interpretations

Respond to your peers' feedback and their concerns or arguments in your own paper.

- You might eliminate counterclaims in your introduction as a lead:
  "While some readers focus on the question of Miss Emily's sanity, it is necessary to focus on the town's contributions to her state of mind."

- You might refute another interpretation in each paragraph:
  "Some readers read 'Then all smiles stopped together' as entirely innocent; however, that reading is not plausible when the title of the poem, the role of the interlocutor, and the last line are considered."
- You might set up specific paragraphs for counterarguments. Writers often set up the section before the conclusion as a location to finally dismiss any counterclaims and to read the text definitely in favor of their interpretation. If your classmates keep concluding that Emily is "just crazy," you might focus an entire paragraph on the evidence that her social environment created her.

Editing and Proofreading Your Argument

- **Focus on Your Audience**. Build a relationship with your readers and try to draw them in. Make them enthusiastic about your topic by including specific and unique examples. Explain your thinking through precise, detailed, vivid language.
- **Make Connections between the Paragraphs** Use smooth and logical transitions that explain the connections between paragraphs and the relationship to the thesis.
- **Repeat Key Words from the Thesis Statement.** Try to balance repetition of words from your thesis statement with a strategic use of synonyms.
- **Proofread.** Again, and it cannot be overemphasized, be certain to be precise in choosing words and constructing sentences. See the proofreading checklist in Chapter 4.

Sample Student Paper

Erin Christian's biography may be found on page 567.

Erin Christian

English 102

October 6 2010

Effects of the Social Environment on Emily Grierson

in "A Rose for Emily"

In Faulkner's "A Rose for Emily," Miss Emily Grierson detested and defied all forms of change. She is completely static, never faltering for a moment in her convictions against the new developments encroaching upon her protected and beloved world. While appearing stubborn, curious, misguided, and even regal by the people of Jefferson, Emily Grierson is but a product of her social environment. Her father's overly controlling nature formed and fueled her ideals of grand Southern ways as well as her aggrandized view of her family status. This status she carried with her into ruin. In all her actions taken and attitudes held she never abandoned it and always strived to preserve it as the townspeople, out of a sort of pitiful reverence for such a curious relic, continued through the years to allow her to wallow in her illusions thereby enabling Miss Emily's tragic demise.

Miss Emily's father was steeped in the traditions and values prized by families with money in the Old South, no matter the fact that his death left his only daughter a pauper. The Griersons had long held themselves in high regard and as a family of privilege. Emily's father used this high self-regard to create an utterly consuming and confining world for Emily that kept its tight hold on her well after his death and up to hers. The people in Jefferson believed, in fact, that "the Griersons held themselves a little too high for what they really were"(223). The scene of "Miss Emily a slender figure in white in the background, her father a straddled silhouette in the foreground, his back to her and clutching a horsewhip" reminded the townsfolk that none "of the young men were quite good enough for Miss Emily and such" (223). Her father fashioned an exclusive world about her, providing her a sense of security and comfort while controlling her in every way.

His death began Emily's struggle to maintain the only world she knew while serving as a catalyst for its degeneration. The demise of her father marked the beginning of her world showing signs of change and her reaction to it showcased her unwilling-ness to accept alteration in her world. For three days after his death she fended off the ladies of the town offering condolence and aid, the ministers, and even the doctors attempting to let her allow them to dispose of the body. She didn't dress in mourn-ing attire, nor did she exhibit grief. She denied the fact that he was even dead until it came to the point where they would have to take him by force. Then, and only then, did she break down and allow them to bury her father. It was this steadfast defiance to change that led the townspeople to remark that it was as "if that quality of her father which had thwarted her woman's life so many times had been too virulent and too furious to die" (225).

While the rest of society moved ahead with the passage of time, Miss Emily needed to keep herself removed from and above society. She needed to maintain the comfort and security present in her world of gentile Southern living, and once left alone, she needed her family status more than ever to maintain her quality of life. Miss Emily was left to "cling to that which robbed her" (223) because she knew of nothing else and was unwilling to adapt. The people of Jefferson recognized this about her and took up feeling responsible for upholding her illusions of grandeur, referring to her as "a tradition, a duty, and a care; a sort of hereditary obligation upon the town" (221). Out of both pity and wonder, they catered to Emily, allowing her to remain an artifact in time against the face of an evolving society. In 1894, following her father's death, Mayor Colonel Sartoris remitted Miss Emily's taxes dating from the death of her father onward. Knowing the Griersons' ways and that Miss Emily would never have accepted charity, he invented a story to tell her that this was just the town's way of repaying her for money her father loaned in years past.

When someone challenged Miss Emily's ways she "vanquished them, horse and foot" (222). She was raised a Grierson, and far be it from the mere townspeople to disrupt her sense of dignity and purpose by attempting to have her alter her ways. When some of the ladies in the town forced the Baptist minister to confront Miss Emily on her disgraceful cavorting with Homer, he "would never divulge what happened during that interview, but he refused to go back again" (224). As the new generation gained power in the town and the postal service became active in Jefferson, Miss Emily remained the only one to blatantly refuse to allow them to place "metal numbers on her door and attach a mailbox to it" (225). They repeatedly sent her tax notices which were always returned unclaimed, and when they came to her home to confront her about it, she coldly referred them to a long dead Colonel Sartoris and sent them on their way.

In so doing, the town allowed Miss Emily to retain her lofty self-image as the last of a dying breed. This treatment of Emily eventually allowed her to get away with sheer murder. She demanded "more than ever the recognition of her dignity as the last Grierson" (224) as she bought the arsenic used to kill Homer, looking the druggist silently in the eyes and obtaining the poison without question. When the smell of Homer's decay permeated the town, the ladies of Jefferson chalked it up to poor kitchen management by Tobe and weren't the least surprised when it developed. The beastly act of murder was an unthinkable act to connect with a Grierson. In response to a suggestion made by a younger man to confront Miss Emily on the offensive odor, Judge Stevens was incensed, saying, "Dammit, sir, will you accuse a lady to her face of smelling bad?" (222). The Board of Aldermen decided that rather than risk offending Miss Emily and hurting her sense of dignity, it would be better to spread lime about the house under cover of darkness to end the smell. Thus, Homer Barron vanished from the world for 40 years. The only other person to know for certain Homer's fate was Tobe, her servant. But his instilled loyalty to Miss Emily and her family, along with his need to care for her well being, prevented him from ever making it known. Only after she died did he relieve himself of his duty and abandon the home to those who discovered Miss Emily's dark secret. Miss Emily knew that her status, and the pity afforded to her by those who whis-pered "poor Emily" behind her back as well as the unfaltering loyalty of Tobe, would allow her to take Homer from the world and thus take a vital step to make sure hers was preserved against change so she could remain to live out her life unmolested.

While the townspeople could have resorted to force and turned the law against her, Miss Emily knew that they would not. In her early years they left her alone out of a desire to not insult her as a Grierson, and as time went on they were merely catering to the whims of a reclusive elderly woman who was doing no harm in being set in her ways. Either way, Miss Emily knew that she had to give in to no one and, thus, did all she could to cling onto the way of life she revered and was raised with. She forever remained the girl who her father controlled so effectively, even keeping his crayon portrait she drew in a place of honor in her parlor until her death where it mused "profoundly over the bier" (226) at her funeral.

And she was aided to remain as such by the people of Jefferson, never forced into changing, and left by them to pass from "generation to generation—dear, inescapable, impervious, tranquil, and perverse" (226).

Work Cited

Faulkner, William. "A Rose for Emily." *Literature: Reading to Write*. Ed. Elizabeth Howells. New York: Pearson, 2010. 220–226. Print.

6
FAMILIES AND THEIR CHARACTERS
Comparing Works of Literature

Family Drama. The First Family (Barack, Sasha, Michelle, and Malia Obama) pose for a family portrait. Family portraits often convey what is ideal about a family. People pose in their best clothes with happy smiles. A favorite topic of literature, however, is to explore what is less than ideal about family dynamics and can disclose the complicated relationships within families. What sorts of ideals do holiday photos or family pictures convey about your family? What stories reside behind those images? Today, we see household dramas on the cover of every single tabloid magazine. Why are private dramas so fascinating to the general public?

Do you have any characters in your family?

Some of the first stories that we hear growing up are family stories, stories like the tragedy of Aunt Lucy's first marriage and the comedy of Uncle Roy's bad dog, stories of grandfather going off to World War I and of the day you were born. Early on, we learn to tell our lives as stories peopled by our families. We begin to understand our identities as individuals because of, or in spite of, these stories.

The rich intense setting of the family is central to many of our most compelling texts, from Shakespeare to *The Simpsons*, from *Gone with the Wind* to *Go Down Moses*. Sitcoms often are situated in family environments, and television families are a staple for programming from *The Waltons* and *Little House on the Prairie* to *The Osbournes* and *The Sopranos*. Tragedy and drama arise when family members become too extreme in their roles, such as the mother in *The Manchurian Candidate,* who is controlling to the point of literally brainwashing her son. Humor is created when family members subvert conventional roles such as Marge, the mother/cop in *Fargo*.

We can look at the texts in this chapter with a special eye toward **character**. Each of the characters in the following literary texts appears in certain family roles: mother, father, sister, brother. Many of them struggle with the responsibilities and limitations of their roles just as real people do. Each role may embody **stereotypes** such as the father as the big, strong provider and the mother as the caring helpmate, and characters may epitomize or challenge these traditional stereotypes. Characters who maintain their roles without changing may be **flat characters** or even **stock characters**. Characters who develop and change over the course of the story are **round** or **dynamic characters**.

It can be useful to compare and contrast characters. In order to recognize the qualities of a good father or mother, we might see those qualities emphasized in one character as opposed to another with different qualities, or in relief against the background of their family. For example, in *The Glass Menagerie*, reprinted in Chapter 4, we see the reaction of children to their mother in the characters of Laura and Tom Wingfield. A secondary character, like Jim O'Connor, might be considered as a foil to Tom or Laura. A **foil** is a minor character who contrasts with a major character and, in so doing, highlights various facets of the main character's personality. This act of comparison and contrast will be a focus of this chapter. It can be useful to compare not only characters in a single work but characters in two works, or two works themselves, to better understand particular themes.

Identify some characters from books or stories, movies or TV shows, who are round or flat family members. Develop a list of some examples. What similarities can you identify among them?

STORIES

The following stories provide useful illustrations of a range of family dynamics and a spectrum of characters within families. Each of the stories focuses specifically on the tensions between children and their parents.

What has frustrated you about your mother through the years?

Flannery O'Connor (1925–1964). *Mary Flannery O'Connor was born in Savannah, Georgia, just across the square from the Catholic Church her family attended. Her father's ill health due to the lupus that she, too, would inherit sent Mary Flannery and her family to Milledgeville, Georgia. After graduating from Peabody High School, O'Connor enrolled in Georgia State College for Women and focused on writing. Publishing under the name Flannery, O'Connor's early success earned her a fellowship to the Iowa Writer's Workshop for an MFA and time at the Yaddo artist's colony in New York. A bout with lupus sent her back to Milledgeville after a few years, but O'Connor continued to write, earning fellowships and grants that enabled her to continue to write the novels and short stories that earned her much acclaim.*

Flannery O'Connor

EVERYTHING THAT RISES MUST CONVERGE [1950]

Her doctor had told Julian's mother that she must lose twenty pounds on account of her blood pressure, so on Wednesday nights Julian had to take her downtown on the bus for a reducing class at the Y. The reducing class was designed for working girls over fifty, who weighed from 165 to 200 pounds. His mother was one of the slimmer ones, but she said ladies did not tell their age or weight. She would not ride the buses by herself at night since they had been integrated, and because the reducing class was one of her few pleasures, necessary for her health, and *free*, she said Julian could at least put himself out to take her, considering all she did for him. Julian did not like to consider all she did for him, but every Wednesday night he braced himself and took her.

She was almost ready to go, standing before the hall mirror, putting on her hat, while he, his hands behind him, appeared pinned to the door frame, waiting like Saint Sebastian for the arrows to begin piercing him. The hat was new and had cost her seven dollars and a half. She kept saying, "Maybe I shouldn't have paid that for it. No, I shouldn't have. I'll take it off and return it tomorrow. I shouldn't have bought it."

Julian raised his eyes to heaven. "Yes, you should have bought it," he said. "Put it on and let's go." It was a hideous hat. A purple velvet flap came down on one side of it and stood up on the other; the rest of it was green and looked like a cushion with the stuffing out. He decided it was less comical than jaunty and pathetic. Everything that gave her pleasure was small and depressed him.

She lifted the hat one more time and set it down slowly on top of her head. Two wings of gray hair protruded on either side of her florid face, but her eyes, sky-blue, were as innocent and untouched by experience as they must have been when she was ten. Were it not that she was a widow who had struggled fiercely to feed and clothe and put him through school and who was supporting him still, "until he got on his feet," she might have been a little girl that he had to take to town.

"It's all right, it's all right," he said. "Let's go." He opened the door himself and started down the walk to get her going. The sky was a dying violet and the houses stood out darkly against it, bulbous liver-colored monstrosities of a uniform ugliness though no two were alike. Since this had been a fashionable neighborhood forty years ago, his mother persisted in thinking they did well to have an apartment in it. Each house had a narrow collar of dirt around it in which sat, usually, a grubby child. Julian walked with his hands in his pockets, his head down and thrust forward and his eyes glazed with the determination to make himself completely numb during the time he would be sacrificed to her pleasure.

The door closed and he turned to find the dumpy figure, surmounted by the atrocious hat, coming toward him. "Well," she said, "you only live once and paying a little more for it, I at least won't meet myself coming and going."

"Some day I'll start making money," Julian said gloomily—he knew he never would—"and you can have one of those jokes whenever you take the fit." But first they would move. He visualized a place where the nearest neighbors would be three miles away on either side.

"I think you're doing fine," she said, drawing on her gloves. "You've only been out of school a year. Rome wasn't built in a day."

She was one of the few members of the Y reducing class who arrived in hat and gloves and who had a son who had been to college. "It takes time," she said, "and the world is in such a mess. This hat looked better on me than any of the others, though when she brought it out I said, 'Take that thing back. I wouldn't have it on my head,' and she said, 'Now wait till you see it on,' and when she put it on me, I said, 'We-ull,' and she said, 'If you ask me, that hat does something for you and you do something for the hat, and besides,' she said, 'with that hat, you won't meet yourself coming and going.'"

Julian thought he could have stood his lot better if she had been selfish, if she had been an old hag who drank and screamed at him. He walked along, saturated in depression, as if in the midst of his martyrdom he had lost his faith. Catching sight of his long, hopeless, irritated face, she stopped suddenly with a grief-stricken look, and pulled back on his arm. "Wait on me," she said. "I'm going back to the house and take this thing off and tomorrow I'm going to return it, I was out of my head. I can pay the gas bill with that seven-fifty."

He caught her arm in a vicious grip. "You are not going to take it back," he said. "I like it."

"Well," she said, "I don't think I ought..."

"Shut up and enjoy it," he muttered, more depressed than ever.

"With the world in the mess it's in," she said, "it's a wonder we can enjoy anything. I tell you, the bottom rail is on the top."

Julian sighed.

"Of course," she said, "if you know who you are, you can go anywhere." She said this every time he took her to the reducing class. "Most of them in it are not our kind of people," she said, "but I can be gracious to anybody. I know who I am."

"They don't give a damn for your graciousness," Julian said savagely. "Knowing who you are is good for one generation only. You haven't the foggiest idea where you stand now or who you are."

She stopped and allowed her eyes to flash at him. "I most certainly do know who I am," she said, "and if you don't know who you are, I'm ashamed of you."

"Oh hell," Julian said.

"Your great-grandfather was a former governor of this state," she said. "Your grandfather was a prosperous landowner. Your grandmother was a Godhigh."

"Will you look around you," he said tensely, "and see where you are now?" and he swept his arm jerkily out to indicate the neighborhood, which the growing darkness at least made less dingy.

"You remain what you are," she said. "Your great-grandfather had a plantation and two hundred slaves."

"There are no more slaves," he said irritably.

"They were better off when they were," she said. He groaned to see that she was off on that topic. She rolled onto it every few days like a train on an open track. He knew every stop, every junction, every swamp along the way, and knew the exact point at which her conclusion would roil majestically into the station: "It's ridiculous. It's simply not realistic. They should rise, yes, but on their own side of the fence."

"Let's skip it," Julian said.

"The ones I feel sorry for," she said, "are the ones that are half white. They're tragic."

"Will you skip it?"

"Suppose we were half white. We would certainly have mixed feelings."

"I have mixed feelings now," he groaned.

"Well let's talk about something pleasant," she said. "I remember going to Grandpa's when I was a little girl. Then the house had double stairways that went up to what was really the second floor - all the cooking was done on the first. I used to like to stay down in the kitchen on account of the way the walls smelled. I would sit with my nose pressed against the plaster and take deep breaths. Actually the place belonged to the Godhighs but your grandfather Chestny paid the mortgage and saved it for them. They were in reduced circumstances," she said, "but reduced or not, they never forgot who they were."

"Doubtless that decayed mansion reminded them," Julian muttered. He never spoke of it without contempt or thought of it without longing. He had seen it once when he was a child before it had been sold. The double stairways had rotted and been torn down. Negroes were living in it. But it remained in his mind as his mother had known it. It appeared in his dreams regularly. He would stand on the wide porch, listening to the rustle of oak leaves, then wander through the high-ceilinged hall into the parlor that opened onto it and gaze at the worn rugs and faded draperies. It occurred to him that it was he, not she, who could have appreciated it. He preferred its threadbare elegance to anything he could name and it was because of it that all the neighborhoods they had lived in had been a torment to him—whereas she had hardly known the difference. She called her insensitivity "being adjustable."

"And I remember the old darky who was my nurse, Caroline. There was no better person in the world. I've always had a great respect for my colored friends," she said. "I'd do anything in the world for them and they'd..."

"Will you for God's sake get off that subject?" Julian said. When he got on a bus by himself, he made it a point to sit down beside a Negro, in reparation as it were for his mother's sins.

"You're mighty touchy tonight," she said. "Do you feel all right?"

"Yes I feel all right" he said. "Now lay off."

She pursed her lips. "Well, you certainly are in a vile humor," she observed. "I just won't speak to you at all."

They had reached the bus stop. There was no bus in sight and Julian, his hands still jammed in his pockets and his head thrust forward, scowled down the empty street. The frustration of having to wait on the bus as well as ride on it began to creep up his neck like a hot hand. The presence of his mother was borne in upon him as she gave a pained sigh. He looked at her bleakly. She was holding herself very erect under the preposterous hat, wearing it like a banner of her imaginary dignity. There was in him an evil urge to break her spirit. He suddenly unloosened his tie and pulled it off and put it in his pocket.

She stiffened. "Why must you look like *that* when you take me to town?" she said. "Why must you deliberately embarrass me?"

"If you'll never learn where you are," he said, "you can at least learn where I am."

"You look like a thug," she said.

"Then I must be one," he murmured.

"I'll just go home," she said. "I will not bother you. If you can't do a little thing' like that for me..."

Rolling his eyes upward, he put his tie back on. "Restored to my class," he muttered. He thrust his face toward her and hissed, "True culture is in the mind, the *mind*," he said, and tapped his head, "the mind."

"It's in the heart," she said, "and in how you do things and how you do things is because of who you are."

"Nobody in the damn bus cares who you are."

"I care who I am," she said icily.

The lighted bus appeared on top of the next hill and as it approached, they moved out into the street to meet it. He put his hand under her elbow and hoisted her up on the creaking step. She entered with a little smile, as if she were going into a drawing room where everyone had been waiting for her. While he put in the tokens, she sat down on one of the broad front seats for three which faced the aisle. A thin woman with protruding teeth and long yellow hair was sitting on the end of it. His mother moved up beside her and left room for Julian beside herself. He sat down and looked at the floor across the aisle where a pair of thin feet in red and white canvas sandals were planted.

His mother immediately began a general conversation meant to attract anyone who felt like talking. "Can it get any hotter?" she said and removed from her purse a folding fan, black with a Japanese scene on it, which she began to flutter before her.

"I reckon it might could," the woman with the protruding teeth said, "but I know for a fact my apartment couldn't get no hotter."

"It must get the afternoon sun," his mother said. She sat forward and looked up and down the bus. It was half filled. Everybody was white. "I see we have the bus to ourselves," she said. Julian cringed.

"For a change," said the woman across the aisle, the owner of the red and white canvas sandals. "I come on one the other day and they were thick as fleas—up front and all through."

"The world is in a mess everywhere," his mother said. "I don't know how we've let it get in this fix."

"What gets my goat is all those boys from good families stealing automobile tires," the woman with the protruding teeth said. "I told my boy, I said you may not be rich but you been raised right and if I ever catch you in any such mess, they can send you on to the reformatory. Be exactly where you belong."

"Training tells," his mother said. "Is your boy in high school?"

"Ninth grade," the woman said.

"My son just finished college last year. He wants to write but he's selling typewriters until he gets started," his mother said.

The woman leaned forward and peered at Julian. He threw her such a malevolent look that she subsided against the seat. On the floor across the aisle there was an abandoned newspaper. He got up and got it and opened it out in front of him. His mother discreetly continued the conversation in a lower tone but the woman across the aisle said in a loud voice, "Well that's nice. Selling typewriters is close to writing. He can go right from one to the other."

"I tell him," his mother said, "that Rome wasn't built in a day."

Behind the newspaper Julian was withdrawing into the inner compartment of his mind where he spent most of his time. This was a kind of mental bubble in which he established himself when he could not bear to be a part of what was going on around him. From it he could see out and judge but in it he was safe from any kind of penetration from without. It was the only place where he felt free of the general idiocy of his fellows. His mother had never entered it but from it he could see her with absolute clarity.

The old lady was clever enough and he thought that if she had started from any of the right premises, more might have been expected of her. She lived according to the laws of her own fantasy world outside of which he had never seen her set foot. The law of it was to sacrifice herself for him after she had first created the necessity to do so by making a mess of things. If he had permitted her sacrifices, it was only because her lack of foresight had made them necessary. All of her life had been a struggle to act like a Chestny without the Chestny goods, and to give him everything she thought a Chestny ought to have but since, said she, it was fun to struggle, why complain? And when you had won, as she had won, what fun to look back on the hard times! He could not forgive her that she had enjoyed the struggle and that she thought *she* had won.

What she meant when she said she had won was that she had brought him up successfully and had sent him to college and that he had turned out so well—good looking (her teeth had gone unfilled so that his could be straightened), intelligent (he realized he was too intelligent to be a success), and with a future ahead of him (there was of course no future ahead of him). She excused his gloominess on the grounds that he was still growing up and his radical ideas on his lack of practical experience. She said he didn't yet know a thing about "life," that he hadn't even entered the real world—when already he was as disenchanted with it as a man of fifty.

The further irony of all this was that in spite of her, he had turned out so well. In spite of going to only a third-rate college, he had, on his own initiative, come out with a first-rate education; in spite of growing up dominated by a small mind, he had ended up with a large one; in spite of all her foolish views, he was free of prejudice and unafraid to face facts. Most miraculous of all, instead of being blinded by love for her as she was for him, he had cut himself emotionally free of her and could see her with complete objectivity. He was not dominated by his mother.

The bus stopped with a sudden jerk and shook him from his meditation. A woman from the back lurched forward with little steps and barely escaped falling in his newspaper as she righted herself. She got off and a large Negro got on. Julian kept his paper lowered to watch. It gave him a certain satisfaction to see injustice in daily operation. It confirmed his view that with a few exceptions there was no one worth knowing within a radius of three hundred miles. The Negro was well dressed and carried a briefcase. He looked around and then sat down on the other end of the seat where the woman with the red and white canvas sandals was sitting. He immediately unfolded a newspaper and obscured himself behind it. Julian's mother's elbow at once prodded insistently into his ribs. "Now you see why I won't ride on these buses by myself," she whispered.

The woman with the red and white canvas sandals had risen at the same time the Negro sat down and had gone farther back in the bus and taken the seat of the woman who had got off. His mother leaned forward and cast her an approving look.

Julian rose, crossed the aisle, and sat down in the place of the woman with the canvas sandals. From this position, he looked serenely across at his mother. Her face had turned an angry red. He stared at her, making his eyes the eyes of a stranger. He felt his tension suddenly lift as if he had openly declared war on her.

He would have liked to get in conversation with the Negro and to talk with him about art or politics or any subject that would be above the comprehension of those around them, but the man remained entrenched behind his paper. He was either ignoring the change of seating or had never noticed it. There was no way for Julian to convey his sympathy.

His mother kept her eyes fixed reproachfully on his face. The woman with the protruding teeth was looking at him avidly as if he were a type of monster new to her.

"Do you have a light?" he asked the Negro.

Without looking away from his paper, the man reached in his pocket and handed him a packet of matches.

"Thanks," Julian said. For a moment he held the matches foolishly. A NO SMOKING sign looked down upon him from over the door. This alone would not have deterred him; he had no cigarettes. He had quit smoking some months before because he could not afford it. "Sorry," he muttered and handed back the matches. The Negro lowered the paper and gave him an annoyed look. He took the matches and raised the paper again.

His mother continued to gaze at him but she did not take advantage of his momentary discomfort. Her eyes retained their battered look. Her face seemed to be unnaturally red, as if her blood pressure had risen. Julian allowed no glimmer of sympathy to show on his face. Having got the advantage, he wanted desperately to keep it and carry it through. He would have liked to teach her a lesson that would last her a while, but there seemed no way to continue the point. The Negro refused to come out from behind his paper.

Julian folded his arms and looked stolidly before him, facing her but as if he did not see her, as if he had ceased to recognize her existence. He visualized a scene in which, the bus having reached their stop, he would remain in his seat and when she said, "Aren't you going to get off?" he would look at her as at a stranger who had rashly addressed him. The corner they got off on was usually deserted, but it was well lighted and it would not hurt her to walk by herself the four blocks to the Y. He decided to wait until the time came and then decide whether or not he would let her get off by herself. He would have to be at the Y at ten to bring her back, but he could leave her wondering if he was going to show up. There was no reason for her to think she could always depend on him.

He retired again into the high-ceilinged room sparsely settled with large pieces of antique furniture. His soul expanded momentarily but then he became aware of his mother across from him and the vision shriveled. He studied her coldly. Her feet in little pumps dangled like a child's and did not quite reach the floor. She was training on him an exaggerated look of reproach. He felt completely detached from her. At that moment he could with pleasure have slapped her as he would have slapped a particularly obnoxious child in his charge.

He began to imagine various unlikely ways by which he could teach her a lesson. He might make friends with some distinguished Negro professor or lawyer and bring him home to spend the evening. He would be entirely justified but her blood pressure would rise to 300. He could not push her to the extent of making her have a stroke, and moreover, he had never been successful at making any Negro friends. He had tried to strike up an acquaintance on the bus with some of the better types, with ones that looked like professors or ministers or lawyers. One morning he had sat down next to a distinguished-looking dark brown man who had answered his questions with a sonorous solemnity but who had turned out to be an undertaker. Another day he had sat down beside a cigar-smoking Negro with a diamond ring on his finger, but after a few stilted pleasantries, the Negro had rung the buzzer and risen, slipping two lottery tickets into Julian's hand as he climbed over him to leave.

He imagined his mother lying desperately ill and his being able to secure only a Negro doctor for her. He toyed with that idea for a few minutes and then dropped it for a momentary vision of himself participating as a sympathizer in a sit-in demonstration. This was possible but he did not linger with it. Instead, he approached the ultimate horror. He brought home a beautiful suspiciously Negroid woman. Prepare yourself, he said. There is nothing you can do about it. This is the woman I've chosen. She's intelligent, dignified, even good, and she's suffered and she hasn't thought it *fun*. Now persecute us, go ahead and persecute us. Drive her out of here, but remember, you're driving me too. His eyes were narrowed and through the indignation he had generated, he saw his mother across the aisle, purple-faced, shrunken to the dwarf-like proportions of her moral nature, sitting like a mummy beneath the ridiculous banner of her hat.

He was tilted out of his fantasy again as the bus stopped. The door opened with a sucking hiss and out of the dark a large, gaily dressed, sullen-looking colored woman got on with a little boy. The child, who might have been four, had on a short plaid suit and a Tyrolean hat with a blue feather in it. Julian hoped that he would sit down beside him and that the woman would push in beside his mother. He could think of no better arrangement.

As she waited for her tokens, the woman was surveying the seating possibilities—he hoped with the idea of sitting where she was least wanted. There was something familiar-looking about her but Julian could not place what it was. She was a giant of a woman. Her face was set not only to meet opposition but to seek it out. The downward tilt of her large lower lip was like a warning sign: DON'T TAMPER WITH ME. Her bulging figure was encased in a green crepe dress and her feet overflowed in red shoes. She had on a hideous hat. A purple velvet flap came down on one side of it and stood up on the other; the rest of it was green and looked like a cushion with the stuffing out. She carried a mammoth red pocketbook that bulged throughout as if it were stuffed with rocks.

To Julian's disappointment, the little boy climbed up on the empty seat beside his mother. His mother lumped all children, black and white, into the common category, "cute," and she thought little Negroes were on the whole cuter than little white children. She smiled at the little boy as he climbed on the seat.

Meanwhile the woman was bearing down upon the empty seat beside Julian. To his annoyance, she squeezed herself into it. He saw his mother's face change as the woman settled herself next to him and he realized with satisfaction that this was more objectionable to her than it was to him. Her face seemed almost gray and there was a look of dull recognition in her eyes, as if suddenly she had sickened at some awful confrontation. Julian saw that it was because she and the woman had, in a sense, swapped sons. Though his mother would not realize the symbolic significance of this, she would feel it. His amusement showed plainly on his face.

The woman next to him muttered something unintelligible to herself. He was conscious of a kind of bristling next to him, a muted growling like that of an angry cat. He could not see anything but the red pocketbook upright on the bulging green thighs. He visualized the woman as she had stood waiting for her tokens—the ponderous figure, rising from the red shoes upward over the solid hips, the mammoth bosom, the haughty face, to the green and purple hat.

His eyes widened.

The vision of the two hats, identical, broke upon him with the radiance of a brilliant sunrise. His face was suddenly lit with joy. He could not believe that Fate had thrust upon his mother such a lesson. He gave a loud chuckle so that she would look at him and see that he saw. She turned her eyes on him slowly. The blue in them seemed to have turned a bruised purple. For a moment he had an uncomfortable sense of her innocence, but it lasted only a second before principle rescued him. Justice entitled him to laugh. His grin hardened until it said to her as plainly as if he were saying aloud: Your punishment exactly fits your pettiness. This should teach you a permanent lesson.

Her eyes shifted to the woman. She seemed unable to bear looking at him and to find the woman preferable. He became conscious again of the bristling presence at his side. The woman was rumbling like a volcano about to become active. His mother's mouth began to twitch slightly at one corner. With a sinking heart, he saw incipient signs of recovery on her face and realized that this was going to strike her suddenly as funny and was going to be no lesson at all. She kept her eyes on the woman and an amused smile came over her face as if the woman were a monkey that had stolen her hat. The little Negro was looking up at her with large fascinated eyes. He had been trying to attract her attention for some time.

"Carver!" the woman said suddenly. "Come heah!"

When he saw that the spotlight was on him at last, Carver drew his feet up and turned himself toward Julian's mother and giggled.

"Carver!" the woman said. "You heah me? Come heah!"

Carver slid down from the seat but remained squatting with his back against the base of it, his head turned slyly around toward Julian's mother, who was smiling at him. The woman reached a hand across the aisle and snatched him to her. He righted himself and hung backwards on her knees, grinning at Julian's mother. "Isn't he cute?" Julian's mother said to the woman with the protruding teeth.

"I reckon he is," the woman said without conviction.

The Negress yanked him upright but he eased out of her grip and shot across the aisle and scrambled, giggling wildly, onto the seat beside his love.

"I think he likes me," Julian's mother said, and smiled at the woman. It was the smile she used when she was being particularly gracious to an inferior. Julian saw everything lost. The lesson had rolled off her like rain on a roof.

The woman stood up and yanked the little boy off the seat as if she were snatching him from contagion. Julian could feel the rage in her at having no weapon like his mother's smile. She gave the child a sharp slap across his leg. He howled once and then thrust his head into her stomach and kicked his feet against her shins. "Behave," she said vehemently.

The bus stopped and the Negro who had been reading the newspaper got off. The woman moved over and set the little boy down with a thump between herself and Julian. She held him firmly by the knee. In a moment he put his hands in front of his face and peeped at Julian's mother through his fingers.

"I see yoooooooo!" she said and put her hand in front of her face and peeped at him.

The woman slapped his hand down. "Quit yo' foolishness," she said, "before I knock the living Jesus out of you!"

Julian was thankful that the next stop was theirs. He reached up and pulled the cord. The woman reached up and pulled it at the same time. Oh my God, he thought. He had the terrible intuition that when they got off the bus together, his mother would open her purse and give the little boy a nickel. The gesture would be as natural to her as breathing. The bus stopped and the woman got up and lunged to the front, dragging the child, who wished to stay on, after her. Julian and his mother got up and followed. As they neared the door, Julian tried to relieve her of her pocketbook.

"No," she murmured, "I want to give the little boy a nickel."

"No!" Julian hissed. "No!"

She smiled down at the child and opened her bag. The bus door opened and the woman picked him up by the arm and descended with him, hanging at her hip. Once in the street she set him down and shook him.

Julian's mother had to close her purse while she got down the bus step but as soon as her feet were on the ground, she opened it again and began to rummage inside. "I can't find but a penny," she whispered, "but it looks like a new one."

"Don't do it!" Julian said fiercely between his teeth. There was a streetlight on the corner and she hurried to get under it so that she could better see into her pocketbook. The woman was heading off rapidly down the street with the child still hanging backward on her hand.

"Oh little boy!" Julian's mother called and took a few quick steps and caught up with them just beyond the lamppost. "Here's a bright new penny for you," and she held out the coin, which shone bronze in the dim light.

The huge woman turned and for a moment stood, her shoulders lifted and her face frozen with frustrated rage, and stared at Julian's mother. Then all at once she seemed to explode like a piece of machinery that had been given one ounce of pressure too much. Julian saw the black fist swing out with the red pocketbook. He shut his eyes and cringed as he heard the woman shout, "He don't take nobody's pennies!" When he opened his eyes, the woman was disappearing down the street with the little boy staring wide-eyed over her shoulder. Julian's mother was sitting on the sidewalk.

"I told you not to do that," Julian said angrily. "I told you not to do that!"

He stood over her for a minute, gritting his teeth. Her legs were stretched out in front of her and her hat was on her lap. He squatted down and looked her in the face. It was totally expressionless. "You got exactly what you deserved," he said. "Now get up."

He picked up her pocketbook and put what had fallen out back in it. He picked the hat up off her lap. The penny caught his eye on the sidewalk and he picked that up and let it drop before her eyes into the purse. Then he stood up and leaned over and held his hands out to pull her up. She remained immobile. He sighed. Rising above them on either side were black apartment buildings, marked with irregular rectangles of light. At the end of the block a man came out of a door and walked off in the opposite direction. "All right," he said, "suppose somebody happens by and wants to know why you're sitting on the sidewalk?"

She took the hand and, breathing hard, pulled heavily up on it and then stood for a moment, swaying slightly as if the spots of light in the darkness were circling around her. Her eyes, shadowed and confused, finally settled on his face. He did not try to conceal his irritation. "I hope this teaches you a lesson," he said. She leaned forward and her eyes raked his face. She seemed trying to determine his identity. Then, as if she found nothing familiar about him, she started off with a headlong movement in the wrong direction.

"Aren't you going on to the Y?" he asked.

"Home," she muttered.

"Well, are we walking?"

For answer she kept going. Julian followed along, his hands behind him. He saw no reason to let the lesson she had had go without backing it up with an explanation of its meaning. She might as well be made to understand what had happened to her. "Don't think that was just an uppity Negro woman," he said. "That was the whole colored race which will no longer take your condescending pennies. That was your black double. She can wear the same hat as you, and to be sure," he added gratuitously (because he thought it was funny), "it looked better on her than it did on you. What all this means," he said, "is that the old world is gone. The old manners are obsolete and your graciousness is not worth a damn." He thought bitterly of the house that had been lost for him. "You aren't who you think you are," he said.

She continued to plow ahead, paying no attention to him. Her hair had come undone on one side. She dropped her pocketbook and took no notice. He stooped and picked it up and handed it to her but she did not take it.

"You needn't act as if the world had come to an end," he aid, "because it hasn't. From now on you've got to live in a new world and face a few realities for a change. Buck up," he said, "it won't kill you."

She was breathing fast.

"Let's wait on the bus," he said.

"Home," she said thickly.

"I hate to see you behave like this," he said. "Just like a child. I should be able to expect more of you." He decided to stop where he was and make her stop and wait for a bus. "I'm not going any farther," he said, stopping. "We're going on the bus."

She continued to go on as if she had not heard him. He took a few steps and caught her arm and stopped her. He looked into her face and caught his breath. He was looking into a face he had never seen before. "Tell Grandpa to come get me," she said.

He stared, stricken.

"Tell Caroline to come get me," she said.

Stunned, he let her go and she lurched forward again, walking as if one leg were shorter than the other. A tide of darkness seemed to be sweeping her from him. "Mother!" he cried. "Darling, sweetheart, wait!" Crumpling, she fell to the pavement. He dashed forward and fell at her side, crying, "Mamma, Mamma!" He turned her over. Her face was fiercely distorted. One eye, large and staring, moved slightly to the left as if it had become unmoored. The other remained fixed on him, raked his face again, found nothing and closed.

"Wait here, wait here!" he cried and jumped up and began to run for help toward a cluster of lights he saw in the distance ahead of him. "Help, help!" he shouted, but his voice was thin, scarcely a thread of sound. The lights drifted farther away the faster he ran and his feet moved numbly as if they carried him nowhere. The tide of darkness seemed to sweep him back to her, postponing from moment to moment his entry into the world of guilt and sorrow.

FOCUSED FREE WRITES

1. What are the motivations and conflicts of the two main characters? Be specific.
2. Are these characters round? Do they undergo an "epiphany"—in other words, a transformation or some sort of realization?
3. In resisting a request to define the "short story" as a genre during a discussion at a University of Scranton symposium, O'Connor commented: "The writer puts us in the middle of some human action and shows it as it is illuminated and outlined by mystery. In every story there is some minor revelation which, no matter how funny the story may be, gives us a hint of the unknown, of death" (Magee, *Conversations with Flannery O'Connor*, 17). How does "Everything That Rises Must Converge" accomplish all this?
4. What is the story's theme? While racism is certainly a topic, what does O'Connor have to say about it?
5. What is distinctive about O'Connor's style in terms of her diction and syntax? Her narration and point of view? Any imagery or symbolism?

LITERARY Contexts

Regionalism and the Grotesque

In her essay, "Some Aspects of the Grotesque in Southern Fiction" (1960), Flannery O'Connor writes about the responsibility of the writer:

Those writers who speak for and with their age are able to do so with a great deal more ease and grace than those who speak counter to prevailing attitudes. I once received a letter from an old lady in California who informed me that when the tired reader comes home at night, he wishes to read something that will lift up his heart. And it seems her heart had not been lifted up by anything of mine she had read. I think that if her heart had been in the right place, it would have been lifted up....

The problem for [the serious innovative] novelist will be to know how far he can distort without destroying, and in order not to destroy,

(continued)

(continued)

> he will have to descend far enough into himself to reach those under-ground springs that give life to his work. This descent into himself will, at the same time, be a descent into his region. It will be a de-scent through the darkness of the familiar into a world where, like the blind man cured in the gospels, he sees men as if they were trees, but walking. This is the beginning of vision, and I feel it is a vision which we in the South must at least try to understand if we want to partici-pate in the continuance of a vital Southern literature. I hate to think that in twenty years Southern writers too may be writing about men in grey flannel suits and may have lost their ability to see that these gentlemen are even greater freaks than what we are writing about now. I hate to think of the day when the Southern writer will satisfy the tired reader. (*Mystery and Manners*, 47, 50)

In this passage, Flannery O'Connor addresses two preoccupations that have come to contextualize her work: regionalism and the grotesque. For O'Connor, the quirky, bizarre, and particular people of the South and their reactions and experiences were a way to under-stand complex, fundamental mysteries about good and evil, life and death, the universe.

Why won't this story "satisfy the tired reader," as O'Connor puts it?

How does this context provide a way to understand this particular story?

COMPARING THEMES: IDENTITY

Family can sometimes obstruct a person's identity. Some characters in the following stories must attempt to negotiate where they come from with who they want to be.

PRE-READING Have you ever tried to hide where you came from? Do you know anyone who has? How so and why?

Alice Walker (1944–). *Alice Walker was born and raised in Eatonton, Georgia, one of seven siblings. She cites her upbringing in the rural South, church, and reading as early influences on her later writing. At the age of eight, Walker lost sight in one eye in a household accident but still managed to become valedictorian of her high school class, which earned her a scholarship to Spelman College in Atlanta. Walker eventually earned a degree from Sarah Lawrence in the Bronx in 1965. Her involvement in the Civil Rights movement coincided with the beginning of her writing career. While widely known for her novels, such as the award-winning The Color Purple (1982), Walker's first book was poetry, and she has published* children's books, nonfiction, literary criticism, and short stories as well. While teaching and lecturing on occasion, Walker resides in San Francisco and continues to write.

Alice Walker

EVERYDAY USE [1973]

for your grandmama

I will wait for her in the yard that Maggie and I made so clean and wavy yesterday afternoon. A yard like this is more comfortable than most people know. It is not just a yard. It is like an extended living room. When the hard clay is swept clean as a floor and the fine sand around the edges lined with tiny, irregular grooves, anyone can come and sit and look up into the elm tree and wait for the breezes that never come inside the house.

Maggie will be nervous until after her sister goes: she will stand hopelessly in corners, homely and ashamed of the burn scars down her arms and legs, eyeing her sister with a mixture of envy and awe. She thinks her sister has held life always in the palm of one hand, that "no" is a word the world never learned to say to her.

You've no doubt seen those TV shows where the child who has "made it" is confronted, as a surprise, by her own mother and father, tottering in weakly from backstage. (A pleasant surprise, of course: What would they do if parent and child came on the show only to curse out and insult each other?) On TV mother and child embrace and smile into each other's faces. Sometimes the mother and father weep, the child wraps them in her arms and leans across the table to tell how she would not have made it without their help. I have seen these programs.

Sometimes I dream a dream in which Dee and I are suddenly brought together on a TV program of this sort. Out of a dark and soft-seated limousine I am ushered into a bright room filled with many people. There I meet a smiling, gray, sporty man like Johnny Carson who shakes my hand and tells me what a fine girl I have. Then we are on the stage and Dee is embracing me with tears in her eyes. She pins on my dress a large orchid, even though she has told me once that she thinks orchids are tacky flowers.

5   In real life I am a large, big-boned woman with rough, man-working hands. In the winter I wear flannel nightgowns to bed and overalls during the day. I can kill and clean a hog as mercilessly as a man. My fat keeps me hot in zero weather. I can work outside all day, breaking ice to get water for washing; I can eat pork liver cooked over the open fire minutes after it comes steaming from the hog. One winter I knocked a bull calf straight in the brain between the eyes with a sledge hammer and had the meat hung up to chill before nightfall. But of course all this does not show on television. I am the way my daughter would want me to be: a hundred pounds lighter, my skin like an uncooked barley pancake. My hair glistens in the hot bright lights. Johnny Carson has much to do to keep up with my quick and witty tongue.

But that is a mistake. I know even before I wake up. Who ever knew a Johnson with a quick tongue? Who can even imagine me looking a strange white man in the eye? It seems to me I have talked to them always with one foot raised in flight, with my head turned in whichever way is farthest from them. Dee, though. She would always look anyone in the eye. Hesitation was no part of her nature.

"How do I look, Mama?" Maggie says, showing just enough of her thin body enveloped in pink skirt and red blouse for me to know she's there, almost hidden by the door.

"Come out into the yard," I say.

Have you ever seen a lame animal, perhaps a dog run over by some careless person rich enough to own a car, sidle up to someone who is ignorant enough to be kind to him? That is the way my Maggie walks. She has been like this, chin on chest, eyes on ground, feet in shuffle, ever since the fire that burned the other house to the ground.

Dee is lighter than Maggie, with nicer hair and a fuller figure. She's a woman now, though sometimes I forget. How long ago was it that the other house burned? Ten, twelve years? Sometimes I can still hear the flames and feel Maggie's arms sticking to me, her hair smoking and her dress falling off her in little black papery flakes. Her eyes seemed stretched open, blazed open by the flames reflected in them. And Dee. I see her standing off under the sweet gum tree she used to dig gum out of; a look of concentration on her face as she watched the last dingy gray board of the house fall in toward the red-hot brick chimney. Why don't you do a dance around the ashes? I'd wanted to ask her. She had hated the house that much.

I used to think she hated Maggie, too. But that was before we raised money, the church and me, to send her to Augusta to school. She used to read to us without pity; forcing words, lies, other folks' habits, whole lives upon us two, sitting trapped and ignorant underneath her voice. She washed us in a river of make-believe, burned us with a lot of knowledge we didn't necessarily need to know. Pressed us to her with the serious way she read, to shove us away at just the moment, like dimwits, we seemed about to understand.

Dee wanted nice things. A yellow organdy dress to wear to her graduation from high school; black pumps to match a green suit she'd made from an old suit somebody gave me. She was determined to stare down any disaster in her efforts. Her eyelids would not flicker for minutes at a time. Often I fought off the temptation to shake her. At sixteen she had a style of her own: and knew what style was.

I never had an education myself. After second grade the school was closed down. Don't ask me why: in 1927 colored asked fewer questions than they do now. Sometimes Maggie reads to me. She stumbles along good-naturedly but can't see well. She knows she is not bright. Like good looks and money, quickness passes her by. She will marry John Thomas (who has mossy teeth in an earnest face) and then I'll be free to sit here and I guess just sing church songs to myself. Although I never was a good singer. Never could carry a tune. I was always better at a man's job. I used to love to milk till I was hooked in the side in '49. Cows are soothing and slow and don't bother you, unless you try to milk them the wrong way.

I have deliberately turned my back on the house. It is three rooms, just like the one that burned, except the roof is tin; they don't make shingle roofs any more. There are no real windows, just some holes cut in the sides, like the portholes in a ship, but not round and not square, with rawhide holding the shutters up on the outside. This house is in a pasture, too, like the other one. No doubt when Dee sees it she will want to tear it down. She wrote me once that no matter where we "choose" to live, she will manage to come see us. But she will never bring her friends. Maggie and I thought about this and Maggie asked me, "Mama, when did Dee ever *have* any friends?"

15   She had a few. Furtive boys in pink shirts hanging about on washday after school. Nervous girls who never laughed. Impressed with her they worshiped the well-turned phrase, the cute shape, the scalding humor that erupted like bubbles in lye. She read to them.

When she was courting Jimmy T she didn't have much time to pay to us, but turned all her faultfinding power on him. He *flew* to marry a cheap city girl from a family of ignorant flashy people. She hardly had time to recompose herself.

When she comes I will meet—but there they are!

Maggie attempts to make a dash for the house, in her shuffling way, but I stay her with my hand. "Come back here," I say. And she stops and tries to dig a well in the sand with her toe.

It is hard to see them clearly through the strong sun. But even the first glimpse of leg out of the car tells me it is Dee. Her feet were always neat-looking, as if God himself had shaped them with a certain style. From the other side of the car comes a short, stocky man. Hair is all over his head a foot long and hanging from his chin like a kinky mule tail. I hear Maggie suck in her breath. "Uhnnnh," is what it sounds like. Like when you see the wriggling end of a snake just in front of your foot on the road. "Uhnnnh."

20   Dee next. A dress down to the ground, in this hot weather. A dress so loud it hurts my eyes. There are yellows and oranges enough to throw back the light of the sun. I feel my whole face warming from the heat waves it throws out. Earrings gold, too, and hanging down to her shoulders. Bracelets dangling and making noises when she moves her arm up to shake the folds of the dress out of her armpits. The dress is loose and flows, and as she walks closer, I like it. I hear Maggie go "Uhnnnh" again. It is her sister's hair. It stands straight up like the wool on a sheep. It is black as night and around the edges are two long pigtails that rope about like small lizards disappearing behind her ears.

"Wa-su-zo-Tean-o!"[1] she says, coming on in that gliding way the dress makes her move. The short stocky fellow with the hair to his navel is all grinning and he follows up with "Asalamalakim,[2] my mother and sister!" He moves to hug Maggie but she falls back, right up against the back of my chair. I feel her trembling there and when I look up I see the perspiration falling off her chin.

"Don't get up," says Dee. Since I am stout it takes something of a push. You can see me trying to move a second or two before I make it. She turns, showing white heels through her sandals, and goes back to the car. Out she peeks next

---

[1] **Wa-su-zo-Tean-o:** greeting common among black Muslims.

[2] **Asalamalakim:** Peace be with you.

with a Polaroid. She stoops down quickly and lines up picture after picture of me sitting there in front of the house with Maggie cowering behind me. She never takes a shot without making sure the house is included. When a cow comes nibbling around the edge of the yard she snaps it and me and Maggie *and* the house. Then she puts the Polaroid in the back seat of the car, and comes up and kisses me on the forehead.

Meanwhile Asalamalakim is going through motions with Maggie's hand. Maggie's hand is as limp as a fish, and probably as cold, despite the sweat, and she keeps trying to pull it back. It looks like Asalamalakim wants to shake hands but wants to do it fancy. Or maybe he don't know how people shake hands. Anyhow, he soon gives up on Maggie.

"Well," I say. "Dee."

25   "No, Mama," she says. "Not 'Dee,' Wangero Leewanika Kemanjo!"

"What happened to 'Dee'?" I wanted to know.

"She's dead," Wangero said. "I couldn't bear it any longer, being named after the people who oppress me."

"You know as well as me you was named after your aunt Dicie," I said. Dicie is my sister. She named Dee. We called her "Big Dee" after Dee was born.

"But who was *she* named after?" asked Wangero.

30   "I guess after Grandma Dee," I said.

"And who was she named after?" asked Wangero.

"Her mother," I said, and saw Wangero was getting tired. "That's about as far back as I can trace it," I said. Though, in fact, I probably could have carried it back beyond the Civil War through the branches.

"Well," said Asalamalakim, "there you are."

"Uhnnnh," I heard Maggie say.

35   "There I was not," I said, "before 'Dicie' cropped up in our family, so why should I try to trace it that far back?"

He just stood there grinning, looking down on me like somebody inspecting a Model A car. Every once in a while he and Wangero sent eye signals over my head.

"How do you pronounce this name?" I asked.

"You don't have to call me by it if you don't want to," said Wangero.

"Why shouldn't I?" I asked. "If that's what you want us to call you, we'll call you."

40   "I know it might sound awkward at first," said Wangero.

"I'll get used to it," I said. "Ream it out again."

Well, soon we got the name out of the way. Asalamalakim had a name twice as long and three times as hard. After I tripped over it two or three times he told me to just call him Hakim-a-barber. I wanted to ask him was he a barber, but I didn't really think he was, so I didn't ask.

"You must belong to those beef-cattle peoples down the road," I said. They said "Asalamalakim" when they met you, too, but they didn't shake hands. Always too busy: feeding the cattle, fixing the fences, putting up salt-lick shelters, throwing down hay. When the white folks poisoned some of the herd the men stayed up all night with rifles in their hands. I walked a mile and a half just to see the sight.

Hakim-a-barber said, "I accept some of their doctrines, but farming and raising cattle is not my style." (They didn't tell me, and I didn't ask, whether Wangero (Dee) had really gone and married him.)

45   We sat down to eat and right away he said he didn't eat collards and pork was unclean. Wangero, though, went on through the chitlins and corn bread, the greens and everything else. She talked a blue streak over the sweet potatoes. Everything delighted her. Even the fact that we still used the benches her daddy made for the table when we couldn't effort to buy chairs.

"Oh, Mama!" she cried. Then turned to Hakim-a-barber. "I never knew how lovely these benches are. You can feel the rump prints," she said, running her hands underneath her and along the bench. Then she gave a sigh and her hand closed over Grandma Dee's butter dish. "That's it!" she said. "I knew there was something I wanted to ask you if I could have." She jumped up from the table and went over in the corner where the churn stood, the milk in it clabber[3] by now. She looked at the churn and looked at it.

"This churn top is what I need," she said. "Didn't Uncle Buddy whittle it out of a tree you all used to have?"

"Yes," I said.

"Un huh," she said happily. "And I want the dasher, too."

50   "Uncle Buddy whittle that, too?" asked the barber.

Dee (Wangero) looked up at me.

"Aunt Dee's first husband whittled the dash," said Maggie so low you almost couldn't hear her. "His name was Henry, but they called him Stash."

"Maggie's brain is like an elephant's," Wangero said, laughing. "I can use the chute top as a centerpiece for the alcove table," she said, sliding a plate over the chute, "and I'll think of something artistic to do with the dasher."

When she finished wrapping the dasher the handle stuck out. I took it for a moment in my hands. You didn't even have to look close to see where hands pushing the dasher up and down to make butter had left a kind of sink in the wood. In fact, there were a lot of small sinks; you could see where thumbs and fingers had sunk into the wood. It was beautiful light yellow wood, from a tree that grew in the yard where Big Dee and Stash had lived.

55   After dinner Dee (Wangero) went to the trunk at the foot of my bed and started rifling through it. Maggie hung back in the kitchen over the dishpan. Out came Wangero with two quilts. They had been pieced by Grandma Dee and then Big Dee and me had hung them on the quilt ftames on the front porch and quilted them. One was in the Lone Star pattern. The other was Walk Around the Mountain. In both of them were scraps of dresses Grandma Dee had worn fifty and more years ago. Bits and pieces of Grandpa Jattell's Paisley shirts. And one teeny faded blue piece, about the size of a penny matchbox, that was from Great Grandpa Ezra's uniform that he wore in the Civil War.

"Mama," Wangero said sweet as a bird. "Can I have these old quilts?"

I heard something fall in the kitchen, and a minute later the kitchen door slammed.

---

[3] **clabber:** turned sour.

"Why don't you take one or two of the others?" I asked. "These old things was just done by me and Big Dee from some tops your grandma pieced before she died."

"No," said Wangero. "I don't want those. They are stitched around the borders by machine."

60 "That'll make them last better," I said.

"That's not the point," said Wangero. "These are all pieces of dresses Grandma used to wear. She did all this stitching by hand. Imagine!" She held the quilts securely in her arms, stroking them.

"Some of the pieces, like those lavender ones, come from old clothes her mother handed down to her," I said, moving up to touch the quilts. Dee (Wangero) moved back just enough so that I couldn't reach the quilts. They already belonged to her.

"Imagine!" she breathed again, clutching them closely to her bosom.

"The truth is," I said, "I promised to give them quilts to Maggie, for when she marries John Thomas."

65 She gasped like a bee had stung her.

"Maggie can't appreciate these quilts!" she said. "She'd probably be backward enough to put them to everyday use."

"I reckon she would," I said. "God knows I been saving 'em for long enough with nobody using 'em. I hope she will!" I didn't want to bring up how I had offered Dee (Wangero) a quilt when she went away to college. Then she had told they were old-fashioned, out of style.

"But they're *priceless*!" she was saying now, furiously; for she has a temper. "Maggie would put them on the bed and in five years they'd be in rags. Less than that!"

"She can always make some more," I said. "Maggie knows how to quilt."

70 Dee (Wangero) looked at me with hatred. "You just will not understand. The point is these quilts, *these* quilts!"

"Well," I said, stumped. "What would *you* do with them?"

"Hang them," she said. As if that was the only thing you *could* do with quilts.

Maggie by now was standing in the door. I could almost hear the sound her feet made as they scraped over each other.

"She can have them, Mama," she said, like somebody used to never winning anything, or having anything reserved for her. "I can 'member Grandma Dee without the quilts."

75 I looked at her hard. She had filled her bottom lip with checkerberry snuff and gave her face a kind of dopey, hangdog look. It was Grandma Dee and Big Dee who taught her how to quilt herself. She stood there with her scarred hands hidden in the folds of her skirt. She looked at her sister with something like fear but she wasn't mad at her. This was Maggie's portion. This was the way she knew God to work.

When I looked at her like that something hit me in the top of my head and ran down to the soles of my feet. Just like when I'm in church and the spirit of God touches me and I get happy and shout. I did something I never done before: hugged Maggie to me, then dragged her on into the room, snatched the quilts out of Miss Wangero's hands and dumped them into Maggie's lap. Maggie just sat there on my bed with her mouth open.

"Take one or two of the others," I said to Dee.

But she turned without a word and went out to Hakim-a-barber.

"You just don't understand," she said, as Maggie and I came out to the car.

"What don't I understand?" I wanted to know.

"Your heritage," she said. And then she turned to Maggie, kissed her, and said, "You ought to try to make something of yourself, too, Maggie. It's really a new day for us. But from the way you and Mama still live you'd never know it."

She put on some sunglasses that hid everything above the tip of her nose and chin.

Maggie smiled; maybe at the sunglasses. But a real smile, not scared. After we watched the car dust settle I asked Maggie to bring me a dip of snuff. And then the two of us sat there just enjoying, until it was time to go in the house and go to bed.

FOCUSED FREE WRITES

1. Map the strengths and weaknesses of the characters introduced here.
2. What conflicts do these characters face? Do they overcome these conflicts or not? Are the characters round or flat?
3. How would you describe the theme of this story?
4. Which particular images or symbols stand out here? Refer to specific moments in the text.
5. This story is told from the mother's point of view. Assume the persona or the voice of another character in the story and write a letter to the mother, Dee, Maggie, or Hakim-a-Barber. What would this character have to say about the quilt incident?

PRE-READING	How do parents put pressure on children? How do children put pressure on themselves because of their parents?

Amy Tan (1952–). *Daughter of Chinese immigrants, Amy Tan and her family moved quite a bit before settling in Santa Clara, California, for a time. While Tan received early praise for her writing, winning an essay contest at age eight, her parents dreamed she would become a successful doctor. After her father and brother died of brain tumors, Tan moved with her mother and brother to Switzerland and confessed to "falling to pieces." Upon returning to the U.S., her mother enrolled her as a pre-med student at a small school in Oregon before Tan eloped with her boyfriend and enrolled as an English major at San Jose City College. After earning a Masters in Linguistics and making a living consulting and freelance writing, Tan began writing down the stories and tragedies that haunted her mother's life. Her cross-cultural novels, children's books, short stories, and essays have earned Tan both popular and critical success.*

🔖 TWO KINDS [1989]

My mother believed you could be anything you wanted to be in America. You could open a restaurant. You could work for the government and get good retirement. You could buy a house with almost no money down. You could become rich. You could be come instantly famous.

"Of course you can be prodigy, too," my mother told me when I was nine. "You can be best anything. What does Auntie Lindo know? Her daughter, she is only best tricky."

America was where all my mother's hopes lay. She had come here in 1949 after losing everything in China: her mother and father, her family home, her first husband, and two daughters, twin baby girls. But she never looked back with regret. There were so many ways for things to get better.

We didn't immediately pick the right kind of prodigy. At first my mother thought I could be a Chinese Shirley Temple. We'd watch Shirley's old movies on TV as though they were training films. My mother would poke my arm and say, "*Ni kan.*" You watch. And I would see Shirley tapping her feet, or singing a sailor song, or pursing her lips into a very round O while saying, "Oh my goodness."

5   "*Ni kan,*" said my mother as Shirley's eyes flooded with tears. "You already know how. Don't need talent for crying!"

Soon after my mother got this idea about Shirley Temple, she took me to a beauty training school in the Mission district and put me in the hands of a student who could barely hold the scissors without shaking. Instead of getting big fat curls, I emerged with an uneven mass of crinkly black fuzz. My mother dragged me off to the bathroom and tried to wet down my hair.

"You look like Negro Chinese," she lamented, as if I had done this on purpose.

The instructor of the beauty training school had to lop off these soggy clumps to make my hair even again. "Peter Pan is very popular these days," the instructor assured my mother. I now had hair the length of a boy's, with straight-across bangs that hung at a slant two inches above my eyebrows. I liked the haircut and it made me actually look forward to my future fame.

In fact, in the beginning, I was just as excited as my mother, maybe even more so. I pictured this prodigy part of me as many different images, trying each one on for size. I was a dainty ballerina girl standing by the curtains, waiting to hear the right music that would send me floating on my tiptoes. I was like the Christ child lifted out of the straw manger, crying with holy indignity. I was Cinderella stepping from her pumpkin carriage with sparkly cartoon music filling the air.

10   In all of my imaginings, I was filled with a sense that I would soon become *perfect*. My mother and father would adore me. I would be beyond reproach. I would never feel the need to sulk for anything.

But sometimes the prodigy in me became impatient. "If you don't hurry up and get me out of here, I'm disappearing for good," it warned. "And then you'll always be nothing."

* * *

Every night after dinner, my mother and I would sit at the Formica kitchen table. She would present new tests, taking her examples from stories of amazing children she had read in *Ripley's Believe It or Not*, or *Good Housekeeping*, *Reader's Digest*, and a dozen other magazines she kept in a pile in our bathroom. My mother got these magazines from people whose houses she cleaned. And since she cleaned many houses each week, we had a great assortment. She would look through them all, searching for stories about remarkable children.

The first night she brought out a story about a three-year-old boy who knew the capitals of all the states and even most of the European countries. A teacher was quoted as saying the little boy could also pronounce the names of the foreign cities correctly.

"What is the capital of Finland?" my mother asked me, looking at the magazine story.

15 All I knew was the capital of California, because Sacramento was the name of the street we lived on in Chinatown. "Nairobi!" I guessed, saying the most foreign word I could think of. She checked to see if that was possibly one way to pronounce "Helsinki" before showing me the answer.

The tests got harder—multiplying numbers in my head, finding the queen of hearts in a deck of cards, trying to stand on my head without using my hands, predicting the daily temperatures in Los Angeles, New York, and London.

One night I had to look at a page from the Bible for three minutes and then report everything I could remember. "Now Jehoshaphat had riches[1] and honor in abundance and . . . that's all I remember, Ma," I said.

And after seeing my mother's disappointed face once again, something inside of me began to die. I hated the tests, the raised hopes and failed expectations. Before going to bed that night, I looked in the mirror above the bathroom sink and when I saw only my face staring back—and that it would always be this ordinary face—I began to cry. Such a sad, ugly girl! I made high-pitched noises like a crazed animal, trying to scratch out the face in the mirror.

And then I saw what seemed to be the prodigy side of me—because I had never seen that face before. I looked at my reflection, blinking so I could see more clearly. The girl staring back at me was angry, powerful. This girl and I were the same. I had new thoughts, willful thoughts, or rather thoughts filled with lots of won'ts. I won't let her change me, I promised myself. I won't be what I'm not.

20 So now on nights when my mother presented her tests, I performed listlessly, my head propped on one arm. I pretended to be bored. And I was. I got so bored. I started counting the bellows of the foghorns out on the bay while my mother drilled me in other areas. The sound was comforting and reminded me of the cow jumping over the moon. And the next day, I played a game with myself, seeing if my mother would give up on me before eight bellows. After a while I usually counted only one, maybe two bellows at most. At last she was beginning to give up hope.

Two or three months had gone by without any mention of my being a prodigy again. And then one day my mother was watching *The Ed Sullivan*

---

[1] *Now Jehoshaphat had riches:* Jing-Mei had been told to report on the Hebrew monarch Jehoshaphat as narrated in the eighteenth chapter of II Chronicles.

Show[2] on TV. The TV was old and the sound kept shorting out. Every time my mother got halfway up from the sofa to adjust the set, the sound would go back on and Ed would be talking. As soon as she sat down, Ed would go silent again. She got up, the TV broke into loud piano music. She sat down. Silence. Up and down, back and forth, quiet and loud. It was like a stiff embraceless dance between her and the TV set. Finally she stood by the set with her hand on the sound dial.

She seemed entranced by the music, a little frenzied piano piece with this mesmerizing quality, sort of quick passages and then teasing lilting ones before it returned to the quick playful parts.

"*Ni kan*," my mother said, calling me over with hurried hand gestures. "Look here."

I could see why my mother was fascinated by the music. It was being pounded out by a little Chinese girl, about nice years old, with a Peter Pan haircut. The girl had the sauciness of a Shirley Temple. She was proudly modest like a proper Chinese child. And she also did this fancy sweep of a curtsy, so that the fluffy skirt of her white dress cascaded slowly to the floor like the petals of a large carnation.

25   In spite of these warning signs, I wasn't worried. Our family had no piano and we couldn't afford to buy one, let alone reams of sheet music and piano lessons. So I could be generous in my comments when my mother bad-mouthed the little girl on TV.

"Play note right, but doesn't sound good! No singing sound," complained my mother.

"What are you picking on her for?" I said carelessly. "She's pretty good. Maybe she's not the best, but she's trying hard." I knew almost immediately I would be sorry I said that.

"Just like you," she said. "Not the best. Because you not trying." She gave a little huff as she let go of the sound dial and sat down on the sofa.

The little Chinese girl sat down also to play an encore of "Anitra's Dance" by Grieg.[3] I remember the song, because later on I had to learn how to play it.

30   Three days after watching *The Ed Sullivan Show*, my mother told me what my schedule would be for piano lessons and piano practice. She had talked to Mr. Chong, who lived on the first floor of our apartment building. Mr. Chong was a retired piano teacher and my mother had traded housecleaning services for weekly lessons and a piano for me to practice on every day, two hours a day, from four until six.

When my mother told me this, I felt as though I had been sent to hell. I whined and then kicked my foot a little when I couldn't stand it anymore.

"Why don't you like me the way I am? I'm *not* a genius! I can't play the piano. And even if I could, I wouldn't go on TV if you paid me a million dollars!" I cried.

My mother slapped me. "Who ask you be genius?" she shouted. "Only ask you be your best. For your sake. You think I want you be genius? Hnnh! What for! Who ask you!"

---

[2] **The Ed Sullivan Show:** Ed Sullivan (1902–1974), originally a newspaper columnist, hosted this popular variety television show from 1948 to 1971.

[3] **"Anitra's Dance" by Grieg:** a portion of the suite composed for Ibsen's *Peer Gynt* by Norwegian composer Edvard Grieg (1843–1907).

"So ungrateful," I heard her mutter in Chinese. "If she had as much talent as she has temper, she would be famous now."

35   Mr. Chong, whom I secretly nicknamed Old Chong, was very strange, always tapping his fingers to the silent music of an invisible orchestra. He looked ancient in my eyes. He had lost most of the hair on top of his head and he wore thick glasses and had eyes that always looked tired and sleepy. But he must have been younger than I thought, since he lived with his mother and was not married.

I met Old Lady Chong once and that was enough. She had this peculiar smell like a baby that had done something in its pants. And her fingers felt like a dead person's, like an old peach I once found in the back of the refrigerator; the skin just slid off the meat when I picked it up.

I soon found out why Old Chong had retired from teaching piano. He was deaf. "Like Beethoven!" he shouted to me. "We're both listening only in our head!" And he would start to conduct his frantic silent sonatas.

Our lessons went like this. He would open the book and point to different things, explaining their purpose: "Key! Treble! Bass! No sharps or flats! So this is C major! Listen now and play after me!"

And then he would play the C scale a few times, a simple chord, and then, as if inspired by an old, unreachable itch, he gradually added more notes and running trills and a pounding bass until the music was really something quite grand.

40   I would play after him, the simple scale, the simple chord, and then I just played some nonsense that sounded like a cat running up and down on top of garbage cans. Old Chong smiled and applauded and then said, "Very good! But now you must learn to keep time!"

So that's how I discovered that Old Chong's eyes were too slow to keep up with the wrong notes I was playing. He went through the motions in half-time. To help me keep rhythm, he stood behind me, pushing down on my right shoulder for every beat. He balanced pennies on top of my wrists so I would keep them still as I slowly played scales and arpeggios. He had me curve my hand around an apple and keep that shape when playing chords. He marched stiffly to show me how to make each finger dance up and down, staccato like an obedient little soldier.

He taught me all these things, and that was how I also learned I could be lazy and get away with mistakes, lots of mistakes. If I hit the wrong notes because I hadn't practiced enough, I never corrected myself. I just kept playing in rhythm. And Old Chong kept conducting his own private reverie.

So maybe I never really gave myself a fair chance. I did pick up the basics pretty quickly, and I might have become a good pianist at that young age. But I was so determined not to try, not to be anybody different that I learned to play only the most ear-splitting preludes, the most discordant hymns.

Over the next year, I practiced like this, dutifully in my own way. And then one day I heard my mother and her friend Lindo Jong both talking in a loud bragging tone of voice so others could hear. It was after church, and I was leaning against the brick wall wearing a dress with stiff white petticoats. Auntie Lindo's daughter, Waverly, who was about my age, was standing farther down the wall about five feet away. We had grown up together and shared all the closeness of two sisters squabbling over crayons and dolls. In other words, for the most part, we hated each other. I thought she was snotty. Waverly Jong had gained a certain amount of fame as "Chinatown's Littlest Chinese Chess Champion."

45   "She bring home too many trophy," lamented Auntie Lindo that Sunday. "All day she play chess. All day I have no time do nothing but dust off her winnings." She threw a scolding look at Waverly, who pretended not to see her.

    "You lucky you don't have this problem," said Auntie Lindo with a sigh to my mother.

    And my mother squared her shoulders and bragged: "Our problem worser than yours. If we ask Jing-Mei wash dish, she hear nothing but music. It's like you can't stop this natural talent."

    And right then, I was determined to put a stop to her foolish pride.

    A few weeks later, Old Chong and my mother conspired to have me play in a talent show which would be held in the church hall. By then, my parents had saved up enough to buy me a secondhand piano, a black Wurlitzer spinet with a scarred bench. It was the showpiece of our living room.

50   For the talent show, I was to play a piece called "Pleading Child" from Schumann's *Scenes from Childhood*.[4] It was a simple, moody piece that sounded more difficult than it was. I was supposed to memorize the whole thing, playing the repeat parts twice to make the piece sound longer. But I dawdled over it, playing a few bars and then cheating, looking up to see what notes followed. I never really listened to what I was playing. I daydreamed about being somewhere else, about being someone else.

    The part I liked to practice best was the fancy curtsy: right foot out, touch the rose on the carpet with a pointed foot, sweep to the side, left leg bends, look up and smile.

    My parents invited all the couples from the Joy Luck Club to witness my debut. Auntie Lindo and Uncle Tin were there. Waverly and her two older brothers had also come. The first two rows were filled with children both younger and older than I was. The little ones got to go first. They recited simple nursery rhymes, squawked out tunes on miniature violins, twirled Hula Hoops, pranced in pink ballet tutus, and when they bowed or curtsied, the audience would sigh in unison, "Awww," and then clap enthusiastically.

    When my turn came, I was very confident. I remember my childish excitement. It was as if I knew, without a doubt, that the prodigy side of me really did exist. I had no fear whatsoever, no nervousness. I remember thinking to myself, This is it! This is it! I looked out over the audience, at my mother's blank face, my father's yawn, Auntie Lindo's stiff-lipped smile, Waverly's sulky expression. I had on a white dress layered with sheets of lace, and a pink bow in my Peter Pan haircut. As I sat down I envisioned people jumping to their feet and Ed Sullivan rushing up to introduce me to everyone on TV.

    And I started to play. It was so beautiful. I was so caught up in how lovely I looked that at first I didn't worry how I would sound. So it was a surprise to me when I hit the first wrong note and I realized something didn't sound quite right. And then I hit another and another followed that. A chill started

---

[4] ***Scenes from Childhood:*** *Scenes from Childhood*, or *Kinderszenen* (1836), is one of the best-known works for piano by Robert Schumann (1810–1856).

at the top of my head and began to trickle down. Yet I couldn't stop playing, as though my hands were bewitched. I kept thinking my fingers would adjust themselves back, like a train switching to the right track. I played this strange jumble through two repeats, the sour notes staying with me all the way to the end.

55   When I stood up, I discovered my legs were shaking. Maybe I had just been nervous and the audience, like Old Chong, had seen me go through the right motions and had not heard anything wrong at all. I swept my right foot out, went down on my knee, looked up and smiled. The room was quiet, except for Old Chong, who was beaming and shouting, "Bravo! Bravo! Well done!" But then I saw my mother's face, her stricken face. The audience clapped weakly, and as I walked back to my chair, with my whole face quivering as I tried not to cry, I heard a little boy whisper to his mother, "That's awful," and the mother whispered back, "Well, she certainly tried."

    And now I realized how many people were in the audience, the whole world it seemed. I was aware of eyes burning into my back. I felt the shame of my mother and father as they sat stiffly throughout the rest of the show.

    We could have escaped during intermission. Pride and some strange sense of honor must have anchored my parents to their chairs. And so we watched it all: the eighteen-year-old boy with a fake mustache who did a magic show and juggled flaming hoops while riding a unicycle. The breasted girl with white makeup who sang from *Madama Butterfly*[5] and got honorable mention. And the eleven-year-old boy who won first prize playing a tricky violin song that sounded like a busy bee.[6]

    After the show, the Hsus, the Jongs, and the St. Clairs from the Joy Luck Club came up to my mother and father.

    "Lots of talented kids," Auntie Lindo said vaguely, smiling broadly.

60   "That was somethin' else," said my father, and I wondered if he was referring to me in a humorous way, or whether he even remembered what I had done.

    Waverly looked at me and shrugged her shoulders. "You aren't genius like me," she said matter-of-factly. And if I hadn't felt so bad, I would have pulled her braids and punched her stomach.

    But my mother's expression was what devastated me: a quiet, blank look that said she had lost everything. I felt the same way, and it seemed as if everybody were now coming up, like gawkers at the scene of an accident, to see what parts were actually missing. When we got on the bus to go home, my father was humming the busy-bee tune and my mother was silent. I kept thinking she wanted to wait until we got home before shouting at me. But when my father unlocked the door to our apartment, my mother walked in and then went to the back, into the bedroom. No accusations. No blame. And in a way, I felt disappointed. I had been waiting for her to start shouting, so I could shout back and cry and blame her for all my misery.

---

[5] *Madama Butterfly:* The girl probably sang "Un Bel Di," the signature soprano aria from the opera *Madama Butterfly* by Giacomo Puccini (1858–1924).

[6] *busy bee:* probably the well-known "Flight of the Bumblebee" by Nikolay Rimsky-Korsakov (1844–1908).

I assumed my talent-show fiasco meant I never had to play the piano again. But two days later, after school, my mother came out of the kitchen and saw me watching TV.

"Four clock," she reminded me as if it were any other day. I was stunned, as though she were asking me to go through the talent-show torture again. I wedged myself more tightly in front of the TV.

"Turn off TV," she called from the kitchen five minutes later.

I didn't budge. And then I decided. I didn't have to do what my mother said anymore. I wasn't her slave. This wasn't China. I had listened to her before and look what happened. She was the stupid one.

She came out from the kitchen and stood in the arched entryway of the living room. "Four clock," she said once again, louder.

"I'm not going to play anymore," I said nonchalantly. "Why should I? I'm not a genius."

She walked over and stood in front of the TV. I saw her chest was heaving up and down in an angry way.

"No!" I said, and I now felt stronger, as if my true self had finally emerged. So this was what had been inside me all along.

"No! I won't!" I screamed.

She yanked me by the arm, pulled me off the floor, snapped off the TV. She was frighteningly strong, half pulling, half carrying me toward the piano as I kicked the throw rugs under my feet. She lifted me up and onto the hard bench. I was sobbing by now, looking at her bitterly. Her chest was heaving even more and her mouth was open, smiling crazily as if she were pleased I was crying.

"You want me to be someone that I'm not!" I sobbed. "I'll never be the kind of daughter you want me to be!"

"Only two kinds of daughters," she shouted in Chinese. "Those who are obedient and those who follow their own mind! Only one kind of daughter can live in this house. Obedient daughter!"

"Then I wish I wasn't your daughter. I wish you weren't my mother," I shouted. As I said these things I got scared. It felt like worms and toads and slimy things crawling out of my chest, but it also felt good, as if this awful side of me had surfaced, at last.

"Too late change this," said my mother shrilly.

And I could sense her anger rising to its breaking point. I wanted to see it spill over. And that's when I remembered the babies she had lost in China, the ones we never talked about. "Then I wish I'd never been born!" I shouted. "I wish I were dead! Like them."

It was as if I had said the magic words. Alakazam!—and her face went blank, her mouth closed, her arms went slack, and she backed out of the room, stunned, as if she were blowing away like a small brown leaf, thin, brittle, lifeless.

It was not the only disappointment my mother felt in me. In the years that followed, I failed her so many times, each time asserting my own will, my right to fall short of expectations. I didn't get straight As. I didn't become class president. I didn't get into Stanford. I dropped out of college.

For unlike my mother, I did not believe I could be anything I wanted to be. I could only be me.

And for all those years, we never talked about the disaster at the recital or my terrible accusations afterward at the piano bench. All that remained unchecked, like a betrayal that was now unspeakable. So I never found a way to ask her why she had hoped for something so large that failure was inevitable.

And even worse, I never asked her what frightened me the most: Why had she given up hope?

For after our struggle at the piano, she never mentioned my playing again. The lessons stopped. The lid to the piano was closed, shutting out the dust, my misery, and her dreams.

So she surprised me. A few years ago, she offered to give me the piano, for my thirtieth birthday. I had not played in all those years. I saw the offer as a sign of forgiveness, a tremendous burden removed.

85 "Are you sure?" I asked shyly. "I mean, won't you and Dad miss it?"

"No, this your piano," she said firmly. "Always your piano. You only one can play."

"Well, I probably can't play anymore," I said. "It's been years."

"You pick up fast," said my mother, as if she knew this was certain. "You have natural talent. You could been genius if you want to."

"No I couldn't."

90 "You just not trying," said my mother. And she was neither angry nor sad. She said it as if to announce a fact that could never be disproved. "Take it," she said.

But I didn't at first. It was enough that she had offered it to me. And after that, every time I saw it in my parents' living room, standing in front of the bay windows, it made me feel proud, as if it were a shiny trophy I had won back.

Last week I sent a tuner over to my parents' apartment and had the piano reconditioned, for purely sentimental reasons. My mother had died a few months before and I had been getting things in order for my father, a little bit at a time. I put the jewelry in special silk pouches. The sweaters she had knitted in yellow, pink, bright orange—all the colors I hated—I put those in moth-proof boxes. I found some old Chinese silk dresses, the kind with little slits up the sides. I rubbed the old silk against my skin, then wrapped them in tissue and decided to take them home with me.

After I had the piano tuned, I opened the lid and touched the keys. It sounded even richer than I remembered. Really, it was a very good piano. Inside the bench were the same exercise notes with handwritten scales, the same secondhand music books with their covers held together with yellow tape.

I opened up the Schumann book to the dark little piece I had played at the recital. It was on the left-hand side of the page, "Pleading Child." It looked more difficult than I remembered. I played a few bars, surprised at how easily the notes came back to me.

95 And for the first time, or so it seemed, I noticed the piece on the right-hand side. It was called "Perfectly Contented." I tried to play this one as well. It had a lighter melody but the same flowing rhythm and turned out to be quite easy. "Pleading Child" was shorter but slower; "Perfectly Contented" was longer, but faster. And after I played them both a few times, I realized they were two halves of the same song.

FOCUSED FREE WRITES

1. What are the strengths and weaknesses of the characters introduced here?
2. What conflicts do these characters face? Do they overcome these conflicts or not? Are the characters round or flat?
3. How would you describe the theme of this story?
4. Which images or symbols stand out here? Refer to specific moments in the text.
5. What do you think Jing-Mei would do or would not do if she were to become a mother?

CRITICAL Contexts

Assimilation versus Acculturation

A literary critic who emphasizes Ethnic Literary Studies or African American studies might examine a text in terms of the domination of one ethnic group over another within the themes, settings, or characterizations of a particular piece of literature. Such critics are interested in examples of **hybridity**, or the interrelationship of cultures, and **resistance to hybridity**, as subordinate cultures are forced to submit.

There is some overlap between these approaches and the **post–colonial approach** discussed in the next chapter, which examines texts with an awareness of the power relations both explicitly and implicitly presented. The post–colonial critic identifies how the dominant or colonial culture is valued and privileged, and how the colonized culture in a text can be devalued or oppressed. Therefore, texts do not present universal values as much as historically and socially contextualized commentaries on cultures. Often, texts reflect these dynamics without awareness or acknowledgment of the imperialist and colonialist relationships between the oppressor and the other. This relationship is naturalized to the extent that **the other** is animalized or "rightfully" subjugated. The post–colonial critic then attempts to reevaluate and reascribe value to difference and otherness and makes apparent the cultural commentary in a text.

The preceding stories can be approached through this critical lens as characters struggle to identify themselves with changing cultures, to modify their identities as cultures transition, and to maintain their identities in spite of cultural clashes. One way to understand this process is in terms of **assimilation** and **acculturation**. Assimilation is the process by which individuals or groups of different ethnic heritages are absorbed into the dominant culture of a society. In the process, outsiders may give up cultural traits to take on new traits that make them indistinguishable from members of the dominant group. Acculturation, however, is a set of processes in which artifacts, customs, and beliefs are interchanged when societies with different cultural traditions come into contact. Such modification can be the result of gradual incorporation or forced directed change.

How do these stories address the themes of assimilation and acculturation?

Are they critical of assimilation or acculturation? Or do they celebrate assimilation or acculturation?

The Act of Comparison

When we compare, we examine the similarities and the differences between two or more things. If we choose to emphasize the similarities, we are comparing, and if we choose to emphasize the distinctions, we are contrasting. In either case, we set two objects side by side to identify the resemblances. We learned in the previous chapter that the act of argument involves interpretation and analysis. The act of comparison, the focus of this chapter, builds on these earlier skills. Readers must interpret and analyze two different texts and then argue for their similarities or differences in a comparison.

Of course, we compare not only literary texts but everyday things on a daily basis. When choosing a cell phone plan, the prospective buyer compares the elements of each plan: the cost, the minutes included, the coverage area, and the kind of phone available. In analyzing these components, he or she can then come to a conclusion about which company to choose.

Similarly, when analyzing literature a reader argues for a particular meaning of a text based on an analysis of the component parts of each text. The point of making comparisons is to see what interesting discoveries you may make about one or both of the texts. So you may start off comparing several different elements of the texts, but wind up thinking that it's really only one element that offers something striking. In that case, you might then go back and examine that one element in more detail.

Describe a time when you had to compare two things to make your case for something. How did comparing the two things help you come to a decision?

Choosing Two Texts to Compare

A useful first step in a comparison may be to analyze each work on its own, or at least free write about works that might be compared. You might ask yourself to write about significant themes, characters, moments, symbols, or images in a handful of works. Reflect on these free writes and circle any common ground. Which two works offer you intriguing overlaps or potential for elaboration? In what two works are there significant resemblances or parallels? You may want to consider the following ideas as you make your decision.

■ Select two texts that are obviously similar, for example, two texts about fathers, then set out to examine significant differences. For example, any of the poems later in this chapter are about children in conflict with their fathers. However, each of the narrators has a different relationship with the past: some have a new vision of their fathers and some have a bitterness that can't be forgotten.

■ Select two obviously different texts and set out to show their similarities. For example, is it possible that Walker's and Tan's texts, while set in different times and places, address a common theme? For example, while Walker's story is about an African American family in the rural south and Tan's story describes Chinese American immigrants in an urban setting, Alice Walker's "Everyday Use" and Amy Tan's "Two Kinds" are both about the struggles of young women in conflict with their mothers to find value in their identities and their cultures. However, Walker's story celebrates the daughter who has always valued her identity, and Tan explores the narrative of the prodigal daughter who strays and finds her way back.

Also, note that if two texts are simply very different, there's not much point in comparing them. It's the combination of similarities and differences that makes for a revealing comparison. Discussing the differences between Tan's and Walker's story does not reveal anything but obvious information. Instead, something new must be revealed when the works are set side by side.

Reflect on potential comparisons in this chapter or in the whole book. Think of reading experiences in which you made a connection to other works or class discussions where students suggested similarities.

Charting Similarities and Differences

It may be useful to brainstorm about similarities and differences using charts like those that follow. The first two focus on similarities and differences while the last one brings those together in one chart.

Similarities between Walker's "Everyday Use" and Tan's "Two Kinds"

Literary Element	Text 1: "Everyday Use"	Text 2: "Two Kinds"
character of the mother	believes her daughters are exceptional: fantasy of reunion with Dee on TV	believes her daughter is exceptional: desire to have her daughter be a piano prodigy
character of the daughter	wants to escape her past and comes to appreciate it: Dee escapes past and comes to appreciate it for the wrong reasons unlike her sister who has always appreciated her past	wants to escape her past and comes to appreciate it: daughter comes to appreciate her mother
symbol	quilt as symbol of heritage	piano as a symbol of the mother's faith and dreams
theme of culture clash	assimilation and acculturation of African heritage	assimilation and acculturation of Chinese heritage

A second chart would be used for differences.

Differences between Walker's "Everyday Use" and Tan's "Two Kinds"

Literary Element	Text 1: "Everyday Use"	Text 2: "Two Kinds"
point of view	from the mother's perspective	from the daughter's perspective
character of the daughter	both daughters are flat characters who do not change	the daughter has a new realization about her past and her mother
setting	poor African American family in the rural south	middle-class Chinese American family in an urban setting

or:

Similarities and Differences between Walker's "Everyday Use" and Tan's "Two Kinds"

Literary Element	Similarities	Differences
mother as character	mothers are in conflict with daughters over their past and future	Walker's story focuses on the mother's perspective and the daughter who has always respected her past is newly appreciated
daughter as character	daughters reject their mothers and their lifestyles and values	Tan's daughter is almost a combination of the two in Walker's: she comes to appreciate the past she had rejected
theme of valuing the past	characters come to value the past and objects that represent the past in new ways	the character that has this revelation is the mother in "Everyday Use" and the daughter in "Two Kinds"

Return to your notes about potential texts for comparison. Construct your own charts to compare two works or elements within works.

Analyzing and Interpreting the Comparisons

After these similarities and differences are organized, you will want to ask what they add up to—what does the comparison reveal that is informative or interesting? This would be a good time to free write your reflections and your observations about these reflections.

For example, in reflecting on these charts, the writer might see that both of these stories contain very similar elements but use them in different ways to argue for a similar theme. In both stories, the main characters must go through conflict to find new value in the past and objects that represent the past. In one story, this main character is the mother; in the other, she is the daughter.

Reflect on the charts you constructed in the focused free write above. What comparisons can be elaborated on? What examples from the texts support these comparisons?

POEMS

The following poems are grouped together with broad suggestions as a beginning point for making specific comparisons between works.

COMPARING THEMES: GROWING UP

Growing up means not only establishing one's own identity but also remembering one's heritage. The following poems address this tension.

PRE-READING Has it been your experience that understanding where you are going means recognizing where you have come from? Discuss.

Rita Dove (1952–).   *The second of four children, Rita Dove was born in Akron, Ohio. A Presidential Scholar in high school, Dove studied English, languages, and music at Miami University in Oxford, Ohio. After a year in Germany on a Fulbright, she earned an MFA in poetry from the Iowa Writer's Workshop and published her first book that same year. Many books of poetry followed, including the 1987 Pulitzer Prize-winning* Thomas and Beulah, *as well as a number of novels, short stories, plays, and essays. Dove continues to win many academic and literary honors, including appointment as the nation's seventh Poet Laureate in 1993.*

Rita Dove

ADOLESCENCE I

In water-heavy nights behind grandmother's porch
We knelt in the tickling grass and whispered:
Linda's face hung before us, pale as a pecan,
And it grew wise as she said:
    "A boy's lips are soft,
     As soft as baby's skin."
The air closed over her words.
A firefly whirred near my ear, and in the distance
I could hear streetlamps ping
Into miniature suns
Against a feathery sky.

ADOLESCENCE III

With Dad gone, Mom and I worked
The dusky rows of tomatoes.
As they glowed orange in sunlight
And rotted in shadows, I too
Grew orange and softer, swelling out
Starched cotton slips.

The texture of twilight made me think of
Lengths of Dotted Swiss. In my room
I wrapped scarred knees in dresses
That once went to big-band dances;
I baptized my earlobes with rosewater.
Along the window-sill, the lipstick stubs
Glittered in their steel shells.

Looking out at the rows of clay
And chicken manure, I dreamed how it would happen:
He would meet me by the blue spruce,
A carnation over his heart, saying,
"I have come for you, Madam;
I have loved you in my dreams."
At his touch, the scabs would fall away.
Over his shoulder, I see my father coming toward us:
He carries his tears in a bowl,
And blood hangs in the pine-soaked air.

PRE-READING "Fathers inspire strong emotions." Discuss an illustrative example of this statement from your own experience.

Judith Ortiz Cofer (1952–). *A writer of poetry and prose, Judith Ortiz Cofer began her early life shuttling between her home in New Jersey and her mother's rich family life in Puerto Rico. Cofer turned to reading and writing at an early age. She earned degrees in English at Augusta College in Georgia and at Florida Atlantic University. While beginning her writing career as a poet, Cofer soon turned to fiction, earning a Pulitzer Prize nomination for her first novel, The Line of the Sun. She continues to write essays, short stories, and children's books while teaching English and Creative Writing at the University of Georgia.*

Judith Ortiz Cofer

COMMON GROUND   [1987]

Blood tells the story of your life
in heartbeats as you live it;
bones speak in the language
of death, and flesh thins
5 with age when up

through your pores rises
the stuff of your origin.

These days,
when I look into the mirror I see
10　my grandmother's stern lips
speaking in parentheses at the corners
of my mouth of pain and deprivation
I have never known. I recognize
my father's brows arching in disdain
15　over the objects of my vanity, my mother's
nervous hands smoothing lines
just appearing on my skin,
like arrows point downward
to our common ground.

FOCUSED FREE WRITES

1. What stories do these poems tell?
2. How are the two poems similar? How are they different?
3. Who peoples these poems? Be specific in describing the "characters" here.
4. What themes are introduced?
5. What words and images are significant? Cite particular moments from the text.
6. What can you identify about the styles of these poems?
7. How and why do they focus on "blood"?

COMPARING THEMES: FATHERS

The following texts are often compared for their contrasting viewpoints of fatherhood.

Robert Hayden (1913–1980).　*Robert Hayden was born in Detroit and raised by foster parents. He showed an early aptitude for reading and writing poetry, and he worked a variety of odd jobs to eventually enroll at Detroit City College. In 1940, Hayden married and began graduate work in creative writing and poetry at the University of Michigan. His first position as assistant professor of English at Fisk University in Nashville was also his first exposure to prejudice and segregation. Nevertheless, he taught at Fisk for twenty-two years before receiving substantial recognition for his poetry. At the time of his death, he was serving as the first African American poetry consultant for the Library of Congress.*

Robert Hayden

THOSE WINTER SUNDAYS　　　　　　　　　　　　[1962]

Sundays too my father got up early
and put his clothes on in the blueblack cold,
then with cracked hands that ached
from labor in the weekday weather made

5 banked fires blaze. No one ever thanked him.
   I'd wake and hear the cold splintering, breaking.
   When the rooms were warm, he'd call,
   and slowly I would rise and dress,
   fearing the chronic angers of that house,

10 Speaking indifferently to him,
   who had driven out the cold
   and polished my good shoes as well.
   What did I know, what did I know
   of love's austere and lonely offices?

FOCUSED FREE WRITES

1. Who is speaking in this poem? Is this narrator static or dynamic?
2. What story does the poem tell?
3. What is the poem's theme? What is its purpose?
4. What words and images are particularly effective in expressing this purpose or theme?
5. What do you notice about this poem's style?

Lucille Clifton (1936–). *Born Thelma Lucile Sayles in Depew, New York, Clifton showed an early interest in reading and writing. After attending Howard University for two years and the State University of New York at Fredonia for a year, she worked at clerical jobs and continued to write poetry. Eventually, she earned a poet-in-residence position at Coppin State College in Baltimore. She taught at the University of California at Santa Cruz and at American University in Washington before assuming the Distinguished Professor of Humanities position at St. Mary's College of Maryland. Clifton has published half a dozen collections of poetry and several children's books. She is the recipient of numerous awards and honors.*

Lucille Clifton

FORGIVING MY FATHER   [1980]

it is friday. we have come
to the paying of the bills.
all week you have stood in my dreams
like a ghost, asking for more time
5 but today is payday, payday old man,
my mother's hand opens in her early grave
and i hold it out like a good daughter.

there is no more time for you. there will
never be time enough daddy daddy old lecher
10 old liar. i wish you were rich so i could take it all
and give the lady what she was due
but you were the only son of a needy father,

the father of a needy son,
you gave her all you had
15 which was nothing. you have already given her
all you had.

you are the pocket that was going to open
and come up empty any friday.
you were each other's bad bargain, not mine.
20 daddy old pauper old prisoner, old dead man
what am i doing here collecting?
you lie side by side in debtor's boxes
and no accounting will open them up.

FOCUSED FREE WRITES

1. Who is speaking here? Is the narrator static or dynamic?
2. What story does this poem tell?
3. What is the poem's theme? What is its purpose?
4. What words and images are particularly effective in expressing this purpose or theme?
5. What do you notice about this poem's style?

Sylvia Plath—biography see Chapter 1.

Sylvia Plath

DADDY   [1962]

You do not do, you do not do
Any more, black shoe
In which I have lived like a foot
For thirty years, poor and white,
5 Barely daring to breathe or Achoo.

Daddy, I have had to kill you.
You died before I had time—
Marble-heavy, a bag full of God,
Ghastly statue with one gray toe[1]
10 Big as a Frisco seal

And a head in the freakish Atlantic
Where it pours bean green over blue
In the waters off the beautiful Nauset.[2]
I used to pray to recover you.
15 Ach, du.[3]

---

[1] Sylvia Plath's father Otto lost a toe to gangrene.

[2] **Nauset:** Cape Cod inlet.

[3] **Ach, du:** Oh, you.

In the German tongue, in the Polish town[4]
Scraped flat by the roller
Of wars, wars, wars.
But the name of the town is common.
20   My Polack friend

Says there are a dozen or two.
So I never could tell where you
Put your foot, your root,
I never could talk to you.
25   The tongue stuck in my jaw.

It stuck in a barb wire snare.
Ich, ich, ich, ich,[5]
I could hardly speak.
I thought every German was you.
30   And the language obscene

An engine, an engine
Chuffing me off like a Jew.
A Jew to Dachau, Auschwitz, Belsen.[6]
I began to talk like a Jew.
35   I think I may well be a Jew.

The snows of the Tyrol, the clear beer of Vienna
Are not very pure or true.
With my gypsy ancestress and my weird luck
And my Taroc pack and my Taroc pack[7]
40   I may be a bit of a Jew.

I have always been scared of *you*,
With your Luftwaffe, your gobbledygoo.[8]
And your neat mustache
And your Aryan eye, bright blue.
45   Panzer-man, panzer-man, O You—[9]

Not God but a swastika
So black no sky could squeak through.
Every woman adores a Fascist,
The boot in the face, the brute
50   Brute heart of a brute like you.

You stand at the blackboard, daddy,
In the picture I have of you,

---

[4] Otto Plath was of German origins and born in Grabow, Poland.

[5] **ich:** I.

[6] Nazi death camps in World War II.

[7] **Taroc pack:** refers to a pack of Tarot cards used for telling fortunes.

[8] **Luftwaffe:** the German air force.

[9] **Panzer-man:** A member of the Nazi tank division.

A cleft in your chin instead of your foot
But no less a devil for that, no not
55 Any less the black man who

Bit my pretty red heart in two.
I was ten when they buried you.
At twenty I tried to die
And get back, back, back to you.
60 I thought even the bones would do.

But they pulled me out of the sack,
And they stuck me together with glue.
And then I knew what to do.
I made a model of you,
65 A man in black with a Meinkampf look

And a love of the rack and the screw.
And I said I do, I do.
So daddy, I'm finally through.
The black telephone's off at the root,
70 The voices just can't worm through.

If I've killed one man, I've killed two—
The vampire who said he was you
And drank my blood for a year,
Seven years, if you want to know.
75 Daddy, you can lie back now.

There's a stake in your fat black heart
And the villagers never liked you.
They are dancing and stamping on you.
They always *knew* it was you.
80 Daddy, daddy, you bastard, I'm through.

FOCUSED FREE WRITES

1. Who is speaking here? Is the narrator static or dynamic?
2. What story does this poem tell?
3. What is the poem's theme? What is its purpose?
4. What words and images are particularly effective in expressing this purpose or theme?
5. What do you notice about this poem's style?

Theodore Roethke (1908–1963). *Theodore Roethke has included aspects of his upbringing in his poetry. Born in Saginaw, Michigan, Roethke excelled in school and sports, particularly tennis. He graduated summa cum laude from the University of Michigan and after some graduate work in literature at Harvard returned to UM for his Masters. Roethke taught at Lafayette, Michigan State, Penn State,* and Bennington before becoming a professor of English at the University of Washington, a post he would hold until the year before his death. While plagued by depression and alcoholism his entire life, Roethke continued to write award-winning poetry, publishing multiple volumes and earning substantial honors and prizes.

Theodore Roethke

MY PAPA'S WALTZ [1942]

The whiskey on your breath
Could make a small boy dizzy;
But I hung on like death:
Such waltzing was not easy.

We romped until the pans
5 Slid from the kitchen shelf;
My mother's countenance
Could not unfrown itself.

The hand that held my wrist
Was battered on one knuckle;
10 At every step you missed
My right ear scraped a buckle.

You beat time on my head
With a palm caked hard by dirt,
Then waltzed me off to bed
15 Still clinging to your shirt.

FOCUSED FREE WRITES

1. Who is speaking in this poem? Is the narrator static or dynamic?
2. What story does this poem tell?
3. What is the poem's theme? What is its purpose?
4. What words and images are particularly effective in expressing this purpose or theme?
5. What do you notice about this poem's style?

Writing a Comparison and Contrast Essay

In this chapter, you have been considering the similarities and differences between texts through the critical thinking act of comparison; now let's translate that thinking into a formal written product. Your assignment is to write an argument comparing two works in this chapter. Your thesis should focus on the particular elements that can be productively compared to come to a new understanding of the meaning of the texts at hand. In other words, you will use comparison to further interpret and analyze these works. Therefore, it will be necessary for you to use the skills of interpretation, analysis, and argumentation to develop this project.

Discovering Similarities and Differences

Your prewriting should engage the two texts in comparisons. You might use the kinds of charts discussed earlier in this chapter in conjunction with focused free writing to explore your thinking about potential works. For example, in reviewing his Focused Free Writes from this chapter, one writer found that his thoughts were the most detailed and thorough when talking about the father poems.

Literary Element	Text 1: "Those Winter Sundays"	Text 2: "forgiving my father"	Text 3: "Daddy"	Text 4: "My Papa's Waltz"
theme	new appreciation for father	forgiveness of father is impossible	trying to move beyond father	coming to terms with father
narrator	learns to reconsider past in new light to appreciate father	is bitterly angry at father	is bitterly angry at father	recognizes that life with father is not what it appeared
figurative language	uses Sunday as illustration of father's care	extended metaphor of payday	multiple metaphors: nazi, vampire...	extended metaphor of dance

Look back at your Focused Free Writes or brainstorm on your own. Construct a chart, mapping the similarities and differences between or among potential texts.

Focusing on What Is Revealed

Using this method, the writer can quickly see similarities and differences. While these poems all address similar topics (fathers), the themes are slightly different and the use of poetic elements is also slightly different. Therefore, comparison of any two of these poems might be useful. The writer could establish the similarities in theme and then elaborate on the contrasting use of poetic elements.

However, I might want to allow for a more focused thesis. In identifying overlaps or similarities in the chart, I might have grounds for a comparison of these similarities and then a discussion of any subtle differences. For example, the narrators of both Clifton and Plath's poems express bitter anger toward the fathers. In the sample essay reprinted at the end of this chapter, Stephanie found it productive to look at how that anger is developed stylistically. While the tone is similar, the execution is quite different.

Upon rereading the poems and then charting out similarities and differences, the writer came to recognize that he had a similar idea about Clifton's poem "forgiving my father" and Roethke's "My Papa's Waltz." Both of these poets feel the same bitterness for their irresponsible fathers and express this bitterness using metaphor in their poems. The writer might think through these similarities and differences in another chart in order to follow this new, more focused thought back through the works.

Focus on what is revealed in the chart you developed a few moments ago. What interesting or unique overlaps do you see? What might make a fruitful focus? What is something you could talk more about?

Shaping a Thesis

A comparison paper will necessarily address both similarities and differences between texts; however, one aspect or another will be more emphasized or developed. When constructing a thesis statement in a comparison paper, you will want to explain which you are focusing on. Be specific.

Your first draft may capture the vague initial thinking for your project:

- There are many similarities and differences between "forgiving my father" and "My Papa's Waltz."
- While "forgiving my father" and "My Papa's Waltz" have many similarities, they are also different.
- While "forgiving my father" and "My Papa's Waltz" are really different, they are also similar in many ways.

All of these potential thesis statements would need to be specified.

A Thesis Focused on Similarities

When constructing a thesis focused on similarities, it is useful to acknowledge the differences. Differences might be addressed in a brief sentence in the introduction or in a dependent clause of the thesis statement. Then you might emphasize the thrust of your argument, the similarities, in the last sentence of your introduction.

> While "Everyday Use" and "Two Kinds" take place among decidedly different people in clearly contrasting settings, Walker's and Tan's stories both describe characters coming to terms with their heritage.

A Thesis Focused on Differences

When constructing a thesis focused on differences, you will want to make the same move, but in the opposite direction. After explaining the similarity, develop the difference:

> While Clifton and Plath angrily and viciously dismiss their fathers in their poems, they use distinct and unique controlled figurative language to do so. Both "forgiving my father" and "My Papa's Waltz" poetically describe tragic experiences with fathers through the use of extended metaphors. These similar themes and devices, however, convey decidedly different tones, one of bitter dismissal and one of understated realization.

Draft a potential thesis for your project.

Writing to Advance the Thesis

There are two main ways to consider organizing a comparison. In a block comparison, each text is discussed on its own on all points, and then the second text is discussed on the same points and in the same order, with references back to the points about the first text. In a point-by-point comparison, one point about both texts are discussed together, then another, and so on. The charts you developed previously may help you imagine your organization.

Block comparison

Text 1

    Character

    Theme

    Setting

    etc.

Text 2

    Character

    Theme

    Setting

    etc.

For example:

Text 1: "Everyday Use"

    Characters of daughters

    Narration

    Theme

Text 2: "Two Kinds"

    Character of daughter

    Narration

    Theme

Point-by-point comparison

Character

    Text 1

    Text 2

Theme

    Text 1

    Text 2

Setting

    Text 1

    Text 2

For example:

Characters

> "Everyday Use"

> "Two Kinds"

Narration

> "Everyday Use"

> "Two Kinds"

Theme

> "Everyday Use"

> "Two Kinds"

Customized comparison:

Often, however, your structure will be based on whatever unique idea you developed from your examination of the similarities and differences between the texts. In fact, you may plan for a paper to be organized using one of the above patterns, and find that in writing it, another model is necessary. Ideally, in successful papers, the ideas should determine the essay's structure. Your thesis should explain that organization. For example, suppose the writer's thesis is as follows:

> Both "forgiving my father" and "My Papa's Waltz" poetically describe tragic experiences with fathers through the use of extended metaphors. These similar themes and devices, however, convey decidedly different tones, one of bitter dismissal and one of understated realization.

The paper would be organized as follows:

1. Extended metaphor of "forgiving my father"
2. Extended metaphor of "My Papa's Waltz"
3. Theme of both poems
4. Tone of "forgiving my father"
5. Tone of "My Papa's Waltz"

STUDENT WRITER *In Stephanie's Words...*

In reflecting on her process, Stephanie explains her struggle with the structure of her essay:

> I had some trouble with organizing my essay, specifically with deciding how to compare and contrast the poems. I asked myself, "Should I write alternating paragraphs—that is alternate my analyses of Clifton and Plath's poems—or lump all the similarities and all differences into separate paragraphs?" To write a paper of this persuasion requires planning. I didn't want to sound too repetitive, saying that "Poem A does this while Poem B does this." Initially, I planned to write about the comparisons between the two poems and then the differences. However, after writing one rough draft,

this approach lacked the ease of transition from one paragraph to another, which affected the overall unity of the essay. After a quick evaluation of my essay, I chose to alternate the comparisons and contrasts to provide a better demonstration of transition and unity as well as make my thesis clearer and paper more interesting.

■ *Develop an outline for your paper using one of the above methods.*

Revising for Coherence

Strong transitions are always important to explain the movement of a paper from one idea to the next. And strong topic sentences will be especially essential here to explain the development of the comparison. Each paragraph should direct the reader to the focus of the paragraphs that follow. Take a look at the following topic sentences from Stephanie's paper. Based on these, identify the topic to follow. Then read her sample paper to see if the topic sentence specifically addresses the information to follow.

- As previously mentioned, "forgiving my father" and "Daddy" are poems united in subject matter. Clifton and Plath present to readers female speakers who address an absent father figure. However, their speakers' methods of address depart greatly from each other.
- The poetic structures of Clifton's and Plath's poems reflect the individualized tones established in the opening stanzas.
- As shown in their language, the speakers share a similar sense of justified anger towards their fathers.
- Even though we can connect these poems through the speakers' attempts at renaming their fathers and reclaiming authority, we need to note the distinctions between Clifton's and Plath's style in the process.
- The significance of these stylistic differences fully manifests itself in last stanzas of "forgiving my father" and "Daddy" as the speakers move towards closure.

■ *Revise the topic sentences of your draft to make them as precise as possible.*

Editing and Proofreading

In a comparison essay, it is necessary to be very clear about which text you are discussing at all times. Consider the following tips:

1. The first time you mention a work, use the author's complete name and the complete title of the work. The introduction should identify both works by title and author.
2. In the paragraphs that follow, you need not include the full name of the author in conjunction with the title of the work:
   - You can refer to the author by his or her **last name**: "Walker's short story," "Plath's poem," and so on.
   - You can refer to just the title of the work. According to MLA style, after stating the title in full at least once, you may use an obvious shortened form. If you are citing a title often in the text of your paper, especially a longer title, this may be useful: "Things" for "The Things They Carried."

3. In the topic sentence of each paragraph, you should identify the topic of focus and the text of focus.
4. Before you quote a text, identify which work you are quoting, and if you are quoting a play, give an approximate location of the material being quoted.

In the first paragraph of O'Connor's short story, the ending is foreshadowed when the reader is introduced to Julian's mother, her high blood pressure, and her "slimming classes."

Proofread your draft to make sure readers will be clear about which text you are discussing.

Integrating Text from a Reading into Your Writing

There are three skills that should serve you well as you integrate text from a reading when writing about literature: **summary, paraphrase,** and **direct quotation.** When you revise, you will want to consider balancing the use of these three techniques.

Summary

When you come home at the end of the day, your roommate, your significant other, or your parents might ask, "How was your day?" You will not give them a minute-by-minute account of what filled the eight hours you were gone. Instead, you will summarize: "I went to class and had a burger with my lab partner. Then, I went to the library and the gym. I had to stop by the drug store on my way home." A summary is an abstract or an abridgement of what happened.

Often, when reading literature, or even when attempting to avoid reading literature, students look for plot summaries—brief descriptions of the events that transpire in a story, play, even a poem. Accounting for what happens can be useful when writing about literature. For example, a reader who was writing about O'Connor's "Everything That Rises Must Converge" might summarize the plot to illustrate the parallels in the characters of the story:

While Julian is intent on his mother learning a lesson about her elitism and small-mindedness, it is Julian who in the end learns a lesson about precisely those things when it comes to his view of his mother.

A summary like this would be used to help the reader further the thesis. When writing about literature, a summary can condense information about plot, character, setting, or theme. Summary can provide evidence and support for your thesis.

Construct your own summary of one of the works in this chapter.

Paraphrase

Sometimes, it isn't enough to simply summarize a series of events. You might want to focus on just a few important events. For example, at the end of a day, your friend might not simply ask you, "How was your day?" but rather "How was your conversation with your English teacher?" You might find yourself paraphrasing the conversation: "Well, he told me that I need to spend more time revising and that I might want to use the Writing Center on my next draft." When paraphrasing, you restate a text or passage from a text using your own words.

When someone leaves a movie for a minute or two, you might find yourself paraphrasing the dialogue when she returns: "He told her that he knows who killed the victim!" Restating the description, dialog, or moments in a story can be useful when writing about literature. For example, a reader might want to paraphrase the ideas in the final paragraph of the story:

> The hat becomes a symbol of the mother's blindness. When she sees it on a black woman's head, she final sees exactly what Julian wanted her to see, and in getting what he so wished for, her enlightenment brings darkness to Julian as the last paragraph suggests.

A paraphrase of the language of the play allows the writer to translate O'Connor's words into his or her own. Then the writer can use the paraphrase as a basis for arguing that the play focuses on "blindness" and uses imagery of light and darkness.

Paraphrase an event from one of the works in this chapter.

Direct Quotation

In some cases, summary and paraphrase don't give enough of the flavor of the text. The writer might need to convey someone's tone or repeat exactly how something was said. Sometimes a character has said something better than the writer ever could in a paraphrase. For example, if someone invites me to go to dinner, I might need to consider the precise language of the invitation to determine if it is a "date." I might look back at the email or listen to the voicemail to see exactly what was said. A direct quotation repeats the language of the text and discusses it to demonstrate an idea or make a point.

A direct quotation might cite a word, line, or whole passage from the text itself to demonstrate exactly how the idea was conveyed or how the character expressed himself or herself. For example, suppose a writer wanted to look at the use of the word "blind" and the imagery of vision and light. He or she would need to discuss passages where such language appears:

> O'Connor uses the language of vision and sight to illustrate a character's experiencing revelation and enlightenment. Here, Julian believes his mother will finally have a true vision of her place in the world: "The vision of the two hats, identical, broke upon him with the radiance of a brilliant sunrise. His face was suddenly lit with joy. He could not believe that Fate had thrust upon his mother such a lesson" (261). In Julian's mind, seeing the black woman in the same hat will force his mother to see her racism and thus her similarity to African American people. He believes he is more enlightened than his mother.

In directly quoting, writers can discuss lines or whole passages to explain what they mean. Consult Chapter 16 for a detailed discussion of how to integrate sources correctly.

Practice a direct quotation of a line or a passage from a work in this chapter.

Sample Student Paper

Stephanie Roberts's biography may be found on page 567.

Stephanie Roberts

Professor Howells

English 102

25 Sept. 2010

Structure and Style in Lucille Clifton's "forgiving my father"

and Sylvia Plath's "Daddy": Renaming and Reclaiming

Given the illustrations of the daughter-father dynamic in
Lucille Clifton's "forgiving my father" and Sylvia Plath's "Daddy,"
readers often examine these poems through a feminist lens. As
their titles suggest, "forgiving my father" and "Daddy" both
involve a female speaker addressing her father. We can extend
this cursory reading to critique the implied power struggle
between the sexes; for instance, we can interpret the daughter
as the symbolic voice of silenced women, finally speaking out
against the father, a repressive agent and clear manifestation of
imposing patriarchal structures. We gravitate toward this particular reading because we identify Clifton and Plath as female poets.
However, when we align the poets' gender with their subject matter, we risk limiting our reading to one generalized interpretation.
Instead of allowing this surface unity to dominate our reading of
Clifton and Plath's poetry, we need to look at the subtle stylistic
differences in structure and language to see how their poems produce distinct meanings concerning communication and power.

As previously mentioned, "forgiving my father" and "Daddy"
are poems united in subject matter. Clifton and Plath present to
readers female speakers who address an absent father figure.
However, their speakers' methods of address depart greatly from
each other. In the opening stanza of "forgiving my father," the

speaker begins, "it is friday. we have come/to the paying of the bills./all week you have stood in my dreams/like a ghost, asking for more time" (lines 1–2). It is evident that in the "we" the speaker implicates both herself and her father. Her tone is inviting yet cautious in delivery. Although the speaker's pronoun usage and tone suggest unity between her and her father, we can detect the distance between the two with the mention of him as a "ghost" in her dreams. The connotations of "dream" and "ghost" point to the father's obvious absence in the poem.

In contrast, Plath's speaker in "Daddy" declares, "You do not do, you do not do/Any more, black shoe" (1–2). The speaker opts for a more direct, albeit initially ambiguous, address to the father. Because the poem is entitled "Daddy," we infer that the pronoun "you" is the speaker's father. The delivery and repetition of "you do not do" is forceful and directed. Like Clifton, Plath incorporates imagery that alludes to the father's absence. In this case, the speaker identifies her subject as a "black shoe." Though more abstract than the "ghost," the black shoe serves to remind us that the father, like the black shoe, is empty, absent, no longer necessary for the speaker. Rather than the unity offered in "forgiving my father," the separation between speaker and subject colors the dynamic of the relationship and sets the tone for the rest of the poem.

The poetic structures of Clifton and Plath's poems reflect the individualized tones established in the opening stanzas. "forgiving my father" is composed of three stanzas, which alternate the septet with the nine-line stanza. In these three stanzas, Clifton's poetic form mimics the ebb and flow of the tide. With the implied unity of "we" and the disunity of imagery and tone with that implication, the poem fluctuates in and out of this pattern, suggesting the potential to enact what the title promises despite his transgressions; we see the speaker struggle between her emotions and the dynamics of her relationship with her father. On the other hand, "Daddy" is composed of sixteen five-line stanzas that clearly deviate from what Clifton does with "forgiving my father." The exactness of the composition mirrors the militancy and repetition that initially open the poem. Although Plath's title "Daddy" implies an informal and seemingly affectionate description of a father, the structure and tone illustrate anything but that assumed understanding; instead, Plath's speaker delivers a strong indictment against her father's oppressive presence in her life. Given these structures, we are further equipped to see how the poets execute similar subject matter in different fashions.

As shown in their language, the speakers share a similar sense of justified anger toward their fathers. In stanza two, Clifton's speaker declares: "there is no time for you. there will/never be time enough daddy daddy old lecher/old liar. i wish you were rich so i could take it all" (8–10). The speaker's bitterness toward her father stems from his inability to provide time for his family. Her desire to steal from him becomes her attempt to reclaim the power he had in their relationship. To amplify her authority and minimize his, she identifies her father through the projection of multiple identities. She first refers to him as "daddy," given readers the sense of affection and familiarity. However, this identification quickly shifts once she calls him "old lecher, old liar." He is no longer "daddy" but a man reduced to pejoratives. For a moment in the second stanza, the speaker relents from the derisive names and identifies her father as "the only son of a needy father" (12). In this personal reference, the speaker returns to the familiarity she previously abandons, establishing a sense of understanding for her father.

Plath's speaker, however, does not offer any such reconciliation to her father or readers. Instead, the speaker follows through with her militancy, asserting "Daddy, I have had to kill you..../Marble-heavy, a bag full of God,/Ghastly statue with one gray toe" (6–8). Although here she projects anger similar to Clifton's speaker, the language Plath's speaker uses in this stanza is remarkably different from Clifton's. And just as the speaker does in "forgiving my father," the speaker in "Daddy" recognizes the familial bond with her father, addressing him as "Daddy." However, the term of endearment holds little weight when paired with "kill." Given the force of the verb "kill," the speaker makes it clear that she wants to erase her father and what he represents. Rather than literally kill him, she does so figuratively by casting him into other identities, such as the "bag full of God" and "ghastly statue," much like what the speaker in "forgiving my father" does with "old lecher/old liar." This act of renaming becomes an act of reclaiming power for Plath's speaker.

Even though we can connect these poems through the speakers' attempts at renaming their fathers and reclaiming authority, we need to note the distinctions between Clifton and Plath's style in the process. Between the omission of capitalization and punctuation and personal references, Clifton's style comes across as informal and intimate. The removal of the formal trappings of writing invites us to see the speaker in personal terms as she addresses her father. Plath's style, however, is more formal and abstract. This becomes apparent halfway through the poem when the speaker announces, "I have always been scared of you,/With your Luftwaffe, your gobbledygoo..../Panzer-man, panzer-man, O You –" (41–5). The combination of repetitive phrases and invented language illustrates the opposite of what Clifton does with her poem. Instead of intimacy, Plath creates distance between speaker, subject, and audience.

The significance of these stylistic differences fully manifests itself in last stanzas of "forgiving my father" and "Daddy" as the speakers move toward closure. Referring to her parents' past relationship, the speaker in the former poem articulates, "you were each other's bad bargain, not mine./ daddy old pauper old prisoner, old dead man/ what am i doing here collecting?" (19–21). This declaration justifies her feelings of bitterness and highlights her recognition of this fact. The subsequent catalog of names for her father illustrates the distance between the pair. He goes from being "daddy" to "old dead man" in her eyes, reflecting a shift from the personal to the impersonal. Her rhetorical question of "what am I doing here collecting?" expresses the realization that demanding for accountability is futile when the accountable is dead. Implied in this understanding is the potential for forgiveness as the poem's title clearly reminds us. The speaker may not be able to forget her father's past misgivings, but she has the option to forgive him for them.

Alternatively, Plath's speaker shows no signs of forgiveness in the concluding stanza. The speaker quietly asserts:

> There's a stake in your fat black heart
> And the villagers never liked you.
> They are dancing and stamping on you.
> They always knew it was you.
> Daddy, daddy, you bastard, I'm through. (76–80)

Resignation from her father is evident. The image of villagers attacking the father reinforces the speaker's final declaration of "I'm through." Closure for her materializes in this vow.

Our tendency to identify Clifton and Plath's poems as one and the same limits our reading and consequently our understanding of the poems. Although "forgiving my father" and "Daddy" convey similar themes concerning power, communication, and distance between daughters and father, the execution of the subject matter is the marker of distinction. When we perform a close comparison of the two poems under this impression, we are able to detect the nuances in structure, style, and theme and realize how remarkably different these poems are.

Works Cited

Clifton, Lucille. "forgiving my father." *Literature: Reading to Write.* Ed. Elizabeth Howells. New York: Pearson, 2010. 289–290. Print.

Plath, Sylvia. "Daddy." *Literature: Reading to Write.* Ed. Elizabeth Howells. New York: Pearson, 2010. 290–292. Print.

7

OPPRESSION AND SOCIAL CHANGE
Using Critical Tools for Analytical Arguments

Fighting Oppression. This photograph from a production of the Theatre of a Two-Headed Calf, in association with the Ontological-Hysteric Incubator in New York City, captures a crucial scene from Susan Glaspell's play *Trifles*. In previous centuries, as this play shows us, it was not always easy for women writers to express themselves publicly. The same holds true for other minority groups. Over time, trailblazers would struggle to make sure silenced voices were heard and unorthodox ideas were considered. What sorts of pioneers are fighting to be heard in our world today? In what forms do their stories get told? What are current issues of oppression in today's society? Are you oppressed? If so, how?

Can writing change the world?

Throughout history, the arts have been an avenue for voicing alternative perspectives. The mainstream point of view is expressed by a variety of cultural institutions, through politics and the mainstream media (TV, newspapers, magazines), in school, and in churches. Writers and artists, however, can provide an alternative voice and alternative space in culture. Literature and art can challenge conventions, protest injustices, or recommend some future course of action. Through art, writers can celebrate or be critical of current events, people, or beliefs, both subtly and overtly, and can suggest possibilities for change. From Aristophanes' anti-war comedy *Lysistrata*, dated 411 B.C. to Picasso's anti-war *Guernica*, painted in 1937, and from Bob Dylan's civil rights lyrics to Charles Moore's civil rights photography in the 1960s, writers and artists of all kinds have used their voices and spotlights, stages and pages, to reach an audience and move them to action.

Throughout literary history, writers have used the page to challenge a dominant way of thinking or give voice to the voiceless. One example, Jonathan Swift's essay "A Modest Proposal: For Preventing the Children of Poor People in Ireland from Being a Burden to their Parents or Country, and for Making them Beneficial to the Public," which was published as a pamphlet in 1729, uses satire to attack the inhumane conditions of the poor. After establishing the dire economic conditions of Ireland, Swift mocks the unfeeling and pragmatic political economists of the day by "modestly" proposing an efficient solution to the problem of the poor: selling their children as food for the wealthy:

> I have been assured by a very knowing American of my acquaintance in London, that a young healthy child well nursed, is, at a year old, a most delicious nourishing and wholesome food, whether stewed, roasted, baked, or boiled; and I make no doubt that it will equally serve in a fricasie, or a ragout.

Using the classical elements of satire, Swift can exaggerate the nation's indifference and shock people into considering the condition of the poor. Similarly, Upton Sinclair's novel *The Jungle*, published in 1906, was written to expose the dangerous and criminal working conditions of immigrants in the U.S. meat-packing industry. His gripping account resulted in a national outcry and political action by the Food and Drug Administration. Many other historical conditions have informed or inspired literary works: Harriet Beecher Stowe, author of the novel *Uncle Tom's Cabin*, was famously described by Abraham Lincoln as "the little lady who made this big war" for the anti-slavery sentiments espoused in her best-selling work and its profound effects on the American public. Certainly, Kate Chopin's novel *The Amakening* explored the "woman question" that had been stirring in the nineteenth century. Her "Story of an Hour," found in Chapter 2, addresses similar themes.

Literature can attempt to overcome oppression in very specific and direct ways. However, challenges to the status quo and oppressive practices can be less focused or directed in questioning conventional ways of thinking or an assumed set of beliefs. Ultimately, all literature can be understood as having an agenda: it normalizes certain behaviors, sanctions certain values, and rewards certain kinds of people. At the same time it marginalizes other behaviors, subordinates other values, and punishes other kinds of people in the development of the narrative. When examining the theme of a certain work of literature, readers can emphasize the message of a work and its acceptance or critique of a culture's way of doing things.

Literature that is extreme to the point of upholding message over art may be categorized as **propaganda**, which is a shortened form of the Latin phrase *congregatio de propaganda fide*, "congregation for propagating the faith." Often used to serve political or religious ends, the term bears a negative connotation when describing, for example, the literature of Russia early in the twentieth century or the literature of Nazi Germany, which was used primarily to disseminate the beliefs of those in power.

Didactic literature is also intended to teach a specific moral lesson, exemplify a doctrine, or provide a model for proper behavior. It too can work to educate more than entertain, to teach more than to delight. In nineteenth-century England, "Condition of England" novels were sometimes accused of heavy-handedness in upholding pedagogy at the expense of art. Novelists such as Elizabeth Gaskell, Benjamin Disraeli, and even Charles Dickens delivered remedies for unfair working conditions, extreme poverty, and rapidly increasing industrialization with the spoonful of sugar found in the novel form.

The writers in this chapter offer a subtle approach to employing the power of literature. While staying true to a particular message, they offer works that also have a high aesthetic value. They establish their works in a particular **setting**, a particular time or place. They establish the particular interrelated conditions in which the text occurs; in other words, they set out a **context**. It then becomes the reader's job to determine the author's tone or attitude toward the subject and to distinguish the characters' attitudes. Finally, literature always inspires engaged readers to consider their own opinions and understandings of the subject at hand.

A common thread among the following texts is that they all challenge oppression, challenge the privileging of one way of thinking. The writers seem to suggest that we should beware of assumptions and consider alternatives when it comes to race, gender, ethnicity, aesthetics, or convention.

What are some examples of writing to overcome or literature with a message you have read in the past?

STORIES

The following stories offer perspectives on scapegoats whom society sacrifices in an exchange of the good of the few for the larger good. You will want to examine how these stories interrogate issues of oppression in terms of race, gender, and more broadly.

| PRE-READING | Describe a time when you were really bored. |

Charlotte Perkins Gilman (1860–1935).   *Born in Hartford, Connecticut to a prominent New England family, Charlotte Anna Perkins' peaceful early childhood was abruptly disrupted when her father abandoned the family. Perkins was left with her mother and siblings to fend for themselves. After marrying a fellow artist and bearing a daughter, she battled depression, eventually turning to Dr. S. Weir Mitchell and his "rest cure" so vividly recounted in "The Yellow Wallpaper." Leaving both the cure and her marriage of obligation for a new life on the west coast, she began to teach, write, lecture, and serve as an activist for the Nationalist Party. Before succumbing to breast cancer in 1935, Charlotte Perkins Gilman had written 186 short stories, 500 poems, a number of novels, and numerous books of nonfiction.*

Charlotte Perkins Gilman

THE YELLOW WALLPAPER [1892]

It is very seldom that mere ordinary people like John and myself secure ancestral halls for the summer.

A colonial mansion, a hereditary estate, I would say a haunted house, and reach the height of romantic felicity—but that would be asking too much of fate!

Still I will proudly declare that there is something queer about it.

Else, why should it be let so cheaply? And why have stood so long untenanted?

5   John laughs at me, of course, but one expects that.

John is practical in the extreme. He has no patience with faith, an intense horror of superstition, and he scoffs openly at any talk of things not to be felt and seen and put down in figures.

John is a physician, and *perhaps*—(I would not say it to a living soul, of course, but this is dead paper and a great relief to my mind)—*perhaps* that is one reason I do not get well faster.

You see he does not believe I am sick! And what can one do?

If a physician of high standing, and one's own husband, assures friends and relatives that there is really nothing the matter with one but temporary nervous depression—a slight hysterical tendency—what is one to do?

My brother is also a physician, and also of high standing, and he says the
10   same thing.

So I take phosphates or phospites—whichever it is—and tonics, and air and exercise, and journeys, and am absolutely forbidden to "work" until I am well again.

Personally, I disagree with their ideas.

Personally, I believe that congenial work, with excitement and change, would do me good.

But what is one to do?

I did write for a while in spite of them; but it *does* exhaust me a good deal—
15   having to be so sly about it, or else meet with heavy opposition.

I sometimes fancy that in my condition if I had less opposition and more society and stimulus—but John says the very worst thing I can do is to think about my condition, and I confess it always makes me feel bad.

So I will let it alone and talk about the house.

The most beautiful place! It is quite alone, standing well back from the road, quite three miles from the village. It makes me think of English places that you read about, for there are hedges and walls and gates that lock, and lots of separate little houses for the gardeners and people.

There is a *delicious* garden! I never saw such a garden—large and shady, full of box-bordered paths, and lined with long grape-covered arbors with seats under them.

20   There were greenhouses, too, but they are all broken now.

There was some legal trouble, I believe, something about the heirs and coheirs; anyhow, the place has been empty for years.

That spoils my ghostliness, I am afraid, but I don't care—there is something strange about the house—I can feel it.

I even said so to John one moonlight evening, but he said what I felt was a draught, and shut the window.

I get unreasonably angry with John sometimes. I'm sure I never used to be so sensitive. I think it is due to this nervous condition.

25   But John says if I feel so I shall neglect proper self-control; so I take pains to control myself—before him, at least, and that makes me very tired.

I don't like our room a bit. I wanted one downstairs that opened on the piazza and had roses all over the window, and such pretty old-fashioned chintz hangings! But John would not hear of it.

He said there was only one window and not room for two beds, and no near room for him if he took another.

He is very careful and loving, and hardly lets me stir without special direction.

I have a schedule prescription for each hour in the day; he takes all care from me, and so I feel basely ungrateful not to value it more.

30   He said he came here solely on my account, that I was to have perfect rest and all the air I could get. "Your exercise depends on your strength, my dear," said he, "and your food somewhat on your appetite; but air you can absorb all the time." So we took the nursery at the top of the house.

It is a big, airy room, the whole floor nearly, with windows that look all ways, and air and sunshine galore. It was nursery first and then playroom and gymnasium, I should judge, for the windows are barred for little children, and there are rings and things in the walls.

The paint and paper look as if a boys' school had used it. It is stripped off— the paper—in great patches all around the head of my bed, about as far as I can reach, and in a great place on the other side of the room low down. I never saw a worse paper in my life. One of those sprawling flamboyant patterns committing every artistic sin.

It is dull enough to confuse the eye in following, pronounced enough to constantly irritate and provoke study, and when you follow the lame uncertain curves for a little distance they suddenly commit suicide—plunge off at outrageous angles, destroy themselves in unheard-of contradictions.

The color is repellent, almost revolting: a smouldering unclean yellow, strangely faded by the slow-turning sunlight. It is a dull yet lurid orange in some places, a sickly sulphur tint in others.

35   No wonder the children hated it! I should hate it myself if I had to live in this room long.

There comes John, and I must put this away—he hates to have me write a word.

We have been here two weeks, and I haven't felt like writing before, since that first day.

I am sitting by the window now, up in this atrocious nursery, and there is nothing to hinder my writing as much as I please, save lack of strength.

John is away all day, and even some nights when his cases are serious.

40 I am glad my case is not serious!

But these nervous troubles are dreadfully depressing.

John does not know how much I really suffer. He knows there is no reason to suffer, and that satisfies him.

Of course it is only nervousness. It does weigh on me so not to do my duty in any way!

I meant to be such a help to John, such a real rest and comfort, and here I am a comparative burden already!

45 Nobody would believe what an effort it is to do what little I am able—to dress and entertain, and order things.

It is fortunate Mary is so good with the baby. Such a dear baby!

And yet I *cannot* be with him, it makes me so nervous.

I suppose John never was nervous in his life. He laughs at me so about this wallpaper!

At first he meant to repaper the room, but afterwards he said that I was letting it get the better of me, and that nothing was worse for a nervous patient than to give way to such fancies.

50 He said that after the wallpaper was changed it would be the heavy bedstead, and then the barred windows, and then that gate at the head of the stairs, and so on.

"You know the place is doing you good," he said, "and really, dear, I don't care to renovate the house just for a three months' rental."

"Then do let us go downstairs," I said, "there are such pretty rooms there."

Then he took me in his arms and called me a blessed little goose, and said he would go down to the cellar, if I wished, and have it whitewashed into the bargain.

But he is right enough about the beds and windows and things.

55 It is as airy and comfortable a room as anyone need wish, and, of course, I would not be so silly as to make him uncomfortable just for a whim.

I'm really getting quite fond of the big room, all but that horrid paper.

Out of one window I can see the garden—those mysterious deep-shaded arbors, the riotous old-fashioned flowers, and bushes and gnarly trees.

Out of another I get a lovely view of the bay and a little private wharf belonging to the estate. There is a beautiful shaded lane that runs down there from the house. I always fancy I see people walking in these numerous paths and arbors, but John has cautioned me not to give way to fancy in the least. He says that with my imaginative power and habit of story-making, a nervous weakness like mine is sure to lead to all manner of excited fancies, and that I ought to use my will and good sense to check the tendency. So I try.

I think sometimes that if I were only well enough to write a little it would relieve the press of ideas and rest me.

60 But I find I get pretty tired when I try.

It is so discouraging not to have any advice and companionship about my work. When I get really well, John says we will ask Cousin Henry and Julia down for a long visit; but he says he would as soon put fireworks in my pillow case as to let me have those stimulating people about now.

I wish I could get well faster.

But I must not think about that. This paper looks to me as if it *knew* what a vicious influence it had!

There is a recurrent spot where the pattern lolls like a broken neck and two bulbous eyes stare at you upside down.

I get positively angry with the impertinence of it and the everlastingness. Up and down and sideways they crawl, and those absurd, unblinking eyes are everywhere. There is one place where two breaths didn't match, and the eyes go all up and down the line, one a little higher than the other.

I never saw so much expression in an inanimate thing before, and we all know how much expression they have! I used to lie awake as a child and get more entertainment and terror out of blank walls and plain furniture than most children could find in a toystore.

I remember what a kindly wink the knobs of our big, old bureau used to have, and there was one chair that always seemed like a strong friend.

I used to feel that if any of the other things looked too fierce I could always hop into that chair and be safe.

The furniture in this room is no worse than inharmonious, however, for we had to bring it all from downstairs. I suppose when this was used as a playroom they had to take the nursery things out, and no wonder! I never saw such ravages as the children have made here.

The wallpaper, as I said before, is torn off in spots, and it sticketh closer than a brother—they must have had perseverance as well as hatred.

Then the floor is scratched and gouged and splintered, the plaster itself is dug out here and there, and this great heavy bed which is all we found in the room, looks as if it had been through the wars.

But I don't mind it a bit—only the paper.

There comes John's sister. Such a dear girl as she is, and so careful of me! I must not let her find me writing.

She is a perfect and enthusiastic housekeeper, and hopes for no better profession. I verily believe she thinks it is the writing which made me sick!

But I can write when she is out, and see her a long way off from these windows.

There is one that commands the road, a lovely shaded winding road, and one that just looks off over the country. A lovely country, too, full of great elms and velvet meadows.

This wallpaper has a kind of sub-pattern in a different shade, a particularly irritating one, for you can only see it in certain lights, and not clearly then.

But in the places where it isn't faded and where the sun is just so—I can see a strange, provoking, formless sort of figure that seems to skulk about behind that silly and conspicuous front design.

There's sister on the stairs!

Well, the Fourth of July is over! The people are all gone and I am tired out. John thought it might do me good to see a little company, so we just had mother and Nellie and the children down for a week.

Of course I didn't do a thing. Jennie sees to everything now.

But it tired me all the same.

John says if I don't pick up faster he shall send me to Weir Mitchell in the fall.

But I don't want to go there at all. I had a friend who was in his hands once, and she says he is just like John and my brother, only more so!

85 Besides, it is such an undertaking to go so far.

I don't feel as if it was worthwhile to turn my hand over for anything, and I'm getting dreadfully fretful and querulous.

I cry at nothing, and cry most of the time.

Of course I don't when John is here, or anybody else, but when I am alone.

And I am alone a good deal just now. John is kept in town very often by serious cases, and Jennie is good and lets me alone when I want her to.

90 So I walk a little in the garden or down that lovely lane, sit on the porch under the roses, and lie down up here a good deal.

I'm getting really fond of the room in spite of the wallpaper. Perhaps *because* of the wallpaper.

It dwells in my mind so!

I lie here on this great immovable bed—it is nailed down, I believe—and follow that pattern about by the hour. It is as good as gymnastics, I assure you. I start, we'll say, at the bottom, down in the corner over there where it has not been touched, and I determine for the thousandth time that I *will* follow that pointless pattern to some sort of a conclusion.

I know a little of the principle of design, and I know this thing was not arranged on any laws of radiation, or alternation, or repetition, or symmetry, or anything else that I ever heard of.

95 It is repeated, of course, by the breadths, but not otherwise.

Looked at in one way each breadth stands alone; the bloated curves and flourishes—a kind of "debased Romanesque" with delirium tremens go waddling up and down in isolated columns of fatuity.

But, on the other hand, they connect diagonally, and the sprawling outlines run off in great slanting waves of optic horror, like a lot of wallowing sea-weeds in full chase.

The whole thing goes horizontally, too, at least it seems so, and I exhaust myself in trying to distinguish the order of its going in that direction.

They have used a horizontal breadth for a frieze, and that adds wonderfully to the confusion.

100 There is one end of the room where it is almost intact, and there, when the crosslights fade and the low sun shines directly upon it, I can almost fancy radiation after all—the interminable grotesques seem to form around a common centre and rush off in headlong plunges of equal distraction.

It makes me tired to follow it. I will take a nap, I guess.

I don't know why I should write this.

I don't want to.

I don't feel able.

105 And I know John would think it absurd. But I *must* say what I feel and think in some way—it is such a relief!

But the effort is getting to be greater than the relief.

Half the time now I am awfully lazy, and lie down ever so much. John says I mustn't lose my strength, and has me take cod liver oil and lots of tonics and things, to say nothing of ale and wine and rare meat.

Dear John! He loves me very dearly, and hates to have me sick. I tried to have a real earnest reasonable talk with him the other day, and tell him how I wish he would let me go and make a visit to Cousin Henry and Julia.

But he said I wasn't able to go, nor able to stand it after I got there: and I did not make out a very good case for myself, for I was crying before I had finished.

110 It is getting to be a great effort for me to think straight. Just this nervous weakness I suppose.

And dear John gathered me up in his arms, and just carried me upstairs and laid me on the bed, and sat by me and read to me till it tired my head.

He said I was his darling and his comfort and all he had, and that I must take care of myself for his sake, and keep well.

He says no one but myself can help me out of it, that I must use my will and self-control and not let any silly fancies run away with me.

There's one comfort—the baby is well and happy, and does not have to occupy this nursery with the horrid wallpaper.

115 If we had not used it, that blessed child would have! What a fortunate escape! Why, I wouldn't have a child of mine, an impressionable little thing, live in such a room for worlds.

I never thought of it before, but it is lucky that John kept me here after all. I can stand it so much easier than a baby, you see.

Of course I never mention it to them any more—I am too wise—but I keep watch of it all the same.

There are things in that paper that nobody knows but me, or ever will.

Behind that outside pattern the dim shapes get clearer every day.

120 It is always the same shape, only very numerous.

And it is like a woman stooping down and creeping about behind that pattern. I don't like it a bit. I wonder—I begin to think—I wish John would take me away from here!

It is so hard to talk with John about my case, because he is so wise, and because he loves me so.

But I tried it last night.

It was moonlight. The moon shines in all around just as the sun does.

125 I hate to see it sometimes, it creeps so slowly, and always comes in by one window or another.

John was asleep and I hated to waken him, so I kept still and watched the moonlight on that undulating wallpaper till I felt creepy.

The faint figure behind seemed to shake the pattern, just as if she wanted to get out.

I got up softly and went to feel and see if the paper *did* move, and when I came back John was awake.

"What is it, little girl?" he said. "Don't go walking about like that—you'll get cold."

130 I thought it was a good time to talk, so I told him that I really was not gaining here, and that I wished he would take me away.

"Why darling!" said he, "our lease will be up in three weeks, and I can't see how to leave before."

"The repairs are not done at home, and I cannot possibly leave town just now. Of course if you were in any danger, I could and would, but you really are better, dear, whether you can see it or not. I am a doctor, dear, and I know. You are gaining flesh and color, your appetite is better, I feel really much easier about you."

"I don't weigh a bit more," said I, "nor as much; and my appetite may be better in the evening when you are here, but it is worse in the morning when you are away!"

"Bless her little heart!" said he with a big hug, "she shall be as sick as she pleases! But now let's improve the shining hours by going to sleep, and talk about it in the morning!"

135 "And you won't go away?" I asked gloomily.

"Why, how can I, dear? It is only three weeks more and then we will take a nice little trip of a few days while Jennie is getting the house ready. Really, dear, you are better!"

"Better in body perhaps—" I began, and stopped short, for he sat up straight and looked at me with such a stern, reproachful look that I could not say another word.

"My darling," said he, "I beg of you, for my sake and for our child's sake, as well as for your own, that you will never for one instant let that idea enter your mind! There is nothing so dangerous, so fascinating, to a temperament like yours. It is a false and foolish fancy. Can you not trust me as a physician when I tell you so?"

So of course I said no more on that score, and we went to sleep before long. He thought I was asleep first, but I wasn't and lay there for hours trying to decide whether that front pattern and the back pattern really did move together or separately.

140 On a pattern like this, by daylight, there is a lack of sequence, a defiance of law, that is a constant irritant to a normal mind.

The color is hideous enough, and unreliable enough, and infuriating enough, but the pattern is torturing.

You think you have mastered it, but just as you get well underway in following, it turns a back somersault and there you are. It slaps you in the face, knocks you down, and tramples upon you. It is like a bad dream.

The outside pattern is a florid arabesque, reminding one of a fungus. If you can imagine a toadstool in joints, an interminable string of toadstools, budding and sprouting in endless convolutions—why, that is something like it.

That is, sometimes!

145 There is one marked peculiarity about this paper, a thing nobody seems to notice but myself, and that is that it changes as the light changes.

When the sun shoots in through the east window—I always watch for that first long, straight ray—it changes so quickly that I never can quite believe it.

That is why I watch it always.

By moonlight—the moon shines in all night when there is a moon—I wouldn't know it was the same paper.

At night in any kind of light, in twilight, candlelight, lamplight, and worst of all by moonlight, it becomes bars! The outside pattern, I mean, and the woman behind it is as plain as can be.

150 I didn't realize for a long time what the thing was that showed behind, that dim sub-pattern, but now I am quite sure it is a woman.

By daylight she is subdued, quiet. I fancy it is the pattern that keeps her so still. It is so puzzling. It keeps me quiet by the hour.

I lie down ever so much now. John says it is good for me, and to sleep all I can. Indeed he started the habit by making me lie down for an hour after each meal.

It is a very bad habit, I am convinced, for you see, I don't sleep.

155   And that cultivates deceit, for I don't tell them I'm awake—oh, no!

The fact is I am getting a little afraid of John.

He seems very queer sometimes, and even Jennie has an inexplicable look.

It strikes me occasionally, just as a scientific hypothesis, that perhaps it is the paper!

.I have watched John when he did not know I was looking, and come into the room suddenly on the most innocent excuses, and I've caught him several times *looking at the paper!* And Jennie too. I caught Jennie with her hand on it once.

160   She didn't know I was in the room, and when I asked her in a quiet, a very quiet voice, with the most restrained manner possible, what she was doing with the paper, she turned around as if she had been caught stealing, and looked quite angry—asked me why I should frighten her so!

Then she said that the paper stained everything it touched, that she had found yellow smooches on all my clothes and John's, and she wished we would be more careful!

Did not that sound innocent? But I know she was studying that pattern, and I am determined that nobody shall find it out but myself!

Life is very much more exciting now than it used to be. You see I have something more to expect, to look forward to, to watch. I really do eat better, and am more quiet than I was.

John is so pleased to see me improve! He laughed a little the other day, and said I seemed to be flourishing in spite of my wallpaper.

165   I turned it off with a laugh. I had no intention of telling him it was *because* of the wallpaper—he would make fun of me. He might even want to take me away.

I don't want to leave now until I have found it out. There is a week more, and I think that will be enough.

I'm feeling ever so much better!

I don't sleep much at night, for it is so interesting to watch developments, but I sleep a good deal in the daytime.

In the daytime it is tiresome and perplexing.

170   There are always new shoots on the fungus, and new shades of yellow all over it. I cannot keep count of them, though I have tried conscientiously.

It is the strangest yellow, that wallpaper! It makes me think of all the yellow things I ever saw—not beautiful ones like buttercups, but old foul, bad yellow things.

But there is something else about that paper—the smell! I noticed it the moment we came into the room, but with so much air and sun it was not bad. Now we have had a week of fog and rain, and whether the windows are open or not, the smell is here.

It creeps all over the house.

I find it hovering in the dining-room, skulking in the parlor, hiding in the hall, lying in wait for me on the stairs.

175   It gets into my hair.

Even when I go to ride, if I turn my head suddenly and surprise it—there is that smell!

Such a peculiar odor, too! I have spent hours in trying to analyze it, to find what it smelled like.

It is not bad—at first—and very gentle, but quite the subtlest, most enduring odor I ever met.

In this damp weather it is awful, I wake up in the night and find it hanging over me.

180 It used to disturb me at first. I thought seriously of burning the house—to reach the smell.

But now I am used to it. The only thing I can think of that it is like is the *color* of the paper! A yellow smell.

There is a very funny mark on this wall, low down, near the mopboard. A streak that runs round the room. It goes behind every piece of furniture, except the bed, a long, straight, even *smooch*, as if it had been rubbed over and over.

I wonder how it was done and who did it, and what they did it for. Round and round and round—round and round and round—it makes me dizzy!

I really have discovered something at last.

185 Through watching so much at night, when it changes so, I have finally found out.

The front pattern *does* move—and no wonder! The woman behind shakes it!

Sometimes I think there are a great many women behind, and sometimes only one, and she crawls around fast, and her crawling shakes it all over.

Then in the very bright spots she keeps still, and in the very shady spots she just takes hold of the bars and shakes them hard.

And she is all the time trying to climb through. But nobody could climb through that pattern—it strangles so: I think that is why it has so many heads.

190 They get through, and then the pattern strangles them off and turns them upside down, and makes their eyes white!

If those heads were covered or taken off it would not be half so bad.

I think that woman gets out in the daytime!

And I'll tell you why—privately—I've seen her!

I can see her out of every one of my windows!

195 It is the same woman, I know, for she is always creeping, and most women do not creep by daylight.

I see her in that long shaded lane, creeping up and down. I see her in those dark grape arbors, creeping all around the garden.

I see her on that long road under the trees, creeping along, and when a carriage comes she hides under the blackberry vines.

I don't blame her a bit. It must be very humiliating to be caught creeping by daylight!

I always lock the door when I creep by daylight. I can't do it at night, for I know John would suspect something at once.

200 And John is so queer now, that I don't want to irritate him. I wish he would take another room! Besides, I don't want anybody to get that woman out at night but myself.

I often wonder if I could see her out of all the windows at once.

But, turn as fast as I can, I can only see out of one at one time.

And though I always see her, she *may* be able to creep faster than I can turn! I have watched her sometimes away off in the open country, creeping as fast as a cloud shadow in a high wind.

If only that top pattern could be gotten off from the under one! I mean to try it, little by little.

205   I have found out another funny thing, but I shan't tell it this time! It does not do to trust people too much.

There are only two more days to get this paper off, and I believe John is beginning to notice. I don't like the look in his eyes.

And I heard him ask Jennie a lot of professional questions about me. She had a very good report to give.

She said I slept a good deal in the daytime.

John knows I don't sleep very well at night, for all I'm so quiet!

210   He asked me all sorts of questions, too, and pretended to be very loving and kind. As if I couldn't see through him!

Still, I don't wonder he acts so, sleeping under this paper for three months.

It only interests me, but I feel sure John and Jennie are secretly affected by it.

Hurrah! This is the last day, but it is enough. John to stay in town over night, and won't be out until this evening.

215   Jennie wanted to sleep with me—the sly thing; but I told her I should undoubtedly rest better for a night all alone.

That was clever, for really I wasn't alone a bit! As soon as it was moonlight and that poor thing began to crawl and shake the pattern, I got up and ran to help her.

I pulled and she shook. I shook and she pulled, and before morning we had peeled off yards of that paper.

A strip about as high as my head and half around the room.

And then when the sun came and that awful pattern began to laugh at me, I declared I would finish it today!

220   We go away tomorrow, and they are moving all my furniture down again to leave things as they were before.

Jennie looked at the wall in amazement, but I told her merrily that I did it out of pure spite at the vicious thing.

She laughed and said she wouldn't mind doing it herself, but I must not get tired.

How she betrayed herself that time!

But I am here, and no person touches this but Me—not *alive*!

225   She tried to get me out of the room—it was too patent! But I said it was so quiet and empty and clean now that I believed I would lie down again and sleep all I could, and not to wake me even for dinner—I would call when I woke.

So now she is gone, and the servants are gone, and the things are gone, and there is nothing left but that great bedstead nailed down, with the canvas mattress we found on it.

We shall sleep downstairs tonight, and take the boat home tomorrow.

I quite enjoy the room, now it is bare again.

How those children did tear about here!

230   This bedstead is fairly gnawed!

But I must get to work.

I have locked the door and thrown the key down into the front path.

I don't want to go out, and I don't want to have anybody come in, till John comes.

I want to astonish him.

235 I've got a rope up here that even Jennie did not find. If that woman does get out, and tries to get away, I can tie her!

But I forgot I could not reach far without anything to stand on! •

This bed will *not* move! •

I tried to lift and push it until I was lame, and then I got so angry I bit off a little piece at one corner—but it hurt my teeth.

Then I peeled off all the paper I could reach standing on the floor. It sticks horribly and the pattern just enjoys it! All those strangled heads and bulbous eyes and waddling fungus growths just shriek with derision!

240 I am getting angry enough to do something desperate. To jump out of the window would be admirable exercise, but the bars are too strong even to try.

Besides I wouldn't do it. Of course not. I know well enough that a step like that is improper and might be misconstrued.

I don't like to *look* out of the windows even—there are so many of those creeping women, and they creep so fast.

I wonder if they all come out of that wallpaper as I did?

But I am securely fastened now by my well-hidden rope—you don't get *me* out in the road there!

245 I suppose I shall have to get back behind the pattern when it comes night, and that is hard!

It is so pleasant to be out in this great room and creep around as I please!

I don't want to go outside. I won't, even if Jennie asks me to.

For outside you have to creep on the ground, and everything is green instead of yellow.

But here I can creep smoothly on the floor, and my shoulder just fits in that long smooch around the wall, so I cannot lose my way.

250 Why there's John at the door!

It is no use, young man, You can't open it!

How he does call and pound!

Now he's crying to Jennie for an axe.

It would be a shame to break down that beautiful door!

255 "John dear!" said I in the gentlest voice, "The key is down by the front steps, under a plantain leaf!"

That silenced him for a few moments.

Then he said very quietly indeed, "Open the door, my darling!"

"I can't," said I. "The key is down by the front door under a plantain leaf!" And then I said it again, several times, very gently and slowly, and said it so often that he had to go and see, and he got it of course, and came in. He stopped short by the door.

"What is the matter?" he cried. "For God's sake, what are you doing!"

260 I kept on creeping just the same, but I looked at him over my shoulder.

"I've got out at last," said I, "in spite of you and Jane. And I've pulled off most of the paper, so you can't put me back! "

Now why should that man have fainted? But he did, and right across my path by the wall, so that I had to creep over him every time!

FOCUSED FREE WRITES

1. Some readers are confused by the ending. How do you understand the plot?
2. What happens to the main character, Jane?
3. How would you characterize the story's style? The point of view?
4. What symbols or themes stand out in this story?
5. What is the purpose or message of this story?
6. Describe the context. What should we understand about the time period to help us understand the story?
7. What was the situation for women at the turn of the twentieth century? How is Charlotte Perkins Gilman addressing that situation?
8. How is this an example of writing to overcome?

CRITICAL Contexts

Feminist Criticism

Feminist literary critics examine the power dynamics of gender in a culture and examine the manifestations of the power imbalance in literature. Feminist critics look at how a given historical, social, and cultural context informs a text and how a gendered reader reads that text. Such critics make visible the assumptions found in a culture's literature and, more fundamentally, in language itself.

Inspired by the work of Simone de Beauvoir, Mary Ellman, and Kate Millett, critics in the 1960s recovered the work of writers like Kate Chopin (see Chapter 2) and Charlotte Perkins Gilman. Since the early work of these scholars, feminist criticism has broadened and deepened, and it is often combined with psychoanalytic, historical, Marxist, post–structuralist, and gender criticism.

In their groundbreaking work of feminist criticism, *The Madwoman in the Attic*, Sandra Gilbert and Susan Gubar describe "The Yellow Wallpaper" as "a striking story of female confinement and escape, a paradigmatic tale which (like *Jane Eyre*) seems to tell *the* story of all literary women..."

What do you think of Gilbert and Gubar's assessment? How might this text be read from a feminist approach?

PRE-READING What do you remember about your parents' lectures? What did they assume about you? What did they expect from you?

Jamaica Kincaid (1949–).   Born in St. John's, Antigua, as Elaine Potter Richardson, Jamaica Kincaid is well known for her semi-autobiographical novels about her childhood. Kincaid left her home in 1966 and arrived in America. There, she worked as a nanny and went to school. In 1975, Kincaid published her first pieces in Ms. magazine. A year later, she became a staff writer for the New Yorker, submitting short fiction and "Talk of the Town" pieces. Kincaid continued writing for the New Yorker until 1990.

Jamaica Kincaid

GIRL

[1978]

Wash the white clothes on Monday and put them on the stone heap; wash the color clothes on Tuesday and put them on the clothesline to dry; don't walk bare-head in the hot sun; cook pumpkin fritters in very hot sweet oil; soak your little cloths right after you take them off; when buying cotton to make yourself a nice blouse, be sure it doesn't have gum on it, because that way it won't hold up well after a wash; soak salt fish overnight before you cook it; is it true that you sing benna[1] in Sunday school?; always eat your food in such a way that it won't turn someone else's stomach; on Sundays, try to walk like a lady and not like the slut you are so bent on becoming; don't sing benna in Sunday school; you mustn't speak to wharf-rat boys, not even to give directions; don't eat fruits on the street—flies will follow you; *but I don't sing benna on Sundays at all and never in Sunday school*; this is how to sew a button; this is how to make a buttonhole for the button you have just sewed on; this is how to hem a dress when you see the hem coming down and so to prevent yourself from looking like the slut I know you are so bent on becoming; this is how you iron your father's khaki shirt so that it doesn't have a crease; this is how you iron your father's khaki pants so that they don't have a crease; this is how you grow okra—far from the house, because okra tree harbors red ants; when you are growing dasheen, make sure it gets plenty of water or else it makes your throat itch when you are eating it; this is how you sweep a corner; this is how you sweep a whole house; this is how you sweep a yard; this is how you smile to someone you don't like too much; this is how you smile to someone you like completely; this is how you set a table for tea; this is how you set a table for dinner; this is how you set a table for dinner with an important guest; this is how you set a table for lunch; this is how you set a table for breakfast; this is how you to behave in the presence of men who don't know you very well, and this way they won't recognize immediately the slut I warned you against becoming; be sure to wash every day, even if it is with your own spit; don't squat to play marbles–you are not a boy, you know; don't pick other people's flowers—you might catch something; don't throw stones at black-birds, because it might not be a blackbird at all; this is how to make bread pudding; this is how to make doukona[2]; this is how to make pepper pot; this is how to make a good medicine for a cold; this is how to make a good medicine to throw away a child before it even becomes a child; this is how to catch a fish; this is how to throw back a fish you don't like, and that way something bad won't fall on you; this is how to bully a man; this is how a man bullies you; this is how to love a

---

[1] **benna:** Calypso or a Caribbean folk-music style.

[2] **doukona:** a pudding made from plantain.

man, and if this doesn't work there are other ways, and if they don't work don't feel too bad about giving up; this is how to spit up in the air if you feel like it, and this is how to move quick so it doesn't fall on you; this is how to make ends meet; always squeeze the bread to make sure it's fresh; *but what if the baker won't let me feel the bread?*; you mean to say that after all you are really going to be the kind of woman who the baker won't let near the bread?

FOCUSED FREE WRITES

1. Is there a plot to this story?
2. What do you understand about the main character and her point of view?
3. What is the effect of the style of this story? Why is it written as a 650-word single sentence?
4. What symbols, images, or motifs are used? How are they used? What other elements of fiction are important to understand in this story?
5. Is there a message we should understand?

PRE-READING   What is a scapegoat?

Ursula LeGuin (1929–).   *LeGuin was born in 1929. Her father and mother, an anthropologist and a writer, respectively, raised her in a highly literate household. After earning degrees from Radcliffe and Columbia, she married historian Charles LeGuin and began to write and publish professionally. Her extensive list of publications is quite varied and impressive, including six books of poetry, twenty novels, over 100 short stories, four books of essays, eleven children's books, and four translations. LeGuin's science fiction and fantasy writing is particularly groundbreaking and extraordinarily popular, yet she has achieved many successes in other literary arenas, including numerous awards.*

Ursula K. LeGuin

THE ONES WHO WALK AWAY FROM OMELAS   [1973]

1   With a clamor of bells that set the swallows soaring, the Festival of Summer came to the city. Omelas, bright-towered by the sea. The rigging of the boats in harbor sparkled with flags. In the streets between houses with red roofs and painted walls, between old moss-grown gardens and under avenues of trees, past great parks and public buildings, processions moved. Some were decorous: old people in long stiff robes of mauve and grey, grave master workmen, quiet merry women carrying their babies and chatting as they walked. In other streets the music beat faster, a shimmering of gong and tambourine, and the people went dancing, the procession was a dance. Children dodged in and out, their high calls rising like the swallows' crossing flights over the music and the

singing. All the processions wound towards the north side of the city, where on the great water-meadow called the Green Fields boys and girls, naked in the bright air, with mud-stained feet and ankles and long, lithe arms, exercised their restive horses before the race. The horses wore no gear at all but a halter without a bit. Their manes were braided with streamers of silver, gold, and green. They flared their nostrils and pranced and boasted to one another; they were vastly excited, the horse being the only animal who has adopted our cere-monies as his own. Far off to the north and west the mountains stood up half encircling Omelas on her bay. The air of morning was so clear that the snow still crowning the Eighteen Peaks burned with white-gold fire across the miles of sunlit air, under the dark blue of the sky. There was just enough wind to make the banners that marked the racehorse snap and flutter now and then. In the silence of the broad green meadows one could hear the music winding through the city streets, farther and nearer and ever approaching, a cheerful faint sweet-ness of the air that from time to time trembled and gathered together and broke out into great joyous clanging of the bells.

2   Joyous! How is one to tell about joy? How describe the citizens of Omelas?

3   They were not simple folk, you see, though they were happy. But we do not say the words of cheer much any more. All smiles have become archaic. Given a description such as this one tends to make certain assumptions. Given a description such as this one tends to look next for the King, mounted on a splen-did stallion and surrounded by his noble knights, or perhaps in a gold litter borne by great-muscled slaves. But there was no king. They did not use swords, or keep slaves. They were not barbarians. I do not know the rules and laws of their society, but I suspect that they were singularly few. As they did without monarchy and slavery, so they also got on without the stock exchange, the adver-tisement, the secret police, and the bomb. Yet I repeat that these were not simple folk, not dulcet shepherds, noble savages, bland utopians. They were not less complex than us. The trouble is that we have a bad habit, encouraged by pen-dants and sophisticates, of considering happiness as something rather stupid. Only pain is intellectual, only evil interesting. This is the treason of the artist: a refusal to admit the banality of evil and the terrible boredom of pain. If you can't lick 'em, join 'em. If it hurts, repeat it. But to praise despair is to condemn delight, to embrace violence is to lose hold of everything else. We have almost lost hold; we can no longer describe a happy man, nor make any celebration of joy. How can I tell you about the people of Omelas? They were not naïve and happy children—though their children were, in fact, happy. They were mature, intelligent, passionate adults whose lives were not wretched. O miracle! but I wish I could describe it better. I wish I could convince you. Omelas sounds in my words like a city in a fairy tale, long ago and far away, once upon a time. Perhaps it would be best if you imagined it as your own fancy bids, assuming it will rise to the occasion, for certainly I cannot suit you all. For instance, how about technol-ogy? I think that there would be no cars or helicopters in and above the streets; this follows from the fact that the people of Omelas are happy people. Happiness is based on a just discrimination of what is necessary, what is neither necessary nor destructive, and what is destructive. In the middle category, however—that of the unnecessary but unrestrictive, that of comfort, luxury, exuberance

etc. —they could perfectly well have central heating, subway trains, washing machines, and all kinds of marvelous devices not yet invented here, floating light-sources, fuelless power, a cure for the common cold. Or they could have none of that: it doesn't matter. As you like it. I incline to think that people from towns up and down the coast have been coming to Omelas during the last days before the Festival on very fast little trains and double-decked trams and that the train station of Omelas is actually the handsomest building in town, though plainer than the Farmers' Market. But even granted trains, I fear that Omelas so far strikes some of you as goody-goody. Smiles, bells, parades, horses, bleh. If so, please add an orgy. If an orgy would help, don't hesitate. Let us not, however, have temples from which issue beautiful nude priests and priestesses already half in ecstasy and ready to copulate with any man or woman, lover or stranger, who desires union with the deep godhead of the blood, although that was my first idea. But really it would be better not to have any temples in Omelas—at least, not manned temples. Religion yes, clergy no. Surely the beautiful nudes can just wander about, offering themselves like divine soufflés to the hunger of the needy and the rapture of the flesh. Let them join the processions. Let tambourines be struck above the copulations, and the glory of desire be proclaimed upon the gongs, and (a not unimportant point) let the offspring of these lovely rituals be beloved and looked after by all. One thing I know there is none of in Omelas is guilt. But what else should there be? I thought at first there were no drugs, but that is puritanical. For those who like it, the faint insistent sweetness of *drooz* may perfume the ways of the city, *drooz* which first brings a great lightness and brilliance to the mind and limbs, and then after some hours of a dreamy languor, and wonderful visions at last of the very arcane and inmost secrets of the Universe, as well as exciting the pleasure of sex beyond all belief; and it is not habit-forming. For more modest tastes I think there ought to be beer. What else, what else belongs in our joyous city? The sense of victory, surely, the celebration of courage. But as we did without clergy, let us do without soldiers. The joy built upon successful slaughter is not the right kind of joy; it will not do; it is fearful and it is trivial. A boundless and generous contentment, a magnanimous triumph felt not against some outer enemy but in communion with the finest and fairest in the souls of all men everywhere and the splendor of the world's summer: this is what swells the hearts of the people of Omelas, and the victory they celebrate is that of life. I really don't think many of them need to take *drooz*.

4   Most of the processions have reached the Green Fields by now. A marvelous smell of cooking goes forth from the red and blue tents of the provisioners. The faces of small children are aimiably sticky; in the benign grey beard of a man a couple of crumbs of rich pastry are entangled. The youths and girls have mounted their horses and are beginning to group around the starting line of course. An old woman, small, fat, and laughing, is passing out flowers from a basket, and tall young men wear her flowers in their shining hair. A child of nine or ten sits at the edge of the crowd, alone, playing on a wooden flute. People pause to listen, and they smile, but they do not speak to him, for he never ceases playing and never sees them, his dark eyes wholly rapt in the sweet, thin magic of the time.

5   He finishes, and slowly lowers his hands holding the wooden flute.

6   As if that little private silence were the signal, all at once a trumpet sounds from the pavilion near the starting line: imperious, melancholy, piercing. The horses rear

on their slender legs, and some of them neigh in answer. Sober-faced, the young riders stroke their horses' necks and soothe them, whispering, "Quiet, quiet, there my beauty, my hope…." They begin to form in rank along the starting line. The crowds along the racecourse are like a field of grass and flowers in the wind. The Festival of Summer has begun.

7   Do you believe? Do you accept the festival, the city, the joy? No? Then let me describe one more thing.

8   In a basement one of the beautiful public buildings of Omelas, or perhaps in the cellar of one of its spacious private homes, there is a room. It has one locked door, and no window. A little light seeps in dustily between cracks in the boards, secondhand from a cobwebbed window somewhere across the cellar. In one corner of the little room a couple of mops, with stiff, clotted, foul-smelling heads, stand near a rusty bucket. The floor is dirt, a little damp to the touch, as cellar dirt usually is. The room is about three paces long and two wide: a mere broom closet or disused tool room. In the room a child is sitting. It could be a boy or girl. It looks about six, but actually is near ten. It is feeble-minded. Perhaps it was born defective, or perhaps it has become imbecile through fear, malnutrition, and neglect. It picks its nose and occasionally fumbles vaguely with its toes or genitals, as it sits hunched in the corner farthest from the bucket and the two mops. It is afraid of the mops. It finds them horrible. It shuts its eyes, but it knows the mops are still standing there; and the door is locked; and nobody will come. The door is always locked; and nobody ever comes, except that sometimes—the child has no understanding of time or interval—sometimes the door rattles open, and a person, or several people, are there. One of them may come in and kick the child to make it stand up. The others never come close, but peer in at it with frightened, disgusted eyes. The food bowl and the water jug are hastily filled, the door is locked, the eyes disappear. The people at the door never say anything, but the child, who has not always lived in the tool room, can remember sunlight and its mother's voice, sometimes speaks. "I will be good," it says. "Please let me out. I will be good!" They never answer. The child used to scream for help at night, and cry a good deal, but now it only makes a kind of whining, "eh-haa, eh-haa," and it speaks less and less often. It is so thin there are no calves to its legs; its belly protrudes; it lives on a half-bowl of corn meal and grease a day. It is naked. Its buttocks and thighs are a mass of festered sores, as it sits in its own excrement continually.

9   They all know it is there, all the people on Omelas. Some of them have come to see it, others are content merely to know it is there. They all know it has to be there. Some of them understand why, and some do not, but they all understand that their happiness, the beauty of their city, the tenderness of their friendships, the health of their children, the wisdom of their scholars, the skill of their makers, even the abundance of their harvest and the kindly weathers of their skies, depend wholly on this child's abominable misery.

10   This is usually explained to children when they are between eight and twelve or whenever they seem capable of understanding; and most of those who come to see the child are young people, though often enough an adult comes, or comes back, to see the child. No matter how well the matter has been explained to them, these young spectators are always shocked and sickened at the sight. They feel disgust, which they had thought themselves

superior to. They feel anger, outrage, impotence, despite all the explanations. They would like to do something for the child. But there is nothing they can do. If the child were brought up into the sunlight out of that vile place, if it were cleaned and fed and comforted, that would be a good thing, indeed; but if it were done, in that day and hour all the prosperity and beauty and delight of Omelas would wither and be destroyed. Those are the terms. To exchange all the goodness and grace of every life in Omelas for that single, small improvement: to throw away the happiness of thousands for the chance of the happiness of one: that would be to let guilt within the walls indeed.

11   The terms are strict and absolute; there may not even be a kind word spoken to the child.

12   Often the young people go home in tears, or in a tearless rage, when they have seen the child and faced this terrible paradox. They may brood over it for weeks or years. But as time goes on they begin to realize that even if the child could be released, it would not get much good of its freedom: a little vague pleasure of warmth and food, no doubt, but little more. It is too degraded and imbecile to know any real joy. It has been afraid too long ever to be free of fear. Its habits are too uncouth for it to respond to humane treatment. Indeed, after so long it would probably be wretched without walls about it to protect it, and darkness for its eyes, and its own excrement to sit in. Their tears at the bitter injustice dry when they begin to perceive the terrible justice of reality, and to accept it. Yet it is their tears and anger, the trying of their generosity and the acceptance of their helplessness, which are perhaps the true source of the splendor of their lives. Theirs is no vapid, irresponsible happiness. They know that they, like the child, are not free. They know compassion. It is the existence of the child, and their knowledge of its existence, that makes possible the nobility of their architecture, the poignancy of their music, the profundity of their science. It is because of the child that they are so gentle with children. They know that if the wretched one were not there snivelling in the dark, the other one, the flute player, could make no youthful music as the young riders line up in their beauty for the race in the sunlight of the first morning of summer.

13   Now do you believe in them? Are they not more credible? But there is one more thing to tell, and this is quite incredible.

14   At times one of the adolescent girls or boys who go to see the child does not go home to weep or rage, does not, in fact, go home at all. Sometimes also a man or woman much older falls silent for a day or two, and then leaves home. These people go out into the street, and walk down the street alone. They keep walking, and walk straight out of the city of Omelas, through the beautiful gates. They keep walking across the farmlands of Omelas. Each one goes alone, youth or girl, man or woman. Night falls; the traveler must pass down village streets, between the houses with yellow-lit windows, and on out into the darkness of the fields. Each alone, they go west or north, toward the mountains. They go on. They leave Omelas, they walk ahead into the darkness, and they do not come back. The place they go toward is a place even less imaginable to most of us than the city of happiness. I cannot describe it at all. It is possible that it does not exist. But they seem to know where they are going, the ones who walk away from Omelas.

The Act of Seeing Through a Critical Perspective

Throughout Part II of this book, you have been building your critical thinking skills. Using the critical thinking acts of interpretation and analysis, you have constructed arguments. Using those skills, you have developed arguments comparing two texts. In this chapter, you will expand your own perspective by using other critical perspectives. Using criticism does not mean the same thing as being "critical" of a text or finding something wrong with it. Rather, when a reader or critic uses literary criticism, he or she is using any of a variety of methods of studying texts for the purpose of analyzing their content or style. Approaching a text from a particular perspective can allow you to focus on certain aspects of a work.

In fact, you have a particular perspective on the texts you consume whether you know it or not. When I watch a movie with my husband, we focus on different things. He pays much more attention to the music than I do. He knows more about music and thinks about the connection between the lyrics or the sounds in relation to the action on screen. His understanding of music impacts how he makes meaning of the film. However, I might tend to understand a movie from my perspective as a woman, or as the mother of young daughters. I might focus intently on the treatment of women or girls. I would view the men or women who oppress these characters in a negative light. I can be said to be taking a feminist perspective of the film. My husband and I might come away from the theater talking about entirely different things. One movie might have multiple meanings based on our perspectives as viewers.

Literature works the same way. In some ways, it is useful to imagine using criticism as viewing a text through a particular lens. If I am viewing a work through a "feminist perspective," I will focus on particular characters, bits of dialogue, and action to making meaning of a text. I might prioritize some information and not others in order to make meaning of the text in this way. This perspective may come "naturally" to me because of my particular interests, identity, experience, or beliefs. However, it may be that a certain text will direct my focus in a certain way. Particular themes may stand out that suggest certain critical perspectives.

These critical perspectives have been discussed throughout the book in various Critical Context boxes, but we can group them together here to revisit how they compare to one another:

Formalist criticism, also described as New Criticism, focuses on the text itself—the *form* of the text—isolated from any other context, even the writer's intention, the historical moment, or the reader's personal response. This critical perspective demands close reading of the text to focus deeply on the structure and style of the work. For instance, a formalist critic might analyze a work in light of its figurative language, point of view, characterizations, and plot. The emphasis will be on the language of the work and how the selection of that language makes meaning. For example, a formalist critic might focus on the point of view of LeGuin's "The Ones Who Walk Away from Omelas" to engage the audience in establishing this no place as any place.

Biographical criticism uses the author's background as a lens through which to understand a piece of literature; thus, it can also be considered a kind of historical criticism or psychoanalytic criticism. A biographical critic might consult the letters, journals, interviews, biographies, or autobiographies of an author to see how his or her life impacted the literary text under examination and to show how understanding the author can make the work more meaningful. The emphasis would be both on what the author intended to convey about his or her own experience as well as material the author inadvertently let into the text as an interpretation of a real-life experience. For example, a biographical critic might examine "The Yellow Wallpaper" in light of Gilman's own experience with S. Weir Mitchell and "the rest cure." This reader might consult Gilman's letters and essays on the topic.

Historical criticism examines a text in its historical context. Such a reader would examine what events in history were reflected in a literary work, whether intentionally or not. This kind of critic would engage in historical research to understand the political, cultural, religious, or other specific milieu to better understand the text. For example, a historical critic might look into the Civil Rights movement and post–Reconstruction racism to better understand the reality O'Connor describes in last chapter's "Everything that Rises Must Converge." **New Historicism** is a version of historical criticism that recognizes that a historical text, like a literary text, is always an interpretation of past events. Therefore, a literary text not only reflects a particular culture, but it also creates our understanding of a culture, the beliefs, assumptions, truths, and values of a society. A New Historicist might look at a text along other historical documents such as letters, editorials, and essays to demonstrate the constitution of racial consciousness in the 1950s.

Marxist criticism recognizes history as the story of the ongoing struggle between socioeconomic classes. For Marxists critics, economics is the "base" or "infrastructure" of a society. All "superstructure"—including politics, religion, and the arts—relies on and is determined by this base. Therefore, the economics of a social order is always reflected in a literary work of art. The values of the dominant class appear as privileged, either directly or indirectly, and the desires of the subordinate class are not valued as highly. The lower classes are subjected, then, to a kind of false consciousness that keeps them from seeing the mechanisms of this disenfranchisement. This kind of critic would examine the economic forces and class struggles implicit in a work of literature and explore how ideology shapes consciousness. For example, a Marxist critic would examine how the monolog in "Girl" promulgates a kind of thinking influenced by class or economic forces. In making the girl "behave," she is kept in "her place" by dominant social forces, not just her mother.

Psychoanalytic (or **psychological**) **criticism** reveals the psychological issues of the author unconsciously included in a text as well as the psychological themes and issues of the characters and readers of a work. This kind of critic might employ Freud's ideas about the parts of the unconscious and the conscious, or the id (the unconscious self), the ego (the conscious self), and the superego (the conscience) to identify the latent or conscious desires of characters, writers, or readers. Central to this notion of the unconscious is the Oedipal complex in which all males must battle their fathers for the affection of the mother. Unconscious desires are expressed, according to Freud, in the creative outpourings of dreams, or even in art. Thus, a text can be understood as a manifestation of the unconscious or as a representation of the psychology of the creator or interpreter. Such a critic might employ Freud's ideas or other psychological theories to make meaning of a text. For example, a psychoanalytic critic could examine LeGuin's short story as an allegory for the story of the psyche: the id must be relegated to the basement for the success of the ego or the conscious, social self.

Feminist criticism focuses on the depiction of women in literature and the revaluation of work by women writers. A feminist critic examines the mechanisms by which gender has been socially constructed in a patriarchal culture to privilege masculinity over femininity. Such a critic might recommend a reconsideration of overlooked writers or a revision of misunderstood characters. Feminist criticism can also be grouped under the broader category of **gender criticism**, whose proponents examine the construction of the genders in literature and demonstrates how gender and sexual codes becomes normalized and reinforced in literary representations. For example, a feminist critic could examine Gilman's "The Yellow Wallpaper" as an account of the oppression of women by a patriarchal culture whose seemingly benevolent institutions—such as marriage or medicine—hurt women in the name of helping them.

Postcolonial criticism approaches literature as the expression of the relationship between cultures, particularly a dominant culture and an "othered" culture. Postcolonial critics are interested in how cultures become stereotyped and how those that are "othered" must negotiate between dominant values and their oppressed culture. The emphasis is on examining the development, maintenance, and ramifications of this marginalization on a person or on cultures. For example, LeGuin's "The Ones Who Walked Away from Omelas" could illustrate how native cultures are made scapegoats and are othered by dominant cultures. Their pain and suffering make others wealthy and successful.

Deconstructive (or **poststructuralist**) **criticism** recognizes the limits of language as a means to translate or represent thinking without ever precisely capturing it. Words have an unstable connection to the things they represent.

Likewise, a text is inherently always deconstructed. While a formalist critic closely reads a text to examine how meaning is constructed, a deconstructive critic would likewise close-read a text to demonstrate how it is already deconstructed. In other words, much like other critics, these critics expose the invisible meanings within a literary work. Texts are necessarily structured based on certain value systems in which a "good" is privileged over "bad" or on other assumptions. Deconstruction forces the reader to recognize this implicit logic and demonstrate how that logic is socially constructed rather than universally valued. For example, Kincaid's "Girl" may be deconstructed to reveal how gender is constructed. The text exposes how female sexuality is both central to and erased from the monolog, something instructed and implied simultaneously.

When approaching a text, a reader might choose to examine it through one of the above lenses to make meaning. A critical perspective should not distract from an interpretation—it should enable the interpretation. It should shed light on a text or make it easier to understand. Not all texts would benefit from all perspectives. Again, it is essential that your perspective makes a text clearer, not more confusing.

These perspectives should be understood as working in combination. For example, to examine "The Yellow Wallpaper" in terms of gender criticism, one would necessarily address history, it seems, and certainly, biographical and psychological criticism would also be useful tools.

Using the critical perspectives above, identify a work that would benefit from analysis for each one of these lenses.

POEMS

Throughout previous chapters, you have been guided through critical, historical, biographical, and textual strategies for contextualizing literary works. When reading these next four poems, what contexts can you determine on your own as necessary to understand the texts? What information should be emphasized? What should you find out more about? What connections can you make to other texts? What critical perspectives can you use? Given your understanding of the genre of poetry and the literary elements of poetry, how do you read these texts?

COMPARING THEMES

Consider the next pairs of poems. How do their different styles allow for different approaches to similar themes?

PRE-READING   Besides the fact that your teacher is making you, why do you write? Why do writers desire to be read?

Anne Bradstreet (1617–1672).   *Acclaimed by some as America's first poet, Anne Bradstreet was born and grew up in England. Her father served as steward to the Earl of Lincolnshire enabling Anne to grow up in aristocratic circles with more liberal views of female education. Soon after she turned sixteen, Anne married Lincoln's assistant Simon Bradstreet, also a devout Puritan, moving with him to Massachusetts where her father became the first governor. Though life was harsh, the family maintained a large library and prominence in the new country. Because of censure of female writers, she began writing poetry privately as she raised eight children. Her brother-in-law would publish her first manuscript in England.*

Anne Bradstreet

THE AUTHOR TO HER BOOK [1678]

Thou ill-formed offspring of my feeble brain,
Who after birth did'st by my side remain,
Till snatched from thence by friends, less wise than true,
Who thee abroad exposed to public view,
5 Made thee in rags, halting to the press to trudge,
Where errors were not lessened, all may judge.
At thy return my blushing was not small,
My rambling brat (in print) should mother call;
I cast thee by as one unfit for light,
10 The visage was so irksome in my sight;
Yet being mine own, at length affection would
Thy blemishes amend, if so I could:
I washed thy face, but more defects I saw,
And rubbing off a spot, still made a flaw.
15 I stretched thy joints to make thee even feet,
Yet still thou run'st more hobbling than is meet;
In better dress to trim thee was my mind,
But nought save homespun cloth in the house I find.
In this array, 'mongst vulgars may'st thou roam;
20 In critic's hands beware thou dost not come;
And take thy way where yet thou art not known.
If for thy Father asked, say thou had'st none;
And for thy Mother, she alas is poor,
Which caused her thus to send thee out of door.

Langston Hughes (1902–1967).   *Hughes wrote and published his first poems in his high school magazine. He received his first award in 1925 in a contest that attracted the interest of editors and Knopf published his first book of poetry, The Weary Blues, in 1926. This collection attracted the attention of Zora Neale Hurston and Countee Cullen, writers known for their work during the Harlem Renaissance. It was through this movement that Hughes' popularity soared. Though famous for his poetry, Hughes also wrote many plays, some short stories, and an autobiography.*

![icon] THEME FOR ENGLISH B

The instructor said,

    Go home and write
    A page tonight.
    And let that page come out of you—
5   Then, it will be true.

I wonder if it's that simple?

I am twenty-two, colored, born in Winston-Salem.[1]
I went to school there, then Durham, then here
to this college on the hill above Harlem.[2]
10 I am the only colored student in my class.
The steps from the hill lead down into Harlem,
through a park, then I cross St. Nicholas,
Eighth Avenue, Seventh, and I come to the Y,
the Harlem Branch Y, where I take the elevator
15 up to my room, sit down, and write this page:

It's not easy to know what is true for you or me
at twenty-two, my age. But I guess I'm what
I feel and see and hear, Harlem, I hear you:
hear you, hear me—we two—you, me, talk on this page.
20 (I hear New York, too.) Me—who?

Well, I like to eat, sleep, drink, and be in love.
I like to work, read, learn, and understand life.
I like a pipe for a Christmas present,
or records—Bessie, bop, or Bach.

25 I guess being colored doesn't make me not like
the same things other folks like who are other races.
So will my page be colored that I write?
Being me, it will not be white.
But it will be
30 a part of you, instructor.
You are white—
yet a part of me, as I am a part of you.
That's American.

Sometimes perhaps you don't want to be a part of me.
35 Nor do I often want to be a part of you.
But we are, that's true!
As I learn from you,

---

[1] Winston-Salem and Durham are towns in North Carolina.

[2] The college in set in New York City.

I guess you learn from me—
although you're older—and white—
40 and somewhat more free.

This is my page for English B.

FOCUSED FREE WRITES

1. What stories do these two poems tell? Describe the person telling the stories—the narrator or persona who narrates the poems.
2. What poetic elements are distinctive? How would you describe the style of these writers? What symbols or imagery are distinctive?
3. How are these very different poems, written at different times, still similar? How do they speak to each other?
4. Discuss the messages of these poems. How are they examples of writing to overcome?
5. What setting or context should we understand?

PRE-READING   Describe a time you were misunderstood.

Wole Soyinka (1934–).   *Soyinka was born in Abeokuta in Southwestern Nigeria. He achieved early success with writing at elite Anglican schools and studied English literature at universities in Nigeria and England. Along the way, Soyinka began writing plays that received much acclaim and earned him a position as a lecturer in English at the University of Ife. His outspoken politics, however, incited a number of arrests and he was forced to write from prison and then from voluntary exile in Europe upon his release. Eventually, as the government changed hands, Soyinka returned to Nigeria, having earned the Nobel Prize for literature and numerous awards and high acclaim internationally.*

Wole Soyinka

TELEPHONE CONVERSATION   [1960]

The price seemed reasonable, location
Indifferent. The landlady swore she lived
Off premises. Nothing remained
But self-confession. "Madam," I warned,
5 "I hate a wasted journey—I am African."
Silence. Silenced transmission of
Pressurized good-breeding. Voice, when it came,
Lipstick coated, long gold-rolled
Cigarette-holder pipped. Caught I was foully.
10 "HOW DARK?"... I had not misheard... "ARE YOU LIGHT
OR VERY DARK?" Button B, Button A. Stench

Of rancid breath of public hide-and-speak.
Red booth. Red pillar-box. Red double-tiered
Omnibus squelching tar. It *was* real! Shamed
15 By ill-mannered silence, surrender
Pushed dumbfoundment to beg simplification.
Considerate she was, varying the emphasis—
"ARE YOU DARK? OR VERY LIGHT?" Revelation came.
"You mean—like plain or milk chocolate?"
20 Her assent was clinical, crushing in its light
Impersonality. Rapidly, wave-length adjusted,
I chose. "West African sepia"—and as afterthought,
"Down in my passport." Silence for spectroscopic
Flight of fancy, till truthfulness clanged her accent
25 Hard on the mouthpiece. "WHAT'S THAT?" conceding
"DON'T KNOW WHAT THAT IS." "Like brunette."
"THAT'S DARK, ISN'T IT?" "Not altogether.
Facially I am brunette, but, madam, you should see
The rest of me. Palm of my hand, soles of my feet
30 Are a peroxide blond. Friction, caused—
Foolishly madam—by sitting down, has turned
My bottom raven black—One moment madam!"—sensing
Her receiver rearing on the thunderclap
About my ears—"Madam," I pleaded, "wouldn't you rather
35 See for yourself?"

Julio Marzán (1946–).   *After earning a BA from Fordham, an MFA from Columbia Teacher's College, and a PhD from New York University, Marzán has become well established as a poet with numerous translations, publications, and books of poetry. His studies of William Carlos Williams and his poetry have received acclaim and international recognition. He is a dedicated teacher and poet making connections among poets of diverse backgrounds and students of all kinds.*

Julio Marzán

ETHNIC POETRY   [1994]

The ethnic poet said: "The earth is maybe
a huge maraca / and the sun a trombone /
and life / is to move your ass / to slow beats."
The ethnic audience roasted a suckling pig.

The ethnic poet said: "Oh thank Goddy, Goddy /
I be me, my toenails curled downward /
deep, deep, deep into Mama earth."
The ethnic audience shook strands of sea shells.

The ethnic poet said: "The sun was created black /
so we should imagine light / and also dream /
a walrus emerging from the broken ice."
The ethnic audience beat on sealskin drums.

The ethnic poet said: "Reproductive organs /
Eagles nesting California redwoods /
Shut up and listen to my ancestors."
The ethnic audience ate fried bread and honey.

The ethnic poet said: "Something there is that
doesn't love a wall / That sends
the frozen-ground-swell under it."
The ethnic audience deeply understood humanity.

FOCUSED FREE WRITES

1. What stories do these poems tell? Describe the characters narrating these poems.
2. What poetic elements are distinctive? How would you describe the style of these writers? What symbols or imagery are distinctive?
3. How are these very different poems, written at different times, still similar? How do they speak to each other?
4. What themes explain the meaning of these poems?
5. What setting or context can inform our understanding of these poems?
6. Look up Robert Frost's poem "Mending Wall" alluded to in the final stanza of "Ethnic Poetry." Why does Marzan allude to Frost's poem? How does this context inform the poem?

PLAY

The following play addresses "the woman question," or the situation of women in the nineteenth century. Read this play to see how the issue of oppression is developed through character, setting, and symbol.

PRE-READING   What are the characteristics of a good detective?

Susan Glaspell (1882–1948).   Born and raised in Davenport, Iowa, the daughter of a feed dealer, Susan Glaspell attended Drake University, where she pursued writing. She made writing a full-time career working as a reporter while publishing stories in magazines and eventually a novel. Glaspell settled in Greenwich Village with her husband, writer George Cram Cook, and began writing plays. While summering in Cape Cod, the couple founded the Provincetown Players, a pioneering small amateur theater company dedicated to producing the work of new American playwrights. Eventually, the Players were moved to New York where Glaspell produced a number of plays. After her husband's untimely death, Glaspell traveled around Europe, remarried, wrote a biography about her first marriage, and returned to the United States to continue to write fiction. She remained involved in theater until her death.

TRIFLES

[1916]

CAST OF CHARACTERS

George Henderson, county attorney
Henry Peters, sheriff
Lewis Hale, a neighboring farmer
Mrs. Peters
Mrs. Hale

SCENE: *The kitchen in the now abandoned farmhouse of* JOHN WRIGHT, *a gloomy kitchen, and left without having been put in order—unwashed pans under the sink, a loaf of bread outside the bread-box, a dish-towel on the table—other signs of incompleted work. At the rear the outer door opens and the* SHERIFF *comes in followed by the* COUNTY ATTORNEY *and* HALE. *The* SHERIFF *and* HALE *are men in middle life, the* COUNTY ATTORNEY *is a young man; all are much bundled up and go at once to the stove. They are followed by the two women—the* SHERIFF'S *wife first; she is a slight wiry woman, a thin nervous face.* MRS. HALE *is larger and would ordinarily be called more comfortable looking, but she is disturbed now and looks fearfully about as she enters. The women have come in slowly, and stand close together near the door.*

COUNTY ATTORNEY: [*Rubbing his hands.*] This feels good. Come up to the fire, ladies.

MRS. PETERS: [*After taking a step forward.*] I'm not—cold.

SHERIFF: [*Unbuttoning his overcoat and stepping away from the stove as if to mark the beginning of official business.*] Now, Mr. Hale, before we move things about, you explain to Mr. Henderson just what you saw when you came here yesterday morning.

COUNTY ATTORNEY: By the way, has anything been moved? Are things just as you left them yesterday?

5 SHERIFF: [*Looking about.*] It's just the same. When it dropped below zero last night I thought I'd better send Frank out this morning to make a fire for us—no use getting pneumonia with a big case on, but I told him not to touch anything except the stove—and you know Frank.

COUNTY ATTORNEY: Somebody should have been left here yesterday.

SHERIFF: Oh—yesterday. When I had to send Frank to Morris Center for that man who went crazy—I want you to know I had my hands full yesterday. I knew you could get back from Omaha by today and as long as I went over everything here myself—

COUNTY ATTORNEY: Well, Mr. Hale, tell just what happened when you came here yesterday morning.

HALE: Harry and I had started to town with a load of potatoes. We came along the road from my place and as I got here I said, "I'm going to see if I can't get John Wright to go in with me on a party telephone." I spoke to Wright about it once before and he put me off, saying folks talked too much anyway, and all he asked was peace and quiet—I guess you know about how much he talked himself; but I thought maybe if I went to the house and talked about it before his wife, though I said to Harry that I didn't know as what his wife wanted made much difference to John—

COUNTY ATTORNEY: Let's talk about that later, Mr. Hale. I do want to talk about that, but tell now just what happened when you got to the house.

HALE: I didn't hear or see anything; I knocked at the door, and still it was all quiet inside. I knew they must be up, it was past eight o'clock. So I knocked again, and I thought I heard somebody say, "Come in." I wasn't sure, I'm not sure yet, but I opened the door—this door [*Indicating the door by which the two women are still standing.*] and there in that rocker—[*Pointing to it.*] sat Mrs. Wright.

[*They all look at the rocker.*]

COUNTY ATTORNEY: What—was she doing?

HALE: She was rockin' back and forth. She had her apron in her hand and was kind of—pleating it.

COUNTY ATTORNEY: And how did she—look?

15 HALE: Well, she looked queer.

COUNTY ATTORNEY: How do you mean—queer?

HALE: Well, as if she didn't know what she was going to do next. And kind of done up.

COUNTY ATTORNEY: How did she seem to feel about your coming?

HALE: Why, I don't think she minded—one way or other. She didn't pay much attention. I said, "How do, Mrs. Wright, it's cold, ain't it?" And she said, "Is it?"—and went on kind of pleating at her apron. Well, I was surprised; she didn't ask me to come up to the stove, or to set down, but just sat there, not even looking at me, so I said, "I want to see John." And then she—laughed. I guess you would call it a laugh. I thought of Harry and the team outside, so I said a little sharp: "Can't I see John?" "No," she says, kind o' dull like. "Ain't he home?" says I. "Yes," says she, "he's home." "Then why can't I see him?" I asked her, out of patience. "Cause he's dead," says she. "*Dead*?" says I. She just nodded her head, not getting a bit excited, but rockin' back and forth. "Why—where is he?" says I, not knowing what to say. She just pointed upstairs—like that. [*Himself pointing to the room above.*] I got up, with the idea of going up there. I walked from there to here—then I says, "Why, what did he die of?" "He died of a rope round his neck," says she, and just went on pleatin' at her apron. Well, I went out and called Harry. I thought I might—need help. We went upstairs and there he was lyin'—

20 COUNTY ATTORNEY: I think I'd rather have you go into that upstairs, where you can point it all out. Just go on now with the rest of the story.

HALE: Well, my first thought was to get that rope off. It looked... [*Stops, his face twitches.*] ... but Harry, he went up to him, and he said, "No, he's dead all right, and we'd better not touch anything." So we went back downstairs. She was still sitting that same way. "Has anybody been notified?" I asked. "No," says she, unconcerned. "Who did this, Mrs. Wright?" said Harry. He said it businesslike—and she stopped pleatin' of her apron. "I don't know," she says. "You don't *know*?" says Harry. "No," says she. "Weren't you sleepin' in the bed with him?" says Harry. "Yes," says she, "but I was on the inside." "Somebody slipped a rope round his neck and strangled him and you didn't wake up?" says Harry. "I didn't wake up," she said after him. We must 'a looked as if we didn't see how that could be, for after a minute she said,

"I sleep sound." Harry was going to ask her more questions but I said maybe we ought to let her tell her story first to the coroner, or the sheriff, so Harry went fast as he could to Rivers' place, where there's a telephone.

COUNTY ATTORNEY: And what did Mrs. Wright do when she knew that you had gone for the coroner?

HALE: She moved from that chair to this one over here [*Pointing to a small chair in the corner.*] and just sat there with her hands held together and looking down. I got a feeling that I ought to make some conversation, so I said I had come in to see if John wanted to put in a telephone, and at that she started to laugh, and then she stopped and looked at me—scared. [*The* COUNTY ATTORNEY, *who has had his notebook out, makes a note.*] I dunno, maybe it wasn't scared. I wouldn't like to say it was. Soon Harry got back, and then Dr. Lloyd came, and you, Mr. Peters, and so I guess that's all I know that you don't.

COUNTY ATTORNEY: [*Looking around.*] I guess we'll go upstairs first—and then out to the barn and around there. [*To the* SHERIFF.] You're convinced that there was nothing important here—nothing that would point to any motive.

25 SHERIFF: Nothing here but kitchen things.

[*The* COUNTY ATTORNEY, *after again looking around the kitchen, opens the door of a cupboard closet. He gets up on a chair and looks on a shelf. Pulls his hand away, sticky.*]

COUNTY ATTORNEY: Here's a nice mess.

[*The women draw nearer.*]

MRS. PETERS: [*To the other woman.*] Oh, her fruit; it did freeze. [*To the* LAWYER.] She worried about that when it turned so cold. She said the fire'd go out and her jars would break.

SHERIFF: Well, can you beat the women! Held for murder and worryin' about her preserves.

COUNTY ATTORNEY: I guess before we're through she may have something more serious than preserves to worry about.

30 HALE: Well, women are used to worrying over trifles.

[*The two women move a little closer together.*]

COUNTY ATTORNEY: [*With the gallantry of a young politician.*] And yet, for all their worries, what would we do without the ladies? [*The women do not unbend. He goes to the sink, takes a dipperful of water from the pail and pouring it into a basin, washes his hands. Starts to wipe them on the roller towel, turns it for a cleaner place.*] Dirty towels! [*Kicks his foot against the pans under the sink.*] Not much of a housekeeper, would you say, ladies?

MRS. HALE: [*Stiffly.*] There's a great deal of work to be done on a farm.

COUNTY ATTORNEY: To be sure. And yet [*With a little bow to her.*] I know there are some Dickson county farmhouses which do not have such roller towels.

[*He gives it a pull to expose its full length again.*]

MRS. HALE: Those towels get dirty awful quick. Men's hands aren't always as clean as they might be.

COUNTY ATTORNEY: Ah, loyal to your sex, I see. But you and Mrs. Wright were neighbors. I suppose you were friends, too.

MRS. HALE: [*Shaking her head.*] I've not seen much of her of late years. I've not been in this house—it's more than a year.

COUNTY ATTORNEY: And why was that? You didn't like her?

MRS. HALE: I liked her all well enough. Farmers' wives have their hands full, Mr. Henderson. And then—

COUNTY ATTORNEY: Yes—?

40 MRS. HALE: [*Looking about.*] It never seemed a very cheerful place.

COUNTY ATTORNEY: No—it's not cheerful. I shouldn't say she had the homemaking instinct.

MRS. HALE: Well. I don't know as Wright had, either.

COUNTY ATTORNEY: You mean that they didn't get on very well?

MRS. HALE: No, I don't mean anything. But I don't think a place'd be any cheerfuller for John Wright's being in it.

45 COUNTY ATTORNEY: I'd like to talk more of that a little later. I want to get the lay of things upstairs now.

[*He goes to the left, where three steps lead to a stair door.*]

SHERIFF: I suppose anything Mrs. Peters does'll be all right. She was to take in some clothes for her, you know, and a few little things. We left in such a hurry yesterday.

COUNTY ATTORNEY: Yes, but I would like to see what you take, Mrs. Peters, and keep an eye out for anything that might be of use to us.

MRS. PETERS: Yes, Mr. Henderson.

[*The women listen to the men's steps on the stairs, then look about the kitchen.*]

MRS. HALE: I'd hate to have men coming into my kitchen, snooping around and criticising.

[*She arranges the pans under the sink which the Lawyer had shoved out of place.*]

50 MRS. PETERS: Of course it's no more than their duty.

MRS. HALE: Duty's all right, but I guess that deputy sheriff that came out to make the fire might have got a little of this on. [*Gives the roller towel a pull.*] Wish I'd thought of that sooner. Seems mean to talk about her for not having things slicked up when she had to come away in such a hurry.

MRS. PETERS: [*Who had gone to a small table in the left rear corner of the room, and lifted one end of a towel that covers a pan.*] She had bread set.

[*Stands still.*]

MRS. HALE: [*Eyes fixed on a loaf of bread beside the breadbox, which is on a low shelf at the other side of the room. Moves slowly toward it.*] She was going to put this in there. [*Picks up loaf, then abruptly drops it. In a manner of returning to familiar things.*] It's a shame about her fruit. I wonder if it's all gone. [*Gets up on the chair and looks.*] I think there's some here that's all right, Mrs. Peters. Yes—here; [*Holding it toward the window.*] this is cherries, too. [*Looking again.*] I declare I believe that's the only one. [*Gets down, bottle in her hand. Goes to the sink and wipes it off on the outside.*] She'll feel awful bad after all her hard work in the hot weather. I remember the afternoon I put up my cherries last summer.

[*She puts the bottle on the big kitchen table, center of the room. With a sigh, is about to sit down in the rocking-chair. Before she is seated realizes what chair it is; with a slow look at it, steps back. The chair which she has touched rocks back and forth.*]

MRS. PETERS: Well, I must get those things from the front room closet. [*She goes to the door at the right, but after looking into the other room, steps back.*] You coming with me, Mrs. Hale? You could help me carry them.

[*They go in the other room; reappear, MRS. PETERS carrying a dress and skirt, MRS. HALE following with a pair of shoes.*]

55 MRS. PETERS: My, it's cold in there.

[*She puts the clothes on the big table and hurries to the stove.*]

MRS. HALE: [*Examining the skirt.*] Wright was close. I think maybe that's why she kept so much to herself. She didn't even belong to the Ladies Aid. I suppose she felt she couldn't do her part, and then you don't enjoy things when you feel shabby. She used to wear pretty clothes and be lively, when she was Minnie Foster, one of the town girls singing in the choir. But that—oh, that was thirty years ago. This all you was to take in?

MRS. PETERS: She said she wanted an apron. Funny thing to want, for there isn't much to get you dirty in jail, goodness knows. But I suppose just to make her feel more natural. She said they was in the top drawer in this cupboard. Yes, here. And then her little shawl that always hung behind the door. [*Opens stair door and looks.*] Yes, here it is.

[*Quickly shuts door leading upstairs.*]

MRS. HALE: [*Abruptly moving toward her.*] Mrs. Peters?
MRS. PETERS: Yes, Mrs. Hale?
60 MRS. HALE: Do you think she did it?
MRS. PETERS: [*In a frightened voice.*] Oh, I don't know.
MRS. HALE: Well, I don't think she did. Asking for an apron and her little shawl. Worrying about her fruit.
MRS. PETERS: [*Starts to speak, glances up, where footsteps are heard in the room above. In a low voice.*] Mr. Peters says it looks bad for her. Mr. Henderson is awful sarcastic in a speech and he'll make fun of her sayin' she didn't wake up.
MRS. HALE: Well, I guess John Wright didn't wake when they was slipping that rope under his neck.
65 MRS. PETERS: No, it's strange. It must have been done awful crafty and still. They say it was such a—funny way to kill a man, rigging it all up like that.
MRS. HALE: That's just what Mr. Hale said. There was a gun in the house. He says that's what he can't understand.
MRS. PETERS: Mr. Henderson said coming out that what was needed for the case was a motive; something to show anger, or—sudden feeling.
MRS. HALE: [*Who is standing by the table.*] Well, I don't see any signs of anger around here. [*She puts her hand on the dish towel which lies on the table, stands*

looking down at table, one half of which is clean, the other half messy.] It's wiped to here. [*Makes a move as if to finish work, then turns and looks at loaf of bread outside the breadbox. Drops towel. In that voice of coming back to familiar things.*] Wonder how they are finding things upstairs. I hope she had it a little more redd-up up there. You know, it seems kind of *sneaking*. Locking her up in town and then coming out here and trying to get her own house to turn against her!

70 MRS. PETERS: But Mrs. Hale, the law is the law.

MRS. HALE: I s'pose 'tis. [*Unbuttoning her coat.*] Better loosen up your things,

MRS. PETERS: You won't feel them when you go out.

[*Mrs. Peters takes off her fur tippet, goes to hang it on hook at back of room, stands looking at the under part of the small corner table.*]

MRS. PETERS: She was piecing a quilt.

[*She brings the large sewing basket and they look at the bright pieces.*]

MRS. HALE: It's log cabin pattern. Pretty, isn't it? I wonder if she was goin' to quilt it or just knot it?

[*Footsteps have been heard coming down the stairs. The SHERIFF enters followed by HALE and the COUNTY ATTORNEY.*]

SHERIFF: They wonder if she was going to quilt it or just knot it!

[*The men laugh; the women look abashed.*]

75 COUNTY ATTORNEY: [*Rubbing his hands over the stove.*] Frank's fire didn't do much up there, did it? Well, let's go out to the barn and get that cleared up.

[*The men go outside.*]

MRS. HALE: [*Resentfully.*] I don't know as there's anything so strange, our takin' up our time with little things while we're waiting for them to get the evidence. [*She sits down at the big table smoothing out a block with decision.*] I don't see as it's anything to laugh about.

MRS. PETERS: [*Apologetically.*] Of course they've got awful important things on their minds.

[*Pulls up a chair and joins MRS. HALE at the table.*]

MRS. HALE: [*Examining another block.*] Mrs. Peters, look at this one. Here, this is the one she was working on, and look at the sewing! All the rest of it has been so nice and even. And look at this! It's all over the place! Why, it looks as if she didn't know what she was about!

[*After she has said this they look at each other, then start to glance back at the door. After an instant MRS. HALE has pulled at a knot and ripped the sewing.*]

MRS. PETERS: Oh, what are you doing, Mrs. Hale?

80 MRS. HALE: [*Mildly.*] Just pulling out a stitch or two that's not sewed very good. [*Threading a needle.*] Bad sewing always made me fidgety.

MRS. PETERS: [*Nervously.*] I don't think we ought to touch things.

Mrs. Hale: I'll just finish up this end. [*Suddenly stopping and leaning forward.*] Mrs. Peters?

Mrs. Peters: Yes, Mrs. Hale?

Mrs. Hale: What do you suppose she was so nervous about?

85 Mrs. Peters: Oh—I don't know. I don't know as she was nervous. I sometimes sew awful queer when I'm just tired. [*Mrs. Hale starts to say something, looks at Mrs. Peters, then goes on sewing.*] Well I must get these things wrapped up. They may be through sooner than we think. [*Putting apron and other things together.*] I wonder where I can find a piece of paper, and string.

Mrs. Hale: In that cupboard, maybe.

Mrs. Peters: [*Looking in cupboard.*] Why, here's a bird-cage. [*Holds it up.*] Did she have a bird, Mrs. Hale?

Mrs. Hale: Why, I don't know whether she did or not—I've not been here for so long. There was a man around last year selling canaries cheap, but I don't know as she took one; maybe she did. She used to sing real pretty herself.

Mrs. Peters: [*Glancing around.*] Seems funny to think of a bird here. But she must have had one, or why would she have a cage? I wonder what happened to it?

90 Mrs. Hale: I s'pose maybe the cat got it.

Mrs. Peters: No, she didn't have a cat. She's got that feeling some people have about cats—being afraid of them. My cat got in her room and she was real upset and asked me to take it out.

Mrs. Hale: My sister Bessie was like that. Queer, ain't it?

Mrs. Peters: [*Examining the cage.*] Why, look at this door. It's broke. One hinge is pulled apart.

Mrs. Hale: [*Looking too.*] Looks as if someone must have been rough with it.

95 Mrs. Peters: Why, yes.

[*She brings the cage forward and puts it on the table.*]

Mrs. Hale: I wish if they're going to find any evidence they'd be about it. I don't like this place.

Mrs. Peters: But I'm awful glad you came with me, Mrs. Hale. It would be lonesome for me sitting here alone.

Mrs. Hale: It would, wouldn't it? [*Dropping her sewing.*] But I tell you what I do wish, Mrs. Peters. I wish I had come over sometimes when she was here. I—[*Looking around the room.*]—wish I had.

Mrs. Peters: But of course you were awful busy, Mrs. Hale—your house and your children.

100 Mrs. Hale: I could've come. I stayed away because it weren't cheerful—and that's why I ought to have come. I—I've never liked this place. Maybe because it's down in a hollow and you don't see the road. I dunno what it is, but it's a lonesome place and always was. I wish I had come over to see Minnie Foster sometimes. I can see now—

[*Shakes her head.*]

Mrs. Peters: Well, you mustn't reproach yourself, Mrs. Hale. Somehow we just don't see how it is with other folks until—something comes up.

MRS. HALE: Not having children makes less work—but it makes a quiet house, and Wright out to work all day, and no company when he did come in. Did you know John Wright, Mrs. Peters?

MRS. PETERS: Not to know him; I've seen him in town. They say he was a good man.

MRS. HALE: Yes—good; he didn't drink, and kept his word as well as most, I guess, and paid his debts. But he was a hard man, Mrs. Peters. Just to pass the time of day with him—[*Shivers.*] Like a raw wind that gets to the bone. [*Pauses, her eye falling on the cage.*] I should think she would 'a wanted a bird. But what do you suppose went with it?

105   MRS. PETERS: I don't know, unless it got sick and died.

[*She reaches over and swings the broken door, swings it again, both women watch it.*]

MRS. HALE: You weren't raised round here, were you? [*Mrs. Peters shakes her head.*] You didn't know—her?

MRS. PETERS: Not till they brought her yesterday.

MRS. HALE: She—come to think of it, she was kind of like a bird herself—real sweet and pretty, but kind of timid and—fluttery. How—she—did—change. [*Silence; then as if struck by a happy thought and relieved to get back to everyday things.*] Tell you what, Mrs. Peters, why don't you take the quilt in with you? It might take up her mind.

MRS. PETERS: Why, I think that's a real nice idea, Mrs. Hale. There couldn't possibly be any objection to it, could there? Now, just what would I take? I wonder if her patches are in here—and her things.

[*They look in the sewing basket.*]

110   MRS. HALE: Here's some red. I expect this has got sewing things in it. [*Brings out a fancy box.*] What a pretty box. Looks like something somebody would give you. Maybe her scissors are in here. [*Opens box. Suddenly puts her hand to her nose.*] Why— [*Mrs. Peters bends nearer, then turns her face away.*] There's something wrapped up in this piece of silk.

MRS. PETERS: Why, this isn't her scissors.

MRS. HALE: [*Lifting the silk.*] Oh, Mrs. Peters—it's—

[*Mrs. Peters bends closer.*]

MRS. PETERS: It's the bird.

MRS. HALE: [*Jumping up.*] But, Mrs. Peters—look at it! Its neck! Look at its neck! It's all—other side *to*.

115   MRS. PETERS: Somebody—wrung—its—neck.

[*Their eyes meet. A look of growing comprehension, of horror. Steps are heard outside. Mrs. Hale slips box under quilt pieces, and sinks into her chair. Enter Sheriff and County Attorney. Mrs. Peters rises.*]

COUNTY ATTORNEY: [*As one turning from serious things to little pleasantries.*] Well, ladies, have you decided whether she was going to quilt it or knot it?

MRS. PETERS: We think she was going to—knot it.

COUNTY ATTORNEY: Well, that's interesting, I'm sure. [*Seeing the bird-cage.*] Has the bird flown?

120 MRS. HALE: [*Putting more quilt pieces over the box.*] We think the—cat got it.

COUNTY ATTORNEY: [*Preoccupied.*] Is there a cat?

[*MRS. HALE glances in a quick covert way at MRS. PETERS.*]

MRS. PETERS: Well, not *now*. They're superstitious, you know. They leave.

COUNTY ATTORNEY: [*To SHERIFF PETERS, continuing an interrupted conversation.*] No sign at all of anyone having come from the outside. Their own rope. Now let's go up again and go over it piece by piece. [*They start upstairs.*] It would have to have been someone who knew just the—

[*MRS. PETERS sits down. The two women sit there not looking at one another, but as if peering into something and at the same time holding back. When they talk now it is in the manner of feeling their way over strange ground, as if afraid of what they are saying, but as if they cannot help saying it.*]

MRS. HALE: She liked the bird. She was going to bury it in that pretty box.

MRS. PETERS: [*In a whisper.*] When I was a girl—my kitten—there was a boy took a hatchet, and before my eyes—and before I could get there—[*Covers her face an instant.*] If they hadn't held me back I would have—[*Catches herself, looks upstairs where steps are heard, falters weakly.*]—hurt him.

125 MRS. HALE: [*With a slow look around her.*] I wonder how it would seem never to have had any children around. [*Pause.*] No, Wright wouldn't like the bird—a thing that sang. She used to sing. He killed that, too.

MRS. PETERS: [*Moving uneasily.*] We don't know who killed the bird.

MRS. HALE: I knew John Wright.

MRS. PETERS: It was an awful thing was done in this house that night, Mrs. Hale. Killing a man while he slept, slipping a rope around his neck that choked the life out of him.

MRS. HALE: His neck. Choked the life out of him.

[*Her hand goes out and rests on the bird-cage.*]

130 MRS. PETERS: [*With rising voice.*] We don't know who killed him. We don't know.

MRS. HALE: [*Her own feeling not interrupted.*] If there'd been years and years of nothing, then a bird to sing to you, it would be awful—still, after the bird was still.

MRS. PETERS: [*Something within her speaking.*] I know what stillness is. When we homesteaded in Dakota, and my first baby died—after he was two years old, and me with no other then—

MRS. HALE: [*Moving.*] How soon do you suppose they'll be through, looking for the evidence?

MRS. PETERS: I know what stillness is. [*Pulling herself back.*] The law has got to punish crime, Mrs. Hale.

135 MRS. HALE: [*Not as if answering that.*] I *wish* you'd seen Minnie Foster when she wore a white dress with blue ribbons and stood up there in the choir and sang. [*A look around the room.*] Oh, I wish I'd come over here once in a while! That was a crime! That was a crime! Who's going to punish that?

MRS. PETERS: [*Looking upstairs.*] We mustn't—take on.

MRS. HALE: I might have known she needed help! I know how things can be—
for women. I tell you, it's queer, Mrs. Peters. We live close together and we
live far apart. We all go through the same things—it's all just a different
kind of the same thing. [*Brushes her eyes, noticing the bottle of fruit, reaches
out for it.*] If I was you I wouldn't tell her her fruit was gone. Tell her it *ain't*.
Tell her it's all right. Take this in to prove it to her. She—she may never
know whether it was broke or not.

MRS. PETERS: [*Takes the bottle, looks about for something to wrap it in; takes petticoat
from the clothes brought from the other room, very nervously begins winding this
around the bottle. In a false voice.*] My, it's a good thing the men couldn't hear us.
Wouldn't they just laugh! Getting all stirred up over a little thing like a—dead
canary. As if that could have anything to do with—with—wouldn't they *laugh*!

[*The men are heard coming down stairs.*]

140 MRS. HALE: [*Under her breath.*] Maybe they would—maybe they wouldn't.

COUNTY ATTORNEY: No, Peters, it's all perfectly clear except a reason for doing it.
But you know juries when it comes to women. If there was some definite
thing. Something to show—something to make a story about—a thing that
would connect up with this strange way of doing it—

[*The women's eyes meet for an instant. Enter* HALE *from outer door.*]

HALE: Well, I've got the team around. Pretty cold out there.

COUNTY ATTORNEY: I'm going to stay here a while by myself. [*To the* SHERIFF.] You
can send Frank out for me, can't you? I want to go over everything. I'm not
satisfied that we can't do better.

SHERIFF: Do you want to see what Mrs. Peters is going to take in?

[*The* COUNTY ATTORNEY *goes to the table, picks up the apron, laughs.*]

COUNTY ATTORNEY: Oh, I guess they're not very dangerous things the ladies have
picked out. [*Moves a few things about, disturbing the quilt pieces which cover the
box. Steps back.*] No, Mrs. Peters doesn't need supervising. For that matter, a
sheriff's wife is married to the law. Ever think of it that way, Mrs. Peters?

145 MRS. PETERS: Not—just that way.

SHERIFF: [*Chuckling.*] Married to the law. [*Moves toward the other room.*] I just
want you to come in here a minute, George. We ought to take a look at
these windows.

COUNTY ATTORNEY: [*Scoffingly.*] Oh, windows!

SHERIFF: We'll be right out, Mr. Hale.

[HALE *goes outside. The* SHERIFF *follows the* COUNTY ATTORNEY *into the other
room. Then* MRS. HALE *rises, hands tight together, looking intensely at* MRS.
PETERS, *whose eyes make a slow turn, finally meeting* MRS. HALE'S. *A moment*
MRS. HALE *holds her, then her own eyes point the way to where the box is concealed. Suddenly* MRS. PETERS *throws back quilt pieces and tries to put the box in
the bag she is wearing. It is too big. She opens box, starts to take bird out, cannot
touch it, goes to pieces, stands there helpless. Sound of a knob turning in the other
room.* MRS. HALE *snatches the box and puts it in the pocket of her big coat. Enter*
COUNTY ATTORNEY *and* SHERIFF.]

COUNTY ATTORNEY: [*Facetiously.*] Well, Henry, at least we found out that she was not going to quilt it. She was going to—what is it you call it, ladies?

150 MRS. HALE: [*Her hand against her pocket.*] We call it—knot it, Mr. Henderson.

CURTAIN

FOCUSED FREE WRITES

1. Imagine Mrs. Wright in jail. Write a soliloquy from her point of view about how she got there.
2. What is significant about the other characters in the play? How would you describe them?
3. What symbols or images stand out in this play?
4. What is the significance of the title?
5. How does this play challenge stereotypes and assumptions?
6. What is a central theme in the play?
7. What is a useful context for understanding this play?

Writing an Analytical Argument from a Critical Perspective

In this chapter, you have been engaged in the critical thinking act of using critical perspectives; now you will use interpretation and analysis to construct an argument about one of the works in this chapter. Your task is to prove your interpretation through your analysis or close reading of a work from a particular critical perspective (or perspectives). You might determine a meaning of the work as a whole or the meaning of some aspect of the text like a character, a scene, or a particular symbol. Your job will be to argue how this critical perspective is useful in making meaning of a text. We'll follow Stephanie's progress as she develops an argument using critical perspectives. Her sample paper will appear at the end of this chapter.

Considering Different Critical Perspectives

Start at the very beginning. In other words, return to your initial interpretations of the text. Return to your Focused Free Writes or your comments in class and consider what meaning you made of a text you were interested in. Free write anew on this text. How do you understand it? What theme is apparent? What is the most important part of the work?

Now, return to the list of critical perspectives beginning on page 329. Did your free writes naturally fall into one of these perspectives? Can any of these perspectives further illustrate the tentative argument you are developing? Try out a couple of these perspectives on your text or your textual focus. Determine which one allows you to develop an argument about important moments in the text. Follow the perspective that opens up possibilities rather than limits your thinking.

After several close readings of Susan Glaspell's 1916 play Trifles,
I had to first decide through which critical lens I would be examining this text. Given the play's central tension between its male
and female characters, I thought this dynamic lends itself to a
feminist reading. Through this perspective, I planned to look
specifically at Glaspell's portrayal of Mrs. Wright, Mrs. Hale,
and Mrs. Peters to see what Glaspell suggests about gender relations in the domestic sphere. To add another dimension to my
research paper, I decided to look at Trifles from a historical
perspective to see if the political and social climate of the early
twentieth century had any impact on Glaspell's subject matter.

Develop tentative arguments using a few of the critical perspectives or a combi-
nation of a number of them. Share your thinking with a partner or in a work
group. Which is most convincing to your classmates?

Rereading the Work in Light of the Perspective

As discussed earlier in this chapter, using a critical perspective is like looking
through a lens. In fact, it might be useful to imagine the lenses as those funny
3D lenses. When you have the right combination of lens and text, amazing
things can appear; but without it, you may get nothing at all. In fact, in viewing with a particular critical approach in mind, certain things will be seen, and
others will not. If a formalist perspective is adopted, then biographical details
of the author's life will not be considered, and Freud may not matter for the
deconstructive critic.

It can be useful to draft writing about the different elements (theme, plot,
style, character, symbol, setting, voice) that are foregrounded when using a
particular perspective. Consider the following questions:

Formalist criticism

What stylistic elements are distinctive? How does the figurative language,
point of view, descriptive language, or structure construct the meaning of
the text?

Biographical criticism

Based on the brief biography in the chapter or on what you know about the
writer, how do the author's life experiences inform or explain the text's meaning?

Historical criticism

Is there a historical context that could shed light on the text? Is there a particular
historical document or set of documents that can work alongside this literary text
to demonstrate how history is constructed? Is there a setting or context you
would like to research to make meaning of the text?

Marxist criticism

What class issues arise in this text? How does the text illustrate how lower classes are oppressed and dominant classes kept in power?

Psychoanalytic criticism

What psychological issues make this text meaningful? Can you diagnose the psychology of the writer, the characters, or readers? How do psychological terminologies figure in the text?

Gender criticism

How is recognizing the construction of gender or sexualities useful in making meaning of the text? Which characteristics of femininity or masculinity are endorsed, and which are marginalized? What kinds of sexualities are normalized, and which are punished?

Postcolonial criticism

Is one culture dominant over another? How is that privileging demonstrated to be necessary or natural? Do any characters have to negotiate competing cultures?

Deconstructive criticism

How is an implied meaning of the text inherently dismantled? What contradictions or ambiguities should be highlighted in the text as meaningful? What can be found in between the lines?

STUDENT WRITER In Stephanie's Words . . .

Before returning to the text for another reading, I did some preliminary research. I searched for books, articles, and essays that would give me some background information on Glaspell's politics and the play's inception, both aspects which would shed some light on whether or not the combination of feminist and historicist approaches would be substantial for this paper. The most useful sources I was able to locate included J. Allen Gainor's book Susan Glaspell in Context: American Theater, Culture, and Politics, 1915–18 and Linda Ben-Zvi's Susan Glaspell: Essays on Her Theater and Fiction. Both books provide critical information the historical events that inspired Glaspell's play and social context in which she lived and experienced.

Test out various critical perspectives by responding to the above questions. Which one encourages the most writing? Which seems to offer the most potential for a paper?

Shaping a Thesis: Establishing the Critical Context

As discussed in the argument chapter, your thesis should be a statement you can prove true with evidence gleaned from the text. In an argument, you might make your case in acknowledging the limitations of counterarguments. When using critical perspectives, you might make your case stronger in employing a particular approach.

It can be useful to directly acknowledge the critical perspective you use:

> Using a postcolonial perspective, Langston Hughes' "Theme for English B" can be understood as a battle between competing cultures.

Or it can be indirectly stated such as in Stephanie's below in which she uses a feminist-historical approach to support the following thesis:

> Considering the way Glaspell constructs the central tension between the men and women in *Trifles*, I want to argue that Glaspell does so to offer audiences two voices on the subject of policing women's identities.

▌ *Develop a thesis statement using one of the above approaches.*

Writing to Advance the Thesis

Once you have a thesis, you will want to outline your topic. Remember, it is essential to focus on just the elements that support your particular argument and are highlighted by your specific critical perspective. Some important moments to the plot or the theme of the text may be left out so that your thesis can be clearly developed. For example, a writer might want to argue the following thesis:

> Using a postcolonial perspective, Langston Hughes' "Theme for English B" can be understood as a battle between competing cultures.

He would brainstorm, listing the following support:

- privileging of academic voice in "Theme for English B"
- role of teacher versus role of student
- othering of black voice in "Theme for English B"
- what is post–colonialism?
- how can post–colonialist perspective work with an American writer?

Once the writer had these ideas, he would need to consider how to arrange them. Based on this thesis, he would have a comparison paper in which he was constructing an argument using a critical perspective. The writer's ideas could be rearranged so that his introduction discusses the critical perspective. Coming up with good ideas for beginnings of papers can be the hardest part; so by discussing the perspective and defining it at the start of the paper, he creates a way in. Each paragraph then would begin with strong transitions showing how similar ideas appear in this poem and essay.

Introduction: what is post–colonialism?
    How can postcolonialist perspective work with American writer?
        thesis: Using a postcolonial perspective, Langston Hughes' "Theme for English B" can be understood as a battles between competing cultures.

A. privileging of academic voice in "Theme for English B"

B. othering of black voice in "Theme for English B"

STUDENT WRITER In Stephanie's Words...

After consulting some background texts, I returned to <u>Trifles</u> for another look to highlight any scenes or lines that would support the direction of my paper. Following this step, I outlined the paper's structure. It is important to have an outline at your disposal when beginning the drafting process. I found it useful in this outline to jot some notes on the historical background of the play and the social understanding of gender divisions at the time before introducing my thesis. I figured that this initial framework gives readers enough information to anchor their understanding of my thesis without feeling overwhelmed. Once I established my introductory material, I was able to outline the remainder of my paper without too much difficulty. The structure of the paper's body alternates textual evidence and my analysis with that of critics to validate my thesis. Although this paper is primarily my thoughts, I used some history and criticism to substantiate those thoughts. As I wrote my rough draft, I tried first to put down all my thoughts before including any critical sources. This approach allows me to focus first on what I'm trying to say before turning to others for support.

Develop a preliminary draft of your outline and revise it as necessary as you develop your support.

Integrating and Citing Source Material

When using a critical perspective broadly, it is not necessary to cite Marx as the father of Marxism or Freud as the founder of psychoanalysis. You can assume a critical perspective generally without citing particular sources. However, you may need to engage in research to pull in particular literary critics or historical documents. In that case, it will be necessary to cite your sources. See Chapter 18 for an expanded discussion of integrating source material and Part IV for an in-depth discussion of the research paper.

The first time you introduce a critic, be certain to state what they wrote and who they are:

In "'Murder, She Wrote': The Genesis of Susan Glaspell's *Trifles*," critic Linda Ben-Zvi explains that Glaspell reported on the murder of John Hossack in Iowa when working as a journalist at the turn of the century.

Here, Stephanie introduced the title of the essay, the name of the critic, and her summary of the history the critic was recounting. Any time she referred to the author subsequently, she was able to cite her by last name with the page number of the quotation located after the end quotation mark:

> Critic Linda Ben-Zvi writes, "At the time she wrote *Trifles* Glaspell was living in a community passionately concerned with socialism and feminism.... [H]er writing acts as a palimpsest for the shifting roles of women in the early twentieth century" (41–2).

The critic is introduced by first and last name, or simply last name, and the quotation appears inside quotation marks. With a short quotation, the parenthetical citation is included after the final quotation mark with the period outside of the closing parenthesis. With a block quotation, no quotation marks are necessary and the punctuation is found before the parenthetical citation (see Chapters 3 and 16.) Stephanie indicated moments where she abbreviated the text with ellipses [...] and adjusted capitalization or punctuation with brackets [].

Review your integration of sources for clarity and correctness.

Revising, Editing, and Proofreading

Sometimes the editing and proofreading stage should be reconsidered to allow more time and energy for substantive revising. The writing of the essay can lead to new ideas, and you'll want to take the time to pursue these new ideas to make your paper as strong as possible.

When the writer got to the end of the draft on Hughes' poem, he found that he didn't have a place to discuss the similar images that arose in the text. The poem addresses the isolation of the protagonist literally and figuratively and how the individual voice of the protagonist was not heard. The writer then needed to rethink the paper's structure and revise the thesis:

> Introduction: what is postcolonialism?
>> How can postcolonialist perspective work with American writer?
>>> thesis: Using a postcolonial perspective, Langston Hughes' "Theme for English B" can be understood as a battle between competing cultures in which the oppressed become isolated and loses individuality.
> A. privileging of academic voice in "Theme for English B"
> B. othering of voice in "Theme for English B"
>> 1. Isolation
>> 2. Individuality lost

Revise, proofread, and edit your draft.

Sample Student Paper

In the following example, Stephanie examines the play *Trifles* from a historical and feminist perspective.

Stephanie Roberts's biography may be found on page 567.

Stephanie Roberts

Dr. Howells

English 102

30 Oct. 2010

Policing Domesticity: Cultural Surveillance

in Susan Glaspell's *Trifles*

Inspired by the circumstances surrounding the murder of John Hossack in 1900, Susan Glaspell makes the surveillance of women the dramatic focal point of her 1916 play *Trifles*. In the play, audiences witness not the actual murder of John Wright but the aftermath. Although the main suspect is John's wife, Minnie Wright, Glaspell deliberately keeps her offstage throughout the entire play. Instead, we learn about what happens offstage through the seemingly objective lenses of the county attorney and sheriff. In sharp contrast to these voices of authority is the presence of Mrs. Peters and Mrs. Hale, friends of Mrs. Wright. As these characters interact, the audience notices an unspoken tension between the genders. This particular grouping of characters demands we question Glaspell's objective in the dichotomous pairing of law enforcement and domestic wives. Considering the way Glaspell constructs the central tension between the men and women in *Trifles*, I want to argue that Glaspell does so to offer audiences two voices on the subject of policing women's identities.

Before delving into the text, it may be useful to consider the historical framework of the early twentieth century in which Glaspell wrote *Trifles*. In "'Murder, She Wrote': The Genesis of Susan Glaspell's *Trifles*," critic Linda Ben-Zvi explains that Glaspell reported on the murder of John Hossack in Iowa when working as a journalist at the turn of the century. In brief, Hossack was killed with two blows to the head while asleep. The accused party of this violent crime was Hossack's wife, Margaret Hossack; the courts found her guilty and sentenced her to life in prison. *Trifles* deviates from this historical depiction; we are not privileged to see Mrs. Wright tried in court. Instead, Glaspell sets up an informal court in Mrs. Wright's kitchen where we watch the voices of authority collide with the voices of domesticity.

This revision of the story stems from Glaspell's social and political position. Critic Linda Ben-Zvi writes, "At the time she wrote *Trifles* Glaspell was living in a community passionately concerned with socialism and feminism.... [H]er writing acts as a palimpsest for the shifting roles of women in the early twentieth century" (41-2). Writing in a time that relied heavily on Victorian ideology and essentialist arguments to maintain women's status in the home, Glaspell concentrated on advertising the oppressive social, economic, and political conditions of women to combat the traditionalists who argued that women's subordination was part of the natural order. As modern readers no longer implicated in this historical context, we have to ask, along with Glaspell, how were these oppressive conditions maintained? What compels people to obey authority? The manifestations of authority—law enforcement, the court system, government—are all accepted as universal principles responsible for maintaining order; we see these systems as natural. I want to contend that in *Trifles* Glaspell sheds light on the identity surveillance and authority maintenance, specifically through the patriarchal structures of law enforcement and marriage.

Although the County Attorney, the Sheriff, Mr. Hale, Mrs. Hale, and Mrs. Peters are all onstage, the play opens with the men specifically recounting and inquiring about the tragic events that unfolded at the Wright farmhouse. During this exchange, we hear very little from the women. As the men inform us that Mr. Wright died from strangulation and that Mrs. Wright responded abnormally to the news, the women stand by idly. It is not until the County Attorney disapproves of Mrs. Wright's housekeeping that the women interrupt the conversation. Upon finding a broken jar of preserves, the County Attorney comments, "Here's a nice mess" (339). To which Mrs. Peters sympathetically responds to the circumstance: "Oh, her fruit; it did freeze. She worried about that when it turned so cold" (339). To counter Mrs. Peters, the Sheriff declares: "Well, can you beat the women! Held for murder and worryin' about her preserves" (339). This brief interaction establishes that tension that pervades the remainder of the play. As a way of controlling the women's responses during the murder investigation, the men make threatening comments to deter them from speaking in Mrs. Wright's defense, which in turn would challenge their authority if they were successful.

The comments that follow assume greater subtlety than the Sheriff's "beating" remark. Surveying the disorder and filth in Mrs. Wright's kitchen, the County Attorney critiques her lack of a "homemaking instinct" (340). Conscious that during this historic time women's domain was the home, that this location shaped her identity as a woman, such a patronizing suggestion implies Mrs. Wright is less than a woman, malformed and unnatural according to society. In another instance of surveillance and control, the Attorney monitors what Mrs. Peters intends to take to Mrs. Wright in the county jailhouse; he makes his surveillance of her behavior clear to her and the audience. There are no questions from Mrs. Peters. She answers affirmatively as the men exit the stage to explore the upstairs bedroom for any evidence. The dynamic here clearly mirrors that of a parent directing his or her disapproval toward a child's misbehavior. According to J. Ellen Gainor, "[Glaspell] overtly establishes tension between male and female modes of interpretation and ties this tension to the larger questions about social codes of law and justice" (47). Because the County Attorney and the Sheriff are representatives of law enforcement and are assumed to be objective and just, there is no questioning their authority. However, the manner in which they conduct business is anything but objective. Their language and tone directed at the women present serve to intimidate them into submission and acceptance of their authority.

Once the men leave the scene, Glaspell reveals to the audience another tool of surveillance: marriage. Mrs. Peters and Mrs. Hale provide us with Mrs. Wright's backstory. Before becoming Mrs. Wright thirty years ago, she was Minnie Foster, a vibrant young woman who "used to wear pretty clothes and be lively...[was] one of the town girls singing in the choir" (341). As brief as this personal history may be, it gives us insight into who Mrs. Wright was before she was actually Mrs. Wright. The women then recount how reserved and isolated Mrs. Wright became as the years passed. With only her canary to keep her company, Mrs. Wright spent most of her time alone. Given these details and the historical understanding of marriage, we can infer that Mrs. Wright's marriage enacted the same surveillance as law enforcement. The common understanding of marriage during the early twentieth century identifies the husband as the head of the household and sole breadwinner, and the wife as the domestic responsible for maintaining an efficient household for the husband. As Karen Alkalay-Gut asserts in "Murder and Marriage: Another Look at *Trifles*": "The significant world for men is elsewhere, but for women it is in the ordering of the scraps of information around the central 'square' of marriage and the total dependence of the wife upon her husband for all physical, emotional, and spiritual fulfillment" (73). Within this dynamic is an embedded master–servant relationship.

To further reinforce the extent to which Mrs. Wright was policed in her marriage, Glaspell includes a number of bird references, such as the canary and the cage as a parallel to Mrs. Wright. Like the canary, Mrs. Wright was once a song bird. An even more startling comparison is how Mrs. Wright is kept in her own cage, first in her home and then in the jailhouse. At home, Mr. Wright was able to monitor her. Even in his absence, Mrs. Wright cannot escape the imprisonment as she waits in jail.

While we speculate on Mrs. Wright's past and future circumstances, Mrs. Hale and Mrs. Peters's exchanges call our attention to the present. Here we distinguish two different voices responding to Mrs. Wright's situation; most notably they are voices that represent two products of surveillance. Despite the women's alliance through gender and their equal exposure to the insensitive attitudes of the County Attorney and the Sheriff, their attitudes are conflicting. After finding Mrs. Wright's beloved canary dead, the women finally speak without reservation. From Mrs. Hale, we detect hostility directed at the officials. She states, "How soon do you suppose they'll be through, looking for evidence?" (345). She begins questioning their presence in a women's domain. In opposition, Mrs. Peters argues it is their duty, that "the law has got to punish crime" regardless of circumstances (345). Enraged at how Mrs. Wright's life turned out, Mrs. Hale ignores Mrs. Peters and laments, "Oh, I wish I'd come over here once in a while! That was a crime! That was a crime! Who's going to punish that?" (345).

Observing these responses, we characterize Mrs. Hale's attitude as recognition of a system that works out of women's favor in order to maintain status quo. On the other hand, we characterize Mrs. Peter's attitude as the internalization of law and order despite the implications for her gender. Unlike Mrs. Hale, she does not want to take on the system in fear of the potential repercussions. However, we do not get the opportunity to see this conflict continue as the scene comes to a close and the men return to assert their authority. Consequently, the women refrain from speaking their opinions in the men's presence as they silently resolve to hide Mrs. Wright's dead canary.

Although Glaspell makes Mrs. Wright the dramatic anchor throughout *Trifles*, audiences gravitate toward Mrs. Hale and Mrs. Peters, women who physically make their voices known on stage. As the law attempts to silence their voices through surveillance and social conditioning, the women speak on behalf of the absent voice—Mrs. Wright. Although the women share an allegiance of gender, Glaspell shows us that this unity is unstable. As illustrated in the responses to the men's presence, the women offer two perspectives for us to consider as we evaluate the degree of surveillance and policing is evident.

Works Cited

Alkalay-Gut, Karen. "Murder and Marriage: Another Look at *Trifles*." *Susan Glaspell: Essays on Her Theater and Fiction*. Ed. Linda Ben-Zvi. Ann Arbor: U of Michigan P, 2002. 71–81. Print.

Ben-Zvi, Linda. "'Murder, She Wrote': The Genesis of Susan Glaspell's *Trifles*." *Susan Glaspell: Essays on Her Theater and Fiction*. Ed. Linda Ben-Zvi. Ann Arbor: U of Michigan P, 2002. 19–47. Print.

Gainor, J. Ellen. *Susan Glaspell in Context: American Theater, Culture, and Politics, 1915–48*. Ann Arbor: U of Michigan P, 2004. Print.

Glaspell, Susan. "Trifles." *Literature: Reading to Write*. Ed. Elizabeth Howells. New York: 2010. 337–347. Pearson/Print.

PART THREE

EXPERIENCING CONTEMPORARY LITERATURE

This innovative section offers five mini-chapters that encourage connections between familiar, popular genres and their less familiar literary counterparts. By focusing on contemporary literature in the forms of comedies, music, graphic novels, horror stories, and experimental literature, the section helps make literature more relatable, identifying the connections between newer works and the classic connections between newer works and the classic "literary" works that are more often assigned. The chapters maintain a fairly standard structure, establishing a kind of literary family tree that defines the genre, includes familiar examples, introduces new texts, identifies the roots of the featured genre, and suggests creative strategies for exploring the form further.

8
LAUGHING OUT LOUD
Getting to Know Comic Literature

Laughing Out Loud. George (Jason Alexander), Elaine (Julia Louis-Dreyfus), and Jerry (Jerry Seinfeld) are interviewed by Kramer (Michael Richards) during this funny scene from the iconic sitcom *Seinfeld*. What makes something funny? Is humor something universal or personal? Who gets to say? Why isn't humor taken seriously when it comes to high art?

Comedy is hard to define. If you have to explain the joke, it probably wasn't that funny. And as for a definition, it seems to be one of those things where we know it when we see it. It is even harder to point to literature that can be characterized as comic. Many of the great works of literature included in this book aren't entirely funny. However, comedy as a genre does have a long and illustrious history.

By design, comedy should amuse. Any literary work (particularly a play) that is not a tragedy—anything less serious or less exalted, usually with a happy ending—is technically considered a comedy. So the genre of comedy is quite broad. Early comedies include Greek plays such as those by Aristophanes and Menander and then Roman plays by Plautus and Terence. In the Middle Ages, the term "comedy" was applied even to narrative poems if they ended happily, such as Dante's *Divine Comedy* (c. 1320). In medieval Italy, the **commedia dell'arte** was the comedy of troupes of professional actors who played stereotyped roles in scenarios about young lovers and clever servants outwitting rich elders. In sixteenth- to seventeenth-century England, Shakespeare's comic plays included low-humor characters and a successful romantic match in the final act. Decades later, Restoration comedies transformed the tradition with **comedies of manners** about the wittiness, intrigues, and romances of sophisticated aristocrats. Today, comedy can be found on the stage in plays or stand-up performances, on the set in films or television, in print in emails and essays as well as on web pages and in comic strips.

From Someone Who Knows

Dave Barry on Being Funny

Bryan Curtis, Slate Magazine

On Dave Barry
Elegy for the Humorist.

Dave Barry, who quit his syndicated humor column last week, has been playing dumb for 22 years. Whenever someone suggests that Barry is our noblest social commentator, that he regularly makes the lions of the *New York Times* editorial page look like bozos, Barry points out that this is impossible, because, unlike most *Times* men, he takes great pride in making booger jokes. Let us ignore that objection and repeat the suggestion. Dave Barry is—was—the most heroic newspaper columnist in America. He hides his considerable candlepower behind a jokester's guise of "Don't trust me, I'm just the comedian!" Or, as Barry once put it, "Readers are sometimes critical of me because just about everything I write about is an irresponsible lie."

Barry began his writing career in humiliating fashion: Slumming for a company called Burger Associates, he flew around the country teaching businessmen how to write interoffice memos. He also produced a syndicated humor column that ran in a few tiny newspapers and that practically nobody read. Barry came to the attention of Gene Weingarten, the editor of *Miami Herald's* Sunday magazine, *Tropic*, after freelancing an article on natural childbirth for a Philadelphia newspaper. "I read it and realized it was the first time in my life I had laughed out loud while reading the printed word," says Weingarten, who now writes a humor column for the *Washington Post*. Barry began freelancing a monthly column for *Tropic*, which became biweekly, then weekly—and eventually landed Barry a full-time job at the *Herald*, where he camped out for the next two decades. Weingarten and his heirs eagerly deployed Barry as humorist, reporter, and quixotic political correspondent, such as the occasion when he began an interview with then-Gov. Bob Graham with a question about harmonica safety.

Weingarten suggests, tantalizingly, that Barry is something of a great brain—a strange thing to say about a man who enjoys covering exploding livestock. "Dave had astonishingly high SAT scores," says Weingarten. "His humor is informed by an astounding intellect." One week, when *Tropic* converted itself into a kind of Devil's Dictionary, Weingarten instructed Barry to come up with a definition for "sense of humor." Barry disappeared from the office for a few days. He came back with this: "A sense of humor is a measurement of the extent to which we realize that we are trapped in a world almost totally devoid of reason. Laughter is how we express the anxiety we feel at this knowledge." Then he promptly went back to writing about exploding livestock.

Barry evades questions about what makes his writing funny. (In a column, he once suggested it was his copious use of the word "weasel.") Weingarten says Barry codified one rule of comedy: "Put the funniest word at the end of sentence." A second rule might be: "Put the funniest sentence at the beginning of the story." Barry writes some of the jazziest opening lines in the business. This is partly out of necessity, since Barry's column usually runs about 800 words. It can take up to a minute or two to unwrap a humor piece by the *New Yorker's* Ian Frazier or Steve Martin, compared to mere seconds for one by Barry. Among Barry's best openers:

> Without my eyeglasses, I have a great deal of trouble distinguishing between house fires and beer signs.

> I have received a disturbing letter from Mr. Frank J. Phillips, who describes himself as both a patriot and a Latin teacher.

> Obviously, we—and when I say "we," I mean people who no longer laugh at the concept of hemorrhoids—need to come up with some kind of plan for dealing with the yuppies.

> Like most Americans, I was thrilled to death last February when our wealthy yachting snots won the coveted America's Cup back from Australia's wealthy yachting snots.

> At the *Miami Herald* we ordinarily don't provide extensive coverage of New York City unless a major news development occurs up there, such as Sean Penn coming out of a restaurant.

Next, we move to Barry's third rule of comedy, which is to change subjects as frequently and jarringly as possible, often beginning with the second sentence of the article. Last July, for example, Barry began a column wondering why breakfast-cereal mascots—Toucan Sam, Cap'n Crunch, et al.—were uniformly male. A few hundred words later, Barry had forgotten about that idea and was asking whether we should ditch the phrase "the birds and the bees" for a zoologically correct expression, "the dogs."

Because he's read by boomers and teenagers alike, Barry is often thought of as a guileless, domestic funnyman. And, true, Barry wrote plenty of sweet columns about his son, his dogs (Earnest and Zippy, themselves comic icons), and his lifelong battle with recalcitrant air conditioners. But Barry wrote an astonishing amount about politics, too. Few know, perhaps, that his book *Dave Barry's Greatest Hits* contains two columns about airline deregulation. And another about tax reform. And another about the defense of Western Europe. And that in his book about American history, *Dave Barry Slept Here*, he inveighed, comically, against the Hawley-Smoot Tariff ("the most terrible and destructive event in the history of Mankind"). And that from the Democratic Convention—he's covered a half-dozen—he wrote that poor John Glenn "couldn't electrify a fish tank if he threw a toaster in it."

In 1987, after the *New York Times* published a bleak article about South Florida ("Can Miami Save Itself?"), Barry's editors dispatched their man to New York to give the *Times* its comeuppance. Barry returned with a wicked 4,000-word story in which he gently pointed out that Ed Koch's Manhattan was a carnival of urban decay and drug paraphernalia, too. Where the *Times'* story had been heavy-handed and sober, Barry was impish and hilarious, reporting, "[W]e immediately detect signs of a healthy economy in the form of people squatting on the sidewalk selling realistic jewelry." The denizens of Times Square, he observed, were "very friendly, often coming right up and offering to engage in acts of leisure with you." After catching a cab at LaGuardia Airport, Barry formulated the three immutable laws of New York taxis:

1. DRIVER SPEAKS NO ENGLISH.
2. DRIVER JUST GOT HERE TWO DAYS AGO FROM SOMEPLACE LIKE SENEGAL.
3. DRIVER HATES YOU.

Barry (not the *Times*) won the Pulitzer Prize for commentary the next year. And perhaps his gifts as a political satirist point toward a second act. In his valedictory, Barry refused to rule out a return to column-writing. Here's an idea: As soon as William Safire shuffles off to the Old Columnists' Home, put Barry smack dab in the middle of the *Times* editorial page. Barry confessed a few years ago that he's a raving libertarian—just the kind of dyspeptic crank who would take pleasure in thumbing Washington in the eye. Give him 14 inches twice a week and let him write whatever he wants. Why settle for another graying libertarian when you can have a libertarian who makes booger jokes? Ultimately, the comedy you love on television, from *Seinfeld* to *The Simpsons*, has its place in the literary canon along with current comic essayists like David Sedaris and Sarah Vowell.

A Genre You Know

Stand-up Comedy

In the 1990s, the stand-up comedy of Jerry Seinfeld provided the opening monolog for his smash show, *Seinfeld*. Think of comedians you are familiar with and stand-up routines you enjoy. Reflect on what makes them funny to you.

Comic Essays

The following essays are by contemporary comedic writers. As you read them, you might consider the definition of comedy from the beginning of the chapter to see if there is any common ground between comedy that is performed and literary comedy.

David Sedaris

THE DRAMA BUG

The man was sent to our class to inspire us, and personally speaking, I thought he did an excellent job. After introducing himself in a relaxed and genial manner, he started toward the back of the room, only to be stopped midway by what we came to know as "the invisible wall," that transparent barrier realized only by psychotics, drug fiends, and other members of the show business community.

I sat enthralled as he righted himself and investigated the imaginary wall with his open palms, running his hands over the seemingly hard surface in hopes of finding a way out. Moments later he was tugging at an invisible rope, then struggling in the face of a violent, fantastic wind.

You know you're living in a small town when you can reach the ninth grade without ever having seen a mime. As far as I was concerned, this man was a prophet, a genius, a pioneer in the field of entertainment—and here he was in Raleigh, North Carolina! It was a riot, the way he imitated the teacher, turning down the corners of his mouth and riffling through his imaginary purse in search of gum and aspirin. Was this guy funny or what!

I went home and demonstrated the invisible wall for my two-year-old brother, who pounded on the very real wall beside his playpen, shrieking and wailing in disgust. When my mother asked what I'd done to provoke him, I threw up my hands in mock innocence before lowering them to retrieve the imaginary baby that lay fussing at my feet. I patted the back of my little ghost to induce gas and was investigating its soiled diaper when I noticed my mother's face assume an expression she reserved for unspeakable horror. I had seen this look only twice before: once when she was caught in the path of a charging, rabid pig and then again when I told her I wanted a peach-colored velveteen blazer with matching slacks.

"I don't know who put you up to this," she said, "but I'll kill you myself before I watch you grow up to be a clown. If you want to paint your face and prance around on street corners, then you'll have to find some other place to live because I sure as hell won't have it in my house." She turned to leave. *"Or in my yard,"* she added.

Fearful of her retribution, I did as I was told, ending my career in mime with a whimper rather than the silent bang I had hoped for.

The visiting actor returned to our classroom a few months later, removing his topcoat to reveal a black body stocking worn with a putty-colored neck brace, the result of a recent automobile accident. This afternoon's task was to introduce us to the works of William Shakespeare, and once again I was completely captivated by his charm and skill. When the words became confusing, you needed only to pay attention to the actor's face and hands to understand that this particular character was not just angry, but vengeful. I loved the undercurrent of hostility that lay beneath the surface of this deceptively beautiful language. It seemed a shame that people no longer spoke this way, and I undertook a campaign to reintroduce Elizabethan English to the citizens of North Carolina.

"Perchance, fair lady, thou dost think me unduly vexed by the sorrowful state of thine quarters," I said to my mother as I ran the vacuum cleaner over the living-room carpet she was inherently too lazy to bother with. "These foul specks, the evidence of life itself, have sullied not only thine shag-tempered mat but also thine character. Be ye mad, woman? Were it a punishable crime to neglect thine dwellings, you, my feeble-spirited mistress, would hang from the tallest tree in penitence for your shameful ways. Be there not garments to launder and iron free of turbulence? See ye not the porcelain plates and hearty mugs waiting to be washed clean of evidence? Get thee to thine work, damnable lady, and quickly, before the products of thine very loins raise their collected fists in a spirit born both of rage and indignation, forcibly coaxing the last breath from the foul chamber of thine vain and upright throat. Go now, wastrel, and get to it!"

My mother reacted as if I had whipped her with a short length of yarn. The intent was there, but the weapon was strange and inadequate. I could tell by the state of my room that she spent the next day searching my dresser for drugs. The clothes I took pride in neatly folding were crammed tight into their drawers with no regard for color or category. I smelled the evidence of cigarettes and noticed the coffee rings on my desk. My mother had been granted forgiveness on several previous occasions, but mess with mine drawers and ye have just made thyself an enemy for life. Tying a feather to the shaft of my ballpoint pen, I quilled her a letter. "The thing that ye search for so desperately," I wrote, "resideth not in mine well-ordered chamber, but in the questionable content of thine own character." I slipped the note into her purse, folded twice and sealed with wax from the candles I now used to light my room. I took to brooding, refusing to let up until I received a copy of Shakespeare's collected plays. Once they were acquired, I discovered them dense and difficult to follow. Reading the words made me feel dull and stupid, but speaking them made me feel powerful. I found it best to simply carry the book from room to room, occasionally skimming for fun words I might toss into my ever fragrant vocabulary. The dinner hour became either unbearable or excruciating, depending on my mood.

"Methinks , kind sir, most gentle lady, fellow siblings all, that this barnyard fowl be most tasty and succulent, having simmered in its own sweet juices for such a time as it might take the sun to pass, rosy and full-fingered, across the plum-colored sky for the course of a twilight hour. 'Tis crisp yet juicy, this plump bird, satisfied in the company of such finely roasted neighbors. Hear me out, fine relations, and heed my words, for me thinks it adventurous, and fanciful, too, to saddle mine fork with both fowl *and* carrot at the exact same time, the twin juices blending together in a delicate harmony which doth cajole and enliven mine tongue in a spirit of unbridled merriment! What say ye, fine father, sisters, and infant brother, too, that we raise our flagons high in celebration of this hearty feast, prepared lovingly and with utmost grace by this dutiful woman we have the good fortune to address as wife, wench, or mother!"

My enthusiasm knew no limits. Soon my mother was literally begging me to wait in the car while she stepped into the bank or grocery store.

I was at the orthodontist's office, placing a pox upon the practice of dentistry, when the visiting actor returned to our classroom.

"You missed it," my friend Lois said. "The man was so indescribably powerful that I was practically crying, that's how brilliant he was." She positioned her hands as if she were supporting a tray. "I don't know what more I can say. The words, they just don't exist. I could try to explain his realness, but you'd never be able to understand it. Never," she repeated. "Never, never, never."

Lois and I had been friends for six months when our relationship suddenly assumed a competitive edge. I'd never cared who made better grades or had more spending money. We each had our strengths; the important thing was to honor each other for the thing that person did best. Lois held her Chablis better than I, and I respected her for that. Her frightening excess of self-confidence allowed her to march into school wearing a rust-colored Afro wig, and I stood behind her one hundred percent. She owned more records than I did, and because she was nine months older, also knew how to drive a car and did so as if she were rushing to put out a fire. *Fine,* I thought, *good for her.* My superior wisdom and innate generosity allowed me to be truly happy for Lois up until the day she questioned my ability to understand the visiting actor. The first few times he visited, she'd been just like the rest of them, laughing at his neck brace and rolling her eyes at the tangerine-sized lump in his tights. *I* was the one who first identified his brilliance, and now she was saying I couldn't understand him? Methinks not.

"Honestly, woman," I said to my mother on our way to the dry cleaner, "to think that this low-lying worm might speak to me of greatness as though it were a thing invisible to mine eyes is more than I can bear. Her words doth strike mine heart with the force of a punishing blow, leaving me both stunned and highly vexed, too. Hear me, though, for I shall bide my time, quietly, and with cunning, striking back at the very hour she doth least expect it. Such an affront shall not go unchallenged, of that you may rest assured, gentle lady. My vengeance will hold the sweet taste of the ripest berry, and I shall savor it slowly"

"You'll get over it," my mother said. "Give it a week or two and I'm sure everything will be back to normal. I'm going in now to get your father's shirts and I want you to wait here, *in the car.* Trust me, this whole thing will be forgotten about in no time."

This had become her answer to everything. She'd done some asking around and concluded I'd been bitten by what her sister referred to as "the drama bug." My mother was convinced that this was a phase, just like all the others. A few weeks of fanfare and I'd drop show business, just like I had the guitar and my private detective agency. I hated having my life's ambition reduced to the level of a common cold. This wasn't a bug, but a full-fledged virus. It might lay low for a year or two, but this little germ would never go away. It had nothing to do with talent or initiative. Rejection couldn't weaken it, and no amount of success would ever satisfy it. Once diagnosed, the prognosis was terminal.

The drama bug seemed to strike hardest with Jews, homosexuals, and portly girls, whose faces were caked with acne medication. These were individuals who, for one reason or another, desperately craved attention. I would later discover it was a bad idea to gather more than two of these people in an enclosed area for any length of time. The stage was not only a physical place but also a state of mind, and the word *audience* was defined as anyone forced to suffer your company. We young actors were a string of lightbulbs left burning twenty-four hours a day, exhausting ourselves and others with our self-proclaimed brilliance.

I had the drama bug and Lois had a car. Weighing the depth of her momentary transgression against the rich rewards of her private chariot, I found it within my bosom to forgive my wayward friend. I called her the moment I learned the visiting actor had scheduled a production of *Hamlet* set to take place in the amphitheater of the Raleigh Rose Garden. He himself would direct and play the title role, but the other parts were up for grabs. We auditioned, and because we were the youngest and least experienced, Lois and I were assigned the roles of the traveling players Hamlet uses to bait his uncle Claudius. It wasn't the part I was hoping for, but I accepted my role with quiet dignity. I had a few decent speeches and planned to work them to the best of my ability.

Our fellow cast members were in their twenties and thirties and had wet their feet in such long-running outdoor dramas as *The Lost Colony* and *Tender Is the Lamb*. These were professionals, and I hoped to benefit from their experience, sitting literally at their feet as the director paced the lip of the stage addressing his clenched fist as "poor Yorick."

I worshiped these people. Lois slept with them. By the second week of rehearsal, she had abandoned Fortinbras in favor of Laertes, who, she claimed, had a "real way with the sword." Unlike me, she was embraced by the older crowd, attending late-night keg parties with Polonius and Ophelia and driving to the lake with the director while Gertrude and Rosencrantz made out in the backseat. The killer was that Lois was nowhere near as committed as I was. Her drama bug was the equivalent of a twenty-four-hour flu, yet there she was, playing bumper pool with Hamlet himself while I practiced lines alone in my room, dreaming up little ways to steal the show.

It was decided that as traveling players, Lois and I would make our entrance tumbling onto the outdoor stage. When she complained that the grass was irritating her skin, the director examined the wee pimples on her back and decided that, from this point on, the players would enter skipping. I had rehearsed my tumble until my brain lost its mooring and could be heard rattling inside my skull, and now, on the basis of one complaint, we were skipping? He'd already cut all my speeches, leaving me with the one line "Aye, my lord." That was it, three lousy syllables. A person could wrench more emotion out of a sneeze than all my dialogue put together. While the other actors strolled the Rose Garden memorizing their vengeful soliloquies, I skipped back and forth across the parking lot repeating, "Aye, my lord," in a voice that increasingly sounded like that of a trained parrot. Lois felt silly skipping and spoke to the director, who praised her instincts and announced that, henceforth, the players would enter walking.

The less I had to do, the more my fellow actors used me as a personal slave. I would have been happy to help them run lines, but instead, they wanted me to polish their crowns or trot over to a car, searching the backseat for a misplaced dagger.

"Looking for something to do? You can help Doogan glow-tape the props," the director said. "You can chase the spiders out of the dressing room, or better yet, why don't you run down to the store and get us some drinks."

For the most part, Lois sat in the shade doing nothing. Not only did she refuse to help out, but she was always the first one to hand me a large bill when placing an order for a thirty-cent diet soda. She'd search through her purse, bypassing the singles in favor of a ten or a twenty. "I need to break this anyway," she'd say. "If they charge you extra for a cup of ice, tell them to fuck themselves." During the rehearsal breaks she huddled in the stands, gossiping with the other actors while I was off anchoring ladders for the technicians.

When it came time for our big scene, Lois recited her lines as if she were reading the words from the surface of some distant billboard. She squinted and paused between syllables, punctuating each word with a question mark. "Who this? Has seen with tongue? In venom steeped?"

If the director had a problem with her performance, he kept it to himself. I, on the other hand, was instructed to remove the sweater from around my neck, walk slower, and drop the accent. It might have been easier to accept the criticism had he spread it around a little, but that seemed unlikely. She could enter the scene wearing sunglasses and eating pizza and that was "fine, Lois. Great work, babe."

By this time I was finding my own way home from rehearsal. Lois couldn't give me a ride, as she was always running off to some party or restaurant with what she referred to as "the gang from Elsinore."

"I can't go," I'd say, pretending I had been invited. "I really need to get home and concentrate on my line. You go ahead, though. I'll just call my mother. She'll pick me up."

"Are we vexed?" my mother would ask, pulling her station wagon into the parking lot.

"We are indeed," I answered. "And highly so."

"Let it go," she said. "Ten years from now I guarantee you won't remember any of these people. Time passes, you'll see." She frowned, studying her face in the rearview mirror. "Enough liquor, and people can forget anything. Don't let it get to you. If nothing else, this has taught you to skim money while buying their drinks."

I didn't appreciate her flippant attitude, but the business with the change was insightful.

"Round everything off to the nearest dollar," she said. "Hand them their change along with their drinks so they'll be less likely to count it—and never fold the bills, keep the money in a wad."

My mother had the vengeful part down. It was the craft of acting I thought she knew nothing about.

We were in dress rehearsal when the director approached Lois regarding a new production he hoped to stage that coming fall. It was to be a musical based on the lives of roving Gypsies. "And you," he said, "shall be my lusty bandit queen."

Lois couldn't sing; everyone knew that. Neither could she act or play the tambourine. "Yours is the heart of a Gypsy," he said, kneeling in the grass. "The vibrant soul of a nomad."

When I expressed an interest, he suggested I might enjoy working behind the scenes. He meant for me to hang lights or lug scenery, to become one of those guys with the lowriding pants, their tool belts burdened with heavy wrenches and thick rolls of gaffer tape. Anyone thinking I might be trusted with electrical wiring had to be a complete idiot, and that's what this man was. I looked at him clearly then, noticing the way his tights made a mockery of his slack calves and dumpy little basket. Vibrant soul of a nomad, indeed. If he were such a big stinking deal, what was he doing in Raleigh? His blow-dried hair, the cheap Cuban-heeled shoes, and rainbow-striped suspenders—it was all a sham. Why wear tights with suspenders when their only redeeming feature was that they stayed up on their own—that's how they got their name, tights. And acting? The man performed as if the audience were deaf. He shouted his lines, grinning like a jack-o'-lantern and flailing his arms as if his sleeves were on fire. His was a form of acting that never fails to embarrass me. Watching him was like opening the door to a singing telegram: you know it's supposed to be entertaining, but you can't get beyond the sad fact that this person actually thinks he's bringing some joy into your life. Somewhere he had a mother who sifted through a shoe box of mimeographed playbills, pouring herself another drink and wondering when her son would come to his senses and swallow some drain cleaner.

I finally saw Hamlet for who he really was and recognized myself as the witless Yorick who had blindly followed along behind him.

My mother attended the opening-night performance. Following my leaden "Aye, my lord," I lay upon the grassy stage as Lois poured a false vial of poison into my ear. As I lay dying, I opened my eyes just a crack, catching sight of my mother stretched out on her hard, stone pew, fighting off the moths that, along with a few dozen seniors, had been attracted by the light.

There was a cast party afterward, but I didn't go. I changed my clothes in the dressing room, where the actors stood congratulating one another, repeating the words "brilliant" and "intense" as if they were describing the footlights. Horatio asked me to run to the store for cigarettes, and I pocketed his money, promising to return "with lightning speed, my lord."

"You were the best in the whole show," my mother said, stopping for frozen pizza on our way home. "I mean it, you walked onto that stage and all eyes went right to you."

It occurred to me then that my mother was a better actor than I could ever hope to be. Acting is different than posing or pretending. When done with precision, it bears a striking resemblance to lying. Stripped of the costumes and grand gestures, it presents itself as an unquestionable truth. I didn't envy my mother's skill, neither did I contradict her. That's how convincing she was. It seemed best, sitting beside her with a frozen pizza thawing on my lap, to simply sit back and learn.

Sarah Vowell

SHOOTING DAD

If you were passing by the house where I grew up during my teenage years and it happened to be before Election Day, you wouldn't have needed to come inside to see that it was a house divided. You could have looked at the Democratic campaign poster in the upstairs window and the Republican one in the downstairs window and seen our home for the Civil War battleground it was. I'm not saying who was the Democrat or who was the Republican—my father or I—but I will tell you that I have never subscribed to *Guns & Ammo*, that I did not plaster the family vehicle with National Rifle Association stickers, and that hunter's orange was never my color.

About the only thing my father and I agree on is the Constitution, though I'm partial to the First Amendment, while he's always favored the Second.

I am a gunsmith's daughter. I like to call my parents' house, located on a quiet residential street in Bozeman, Montana, the United States of Firearms. Guns were everywhere: the so-called pretty ones like the circa 1850 walnut muzzleloader hanging on the wall, Dad's clients' fixer-uppers leaning into corners, an entire rack right next to the TV. I had to move revolvers out of my way to make room for a bowl of Rice Krispies on the kitchen table.

I was eleven when we moved into that Bozeman house. We had never lived in town before, and this was a college town at that. We came from Oklahoma— a dusty little Muskogee County nowhere called Braggs. My parents' property there included an orchard, a horse pasture, and a couple of acres of woods. I knew our lives had changed one morning not long after we moved to Montana when, during breakfast, my father heard a noise and jumped out of his chair. Grabbing a BB gun, he rushed out the front door. Standing in the yard, he started shooting at crows. My mother sprinted after him screaming, "Pat, you might ought to check, but I don't think they do that up here!" From the look on his face, she might as well have told him that his American citizenship had been revoked. He shook his head, mumbling, "Why, shooting crows is a national pastime, like baseball and apple pie." Personally, I preferred baseball and apple pie. I looked up at those crows flying away and thought, I'm going to like it here.

Dad and I started bickering in earnest when I was fourteen, after the 1984 Democratic National Convention. I was so excited when Walter Mondale chose Geraldine Ferraro as his running mate that I taped the front page of the newspaper with her picture on it to the refrigerator door. But there was some sort of mysterious gravity surge in the kitchen. Somehow, that picture ended up in the trash all the way across the room.

Nowadays, I giggle when Dad calls me on Election Day to cheerfully inform me that he has once again canceled out my vote, but I was not always so mature. There were times when I found the fact that he was a gunsmith horrifying. And just *weird*. All he ever cared about were guns. All I ever cared about was art. There were years and years when he hid out by himself in the garage making rifle barrels and I holed up in my room reading Allen Ginsberg poems, and we were incapable of having a conversation that didn't end in an argument.

Our house was partitioned off into territories. While the kitchen and the living room were well within the DMZ, the respective work spaces governed by my father and me were jealously guarded totalitarian states in which each of us declared ourselves dictator. Dad's shop was a messy disaster area, a labyrinth of lathes. Its walls were hung with the mounted antlers of deer he'd bagged, forming a makeshift museum of death. The available flat surfaces were buried under a million scraps of paper on which he sketched his mechanical inventions in blue ball-point pen. And the floor, carpeted with spiky metal shavings, was a tetanus shot waiting to happen. My domain was the cramped, cold space known as the music room. It was also a messy disaster area, an obstacle course of musical instruments—piano, trumpet, baritone horn, valve trombone, various percussion doodads (bells!), and recorders. A framed portrait of the French composer Claude Debussy was nailed to the wall. The available flat surfaces were buried under piles of staff paper, on which I penciled in the pompous orchestra music given titles like "Prelude to the Green Door" (named after an O. Henry short story by the way, not the watershed porn flick *Behind the Green Door*) I starting writing in junior high.

It has been my experience that in order to impress potential suitors, skip the teen Debussy anecdotes and stick with the always attention getting line "My dad makes guns." Though it won't cause the guy to like me any better, it will make him handle the inevitable breakup with diplomacy—just in case I happen to have any loaded family heirlooms lying around the house.

But the fact is, I have only shot a gun once and once was plenty. My twin sister, Amy, and I were six years old—six—when Dad decided that it was high time we learned how to shoot. Amy remembers the day he handed us the gun for the first time differently. She liked it.

Amy shared our father's enthusiasm for firearms and the quick draw cowboy mythology surrounding them. I tended to daydream through Dad's activities—the car trip to Dodge City's Boot Hill, his beloved John Wayne Westerns on TV. My sister, on the other hand, turned into Rooster Cogburn Jr., devouring Duke movies with Dad. In fact, she named her teddy bear Duke, hung a colossal John Wayne portrait next to her bed, and took to wearing one of those John Wayne shirts that button on the side. So when Dad led us out to the backyard when we were six and, to Amy's delight, put the gun in her hand, she says she felt it meant that Daddy trusted us and that he thought of us as "big girls."

But I remember holding the pistol only made me feel small. It was so heavy in my hand. I stretched out my arm and pointed it away and winced. It was a very long time before I had the nerve to pull the trigger and I was so scared I had to close my eyes. It felt like it just went off by itself, as if I had no say in the matter, as if the gun just had this *need*. The sound it made was as big as God. It kicked little me back to the ground like a bully, like a foe. It hurt. I don't know if I dropped it or just handed it back over to my dad, but I do know that I never wanted to touch another one again. And, because I believed in the devil, I did what my mother told me to do every time I felt an evil presence. I looked at the smoke and whispered under my breath, "Satan, I rebuke thee."

It's not like I'm saying I was traumatized. It's more like I was decided. Guns: Not For Me. Luckily, both my parents grew up in exasperating households where children were considered puppets and/or slaves. My mom and dad were hell-bent on letting my sister and me make our own choices. So if I decided that I didn't want my father's little death sticks to kick me to the ground again, that was fine with him. He would go hunting with my sister, who started calling herself "the loneliest twin in history" because of my reluctance to engage in family activities.

Of course, the fact that I was allowed to voice my opinions did not mean that my father would silence his own. Some things were said during the Reagan administration that cannot be taken back. Let's just say that I blamed Dad for nuclear proliferation and Contra aid. He believed that if I had my way, all the guns would be confiscated and it would take the commies about fifteen minutes to parachute in and assume control.

We're older now, my dad and I. The older I get, the more I'm interested in becoming a better daughter. First on my list: Figure out the whole gun thing.

Not long ago, my dad finished his most elaborate tool of death yet. A cannon. He built a nineteenth-century cannon. From scratch. It took two years.

My father's cannon is a smaller replica of a cannon called the Big Horn Gun in front of Bozeman's Pioneer Museum. The barrel of the original has been filled with concrete ever since some high school kids in the '50s pointed it at the school across the street and shot out its windows one night as a prank. According to Dad's historical source, a man known to scholars as A Guy at the Museum, the cannon was brought to Bozeman around 1870, and was used by local white merchants to fire at the Sioux and Cheyenne Indians who blocked their trade access to the East in 1874.

"Bozeman was founded on greed," Dad says. The courthouse cannon, he continues, "definitely killed Indians. The merchants filled it full of nuts, bolts, and chopped -up horseshoes. Sitting Bull could have been part of these engagements. They definitely ticked off the Indians, because a couple of years later, Custer wanders into them at Little Bighorn. The Bozeman merchants were out to cause trouble. They left fresh baked bread with cyanide in it on the trail to poison a few Indians."

Because my father's sarcastic American history yarns rarely go on for long before he trots out some nefarious ancestor of ours—I come from a long line of moonshiners, Confederate soldiers, murderers, even Democrats—he cracks that the merchants hired some "community-minded Southern soldiers from North Texas." These soldiers had, like my great-great-grandfather John Vowell, fought under pro-slavery guerilla William C. Quantrill. Quantrill is most famous for riding into Lawrence, Kansas, in 1863 flying a black flag and commanding his men pharaohlike to "kill every male and burn down every house."

"John Vowell," Dad says, "had a little rep for killing people." And since he abandoned my great-grandfather Charles, whose mother died giving birth to him in 1870, and wasn't seen again until 1912, Dad doesn't rule out the possibility that John Vowell could have been one of the hired guns on the Bozeman Trail. So the cannon isn't just another gun to my dad. It's a map of all his obsessions—firearms, certainly, but also American history and family history, subjects he's never bothered separating from each other.

After tooling a million guns, after inventing and building a rifle barrel boring machine, after setting up that complicated shop filled with lathes and blueing tanks and outmoded blacksmithing tools, the cannon is his most ambitious project ever. I thought that if I was ever going to understand the ballistic bee in his bonnet, this was my chance. It was the biggest gun he ever made and I could experience it and spend time with it with the added bonus of not having to actually pull a trigger myself.

I called Dad and said that I wanted to come to Montana and watch him shoot off the cannon. He was immediately suspicious. But I had never taken much interest in his work before and he would take what he could get. He loaded the cannon into the back of his truck and we drove up into the Bridger Mountains. I was a little worried that the National Forest Service would object to us lobbing fiery balls of metal onto its property. Dad laughed, assuring me that "you cannot shoot fireworks, but this is considered a fire*arm*."

It is a small cannon, about as long as a baseball bat and as wide as a coffee can. But it's heavy—110 pounds. We park near the side of the hill. Dad takes his gunpowder and other tools· out of this adorable wooden box on which he has stenciled "PAT G. VOWELL CANNONWORKS." Cannonworks: So that's what NRA members call a metalstrewn garage.

Dad plunges his homemade bullets into the barrel, points it at an embankment just to be safe, and lights the fuse. When the fuse is lit, it resembles a cartoon. So does the sound, which warrants Ben Day dot words along the lines of *ker-pow!* There's so much Fourth of July smoke everywhere I feel compelled to sing the national anthem.

I've given this a lot of thought—how to convey the giddiness I felt when the cannon shot off. But there isn't a sophisticated way to say this. It's just really, really cool. My dad thought so, too.

Sometimes, I put together stories about the more eccentric corners of the American experience for public radio. So I happen to have my tape recorder with me, and I've never seen levels like these. Every time the cannon goes off, the delicate needles which keep track of the sound quality lurch into the bad, red zone so fast and so hard I'm surprised they don't break.

The cannon was so loud and so painful, I had to touch my head to make sure my skull hadn't cracked open. One thing that my dad and I share is that we're both a little hard of hearing—me from Aerosmith, him from gunsmith.

He lights the fuse again. The bullet knocks over the log he was aiming at. I instantly utter a sentence I never in my entire life thought I would say. I tell him, "Good shot, Dad."

Just as I'm wondering what's coming over me, two hikers walk by. Apparently, they have never seen a man set off a homemade cannon in the middle of the wilderness while his daughter holds a foot-long microphone up into the air recording its terrorist boom. One hiker gives me a puzzled look and asks, "So you work for the radio and that's your dad?"

Dad shoots the cannon again so that they can see how it works. The other hiker says, "That's quite the machine you got there." But he isn't talking about the cannon. He's talking about my tape recorder and my microphone—which is called a *shotgun* mike. I stare back at him, then I look over at my father's cannon, then down at my microphone, and I think, Oh. My. God. My dad and I are the same person. We're both smart-alecky loners with goofy projects and weird equipment. And since this whole target practice outing was my idea, I was no longer his adversary. I was his accomplice. What's worse, I was liking it.

I haven't changed my mind about guns. I can get behind the cannon because it is a completely ceremonial object. It's unwieldy and impractical, just like everything else I care about. Try to rob a convenience store with this no-pound Saturday night special, you'd still be dragging it in the door Sunday afternoon.

I love noise. As a music fan, I'm always waiting for that moment in a song when something just flies out of it and explodes in the air. My dad is a one-man garage band, the kind of rock' n' roller who slaves away at his art for no reason other than to make his own sound. My dad is an artist—a pretty driven, idiosyncratic one, too. He's got his last *Gesamtkunstwerk* all planned out. It's a performance piece. We're all in it—my mom, the loneliest twin in history, and me.

When my father dies, take a wild guess what he wants done with his ashes. Here's a hint: It requires a cannon.

"You guys are going to love this," he smirks, eyeballing the cannon. "You get to drag this thing up on top of the Gravellies on opening day of hunting season. And looking off at Sphinx Mountain, you get to put me in little paper bags. I can take my last hunting trip on opening morning."

I'll do it, too. I will have my father's body burned into ashes. I will pack these ashes into paper bags. I will go to the mountains with my mother, my sister, and the cannon. I will plunge his remains into the barrel and point it into a hill so that he doesn't take anyone with him. I will light the fuse. But I will not cover my ears. Because when I blow what used to be my dad into the earth, I want it to hurt.

FOCUSED FREE WRITES

1. What makes these essays funny? How do they fulfill the definition of comedy?
2. What is the difference between stand-up comedy and written comedy? What should a writer do to be funny on the page?
3. Do you see any similarities between these humorous essays? What are some differences?
4. Both of these essays still have a serious purpose or thesis even though they use humor to achieve it. What is the purpose of each essay?
5. Is the nonfiction essay a good medium for comedy? Why or why not?

Knowing Where We Come From

Comedy in the Theatre

Comedy has a long, illustrious history in the theater from Restoration comedies of eighteenth-century England to the Victorian plays of Oscar Wilde to the modern-day musical theater found in plays like *Spamalot*. If you are interested in the ancestors of today's stand-up comics and are intrigued by the comic essays of the writers included here, you might travel back in time to these early moments of comedy on stage.

Want to Know More?

The Language of Comedy

There isn't only one kind of funny—comedy includes a variety of sub-genres. Some categories of comedy and terms that apply to comedy include the following.

- **Satire** is the ridicule of a subject, idea, institution, person, or group of people to amuse people in exposing its failings. Jonathan Swift is famous for his satires like "A Modest Proposal" in which he mocked contemporary governments and current policies.

- **Parody** mocks the style of a particular work creating humor in imitating it in an exaggerated way. Comedy Central's *The Daily Show* is a parody that creates "fake news" in imitation of other mainstream news shows.
- **Irony** creates humor through inconsistency by communicating an implied meaning through an apparently opposite statement. In other words, it involves a discrepancy between what is said and what is really meant (**verbal irony**). Irony can also be achieved when the audience knows more about a situation than the characters (**dramatic irony**). Jane Austen is said to be a master of irony; she lets her characters skewer themselves as they betray their silliness in their own words.
- **Black comedy** addresses a disturbing subject through bitter amusement. Horrifying elements are sharply juxtaposed with humorous ones in works such as Joseph Heller's *Catch-22*, where the logic of war is mocked and made comic.
- **Romantic comedy** has earned a place as a contemporary film genre but historically has been applied to any comedy focused on the misadventures of young lovers who live happily ever after. Shakespeare's *A Midsummer Night's Dream* is probably the most famous example.
- **Light verse** describes comic poetry. Humorous poetry that focuses on trivial subjects is categorized as light verse and might include such forms as epigrams, jingles, limericks, and mock epics.

Writing About Your Experience with Literature

Be funny

Many people think they are funny, but it can be challenging to write comedy. Working in groups, pairs, or individually, try your hand at one of the above forms: the monolog, the comic essay, a comic dialog, or those listed in the box above. Use some of the lessons learned from the examples you've read and attempt to walk that fine line between comic method and serious message.

Research comedy in literature

Why is there so much tragedy in literature? What are some examples of quality literature that is funny? Working in groups, pairs, or individually, look into the history of the genre through research. Develop a brief paper or presentation on one of the following topics:

- Make a case for one or two comic works and writers that should be added to this textbook or textbooks like it. Discuss how they maintain a focused purpose and literary craft while using humor. Demonstrate how this work or these works illustrate the duality of comedy and tragedy.

- Develop a timeline of the comedy genre. Identify important figures in the history of the genre and highlight one or two.

9

VIEWING WORDS AND READING PICTURES
Getting to Know Graphic Novels

Viewing Words and Reading Pictures. This scene from the graphic novel *Maus* by Art Spiegelman tells the story visually as well as with words. While a variation on previous genres, graphic novels are a new genre for the most part. Are they a form of literature? Should they be taken seriously? Why or why not?

Even before we can read words, as children we understand that stories can be told with pictures. We follow the narratives of picture books, and Saturday mornings are filled with cartoons. As we get a little older, we follow the adventures of Dennis the Menace in the newspaper comics and later read the visual political commentary of Doonesbury. Where literature creates stories in our minds' eyes, in comics and cartoons we first learn to lose ourselves in the imagination of others.

Increasingly, our world requires an advanced level of visual literacy to deal with the onslaught of images from the Internet and television, advertising and messaging, as well as from video games, movies, magazines, and books. Lessons learned from viewing picture books might be becoming more essential for thoughtful civic participation. Even the nature of text publishing has been transformed since the advent of the Internet. Now, books, magazines, and newspapers that once published "walls of print" on their pages invite readers into the text through "chunked" articles that have more images than text. Print appears in sound bites, not pages. It is not surprising then that the next generation of literature would court the visual as much as the verbal. The graphic novel may represent a new permutation of the novel form that will continue to receive accolades and attention as a venue for serious literature, as a teaching opportunity, and as a frontier to explore.

From Someone Who Knows

Scott McCloud on Understanding Comics

In his comic book, *Understanding Comics*, Scott McCloud goes to great lengths to explain people's attraction to comics and recommends revising our attitude toward them as child's play. He begins by defining comics broadly as "sequential art." He then outlines the long history of comics as far back as the Egyptians before trying to distill some of the fundamental premises of comics.

As McCloud's summary suggests, the attraction to and value of comics can be boiled down to three ideas:

- **Iconography:** In amplification through simplification, we abstract an image through cartooning to focus on specific details. We "strip down an image to its essential 'meaning'" to "amplify that meaning." We become a caricature of ourselves when we become a cartoon.
- **Universality:** We see the world in images in cartoons and no one is excluded. A smiley face can represent anyone and can be found in anything.
- **Audience identification:** These simplistic images can become vehicles for our own escape. We become the characters crudely represented. That smiley face is me.

According to McCloud, the work that goes into creating comics is not unlike the work that goes into creating any art or functioning in the world as a human: "Simplifying characters and images toward a purpose can be an effective tool for storytelling in any medium. Cartooning isn't just a way of drawing. It's a way of seeing" (483). As we have seen in this book, literature too creates a vision of an alternative world and lets us glimpse it and learn from it. Characters and storylines are condensed and crafted, simplified and streamlined, to envision this world. Creating comics is another form of storytelling.

380

TINTIN © EDITIONS CASTERMAN.

THIS COMBINATION ALLOWS READERS TO *MASK* THEMSELVES IN A CHARACTER AND SAFELY ENTER A SENSUALLY STIMULATING WORLD.

ONE SET OF LINES TO *SEE.* ANOTHER SET OF LINES TO *BE.*

IN THE WORLD OF *ANIMATION,* WHERE THE EFFECT HAPPENS TO BE A PRACTICAL *NECESSITY,* DISNEY HAS USED IT WITH IMPRESSIVE RESULTS FOR OVER *50 YEARS!*

IN *EUROPE* IT CAN BE FOUND IN MANY POPULAR COMICS, FROM *ASTERIX* TO *TINTIN* TO WORKS OF *JACQUES TARDI.*

IN *AMERICAN* COMICS, THE EFFECT IS USED FAR LESS *OFTEN,* ALTHOUGH IT HAS CREPT UP IN THE WORKS OF ARTISTS AS DIVERSE AS *CARL BARKS, JAIME HERNANDEZ* AND IN THE TEAM OF *DAVE SIM* AND *GERHARD.*

CEREBUS © DAVE SIM.

IN *JAPAN,* ON THE OTHER HAND, THE MASKING EFFECT WAS, FOR A TIME, VIRTUALLY A *NATIONAL STYLE!*

THANKS TO THE *SEMINAL INFLUENCE* OF COMICS CREATOR *OSAMU TEZUKA,* JAPANESE COMICS HAVE A LONG, RICH HISTORY OF ICONIC CHARACTERS.

BUT, IN RECENT DECADES JAPANESE FANS ALSO DEVELOPED A TASTE FOR *FLASHY, PHOTO-REALISTIC ART.*

CLIK!

ART © HAYASI AND OSIMA.

Graphic Novels versus Literature

If reading graphic novels is not so dissimilar from reading other forms of literature, many of the same tools can be used to understand them such as theme, plot, character, setting, and symbols. Author Marjane Satrapi wrote *Persepolis*, an award-winning graphic novel in French about growing up in Iran after the revolution. Here, she describes to her editorial staff at Pantheon comics her decision to write a graphic novel and compares it to making a movie:

> People always ask me, "Why didn't you write a book?" But that's what *Persepolis* is. To me, a book is pages related to something that has a cover. Graphic novels are not traditional literature, but that does not mean they are second-rate. Images are a way of writing. When you have the talent to be able to write and to draw it seems a shame to choose one. I think it's better to do both.
>
> We learn about the world through images all the time. In the cinema we do it, but to make a film you need sponsors and money and 10,000 people to work with you. With a graphic novel, all you need is yourself and your editor.
>
> Of course, you have to have a very visual vision of the world. You have to perceive life with images, otherwise it doesn't work. Some artists are more into sound; they make music. The point is that you have to know what you want to say, and find the best way of saying it. It's hard to say how *Persepolis* evolved once I started writing. I had to learn how to write it as a graphic novel by doing.

As Satrapi suggests, graphic novels are not unlike literature; however, she compares them more to cinema. While there are some similarities between films and literature, significant differences remain. While many students are now more knowledgable than their teachers about the graphic novel, this form may be new to some of you. When reading graphic novels, remember the following points.

- **Style:** The form of a graphic novel will necessitate a different reading style in which you absorb picture and words simultaneously. This kind of dual reading may not come easy at first, but with practice, you will learn to develop a kind of parallel focus. If you just read the words or just look at the pictures, you will only get half the story. Often, the pictures indicate shifts in time or changes in mood that cannot be captured in dialog. Such inflections are expressed by the actors themselves. Just as you wouldn't watch a film without the sound, you wouldn't read a graphic novel paying attention only to the words.
- **Episodic narratives:** Like soap operas, graphic novels can be episodic narratives with particular distinct scenes or episodes reminiscent of the serial form of comics. You will have to pay attention to shifts in time and flashbacks within scenes that trace out past experiences and inform characters' stories and motivations.
- **Reading between the lines:** As in film, action happens between scenes: time passes, locations change, and people enter and exit. As a reader,

you will want to read between the lines in order to recognize the invisible action as well as the visible action, as McCloud describes it.

■ **Different genres of graphic novels:** Fans of graphic novels will tell you that not all are alike, so if you find you don't enjoy one example, you might try another. Graphic novels can include superheroes or not, can be adaptations or spinoffs, can be human-interest-focused or nonfiction, or may be examples of the popular Japanese *anime* in the comic form called *manga*. Just as there are many kinds of stories, plays, or poems, there are different kinds of graphic novels.

In this chapter, you will be reminded of the genre you know in the examples of comic strips, then you will be introduced to two forms of the graphic novel through the award-winning example of Alan Moore and David Lloyd's *V. for Vendetta*, and the example of Art Spiegelman's *Maus*, before we take a quick glimpse at where these forms may have come from.

A Genre You Know

Comic Strips

Before there were graphic novels, we knew comic strips. Read the following examples of a classic and contemporary comic strip.

SNOOPY by Charles Schulz

Peanuts: © United Feature Syndicate, Inc.

THE BOONDOCKS by Aaron McGruder

FOCUSED FREE WRITES

1. Can you identify elements of literature in these comic strips? Is there a plot? Are there characters? How would you characterize them?
2. As in a graphic novel, the "childish" and playful form of comic strips can address a serious theme. Is there a theme in any of these? What is it?
3. How do the images and words relate? In which places do the pictures express more than the words?
4. Discuss your reading process. How do you go about reading both words and pictures simultaneously?

A Genre You Might Like to Know

The Superhero Graphic Novel

Alan Moore first developed *V for Vendetta* as a black and white comic in collaboration with David Lloyd when he was working for British publisher *Warrior*. After his success with comics for *2000 AD, Marvel UK,* and *Warrior,* Moore began developing projects for American giant *DC Comics*. There, he made a name for himself with *Swamp Thing* and *Hellboy* as well as the color graphic novel version of *V for Vendetta*. The publication of *Watchmen*, a DC monthly series starting in 1986 won him critical acclaim and established him as the master of the graphic novel. Since then, *V for Vendetta, Watchmen,* and *The League of Extraordinary Gentlemen,* all Moore projects, have gained wider audiences as major motion pictures. *V for Vendetta* tells the story of a grim future British cityscape overseen by a totalitarian government. V, an anarchist revolutionary in a Guy Fawkes mask, arrives on the scene to save the day, overthrow the government, and free the people from this perverse police state. Pay attention to the reading process as you try to identify the literary elements in this celebrated graphic novel *V for Vendetta*.

Excerpt from Alan Moore and David Lloyd's
V for Vendetta

From *V for Vendetta* © 1989 DC Comics. All Rights Reserved. Used with Permission.

From *V for Vendetta* © 1989 DC Comics. All Rights Reserved. Used with Permission.

From *V for Vendetta* © 1989 DC Comics. All Rights Reserved. Used with Permission.

From *V for Vendetta* © 1989 DC Comics. All Rights Reserved. Used with Permission.

From *V for Vendetta* © 1989 DC Comics. All Rights Reserved. Used with Permission.

From *V for Vendetta* © 1989 DC Comics. All Rights Reserved. Used with Permission.

From *V for Vendetta* © 1989 DC Comics. All Rights Reserved. Used with Permission.

From *V for Vendetta* © 1989 DC Comics. All Rights Reserved. Used with Permission.

From *V for Vendetta* © 1989 DC Comics. All Rights Reserved. Used with Permission.

FOCUSED FREE WRITES

1. How can you interpret this as you would another form of literature? What is the theme? How would you analyze the parts that make up and support this theme? What characters, symbols, or settings are important for this theme?
2. How do the images and the words relate? Are there moments in which the pictures say more than the words can or do?
3. One of the characteristics of **postmodern literature** is its ironic referentiality—an aware recycling of something old to make it new again. Postmodern literature challenges traditional forms, not by breaking with them but by revisiting them in pastiche form (borrowing from them) or parody form (mocking or critiquing them). Given this brief definition, how is this excerpt an example of postmodern literature?

Another Kind of Graphic Novel: A Memoir

Winner of the 1992 Pulitzer Prize Special Award, *Maus: A Survivor's Tale* was groundbreaking as the first graphic novel to receive literary acclaim. In fact, the *New York Times* reported that the Pulitzer Prize committee found the novel "hard to classify." In this novel, Art Spiegelman records the story of his father Vladek, a Holocaust survivor; however, he also travels from Poland to Rego Park, New York, to tell the story of his own coming to terms with his father and his experience. Depicting the Jews as mice and the Nazis as cats, Spiegelman attempts to express the inexpressible. Graphic novelists like Moore and Gibbons and Satrapi cite Spiegelman's inspiration and influence and so you might check out this "founding father" of the popular genre.

Excerpt from Art Spiegelman's
Maus: A Survivor's Tale

EVERYONE CAME VERY NICE DRESSED. THEY TRIED SO THAT THEY WOULD LOOK YOUNG AND ABLE TO WORK, IN ORDER TO GET A GOOD STAMP ON THEIR PASSPORT.

WHEN WE WERE EVERYBODY INSIDE, GESTAPO WITH MACHINE GUNS SURROUNDED THE STADIUM.

LINE UP BY FAMILY AT THE TABLES TO REGISTER! QUICKLY!

THEN WAS A SELECTION, WITH PEOPLE SENT EITHER TO THE LEFT, EITHER TO THE RIGHT.

OLD PEOPLE, FAMILIES WITH LOTS OF KIDS, AND PEOPLE WITHOUT WORK CARDS ARE ALL GOING TO THE LEFT!

WE UNDERSTOOD THIS MUST BE VERY BAD.

ME AND ANJA CAME TO THE TABLE WHERE MY COUSIN WAS SITTING...

AH, YOU WORK AT THE CARPENTRY SHOP. GO TO THE RIGHT.

SO WE GOT STAMPED OUR PASSPORTS AND CAME QUICK TO THE GOOD SIDE OF THE STADIUM. THOSE THEY SENT LEFT, THEY DIDN'T GET ANY STAMP.

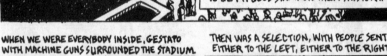

The Evolution of Comics

In his textbook on comics, Scott McCloud constructs a timeline of the earliest forms of comics, including pre-Columbian picture manuscripts "discovered" by Cortes around 1519, the French Bayeux Tapestries of the Norman Conquest of 1066, and even Hogarth's six-plate picture-story "A Harlot's Progress" published in 1731. He highlights the complete scene from the tomb of "Menna," ancient Egyptian scribe, painted over thirty-two centuries ago, included here.

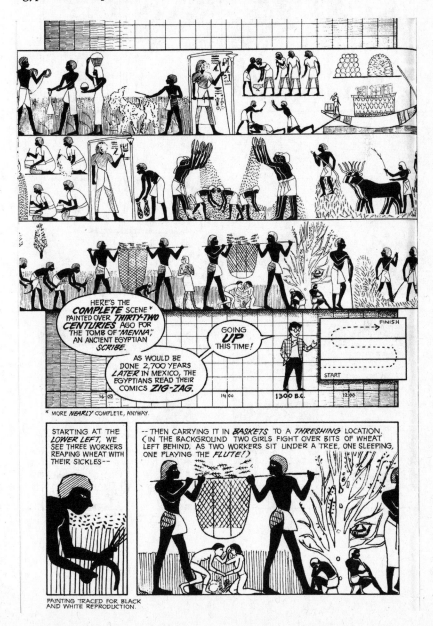

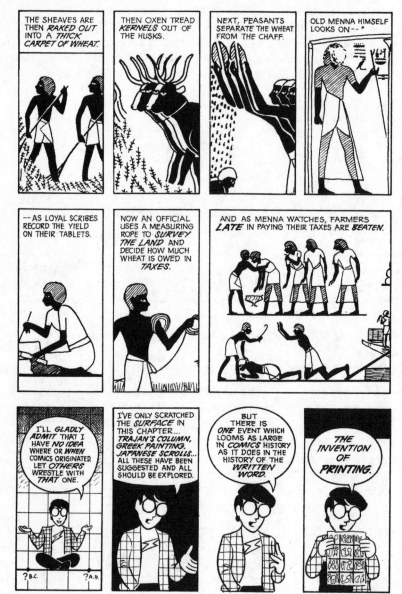

* FACE GOUGED OUT BY FUTURE GENERATIONS OF LEADERS

FOCUSED FREE WRITES

1. How does McCloud make a convincing case for the Egyptian tomb painting as an early comic? What qualities does it share with the comic form?
2. Since the graphic novel is a new genre, its critical history is also new. What other kinds of texts might make up the graphic novel's literary family tree?

Writing About Your Experience with Literature

Construct a comic

Working in groups, pairs, or individually, determine what story might best be communicated visually. Will you create a superhero story or try your hand at a memoir? How can you use both the visual and the verbal to communicate a narrative and a message simultaneously?

Research the history of the graphic novel

Follow the lead of Scott McCloud and look into the history of the genre. Working in groups, pairs, or individually, look into the history of the genre yourself through research and choose an aspect of the form to investigate. Develop a brief paper or presentation on one of the following topics.

- What are some of the earliest examples of comics?
- Who are some of the most important comic writers to consider when constructing a genealogy of the genre?
- Choose one graphic novelist or comic artist to study. Demonstrate his or her importance to the canon of comics. Using examples of his or her art, demonstrate its literary value.
- Identify the range of subgenres of the comic form or choose one subgenre for further investigation.

10 THRILLED AND CHILLED
Getting to Know Horror in Literature

Thrilled and Chilled. Here is a photograph of the film version of Oates's story "Where Are You Going, Where Have You Been?" The film entitled *Smooth Talk* (1985) starred Laura Dern and Treat Williams and was categorized as a psychological drama or thriller. Do all people like being scared? Why or why not? Should horror literature be valued like other forms of literature? Are there different categories of scary stories? What are they?

What is it that draws us to horror at the same time we flinch and turn our heads in terror? We can't help ourselves. We beg for ghost stories at summer camp even though they keep us up all night. We ride roller coasters even though our hearts beat out of our chest as our stomachs drop at the pinnacle of that impossibly steep hill. At the movies, we peek through the fingers covering our eyes as the damsel in distress investigates the noise downstairs while we cry out "Don't do it! Don't go in there!" We are magnetically drawn to horror yet can barely stand the fear; we are thrilled and chilled.

The *Oxford English Dictionary* describes this dual desire for horror in defining it through its earliest usage as "a shuddering or shivering" and then a "strong aversion mingled with dread; the feeling excited by something shocking or frightful." This combination of excitement and dread, this unique form of anticipation and anxiety, has spawned an incredibly powerful and popular form of literature. **Horror** fiction encompasses a number of characteristics and themes and may include murder, suicide, torture, fear, madness, ghosts, vampires, *doppelgangers* (a double, literally, "double-goer"—a ghostly double), poltergeists, demons, witchcraft, or any of a number of evil machinations. Horror confronts otherworldly death and evil as well as the darkness within the psyche. Much more than child's play, the horror story has a long and complex literary history with classical roots, connections to the eighteenth-century gothic novel, as well as prevalence in science fiction today. The horror story also contributed to the development of the short story, mystery stories, and crime-themed fictions.

The form's illustrious history, however, certainly doesn't explain its immense popularity. As Aristotle before him discussed the cathartic power of literature, Stephen King suggests horror taps into some fundamental human desires:

From Someone Who Knows

Stephen King on Horror

By Stephen King

WHY WE CRAVE HORROR MOVIES

1   I think that we're all mentally ill; those of us outside the asylums only hide it a little better—and maybe not all that much better, after all. We've all known people who talk to themselves, people who sometimes squinch their faces into horrible grimaces when they believe no one is watching, people who have some hysterical fear—of snakes, the dark, the tight place, the long drop...and, of course, those final worms and grubs that are waiting so patiently underground.

2   When we pay our four or five bucks and seat ourselves at tenth-row center in a theater showing a horror movie, we are daring the nightmare.

3   Why? Some of the reasons are simple and obvious. To show that we can, that we are not afraid, that we can ride this roller coaster. Which is not to say that a really good horror movie may not surprise a scream out of us at some point, the way we may scream when the roller coaster twists through a complete 360 or plows through a lake at the bottom of the drop. And horror movies, like roller coasters, have always been the special province of the young; by the time one turns 40 or 50, one's appetite for double twists or 360-degree loops may be considerably depleted.

4   We also go to re-establish our feelings of essential normality; the horror movie is innately conservative, even reactionary. Freda Jackson as the horrible melting woman in *Die, Monster, Die!* confirms for us that no matter how far we may be removed from the beauty of a Robert Redford or a Diana Ross, we are still light-years from true ugliness.

5   And we go to have fun.

6   Ah, but this is where the ground starts to slope away, isn't it? Because this is a very peculiar sort of fun indeed. The fun comes from seeing others menaced—sometimes killed. One critic has suggested that if pro football has become the voyeur's version of combat, then the horror film has become the modern version of the public lynching.

7   It is true that the mythic "fairytale" horror film intends to take away the shades of grey.... It urges us to put away our more civilized and adult penchant for analysis and to become children again, seeing things in pure blacks and whites. It may be that horror movies provide psychic relief on this level because this invitation to lapse into simplicity, irrationality and even outright madness is extended so rarely. We are told we may allow our emotions a free rein...or no rein at all.

8   If we are all insane, then sanity becomes a matter of degree. If your insanity leads you to carve up women like Jack the Ripper or the Cleveland Torso Murderer, we clap you away in the funny farm (but neither of those two amateur-night surgeons was ever caught, heh-heh-heh); if, on the other hand, your insanity leads you only to talk to yourself when you're under stress or to pick your nose on your morning bus, then you are left alone to go about your business...though it is doubtful that you will ever be invited to the best parties.

9   The potential lyncher is in almost all of us (excluding saints, past and present; but then, most saints have been crazy in their own ways), and every now and then, he has to be let loose to scream and roll around in the grass. Our emotions and our fears form their own body, and we recognize that it demands its own exercise to maintain proper muscle tone. Certain of these emotional muscles are accepted—even exalted—in civilized society; they are, of course, the emotions that tend to maintain the status quo of civilization itself. Love, friendship, loyalty, kindness—these are all the emotions that we applaud, emotions that have been immortalized in the couplets of Hallmark cards...

10   When we exhibit these emotions, society showers us with positive reinforcement; we learn this even before we get out of diapers. When, as children, we hug our rotten little puke of a sister and give her a kiss, all the aunts and uncles smile and twit and cry, "Isn't he the sweetest little thing?" Such coveted treats as chocolate-covered graham crackers often follow. But if we deliberately slam the rotten little puke of a sister's fingers in the door, sanctions follow—angry remonstrance from parents, aunts and uncles; instead of a chocolate-covered graham cracker, a spanking.

11   But anticivilization emotions don't go away, and they demand periodic exercise. We have such "sick" jokes as, "What's the difference between a truck-load of bowling balls and a truckload of dead babies?" (You can't unload a truckload of bowling balls with a pitchfork...a joke, by the way, that I heard originally from a ten-year-old.) Such a joke may surprise a laugh or a grin out

of us even as we recoil, a possibility that confirms the thesis: If we share a brotherhood of man, then we also share an insanity of man. None of which is intended as a defense of either the sick joke or insanity but merely as an explanation of why the best horror films, like the best fairy tales, manage to be reactionary, anarchistic, and revolutionary all at the same time.

12   The mythic horror movie, like the sick joke, has a dirty job to do. It deliberately appeals to all that is worst in us. It is morbidity unchained, our most base instincts let free, our nastiest fantasies realized…and it all happens, fittingly enough, in the dark. For those reasons, good liberals often shy away from horror films. For myself, I like to see the most aggressive of them—*Dawn of the Dead*, for instance—as lifting a trap door in the civilized forebrain and throwing a basket of raw meat to the hungry alligators swimming around in that subterranean river beneath.

13   Why bother? Because it keeps them from getting out, man. It keeps them down there and me up here. It was Lennon and McCartney who said that all you need is love, and I would agree with that.

14   As long as you keep the gators fed.

Based on King's argument here, we are "daring the nightmare," as he put it, to show we are not afraid, to confirm our normality, and to have fun. The fun can be described as psychic relief, catharsis, or as permissible forays into innate human insanity, a universal condition shared by all and admitted to by few.

Want to Know More?

Kinds of Horror

As with any genre, horror can take on a variety of forms, from classical depictions of human suffering by Seneca to the violence of *Gilgamesh* and *Beowulf*, from Chaucer's *Pardoner's Tale* to Marlowe's *Dr. Faustus*, from Gothic novels to Romantic-era vampires. The prolixity and range would surprise most modern-day connoisseurs of the form. Put most simply, horror fiction can be divided into two types.

- **Psychological horror** relies on character fears, guilt, failings, evil, and mental instability to build tension or further the plot. The evil "Other" may be found in those childhood horror stories of the escapee from a mental asylum or the twisted evil of the suave Dr. Hannibal Lecter who is not what he seems. The darkness could also be located within. By way of an unreliable narrator such as Jane in "The Yellow Wallpaper" or Humbert Humbert in Nabokov's *Lolita*, the reader can feel the horror of a disturbed psyche through his or her own words.
- **Supernatural horror** introduces some form of otherworldly or supernatural evil into everyday experience. Such horror takes on a more physical form and may incorporate gore or violence. Supernatural figures may be introduced: the devil as in Mephistophilis; doppelgangers as in Dr. Jekyll and Mr. Hyde; vampires in a range of incarnations from Polidori's to Bram Stoker's; and creatures such as ghosts, werewolves, or Mary Shelley's monster.

Many times, however, horror stories invoke both kinds of horror or even leave it to the reader to decide the source of evil, as, for instance, Henry James does in the novella *The Turn of the Screw*.

A Genre You Know

The Ghost Story

Stephen King may be a writer who needs no introduction. Readers young and old often name him as their favorite author. He has published classic horror fiction such as *Carrie*, *The Shining*, and *The Stand*, over fifty best-selling novels, and a number of projects for cinema and television. If you return to King's writing, you will notice how he often uses the foibles of ordinary humanity to build tension before introducing supernatural horror. What ghost stories are you familiar with?

A Horror Story You Might Like

A Real-Life Devil

Joyce Carol Oates is not famous as a horror writer, per se. However, she is renowned as a prolific writer of fiction, poetry, and criticism. Critic Laura Kalpakian described her as an unlikely figure for "willingly, knowingly smash[ing] up the conventions of narrative" and "unmask[ing] the evil of every-day life, who will see allegory in the backyard and real darkness among the metaphoric daisies." Therein lies the horror, perhaps. What follows is Oates's most anthologized short story.

Joyce Carol Oates

WHERE ARE YOU GOING, WHERE HAVE YOU BEEN? [1970]

For Bob Dylan

Her name was Connie. She was fifteen and she had a quick, nervous giggling habit of craning her neck to glance into mirrors, or checking other people's faces to make sure her own was all right. Her mother, who noticed everything and knew everything and who hadn't much reason any longer to look at her own face, always scolded Connie about it. "Stop gawking at yourself. Who are you? You think you're so pretty?" she would say. Connie would raise her eyebrows at these familiar old complaints and look right through her mother, into a shadowy vision of herself as she was right at that moment: she knew she was pretty and that was everything. Her mother had been pretty once too, if you could believe those old snapshots in the album, but now her looks were gone and that was why she was always after Connie.

"Why don't you keep your room clean like your sister? How've you got your hair fixed—what the hell stinks? Hair spray? You don't see your sister using that junk."

Her sister June was twenty-four and still lived at home. She was a secretary in the high school Connie attended, and if that wasn't bad enough—with her in the same building—she was so plain and chunky and steady that Connie had to hear her praised all the time by her mother and her mother's sisters. June did this, June did that, she saved money and helped clean the house and cooked and Connie couldn't do a thing, her mind was all filled with trashy daydreams. Their father was away at work most of the time and when he came home he wanted supper and he read the newspaper at supper and after supper he went to bed. He didn't bother talking much to them, but around his bent head Connie's mother kept picking at her until Connie wished her mother was dead and she herself was dead and it was all over. "She makes me want to throw up sometimes," she complained to her friends. She had a high, breathless, amused voice that made everything she said sound a little forced, whether it was sincere or not.

There was one good thing: June went places with girl friends of hers, girls who were just as plain and steady as she, and so when Connie wanted to do that her mother had no objections. The father of Connie's best girl friend drove the girls the three miles to town and left them at a shopping plaza, so they could walk through the stores or go to a movie, and when he came to pick them up again at eleven he never bothered to ask what they had done.

5   They must have been familiar sights, walking around the shopping plaza in their shorts and flat ballerina slippers that always scuffed the sidewalk, with charm bracelets jingling on their thin wrists; they would lean together to whisper and laugh secretly if someone passed who amused or interested them. Connie had long dark blond hair that drew anyone's eye to it, and she wore part of it pulled up on her head and puffed out and the rest of it she let fall down her back. She wore a pull-over jersey blouse that looked one way when she was at home and another way when she was away from home. Everything about her had two sides to it, one for home and one for anywhere that was not home: her walk that could be childlike and bobbing, or languid enough to make anyone think she was hearing music in her head, her mouth which was pale and smirking most of the time, but bright and pink on these evenings out, her laugh which was cynical and drawling at home—"Ha, ha, very funny"—but highpitched and nervous anywhere else, like the jingling of the charms on her bracelet.

Sometimes they did go shopping or to a movie, but sometimes they went across the highway, ducking fast across the busy road, to a drive-in restaurant where older kids hung out. The restaurant was shaped like a big bottle, though squatter than a real bottle, and on its cap was a revolving figure of a grinning boy holding a hamburger aloft. One night in mid-summer they ran across, breathless with daring, and right away someone leaned out a car window and invited them over, but it was just a boy from high school they didn't like. It made them feel good to be able to ignore him. They went up through the maze of parked and cruising cars to the bright-lit, fly-infested restaurant, their faces pleased and expectant as if they were entering a sacred building that loomed up out of the night to give them what haven and blessing they yearned for. They sat at the counter and crossed their legs at the ankles, their thin shoulders rigid with excitement, and listened to the music that made everything so good: the music was always in the background like music at a church service, it was something to depend upon.

A boy named Eddie came in to talk with them. He sat backwards on his stool, turning himself jerkily around in semi-circles and then stopping and turning again, and after a while he asked Connie if she would like something to eat. She said she did and so she tapped her friend's arm on her way out—her friend pulled her face up into a brave droll look—and Connie said she would meet her at eleven, across the way. "I just hate to leave her like that," Connie said earnestly, but the boy said that she wouldn't be alone for long. So they went out to his car and on the way Connie couldn't help but let her eyes wander over the windshields and faces all around her, her face gleaming with a joy that had nothing to do with Eddie or even this place; it might have been the music. She drew her shoulders up and sucked in her breath with the pure pleasure of being alive, and just at that moment she happened to glance at a face just a few feet from hers. It was a boy with shaggy black hair, in a convertible jalopy painted gold. He stared at her and then his lips widened into a grin. Connie slit her eyes at him and turned away, but she couldn't help glancing back and there he was, still watching her. He wagged a finger and laughed and said, "Gonna get you, baby," and Connie turned away again without Eddie noticing anything.

She spent three hours with him, at the restaurant where they ate hamburgers and drank Cokes in wax cups that were always sweating, and then down an alley a mile or so away, and when he left her off at five to eleven only the movie house was still open at the plaza. Her girl friend was there, talking with a boy. When Connie came up the two girls smiled at each other and Connie said, "How was the movie?" and the girl said, "*You* should know." They rode off with the girl's father, sleepy and pleased, and Connie couldn't help but look at the darkened shopping plaza with its big empty parking lot and its signs that were faded and ghostly now, and over at the drive-in restaurant where cars were still circling tirelessly. She couldn't hear the music at this distance.

Next morning June asked her how the movie was and Connie said, "So-so."

10   She and that girl and occasionally another girl went out several times a week that way, and the rest of the time Connie spent around the house—it was summer vacation—getting in her mother's way and thinking, dreaming, about the boys she met. But all the boys fell back and dissolved into a single face that was not even a face, but an idea, a feeling, mixed up with the urgent insistent pounding of the music and the humid night air of July. Connie's mother kept dragging her back to the daylight by finding things for her to do or saying, suddenly, "What's this about the Pettinger girl?"

And Connie would say nervously, "Oh, her. That dope." She always drew thick clear lines between herself and such girls, and her mother was simple and kind enough to believe her. Her mother was so simple, Connie thought, that it was maybe cruel to fool her so much. Her mother went scuffling around the house in old bedroom slippers and complained over the telephone to one sister about the other, then the other called up and the two of them complained about the third one. If June's name was mentioned her mother's tone was approving, and if Connie's name was mentioned it was disapproving. This did not really mean she disliked Connie and actually Connie thought that her mother preferred her to June because she was prettier, but the two of them kept up a pretense of exasperation, a sense that they were tugging and struggling over something of little value to either of them. Sometimes, over coffee, they were almost friends, but something would come up—some vexation that was like a fly buzzing suddenly around their heads—and their faces went hard with contempt.

One Sunday Connie got up at eleven—none of them bothered with church—and washed her hair so that it could dry all day long, in the sun. Her parents and sister were going to a barbecue at an aunt's house and Connie said no, she wasn't interested, rolling her eyes to let her mother know just what she thought of it. "Stay home alone then," her mother said sharply. Connie sat out back in a lawn chair and watched them drive away, her father quiet and bald, hunched around so that he could back the car out, her mother with a look that was still angry and not at all softened through the windshield, and in the back seat poor old June all dressed up as if she didn't know what a barbecue was, with all the running yelling kids and the flies. Connie sat with her eyes closed in the sun, dreaming and dazed with the warmth about her as if this were a kind of love, the caresses of love, and her mind slipped over onto thoughts of the boy she had been with the night before and how nice he had been, how sweet it always was, not the way someone like June would suppose but sweet, gentle, the way it was in movies and promised in songs; and when she opened her eyes she hardly knew where she was, the back yard ran off into weeds and a fence-line of trees and behind it the sky was perfectly blue and still. The asbestos "ranch house" that was now three years old startled her—it looked small. She shook her head as if to get awake.

It was too hot. She went inside the house and turned on the radio to drown out the quiet. She sat on the edge of her bed, barefoot, and listened for an hour and a half to a program called XYZ Sunday Jamboree, record after record of hard, fast, shrieking songs she sang along with, interspersed by exclamations from "Bobby King": "An' look here you girls at Napoleon's—Son and Charley want you to pay real close attention to this song coming up!"

And Connie paid close attention herself, bathed in a glow of slow-pulsed joy that seemed to rise mysteriously out of the music itself and lay languidly about the airless little room, breathed in and breathed out with each gentle rise and fall of her chest.

15   After a while she heard a car coming up the drive. She sat up at once, startled, because it couldn't be her father so soon. The gravel kept crunching all the way in from the road—the driveway was long—and Connie ran to the window. It was a car she didn't know. It was an open jalopy, painted a bright gold that caught the sunlight opaquely. Her heart began to pound and her fingers snatched at her hair, checking it, and she whispered, "Christ. Christ," wondering how bad she looked. The car came to a stop at the side door and the horn sounded four short taps as if this were a signal Connie knew.

She went into the kitchen and approached the door slowly, then hung out the screen door, her bare toes curling down off the step. There were two boys in the car and now she recognized the driver: he had shaggy, shabby black hair that looked crazy as a wig and he was grinning at her.

"I ain't late, am I?" he said.

"Who the hell do you think you are?" Connie said.

"Toldja I'd be out, didn't I?"

20   "I don't even know who you are."

She spoke sullenly, careful to show no interest or pleasure, and he spoke in a fast bright monotone. Connie looked past him to the other boy, taking her time. He had fair brown hair, with a lock that fell onto his forehead. His sideburns gave him a fierce, embarrassed look, but so far he hadn't even bothered to glance at her. Both boys wore sunglasses. The driver's glasses were metallic and mirrored everything in miniature.

"You wanta come for a ride?" he said.

Connie smirked and let her hair fall loose over one shoulder.

"Don'tcha like my car? New paint job," he said. "Hey."

"What?"

25 "You're cute."

She pretended to fidget, chasing flies away from the door.

"Don'tcha believe me, or what?" he said.

"Look, I don't even know who you are," Connie said in disgust.

30 "Hey, Ellie's got a radio, see. Mine broke down." He lifted his friend's arm and showed her the little transistor radio the boy was holding, and now Connie began to hear the music. It was the same program that was playing inside the house.

"Bobby King?" she said.

"I listen to him all the time. I think he's great."

"He's kind of great," Connie said reluctantly.

"Listen, that guy's great. He knows where the action is."

35 Connie blushed a little, because the glasses made it impossible for her to see just what this boy was looking at. She couldn't decide if she liked him or if he was just a jerk, and so she dawdled in the doorway and wouldn't come down or go back inside. She said, "What's all that stuff painted on your car?"

"Can'tcha read it?" He opened the door very carefully, as if he was afraid it might fall off. He slid out just as carefully, planting his feet firmly on the ground, the tiny metallic world in his glasses slowing down like gelatine hardening and in the midst of it Connie's bright green blouse. "This here is my name, to begin with," he said. ARNOLD FRIEND was written in tarlike black letters on the side, with a drawing of a round grinning face that reminded Connie of a pumpkin, except it wore sunglasses. "I wanta introduce myself, I'm Arnold Friend and that's my real name and I'm gonna be your friend, honey, and inside the car's Ellie Oscar, he's kinda shy." Ellie brought his transistor radio up to his shoulder and balanced it there. "Now these numbers are a secret code, honey," Arnold Friend explained. He read off the numbers 33, 19, 17 and raised his eyebrows at her to see what she thought of that, but she didn't think much of it. The left rear fender had been smashed and around it was written, on the gleaming gold background: DONE BY CRAZY WOMAN DRIVER. Connie had to laugh at that. Arnold Friend was pleased at her laughter and looked up at her. "Around the other side's a lot more —you wanta come and see them?"

"No."

"Why not?"

"Why should I?"

40 "Don'tcha wanta see what's on the car? Don'tcha wanta go for a ride?"

"I don't know."

"Why not?"

"I got things to do."

"Like what?"

45 "Things."

He laughed as if she had said something funny. He slapped his thighs. He was standing in a strange way, leaning back against the car as if he were balancing himself. He wasn't tall, only an inch or so taller than she would be if she came down to him. Connie liked the way he was dressed, which was the way all of them dressed: tight faded jeans stuffed into black, scuffed boots, a belt that pulled his waist in and showed how lean he was, and a white pull-over shirt that was a little soiled and showed the hard small muscles of his arms and shoulders. He looked as if he probably did hard work, lifting and carrying things. Even his neck looked muscular. And his face was a familiar face, somehow: the jaw and chin and cheeks slightly darkened, because he hadn't shaved for a day or two, and the nose long and hawk-like, sniffing as if she were a treat he was going to gobble up and it was all a joke.

"Connie, you ain't telling the truth. This is your day set aside for a ride with me and you know it," he said, still laughing. The way he straightened and recovered from his fit of laughing showed that it had been all fake.

"How do you know what my name is?" she said suspiciously.

"It's Connie."

50 "Maybe and maybe not."

"I know my Connie," he said, wagging his finger. Now she remembered him even better, back at the restaurant, and her cheeks warmed at the thought of how she had sucked in her breath just at the moment she passed him—how she must have looked to him. And he had remembered her. "Ellie and I come out here especially for you," he said. "Ellie can sit in back. How about it?"

"Where?"

"Where what?"

"Where're we going?"

55 He looked at her. He took off the sunglasses and she saw how pale the skin around his eyes was, like holes that were not in shadow but instead in light. His eyes were chips of broken glass that catch the light in an amiable way. He smiled. It was as if the idea of going for a ride somewhere, to some place, was a new idea to him.

"Just for a ride, Connie sweetheart."

"I never said my name was Connie," she said.

"But I know what it is. I know your name and all about you, lots of things," Arnold Friend said. He had not moved yet but stood still leaning back against the side of his jalopy. "I took a special interest in you, such a pretty girl, and found out all about you like I know your parents and sister are gone somewheres and I know where and how long they're going to be gone, and I know who you were with last night, and your best girl friend's name is Betty. Right?"

He spoke in a simple lilting voice, exactly as if he were reciting the words to a song. His smile assured her that everything was fine. In the car Ellie turned up the volume on his radio and did not bother to look around at them.

60 "Ellie can sit in the back seat," Arnold Friend said. He indicated his friend with a casual jerk of his chin, as if Ellie did not count and she should not bother with him.

"How'd you find out all that stuff?" Connie said.

"Listen: Betty Schultz and Tony Fitch and Jimmy Pettinger and Nancy Pettinger," he said, in a chant. "Raymond Stanley and Bob Hutter—"

"Do you know all those kids?"

"I know everybody."

65 "Look, you're kidding. You're not from around here."

"Sure."

"But—how come we never saw you before?"

"Sure you saw me before," he said. He looked down at his boots, as if he were a little offended. "You just don't remember."

"I guess I'd remember you," Connie said.

70 "Yeah?" He looked up at this, beaming. He was pleased. He began to mark time with the music from Ellie's radio, tapping his fists lightly together. Connie looked away from his smile to the car, which was painted so bright it almost hurt her eyes to look at it. She looked at that name, ARNOLD FRIEND. And up at the front fender was an expression that was familiar—MAN THE FLYING SAUCERS. It was an expression kids had used the year before but didn't use this year. She looked at it for a while as if the words meant something to her that she did not yet know.

"What're you thinking about? Huh?" Arnold Friend demanded. "Not worried about your hair blowing around in the car, are you?"

"No."

"Think I maybe can't drive good?"

"How do I know?"

75 "You're a hard girl to handle. How come?" he said. "Don't you know I'm your friend? Didn't you see me put my sign in the air when you walked by?"

"What sign?"

"My sign." And he drew an X in the air, leaning out toward her. They were maybe ten feet apart. After his hand fell back to his side the X was still in the air, almost visible. Connie let the screen door close and stood perfectly still inside it, listening to the music from her radio and the boy's blend together. She stared at Arnold Friend. He stood there so stiffly relaxed, pretending to be relaxed, with one hand idly on the door handle as if he were keeping himself up that way and had no intention of ever moving again. She recognized most things about him, the tight jeans that showed his thighs and buttocks and the greasy leather boots and the tight shirt, and even that slippery friendly smile of his, that sleepy dreamy smile that all the boys used to get across ideas they didn't want to put into words. She recognized all this and also the singsong way he talked, slightly mocking, kidding, but serious and a little melancholy, and she recognized the way he tapped one fist against the other in homage to the perpetual music behind him. But all these things did not come together.

She said suddenly, "Hey, how old are you?"

His smiled faded. She could see then that he wasn't a kid, he was much older—thirty, maybe more. At this knowledge her heart began to pound faster.

80 "That's a crazy thing to ask. Can'tcha see I'm your own age?"

"Like hell you are."

"Or maybe a coupla years older, I'm eighteen."

"Eighteen?" she said doubtfully.

He grinned to reassure her and lines appeared at the corners of his mouth. His teeth were big and white. He grinned so broadly his eyes became slits and she saw how thick the lashes were, thick and black as if painted with a black tarlike material. Then he seemed to become embarrassed, abruptly, and looked over his shoulder at Ellie. "*Him,* he's crazy," he said. "Ain't he a riot, he's a nut, a real character." Ellie was still listening to the music. His sunglasses told nothing about what he was thinking. He wore a bright orange shirt unbuttoned halfway to show his chest, which was a pale, bluish chest and not muscular like Arnold Friend's. His shirt collar was turned up all around and the very tips of the collar pointed out past his chin as if they were protecting him. He was pressing the transistor radio up against his ear and sat there in a kind of daze, right in the sun.

85   "He's kinda strange," Connie said.

"Hey, she says you're kinda strange! Kinda strange!" Arnold Friend cried. He pounded on the car to get Ellie's attention. Ellie turned for the first time and Connie saw with shock that he wasn't a kid either—he had a fair, hairless face, cheeks reddened slightly as if the veins grew too close to the surface of his skin, the face of a forty-year-old baby. Connie felt a wave of dizziness rise in her at this sight and she stared at him as if waiting for something to change the shock of the moment, make it all right again. Ellie's lips kept shaping words, mumbling along, with the words blasting in his ear.

"Maybe you two better go away," Connie said faintly.

"What? How come?" Arnold Friend cried. "We come out here to take you for a ride. It's Sunday." He had the voice of the man on the radio now. It was the same voice, Connie thought. "Don'tcha know it's Sunday all day and honey, no matter who you were with last night today you're with Arnold Friend and don't you forget it!—Maybe you better step out here," he said, and this last was in a different voice. It was a little flatter, as if the heat was finally getting to him.

"No. I got things to do."

90   "Hey."

"You two better leave."

"We ain't leaving until you come with us."

"Like hell I am—"

"Connie, don't fool around with me. I mean—I mean, don't fool *around*," he said, shaking his head. He laughed incredulously. He placed his sunglasses on top of his head, carefully, as if he were indeed wearing a wig, and brought the stems down behind his ears. Connie stared at him, another wave of dizziness and fear rising in her so that for a moment he wasn't even in focus but was just a blur, standing there against his gold car, and she had the idea that he had driven up the driveway all right but had come from nowhere before that and belonged nowhere and that everything about him and even about the music that was so familiar to her was only half real.

95   "If my father comes and sees you—"

"He ain't coming. He's at a barbecue."

"How do you know that?"

"Aunt Tillie's. Right now they're uh—they're drinking. Sitting around," he said vaguely, squinting as if he were staring all the way to town and over to Aunt Tillie's back yard. Then the vision seemed to get clear and he nodded energetically. "Yeah. Sitting around. There's your sister in a blue dress, huh? And high heels, the poor sad bitch—nothing like you, sweetheart! And your mother's helping some fat woman with the corn, they're cleaning the corn—husking the corn—"

"What fat woman?" Connie cried.

100 "How do I know what fat woman. I don't know every goddam fat woman in the world!" Arnold Friend laughed.

"Oh, that's Mrs. Hornsby.... Who invited her?" Connie said. She felt a little light-headed. Her breath was coming quickly.

"She's too fat. I don't like them fat. I like them the way you are, honey," he said, smiling sleepily at her. They stared at each other for a while, through the screen door. He said softly, "Now, what you're going to do is this: you're going to come out that door. You're going to sit up front with me and Ellie's going to sit in the back, the hell with Ellie, right? This isn't Ellie's date. You're my date. I'm your lover, honey."

"What? You're crazy—"

"Yes, I'm your lover. You don't know what that is but you will," he said. "I know that too. I know all about you. But look: it's real nice and you couldn't ask for nobody better than me, or more polite. I always keep my word. I'll tell you how it is, I'm always nice at first, the first time. I'll hold you so tight you won't think you have to try to get away or pretend anything because you'll know you can't. And I'll come inside you where it's all secret and you'll give in to me and you'll love me—"

105 "Shut up! You're crazy!" Connie said. She backed away from the door. She put her hands up against her ears as if she'd heard something terrible, something not meant for her. "People don't talk like that, you're crazy," she muttered. Her heart was almost too big now for her chest and its pumping made sweat break out all over her. She looked out to see Arnold Friend pause and then take a step toward the porch lurching. He almost fell. But, like a clever drunken man, he managed to catch his balance. He wobbled in his high boots and grabbed hold of one of the porch posts.

"Honey?" he said. "You still listening?"

"Get the hell out of here!"

"Be nice, honey. Listen."

"I'm going to call the police—"

110 He wobbled again and out of the side of his mouth came a fast spat curse, an aside not meant for her to hear. But even this "Christ!" sounded forced. Then he began to smile again. She watched this smile come, awkward as if he were smiling from inside a mask. His whole face was a mask, she thought wildly, tanned down to his throat but then running out as if he had plastered makeup on his face but had forgotten about his throat.

"Honey—? Listen, here's how it is. I always tell the truth and I promise you this: I ain't coming in that house after you."

"You better not! I'm going to call the police if you—if you don't—"

"Honey," he said, talking right through her voice, "honey, I'm not coming in there but you are coming out here. You know why?"

She was panting. The kitchen looked like a place she had never seen before, some room she had run inside but that wasn't good enough, wasn't going to help her. The kitchen window had never had a curtain, after three years, and there were dishes in the sink for her to do—probably—and if you ran your hand across the table you'd probably feel something sticky there.

"You listening, honey? Hey?"

"—going to call the police—"

"Soon as you touch the phone I don't need to keep my promise and can come inside. You won't want that."

She rushed forward and tried to lock the door. Her fingers were shaking. "But why lock it," Arnold Friend said gently, talking right into her face. "It's just a screen door. It's just nothing." One of his boots was at a strange angle, as if his foot wasn't in it. It pointed out to the left, bent at the ankle. "I mean, anybody can break through a screen door and glass and wood and iron or anything else if he needs to, anybody at all and specially Arnold Friend. If the place got lit up with a fire honey you'd come running out into my arms, right into my arms and safe at home—like you knew I was your lover and'd stopped fooling around. I don't mind a nice shy girl but I don't like no fooling around." Part of those words were spoken with a slight rhythmic lilt, and Connie somehow recognized them—the echo of a song from last year, about a girl rushing into her boyfriend's arms and coming home again—

Connie stood barefoot on the linoleum floor, staring at him. "What do you want?" she whispered.

"I want you," he said.

"What?"

"Seen you that night and thought, that's the one, yes sir. I never needed to look anymore."

"But my father's coming back. He's coming to get me. I had to wash my hair first—" She spoke in a dry, rapid voice, hardly raising it for him to hear.

"No, your daddy is not coming and yes, you had to wash your hair and you washed it for me. It's nice and shining and all for me, I thank you, sweetheart," he said, with a mock bow, but again he almost lost his balance. He had to bend and adjust his boots. Evidently his feet did not go all the way down; the boots must have been stuffed with something so that he would seem taller. Connie stared out at him and behind him at Ellie in the car, who seemed to be looking off toward Connie's right, into nothing. This Ellie said, pulling the words out of the air one after another as if he were just discovering them, "You want me to pull out the phone?"

"Shut your mouth and keep it shut," Arnold Friend said, his face red from bending over or maybe from embarrassment because Connie had seen his boots. "This ain't none of your business."

"What—what are you doing? What do you want?" Connie said. "If I call the police they'll get you, they'll arrest you—"

"Promise was not to come in unless you touch that phone, and I'll keep that promise," he said. He resumed his erect position and tried to force his shoulders back. He sounded like a hero in a movie, declaring something important. He spoke too loudly and it was as if he were speaking to someone behind Connie. "I ain't made plans for coming in that house where I don't belong but just for you to come out to me, the way you should. Don't you know who I am?"

"You're crazy," she whispered. She backed away from the door but did not want to go into another part of the house, as if this would give him permission to come through the door. "What do you...you're crazy, you..."

"Huh? What're you saying, honey?"

Her eyes darted everywhere in the kitchen. She could not remember what it was, this room.

"This is how it is, honey: you come out and we'll drive away, have a nice ride. But if you don't come out we're gonna wait till your people come home and then they're all going to get it."

"You want that telephone pulled out?" Ellie said. He held the radio away from his ear and grimaced, as if without the radio the air was too much for him.

"I toldja shut up, Ellie," Arnold Friend said, "you're deaf, get a hearing aid, right? Fix yourself up. This little girl's no trouble and's gonna be nice to me, so Ellie keep to yourself, this ain't your date—right? Don't hem in on me. Don't hog. Don't crush. Don't bird dog. Don't trail me," he said in a rapid meaningless voice, as if he were running through all the expressions he'd learned but was no longer sure which of them was in style, then rushing on to new ones, making them up with his eyes closed. "Don't crawl under my fence, don't squeeze in my chipmunk hole, don't sniff my glue, suck my popsicle, keep your own greasy fingers on yourself!" He shaded his eyes and peered in at Connie, who was backed against the kitchen table. "Don't mind him honey he's just a creep. He's a dope. Right? I'm the boy for you and like I said you come out here nice like a lady and give me your hand, and nobody else gets hurt, I mean, your nice old bald-headed daddy and your mummy and your sister in her high heels. Because listen: why bring them in this?"

"Leave me alone," Connie whispered.

"Hey, you know that old woman down the road, the one with the chickens and stuff—you know her?"

"She's dead!"

"Dead? What? You know her?" Arnold Friend said.

"She's dead—"

"Don't you like her?"

"She's dead—she's—she isn't here any more—"

"But don't you like her, I mean, you got something against her? Some grudge or something?" Then his voice dipped as if he were conscious of a rudeness. He touched the sunglasses perched up on top of his head as if to make sure they were still there. "Now, you be a good girl."

"What are you going to do?"

"Just two things, or maybe three," Arnold Friend said. "But I promise it won't last long and you'll like me the way you get to like people you're close to. You will. It's all over for you here, so come on out. You don't want your people in any trouble, do you?"

She turned and bumped against a chair or something, hurting her leg, but she ran into the back room and picked up the telephone. Something roared in her ear, a tiny roaring, and she was so sick with fear that she could do nothing but listen to it—the telephone was clammy and very heavy and her fingers groped down to the dial but were too weak to touch it. She began to scream into the phone, into the roaring. She cried out, she cried for her mother, she felt her breath start jerking back and forth in her lungs as if it were something Arnold Friend was stabbing her with again and again with no tenderness. A noisy sorrowful wailing rose all about her and she was locked inside it the way she was locked inside this house.

145 After a while she could hear again. She was sitting on the floor with her wet back against the wall.

Arnold Friend was saying from the door, "That's a good girl. Put the phone back."

She kicked the phone away from her.

"No, honey. Pick it up. Put it back right."

She picked it up and put it back. The dial tone stopped.

150 "That's a good girl. Now, you come outside."

She was hollow with what had been fear, but what was now just an emptiness. All that screaming had blasted it out of her. She sat, one leg cramped under her, and deep inside her brain was something like a pinpoint of light that kept going and would not let her relax. She thought, I'm not going to see my mother again. She thought, I'm not going to sleep in my bed again. Her bright green blouse was all wet.

Arnold Friend said, in a gentle-loud voice that was like a stage voice, "The place where you came from ain't there any more, and where you had in mind to go is cancelled out. This place you are now—inside your daddy's house—is nothing but a cardboard box I can knock down any time. You know that and always did know it. You hear me?"

She thought, I have got to think. I have got to know what to do.

"We'll go out to a nice field, out in the country here where it smells so nice and it's sunny," Arnold Friend said. "I'll have my arms tight around you so you won't need to try to get away and I'll show you what love is like, what it does. The hell with this house! It looks solid all right," he said. He ran a fingernail down the screen and the noise did not make Connie shiver, as it would have the day before. "Now, put your hand on your heart, honey. Feel that? That feels solid too but we know better, be nice to me, be sweet like you can because what else is there for a girl like you but to be sweet and pretty and give in?—and get away before her people come back?"

155 She felt her pounding heart. Her hand seemed to enclose it. She thought for the first time in her life that it was nothing that was hers, that belonged to her, but just a pounding, living thing inside this body that wasn't really hers either.

"You don't want them to get hurt," Arnold Friend went on. "Now get up, honey. Get up all by yourself."

She stoodup.

"Now turn this way. That's right. Come over here to me—Ellie, put that away, didn't I tell you? You dope. You miserable creepy dope," Arnold Friend said. His words were not angry but only part of an incantation. The incantation was kindly. "Now come out through the kitchen to me honey and let's see a smile, try it, you're a brave sweet little girl and now they're eating corn and hot dogs cooked to bursting over an outdoor fire, and they don't know one thing about you and never did and honey you're better than them because not a one of them would have done this for you."

Connie felt the linoleum under her feet; it was cool. She brushed her hair back out of her eyes. Arnold Friend let go of the post tentatively and opened his arms for her, his elbows pointing in toward each other and his wrists limp, to show that this was an embarrassed embrace and a little mocking, he didn't want to make her self-conscious.

She put out her hand against the screen. She watched herself push the door slowly open as if she were back safe somewhere in the other doorway, watching this body and this head of long hair moving out into the sunlight where Arnold Friend waited.

"My sweet little blue-eyed girl," he said in a half-sung sigh that had nothing to do with her brown eyes but was taken up just the same by the vast sunlit reaches of the land behind him and on all sides of him, so much land that Connie had never seen before and did not recognize except to know that she was going to it.

FOCUSED FREE WRITES

1. What makes this story a horror story? What is scary about it? How does the story build tension or suspense?
2. Some readers identify Arnold Friend as a kind of devil figure. How is that so? How does he compare to other devil figures you have encountered in literature or film?
3. Critics have also identified elements of fairy tales in this story. Do you see any such allusions here? Where? Which ones?
4. An allegory is a story with a double meaning, a surface meaning and a second, under-the-surface meaning. Oates is known for her allegories, as the Kalpakian quotation before the story suggests. Is this story an allegory? How so?
5. Is this a feminist story? How so? How is it not?
6. The title comes from a very disturbing and problematic chapter in the Bible, chapter 19, verse 17 of Judges, which tells the story of a wife raped, killed, and left for dead while traveling home with her husband. What is the meaning of this title in relation to the themes of the story?

Want to Know More?

Source Material for Oates's Story

This story has enjoyed tremendous critical success as many scholars have made connections between it and its source material. Below you will find excerpts from some of these sources. Which do you find most informative in opening of the meaning of the story and why?

Excerpt from Don Moser's "The Pied Piper of Tucson"

According to her biographer, Greg Johnson, Oates read the opening of a *Life* magazine article about Charles Schmid, an Arizona serial killer of teenage girls. Immediately, she envisioned a short story based on this material and stopped reading, not wanting "to be distracted by too much detail." Often, though, real life events from the newspaper were sources of inspiration for Oates: "It is the very skeletal nature of the newspaper, I think, that attracts me to it, the need it inspires in me to give flesh to such neat and thinly-told tales." What in these paragraphs may have provided Oates with her inspiration?

At dusk in Tucson, as the stark, yellow-flared mountains begin to blur against the sky, the golden car slowly cruises Speedway. Smoothly it rolls down the long, divided avenue, past the supermarkets, the gas stations and the motels; past the twist joints, the sprawling drive-in restaurants. The car slows for an intersection, stops, then pulls away again. The exhaust mutters against the pavement as the young man driving takes the machine swiftly, expertly through the gears. A car pulls even with him; the teenage girls in the front seat laugh, wave and call his name. The young man glances toward the rearview mirror, turned always so that he can look at his own reflection, and he appraises himself.

The face is his own creation: the hair dyed a raven black, the skin darkened to a deep tan with pancake make-up, the lips whitened, the whole effect heightened by a mole he has painted on one cheek. But the deep-set blue eyes are all his own. Beautiful eyes, the girls say.

Approaching the Hi-Ho, the teenagers' nightclub, he backs off on the accelerator, then slowly cruises on past Johnie's Drive-in. There the cars are beginning to orbit and accumulate in the parking lot—neat sharp cars with deep-throated mufflers and Maltese-cross decals on the windows. But it's early yet. Not much going on. The driver shifts up again through the gears, and the golden car slides away along the glitter and gimcrack of Speedway. Smitty keeps looking for the action.

"The Pied Piper of Tucson," *Life*, March 4, 1966: 19–24, 80c–90

This story is full of references to music, is dedicated to Bob Dylan, and was said to have been inspired by this song in particular. Why does music generally and this song in particular figure so prominently in this story?

Bob Dylan

IT'S ALL OVER NOW, BABY BLUE

You must leave now, take what you need, you think will last
But whatever you wish to keep, you better grab it fast
Yonder stands your orphan with his gun
Crying like a fire in the sun
Look out the saints are comin' through
And it's all over now, Baby Blue

The highway is for gamblers, better use your sense
Take what you have gathered from coincidence
The empty-handed painter from your streets
Is drawing crazy patterns on your sheets
This sky, too, is folding under you
And it's all over now, Baby Blue

All your seasick sailors, they are rowing home
All your reindeer armies, are all going home
The lover who just walked out your door
Has taken all his blankets from the floor
The carpet, too, is moving under you
And it's all over now, Baby Blue

Leave your stepping stones behind, something calls for you
Forget the dead you've left, they will not follow you
The vagabond who's rapping at your door
Is standing in the clothes that you once wore
Strike another match, go start anew
And it's all over now, Baby Blue

There is a lot of controversy about the meaning of the ending. In fact, the film version of the story, *Smooth Talk*, revises the ending in its adaptation. How do you interpret the ending?

Edgar Allan Poe

Edgar Allan Poe's life story almost reads as material from fiction, maybe even from a horror story. However, he is most famous for his own short, intense, sensational tales of horror and terror. In a review of Hawthorne's *Twice-Told Tales*, he describes what makes a story successful:

> A skilful literary artist has constructed a tale. If wise, he has not fashioned his thoughts to accommodate his incidents; but having conceived, with deliberate care, a certain unique or single effect to be wrought out, he then invents such incidents—he then combines such events as may best aid him in establishing this preconceived effect. If his very initial sentence tend not to the outbringing of this effect, then he has failed in his first step. In the whole composition there should be no word written, of which the tendency, direct or indirect, is not to the one pre-established design. And by such means, with such care and skill, a picture is at length painted which leaves in the mind of him who contemplates it with a kindred art, a sense of the fullest satisfaction. The idea of the tale has been presented unblemished, because undisturbed; and this is an end unattainable by the novel. Undue brevity is just as exceptionable here as in the poem; but undue length is yet more to be avoided.

Poe's literary criticism as well as his command of the genre has established his long-term influence on horror fiction. In famous stories like "The Tell-Tale Heart" and "Cask of Amontillado," for example, you should be able to identify this "certain unique or single effect" as well as the influence of Poe's effect on the writers in this chapter and in this genre.

Writing About Your Experience
with Literature

Write a horror story

Using the advice and examples illustrated here, as well as your own experience with the genre, try your hand at writing horror fiction. Work in groups, pairs, or individually to determine what kind of horror story you will write. How will you thrill and chill? What elements of horror fiction will you include? What sort of catharsis will you offer your readers as a vacation from sanity? Will you write a psychological or supernatural horror story? Is there an actual event that can inspire your vision? What "certain unique or single effect" will you convey in your story?

Research the history of horror

This chapter only skimmed the surface of the rich and complex history of the horror genre. Working in groups, pairs, or individually, look into the history of the genre through research. Choose an aspect of the form to investigate and write a brief paper or develop a presentation. You might consider one of the following questions:

- What are some of the earliest forms of horror in literature?
- Who are some of the most important horror writers in constructing a genealogy of horror fiction?
- What is the literary history of one of the central horror figures: vampires, werewolves, monsters, or ghosts?
- Identify the range of subgenres of the form.
- What does *gothic* mean? How did the gothic novel beget horror fiction?

11
LISTENING
TO MUSIC
Experiencing Stories in Rhythm

Listening to Music. Here is a photograph of legend Bob Dylan, celebrated as a bard, a poet, and a singer. Are songs a form of literature? In what way are they a form of poetry? Which contemporary musicians should be considered poets? What characteristics do their songs share?

In the 1995 film, *Dangerous Minds*, Michelle Pfeiffer plays an inner-city English teacher who attempts to reach her students by using the music of Bob Dylan to teach poetry. In her classroom, students come to realize the poetry of music and the music of poetry. In our own lives, we may have heard lyrics on the radio that sounded like poetry because of their careful or surprising word choices, their depth of feeling, or their catchy rhythms. We might even have run across a bit of poetry that sounded like a song or have seen a hymn in church that was written by a poet whose name we recognize. Songwriters like Jim Morrison or Jewel often have dabbled in poetry along with writing music. In fact, Bob Dylan has his own entry at the Academy of American Poets' official website, www.poets.org.

Poetry and music go hand in hand. In fact, any **poem** may technically be called a song, though the term **song** usually refers to a poem that has a regular metrical pattern and that is designed to be sung. Both poetry and music rely on the persuasive power of language, both require a skilled use of sound and rhyme, and both engage readers or listeners emotionally.

Clearly, however, there are distinctions to be drawn between the two genres. A **poem** can be any length. Since poems are designed to be read silently and contemplated at length, they may be dense in ideas and structurally complex. **Song lyrics**, on the other hand, are often more concise. They are designed to work with the rhythm and structure of the accompanying music; together, words and music must impart a message and a mood to listeners in a matter of minutes.

Early poetry, a kind of storytelling set to music, was meant to be sung or chanted. Over time, poetry and songs developed their own traditions not entirely dependent on storytelling and seemed to veer away from each other. Poems that tell stories, like epics and ballads, gave way to lyric poetry and free-verse forms, but the rise of spoken-word poetry is bringing back the oral tradition of the poem form. Great music can be produced by attending to the poetry of the language. Great poetry can be produced by considering the music of the language and the power of the performance.

From Someone Who Knows

Paul Simon on Songwriting

In the article that follows, legendary singer and songwriter Paul Simon describes the process of matching music with lyrics.

Richard Harrington

Music, Lyrics in Their Best Order
The Washington Post, Friday, May 18, 2007

For Paul Simon, songwriting has always been a meld of craft and inspiration, intellect and emotion, a process of endless revising, rewriting, arranging and production in pursuit of a more perfect union of lyric, melody and rhythm—all to ensure that his songs do not come back and haunt him "in shades of mediocrity."

"What happens is there's some problem that's really interesting and I begin to first describe the problem to myself and then I try and solve the problem," Simon says. "In a certain sense, the whole thing is about pleasure—the inference is that because of the degree to which I rewrite or how long it takes, that there's some sort of suffering going on. There's not. Once I find the description of the problem, that's my favorite time because now I'm working on something that I'm really interested in. That's fun.

"The solutions to the problems are sometimes satisfying, sometimes not, and at this point in time—really for quite some time now—I've been perfectly willing to say, 'Well, that's as good as I can do on that' and move on to the next thing, and I won't have any judgment about it because you can't tell anyways whether what you've done is extraordinary or not. It's all about some sound I heard in my head and how close I got to it. You can't get a hit every time you're up at bat."

As for his finely wrought and beautifully observed lyrics, he says, "they come after the music, and what happens is that sometimes if the words aren't right, it doesn't mean that the words aren't right, it means that the rhythm is wrong or that the melody wants to be less notes or more notes. When the melody is natural, like the way you speak when you have something to say and everything is just flowing out of you naturally, you don't have to struggle with your phrases the way I'm doing now.

"At a certain point, it is effortless, and that's the point where I know I can leave it and move on to the next problem, whether it's the next verse or the next song or whatever....It's the same with the lyrics—once the pattern and the flow of how you're going to sing it is established, then most of the time, the words that fit into that flow, they're going to be interesting, to me anyway, because I'm sort of writing about what's on my mind. I'm not researching—it's what's going on. The only thing that I look for, and the only thing that I actually work at in a way, is the imagery, but I do that independent of the songwriting.

"I keep a notebook, and if some image or thought or phrase comes to me, I put it down in the notebook. And then when I'm working on my songs, I look through my notebook and see if any of those phrases apply to the song that I'm working on in a rhythmic way that you can sing it."

In discussing his process, legendary songwriter Paul Simon describes writing songs as problem-solving. The writers that follow would most likely agree with Simon. All of these writers address a problem that many songwriters (and poets, for that matter) are familiar with: "Love hurts." In the songs that follow, we will witness how contemporary songwriters attempt the literary in their lyrics. If the stereo is more your style, you might connect with the lyrics of some of the spoken-word poets that follow. Finally, understanding the song-writing and poetry tradition might inform where you might go next in your journey into listening to music. And if you wonder if lyrics really are literary, then take note of the literary references in the verses included here.

A Genre You Know

Songs

The following lyrics illustrate the literary in songwriting. Each of the five songs incorporates allusions or references to other texts. The Zombies rewrite Faulkner's short story "A Rose for Emily." In her title "Sleep to Dream," Fiona Apple makes a fleeting reference to Hamlet's most famous soliloquy. The Magnetic Fields allude to Camus in "I Don't Want to Get Over You," and The Arctic Monkeys make mention of Shakespeare's Montagues and Capulets in "I Bet You Look Good on the Dancefloor." The Decemberists received much critical acclaim for their 2006 album *Crane Wife*, which retells the old Japanese tale of the same name in the song "The Crane Wife 1 & 2." All of these songs address love and desire, but in new ways. They illustrate how stories can be told in the briefest of lines. As you read, determine if there is something more literary than just the allusions in these songs.

The Zombies

A ROSE FOR EMILY

The summer is here at last
The sky is overcast
And no one brings a rose for Emily

She watches her flowers grow
While lovers come and go
To give each other roses from her tree
But not a rose for Emily...

Emily, can't you see
There's nothing you can do?
There's loving everywhere
But none for you...

Her roses are fading now
She keeps her pride somehow
That's all she has protecting her from pain

And as the years go by
She will grow old and die
The roses in her garden fade away
Not one left for her grave
Not a rose for Emily...

Emily, can't you see
There's nothing you can do?
There's loving everywhere
But none for you...

Her roses are fading now
She keeps her pride somehow
That's all she has protecting her from pain

And as the years go by
She will grow old and die
The roses in her garden fade away
Not one left for her grave
Not a rose for Emily...

—from the album *Odyssey and Oracle* (1967)

SLEEP TO DREAM

I tell you how I feel, but you don't care.
I say tell me the truth, but you don't dare.
You say love is a hell you cannot bear.
And I say gimme mine back and then go there—for all I care.

I got my feet on the ground and I don't go to sleep to dream.
You got your head in the clouds and you're not at all what you seem.
This mind, this body, and this voice cannot be stifled by your deviant ways.
So don't forget what I told you, don't come around, I got my own hell to raise.

I have never been insulted in all my life.
I could swallow the seas to wash down all this pride.
First you run like a fool just to be at my side.
And now you run like a fool, but you just run to hide, and I can't abide.

I got my feet on the ground and I don't go to sleep to dream.
You got this head in the clouds and you're not at all what you seem.
This mind, this body, and this voice cannot be stifled by your deviant ways.
So don't forget what I told you, don't come around, I got my own hell to raise.

Don't make it a big deal, don't be so sensitive.
We're not playing a game anymore, you don't have to be so defensive.
Don't you plead me your case, don't bother to explain.
Don't even show me your face, cuz it's a crying shame.
Just go back to the rock from under which you came.
Take the sorrow you gave and all the stakes you claim—
And don't forget the blame.
I got my feet on the ground and I don't go to sleep to dream.
You got this head in the clouds and you're not at all what you seem.
This mind, this body, and this voice cannot be stifled by your deviant ways.
So don't forget what I told you, don't come around, I got my own hell to raise.

—from the album _Tidal_ (1996)

I DON'T WANT TO GET OVER YOU

I don't want to get over you.
I guess I could take a sleeping pill and sleep at will
And not have to go through what I go through.
I guess I should take Prozac, right,
And just smile all night at somebody new,
Somebody not too bright but sweet
And kind who would try to get you off my mind.
I could leave this agony behind which is just what I'd do if I wanted to,
But I don't want to get over you cause
I don't want to get over love.

I could listen to my therapist, pretend you don't exist
And not have to dream of what I dream of;

I could listen to all my friends and go out again
and pretend it's enough,
Or I could make a career of being blue
I could dress in black and read Camus,
Smoke clove cigarettes and drink vermouth like I was 17 that
would be a scream
But I don't want to get over you.

—from the album 69 Love Songs (1999)

Arctic Monkeys

I BET YOU LOOK GOOD ON THE DANCEFLOOR

Stop making the eyes at me
I'll stop making the eyes at you
What it is that surprises me
Is that I don't really want you to
When your shoulders are frozen (cold in the night)
Oh but you're an explosion (you're dynamite)
Your name isn't Rio, but I don't care for sand
And lighting the fuse might result in a bang, ba-ba bang go

I bet that you look good on the dancefloor
I don't know if you're looking for romance or...
I don't know what you're looking for

Well I bet that you look good on the dancefloor
Dancing to electro-pop like a robot from 1984
From 1984

I wish you'd stop ignoring me
Because you're sending me to despair
Without a sound yeah you're calling me
And I don't think it's very fair
That your shoulders are frozen (cold in the night)
Oh but you're an explosion (you're dynamite)
Your name isn't Rio, but I don't care for sand
And lighting the fuse might result in a bang, ba-ba bang go

I bet that you look good on the dance floor
I don't know if you're looking for romance or...
I don't know what you're looking for
Well I bet that you look good on the dancefloor
Dancing to electro-pop like a robot from 1984
From 1984

Oh there ain't no love
No Montagues or Capulets

We're just banging tunes and DJ sets and
Dirty dance floors and dreams of naughtiness

Well I bet that you look good on the dance floor
I don't know if you're looking for romance or...
I don't know what you're looking for

I said that I bet that you look good on the dance floor
Dancing to electro-pop like a robot from 1984
From 1984

—from the album *Whatever People Say I Am, That is What I'm Not* (2006)

The Decemberists

THE CRANE WIFE 1 & 2

It was a cold night
And the snow lay around
I pulled my coat tight
Against the falling down
And the sun was all
And the sun was all down
And the sun was all
And the sun was all down

I am a poor man
I haven't wealth nor fame
I have my two hands
And a house to my name
And the winter's so
And the winter's so long
And the winter's so
And the winter's so long

And all the stars were crashing 'round
As I laid eyes on what I'd found

It was a white crane
It was a helpless thing
Upon a red stain
With an arrow in its wing
And it called and cried
And it called and cried so
And it called and cried
And it called and cried so

And all the stars were crashing 'round
As I laid eyes on what I'd found
My crane wife, my crane wife
My crane wife, my crane wife

Now I helped her
And I dressed her wounds
And how I held her
Beneath the rising moon
And she stood to fly
And she stood to fly away
And she stood to fly
She stood to fly away

And all the stars were crashing 'round
As I laid eyes on what I'd found
My crane wife, my crane wife
My crane wife, my crane wife

[2]

My crane wife arrived at my door in the moonlight
All star bright and tongue-tied, I took her in
We were married and bells rang sweet for our wedding
And our bedding was ready, we fell in

Sound the keening bell
And see it's painted red
Soft as fontenelle
The feathers in the thread
And all I ever meant to do was to keep you
My crane wife
My crane wife
My crane wife

We were poorly, our fortunes fading hourly
And how she avowed me, she could bring it back
But I was greedy, I was vain and I forced her to weaving
On a cold loom, in a closed room with down and wool

Sound the keening bell
And see it's painted red
Soft as fontenelle
The feathers in the thread
And all I ever meant to do was to keep you
My crane wife
My crane wife
MY crane wife

There's a bend in the wind and it rakes at my heart
There is blood in the thread and it rakes at my heart
It rakes at my heart

—from the album *The Crane Wife* (2006)

FOCUSED FREE WRITES

1. What are the themes of these songs? How would you summarize their meanings?
2. What kinds of stories do these songs tell? If all these songs address love and desire in some way, how do they address this old theme in new ways?
3. Can you distinguish any literary elements in these songs, such as figurative language like similes or metaphors, imagery, symbols, rhyme, meter, alliteration?
4. How are these songs like poetry? What makes a song poetic? How are these not examples of poetry?

A Genre You Might Like to Know

Spoken-Word Poetry

Spoken-word poetry is written to be spoken, or more accurately, performed, and thus it emphasizes rhythm, repetition, and rhyme, some of the very elements that characterize music and traditional poetry. Cristin O'Keefe Aptowicz and Vince Cavasin allude to the literary stylistically and literally. Both address heartbreak and loss in the spoken-word form. As poets and songwriters for centuries have addressed the loss of love, so too has the new form of spoken word in its recovery of the original oral tradition of poetry.

In the mid-1980s, Mark Smith launched a revolution in Chicago at the Green Mill jazz club and lounge. After a number of boring poetry readings at an open-mic night, Smith created a new forum and format for spoken-word poetry called a poetry slam. At a poetry slam, poets perform lyrics, poems, or stories that are then judged by the audience. This relatively new form of poetry has now developed a twenty-year tradition of annual national slam competitions (http://www.poetryslam.com/) and the *Def Poetry* series on HBO. The four poets featured here are nationally known in the spoken-word world.

- **Cristin O'Keefe Aptowicz** (http://www.aptowicz.com), the author of three books of poetry and three screenplays, is founder and host of the three-time National Poetry Slam Championship Venue, NYC Urbana.
- **Vince Cavasin** served as one of the editors of the Ann Arbor Poetry Slam Anthology entitled *(off the mic)*.
- **Debora K. Marsh** (http://a2slam.com/poet-bios/deb-marsh/) is celebrated as a poet, teacher, and mother as well as a SlamMaster, coach, and mentor. She has been active in spoken-word poetry in Ann Arbor and around the country since 1991.
- **Scott Woods** (http://www.blackair.org), a prolific poet and performer, founded the poetry performance group The Black Air Poets, serves as a

member of the Executive Council of Poetry Slam, Inc., and emcees a weekly open mic series in Columbus, Ohio.

Cristin O'Keefe Aptowicz

LIT
(Or For The Scientist To Whom
I'm Not Speaking Anymore)

Don't say you didn't see this coming, Jason.

Don't say you didn't realize this would be my reaction
and that you never intended for me to get all worked up,
because if that were true, then you are dumber
than Lenny from Mice and Men, blinder than Oedipus
and Tiresias put together and can feel less
than a Daulton Trumbo character.

You put the Dick in Dickens and the Boo in kowski
and are more Coward-ly than Noël.

But you don't understand any of these references,
Do you, Jason? Because you "don't read."
You are a geology major and you once told me
that "scientists don't read popular literature,
Cristin, we have more important things to do."

Well, fuck you.

Be glad you don't read, Jason,
because maybe you won't understand this
as I scream it to you on your front lawn,
on Christmas Day, brandishing
three hypodermic needles, a ginsu knife
and a letter of permission
from Bret Easton Ellis.

Jason, you are more absurd than Ionesco.
You are more abstract than Joyce,
more inconsistent than Agatha Christie
and more Satanic than Rushdie's verses.

I can't believe I used to want to Sappho you, Jason.
I used to want to Pablo Neruda you,
to Anaïs Nin and Henry Miller you. I used to want
to be O for you, to blow for you in ways
that even Odysseus' sails couldn't handle.
But self-imposed illiteracy isn't a turn-on.

You used to make fun of me being a writer,
saying "Scientists cure diseases,
what do writers do?"

But of course, you wouldn't understand, Jason.
I mean, have you ever gotten an inner thirsting
for Zora Neale Hurston?
Or heard angels herald for you
to read F. Scott Fitzgerald?
Have you ever had a beat attack for Jack Kerouac?
The only Morrison you know is Jim, and you think
you're the noble one?

Go Plath yourself.

Your heart is so dark, that even Joseph Conrad
couldn't see it, and it is so buried under bullshit
that even Poe's cops couldn't hear it.

Your mind is as empty as the libraries in Fahrenheit 451.
Your mind is as empty as Silas Marner's coffers.
Your mind is as empty as Huckleberry Finn's wallet.
And some people might say that this poem
is just a pretentious exercise
in seeing how many literary references
I can come up with.

And some people might complain that this poem is,
at its core, shallow, expressing the same emotion again,
and again, and again. I mean, how many times
can you articulate your contempt for Jason,
before the audience gets a little bored.

But you know what, Jason? Those people
would be wrong. Because this is not the poem
I am writing to express my hatred for you.

This poem is the poem I am writing because
we aren't speaking, and it is making my heart hurt
so bad, that sometimes I can't make it up off the floor.

And this is the poem I am writing instead of writing
the *I miss having breakfast with you* poem, instead
of the *Let's walk dogs in our old schoolyard
again* poem. Instead of the *How are you doing?* poem,
the *I miss you* poem, the *I wish I was making fun
of how much you like Garth Brooks while sitting
in front of your parents' house in your jeep* poem,
instead of the *Holidays are coming around and
you know what that means: SUICIDE!* poem.

I am writing this so that I can stop wanting to write
the *I could fall in love with you again so quickly
if only you would say one more word to me* poem.

But I am tired of loving you, Jason
'cause you don't love me right.

And if some pretentious ass poem can stop me
From thinking about the way your laugh sounds,
about the way your skin feels in the rain,
about how I would rather be miserable with you,
than happy with anyone else in the world,

If some pretentious ass poem can do all that?

Then I am gone with the wind, I am on the road,
I have flown over the fucking cuckoo's nest,
I am gone, I am gone, I am gone.

I am.

FOCUSED FREE WRITES

1. Is this a poem? How so? What elements of poetry can you identify here?
2. How is this work different from a traditional poem? How is it like a song or another form of poetry? What makes it work as a performance piece?
3. This poem is full of literary allusions. How many can you identify, and how do they work as insults?
4. How does this poem compare to other poetry in this book about the pain of love?

Vince Cavasin

I HAVE NOT GONE MARKING
(With Apologies To Pablo Neruda)

i have not gone marking
the days since you left
swirling like an ebb tide
from my receding shore

i have not gone crying
frozen tears to shatter on the sand
from which the wind carries off gently, silently
all traces of snow and frost

i have not gone wandering
about the hills of your future
through the laughter of the children
who might see through your dark eyes

i have not gone feeling
the absence of your fingertips
against my flesh
burning with what has become cold

i have not gone alone into this winter
warmed by the bits of you left in me
my frozen heart still beating
in irregular rhytms as it always has

i have not forgotten
the seasons
of your touch

FOCUSED FREE WRITES

1. Does this poem read like poetry or music? Why?
2. What elements of literature are evident here? What is the poem's theme?
3. In this poem, Cavasin responds to one of Pablo Neruda's most famous love poems. The sensual first stanza reads:

   I have gone marking the atlas of your body
   with crosses of fire.
   My mouth went across: a spider, trying to hide.
   In you, behind you, timid, driven by thirst.

   Why would Cavasin choose to revise the words of this famous love poet?

Debora Marsh

UNBREAKABLE GLASS—A POEM
FOR MY DAUGHTER

I used to think she was like Laura—dainty, beautiful to look at,
but not to touch.
The unicorn on the shelf, horn in tact,
in a place of prominence,
for all to see.
I used to think I had to protect her
from gum chewing gentleman callers
who would whirl her away,
Breaking her delicate glass into shards.
But now I see her clearly—the rose colored glass is rose quartz instead.
She is strong and beautiful but unlikely to break
When spun and twirled while dancing.
Dance my darling daughter,
Spin and dance and whirl.
Although the world is lit by lightning,
Don't be afraid to light your candles and dance!

FOCUSED FREE WRITES

1. What is the poem's theme? Identify other literary elements in this spoken-word poem: figurative language like similes or metaphors, imagery, symbols, rhyme, meter, or alliteration.
2. Why does Marsh use the allusion to Williams's *The Glass Menagerie*? How does the comparison serve to describe Marsh's daughter more fully?

Scott Woods

I, NIGHTMARE

The other day I stepped into an elevator with an old white woman
    and she smiled at me and asked, "what floor you going to?"
The other day I walked into a clothing store at the mall
    and no one followed me around to see if I needed any "help"
The other day, I went to Denny's and got
    service with a smile
Just yesterday I got pulled over for ACTUALLY speeding.

Oh, I know what the problem is:
white people aren't scared of brothers anymore, but it's our own fault.
It's the BET
It's the UPN
It's the WB
It's all of the hip-hop.

The MEDIA has made being Black "not so bad"
The MEDIA has shown the world we're not REALLY that scary
The MEDIA has revealed our dancing, smiling, cartoon underbellies, and now?
NOW I can't even get a decent scare out of people on the street anymore.

Oh, you can still find the random thug now and then;
Ol' Dirty Bastard will carry the torch to his grave,
but I NEEDED the mystery
Brothers like me NEEDED that/ we NEEDED the quiet fear of our skin.

Hip-hop has made us too cool and given away too many secrets,
and yet I have cracked the code
I have broken the chain
I have shucked a lump of coal into the engine of the new Underground
    Railroad,
    and you know what the destination is?
N.P.R.
I listen to National Public Radio.
I only watch movies with subtitles in them.
I watch the BBC.
I got season tickets to the opera.
I use Head & Shoulders.

I own Barry Manilow on vinyl.
Because making gangbanger madfaces doesn't work anymore!
Baggy pants and Air Jordans simply brand thee "fellow consumer"!

Because madfaces don't work anymore.
Now you have to stand against the wall at the nightclub
   staring at things
   with a small smile playing at the corners of your lips,
   looking
     pensive.
   Like BIG WORDS could fall out your mouth at anytime.
Sometimes I just walk into a store and shout out:
"SUBSISTENCE!"
   and watch, as in-store security trips over themselves to assist me.

I don't even know what that MEANS.

Because THAT'S what's scary now.
Willie Horton is passé.
Gangsta rap is a cartoon.
But intelligence?
Wearing intelligence is the scariest thing I can do.

FOCUSED FREE WRITES

1. What is the "nightmare"? How would you characterize the tone of this poem?
2. While this poem does not include literary allusions, it does include cultural references. What are they, and what do they mean in this poem?
3. How does this example demonstrate that spoken-word poetry is distinctly different from other forms of poetry? How is it similar?

Knowing Where We Come From

Oral Literature

The earliest known examples of literature were poems and songs performed orally, such as the *Odyssey* and the *Iliad*, attributed to Homer in the 8th century B.C.E. **Ballads** are another oral form of poetry with an equally long tradition though they rose to prominence in Europe in the late Middle Ages. **Ballads** are songs that tell a focused, sparse story in simple language characterized by repetition and dialog. The themes are often tragic, characterization is minimal, and tales usually include adventure, war, love, death, or the supernatural. A famous traditional British ballad from the seventeenth century is "The Daemon Lover," also known as "James Harris," "James Herries," or "The House Carpenter." This popular ballad tells the story of a devil figure who returns to a lover he had abandoned, only to find her with a carpenter husband and child. After enticing her to leave them both, they travel away by ship over the seas where she mourns what she has lost and where a darker horizon awaits.

Ballads like this one are often subject to collaboration; singers create a version and pass it on to other singers, who remake the song according to their own visions. This particular ballad has been recorded by at least thirty different artists. Songwriter Bob Dylan sang his version of the popular ballad on his 1991 album *The Bootleg Series*. Dylan has been celebrated as a songwriter with countless awards, and he is respected by musicians, critics, and the general public alike with dozens of informal monikers like "The Bard." His songs define a generation with anthems like "Blowin' in the Wind," "The Times They Are A-Changing," and "Like a Rolling Stone." His understanding of the history of music informs his compositions and has earned him respect as a poet. The Academy of the American Society of Poets summarizes the debate over Dylan's designation as songwriter or as a poet in their profile of him at www.poets.org, ultimately citing Dylan's own answer to the question: "Anything I can sing, I call a song. Anything I can't sing, I call a poem."

Writing About Your Experience with Literature

Develop a spoken-word poem

In groups, pairs, or individually, use the information and examples from this chapter to compose your own spoken-word poem, perhaps on the "love hurts" theme or perhaps incorporating allusions to literature as many of these songs and poems have. Your poem should emphasize rhythm, repetition, and rhyme. Its success should depend on your performance of the words, not just the words themselves, so be sure to practice performing it rather than just writing it.

Research the history of spoken-word poetry or a spoken-word poet

This chapter only introduced the genre of spoken-word poetry. Do some research into spoken-word poetry. Investigate the history of the form and some of the key figures, or choose one important figure to look into. Find examples of the poetry and listen to them performed. Working in groups, pairs, or individually, write a brief paper or develop a presentation discussing the historical timeline of the form, the nature of the genre, or the significance of this figure.

Analyze the poetry of a song that tells a story

Don McLean wrote "American Pie" about the "day the music died." Eric Clapton wrote "Tears in Heaven" about the death of his son. And urban legends have arisen over what Phil Collins's "In the Air Tonight" is supposedly about. Songs have a long history as means for telling stories. Working in groups, pairs, or individually, use the critical tools you have been developing in this course to analyze the story told by a song. You might choose a Beatles or a Bob Dylan song or something more contemporary; for example,

(continued)

the songs listed below all contain some kind of literary reference. Do some research into the origin of the allusion or meaning of the song and in a brief paper or presentation identify the theme, plot, characters, figurative language, and any other elements used to support this theme.

Listening for the literary in music

As this chapter illustrated, music and literature are closely related. All of the songs in this chapter, in fact, include literary allusions. However, there are many more out there on websites such as www.artistsforliteracy.org/home.html. Find your own song about literature to study. Develop a brief paper or presentation explicating these literary allusions and demonstrate how understanding the literary allusions can help you listen to the music. Identify the theme, plot, characters, figurative language, and any other literary elements that could be useful in understanding the meaning of the song.

Songs with Literary References: A Selective List

Many of these songs were found online at a query entitled: "She reads Simone de Beauvoir in her American circumstance," located at http://ask.metafilter.com/37294/. However, the Songs Inspired by Literature project (http://www.siblproject.org/) and Wikipedia have compiled their own lists as well:

Ryan Adams, "Sylvia Plath"
The Ataris, "If You Really Want to Hear about It"
Bad Religion, "Stranger than Fiction"
The Beatles, "Paperback Writer"
Belle and Sebastian, "Wrapped Up in Books"
Kate Bush, "Wuthering Heights"
Cake, "Open Book"
Nick Cave, "There She Goes"
The Clean, "Franz Kafka at the Zoo"
The Decemberists, "Myla Goldberg"
Dire Straits, "Lady Writer"
Dire Straits, "Romeo and Juliet"
Divine Comedy, "Booklovers"
Divine Comedy, "Lucy"
Elvis Costello & The Attractions, "Everyday I Write the Book"
The Cure, "Killing an Arab"
Gordon Lightfoot, "Don Quixote"
Green Day, "Who Wrote Holden Caufield?"
Husker Du, "Books about UFOs"
Indigo Girls, "Virginia Woolf"
Indigo Girls, "Romeo and Juliet"

Iron Maiden, "Rime of the Ancient Mariner"
Manic Street Preachers, "The Girl Who Wanted to Be God"
Modest Mouse, "Bukowski"
Morrissey, "Reader Meet Author"
Moxy Früvous, "My Baby Loves a Bunch of Authors"
Alan Parsons Project, "Tales of Mystery and Imagination"
The Police, "Don't Stand So Close to Me"
The Shins, "Pressed in a Book"
Simon & Garfunkel, "Bookends"
Simon & Garfunkel, "Richard Corey"
The Smiths, "Cemetery Gates"
Sparklehorse, "London"
Soul Coughing, "Screenwriter's Blues"
The Story, "Love Is More Thicker Than Forget"
Talking Heads, "The Book I Read"
Toad the Wet Sprocket, "Windmills"
Tsunami, "David Foster Wallace"
The Verve, "History"
Weezer, "Holiday"
Paul Westerberg, "Bookmark"

12

EXPLORING THE ALTERNATIVE
Getting to Know Experimental Literature

Exploring the Alternative. This is a photograph of Claes Oldenberg and Coosje Van Bruggen's *Spoonbridge and Cherry* (1985–1988) located in the Minneapolis Sculpture Garden. What are we supposed to think or feel when experiencing this sculpture? What is it saying? What examples of alternative art you are familiar with? Why should they be valued as art? What purpose do they serve?

(Accession number: 1988.385. Artist: Oldenburg, Claes and Coosje van Bruggen. Title: Spoonbridge and Cherry; Date:1985–1988. Medium: aluminum, stainless steel, paint. 354 x 618 x 162. Collection Walker Art Center, Minneapolis. Gift of Frederick R. Weisman in honor of his parents, William and Mary Wesiman, 1988. © Claes Oldenburg and Coosje van Bruggen.)

John Cage is a musician, but his most famous work, entitled 4'33", and first performed in 1952, is composed entirely of silence, just over four and half minutes of silence divided into three movements. Those who have heard it performed are amazed by the sounds they hear in this choreographed silence.

Cage's composition was influenced by artist Robert Rauschenberg's "white paintings" of 1951, blank canvases that contain no paint at all. Rauschenberg once said that "An empty canvas is full only if you want it to be full." In other words, art can be found in silence or on blankness, in echoes and shadows and by chance.

Both Cage and Rauschenberg can be described as experimental artists. Experimental art is any intellectual, imaginative, or creative activity that explores new concepts and techniques, new styles and statements, that move beyond what is considered popular by the public or conventional in literary circles. Experimental art, sometimes called *avant-garde,* challenges the status quo in music, art, and literature, and in so doing, forces the audience to actively question not only the meaning of the individual work, but also the nature of that genre, art generally, and the act of interpretation.

Experimental literature challenges and even dismantles literary conventions. If it's conventional in a short story to have a beginning, a middle, and an end, to have believable characters, and to have a conflict and a resolution, then an experimental story might reject those formulaic elements. It might focus on style rather than narrative, it might not have a narrative structure at all, or it might emphasize other elements like mood or language.

In *The Anchor Book of New American Short Stories*, an anthology that celebrates experimental literature, editor Ben Marcus writes:

> Stories keep mattering by reimagining their own methods, manners, and techniques. A writer has to believe, and prove, that there are, if not new stories, then new ways of telling the old ones. A stylist is an artist of diction, a grammarist, a shaper of sentences, who recognizes language as the sole technology at work in a story. A stylist seeks to master that technology, to not let it lead or dictate terms, but to control it and make it produce whatever effects the stylist desires. (xiii)

Whether stylists of fiction or poetry or drama, experimental writers create something innovative. This revolution in writing style then forces a new approach to reading as well. The reader is often shocked and surprised by this unique form and must rethink how to interpret and consume it.

From Someone Who Knows

Claes Oldenberg on Experimental Art

Often the notion of experimentalism is discussed in the context of experimental art. The avant-garde, impressionism, expressionism, surrealism, Dadaism—all were forms of art that challenged convention and were initially conceived as experimental. But the experimental often becomes the new convention, and once these forms of artistic expression became movements, new forms of art developed to challenge them. Thus, art continually rebels and transforms, challenging norms and continually recreating itself.

Sculptor Claes Oldenberg is one such artist whose monumental sculptures and installations memorializing everyday objects dismantled conventional notions of what art is, where it is, how big it is, and who sees it. The following excerpt of Oldenberg's essay/manifesto/poem/statement "I am for an art…" can perhaps illustrate the essence of experimental art:

> I am for an art that is political-erotical-mystical, that does something other than sit on its ass in a museum.
>
> I am for an art that grows up not knowing it is art at all, an art given the chance to have a starting point of zero.
>
> I am for an art that embroils itself with the everyday crap and still comes out on top. I am for the art that imitates the human, that is comic, if necessary, or violent, or whatever is necessary.
>
> I am for the art that takes its form from the lines of life itself, that twists and extends and accumulates and spits and drips, and is heavy and coarse and blunt and sweet and stupid as life itself.
>
> I am for the art that a kid licks, after peeling away the wrapper…
>
> I am for art that coils and grunts like a wrestler…
>
> I am for the blinking arts, lighting up the night. I am for the falling, splashing, wiggling, jumping, going on and off.
>
> I am for the art of fat tires and black eyes.
>
> I am for Kool-art, 7-Up art, Pepsi art Sunshine art, 39 cents art, 15 cents art, Vatronol Art, Dro-bomb art, Vam art, Menthol art, L & M art Ex-lax art, Venida art, Heaven Hill art, Pamryl art, San-o-med art, RX art, 9.99 art, Now art, New art, How art, Fire sale art, Last Chance art, Only art, Diamond art, Tomorrow art, Franks art, Ducks art, Meat-o-rama art.'…
>
> I am for U.S. Government Inspected Art, Grade A art, Regular Price art, Yellow Ripe art, Extra Fancy art, Ready-to-eat art, Best-for-less art, Ready-to-cook art, Full cleaned art, Spend Less art, Eat Better art, Ham art, Pork art, chicken art, tomato art, banana art, apple art, turkey art, cake art, cookie art.

Clearly, Oldenberg's conception dismantles any high-falutin' notions of museum art and re-envisions art as of the masses and for the masses, as messy and confrontational, as funny and available, as surprising and thought provoking. The experimental literature in this chapter will illustrate those qualities. In the examples that follow, we will be introduced to literary experimentation in reference to Eve Ensler's dramatic composition *The Vagina Monologues*, in samples of the experimental fiction of Lydia Davis and Chris Bachelder and, finally, in a discussion of Gertrude Stein's groundbreaking poem *Tender Buttons*. As you read, try to figure out how these unconventional forms challenge conventional narratives and how their content necessitates this rebellion. Also, consider what works you might categorize as experimental or alternative.

Eve Ensler, Dramatist

Many college campuses and communities across the country have staged productions of *The Vagina Monologues*. Some have even boycotted such productions. The play has been in the news and has been parodied; it has charged controversies and it has changed lives. Actresses have had transformative experiences performing in it and people have lost jobs over it. Based on interviews with over 200 women, Eve Ensler composed *The Vagina Monologues* as a series of scenes in which a female performer remembers her own experiences with sexuality. This piece of performance art is a kind of collage with monologues in different voices, facts from references books, and litanies of responses to interview questions. In making public what has been shameful, embarrassing, or painful, Ensler has described her mission as revelatory and revolutionary.

Lydia Davis and Chris Bachelder

What follows aren't stories at all, or are they? They could be called experimental fiction. They may not even be fiction, though, since they are partly based on real life. And according to Lydia Davis, the term "experimental" is problematic. In an interview in *The Boston Globe* with Kate Bolick, published on April 29, 2007, Davis commented: "I haven't met a so-called experimental writer who likes the term. It must be people who aren't experimental writers who call people experimental. It's just the wrong word. 'Experiment' carries the suggestion that it may not work. I prefer the idea of being adventurous, exploring forms." As you read, consider how these examples are "adventurous" or how they "explore forms." Think back to the elements of fiction discussed in this book: plot, character, theme, setting, symbols, and style. Do these stories or essays include these elements?

Lydia Davis

BORING FRIENDS

We know only four boring people. The rest of our friends we find very interesting. However, most of the friends we find interesting find us boring: the most interesting find us the most boring. The few who are somewhere in the middle, with whom there is reciprocal interest, we distrust: at any moment, we feel, they may become too interesting for us, or we too interesting for them.

A MOWN LAWN

She hated a *mown lawn*. Maybe that was because *mow* was the reverse of *wom*, the beginning of the name of what she was—a *woman*. A *mown lawn* had a sad sound to it, like a *long moan*. From her, a *mown lawn* made a *long moan*. *Lawn* had some of the letters of *man*, though the reverse of *man* would be *Nam*, a bad war. A *raw war*. *Lawn* also contained the letters of *law*. In fact, *lawn* was a contraction of *lawman*. Certainly a *lawman* could and did *mow* a *lawn*. *Law and order* could be seen as starting from *lawn order*, valued by so many Americans. *More lawn* could be made using a *lawn mower*. A *lawn mower* did make *more lawn*. *More lawn* was a contraction of *more lawmen*. Did *more lawn* in America make *more lawmen* in America? Did *more lawn* make *more Nam*? *More mown lawn* made *more long moan*, from her. Or a *lawn mourn*. So often, she said, Americans wanted *more mown lawn*. All of America might be one *long mown lawn*. A *lawn* not *mown* grows *long*, she said: better a *long lawn*. Better a *long lawn* and a *mole*. Let the *lawman* have the *mown lawn*, she said. Or the *moron*, the *lawn moron*.

INTERESTING

My friend is interesting but he is not in his apartment.

Their conversation appears interesting but they are speaking a language I do not understand.

They are both reputed to be interesting people and so I'm sure their conversation is interesting, but they are speaking a language I understand only a little, so I catch only fragments such as "I see" and "on Sunday" and "unfortunately."

This man has a good understanding of his subject and says many things about it that are probably interesting themselves, but I am not interested because the subject does not interest me.

Here is a woman I know coming up to me. She is very excited, but she is not an interesting woman. What excites her will not be interesting, it will simply not be interesting.

At a party, a highly nervous man talking fast says many smart things about subjects that do not particularly interest me, such as the restoration of historic houses and in particular the age of wallpaper. Yet, because he is so smart and because he gives me so much information per minute, I do not get tired of listening to him.

Here is a very handsome English traffic engineer. The fact that he is so handsome, and so animated, and has such a fine English accent makes it appear, each time he begins to speak, that he is about to say something interesting, but he is never interesting, and he is saying something, yet again, about traffic patterns.

THE OLD DICTIONARY

I have an old dictionary, about one hundred and twenty years old, that I need to use for a particular piece of work I'm doing this year. Its pages are brownish in the margins and brittle, and very large. I risk tearing them when I turn them. When I open the dictionary I also risk tearing the spine, which is already split more than halfway up. I have to decide, each time I think of consulting it, whether it is worth damaging the book further in order to look up a particular word. Since I need to use it for this work, I know I will damage it, if not today, then tomorrow, and that by the time I am done with this work it will be in poorer condition than it was when I started, if not completely ruined. When I took it off the shelf today, though, I realized that I treat it with a good deal more care than I treat my young son. Each time I handle it, I take the greatest care not to harm it: my primary concern is not to harm it. What struck me today was that even though my son should be more important to me than my old dictionary, I can't say that each time I deal with my son, my primary concern is not to harm him. My primary concern is almost always something else, for instance to find out what his homework is, or to get supper on the table, or to finish a phone conversation. If he gets harmed in the process, that doesn't seem to matter to me as much as getting the thing done, whatever it is. Why don't I treat my son at least as well as the old dictionary? Maybe it is because the dictionary is so obviously fragile. When a corner of a page snaps off, it is unmistakable. My son does not look fragile, bending over a game or manhandling the dog. Certainly his body is strong and flexible, and is not easily harmed by me. I have bruised his body and then it has healed. Sometimes it is obvious to me when I have hurt his feelings, but it is harder to see how badly they have been hurt, and they seem to mend. It is hard to see if they mend completely or are forever slightly damaged. When the dictionary is hurt, it can't be mended. Maybe I treat the dictionary better because it makes no demands on me, and doesn't fight back. Maybe I am kinder to things that don't seem to react to me. But in fact my house plants do not seem to react much and yet I don't treat them very well. The plants make one or two demands. Their demand for light has already been satisfied by where I put them. Their second demand is for water. I water them but not regularly. Some of them don't grow very well because of that and some of them die. Most of them are strange-looking rather than nice-looking. Some of them were nice-looking when I bought them but are strange-looking now because I haven't taken very good care of them. Most of them are in pots that are the same ugly plastic pots they came in. I don't actually like them very much. Is there any other reason to like a houseplant, if it is not nice-looking? Am I kinder to something that is nice-looking? But I could treat a plant well even if I didn't like its looks. I should be able to treat my son well when he is not looking good and even when he is not acting very nice. I treat the dog better than the plants, even though he is more active and more demanding. It is simple to give him food and water. I take him for walks, though not often enough. I have also sometimes slapped his nose, though the vet told me never to hit him anywhere near the head, or maybe he said anywhere at all. I am only sure I am not neglecting the dog when he is asleep. Maybe I am kinder to things that are not alive. Or rather if they are not alive there is no question of kindness. It does not hurt them if I don't pay attention to them, and that is a great relief. It is such a relief it is even a pleasure. The only change they show is that they gather dust. The dust won't really hurt them. I can even get someone else to dust them. My son gets dirty, and I can't clean him, and I can't pay someone to clean him. It is hard to keep him clean, and even complicated trying to feed him. He doesn't sleep enough, partly because I try so hard to get him to sleep. The plants need two things, or maybe three. The dog needs five or six things. It is very clear how many things I am giving him and how many I am not, therefore how well I'm taking care of him. My son needs many other things besides what he needs for his physical care, and these things multiply or change constantly. They can change right in the middle of a sentence. Though I often know, I do not always know just what he needs. Even when I know, I am not always able to give it to him. Many times each day I do not give him what he needs. Some of what I do for the old dictionary, though not all, I could do for my son. For instance, I handle it slowly, deliberately, and gently. I consider its age. I treat it with respect. I stop and think before I use it. I know its limitations. I do not encourage it to go farther than it can go (for instance to lie open flat on the table). I leave it alone a good deal of the time.

FOCUSED FREE WRITES

1. Are these short stories, essays, monologs, or poems? How and why?
2. How are these pieces experimental? How do they challenge conventional narrative forms?
3. If these narratives are not plot based, if they do not move forward based on linear narrative concerns, then how are they organized or structured? What do they emphasize instead of plot?
4. Do any of these pieces have a theme? If so, what is it? How is it illustrated or supported in the text?

Chris Bachelder

Author of the novels *Bear v. Shark* and *U.S.!*, as well as short fiction and essays, Chris Bachelder writes stories that aren't stories, or are they? Included here, one appears as a newspaper article, one as Amazon reviews, and the third as a list of notes for a scientific report. However, these texts still convey a narrative, include characters, and use many of the elements of fiction. Here, Bachelder described for me why he writes experimental fiction:

> Most so-called experimental fiction writers are formalists—that is, writers who are interested in the constraints and possibilities of literary form. I am a great admirer of the realist narrative tradition, but what excites me as an artist is the overt manipulation of non-fictional forms to serve the purposes of fiction. There is an exciting friction (and comic potential) in the connection between the WHAT and HOW of a story. Fiction is a grand borrower and stealer of forms; it can use letters, scientific reports, diaries, email messages, confessions, lists. Looking up at my shelves now I see a book written in the form of a high school alumni newsletter, and another written as a collection of fast food restaurant response cards. When this kind of experimentation is done for its own sake, it can seem gimmicky and insubstantial. But when the form is fully integrated with the thematic and emotional components of the story, I think that experimentation can be exhilarating.

Like Davis, Bachelder is interested in the adventure of exploring forms. The stories that follow offer the exhilaration he describes. The first story appeared in *New Stories from the South* in 2006 and here, he describes his process:

> For "Blue Knights," I began with form, as I generally do. I was interested to find out what kind of story could be told in the form of a newspaper article, or what might happen when a strong authorial voice broke through journalistic style, convention, and standards of objectivity. I played sports in high school and later I covered a lot of games as a sportswriter. There is a glory and sadness to

small-town high school athletics, and I suppose I wanted to create a reporter who refused to narrow his report of a basketball game to the game itself.

As you read, consider how Bachelder captures the "glory and sadness" of small-town sports in this particular form.

Chris Bachelder

BLUE KNIGHTS BOUNCED FROM CVD TOURNEY

STARKE—It was perhaps a fitting end to a tumultuous and frustrating season for the Perlis High School boys' basketball team.

Friday night, in the first round of the Cedar Valley District Tournament, Perlis surrendered the game and its entire season—without firing a single shot.

Trailing Starke by a point with less than a minute to go, the Blue Knights had the ball but failed to attempt a shot before time expired, falling 64–63 to their cross-valley rivals.

"We just passed it and passed it," said Perlis coach Doug Way of the final 48 seconds. There must have been nine, ten, eleven passes there. Maybe more. I'll have to check the film. There was so much [frigging] passing. It was like a hot potato. I don't want it, you take it! Everybody touched it, but nobody wanted to step up and take that big shot. It's a thing now, a type of deal where I just want to throw up."

Perlis took a timeout with 48 seconds remaining, another timeout with 21 seconds remaining, and its third and final timeout with nine seconds left.

"Each time, we drew up a good play," said Way, whose daughter, Cassandra, was born in November without arms. "But I could see my guys were rattled, I could see the fear [in their faces and in their hearts]. These guys don't have any guts. They have two arms but it's a situation where they have no guts."

When the buzzer sounded, the ball was in the hands of Blue Knight senior captain Trevor Basham, who led the team in scoring with 19 points and whose mother and father sat in different sections of the gymnasium. "I got the ball with about four or five seconds left," said Basham, who sobbed inconsolably in the musty visitors' locker room after the game. "I was just scared to shoot. Just really scared. I kind of locked up. Then I tried to find someone to pass to, but it was too late."

"Winning is boring," said Clarence Block, my first editor, before he died alone at age 54 from a heart attack. "You want the story, go to the losers' locker room."

For most of the game, it looked like it was going to be the Blue Knights' night. Basham, whose father has been sleeping on a cot in the basement for about a year, scored 11 points in the third quarter and Perlis opened up a 59–46 lead with one quarter to go.

"[Golly Moses], I love that little girl of mine," said Way, rubbing away tears with the palm of his hand. "You can't tell me she's not perfect. To me, she's a perfect angel from Heaven."

Seldom-used reserve Nathan Kraft gave the Knights a spark off the bench by hitting two 3-pointers in the third quarter as Perlis improved on its six-point halftime lead. Kraft, a junior, has a funny-looking release, and both of his shots banked in hard off the glass. Many of the Starke students and parents jeered him and chanted "homo."

"It didn't really bother me," said Kraft, who does look like he might be gay. *I'm leaving this valley first chance I get*, he thought.

"Nathan should have started and he should have been playing the whole game," said Kraft's father, Nelson, after the game and pretty much after every game this season. "Way is an idiot. Way is a [frigged-up] idiot who couldn't coach a team of girls."

"Nelson, *please*," said Nelson's gaunt and mousy wife, Carol. But Starke roared back in the final quarter behind the strong interior play of the Cedar Valley District MVP, Josh Stetson, a fundamentally sound and nicely proportioned center who scored 13 in the quarter and finished with game-high totals in both points (24) and rebounds (14).

"We had no answer for Stetson," Way said of the Bobcats' 6'8" forward. "That kid is good. I always look for a reason to hate that guy and it's a deal where I can't find one. He seems like a nice kid and he's a heck of a player. But I have to say, our guys were cowardly on defense and the refs, Christ, don't even get me started on those [turds]."

Told that Stetson had set a CVD single-season scoring record with his performance, Basham said, "What do you want me to say? He's a stud. And he's a nice guy, too. I hear he's got a [turd] load of AP credit. News flash, Stetson is a model citizen. Next year, he'll be playing D-I ball while I'm on some intramural team at that mid-tier school I'll be lucky to get into with my test scores."

Told that he had snot in his nose from his crying jag, Basham said, "Oh, thank you."

With 6:34 remaining in the fourth quarter, Stetson tipped in a missed shot to break the CVD season scoring mark set by Perlis star Johnny Dill in 1978. Dill was not in attendance on Thursday. He lives in a trailer in the woods and rarely comes into town anymore. He makes dioramas, which are these little scenes in boxes.

"When I see people or when I get out into open spaces, my heart just starts racing and I feel like I'm going to pass out," said Dill in a rare interview conducted two years ago through an open window in his trailer. "I have my dogs and my dioramas. I do OK out here. You should go now."

Stetson then scored on Starke's next four possessions to pull the Bobcats to within four points at 61–57 with 3:43 remaining.

"I just want to thank my teammates and hopefully return to Starke after college and set up a car dealership," Stetson might have said to the throng of people surrounding him at the conclusion of the game.

The Blue Knights' second-leading scorer, sophomore guard Jeff Lassiter, who came into the tournament averaging 15.6 points per game, missed four free throws down the stretch and finished with just two points on 1-for-7 shooting and six turnovers.

"Lassiter was sleepwalking out there," said Way, who has guided Perlis to three consecutive 11–13 seasons. "He was a nonfactor, completely out of it. You could stare into his eyes and you just knew it was a thing where he wasn't there. Off the record? It's [coochie], I guarantee it."

"I've been struggling," said Lassiter, who earlier in the week touched junior Stephanie Conley's bare breast beneath her department-store blouse while the couple made out on the couch at Stephanie's house after school. "Stephanie took off her bra and I couldn't believe it. Don't write this down. After I touched her [boob], everything was just different. Do you know what I mean? Like everything just changed. I can't explain it. I went home and my mom and sister and me all had dinner, and they were talking to me but it was like they were five miles away. The way it felt in my hand. God, it's just like nothing is the same now. Do you know what I mean?"

After two missed free throws by Lassiter, Starke guard J. R. Stein, a Jewish player, hit a 3-pointer with 2:30 left to pull to 61–60. The Starke fans, many of whom were laid off from the canning factory earlier this winter, began stomping on the metal bleachers, and I think many of us felt the ancient gymnasium would crumble to the ground, killing us all. There are things I want to tell my ex-wife. There are things she needs to know before I go to my grave, and I wrote some of them down on my stat sheet.

"This game is a big deal for us," said one unemployed factory worker. "We hate Perlis. We hate Perlis and everything it stands for."

The Blue Knights silenced the crowd momentarily when center Donny Weddle got away with a travel and then hit a 17-foot fadeaway he had no business taking to give Perlis a 63–60 advantage.

"Obviously, that's a deal where that's not the shot we wanted in that situation," said Way. "That's a kid who has zero touch. But hell, at least he *shot* it. You can't score if you don't even shoot."

Weddle refused to talk to me or to the reporter from the *Starke Eagle* after the game. "No, we *lost*, grandma," he said into his cell phone, naked.

It may or may not have occurred to Donny, a senior, that he'll probably never play another game of organized basketball in his life. He'll gain weight and his feet will hurt all the time. He's a big guy. He'll have dreams at night, like I do, that he discovers that he somehow has one more year of high school basketball eligibility and he gets to put on the uniform again and play another season, but then he will wake up and see the fake varnished wood of his bedside table.

Stetson hit a pair of free throws to cut the lead to 63–62 with 2:02 left, and then 20 seconds later Lassiter turned the ball over on a double dribble.

"[Turd], I might have *triple* dribbled, if there's such a thing as that," said Lassiter, lying on the locker room bench and staring upward at the ceiling. None of today's players seem to wear a jockstrap, whereas when I played we all wore one.

"You try coaching kids who want to play basketball in *boxer shorts*," said Way, who conjectured that Stetson wore a jockstrap.

"Tell me what it feels like to do it," Lassiter said, "I mean, if her left [boob] felt that good, I just can't even imagine. Tell me what it's like."

"No," I said. I wanted to tell him that any act he could imagine committing with Stephanie or any other person could be either lovely or grotesque, depending on the context, but I didn't say anything.

After Lassiter's turnover, the Starke fans were out of their minds, and it was pretty clear to everyone in the old gym that Perlis was going to lose to the Bobcats again.

"Sexuality is on a continuum," Kraft said. "It's not this either/or thing."

Starke guard Chuck Jasper hit a driving layup with 48 seconds left to give the Bobcats their first lead since early in the first quarter.

That set up the Blue Knights' final possession, which resulted in three time-outs, 13 passes, and, as I mentioned at the top, zero shots.

"You suck," said a Starke fan as the Perlis players left the floor. "You're a bunch of skirts."

Starke advances to play the winner of Cambria and Emmitt in the semifinals of the Cedar Valley District Tournament.

"So we don't play again?" Lassiter asked.

Outside, after the game, the night was so cold it hurt your throat to breathe. The team bus idled depressingly. I remembered the way it smelled inside, the rips in the seats, the bad sandwiches that someone's mother made with Miracle Whip instead of mayonnaise.

From what I could gather, most of the Starke kids were going to hang out in the Hardee's parking lot.

And now it's pretty clear that the cedars along the road back to Perlis are all dying.

"It's a disease," said Fred Owen, a county extension agent. "There's nothing we can do about it."

MY BEARD, REVIEWED

Average Customer Rating: *** (Based on 9 reviews)

**** Must-see beard!!!

Reviewer: A. Dawson from San Antonio, TX, USA
This is the best beard I've seen all year. It's one of those beards where you just never want it to end. If you get a chance, CHECK OUT THIS BEARD. You won't be sorry. I guarantee it.

** Disappointing

Reviewer: Monster Man from Baltimore, MD, USA
I see a lot of beards, and I usually really like first beards, so I was excited about seeing Mr. Bachelder's beard, especially after a friend of mine recommended it to me. But I'm sorry to say that this beard was a big disappointment. You can see that it has potential, but it's a little patchy and it just isn't doing anything new or interesting.

**** Not for everyone

Reviewer: Melissa T. from Eugene, OR, USA
This is one of those beards that not everyone is going to love, but I think it will find a cult following. It's a really funny and quirky beard. It's not completely full, but that almost makes it better somehow. Yes it's uneven and things get stuck in it, but it's a first beard people! Congratulations, Mr. Bachelder, I can hardly wait for your next beard!!

***** AMAZING!!!

Reviewer: JD Vulture from Greenville, NC, USA
Oh my God this is an incredible beard!!! I saw a small part of Chris Bachelder's beard on the Internet and I just had to go see the whole thing. I was blown away. It's a hilarious beard, but it's also sad and touching. This girl beside me was crying because the beard was so emotional. I can't do it justice. Just do yourself a favor and see this beard. It's an instant classic, and I know you'll love it as much as I did.

* Don't believe the hype

Reviewer: Paul Russell from Lexington, KY, USA
I am baffled by the hype surrounding this beard. I decided to check the beard out after I read reviews calling it a "daring" beard, a "shockingly original" beard, "one of our best young beards." Some reviewers went so far as to compare it to Vonnegut's first beard. Well, nothing could be further from the truth. With Vonnegut, you never lose sight of the integrity and sincerity underlying the beard, but Bachelder's beard is just a tangled joke, and not even very funny, much less deep or substantive. Right now, the last thing this country needs is more smart-ass facial hair. At a time like this we need authentic beards. Bachelder's beard is the same beard we've been seeing for the last fifteen or twenty years, and it's getting old. Either do it right or shave.

*** Not great, not horrible

Reviewer: RW from Jacksonville, FL, USA
Let's not get carried away on either end. It's not a National Beard Award winner, but it's not trash, either. Bachelder's got a decent beard. It has a certain ragged charm, though I agree with others who have said it could have used a trim.

* pathetic

Reviewer: Jennifer K. from Rochester, NY, USA
I just can't believe what passes for a good beard these days. I teach junior high English, and I've seen better beards on my eighth-graders. Don't waste your time. I'll take Hemingway's beard every time over today's beards.

**** A first look at an up-and-coming beard

Reviewer: Night Train from Silver City, CO, USA
Even though Mr. Bachelder won't let you touch his beard, his beard will touch you!! See it TODAY!!!!

**** Surprisingly deep

Reviewer: M-Dog from Tempe, AZ, USA
I was prepared to hate this beard after I found out about the huge advance that Bachelder got for it. And to be honest, I didn't think much of the beard when I first saw it, and I almost didn't finish looking at it. But I stuck with it and I'm glad I did. This beard has a way of sneaking up on you. Before I knew it, I was

completely engrossed. It has a deceptively simple appearance, but this beard is actually very complicated and challenging. If you devote some time and careful attention to Bachelder's beard, it will pay you back, but you have to be willing to work.

NOTES TOWARD A LAY REPORT ON THE JOY DEBT

1. Joy Debt, over half century reigning model for joy/pain science, challenged by new evidence. Discoveries at frontiers of joy/pain research leading some scientists to adopt new theories of suffering
2. Lead: given nature of debt, we shud declare bankruptcy (tone?)
3. Dr. Bill Cromer, sr. researcher at the Martin-Collins Inst. of Despair: "It's just a really exciting time to be studying pain. What we're finding out is that pain may be unquantifiable, infinite, all-pervasive. It might even be possible now to speak of pain as part of the very stuff that makes up the universe."
4. Dr. Mary Anne Settle, Natl. Ctr. for the Study of Misery: "There's a danger in speaking prematurely, but I think we're on the verge of something very big. If these new findings are borne out, what we'll see is a paradigm shift in joy/pain science over the next five to ten years."
5. 1 yr. ago (8/12)—neighbors' child drowned in pool
6. Current debt model in place more than 60 years. 1936—Lucius Brant's definitive paper on Asymmetrical Model: pain exists far greater amts. than joy. Brant Asymmetrical Model (BAM) initially met w/skepticism but eventually won acceptance. Overturned trad. symmetrical (balanced) model: joy + pain exist in constant precise balance
7. Symm. model dev. by Simon Wells (UK) early 19th c.—any fluctuation in joy or pain, however small/large, necessarily + simultaneously accompanied by same degree fluctuation in counterpart. Thus: universe maintains perfect joy/pain symmetry at all times acc. to Wellsian model
8. Symm. Model simple, elegant. But Brant + others dislodged in 1940s by demonstrating pain far outstrips joy, suffering exists in sig. greater quantities than happiness/pleasure. Brant, '49: "The Law of Balance is a myth, a fiction.... Those who adhere to the ancient system are rather more like religious zealots than scientists. Those who are interested in truth and progress must undoubtedly see that ours is an asymmetrical universe."
9. Thru open windows still the crying + yelling at night nxt dr + Anna gone from our bed
10. Brant: Happiness remains frly constant while pain expands steadily, oft. precipitously. George Melvin, student of Brant, devised Melvin Pain Index (MPI) in '50s to quantify grief, calculate expansion, measure imbalance between j. + p.
11. Imbalance came to be known as JOY DEBT. Term coined by NYT science writer Maxwell Loots in 62
12. Generation of scientists following Brant argued humans might mitigate universal JD thru technology, medicine, social planning. Some said JD cud be eradicated—never widely believed in sci. comm.
13. Idea of severe but adjustable asymmetry has held sway for several decades

14. Floating, dead, a star-shaped boy in the sun
15. Nicholas.
16. **Recent discoveries challenge notion that humans can mitigate JD—also demonstrate self-correcting nature of science
17. On science, bootstrapping: BAM generated research prgrms that produced evidence that calls into question the model's own principles, assumptions—leads to revision of model, which leads to new forms of evidence, etc.
18. Dr. Lindsay Bahl-Smith, M-C Inst.: "I'm not sure it makes sense to continue speaking of the Joy Debt. The debt model or metaphor is not apt anymore. When we talk about the pain of the universe, we're not talking of something that can be quantified. We're not talking about something that can be reduced or, well, repaid."
19. Bahl-Smith's commts based on 3 recent discov. 1st involves research on atomic particles. Mich. team concluded in journal *J/P* that pain exists at atomic and sub-atomic levels
20. Team ldr Dr. Rachel Tomlin: "What we've found is fairly convincing evidence of sub-atomic suffering. One way of explaining the potentially awesome power contained within the atom is in terms of *anguish*."
21. 2 a.m.: Anna kneeling by black pool, staring
22. 2nd finding involves opp. extreme, deep space: Using most soph. detection equip. researchers picked up "pain waves" from far reaches of galaxy, perhaps neighboring gal.
23. Dr. David Sayers, ed. of *P/J* and head of Interstellar Grief Div. at Calif. Observatory: "We're starting to believe that suffering is part of the very fabric of the universe, as fundamental as time and space." Admits not sure about orig. of cosmic pain. Competing views. "The theory that I think is most likely true is that this energy was unleashed in the Big Bang." (Call BB the birth of pain.) "If this is so, the Big Bang might be regarded as an expression of pain so immense and total that it exceeds our current understanding. All we can say is that after the Big Bang, grief became one of the core elements of the cosmos. It pervades all space and time."
24. Music of spheres is dirge (too glib?)
25. Boy's father sits in driveway for hrs + Anna found him in bright pool
26. 3rd discovery challenging JD—Galax, VA—Otis Shepherd, mailman + amateur pain observer, claims saw hand-painted sign nailed to tree along gravel road. Sign:
    > lost Dog—
    > gold Lab
    > "Murphy"!
    > old + blind
27. State officials sent sci. team to investigate. Team will pub. report in forthcoming *Quart. Journal of World Pain*
28. Cromer: "We're not sure about the Galax evidence, but if it checks out to be true—if there is really someone out there in rural Virginia looking for Murphy—then that just fits in with all the rest we're learning about grief. It's irreducible. It's measureless."
29. 3 a.m.: alone in bed + smell of bread baking

30. Sayers: "If we're right about all of this, then we'll have to re-think the universe. Everything we know, or think we know, about the universe might be reinterpreted within this framework, this Pain Paradigm, as some are calling it. Black holes might be seen as vast engines of sorrow, entropy can be seen as the tendency of all closed systems to move toward despair and wretchedness, quantum weirdness may be recast as quantum sadness, erratic and paradoxical. The answer to the so-called GUT [grand unifying theory] or TOE [theory of everything] that physicists and mathematicians have long sought might very well be found in pain."

31. Ldr of Norwegian team wrkng on pain waves comm. suicide last month (7th pain researcher in 14 months)

32. Pool: a yr. w/out cleaning—a layer of leaves on dark water + the rotten smell thru window

33. Dr. Paul Thornwood, Chair, Dept. of Abject Studies, Penn State: "Some of us are not quite ready to bury the debt model. And even if it is to be superceded, as most scientific models eventually are, we need to recognize what an extraordinarily fecund program it has been."

34. Back in bed, slow breath, slatted shadow on her hip + neck—her pulse on my lips + her hands on me then, warm from the oven—come back, Anna.

35. "Come back and never leave."

36. Dr. Elaine Mays, Prof. of astron. + beauty, Univ. of Chicago: "Look, this new evidence about suffering simply confirms what many of us have long thought and felt. It's a disturbing conclusion, yes, but it's not shocking or counterintuitive. Now sure, I could go on ahead and make my career in pain. Many scientists are doing exactly that. But I'm more interested in how this new information will lead us to think in new ways about grace and happiness."

FOCUSED FREE WRITES

1. How are Bachelder's pieces experimental?
2. How are these texts narrative? What stories are told? What characters are described? What literary elements are employed?
3. All of these works parody other written forms. What are they? How do these pieces revise those forms? What are the effects of these revisions?
4. So what? Does Bachelder make a point here? Have a theme? What is it?

Knowing Where We Come From

The Experimental Poetry of Gertrude Stein

Gertrude Stein was one of the key figures in the "Lost Generation" of American artists living as expatriates in Paris early in the twentieth century. She was tremendously influential on the artists of her era, including writer Ernest Hemingway and painter Pablo Picasso. For example, in an excerpt entitled "Objects" from her lengthy three-part poem *Tender Buttons: Objects, Food,*

Rooms, Stein challenges conventional conceptions of poetry in juxtaposing words by sounds and rhythm rather than by sense. Capturing "moments of consciousness," she challenges poetic structure and forces the reader to confront his or her understanding of language when facing it out of context.

Want to Know More?

A Suggested Reading List of Experimental Writers

People You May Know
Charles Bukowski
William S. Burroughs
Don Delillo
Dave Eggers
Jack Kerouac
Chuck Palahniuk
David Foster Wallace

People You Might Want to Know
Kathy Acker
Martin Amis
Gloria Anzaldua
Margaret Atwood
John Barth
Donald Barthelme
T.C. Boyle
Italo Calvino
Henry Miller
Thomas Pynchon
Salman Rushdie
Kurt Vonnegut

Knowing Where We Come From
Charles Baudelaire
Samuel Beckett
Albert Camus
T.S. Eliot
Joseph Heller
Franz Kafka
James Joyce
Stephen Mallarme
Gabriel Garcia-Marquez
Laurence Sterne
Oscar Wilde
Virginia Woolf

Writing About Your Experience with Literature

Develop a piece of experimental literature

Working in groups, pairs, or individually, compose a poem, play, or piece of short fiction. Consider first what meaning you want to convey to your readers. Determine a theme or message you might like to deliver. For example, what conventional belief or status quo notion would you like to challenge? What assumption would you like to force people to reconsider? Next, determine how best to convey this message. What form will challenge this assumed belief? How will you shake your reader from complacent viewing to actively engage with your text?

Research a significant figure in the world of experimental literature

In groups, pairs or individually, do some research into one of the writers listed in the Want to Know More box. Find some examples of their work to read. Write a brief paper or develop a presentation about one experimental writer. Address the following questions: How is this writer's work experimental? What conventions does the writer challenge and how does he or she challenge them? How does the writer force the reader to revise, rethink, and re-envision an idea, literature, or way of reading?

PART FOUR

RESEARCH FOR WRITING

I n this five-chapter section, the research process is thoroughly outlined and modeled. Entire chapters are broken down into the detailed steps necessary for establishing a topic, stating a thesis, finding and evaluating sources, understanding critical perspectives, integrating primary and secondary sources, and using the MLA style of documentation. The progression of a sample student project is used to demonstrate the assigned tasks, including the proposal, an annotated bibliography, the research paper itself, and the works cited list. The section also introduces a step-by-step process for developing either a literary or historical research project. Three critical casebooks offer excerpts from literary criticism to showcase the acts of synthesizing and incorporating criticism. With detailed attention to everything from brainstorming on a topic to the logistics of citing sources, Part IV provides guidance for every step of the research project.

13

DEVELOPING A TOPIC AND STATING A THESIS

In earlier chapters, you were asked to compose formal responses, interpretations, analyses, arguments, and comparisons of literary works. In developing these projects, you wrote informally through Focused Free Writes or other kinds of prewriting to determine your topic, and then you used close reading to make your case about the meaning of a text. Another kind of formal project you may be asked to produce is a literary analysis or interpretation that includes research. This chapter and the four that follow will take you through the different steps required to develop an argument supported by close reading and research, an essential skill for any well-educated person. This illustration will also be of use as you develop topics in other courses, many of which will also require you to write arguments based on research. Even though the kinds of sources you consult will be different in each field of study, researched writing is valued across the curriculum. If you need additional information to complete this or any other research paper, you can find expanded discussions of research and citation through your university library, your handbook, and the Pearson online resources.

As we discussed in Chapter 1, it is important to develop your own individual writing process. Similarly, you will want to develop a personal process for research. Writing a research paper is a hefty project made up of a number of steps. Above all, it takes time and organization. You will want to create your own personal step-by-step process, thereby learning to write and research more successfully and most efficiently.

A sample process might look something like this:

- **Reading.** In order to identify a possible text for focus, your first step should involve re-reading the text in question, marking it for significant moments and compelling ideas. Erin Christian, whose writing and research process on the poem "One Art" will illustrate the research chapters, returned to Elizabeth Bishop's poem "One Art" and reread it multiple times. She made a photocopy of the poem so she could mark it up with questions about the poem and comments about its meaning.
- **Question, Topic, and Thesis Development.** The next step is determining what you might have to say about the work. What questions do you have

about what the text means or how it means? What is a moment, scene, or character that merits focus? What assertion can you make about the meaning of the text? In answering these questions, you begin to focus your research. Erin was curious about why Bishop used repetition in her poem. She found herself commenting on and questioning the pattern of the poem. She wondered how this repetitive pattern worked to convey the poem's meaning.

- **Research and Information Gathering.** Once you have a text and topic, you can use library databases to gather resources. After you find a number of articles about your work, you can read them and take notes about them to determine how they can provide support for your argument. Erin found a few articles about the poem and a collection of the letters of Bishop of the same title as the poem. It was challenging to find any substantial commentary that focused on this single poem so she had to really dig. She did turn up some brief analyses in critical books on women poets.

- **The Reading/Research Dialectic.** As you are researching and reading, you will be able to fine-tune and focus your thesis. Sometimes reading more will mean you must go back and follow up on resources cited by other critics. Sometimes you will have to revise your thesis in light of new findings. The cycle of reading and searching can seem eternal; however, at some point, you will move on to the writing. Erin thought she had completed her research when her classmate ran across a source that offered a number of books she had not found. She went back to read these sources and found them stronger than those she had initially identified. She was excited to employ these critics to make her argument stronger.

- **Understanding Critical Perspectives.** You might be able to identify a particular slant or focus in the research on your text. Critics might focus on how the author's life is reflected in the work or may emphasize a particular character, symbol, or conflict in the text. Erin was able to determine that most critics did discuss the poem as a villanelle while talking about it in comparison to Bishop's other works and her larger poetic vision.

- **Drafting Your Ideas.** At a certain point (and sometimes that moment might seem arbitrary and be induced by deadlines), you must put the research down and begin the writing process. Erin found herself enjoying what others were saying about the poem and anxious about writing about it herself. Since she had done thorough research, however, she found she was able to sit down and draft fairly confidently.

- **Integrating and Documenting Primary and Secondary Sources.** When you write a research paper, imagine yourself entering into a conversation with others who wrote about the text at hand. It is important to involve these previous critics in your conversation—to gracefully engage them in your own project. Integrating your sources can seem intimidating (see Chapter 16 for details). Erin, for example, found herself continually checking and rechecking how she punctuated her quotations.

- **Revising and Editing Your Draft.** Once you have a draft, you are going to want to revise it for purpose, structure, support, and clarity. However, you may also want to involve others in the revision process: peers, your instructor, a writing center tutor, and so on. Even though her friend Leona is a Law and Society major, Erin had her read her draft and give feedback. She helped her see things she had overlooked.

The chapters that follow will examine each part of this process in depth.

Choosing a Text

Your first step in developing a research project is deciding on the poem, play, story, or essay you will write about. Select a text you want to work with, one that interests you enough so that you will want to spend time with it, investigate it, and think about it.

You may be considering several works. To decide which one to focus on, you might want to reread the texts and formulate questions about them. Look back at your informal and formal writing and see what ideas pop up. Which text do you have the most interest in or most interesting questions about? What do you want to know to understand the text better? Do you want to persuade someone what this text means? Now is also a good time to schedule a conference with your instructor to discuss possible directions.

FOCUSED FREE WRITE

If you are having trouble choosing a text, look back at the works you have read this semester. Do a focused free write in response to the following questions to discover your interests.

1. Which ones have stayed with you? What characters continue to whisper in your ear? Which stories are you still reminded of? What bits of dialog or lines of poetry still resonate for you?
2. Which ones did you walk away from class thinking more about? Which class discussions of a work engaged or irritated you?
3. Which ones did you tell someone else about?

STUDENT WRITER In Erin's Words: On Choosing a Text...

No matter whether fiction, nonfiction, plays, or poetry is available for me to write on at the end of a given term, I always look for a text that I can relate to in some way. If there is a line, character, or scene in a text that strikes a familiar chord with me, I generally want to explore the text further to see if I can prove that the meaning that first glimmered out to me is really what I perceive it to be. If I feel strongly about connecting to meaning in a text, then I become excited about sharing my interpretation with others through writing.

Because of personal preference, I always jump at an opportunity to write about poetry. Poems are often like compact riddles or puzzles, and I look at a chance to write about a poem as a chance to prove that I can tease out meaning from the complex structure of the poem. So if there is a poem that has an image, line, or stanza that I feel I can relate to, then I become excited about pulling apart the puzzle to develop my own interpretation.

Read. Reread. Read Again.

Once you have your chosen text, read that work. Reread it. Then read it again. Look back at the discussion about marking a text in Chapter 2. Mark up the work. Ask questions. Make comments. Identify significant scenes, moments, lines, people, or objects that are emphasized. Write in the margins or take notes alongside your reading. You might consider the following:

- What is the theme of the text?
- What is the most important plot point? What moment or scene stands out?
- Are there any characters who are particularly interesting or significant? Identify any characters that are surprisingly similar or different. Is there a crucial plot point or speech by a character that stands out?
- Are there any objects, symbols, or motifs that seem meaningful or memorable?
- Are there any stylistic patterns of note? Do you notice any repetitions? Are there any words or lines that bear investigation?
- Who is the narrator? Is the point of view distinctive?
- Why is the work set when and where it is? Could you find out more about the setting to help you understand the meaning better?
- What questions do you have? What information would you need to enrich your understanding of this text? What do you want to find out more about?
- In your re-reading, did you notice something that you and your classmates did not notice the first time through?

The best research projects begin with a question about the text that arouses your curiosity.

FOCUSED FREE WRITE

Respond to some of the preceding questions by writing several sentences on what could lead you to decide on a particular work on which to write a research paper. Identify as well as you can which aspects of the work spark your curiosity.

STUDENT WRITER In Erin's Words: On Reading and Re-reading...

In this case, it only takes me one full read-through to come to the understanding that the major theme of "One Art" is dealing with loss. Two opposite approaches to loss, that of mastery and that which constitutes loss as a disaster, are presented through the end-rhyme repetition throughout the poem. Another motif of this villanelle is that the examples of loss begin as trivial daily losses and, as the poem moves toward becoming a first person narrative, the examples grow in importance and scale until the poem ends with the loss of a loved one.

While the identity of the narrator is not explicit, certain clues within the text of the poem suggest Bishop as a likely candidate for the voice of the speaker. If Bishop is indeed to be interpreted as the narrator, questions arise as to who the "you" is in the final stanza. Only this "you" has brought Bishop to the point of contemplating loss as disaster, yet the identity of the "you" is not clearly revealed. To perhaps uncover possible identities of the narrator and the "you," research into Bishop's personal life would be necessary. The main thing that I was left wanting to know more about after reading the poem was the identity of the "you" and the circumstances revolving around the loss of the loved one in the poem.

Posing a Research Question

The next step is determining what you might have to say about the work. This may work best by beginning with a preliminary research question. These questions may be "what," "why," or "how" questions. They may focus on the work itself or examine the text's context. However, the most important thing is that these questions are not simple "yes" or "no" questions. They should demand greater engagement and deeper investigation. They should set out to solve a problem, in a way. For example, Erin considered the following questions:

- What does "One Art" mean? How is it trying to saying something different from what it seems to say?
- Why is the poem written in this pattern? How does the repetition relate to the meaning of the poem?
- Why is the poem ordered in the way it is? Why does one stanza follow the next in this particular order?
- Why is *(Write it!)* in the last line?
- What was going on in Elizabeth Bishop's life to inspire her to write this poem?
- Is this similar to or different from Bishop's other poetry? Was she influenced by any other writers?

FOCUSED FREE WRITE

After looking back at your reading notes, create a jot list—or a Free Write listing all of the possible research questions that might interest you. Don't limit this list; rather, brainstorm all possible questions. Read over your list and circle the question or questions you find most intriguing.

Answering Your Question with a Tentative Thesis

Once you have a question you want to pursue, try to answer it for yourself through close reading the poem, play, story, or essay. To help determine a direction for your thesis, pay attention to and take notes in response to some of the previous questions during your close reading. This preliminary answer, or tentative thesis, should be in the form of a statement. It should be an assertion, a specific claim you are staking. It is not enough to write: "This story is interesting." Instead, you should make a case: "Chopin's 'Story of an Hour' uses irony to pique the reader's interest and build suspense and surprise in the story." For further discussion, see Chapter 3 "Shaping a Thesis: Constructing a Statement."

FOCUSED FREE WRITE

Make a statement about the work in answer to one of the questions you asked. The statement should be constructed as an assertion or something you want to prove. The statement will be the first draft of your tentative thesis statement. You may later revise it as you conduct research, but it will give you a starting point and a means to focus.

STUDENT WRITER In Erin's Words: On Constructing a Tentative Thesis...

When I begin to construct my thesis statement, I always think back to my original reasons for picking the text and focus on the meaning that I want to tease out first. What interested me about it? What questions did I want answered? I then list the answers to these questions out and pick around 2 or 3 to focus on during my argument.

Once I have established for myself what I want to prove about the meaning of the text, I then begin to focus on what devices the author uses to convey that meaning. In poetry especially, did the author use any repetition or figurative language? Did they manipulate the form of a sonnet, villanelle, or even haiku to get meaning across? To finally begin a thesis statement, I take my options concerning what I want to prove about the meaning of the work and assert that the author uses structural methods A, B, and C to convey such meaning.

Conducting Preliminary Research

You might want to do a bit of preliminary research at this point. Search your school's library catalog or an online database to see how many "hits" you get when you enter the author's name, title, and a key word related to your topic. Do you find thousands of articles or a few hundred? You may want to choose a text or topic that allows for focused research. For example, when a student researcher used the MLA database online and plugged in Shakespeare and the character Hamlet, she found over 3000 sources. The research question about the play *Hamlet* needs to be more focused, perhaps by looking at Ophelia as a foil to Hamlet. By searching using the terms Hamlet AND Ophelia, just over 100 results appear. In Erin's preliminary database search, she located fewer than 100 on Bishop's poem "One Art," a manageable number to start with. Preliminary research can help you determine whether you have a manageable and focused topic and tentative thesis.

A preliminary search can also introduce you to the range of approaches to your topic. As you scroll through the titles listed as results for your search, you might identify particular patterns and recurring themes. For example, in reflecting on the Hamlet and Ophelia titles, the researcher realized that topics like madness, sexuality, and gender recur. This brief overview can offer a general idea of the plausibility of your topic. A few critics seem to compare Hamlet and Ophelia, but quite a few do not. Ideally, your topic should be manageable—with a reasonable number of hits, supportable—with critics who address the same issue, yet original—with not too many addressing precisely the same topic. Of course, your preliminary search will give you only a general sense based on browsing titles. The next chapter, however, will explore searching more in depth.

FOCUSED FREE WRITE

Do a preliminary search using your author and title. How many hits do you get? Scroll through the titles found through your search. What are some of these articles or books about? When critics write about your work, what do they focus on?

Once I have a tentative thesis, I pluck a couple of key words from it, including of course the title of the text that I am working with, and start at article databases. If I find too many articles popping up on my topic, I try to narrow the search field by making my search even more specific to my thesis. On the other hand, if I think I have found just enough to warrant a further look, I bookmark the articles and begin reading the abstracts to get an idea as to what they are about. Some databases, such as JSTOR, will actually highlight your search words within the text of the article. This can be a big help when doing a quick scan through to see if the article is actually discussing aspects of my search keywords that will be helpful to me.

Once I feel that I have found an adequate amount of support from article databases, I then begin searching my university's library online catalog for books. I find titles that seem to be geared toward subjects that would be of aid to me, and then I see if there is an option to view the book's table of contents. That alone has saved me countless minutes searching the shelves only to find books that sound promising but are actually worthless to my cause. Once I feel that I have a list of books that suits my needs, I run down to the library and browse through them before checking out the ones that I feel will be the most helpful.

Assignment: Drafting a Proposal

A proposal can be a useful tool for articulating your developing project. You may be required to submit a proposal, or you may want your instructor to review your proposal to see if you are on the right track or to ask for advice on references. In a proposal, you might do the following:

- Name and briefly summarize the text you are examining.
- Articulate your proposed thesis.
- Describe what evidence you currently have to support this thesis. What did you discover in your close reading that can help make your case?
- Discuss your plan for research. What databases will you use? Write out the steps you will take in your search.
- Discuss your preliminary research, giving an overview of the range of topics based on your cursory search. Situate your project in terms of the range of current research. Based on your preliminary reflections,

(continued)

your project should be plausible. It should react to current research without parroting it directly. How is your project unique when compared to what else is out there? Are you synthesizing a debate popular in current research? Have you identified a gap in the research that should be examined? While you will not be able to answer these questions completely at this time, you will want to state what you know at this point.

In essence, your proposal can act as a kind of hypothesis or working introduction. It can force you to begin the process of drafting your paper and can demand you fine-tune your idea. Your proposal will likely be several paragraphs in length. You can imagine it as something you might return to or revise once you have more information. A proposal can be useful at any of the beginning stages of a project as it forces you to crystallize your thinking and communicate it to someone else.

Sample Student Paper

Erin Christian's biography can be found on page 567.

Erin Christian

A Research Proposal

Elizabeth Bishop addresses the theme of loss in her villanelle "One Art" through the motif of a lesson to her readers. Encouraging her audience to practice the "art of losing," Bishop uses the two rhyming sounds of the villanelle form, evident in the repetition of "master" and "disaster," to promote the idea that losing is a common human habit, in which countries and keys can be lost with equal ease, and that the loss of a person's companion is the closest thing to disaster that can be known. Initially, Bishop attempts to mute the pain of her loss with irreverence, but this stance gradually falls apart.

In my paper, I plan to show that Bishop means for readers to become aware of the shifts of mood regarding loss in the poem through her manipulation of the sound scheme, enjambment, and syntax; the shift from third person to first person; and, in the final stanza, the disruption of the poem's rhythm and the introduction of parenthetical asides. Through analyzing the text closely in my reading and rereading, I discovered that Bishop puts the structure of the villanelle to work for her as she presents the various takes on loss that echo throughout the poem. Research into the methods used by Bishop, such as point of view shifts and repetition within the rhyme scheme, has shown that Bishop's construction of the poem's very structure leaves room for layers of interpretation of loss; I plan to use this research to help me prove that Bishop means for the poem to highlight the impact of the loss of love as something, contrary to what the initial mood of the poem implies, difficult to master. Based on my preliminary research, there seem to be

limited discussions about this specific poem so mine should
be original. Most of the research addresses biography or other
poems or books of poetry. There is quite a bit of gender
criticism as well so I imagine I might incorporate some of these
analyses.

The chapters that follow will build on your work here. You will tackle finding
and evaluating sources, understanding critical perspectives, integrating and
documenting primary and secondary sources, as well as drafting and revising
your final paper.

14

FINDING AND EVALUATING SOURCES

Once you have your text and topic, you will want to begin searching for sources. The first step should be visiting your university library, either in person or virtually through your computer. If you have not already participated in a library orientation, you can save yourself quite a bit of time by doing so. Your local librarians can introduce you to useful resources and their locations since each library is set up a little bit differently. You will also want to use your local reference desk as a resource when you need to solve problems during your process. With this Pearson textbook, you also have access to My Literature Lab and Research Navigator to supplement your on-campus resources. Use the access code that came with this textbook to use these online resources.

Considering Research Sources

As you work on your research project, you are going to consult two kinds of sources: **primary sources** and **secondary sources.** The work you are going to write about is your **primary source** or **primary material.** My primary source might be Susan Glaspell's play *Trifles* or Kate Chopin's "Story of an Hour." Erin's primary source is Elizabeth Bishop's poem "One Art." According to the *MLA Handbook,* primary research "is the study of a subject through firsthand observation" (3). Your work in analyzing the text at hand constitutes primary research.

In addition to studying your primary source, you will be looking for **secondary sources,** that is, works in which others discuss your primary source or discuss matters related to your primary source. Examples of secondary sources can include books or articles about your primary source, and you should expect to cite both books and articles in your paper. Any historical, biographical, or critical document used to support your claims can be considered a secondary source. This chapter will focus on your selection of reliable secondary sources.

Your tentative thesis will determine the kind of research you might engage in. For this project, it is most likely that your research will lead you in the following directions:

- **Literary Criticism.** If you are undertaking an analytical argument about a particular text or a pair of texts in order to make a case about its (or their) meaning, you will want to consult literary criticism to see how other critics have interpreted the poem, play, story, or essay you are studying. Erin is undertaking literary criticism in analyzing how the form of "One Art" reinforces the poem's theme.

- **Historical or Cultural Context.** You might try to explain the meaning of your text in its appropriate historical or cultural context. This would necessitate understanding the setting of the work and consulting history books, biographies, newspapers, magazines, or other cultural documents to inform the meaning of your work. For example, a student might try to understand the "rest cure" that Gilman was discussing in "The Yellow Wallpaper."
- **Both Approaches.** You might find yourself combining the literary approach with the historical-cultural approach. One student might want to look at the critical reception of Williams's play *The Glass Menagerie*.

The approach you take will determine the kinds of resources you will consult. Therefore, again, it can be very useful to solicit specific help about your particular library's resources.

Beginning Your Research and Developing Search Terms

The first step in beginning your research is developing search terms. Books are situated in libraries according to the Library of Congress Classification System. Each book has a specific call number that begins with certain letters. For the purposes of this project, you might want to know that Language and Literature is shelved under P, with British literature located at PR and American literature at PS. Within these categories, books are arranged chronologically by century, topically by genre, and alphabetically by subject and author. Each book has a particular call number that places it in the right spot in the P section. For example, when searching for books at the library on Elizabeth Bishop, Erin finds them in the vicinity of *PS3503.I785*. You might want to locate the section of the library devoted to the text you are working on. Browse through the titles there and see if any strike you as useful for your project.

You will also want to identify appropriate Library of Congress Subject Headings (LCSH) for your topic for the most precise searches. It is important to know the LCSH for your topic because indexes list topics in different ways. If I wanted to go to the movies, I would not look up "movies" in the Yellow Pages or even "movie theatre." Instead, I would need to look up "theatres—movies" according to the Yellow Pages terminology. Knowing the library's terminology can also be infinitely helpful.

Subject headings can be found in the Library of Congress Subject Heading (LCSH) reference book in your local library or online at http://authorities. loc.gov/. You can also identify the appropriate subject heading through a preliminary search in your own library's catalog.

- Start with a keyword search using the author or title you are focusing on.
- Browse through the results list looking for sources that might be useful.
- Notice the Subject or Descriptors listed in those records and note the terms used.
- Search again using this precise terminology or use the hyperlink to the appropriate LCSH term.

Keyword searches allow you to use natural language for a broader search, and they can lead you to more precise subject searches. For this project, you might begin with a keyword search for your author, title, or subject and then identify the search heading standardized for a subject search by libraries. For example, after using *Bishop, Elizabeth* as my keyword, I found the subject heading <u>Bishop, Elizabeth, 1911–1979</u> and the subject heading for criticism on her work, <u>Bishop, Elizabeth, 1911–1979 Criticism and interpretation</u>. Or I might enter in the important words in my author's name and title as keywords to determine the subject. When I enter *Faulkner AND Emily AND Rose,* I learn that the appropriate subject heading is <u>Faulkner, William, 1897–1962. Rose for Emily</u>. Once you have these subject headings, you know you are entering the appropriate terms and can search more efficiently.

Whether you are using your library's catalog or an academic database, you might begin by entering the author's name as a subject heading or the Library of Congress Subject Heading as a subject search term; for example, try *Welty, Eudora* or *Faulkner, William*. Search the subheadings (characters, criticism and interpretation, title of a specific work) attached to your author's name for your topic. When searching for criticism on Elizabeth Bishop, I might cast a wider net by using her name as my search term. However, if I were searching for criticism on Tennessee Williams, a writer on whom there is a great deal of criticism, I might limit my search by combining author and title of the work and use the Library of Congress Subject Heading <u>Williams, Tennessee, 1911–1983. Glass menagerie.</u>

Keep a list of useful subject headings or keyword terms you have tried as well as those you would like to try. Devote a legal pad, a section of a notebook, or a document in your computer to each project to keep track of the search terms you checked, the number of hits received, notes on useful information, and a "to do" list of searches that need to be done.

Interlibrary Loan

While some libraries may have larger collections than others, no library will have everything; therefore, it is important to start early on your research to locate and obtain the sources you need. Through interlibrary loan, your local librarians can work to find the sources you need in a few days or weeks. Request sources you cannot find locally while there is still plenty of time before your deadline.

Locating Background Information

You may want to begin your research by locating background information about your author. In that case, some of the following materials may be of use to you.

Reference Books and Guides

Talk to your reference librarian. He or she will help you locate the reference section of your library and browse the appropriate sources for your project. You may start by consulting encyclopedias or dictionaries such as the *Encyclopedia of the Novel*, the *New Princeton Encyclopedia of Poetry and Poetics*, the *Reference*

Guide to Short Fiction, or *The New York Public Library Literature Companion*. For example, the *Dictionary of Literary Biography* is made up of over 300 volumes organized by topic and time period such as British Poets 1880–1914, German Fiction Writers 1914–1945, American Newspaper Journalists 1901–1925, and so on. Each volume consists of general summaries about the lives and works of writers. You may find some of these volumes in your library's holdings. While these entries are general and offer more summary than criticism, they can be a good starting point for understanding the general knowledge about your topic. Sources like this will inform your understanding more than they will provide specific information for your paper. In other words, these kinds of references will most likely be "works consulted" in your project, not "works cited." Your library's reference section may also hold research guides such as the *Literary Research Guide: A Guide to Reference Sources for the Study of Literatures in English and Related Topics* by James Harner, *A Reference Guide for English Studies* by Michael Marcuse or the *Oxford Guide to Library Research* by Thomas Mann, and these resources can really guide you in your search for useful and reliable references.

Search Your Library's Online Catalog

Look in the section of the library devoted to your work and see if you find any books that offer an introduction or a guide to your author or work. Sometimes the books published by Twayne Publishers, for example, can give you a general overview of the author and background for the text you are studying.

Online Literary Index

It is an excellent idea to use Gale's Literary Index (www.galenet.com), a master index to the major literature products published by Gale that includes a number of reference books such as the *Dictionary of Literary Biography* and imprints from Scribner's Sons, St. James Press, and Twayne Publishers. The books found here will offer you biographical profiles as well as excerpts and citations of other critical sources.

Web Resources

As will be discussed later in this chapter, reliable web resources can be tricky to identify. When conducting research at the library or through the library databases, you can be fairly confident in the reliability of your sources; however, it can be frustrating for new researchers on their own to find online sources that can be trusted. But they are out there, and through resources like Research Navigator's Link Library for Literature, you could identify reliable and maintained web resources like *Voice of the Shuttle: Web Page for Humanities Research* (http://vos.ucsb.edu/), university pages, publisher pages, and pages by authorities like the Modern American Poetry Society (http://www.english.uiuc.edu/maps/) or the Academy of American Poets (www.poets.org). Bartleby.com can also offer access to a number of reference sources as well as full texts of literary works.

Indexes and Databases

Your library may subscribe to useful databases or indexes that can help you begin your search. In fact, many of the most useful websites are only accessible with a subscription through your institution's library. Using a terminal at your library or a special student password for accessing your library's databases from home, you can search your library's listings for electronic indexes or databases like *Literature OnLine Reference Edition*, the *Literature Resource Center*, or specialized databases such as the *African American Biographical Database* for general biographical information as well as some literary criticism.

Subject Guides

Subject guides available in or through your local library direct you to the information resources in major teaching areas and can be an incredibly useful starting point for researching a subject. You will want to see if your library has subject guides for research locally. Our local university has a useful listing of accessible resources for literary criticism: http://library.armstrong.edu/subjectguides.html. Or take a look at MIT's Subject Guide for Literature: http://libraries.mit.edu/guides/subjects/literature/index.html. While many of the listed resources are available at or through MIT, your library can help you obtain useful resources accessible through your local institution.

Bibliographies

A good researcher learns how to save time by capitalizing on the work of other researchers. Always read the bibliographies of sources you consult. Write down any sources that could be of use to you. You might run across a source that does not seem useful at all, but check the bibliography anyway. That writer could direct you to a much more useful source. Furthermore, you can locate specialized bibliographies through your catalog searches or reference sections at your local library. While a bibliography is a list of citations that appear at the end of a paper, article, chapter or book, there are also books entirely made up of bibliographies. These are usually compilations of citations on a particular subject or a particular author and may include helpful annotations summarizing the content of the citations.

Locating Literary Criticism

Literary critics examine **how** the text in question makes meaning—in other words, they analyze texts, just as you have been doing in this course. However, literary critics are experts in the field with academic credentials whose job it is to write about authors and literature. It can be challenging to read literary criticism because of the advanced level of the criticism and the use of jargon particular to the field of study. However, with patience and persistence when researching and reading, you should be able to identify useful resources:

Reference Books and Guides

In the reference section of your of your library, you will be able to locate reference guides or online sources of those guides that offer citations or excerpts of significant literary criticism such as *Contemporary Literary Criticism* if your author is living or was alive after 1960; *Twentieth-Century Literary Criticism* if your author died after 1900 but before 1960; *Nineteenth-Century Literature*

Criticism, Readers' Guide to Literature in English; or guides organized by genre such as in the lists below.

Selected Guides by Genre:

> ### Guides to Criticism of Fiction
> *Critical Survey of Long Fiction*
> *Critical Survey of Short Fiction*
> *Short Story Criticism*
>
> ### Guides to Criticism of Poetry
> *Critical Survey of Poetry*
> *Poetry Criticism*
> *Poetry Explication*
>
> ### Guides to Criticism of Drama
> *Dramatic Criticism Index*
> *A Guide to Critical Reviews*
> *New York Times Theatre Reviews*

Once you find a list of citations that seem promising, use your library's online catalog or interlibrary loan options to locate these sources.

Search Your Library's Online Catalog

Identify the Library of Congress Subject Heading for Criticism and Interpretation on your author and determine the LC classification number. Once you have identified this location in your library, go and browse the titles looking for texts that can relate to your project. You may find edited collections of literary criticism under titles like *Faulkner* and *New Perspectives* or something similar like *Critical Perspectives* or *Critical Interpretations*. Titles like this contain a collection of a dozen or so essays. You may find a few useful resources in a volume like this.

Web Resources

Return to the literary index discussed above, www.galenet.com, and identify potentially useful citations. Another good starting point to find literary criticism is the *Internet Public Library* (http://www.ipl.org/div/litcrit), where you can search for criticism based on the title and author of the work you are writing about. Consult the Online Literary Criticism Collection. Be sure to look both by author and title, since different resources are listed under each. The *Voice of the Shuttle: Web Page for Humanities Research* (http://vos.ucsb.edu) is also a useful annotated guide to literary resources online. Jack Lynch's *Literary Resources on the Net* (http://andromeda.rutgers.edu/~jlynch/Lit/) is a collection of links to appropriate literary resources as well. Through Yahoo!, you can select from a menu of categories and follow the appropriate paths to avoid the plethora of hits you might get when entering Kate Chopin directly in Yahoo! and Google with records including syllabi, books for sale, and papers to plagiarize. Instead, customize your search for Chopin in Yahoo! and follow the links for Arts/Humanities/Literature/Authors/Literary Fiction/Chopin, Kate and so on to find useful biographical and critical websites.

Indexes and Databases

There are a number of academic databases that can help you find reliable sources. These databases are not free on the web but are subscribed to by your library; therefore, they are free to you as a member of that library system. The standard database in the field of literary studies is the **MLA International Bibliography**, published by the Modern Language Association. You should be able to search this online database, listing sources published since 1963, through your library's website. You may also have access to other databases for Language, Literature, and Criticism such as *Literature Online Reference Edition, Infotrac, Academic Search Premier, Research Library*, and so on. Once you locate the appropriate database, enter your search terms and these databases will then list matching citation records. Mark which records are most appropriate to create a list of potential resources. Those citations can be printed or emailed to you, and these lists of records can help you keep track of sources found, selected, and discarded. Search for the marked journal or book at your library, through online resources, or through interlibrary loan. Many students rely on full text databases like *Jstor, Project MUSE*, or *Humanities Full Text* to locate references and pdf articles in one step. It is important, however, to avoid limiting yourself just to full text articles. Be sure to conduct a comprehensive search and take the extra time and effort to request a source or copy one not available online. In a few cases, you may be able to identify a specialized database such as the *American Literary Scholarship, World Shakespeare Bibliography Online*, or *Contemporary Authors*. Locate these by browsing through your library's list of databases or ask your librarian for guidance.

Bibliographies

As you gather sources, you will accumulate a number of bibliographies. Remember to consult them to identify useful sources. If there is a source that is repeatedly cited, you should be sure to consult it. Furthermore, you can also locate specialized bibliographies or entire books made up of bibliographies about certain fields, time periods, or even authors. These bibliographies list citations for resources and sometimes offer annotations describing the content of these resources. You should search for bibliographies dedicated to writers on whom there is a great deal of criticism. You can also consult specialized bibliographies that appear in multiple volumes with supplements in categories such as *American and British Poetry: A Guide to the Criticism, Guide to American Poetry Explication, Guide to British Poetry Explication*, and *Twentieth-Century Short Story Explication*. In fact, *Short Fiction: A Critical Companion* provides lengthy annotations for selected articles in journals and books. Again, once you identify potential sources, use your library's online catalog , databases, or ILL to search for the actual text.

Locating Historical and Cultural Works

If your potential project addresses historical or cultural contexts, you might need to consult historical or cultural histories, newspapers, magazines, or other cultural documents of the time period. For example, my student Ashley Walden, who is writing about "The Story of an Hour," may choose to expand her project on Kate Chopin by looking at the text in context by exploring the situation of women in turn-of-the-century America. (Her essay is shown on page 48.) In a case like this, while you could certainly use the literary resources discussed above, additional resources outside of the field of literature might be welcome.

Again, Library of Congress Subject Headings constitute a very powerful way to search for books and information in books. Coming up with the possible fruitful subject headings can be difficult, so brainstorm your topic with a librarian who will be able to identify several possible subject headings for you to search for books related to your topic. When Ashley consulted her local librarian to find out background information on Chopin, they honed in on the following Subject Headings:

Women-Southern States-History

Women-United States-Social Conditions

Women-United States-History-19th Century

Women's rights-United States-History

Searching with these terms, Ashley was able to identify a number of useful reference books.

Reference Books

When attempting to determine the historical or cultural context for a work, you may be best off using reference books to locate general information about significant events. Begin by consulting general guides like Robert Balay's *Guide to Reference Books*, Ron Blazek and Elizabeth Aversa's *The Humanities: A Selective Guide to Information Sources*, *ARBA Guide to Subject Encyclopedia and Dictionaries*, or *First Stop: The Master Index to Subject Encyclopedias*. Such guides or your reference librarian can direct you to the reference section of the library where a number of specific dictionaries, encyclopedias, or companions are located in D for General History and History of Europe, E-F for History: America, or H for Social History. Titles like *Social History through the Ages*, *Dictionary of American History*, *Encyclopedia of American Social History*, *Columbia Guides* or the *Oxford Companions* can offer overviews of particular historical or cultural contexts, significant events, or important figures. In the P reference section, you may be able to locate encyclopedias, dictionaries, companions, or other reference books that situate literary contexts, books such as *Identities and Issues in Literature* and *Literature and Its Times*. Such references would be organized by country or time period and may offer the general knowledge you need to contextualize a work without in-depth interpretation extraneous for literary research at this level. Furthermore, any of them also include bibliographies useful in directing you to other reliable and useful sources.

Search Your Library's Online Catalog

You might also visit the appropriate section of your library to locate other companions specific to literature at the time and browse the stacks. Locate the general section about the time period and genre you are working on, and there you will find a number of volumes that offer an overview of the historical context: for example, in writing about Browning's poem, "My Last Duchess," I could locate Richard Altick's *Victorian People and Ideas* or *The Presence of the Present* at the beginning of the Victorian literature section (PR878.R4 A48). It is also useful to consult various of the companions such as the *Cambridge Companions To Literature*, *Blackwell Companion to Literature and Culture*, *The Oxford Companion to African American Literature*, or any other companion to reading or teaching your author or work. Use keywords like "companion" and "guide" alongside your author's name to locate series such as *Historical Guides to Teaching American Authors* which has individual volumes on writers like Poe, Dickinson, or Hughes as well as many others. For example, when I enter "hansberry AND historical and context," I get Lynn Domina's *Understanding A Raisin in the Sun: A Student Casebook to Issues, Sources, and Historical Documents*, an incredibly useful resource to contextualize the play. When Ashley searches using "Chopin and historical and context," she gets *Critical Essays on Kate Chopin*, edited by Alice Hall Petry, which offers a great deal of information about the reception of Chopin's work at the time.

Web Resources

Your best resources are going to be the dictionaries, encyclopedias, companions, and guides already mentioned. They are going to offer you general overviews of basic facts that can allow you to focus your research. Since your search terms are broad, web research is going to be extremely difficult. You might consult the Pearson's Link Library in Research Navigator to track reliable links to your author to see if any web resources discuss historical context. In general, however, you are best off sticking to reliable resources located through your library.

Indexes and Databases

In the same way, searching through indexes and databases can be extremely frustrating. Using broad terms like the author's name and words like "historical" and "context," you will turn up large numbers of hits but few relevant ones. Many will be too detailed or more appropriate for historical scholars. However, you can try general databases like *Academic Search Premier*, *Proquest*, or *Research Library*. To get a general sense of the historical context, you might consult the online or print version of *Facts on File*, a summary of the news stories of a particular week or month or year. Consult the Subject Guides at your library to locate appropriate and available databases for general information.

If you were doing a project on the reception of Williams's *The Glass Menagerie*, you would want to locate contemporary reviews in magazines or newspapers. *The American Periodicals Series*, the *Readers' Guide to Periodical Literature*, or *Infotrac* would direct you to useful sources. Work with your librarians to locate these sources.

Evaluating Sources

Your librarians and your instructors will remind you that not all information is created equal! Quality will vary. In the course of your research, you will encounter lots of information and you will be responsible for determining whether your resources are reliable. Are they to be trusted or discarded? Unfortunately, resources like Google and Wikipedia are often not selective enough to give you reliable information. General search engines like Google list all of the online mentions on a particular topic without evaluating their contents or categorizing their purposes in any way, and resources like Wikipedia are not necessarily accurate. The information you may find there is not always provided by authorities in the field or people with credentials. For example, a high school student's thoughts about Kate Chopin do not carry the same weight as those of a scholar who wrote a book about Chopin, but that high school student's essay may appear when you Google "Story of an Hour," and his opinions could be incorporated into a Wikipedia entry. The best and most reliable resources are fairly recent books or articles published by academic, government, or official institutions and articles in prominent, reputable newspapers and magazines. However, you may encounter a resource that you would like to include. If that is the case, librarians and instructors will want you to ask some of the following questions, particularly when assessing web sources:

Authority
- Who are the authors? Can you tell if they are recognized, qualified, or credible?
- With whom are they affiliated? Does that affiliation seem credible?
- Can you determine the publisher? Is the source published in a respectable location?

Accuracy
- Is the information accurate? Reliable and error-free?
- Are the interpretations and implications reasonable, sound, and thoughtful?
- Is there verifiable evidence to support the author's conclusion?
- Is there a citation, reference, or works cited page?

Objectivity
- What is the purpose of the resource?
- What do the authors hope to accomplish?
- Is there apparent bias?
- Is the information appropriately fact or opinion?

Currency
- Is the information current?
- Is the validity of the information likely to have changed significantly over time?

If you do not know the answer to many of these questions or answer "no" to a number of them, it may be in your best interest to reconsider using the source. With the wide range of resources out there, you should be able to locate sources that are accurate, reliable, and authoritative.

Ask the Expert!

Whenever you have a question about the reliability of your source, especially an online source, ask your instructor. He or she will be able to help you answer questions to decide whether or not you can trust a source. You may also want to consult your instructor about print sources. For example, does your teacher want you to avoid using encyclopedias or explications? Are there other sources that should be avoided? Are there sources you must include? You might want to make an appointment to review the works you are planning to cite with your instructor. He or she may be able to direct you to essential sources as well.

Taking Good Notes

Time and again, most of us have found ourselves at the last hour of deadlines without all of the citation information necessary for our bibliographies. The first step in gathering resources is to make certain you record the appropriate citation information that might include the following: author(s), title, edition or journal title, volume number, editor(s), publication location, publisher, date of publication, database name, service name of database, location accessed, and date accessed. A good tip is to copy the title page of the book or journal you are using and note all of the publication information on the copy so you can easily return to your research materials for your works cited. If you are taking notes and not making copies, be certain to record the publication information on a notecard or before you begin your notes in your notebook, on your legal pad, or on your computer. These few minutes early on can save you a lot of frantic minutes in the final hours.

Record insights and ideas from your research that relate to your focused topic. Just like other papers you have written for this course, your research paper needs to stay focused, so only take notes on what critics have said that seem pertinent to your tentative thesis.

Develop a process for taking notes—a way to organize and collect the information you have found. Consider these suggestions:

1. Use note cards to record new pieces of information. Code each card to identify each new source.
2. Take notes in your word processor. Be certain to record the bibliographic information for each new source.
3. My personal favorite is legal pads. I find legal pads indispensable and use a new one for each project. I record the bibliographic information (author, title, publishing information) at the top of the page as a header. I use the left margin for page numbers that relate to the notes I'm taking. In the right margin, I make comments about how I might use the information I am gathering.
4. Devote a section of your spiral-bound notebook to your research project. Devote a new page to each source and record your bibliographic information as a header and page numbers in the margins.

At this point, you may have a sense of how critics have responded to this author, text, and topic. You are not just looking for critics who have said exactly what you already think! Instead, you want to provide a new perspective on the topic or text, grounded in close reading and in reaction to what has already been said. Understanding the current commentary on the work at hand can help you formulate your thesis still more specifically.

Chapter 15 will help you understand critical perspectives, and Chapter 16 will teach you how to integrate critical perspectives into your essay. Then, Chapter 17 will show you how to document your research sources correctly.

The Reading/Research Dialectic

Keep a to-do list. You should also keep a list of sources you want to consult as you identify possibilities in bibliographies and other references. Check off sources as you consult them and add new ones as they arise. There is a good chance that your research is going to send you back to the drawing board, so to speak, to reread certain passages and to seek out certain resources. Be prepared to keep an ongoing list of not only sources to investigate but also search terms and lines of inquiry to pursue. You may find you need to reread information, not having realized its import the first time through. An article may direct you to a certain passage in the text you might not have initially considered significant but should. Be prepared to engage in cycles of reading, writing, and research as your gather your materials.

A Tentative Timeline: 10 Steps to a Successful Research Project

You will find subject headings throughout Chapters 13–17 in Part IV of this book that correspond with the ten steps listed below. While every researcher should develop a customized process, you may find the following structure useful:

1. Choose a text and reread it, then reread it again. (Chapter 13)
2. Pose a research question. (Chapter 13)
3. Answer your question with a tentative thesis. (Chapter 3 and Chapter 13)
4. Conduct preliminary research and refine your topic. (Chapter 13)
5. Begin your research and develop search terms. (Chapter 14)
6. Engage in the reading/research dialectic. (Chapter 14)
7. Read and synthesize resources. (Chapter 15)
8. Draft. (Chapter 16)
9. Check citations. (Chapter 17)
10. Revise and revise again.

STUDENT WRITER In Erin's Words: On the Research Process...

When I begin to research for a paper, I generally start with article databases where I can easily type in keywords and see the results of my search immediately through the HTML or PDF representations of the articles that I find. Unlike searching an online database for books, searching for PDF or HTML articles on databases such as JSTOR or EBSCOhost yields results that allow me to read the shorter articles from my screen and determine quickly whether or not they will prove to be beneficial to my writing process. When I find an adequate number of articles to begin my collection of research, I then look at the bibliographies of the articles to help guide my search through my university's online database of books.

Once I have compiled a list of articles and books that I feel will be useful to me in my research process, I then go through them carefully, underlining and taking notes to remind myself as to what each text offers me. Occasionally I find that an article or book is not going to offer me the aid that I had hoped, and in those instances it is back to the computer to find more a suitable source. When a situation like that occurs, I sometimes find myself having to reevaluate my focus or certain parts of the text with which I am working because the new sources I find may inspire me to take a second, closer, glance at a line or paragraph that I may have previously neglected. For instance, when writing my paper on "One Art," I found that after I thought my research process was complete, new sources were brought to my attention that worked better than a few of the earlier sources that I found. Even though this cost me some time and effort to go back and incorporate the new sources while doing away with the less helpful ones, it was worth it to have stronger support for my points.

Assignment: Writing an Annotated Bibliography

An annotated bibliography can be a useful tool for you and your instructor to keep track of the progress you are making on your research. It can also help you identify the value of each of your sources as a reminder of how and why it fits into your argument and your project.

To write an annotated bibliography, you develop your works cited list—that is, the list of sources you plan to mention in your paper—and under each citation, you provide an annotation. The annotation summarizes the purpose of the text referenced and then justifies its use in your particular project. In other words, you should have a sense of the main idea of the article you have cited and then be able to argue for its use in your paper. Each annotation may be five to seven sentences in length.

Sample Student Paper
An Annotated Bibliography

Erin Christian

Annotated Bibliography

Blackmer, Corrine E. "Writing Poetry like a 'Woman.'" *American Literary History* 8.1 (1996): 130–153. *JSTOR* Web. 26 Apr 2010.

Throughout her article, "Writing Poetry like a 'Woman,'" Corrine E. Blackmer discusses the evolution of recent feminist literary history in regard to women's poetry. Blackmer traces the development of feminist literary criticism and how it has addressed, among other issues, female war poets, lesbianism, and the gender roles that have confined both men and women over time. Focusing in on Elizabeth Bishop as a "twentieth-century female icon," Blackmer examines how Bishop's unease in America and the pervasive homophobia that existed during the McCarthy era influenced her move to Brazil and her writing as a lesbian American woman. I will use Blackmer's discussion of the self-consciousness, discretion, and modesty that the poet embraced in the face of her several displacements and losses to help me illustrate that while "One Art" seems to advocate learning to relinquish one's claims of ownership with emotional restraint, Bishop's structuring of the poem discloses her collapse of reserve in the face of the "disaster" of human loss.

Blasing, Mutlu Konuk. "'Mount d'Espoir' or 'Mount Despair' : The Re-Verses of Elizabeth Bishop." *Contemporary Literature* 25.3 (1984): 341–353. *JSTOR* Web. Apr 2010.

Mutlu Konuk Blasing observes the contradictory nature of Elizabeth Bishop as an autobiographical poet with an "impersonal touch" in her formalist designs in "'Mount d'Espoir' or 'Mount Despair': The Re-Verses of Elizabeth Bishop." Blasing asserts that Bishop means for her readers to view both writing and losing as one in "One Art," and that the formal repetition of the villanelle both promises mastery and finalizes disaster. Using Blasing's notes regarding the repetition in "One Art," I will seek to prove that the "disaster" and "master" placements in each stanza reflect Bishop's own perceptions of what she felt could be coped with adequately in comparison to that which seemed more devastating. Following up on an observation made by Blasing regarding the negative prefix "dis-," as well as the information from other sources regarding the "aster" blue of her lover Methfessel's eyes, I will argue that the true disaster for Bishop was the loss of Alice Methfessel and her way of illustrating her private pain in an appropriately distant public manner was the subversion of this detail into her repetition.

Costello, Bonnie. *Elizabeth Bishop: Questions of Mastery*.
    Cambridge: Harvard University Press, 1991. Print.

In *Elizabeth Bishop: Questions of Mastery*, Bonnie Costello examines the questions of mastery that she claims Elizabeth Bishop concerned herself with during her career as a poet. Costello seeks to illustrate that the poems of Elizabeth Bishop "portray both the desire for mastery and the dangers and illusions to which such desire is prone." In my argument regarding the theme of loss in "One Art," I will use Costello's examination of what she perceives as Bishop's urge for order to contend with both the unruly world and her difficult personal life to help me illustrate the face that Bishop's particular structure in "One Art," such as her uses of enjambment or the deliberate metric disruption of villanelle form in the final stanza, is a plea for control hidden in her flippant lesson on loss.

Dickie, Margaret. "Elizabeth Bishop: Text and Subtext." *South Atlantic Review* 59.4 (1994): 1–19. *JSTOR* Web. 26 Apr 2010.

Margaret Dickie explores the connections between Bishop's style and her politics as well as her interest in art and her social concerns throughout her article "Elizabeth Bishop: Text and Subtext." Noting that many of Bishop's rhymed tercets, sestinas, and villanelles fail to fit solely into to her themes of social awareness or politics, Dickie asserts that Bishop used highly complicated forms as a means of layering varied meanings. Regarding the poem "One Art," Dickie claims that its patterns afford Bishop a way to "exteriorize" the interior. I will use Dickie's claims of Bishop using form in "One Art" to allow her to safely write about those parts of her which she felt could not be openly explored: factors dealing with her lesbianism, alcoholism, and sense of isolation. The reticence of Bishop's language in "One Art" lends little to exposing the events in her personal life that may have prompted the poem, but I will seek to prove that Bishop's manipulation of the form of the poem lays bare a more personal subtext.

Diehl, Joanne Feit. *Women Poets and the American Sublime*. Bloomington: Indiana UP, 1990. Print.

In *Women Poets and the American Sublime*, Joanne Feit Diehl argues that Elizabeth Bishop, in "One Art," articulates the "tension between discipline in life and the force of circumstance." Diehl explores how Bishop's form keeps even the blatantly autobiographical section of "One Art," once she begins to utilize first person narrative, distanced as an artistic expression rather than a bleeding heart confession. Diehl asserts that the flippant tone in the villanelle functions as a "disarming form of humor that undercuts the potential self-pity otherwise latent in the poem's subject." Utilizing Diehl's analysis of the breakdown of Bishop's

traditional villanelle form in the final stanza to support my assertion that Bishop's pedantic lesson on the art of losing becomes a
self-directed lesson for the writer, I will illustrate how the syntax
of the poem by the end truly reveals the pain that the poet has
been attempting to hide.

Dodd, Elizabeth. *The Veiled Mirror and the Woman Poet: H.D.,*
Louise Bogan, Elizabeth Bishop, and Louise Glück. Columbia:
University of Missouri Press, 1992. Print.

In the section on Elizabeth Bishop, Elizabeth Dodd explores
the connections between her style and her tendency toward
personal reticence in *The Veiled Mirror and the Woman Poet: H.D.,*
Louise Bogan, Elizabeth Bishop, and Louise Glück. Regarding the
poem "One Art," Dodd claims that the patterns within the
villanelle afford Bishop a way to safely express the interior. I will
build upon Dodd's claims, concerning Bishop's use of the villanelle
form in "One Art," by illustrating that her conversational tone in
this form allowed her to write about those parts of her which
she felt could not be openly explored: factors dealing with her
lesbianism and sense of isolation.

Doreski, C.K. *Elizabeth Bishop: The Restraints of Language.*
New York: Oxford University Press, 1993. Print.

C. K. Doreski contemplates the entirety of Elizabeth Bishop's
career in *Elizabeth Bishop: The Restraints of Language.* Doreski
believes that the restraint in language that Bishop shows
throughout her work shapes the tone, tensions and topics of her
poetry. Looking at Bishop's restraint as a positive virtue, Doreski
examines the lesson on loss that Bishop asserts in "One Art" and
how her diction, use of refrains, and well-executed punctuation all
serve to demonstrate her reticence and self-knowledge in the face

of loss. I will use Doreski's stylistic approach to "One Art" to support my own stylistic analysis of the poem as I examine the autobiographical aspects of "One Art" and how Bishop manipulates the villanelle form to convey her theme that the art of losing can be learned, but that losing a person can never be anticipated or equal in impact to our daily losses.

Harrison, Victoria. *Elizabeth Bishop's Poetics of Intimacy*.
New York: Cambridge University Press, 1993. Print.

Throughout *Elizabeth Bishop's Poetics of Intimacy*, Victoria Harrison examines Bishop's private life and its relationship to her poetry. When Harrison discusses "One Art," she illustrates the changes that the poem underwent through more than fifteen drafts by showing her readers transcripts of pertinent drafts and explaining the significance behind the changes. Harrison asserts that the "you" in the final stanza of the poem is meant to be Alice Methfessel, and that the several drafts in which Bishop endeavors to include mention of Methfessel's blue eyes into the rhyme scheme serve as proof of the identity of the "you." I will use this hypothesis of Harrison's regarding Methfessel to support the idea that not only does Bishop's punctuation, diction, and form support her lesson on loss to the climax of the loss of a person, but Bishop also managed to keep in that personal detail of the blue eyes in her rhyme by subversively including "disaster" with the negative prefix "dis-" and the "aster" color that she tried to include in her earlier drafts.

Miller, Brett C. *Elizabeth Bishop: Life and the Memory of It*.
Los Angeles: University of California Press, 1993. Print.

Brett C. Miller's book *Elizabeth Bishop: Life and the Memory of It* is a critical biography that uses literary criticism to tell the story of Elizabeth Bishop's life and explain the poems that she wrote. Miller examines Bishop's life with the aid of her letters, drafts, and journal entries, and his analysis of "One Art" is largely supported by his discussion of a dark moment in Bishop's life due to her alcoholism. At the time that "One Art" was written, in the fall of 1975, Bishop feared that her companion Alice Methfessel was abandoning her. In the fall of 1975, Bishop wrote almost nothing aside from "One Art," and this points strongly to the idea that the poem was written particularly about Methfessel's distancing from Bishop and the use of "twos" throughout the piece highlights the lament of the lover not being "two" anymore. I will use Miller's close analysis of Bishop's various drafts of "One Art" in my exploration of how Bishop allowed form to reveal meaning in the poem as each draft depersonalized her pain a little more while simultaneously retaining evidence of being a "crisis" lyric that is not "emotion recollected in tranquility but is a live moment of awful fear."

15
UNDERSTANDING CRITICAL PERSPECTIVES

While the last chapter explored how to locate appropriate secondary sources, this chapter explains how to understand the critical perspectives of the sources you find. The secondary sources provide support for the topic you are developing, which is based on your close reading of the primary text. To help make your case, cite passages from literary critics, whether they are full paragraphs, sentences, phrases, or words, as you did from your primary literary text. You can bring up a critic's point to discredit it and argue against it. You can also cite a critic's point to support the case you are making. You need not argue with the entirety of a critic's own argument to use their close reading in support of yours. You should not, however, take a critic's comments out of context to better make your case.

Finally, understanding critical perspectives and using them correctly can keep you out of trouble. Plagiarism is the act of using another person's ideas without citing them. You should never plagiarize, and it is never necessary to plagiarize. Remember: citing another authority only lends you credibility. Using someone else's ideas and citing them—especially really smart ideas—demonstrates your intelligence in seeking the idea out and identifying it. Unfortunately, there are also many inappropriate "sources" out there. For example, essays from online paper mills do not have credibility and, when plagiarized, can put you in serious academic jeopardy.

Reading the Critics

Once you have identified a source that seems to address the author, work, and topic of your project, read it carefully. With your own preliminary thesis in mind, try to identify the following elements and answer the following questions.

The Scope of the Criticism
- Is the critic discussing the whole work?
- Is the critic discussing just a part of the text? Which part?
- How does the critic's discussion overlap with your discussion?
- Can you characterize the kind of criticism? Is it historical, gender, or another school of criticism?

The Critic's Thesis
- What is the critic's thesis? Restate it in your own words.

- What is the argument?
- What point is he or she making in the article or chapter?

The Critic's Analysis and Interpretation
- Try to outline the critic's argument. Map out the logic of the discussion.
- Mark each new section on your photocopy or list the order of topics addressed on separate paper. You might try to identify the purpose of each paragraph and section to show the purpose and relationship of ideas. Look for transition words like "finally," "furthermore," "in addition," "moreover," "then," "however," "certainly," or "also" as indications of new ideas emphasized.

The Critic's Language
- Identify confusing language and look it up. Have a reliable dictionary on hand, or use the dictionary affiliated with your library's website such as the Merriam-Webster Online dictionary.
- Look up unfamiliar language. However, you may encounter words like "existential," "evaluative equation," "common auditor," and other jargon. It may be useful to take a particularly sticky passage to your librarian or instructor for assistance.

The Relationship Between the Critics' Arguments and Your Own

You will want to compare your argument with the arguments of the critics you are reading. It might be useful to create a chart based on the questions above to allow for comparison of your own argument with the critic's.

Textual Moment of Focus (character, scene, passage, line, symbol)	Your Interpretation of Textual Moment of Focus	Name of Critic and Location of Source	Critic's Analysis or Interpretation of Textual Moment of Focus

A Quick Look Back at Schools of Critical Thought

Throughout this book, you were introduced to context boxes about various critical perspectives. While some articles and books can be categorized as one or another kind of criticism, often you will find that critics employ multiple perspectives to make meaning of a text. As you examine the criticism that follows, it can be useful to identify the kinds of critical perspectives at work and you might employ one of the following lenses to better understand your own critical analysis, (See Chapter 7, pages 328–331, if you need fuller explanations.)

Formalist criticism seeks to examine the text in isolation by focusing on the formal elements of the text itself, the work as it appears on the page, in order to determine its meaning.

Biographical criticism views a literary text in light of the life of the author.

Historical criticism looks at the historical context of a work of literature to better understand it.

Marxist criticism studies a text in light of the economic forces and class relationships, struggles, and issues that must be present in any cultural construction.

Psychoanalytic criticism reveals the psychological issues of the author unconsciously expressed in a text as well as the psychological themes and issues of the characters and readers of a work.

Feminist criticism focuses on the depiction of women in literature and the revaluation of work by women writers.

Gender criticism examines the construction of the genders in literature and demonstrates how gender and sexuality becomes normalized, codified, and reinforced in literary representations.

Postcolonial criticism approaches literature as the expression of the relationship between cultures, particularly a dominant culture and an "othered" culture.

Deconstructive criticism exposes the already deconstructed nature of the literary text, recognizes the implicit logic of a work, and demonstrates how that logic is constructed and is far from stable.

In the three casebooks that follow, you will have a chance to encounter critical perspectives and practice the reading skills discussed above.

A Critical Casebook on Elizabeth Bishop's "One Art"

You may wish to read the poem "One Art" (on page 106) before you read the materials in the casebook. This casebook includes excerpts of literary criticism from books on Elizabeth Bishop or books on women poets.

Reading 1: Excerpt from Joanne Fiet Diehl, *Women Poets and the American Sublime*. (Bloomington: Indiana University Press, 1990).

Bishop's late poem, "One Art" (whose title conveys the implicit suggestion that mastery sought over loss in love is closely related to poetic control), articulates the tension between discipline in life and the force of circumstance.
The poem speaks in the tones of the survivor:

> the art of losing isn't hard to master:
> so many things seem filled with the intent
> to be lost that their loss is no disaster.

The opening line, with its echo of a folk prescription such as "an apple a day," leads into the specifics of daily loss—of keys, of time— the syntactic parallelism suggesting an evaluative equation of what we immediately recognize as hardly equal realities. Such parallelism, by providing a temporary distraction that draws the reader away from the force building in the poem, functions as a disarming form of humor that undercuts the potential self-pity otherwise latent in the poem's subject.

Lose something every day. Accept the fluster
of lost door keys, the hour badly spent.
The art of losing isn't hard to master.

"One Art" presents a series of losses as if to reassure both its author and its reader that control is possible—an ironic gesture that forces upon us the tallying of experience cast in the guise of reassurance. By embracing loss as Emerson had Fate (the Beautiful Necessity), Bishop casts the illusion of authority over the inexorable series of losses she seeks to master.

Then practice losing farther, losing faster:
places, and names, and where it was you meant
to travel. None of these will bring disaster.

The race continues between "disaster" and "master" as the losses include her mother's watch, houses, cities, two rivers, a continent, and, perhaps, in the future, an intimate friend whom, breaking out of the pattern of inanimate objects, the poem directly addresses:

—Even losing you (the joking voice, a gesture
I love) I shan't have lied. It's evident
The art of losing's not too hard to master
though it may look like (Write it!) like disaster.

Here conflict explodes as the verbal deviations from previously established word patterns reflect the price of the speaker's remaining true to her initial claim that experience of loss can yield to mastery. With a directness that comes to predominate in Bishop's later work, "One Art" delineates the relationship between the will and the world. Note the split of "a gesture / I love" across two lines; the profession stands by itself as it turns back toward the beloved gesture. Syntax reveals the pain "One Art" has been fighting, since its beginnings, to suppress as the thought of losing "you" awakens an anxiety the poem must wrestle with down to its close. This last time, the refrain varies its form, assuming an evidentiary structure that challenges as it expresses what has hitherto been taken as a fact recognized from within the poet's consciousness. Coupled with the addition of "it's evident" is the adverbial "too" (It's evident / the art of losing's not too hard to master"), which increases the growing tension within the desire to repeat the poem's refrain while admitting growing doubts as to its accuracy. In the end, the pressure to recapitulate the by-now-threatened refrain betrays itself in the sudden interruption of the closing line by an italicized hand that enforces the completion of the "master" / "disaster" couplet that the poem itself has made, through its formal demands, an inevitable resolution: "the art of losing's not too hard to master / though it may look like (Write it!) like disaster." The repetition of "like" postpones, ever so fleetingly, the final word that hurts all the more. The inevitability of "disaster" ironically recalls the fatalism of such childhood rituals as "he loves me; he loves me not"—in which the child's first words, "he loves me," and the number of petals on the flower determine the game's outcome. In its earlier evocation of folk ritual and in the villanelle's rhyme scheme, "One Art" reveals an ironic playfulness that works in collusion with high seriousness, a strategy that proliferates throughout Bishop's work.

FOCUSED FREE WRITES

1. How does Diehl address the theme of "loss of control" in Bishop's poem?
2. What parts of the poem does this critic focus on?
3. Identify the critic's thesis.
4. List the topics addressed by the critic.
5. Is any of the language unfamiliar or unclear? List confusing words or phrases and use resources such as dictionaries, librarians, peers, or instructors to untangle them.
6. What is the relationship between the critic's argument and your own? What is your argument about the poem's meaning? How does the critic confirm, extend, or challenge your argument?

Reading 2: Excerpt from Elizabeth Dodd, *The Veiled Mirror and the Woman Poet: H.D., Louise Bogan, Elizabeth Bishop, and Louise Glück.* (Columbia: University of Missouri Press, 1992).

"One Art" is Bishop's one example of a villanelle, a form she admired and tried to work with for years. It is widely considered a splendid achievement of the villanelle.

The art of losing isn't hard to master;
so many things seem filled with the intent
to be lost that their loss is no disaster.

Lose something every day. Accept the fluster
of lost door keys, the hour badly spent.
The art of losing isn't hard to master.

Then practice losing farther, losing faster:
places, and names, and where it was you meant
to travel. None of these will bring disaster.

I lost my mother's watch. And look! my last, or
next-to-last, of three loved houses went.
The art of losing isn't hard to master.

I lost two cities, lovely ones. And, vaster,
some realms I owned, two rivers, a continent.
I miss them, but it wasn't a disaster.

—Even losing you (the joking voice, a gesture
I love) I shan't have lied. It's evident
the art of losing's not too hard to master
though it may look like (*Write* it!) like disaster.
                    (*The Complete Poems*, 178)

Loss is its subject, but the poem begins almost trivially. The first line, casual and disarming, returns throughout the poem. The natural-sounding contraction helps to create the semblance of real speech even within this complex form, and the details and examples that follow immediately do not, indeed, seem like great losses. Door keys, a wasted hour, even forgotten names certainly do not warrant the term consistently invoked by the rhyme: "disaster." But the poem builds, until "cities" and "realms"—of great import to this geographically inclined poet implied by this and all her books—have been lost.

Not until the final quatrain, bringing the villanelle to the completion of its required form, does the real occasion of the poem appear. Here the loss is very personal, a person, "you." Yet the details and attributes here too are muted. Only parenthetically does Bishop reveal the importance of the you: "(the joking voice, a gesture / I love)," yet love is evident through the speaker's difficulty in revealing herself. There is a slight change, too, in the refrain line: "the art of losing's not too hard to master," qualifying that original assertion that loss "isn't hard to master." And in the final line the speaker must even exhort herself to complete the rhyme—(*Write* it!)—since disaster looms very large indeed. Yes, says the poem, this is a great loss, which I am still working to master. After the suicide of Macedo Soares, Bishop returned to the United States, and so the loss of lands and love compound one another. At least in part, "One Art" is a deeply felt elegy, but Bishop uses both a strict and difficult form and a casual, conversational tone to hush the emotional intensity. In this fine poem, her attempt to mute serves also to heighten the poignancy.

FOCUSED FREE WRITES

1. How does Dodd make this poem personal for Bishop?
2. What parts of the poem does this critic focus on?
3. Identify the critic's thesis.
4. List the topics addressed by the critic.
5. Is any of the language unfamiliar or unclear? List confusing words or phrases and use resources such as dictionaries, librarians, peers, or instructors to untangle them.
6. What is the relationship between the critic's argument and your own? What is your argument about the poem's meaning? How does the critic confirm, extend, or challenge your argument?

Reading 3: Excerpt from Susan McCabe, *Elizabeth Bishop: Her Poetics of Loss.* (University Park: Pennsylvania State University Press, 1994).

III

Though personal loss is often not explicitly confronted in Bishop's poems, it pervades them. Readers of Bishop frequently turn to "One Art" in *Geography III* as distinctively Bishopian in its restraint, formality, classicism. Yet this poem deals openly with loss and has been rightly called by J. D. McClatchy "painfully autobiographical." The formal demands of the villanelle keep "squads of undisciplined emotion" from overwhelming the poem, while James Merrill has spoken of "One Art" as resuscitating the villanelle in that its "key lines seem merely to approximate themselves, and the form, awakened by a kiss, simply toddles off to a new stage in its life, under the proud eye of Mother, or the Muse." Personal expression makes the form looser, more pliant and intimate. In fact, Bishop uses form frequently, and especially here, to show its arbitrariness, its attractive flimsiness. Bishop claims that she had not been able to write a villanelle before but that "One Art," possessing a somewhat diaristic dating through its metrics and tone, "was like writing a letter." It is a form tellingly imitative of the obsessional behavior of mourners with their need for repetition and ritual as resistance to "moving on" and their inevitable search for substitutions.

We are ultimately left not with control but with the unresolved tension between mastery and a world that refuses to be mastered; we are left with language. Restraint is tense hilarity here:

> —Even losing you (the joking voice, a gesture
> I love) I shan't have lied. It's evident
> the art of losing's not too hard to master
> though it may look like (*Write* it!) like disaster.

The imperative self-prompt "(*Write* it!)" conveys the immense energy needed to utter the last word of "disaster." From the beginning, Bishop presents "the art of losing" as perverse rejection of the desire to win. In the poem's alternating rhyme of "master" with "disaster," disaster has the last word. "The art of losing isn't hard to master" is true because losing is all we do. The poem reveals a struggle for mastery that will never be gained. We can only make loss into therapeutic play. One does try to master loss, but Bishop recommends that we recognize our powerlessness and play with the conditions of loss: the blurring and splitting of presence and absence, being and nonbeing.

Bishop's "art of losing" resembles what Freud in *Beyond the Pleasure Principle* calls the rule of "fort-da" (gone / there), after a game his grandson constructed in his mother's absence:

> The child had a wooden reel with a piece of string tied round it. It never occurred to him to pull it along the floor behind him, for instance, and play at its being a carriage. What he did was to hold the reel by the string and very skillfully throw it over the edge of his curtained cot, so that it disappeared into it, at the same time uttering the expressive "o-o-o-o." He then pulled the reel out of the cot again by the string and hailed its reappearance with a joyful "da" ("there"). This, then, was the complete game—disappearance and return.

At first perplexed by an impulse seemingly opposed to the pleasure principle, by a symbolic repetition of the distressing experience of the mother's departure, Freud offers two explanations for the child's apparent gratification in this loss game.

> At the outset he was in a passive situation—he was overpowered by the experience; but, by repeating it, unpleasurable though it was, as a game, he took on an active part. These efforts might be put down to an instinct for mastery acting independently of whether the (repeated) memory were in

itself pleasurable or not. But still another interpretation may be attempted. Throwing away the object so that it was "gone" might satisfy an impulse of the child's, which was suppressed in his actual life, to revenge himself on his mother for going away from him. In that case it would have a defiant meaning: "All right, then, go away! I don't need you. I'm sending you away myself." (10)

Freud finally hands over to a "system of aesthetics" (17) the consideration of how pleasure can come from repeating traumatic moments of dissatisfaction. The child's rendering of loss in symbolic terms with the accompanying verbalization "fort-da" suggests that loss marks entry into language, as language marks entry into the awareness of the presence of absence. The shifting between such appearance and disappearance, as we have seen, becomes quite vivid through abruptly sequential sentences of "In the Village":

> First, she had come home, with her child. Then she had gone away again, alone, and left the child. Then she had come home. Then she had gone away again, with her sister; and now she was home again.

In a sense, Bishop practices the "instinctual renunciation" Freud points to in her poem not only by making loss an intention and active practice (as she does by swallowing the coins and burying the needles in the story) but by losing and recuperating words in rhyme. Poetry can imitate through refrain the experience of "fort-da."

The poet's "one art" handles plural loss; but the expansion of this phrase to include so much validates such activity as the one and only one possible—with death as the ultimate project to be undertaken even as it is postponed within language. The middle line endings weave together to spell ultimate "evident" loss—"intent" / "spent," "meant" / "went": the other side of will and choice must always be loss of control, abandon, renunciation. Bishop instructs us: "Lose something every day," and in the third stanza, "Then practice losing farther, losing faster." The tercets logically build up from small (keys) to big (continent) with demonic precision and momentum. We are reassured by the second stanza that mastery will come to the novice in time, that we will develop the ability to "[a]ccept the fluster." Yet the items lost become increasingly personal with her "mother's watch" at the center, deliberately at the beginning of a line as if to skip over it with a distracting exclamation, one that further heightens the way the poem presents a consciousness in process:

> I lost my mother's watch. And look! my last, or
> next-to-last, of three loved houses went.
> The art of losing isn't hard to master.

Still a potentially "last" or "yet-to-be-dismantled" house remains for us to see slip away from the poet, but there will always, one senses, be a further house, the never-to-be-secure home of her childhood that must be continually refigured, the child of "Sestina" drawing yet "another inscrutable house." As we move forward, we also step backwards. The watch stands in for her mother's absence and loss—a timekeeper that reflects its inability to "keep" time.

Embedded in the loss of the watch is also the loss of her mother's caretaking and vigilance, as well as her father's position as timekeeper.

In the penultimate stanza, she leaps from the moment of initial loss:

> I lost two cities, lovely ones. And, vaster,
> some realms I owned, two rivers, a continent.
> I miss them, but it wasn't a disaster.

She can afford to let go of these "realms" because her imagination can provide new ones. She travels from one tercet to the next, pushing the poem in opposing directions with rhyme. Crisis occurs just when we might expect "mastery." Even within lines there emerges the desire for mastery along with its inevitable breakdown. Enjambed lines in all stanzas but the next to last indicate slippage. A complete sentence occupies only part of a line in stanzas 2, 4, and 5 and so disintegrates any effect of finality or surety. Movement in time—"losing farther, losing faster"—is loss, and Bishop reinforces her theme of displacement with "farther" liminally haunted by "father."

Bishop's characteristic dash emphasizes breakage and propels us forward into the last enjambed four lines:

> —Even losing you (the joking voice, a gesture
> I love) I shan't have lied. It's evident
> the art of losing's not too hard to master
> though it may look like (*Write* it!) like disaster.

Loss and love are significantly enjambed with the first two lines of this final stanza, but they not only confess how loss and love are bound, but give continuing evidence of "I love)," risked with a solitary parenthesis in the line. The most intimate words are not deemphasized by being parenthesized but blaze out as a temporary withholding, as her most prominent resistance to and acceptance of losing. We no longer have an object such as the timepiece standing in for a person but an evanescent voice and gesture, silhouette and trace. There appears a breakdown also in the certainty of the declaration "The art of losing isn't hard to master" by the addition of "not too hard" and an admission of strain with the fiercely whispered "(*Write* it!)" between the stuttered double "like." Her "write it" is another way of saying "don't lose it. " But disaster exceeds troping. Writing reveals a doubleness: Bishop wants language to gain mastery, but writing brings us back to the recognition of displacement and loss. Rhyming, dashing, parenthesizing, joking—all these are activities meant to contain but in emphatic practice remind only how such strategies finally fail. They can lead to renunciation not by making "disaster" into reified form but by accepting it as process and reenactment.

The "work of mourning," explains Freud, involves a gradual withdrawal of investment from a loved and lost object but against such a necessity "a struggle of course arises—as may be universally observed that man never willingly abandons a libido position, not even when a substitute is already beckoning to him." Bishop's art is one that gives up fixed positions. We can now understand, perhaps, how "One Art" is only seemingly far removed from *The Diary* or "In the Village": these texts demonstrate as well, as we have seen,

Bishop's concern with absence as it participates in writing. Language insists upon presence but always keeps loss in sight through its movement; ultimately it cannot hold back the fluid self and reminds us of the space left between us and our words.

FOCUSED FREE WRITES

1. According to McCabe, how is this poem about mourning?
2. What parts of the poem does this critic focus on?
3. Identify the critic's thesis.
4. List the topics addressed by the critic.
5. Is any of the language unfamiliar or unclear? List confusing words or phrases and use resources such as dictionaries, librarians, peers, or instructors to untangle them.
6. What is the relationship between the critic's argument and your own? What is your argument about the poem's meaning? How does the critic confirm, extend, or challenge your argument?

Reading 4: Excerpt from Anne Colwell, "*Geography III*: The Art of Losing," Chapter 4 in *Inscrutable Houses: Metaphors of the Body in the Poems of Elizabeth Bishop* (Tuscaloosa: University of Alabama Press, 1997).

By embodying uncontrollable emotion in a form meant to control it, and in an utterance meant to deny it, Bishop can create tension, ambivalence, and a poignant recognition of the pathos of human attempts to control the uncontrollable.

In the earlier drafts of this stanza, Bishop struggled with the desire to say and unsay, to say two things at once, both admitting to the truth of the argument that the villanelle has established and admitting to the evasion of the truth that the tone has insisted on. To accomplish this she tried lines such as "of course, I'm lying" and "it's evident I'm telling the truth"; one draft of one verse completely explodes the villanelle form:

> All that I write is false, it's evident
> The art of losing isn't hard to master
> oh no
> anything at all anything but one's love. (Say it: disaster). (Vassar Box 30)

This duality that Bishop works so hard to achieve in draft after draft (there are seventeen drafts of "One Art" in Vassar's manuscript collection) she finally finds in one word, "shan't." This word, with its overformal stiffness, its anachronistic sound, its school-marmish precision, says both "I'm lying" and "I'm not lying." Using the future perfect tense allows an ambiguity that no other grammatical structure can provide. Bishop accomplished the feat of expressing her ambivalence about her own endeavor; in the word "shan't" she combined opposite meanings in one utterance.

FOCUSED FREE WRITES

1. According to Colwell, how do the multiple drafts inform our understanding of the poem?
2. What parts of the poem does this critic focus on?
3. Identify the critic's thesis.
4. List the topics addressed by the critic.
5. Is any of the language unfamiliar or unclear? List confusing words or phrases and use resources such as dictionaries, librarians, peers, or instructors to untangle them.
6. What is the relationship between the critic's argument and your own? What is your argument about the poem's meaning? How does the critic confirm, extend, or challenge your argument?

"ONE ART" CRITICAL CASEBOOK: FOCUSED FREE WRITES

1. How do these critics relate to one another? Do any contradict each other?
2. How do these critics support or challenge your argument about the meaning of the poem?
3. Fill out the following chart to envision the critical conversation about a particular moment in the poem.

Textual Moment of Focus (character, scene, passage, line, symbol)	Your Interpretation of Textual Moment of Focus	Name of Critic and Location of Source	Critic's Analysis or Interpretation of Textual Moment of Focus
The final stanza of Bishop's "One Art"		Joanne Fiet Diehl from *Women Poets and the American Sublime*	
		Elizabeth Dodd from *The Veiled Mirror and the Woman Poet*	
		Susan McCabe from *EB: Her Poetics of Loss*	
		Anne Colwell from ch. 4 *Inscrutable Houses*	

A Critical Casebook on Toni Cade Bambara's "The Lesson"

The story "The Lesson" begins on page 170. You may wish to read it before you read the materials in the casebook. The casebook includes excerpts of literary criticism from articles about "The Lesson" and about short stories.

Reading 1: Jerome Cartwright, "Bambara's 'The Lesson'" *Explicator* 47.3 (1989): 61–63.

Jerome Cartwright, Utica College of Syracuse University

BAMBARA'S THE LESSON

Readers of Toni Cade Bambara's "The Lesson" tend to understand the story incompletely. Nancy D. Hargrove, for example, in her valuable essay on *Gorilla, My Love* asserts that Sylvia, the first-person narrator, experiences a "painful ... disillusionment" that forces her "to realize the unfairness of life and, as a black girl, her often low position in the scheme of things."[1] Although her assertion is not incorrect, it is incomplete and misleading. Sylvia is not merely disillusioned at the end of the story: she is changed in a way that promises hope for her ability to respond effectively to the newly discovered reality she faces. Hargrove, further, is mistaken in believing the story to be primarily about economic injustice and larger social injustices that it implies (Hargrove 222). Rather than simply teaching a single lesson, the story is essentially about the value of lessons themselves, the value of learning and thinking.

Although Miss Moore's lesson for the day—the conflict between rich and poor and the economic injustice it reveals—is obviously significant, the story makes it clearly and explicitly only one lesson among many. When Big Butt expresses his yearning for the microscope the children see at F. A. O. Schwarz, Miss Moore seizes the occasion to teach science and launches into a lecture on the invisible world around us. And when Sylvia makes a crack about terrorizing the West Indian kids, she knows that Miss Moore has filed her "remark away for next week's lesson on brotherhood."[2] Implicitly, the children do not simply need to learn one lesson: they need an education. Furthermore, the rich-poor conflict does not provide the dramatic tension, the force that drives the story forward. Hargrove seems to believe that it does, when she objects to the following comment from Miss Moore near the end of the story as "a blunt and heavy-handed statement of theme" (Hargrove 222): "Imagine for a minute what kind of society it is in which some people can spend on a toy what it would cost to feed a family of six or seven" (95). Miss Moore, in fact, has said much the same thing before she and the children even depart for F. A. O. Schwarz. Sylvia describes it this way: "So we heading down the street and she's boring us silly

---

[1] Nancy D. Hargrove, "Youth in Toni Cade Bambara's *Gorilla, My Love*," *Women Writers of the Contemporary South*, ed. Peggy Witman Prenshaw (Jackson: U of Mississippi P, 1984) 220.

[2] Toni Cade Bambara, "The Lesson," *Gorilla, My Love* (New York: Vintage, 1981) 88–89. Subsequent quotations are from this edition, and references will appear in the text.

about what things cost and what our parents make and how much goes for rent and how money ain't divided up right in this country" (94). The reader knows the object of the lesson, which is baldly stated at several points, as soon as the lesson gets underway.

The initial and primary conflict of the story is not that of rich versus poor, but that between Miss Moore and Sylvia, the spunky leader of the gang of ghetto kids that Miss Moore generously tries to teach. The opening sentence of the story describes the opposing forces: "Back in the days when everyone was old and stupid or young and foolish and me and Sugar were the only ones just right, this lady moved on our block with nappy hair and proper speech an no makeup" (87). "This lady," significantly named Miss Moore, has been to college and, of her own volition, has taken on the responsibility for the children's education. Her distinguishing quality is that she knows more than the children. And, evidently as a consequence of her knowledge, she has more money— enough to hire two cabs to take the kids to F. A. O. Schwarz and not worry about the $4.00 change that Sylvia has kept and which Miss Moore surely has not forgotten. Finally, by virtue of her knowledge and money, she enjoys more freedom. Sylvia, by contrast, is stubbornly ignorant, abjectly poor, and so unaware of any existence beyond her own that she is angered when Miss says that she and the children are "poor and live in the slums" (89). Although the cause of the plight may be traceable to an unjust society, one that seems to remain indifference at best, it is her ignorance, conspiring with circumstances, that makes change impossible. The story is essentially about Miss Moore's efforts to teach the children and their resistance, especially Sylvia's, to learning anything. The beginning of the second paragraph sets forth this central conflict with direct clarity: "So this one day Miss Moore rounds us all up at the mailbox and it's puredee hot and she's knockin herself out about arithmetic. And school suppose to let up in summer I heard, but she don't never let up. And the starch in my pinafore scratching the shit outta me and I'm really hating this nappy-head bitch and her goddamn college degree" (88). The dramatic question that powers the story, that moves it forward, is whether Miss Moore will succeed in teaching anything to Sylvia.

The question is answered conclusively at the end of the story. When she and the children return from F. A. O. Schwarz, Miss Moore brings her lesson to a close, and she is delighted to hear Sylvia's cousin Sugar say, "You know, Miss Moore, I don't think all of us here put together eat in a year what the sailboat costs …. Think … that this is not much of a democracy if you ask me. Equal chance to pursue happiness means an equal crack at the dough, don't it?" (95). This, of course, is exactly what Miss Moore wants to hear, but it is no more than Sylvia has already figured out. On the train ride home she calculates what $35, the cost of a clown that has caught her attention, would mean to her family, and she wonders, "Who are these people that spend that much for performing clowns and $1000 for toy sailboats? What kinda work they do and how they live and how come we ain't in on it?" (94). Hoping for something more than Sugar's summary statement, Miss Moore look directly at Sylvia and asks the climatic question the story: "Anybody else learn anything today?" (95). Sylvia, refusing to give Miss Moore the satisfaction of an answer, walks away. Ironically, Sugar, who has stated the object of the day's lesson, can think of nothing but spending the $4.00 left over from cab fare on half a chocolate layer cake, potato chips, and ice cream sodas. But Sylvia has more important things on her mind and ignores Sugar's challenge to race to Hascombs: "We start down the block and she gets ahead which is O.K. by me cause I'm going to the West end and then over to the Drive to think this day through. She can run if she want to and even run faster. But ain't nobody gonna beat me at nuthin'" (96). Of course, nothing could make Miss Moore happier than Sylvia's commitment "to think this day through." Although the story does not allow her to know it, she has succeeded in initiating Sylvia into the world of knowledge and educated perception. With the power that comes from learning lessons and thinking about them, Sylvia has a change of making good on her boast that "nobody gonna beat me at nuthin."

FOCUSED FREE WRITES

1. How does this critic's perspective affect your understanding of the story's meaning?
2. What is the critic's thesis? Why does he disagree with Hargrove?
3. What parts of the story does this critic focus on? List the topics he addresses.
4. Is any of the language unfamiliar or unclear? List any confusing words or phrases.
5. How do the author's comments connect to your argument?

Reading 2: Excerpt from Janet Carey Eldred, "Narratives of Socialization: Literacy in the Short Story" in *College English* 53.6 (1991): 692–695.

Toni Cade Bambara's "The Lesson," from her 1972 collection, *Gorilla, My Love*, provides yet another example of arrested socialization in short fiction. In the story, Sylvia—a young, poor, black girl—collides with Miss Moore, a middle-class, black school teacher who has returned to educate the neighborhood children about white class and power structures. To teach her lesson, Miss Moore takes the children on a field trip to an exclusive toy store, where mechanical clowns sell for $35 and toy sail boats for $1,195. The confident Sylvia resists the lessons of Miss Moore, but finally the toy store overwhelms her, pushing her to question her fixed definitions of self and environment.

In the opening sentence of the story, Bambara defines the central conflict—that between Sylvia and Miss Moore—at least in part as a conflict between language conventions:

> Back in the days when everyone was old and stupid or young and foolish and me and Sugar were the only ones just right, this lady moved on our block with nappy hair and proper speech and no makeup. And quite naturally we laughed at her, laughed the way we did at the junk man who went about business like he was some big-time president and his sorry-ass horse his secretary. (87)

Sylvia hears Miss Moore's proper speech as an affectation, a noise that resounds with aspirations that cannot be realized. Miss Moore is, after all, "black as hell," even if she has a college education and is "the only woman on the block with no first name." The introduction thus establishes the two competing voices and ideologies in the text: 1) Miss Moore's black white-educated voice and 2) Sylvia's youthful, black urban voice.

Miss Moore begins the lesson by "knockin herself out about arithmetic" and by trying to exact from her students a definition of money (88). Specifically, Miss Moore tells them the story of their poverty and oppression, a story whose language Sylvia absorbs, notwithstanding considerable resistance, so that we hear Miss Moore through Sylvia just as we hear Abner through Sarty: "So we heading down the street and she's boring us silly about what things cost and what our parents make and how much goes for rent and how money ain't divided up right in this country. And then she gets to the part about we all poor and live in the slums, which I don't feature" (89). During the field trip, Miss Moore continues her lecture, teaching them with "the voice she uses at the museum" (89). When they see the microscope from outside the store window, Miss Moore describes "the thousands of bacteria in a drop of water and the somethinorother in a speck of blood and the million and one living things in the air around us . . . invisible to the naked eye" (90). Sylvia does not "feature" these details; however, the price tag—$300—catches her off guard. And the $480 paperweight "made of semi-precious stones" garners her attention as well. But the fiberglass boat for $1,195 moves Sylvia outside herself, and for the first time she speaks in an uncharacteristically Miss Moore voice: "'Unbelievable,' I hear myself say and am really stunned. I read it again for myself just in case the group recitation put me in a trance. Same thing" (92). Despite herself and her resistance to group pressure, the price tag on the boat makes Sylvia curious to know more. And so she finds herself dropping her usual posture for long enough to pose a question: "'What I want to know is,' I says to Miss Moore though I never talk to her, I wouldn't give the bitch that satisfaction, 'is how much a real boat costs? I figure a thousand'd get you a yacht any day'" (93). When Miss Moore suggests in her best teacherly voice that Sylvia find the answer to her question and report it to the group, the young girl cuts the dialogue short and resorts to silence.

But something has changed. Sylvia feels "funny, shame" for reasons she can't articulate even to herself, she does not want to enter the expensive toy store. Once in the store, Sylvia finds her behavior even more uncharacteristic. She and her best friend Sugar move quietly, silently, on tip-toe. Then Sylvia finds herself angered, like she wants "to punch somebody in the mouth," although again, she cannot articulate why. Sylvia responds to the violence done by the economic system, by those in power: "With the establishment of a relationship of oppression, violence has *already* begun. Never in history has violence been initiated by the oppressed. How could they be the initiators, if they themselves are the result of violence?" (Freire 61). It is this violence—violence that creates and sustains unjust systems—that Sylvia is just beginning to articulate and "know." And indeed, Bambara herself locates the kernel for "The Lesson" in the awareness and rage against racial and economic injustice.

Many stories are provoked into being by observed violations of the Law—"Gorilla, My Love" (broken child-adult contract), "The Lesson" (race/class inequities), "Wall of Respect" (police brutality), "Madame Bai and the Taking of

Stone Mountain" (the missing and murdered children of Atlanta)—then edited when the poker-hot rage abates. ("Salvation" 46)

Sylvia's rage is the anger that comes with awareness of an injustice. Caught between the old stories and a newly emerging one, trapped between languages, Sylvia—like Robin and Sarty (and Abner)—reacts to this "reframing" of experience with rage, anger, and the impulse to respond violently, to "punch somebody."

By the end of the lesson, the gap between Miss Moore and Sylvia's best friend, Sugar, closes. Sugar volunteers, "You know, Miss Moore, I don't think all of us here put together eat in a year what that sailboat costs." Miss Moore is pleased by Sugar's statement. And though Sylvia tries to silence her friend, Sugar continues, "I think ... that this is not much of a democracy if you ask me. Equal chance to pursue happiness means an equal crack at the dough, don't it?" (95). Other than the "crack at the dough" and "don't it," the words as well as the content of the statement echo Miss Moore. Sugar begins to learn to speak a new discourse and to lean toward a different world view; she has been "saved," assimilated almost completely into Miss Moore's verbal world. Sylvia feels betrayed and confused by Sugar's words. Words are, in Bambara's fictional world, "barriers" (Burks 49).

Just as critics argue for the protagonist's choice at the end of "My Kinsman" and "Barn Burning," so they argue for Sylvia's clear acceptance or rejection of Miss Moore's ideas at the end of "The Lesson." Indeed, Sylvia does distance herself from the lesson, one that challenges the way she views and controls her world. But "somethin weird is goin on"; she feels her chest tightening. Sylvia, like many of Bambara's characters, must learn to compose herself "within the divergent, often conflicting strata" that make up her world (Vertreace 156). "The Lesson" ends with Sylvia brooding over the day's events. She races with Sugar, but doesn't feel bothered when her friend begins to pull ahead. Sylvia, it seems, has learned from Miss Moore about a different "competition," another race that she is losing. Still, she is not ready to speak about it, particularly if this means using Miss Moore's words as Sugar has done. Sylvia's silence is a defense: "her only protection against further pain and humiliation seems to be in not acknowledging formally, aloud, what has been so powerfully demonstrated to her" (Hargrove 89). Sylvia is going to "think this day through." But finally, she resolves, in a voice still her own, not Miss Moore's, "ain't nobody gonna beat me at nuthin" (96).

As with all retrospective narration, we also hear faintly the voice of an experienced, wisened narrator, the voice we hear in "Back in the days when ..." This third voice is important because it combines Sylvia's black urban speech with Miss Moore's knowledge of the relationship between education, money, race, and power. As linguist Geneva Smitherman argues through and in her own prose, the choice African-Americans face in education involves more than simply "dialects," more than simply learning to speak properly, more than simply exchanging one dialect for another. Discussing the repercussions of black assimilation into the dominant white culture, Smitherman warns: "As black people go moving on up toward separation and cultural nationalism, the question of the movement is not which dialect, but which culture, not whose vocabulary, but whose values, not I *am* vs. I *be*, but WHO DO I BE?" (38). In "The Lesson," Sylvia by choice gives up on the words of Miss Moore, by necessity gives up on her own in the toy store. Yet the third narrative voice combines Miss Moore's values with Sylvia's words. Bambara thus makes the same stylistic choice as Smitherman: both assume a "double-edged" voice that appropriates the values of education without erasing the language of African-American identity and, more importantly, that dramatizes the tensions between these coexisting discursive worlds. Faulkner makes much the same choice when he weaves a variety of Southern voices and speech patterns into his texts. Though much of what Ab may say is "unprintable and vile," some of his thoughts and views do indeed make their way into the language of "Barn Burning"; Faulkner allows us "to inhabit Ab's point of view" to hear Ab speak (Zender 54). Character, speech, and community values are intertwined, inseparable.

FOCUSED FREE WRITES

1. How does this critic's perspective affect your understanding of the story's meaning?
2. What is the critic's thesis?
3. What parts of the story does this critic focus on? List the topics she addresses.
4. Is any of the language unfamiliar or unclear? List any confusing words or phrases.
5. How do the author's comments connect to your argument?
6. How does this critic interpret the ending of the story?

Reading 3: Excerpt from Janet Ruth Heller, "Toni Cade Bambara's Use of African American Vernacular English in 'The Lesson'" *Style* 37.3 (2003): 279–93.

In Toni Cade Bambara's short story, "The Lesson" (1972), the narrator, Sylvia, speaks and narrates in African American Vernacular English (AAVE). This is an appropriate dialect for Sylvia, who lives in a New York ghetto, is a working-class black child about twelve years old, and has a strong feminist attitude. AAVE is also a dialect that Bambara herself would have learned growing up during the 1940s and 1950s in New York City's Harlem and Bedford-Stuyvesant communities. AAVE adds realism and humor to Sylvia's narrative. The dialect also reflects Bambara's pride in her ethnic heritage. Finally, AAVE fits the story's themes, one of which is that the black children in the story need to learn about the world outside their ghetto and another that wealth is unequally and unfairly distributed in American society. In "The Lesson," most of the have-not children in need of education speak AAVE. This dialect emphasizes the children's distance from mainstream white bourgeois culture and economic power. However, Bambara also celebrates AAVE as a vehicle for conveying black experience: Sylvia uses AAVE to express her self-confidence, assertiveness, and creativity as a young black woman.

Gavin Jones points out that, by the late nineteenth century, ethnic dialects provided American writers with "a voice for social commentary and political satire" (5). Dialect literature questions "sociolinguistic wholeness" (51). Writers like Paul Laurence Dunbar valued dialect for its realism as well as "its power to structure a political response to larger social, cultural, and racial issues" (Jones 20). Such writing implies resistance to the dominant culture, destabilizes the privileged dialect/discourse, and portrays "subversive voices" that present "alternative versions of reality" (11, 13, 46).

Bambara's fiction reflects the perspective of her black contemporaries. Sylvia Wallace Holton explains that, by the 1960s, many African Americans were alienated from aspects of life in the United States. Especially traumatic for blacks were "White resistance to Civil Rights legislation, the loss of a number of important leaders," and the Vietnam War, which blacks considered racist. African Americans became interested in the movements that emphasized Black Power, Black Pride, and black nationalism (144–45). Holton analyzes the work of black writers like Amiri Baraka who experimented with AAVE in fiction. "Committed to writing for a black rather than a white audience, Baraka [...] refuses to be bound by the rules of 'white' literature and language. Instead, he expresses himself [...] in a normative but distinctive black speech" (180). Bambara carries on this tradition of cultural nationalism in her fiction and essays.

Barbara Hill Hudson's research indicates that in literature by African-American women writers, "the Standard speakers display conformist behavior, while the Vernacular speakers use more creative, individualistic behavior." Colorful, striking language is part of this individualism (120,161,185,192). Denise Troutman argues that black women often use an assertive, outspoken style of speech (219). In general, the African-American community values sophisticated verbal skills and associates such ability with intelligence (223,234). Furthermore, Richard O. Lewis has pointed out that African-American writers use AAVE to emphasize their political and social commentary. AAVE can effectively convey the characters' "strong emotion. The language of these characters marks impropriety; it signals commission of some taboo act that transgresses society's limits. These challenge phrases indicate conflict between authority figures and subordinate figures" (27). Lewis's analysis applies to Sylvia: she is a rebellious youngster who dislikes having to learn summer lessons from Miss Moore, an older woman and the authority figure in the story. Sylvia's language, which includes cursing, expresses her self-confidence, nonconformity, anger, frustration, and inventiveness.

In the opening sentence of "The Lesson," Bambara clearly indicates that Sylvia is narrating in AAVE. Here, Sylvia describes Miss Moore as an adult with "nappy hair" (87). The word *nappy*, of course, originated in AAVE, though it has passed into standard usage (see *nappy*, Major 315; Smitherman 64; and *nappy*, the first lexical definition, *The American Heritage College Dictionary*, 3d ed., 1993). Sylvia also notices that Miss Moore has "proper speech" (87). In contrast to the children in the story, Miss Moore is college-educated and speaks Standard American English. According to Sylvia, the other blacks in the neighborhood tended to "laugh" at Miss Moore, made fun of her behind her back, and even "kinda hated her" because she seemed to them to be putting on airs. However, the black adults respect Miss Moore's education and allow her to teach their children in an informal summer school session. At first, Sylvia and the other kids view Miss Moore's lessons as "boring-ass," but by the end of the story, they have greater respect for her because a field trip that originally seems to be about arithmetic turns out to be quite revolutionary: by showing them the pricey toy store F. A. O. Schwarz, Miss Moore has made them question the fairness of social and economic class stratification in America.

In creating the character of Miss Moore, Bambara may have been influenced by the writings of Brazilian educator Paolo Freire, whose work she admired. Bambara praises Freire's "activist pedagogy" and quotes Freire's dictum, "The purpose of educational forms is to reflect and encourage the practice of freedom" (Bambara, "Education" 250). Also, as a child, Bambara had an older friend whom she called Grandma Dorothy who "steeped me in the tradition of Afrocentric aesthetic regulations, who trained me to understand that a story should be informed by the emancipatory impulse. [...] She taught that a story [...] should be grounded in cultural specificity and shaped by the modes of Black art practice" (249–50). Thus, Miss Moore may also be modeled on Bambara's mentor, Grandma Dorothy. In the 1974 essay "On the Issue of Black English," Bambara writes that the goal of teachers of black children should not be to force-feed Standard American English, white conversational rituals, or mindless answers to questions. Rather, teachers should strive "to develop question-oriented students. Inquiring. Explanatory. Curious. Critical. Analytical. An informed citizenry is one that can raise the intelligent question itself" (111). Miss Moore may represent one aspect of Bambara herself.

Sylvia represents another aspect of Bambara. "On the Issue of Black English" conveys the spirit, pride, and combativeness of an adult version of Sylvia. Bambara fills this essay with sentence fragments, AAVE vocabulary, AAVE syntax, taboo words, and in-your-face confrontation of traditional methods of indoctrinating black students with standard English. The piece is also full of humor, as is "The Lesson." Bambara even inserts a mini-drama in the middle with a black educator trying hard to explain AAVE to a group of prejudiced white teachers. Bambara comments after the dialogue, "You can lead a fool to water but the trip'll be a thorough drag" (110).

In "The Lesson," Sylvia's consistent narration in AAVE enables Bambara to indicate that Sylvia is an African-American child without the author's having to state this explicitly. However, Bambara does have Sylvia comment on the shade of Miss Moore's skin ("And she was black as hell"), and Sylvia refers to her own family members' having "all moved North the same time" (87). These comments also give clues about the characters' race and their recent move to New York from the South.

The young narrator's language makes her ethnicity quite clear in its phonology, morphology, lexicon, and syntax. An example of Sylvia's use of AAVE phonological rules is that she often simplifies consonant clusters (apocope) in words like *ole* for *old* (88). Sylvia occasionally adds extra syllables to words to avoid consonant clusters such as *pr*, using *"puredee"* (88) for *pretty*. At other times, she simply engages in syllable contraction, which is a feature of AAVE and of many vernacular American dialects. Sylvia shortens *because* to *cause* (87, 89, 94, 95, 96), *before* to *fore* (91), *ashamed* to *shamed* (93), *especially* to *'specially* (94). John Baugh transcribes the sounds in *cause* as/kawz/(61). Guy Bailey and Erik Thomas list "unstressed syllable deletion (initial and medial syllables)" as a feature of AAVE phonology. They argue that this feature is present in "most English varieties; more frequent in AAVE" (88). Another common example in "The Lesson" is *cept* for *except* (87). Baugh gives *cept* as an example of "syllable contraction" in what he calls "black street speech." In fact, Baugh notes that the word can be further shortened to be pronounced/sop/(61). He observes, "Speakers reduce syllables quite regularly in the vernacular" (62). Sylvia usually changes [ŋ] to [n]. For example, she describes Miss Moore "knockin herself out about arithmetic" (88), Junebug "punchin on Q.T.'s arm for potato chips" (88), the children "hangin out the window" of a taxicab (89), Sylvia and Sugar "screamin" (90), Miss Moore explaining "the somethinorother in a speck of blood" (90).

Some writers use "eye dialect" to emphasize AAVE. Holton defines eye dialect as "variations from normal spelling that do not indicate significant dialectal differences in pronunciation" (58). However, Bambara avoids eye dialect in "The Lesson." The only exception is in the last sentence, where Sylvia uses the word "nuthin" for *nothing* (96). Bambara's avoidance of eye dialect gives Sylvia more dignity than the black characters of white authors like Joel Chandler Harris and Mark Twain. Toni Morrison has complained in *Playing in the Dark* that eye dialect distorts characters: "the dialogue of black characters is construed as an alien, estranging dialect made deliberately unintelligible by spellings contrived to disfamiliarize it" (52). Similarly, Holton argues, "Eye dialect calls the reader's attention to the 'difference' of the speech without really contributing to its 'realism.' [...] Often eye dialect is added in the represented speech of a character who is to be patronized by the reader" (58). Eye dialect can even make a character appear stupid. William Dahill-Baue believes that eye dialect can "misrepresent and minstrelize" black characters and that it also has racist connotations (461, 463). Gavin Jones agrees, calling eye dialect "orthographic buffoonery that inscribed the semiliterate status of the speaker" (38). Jones points out that some dialect writers reveal "a racist logic of black difference and inferiority" related to the notion "that intellectual capacity was strictly limited by nonstandard speech" (45–46). Bambara does not want to use eye dialect because it may distance the reader from her characters and degrade them. While "The Lesson" uses humor, Bambara wishes readers to take her ideas seriously and respect her intelligent characters.

FOCUSED FREE WRITES

1. How does this critic's perspective affect your understanding of the story's meaning?
2. What is the critic's thesis?
3. What parts of the story does this critic focus on? List the topics she addresses.
4. Is any of the language unfamiliar or unclear? List any confusing words or phrases.
5. How do the author's comments connect to your argument?
6. How does this critic address the use of dialect in the story?

"THE LESSON" CRITICAL CASEBOOK: FOCUSED FREE WRITES

1. How do these critics relate to one another? Do any contradict each other?
2. How do these critics support or challenge your argument about the meaning of the story?
3. Fill out the following chart to envision the critical conversation about a particular moment in the story.

Textual Moment of Focus (character, scene, passage, line, symbol)	Your Interpretation of Textual Moment of Focus	Name of Critic and Location of Source	Critic's Analysis or Interpretation of Textual Moment of Focus
		Cartwright's "Bambara's THE LESSON"	
		Eldred's "Narratives of Socialization"	
		Heller's "Bambara's Use of the African American Vernacular"	

A Critical Casebook on Tennessee Williams' *The Glass Menagerie*

The play *The Glass Menagerie* appears on page 117. You may want to read it before you read the materials in this casebook. The casebook includes both historical documents and literary criticism from articles and books about *The Glass Menagerie*.

Reading 1: Excerpt from Tennessee Williams, "How to Stage *The Glass Menagerie*" Author's Production Notes (Preface to the Published Edition)

Being a "memory play," *The Glass Menagerie* can be presented with unusual freedom of convention. Because of its considerably delicate or tenuous material, atmospheric touches and subtitles of direction play a particularly important part. Expressionism and all other unconventional techniques in drama have only one valid aim, and that is a closer approach to truth. When a play employs unconventional techniques, it is not, or certainly shouldn't be, trying to escape its responsibility of dealing with reality, or interpreting experience, but is actually or should be attempting to find a closer approach, a more penetrating and vivid expression of things as they are. The straight realistic play with its genuine Frigidaire and authentic ice-cubes, its characters who speak exactly as its audience speaks, correspond to the academic landscape and has the same virtue of a photographic likeness. Everyone should know nowadays the unimportance of the photographic in art: that truth, life, or reality is an organic thing which the poetic imagination can represent or suggest, in essence, only through transformation, through changing into other forms than those which were merely present in appearance.

These remarks are not meant as a preface only to this particular play. They have to do with a conception of a new, plastic theater which must take the place of the exhausted theatre of realistic conventions if the theatre is to resume vitality as a part of our culture.

THE SCREEN DEVICE: There is *only one important difference between the original and acting version of the play* and that is the *omission* in the latter of the device which I tentatively included in my *original* script. This device was the use of a screen on which were projected magic-lantern slides bearing images or titles. I do not regret the omission of this device from the original Broadway production. The extraordinary power of Miss Taylor's performance made it suitable to have the utmost simplicity in the physical production. But I think it may be interesting to some readers to see how this device was conceived. So I am putting it into the published manuscript. These images and legends, projected from behind, were cast on a section of wall between the front-room and dining-room areas, which should be indistinguishable from the rest when not in use.

The purpose of this will probably be apparent. It is to give accent to certain values in each scene. Each scene contains a particular point (or several) which is structurally the most important. In an episodic play, such as this, the basic structure or narrative line may be obscured from the audience; the effect may seem fragmentary rather than architectural. This may not be the fault of the play so much as a lack of attention in the audience. The legend or image upon the screen will strengthen the effect of what is merely allusion in the writing and allow the primary point to be made more simply and lightly than if the entire responsibility were on the spoken lines. Aside from this structural value, I think the screen will have a definite emotional appeal, less definable but just as important. An imaginative producer or director may invent many other uses for this device than those indicated in the present script. In fact the possibilities of the device seem much larger to me than the instance of this play can possibly utilize.

THE MUSIC: Another extra-literary accent in this play is provided by the use of music. A single recurring tune, "The Glass Menagerie," is used to give emotional emphasis to suitable passages. This tune is like circus music, not when you are on the grounds or in the immediate vicinity of the parade, but when you are at some distance and very likely thinking of something else. It seems under those circumstances to continue almost interminably and it weaves in and out of your preoccupied consciousness; then it is the lightest, most delicate music in the world and perhaps the saddest. It expresses the surface vivacity of life with the underlying strain of immutable and inexpressible sorrow. When you look at a piece of delicately spun glass you think of two things: how beautiful it is and how easily it can be broken. Both of those ideas should be woven into the recurring tune, which dips in and out of the play as if it were carried on a wind that changes. It serves as a thread of connection and allusion between the narrator with his separate point in time and space and the subject of his story. Between each episode it returns as reference to the emotion, nostalgia, which is the first condition of the play. It is primarily Laura's music and therefore comes out most clearly when the play focuses upon her and the lovely fragility of glass which is her image.

THE LIGHTING: The lighting in the play is not realistic. In keeping with the atmosphere of memory, the stage is dim. Shafts of light are focused on selected areas or actors, sometimes in contradistinction to what is the apparent center. For instance, in the quarrel scene between Tom and Amanda, in which Laura has no active part, the clearest pool of light is on her figure. This is also true of the supper scene, when her silent figure on the sofa should remain the visual center. The light upon Laura should be distinct from the others, having a peculiar pristine clarity such as light used in early religious portraits of female saints or madonnas. A certain correspondence to light in religious paintings, such as El Greco's, where the figures are radiant in atmosphere that is relatively dusky, could be effectively used throughout the play. (It will also permit a more effective use of the screen.) A free, imaginative use of light can be of enormous value in giving a mobile, plastic quality to plays of a more or less static nature.

Tennessee Williams

FOCUSED FREE WRITES

1. How does the author's perspective on his intention affect your understanding of the play's theme?
2. What is Williams' purpose here? Is there a thesis?
3. List the topics he addresses.
4. How do the author's comments connect to your argument? Does he emphasize any textual moments that could support your interpretation of the play?

Reading 2: Excerpt from a review by Lewis Nichols that originally appeared in *The New York Times* on April 2, 1945 upon the play's opening. Source: *On Stage: Selected Theater Reviews from The New York Times*, 1920–1970, edited by Bernard Beckerman and Howard Siegman. Arno Press, 1973.

The theatre opened its Easter basket the night before and found it a particularly rich one. Preceded by warm and tender reports from Chicago, *The Glass Menagerie* opened at the Playhouse on Saturday, and immediately it was clear that for once the advance notes were not in error. Tennessee Williams' simple play forms the framework for some of the finest acting to be seen in many a day. "Memorable" is an overworked word, but that is the only one to describe Laurette Taylor's performance. March left the theatre like a lioness.

Miss Taylor's picture of a blowsy, impoverished woman who is living on memories of a flower-scented Southern past is completely perfect. It combines qualities of humor and human understanding. The Mother of the play is an amusing figure and a pathetic one. Aged, with two children, living in an apartment off an alley in St. Louis, she recalls her past glories, her seventeen suitors, the old and better life. She is a bit of a scold, a bit of a snob; her finery has worn threadbare, but she has kept it for occasions of state. Miss Taylor makes her a person known by any other name to everyone in her audience. That is art.

In the story the Mother is trying to do the best she can for her children. The son works in a warehouse, although he wants to go to far places. The daughter, a cripple, never has been able to finish school. She is shy, she spends her time collecting glass animals—the title comes from this—and playing old phonograph records. The Mother thinks it is time she is getting married, but there has never been a Gentleman Caller at the house. Finally the son brings home another man from the warehouse and out comes the finery and the heavy if bent candlestick. Even the Gentleman Caller fails. He is engaged to another girl.

Mr. Williams' play is not all of the same caliber. A strict perfectionist could easily find a good many flaws. There are some unconnected odds and ends which have little to do with the story: Snatches of talk about the war, bits of psychology, occasional moments of rather flowery writing. But Mr. Williams has a real ear for faintly sardonic dialogue, unexpected phrases and an affection for his characters. Miss Taylor takes these many good passages and makes them sing. She plays softly and part of the time seems to be mumbling-a mumble that can be heard at the top of the gallery. Her accents, like the author's phrases, are unexpected; her gestures are vague and fluttery. There is no doubt she was a Southern belle; there is no doubt she is a great actress.

Eddie Dowling, who is co-producer, and, with Margo Jones, co-director, has the double job of narrator and the player of The Son. The narration is like that of *Our Town* and *I Remember Mama* and it probably is not essential to *The Glass Menagerie*. In the play itself Mr. Dowling gives his quiet, easy performance. Julie Haydon, very ethereal and slight, is good as the daughter, as is Anthony Ross as the Gentleman Caller. The Caller had been the hero in high school, but he, too, had been unsuccessful. Jo Mielziner's setting fits the play, as does Paul Bowles' music. In fact, everything fits. The Glass Menagerie, like spring, is a pleasure to have in the neighborhood.

FOCUSED FREE WRITES

1. Theatre critics review plays and also interpret them. How is this a review of the play? How is it an interpretation? In other words, how is this critic emphasizing his own understanding of the play's meaning?
2. How does this historical document connect with your discussion of the play and your interpretation?

Reading 3: Excerpt from Nancy M. Tischler, *Student Companion to Tennessee Williams*. Source: *Student Companion to Tennessee Williams* by Nancy M. Tischler. Copyright © 2000 by Nancy M. Tischler. Reproduced with permission of ABC-CLIO, LLC.

Williams loved symbols. Having started his writing as a lyric poet, he explained that he had a "poet's weakness for symbols." This trait was undoubtedly also a result of his early saturation with the symbolism and thought of the Episcopal Church. He came to see almost every aspect of life as symbolic of some greater truth.

He had originally designed *The Glass Menagerie* as a Christmas story (Letter to Audrey Wood, 12/43), with the opening scene one of gift giving. The change in his point of attack to a family meal, though more secular, is nonetheless introduced by a demand that Tom come to the table so that they can say "grace," which incidentally, they then omit; but it is also to make his failed, secular "communion" a commentary on the painful relationship in this community of believers. Nothing should be more ordinary and comfortable than breaking bread together, yet the Wingfield children can perform no function without scrutiny and advice from the hovering mother. An echo of this scene is a second announcement of the impending blessing, this time a summons for Laura to come to the table when Jim O'Connor is their guest for dinner. Pretending that Laura has prepared the meal for their visitor, Amanda again dominates the event, making it her solo performance rather than a shared experience of hospitality. She turns the ritual of eating into a contest of wills. She has transformed a communion into a celebration of her personal sacrifices and a reinforcement of her children's obligations to her as their appropriately grateful response.

Amanda soon reveals herself as a symbol of the "devouring mother." Though apparently nurturing, she thwarts and hobbles her children, dominating not only their eating habits, but their entire lives, keeping them safely in the nest with her. Portraying herself as a martyr to their needs, she actually requires their submission to feed her own pride, crippling Laura by her outrageous expectations. If she could, she would emasculate Tom as well. As her own beauty fades, her appetite for adulation increases, making her a harpy rather than a saint. In a fit of anger, Tom calls his mother an ugly old "witch." Williams was to continue embellishing his archetypal monster-woman as he met more complex and powerful ogres throughout his career.

The central image in this play, from which the work takes its name, is Laura's glass menagerie. Williams' biographers have traced the origins of this image to a tragic young woman in Clarksdale, Mississippi (Leverich 1995, 55). Within the play, it allows us to see the childlike fixation on a private world of make-believe animals, and delicacy of this isolated girl.

Taking it as a symbol of Laura herself, fragile and beautiful, the author plays with the more specific figure of the unicorn. Here we see the complete development of a complex idea, hinted at in the dialogue. We know from medieval iconography that this mythical figure is identified with virgins and therefore with sexuality. Although it looks like a horse the unicorn not a horse, but is a unique (if mythical) creature. Thus, when Jim accidentally breaks off its horn, he has not transformed it into a horse: it remains a unicorn, but is now a damaged unicorn that manages to look like an ordinary horse. In some ways, this is what Amanda has done to Laura, distorted her true childish nature to make her seem like all the normal young ladies being courted by nice young gentlemen. (The "gay deceivers" are delightful symbols of Laura's underdeveloped sexuality and Amanda's pressures to appear sexy.) Laura's pained responses to her mother's cruel questions about her plans for the evening expose the anguish that this teasing causes the sensitive girl.

The mock-courtship scene between Laura and Jim contains another cluster of images. Tom, having misused the money for the electric bill, has plunged them into darkness. Amanda, always eager to adopt romantic attitudes, furnishes them with a candelabra, a relic from a church fire, and thereby returns them to the nineteenth century—the family's native habitat. Jim briefly enters into their game of playing at pre-electric life, settles on the floor, and enjoys a childlike moment of shared memories with Laura. But we soon learn that he lives fully in the "Century of Progress," which Laura is blocked from entering. Jim tries, in an act of egocentric kindness, to move her into the adult world of dancing and kissing, but Laura remains a lonely little girl who had a playmate over to visit for the evening. That scene foreshadows the final words, "For nowadays the world is lit by lightening! Blow out your candles, Laura—and so goodbye" (237).

Other images also populate the play. Williams loved the ocean and frequently used the sea as an escape symbol. His sailors, pirates, and buccaneers are the gallant figures who sail away form the dreary land to have adventures denied to most of mankind. Certainly Americans have known this imagery from their earliest days, America itself being the grand adventure for most of our ancestors. For at least three of Williams' literary heroes—Melville, O'Neill, and Crane—the sea voyage was also the escape into the life of literature.

Tennessee Williams' delight in earlier poets, novelists, and dramatists gives additional richness to the texture of the phrasing in *The Glass Menagerie*. For example, Tom's final portrayal of cities as leaves blown by the wind, "brightly colored, but torn away from the branches" echoes Shelley's "Ode to the West Wind." Fortunately, such similes work effectively even if the listener fails to pick up the source of the allusion. We need not picture the famous medieval unicorn tapestry in order to delight in the unicorn reference. Nor do we need to know about D. H. Lawrence's rainbow of sexuality in order to understand the rainbow colors at the Paradise Dance Hall. Blue Mountain is the right name for a romantic past, and Moon Lake is the ideal name for adventures in love. The words carry the message, regardless of our specific knowledge of Clarksdale's geography. Williams lets his words tell their own stories. The viewer can delight in the surface brilliance or dig deep into allusions, allowing several levels of possible resonance.

Like Clifford Odets, Eugene O'Neill, Arthur Miller, Lillian Hellman, and Lorraine Hansberry, Williams was trying to capture the dynamics of the twentieth-century American family, endowing the everyday speech and activities and concerns of these people with a kind of tragic grandeur. Unlike most of his contemporaries, he sought to broaden the range of American theatrical dialogue. For this, he blended the colloquialism of Southern dialect, Midwestern popular speech, and poetic diction. He juxtaposed Amanda's rhetorical flourishes, her monologues, and her lyrical recollections of an idyllic past with Tom's flat, often comic responses. Even more mundane are the words and gestures of Jim

O'Connor, who talks of cattle, chewing gum, the Century of Progress, and self-improvement in a sharp parody of American popular culture. His comic strip quality of speech contrasts neatly with the romanticized language of the Wingfield family.

In addition to the wide range of styles and multiple levels of meaning, Williams also uses varied pace and quantity of speech for effect. Amanda is a compulsive talker, Tom a reluctant one, angry and frustrated, silent at times, bursting into overwrought expression under pressure. Laura speaks gently and at her own pace, using her simple vocabulary, refusing to respond to the usual signals, marked primarily by her quiet withdrawal. When she does speak, we attend to her words. More often, she substitutes music or gesture for language. By contrast, Jim has the skills of the social talker who is delighted with his own ability to make conversation, no matter how awkward the situation or how banal the message. His preference for the sports section of the paper (though Tom expects him to choose the comics) is a perfect summation of the strategy that American men use to avoid embarrassing silences or personal, intrusive conversation. The shared commentary on Dizzy Dean can fill the air with chatter without revealing much about the individual speaker.

The narrative voice that frames this group of players moves the range of language even further, giving a broader dimension to the domestic drama, universalizing the specifics, and lending a poignancy to the actions. Sometimes the narrator is ironic about himself and his family, sometimes he pontificates about the nature of the world, and sometimes he is sentimental. At the end, we hear Tom's voice breaking through, merging with the narrator's. It is now poetic and delicate, void of its earlier ironic sharpness. In telling the tale, he has become more sympathetic. If the play succeeds, we have also found ourselves increasingly reflective and gentle, finally moved to tears.

FOCUSED FREE WRITES

1. What parts of the play does Tischler focus on? List the topics addressed by the critic.
2. Identify the thesis.
3. Is any of the language unfamiliar or unclear? List confusing words or phrases and use resources such as dictionaries, librarians, peers, or instructors to untangle them.
4. What is the relationship between the critic's argument and your own? What is your argument about the poem's meaning? How does the critic confirm, extend, or challenge your argument?

Reading 4: Excerpt from C. W. E. Bigsby, "Entering *The Glass Menagerie*." *The Cambridge Companion to Tennessee Williams.* Ed. Matthew C. Roudane. Cambridge: Cambridge University Press, 1997.

The play is set at a moment of change, change in the private world of the characters but also in the public world, as though it resonated this private pain.

As Tom tells us, "Adventure and change were imminent in this year. They were waiting around the corner for all these kids. Suspended in the mist over Berchtesgarden, caught in the folds of Chamberlain's umbrella. In Spain there was Guernica! ... All the world was waiting for bombardments!" (179). It is a speech which does more than situate the play, provide a context for what, by contrast, must seem a minor drama. It is an invitation to read the events ironically, and to see in the desire to live with comforting fictions, rather than confront brutal truths, a doomed and ultimately deadly strategy. For, as Tom indicates in the same speech, whatever consolations or distractions existed— hot swing music, liquor, movies, sex, glass menageries (the last hinted at by his reference to a chandelier)—flooded the world with rainbows which he characterizes as "brief" and "deceptive."

The Glass Menagerie is more than a lament for a tortured sister (Laura is based on Williams's mentally damaged sister, Rose); it is an elegy for a lost innocence. The Depression had already destroyed one American dream; the war destroyed another, and Tom looks back on the events which he stages in his memory and imagination from the perspective of an immediately post-war world. Neville Chamberlain's piece of paper promising "peace in our time" was no less a product of desperation, no less a symbol of the triumph of hope over despair, than Laura's glass menagerie. Chamberlain's piece of theatre, as he emerged from an aircraft and waved the flag of surrender, believing it to be evidence of his triumph, was no less ironic than Amanda's stage-managed drama of the gentleman caller. In the end brute reality trampled on both.

The Glass Menagerie is no more a play of purely private emotions and concerns than Chekhov's The Cherry Orchard. In both cases society, no less than the characters who are its expression and in some senses its victims, is caught at a moment of change. Something has broken. We even hear its sound. In Chekhov "A distant sound is heard, coming as if out of the sky, like the sound of a string snapping, slowly and sadly dying away." In The Glass Menagerie "There is an ominous cracking sound in the sky ... The sky falls" (233). The snapping of the horn from a glass unicorn thus stands for something more than the end of a private romantic myth. It marks the end of a phase of history, of a particular view of human possibility.

The origins of The Glass Menagerie lie in a short story which Williams wrote around 1941. "Portrait of a Girl in Glass" differs in certain respects from the final play version, not least in the absence of that detailed social and political context which broadened the metaphoric significance of The Glass Menagerie. The character of Laura is much closer to being a portrait of his sister, Rose. In the play she suffers from a deformed foot; in the story the flaw is more cruel. She is mentally rather than physically fragile. At the age of twenty she believes that stars are five-pointed because they are represented as such on the Star of Bethlehem which she fixes to the top of her Christmas tree. She treats the characters in her favorite book as real and responds to her gentleman caller not because they had shared the same high school but because, in her mind, he resembles a character from that book, though there is an echo of that in the play when Laura suddenly addresses Jim as Freckles, the protagonist of the novel which is no longer alluded to.

The setting is similar though with certain crucial differences. There is no dance hall across the street, with its overtones of a smoldering sexuality. Instead the alleyway is a scene of death as a dog regularly attacks and kills stray cats in a cul-de-sac which mirrors that confronting the characters in the story. That sense of entrapment, social and metaphysical, survives into the play version, though without this reminder of mortality.

Other elements fed into *The Glass Menagerie*. A projected series of plays, to be called "Mississippi Sketches," included a comedy entitled "The Front Porch Girl," in which a shy girl ultimately finds companionship with one of the lodgers in her mother's boarding house. Expanded into a play called *If You Breathe, it Breaks! or Portrait of a Girl in Glass*, it featured a girl who sat on the front porch of her house awaiting gentlemen callers while finding consolation in a menagerie of glass animals, which becomes an expression of the fragility she believes characterizes those so easily broken by the world. Finally, under contract to Metro-Goldwyn-Mayer in Hollywood, Williams worked on a script, then titled *The Gentleman Caller*, about a woman awaiting a gentleman caller. This, revised, became *The Glass Menagerie*.

Story and play are rooted firmly in Williams's own life. As he explained, speaking in the year of the play's first production, his family had lived in an apartment not essentially different from that featured in his drama. He recalled his sister's room which was "painted white" with shelves which he had helped her fill "with the little glass animals" which constituted her menagerie. "She was the member of the family with whom I was most in sympathy and, looking back, her glass menagerie had a meaning for me ... and as I thought about it the glass animals came to represent the fragile, delicate ties that must be broken, that you inevitably break, when you try to fulfill yourself."

This, indeed, is a clue to why Tom, the narrator who shares Tennessee Williams's first name, chooses to "write" the play, in the sense of recalling what seem to him to have been key moments in his past life. For the fact is that the play does have a narrator and his values and perceptions shape the way we see the action, indeed determine what we see. The story is told for a purpose and serves a need outside that story. Tom Wingfield recalls the past for much the same reason that Willy Loman does in *Death of a Salesman*: guilt. He revisits the past because he knows that his own freedom, such as it is, has been purchased at the price of abandoning others, as Williams had abandoned his mother and, more poignantly, his sister. He "writes" the play, more significantly, perhaps, because he has not effected that escape from the past which had been his primary motive for leaving. The past continues to exert a pull on him, as it does on his mother and sister, as it does on the South which they inhabit.

For his mother, Amanda, the past represents her youth, before time worked its dark alchemy. Memory has become myth, a story to be endlessly repeated as a protection against present decline. She wants nothing more than to freeze time; and in this she mirrors a region whose myths of past grace and romantic fiction mask a sense of present decay. In Williams's words, she clings "frantically to another time and place" (129). The South does no less and Williams (here and in *A Streetcar Named Desire*), like William Faulkner, acknowledges the seductive yet destructive power of a past reconstituted as myth. At the same time she knows that compromise is necessary. Survival has its price and

Amanda is one of Williams's survivors. She survives, ironically, by selling romantic myths, in the from of romance magazines, to other women.

For her daughter, the glass animals of her menagerie transport her into a mythical world, timeless, immune from the onward rush of the twentieth century. It is an immunity, however, which she buys at too high a price for, in stepping into the fictive world of her glass animals, she steps out of any meaningful relationship with others in the present. She becomes one more beautiful but fragile piece in the collection, no longer vulnerable to the depredations of social process or time but no longer redeemed by love.

Tom, meanwhile, prefers the movies, or, more importantly, his poetry. A poet in an unpoetic world, he retreats into his writing because there he can abstract himself from the harsh truths of his existence in a down-at-heel St. Louis apartment. It is not, however, a strategy which has brought him success or peace of mind. He narrates the play in the uniform of the Merchant Marine. He has traded a job in the warehouse for one at sea. There is no suggestion that his desertion of mother and sister has been sanctified by the liberation, or public acknowledgement, of his talent. Like his father before him he has fallen in love with long distance, mistaking movement for progress. Williams himself may have seen Laura's glass animals as representing the fragile, delicate ties that must be broken "when you try to fulfull yourself," but it is clear that in *The Glass Menagerie*. Tom has not fulfulled himself. Tennessee Williams may have felt guilty that his success with the play was built on the exploitation of others; Tom lacks even the consolation of success. Fired from his job in the shoe warehouse, he wanders from city to city, looking for the companionship he had failed to offer his sister. In the story version he tells us that he has grown "firm and sufficient." In the play there is no such assurance as, in that Merchant Marine uniform which is the very symbol of his homelessness, he returns, in his memory, to the home he deserted for the fulfillment he failed to find. When his mother asks him to "look out for your sister ... because she's young and dependent" (175), she identifies an obligation which Tom refuses. In his own life Williams never quite absolved himself of a feeling of guilt with respect to his sister.

For Tom, memories of the past are a distraction from present failure for though situated in time they exist outside of time. In summoning those memories into existence, he transposes experience into a series of images, transforms life into art, and in so doing mimics the process which his namesake Tom Williams adopts in creating plays, for, as Williams has remarked, the virtue of a play lies in the fact that it occurs "*outside of time*," indeed that it is "*a world without time*." It is, to his mind, time which renders experience and, indeed, people, inconsequential. Art ascribes meaning to the moment, neutralizes a fear of "*not meaning*." It is a world in which "emotion and action have a dimension and a dignity that they would ... have in real existence, if only the shattering intrusion of time could be locked out" (52). The theatrical metaphor, indeed, is central, with Tom as author of a metadrama in which he self-consciously stages his memories as a play in which he performs as narrator. But if he is the primary author, he acknowledges the centrality of Amanda as director, designer, and lighting technician of the drama which has been his life and the life of his tortured sister.

Early in the play Amanda is presented as an actress, self-dramatizing, self-conscious. Her first part is that of martyred mother. When she removes her hat and gloves she does so with a theatrical gesture ("a bit of acting" [151]). She dabs at her lips and nostrils to indicate her distress before melodramatically tearing the diagram of a typewriter keyboard to pieces. When the gentleman caller arrives for her daughter she changes roles, dressing herself in the clothes of a young woman and becoming a Southern belle, rendered grotesque by the distance between performer and role. But at the end of the play all such pretences are abandoned. As we see but do not hear her words of comfort to her daughter, so her various roles—shrewish mother, coquettish belle, ingratiating saleswoman—are set aside. The tableau which we see as Tom delivers his final speech is one in which mother and daughter are reunited in their abandonment. "Her silliness is gone," Williams tell us. Amanda "withdraws through the portiere," retreating from the stage which Tom has summoned into being but also from the arena in which she has chosen to play out her own drama. Just as Stanislavsky had rejected those who try to "act" or "pretend" in a Chekhov play, praising only those who "live them … and follow the deeply buried arteries through which their emotions flow," so Williams presents Amanda as most completely human when she lays aside her performance and allows simple humanity to determine her actions.

Laura, too, is an actress, though of a different kind. If she has learned "to live vitally in her illusions," (129) she is forced to deceive when her enrollment in a typewriting course ends in fiasco. Each day she leaves home supposedly to go to the business college but in fact to watch movies, visit museums, the zoo, or the botanical gardens. At home she pretends to study a keyboard chart. When this performance proves futile she is cast in a part of her mother's making for the visit of Tom's friend, Jim, the gentleman caller. Laura is costumed by Amanda ("The dress is colored and designed by memory," her breasts enhanced by powder puffs). She is made up ("The arrangement of Laura's hair is changed; it is softer and more becoming") and placed center stage ("Laura stands in the middle of the room"). The stage has been set and the lighting adjusted by Amanda as stage manager ("The new floor lamp with its rose silk shade is in place, a colored paper lantern conceals the broken light fixture in the ceiling, new billowing white curtains are at the windows, chintz covers are on the chairs and sofa … " [191]). She even directs the action ("Laura Wingfield, you march right to that door!" [197]). The failure of this performance, however, leaves Laura with only one theatre in which to live out her life, that of her glass menagerie.

FOCUSED FREE WRITES

1. How is this a play about acting or deception, according to Bigsby?
2. What parts of the play does Bigsby focus on?
3. Identify this critic's thesis.
4. Is any of the language unfamiliar or unclear? List confusing words or phrases and use resources such as dictionaries, librarians, peers, or instructors to untangle them.
5. What is the relationship between the critic's argument and your own? What is your argument about the poem's meaning? How does the critic confirm, extend, or challenge your argument?

Reading 5: Excerpt from Judith J. Thompson, *Tennessee Williams' Plays: Memory, Myth, and Symbol*. Revised Edition. New York: Peter Lang, 2002.

A "MEMORY PLAY"

Memory structures both the form and content of *The Glass Menagerie* (1944–45), Williams' earliest successful play. Consisting of seven memory scenes framed by the present-time monologues of Tom Wingfield, "the narrator of the play, and also a character in it," (I, 145), the play focused on Tom's remembered experience of the single momentous event in the drab life of his mother, Amanda, and his sister, Laura; the arrival of a gentleman caller, Jim O'Connor. Within the "memory play" (p. 145) recalled by Tom, Amanda's reminiscences of a happier past mythicize its main event, imbuing both the ordinary social occasion and its caller with portentous symbolic significance.

Amanda's memory-stories of her Southern girlhood and, especially, of her courtship by numerous "gentlemen callers" (p. 148) transport the play's events beyond the commonplace to evoke what Northrop Frye calls "the idyllic world" of romance: "a world associated with happiness, security, and peace; the emphasis is often thrown on childhood or on an 'innocent' or pre-genital period of youth, and the images are those of spring and summer, flowers and sunshine." Implicit in Amanda's romantic recollections of courtship, however, is their inevitably disappointing outcome, evoking the equally unforgettable memory of her last caller—the husband who left her—and the "demonic" images of "separation, loneliness, humiliation, [and] pain." From idealized beginning to realized end, Amanda's memories form a paradigm of experience that underlines the structure of the entire play—an ironic pattern of romantic expectations, momentary fulfillment, and ultimate loss.

It is, specifically, Amanda's mythicized memory of "One Sunday afternoon in Blue Mountain" when she received "*seventeen!*—gentleman callers!" (p. 148) that is reenacted in a demythicized version by Laura and Jim. Their ironic romance thus merges the illusion of fulfilling romantic dreams with the reality of reenacting their loss. In the process of the memory's reenactment, Amanda is divested of her hopes of recapturing an idyllic past or of transforming existential reality. The juxtaposition of Amanda's memory of idyllic romance to its ironic reenactment by Laura and Jim ultimately gives the play its nostalgic mood, deepens the meaning of its mundane events, and defines its archetypal pattern: the inevitable fall of romantic aspirations to existential limitations.

Not only the meeting between Laura and Jim but every other event in the play also reflects this pattern of disillusionment. A similar pattern of great expectations and subsequent despair informs the experience of Tom, the aspiring poet ("Shakespeare" [p. 190]), whose dreams of life as a meaningful voyage (or "sea-change") end only in aimless drifting. Although Jim O'Connor's ability to compromise with a diminished reality distinguishes him from the members of the Wingfield family, the pattern also informs his experience, for he is the high-school hero—the "Pirate of Penzance" (p. 156)—who is reduced to a clerk in a warehouse, his romantic libretto exchanged for a paean to capitalistic enterprise. The pattern of initial anticipation and ultimate loss is capsulated at the very beginning of the play in the sardonic message contained in the father's picture postcard: "Hello—Goodbye!" (p. 145), a microcosmic image of the play's fleeting dreams.

The cumulative effect of the pattern's recurrence is to render life itself a series of losses, beginning with inflated expectations of its infinite possibilities and ending in confrontation with its inherent limitations. At the play's end, both Amanda's and Tom's romantic aspirations converge as understood experience: Amanda's failure to recapture a romantic past for Laura coincides with Tom's futile efforts to escape an inescapable reality, circumstances to which all three Wingfields respond with a mixture of bitterness, compassion, and "ever-lasting regret." (p. 185).

The Glass Menagerie as Symbol

Like the play's pattern, its symbols and images evoke a world that is at once metaphorically expansive and existentially constrictive. Even as the archetypal images inflate the characters to mythic dimensions, concrete symbols define their human limitations. The principal concrete symbol in the play is, as the title suggests, the glass menagerie. It is, specifically, Laura's symbols, the objective correlative of her fragile, otherworldly beauty. Its frozen animal forms image her own immobilized animal or sexual nature, her arrested emotional development, and her inability to cope with the demands of a flesh-and-blood world. Given broader implications, the separate pieces of the glass collection reflect the respective fixations of all the members of the Wingfield family as well as their insular natures. Presented as crystallized forms in Tom's memory, each character is shown to be encased psychologically in a world of his or her own. Seeking escape, refuge, or rejuvenation, each imagines a different version of a transcendent reality. Together, they comprise a collection of "isolatoes" condemned to existential isolation and mutual misunderstanding. Ultimately, the glass menagerie is symbolic of all their shattered dreams. Failing to fulfill their transcendent aspirations, the Wingfields find themselves confined to a Wasteland reality, their dreams become "a heap of broken images."

FOCUSED FREE WRITES

1. Thompson goes on to identify how each character functions as a symbol or archetype. How might each character be representative of a certain kind of person, a common image or symbol?
2. Thompson argues disillusionment recurs throughout the play as a kind of theme and structural pattern. Is that true? Identify examples of disillusionment in the play: of high "expectations, momentary fulfillment, and ultimate loss."
3. What parts of the play does Thompson focus on?
4. Identify the thesis.
5. Is any of the language unfamiliar or unclear? List confusing words or phrases and use resources such as dictionaries, librarians, peers, or instructors to untangle them.
6. What is the relationship between the critic's argument and your own? What is your argument about the play's meaning? How does the critic confirm, extend, or challenge your argument?

THE GLASS MENAGERIE CRITICAL CASEBOOK: FOCUSED FREE WRITES

1. How do these critics relate to one another? Do any contradict each other?
2. How do these critics support or challenge your argument about the meaning of the story?
3. Fill out the following chart to envision the critical conversation about a particular moment in the story.

Textual Moment of Focus (character, scene, passage, line, symbol)	Your Interpretation of Textual Moment of Focus	Name of Critic and Location of Source	Critic's Analysis or Interpretation of Textual Moment of Focus
		Williams on Staging *TGM*	
		Nichols from review of *TGM*	
		Tischler from *Student Companion to TW*	
		Bigsby from "Entering *TGM*"	
		Thompson from *TW's Plays*	

16

INTEGRATING PRIMARY AND SECONDARY SOURCES

You've read and taken notes on the literary work you plan to do your research project on, researched what the critics have to say about it, and drafted a proposal and perhaps an annotated bibliography. How do you organize and integrate these diverse materials?

Some Organizing Principles

Now that you have collected your notes, sit down and determine how to organize your draft. Start by articulating your thesis, or main claim (Chapter 13). This is your starting point and should be kept in mind as you lay out the different pieces of evidence in support of the thesis. Evidence from the literary work may include discussion of literary elements and any scenes, lines, or words that illustrate your thesis. These points may be discussed in individual paragraphs or developed over several paragraphs. A topic sentence at the beginning of each paragraph shows how the idea at hand connects back to the thesis. The same writing lessons discussed in Parts I and II of this book should apply here.

In the first paragraph of the introduction, name the author and work you are examining. Consider starting with an overview of the research you've done and how your thesis varies from what has already been said by the critics: "While critics have offered varied and prolific responses to T. S. Eliot's 'The Love Song of J. Alfred Prufrock' such as..., the poem can be best be understood in this way..." The first few sections of your essay are an ideal place to share the range of responses to your topic in order to present your assertion as particularly unique and insightful. You might return to your initial proposal (Chapter 13) as a starting point.

The sections of the research essay that follow use two kinds of evidence as support: textual evidence developed by close reading and critical evidence identified by research. The information used should support your thesis in a persuasive manner.

Drafting Body Paragraphs

Your body paragraphs should each include a topic sentence that supports your thesis. In turn, that topic sentence should be supported by two kinds of evidence.

The first kind is textual evidence. Summarize, paraphrase, or directly quote your primary source. As you make the case for your interpretation, emphasize the moments in the literary work that seem to offer the greatest support for your point of view.

The second kind of evidence—critical evidence—works in a similar way. Identify critical information you can use to further your argument. There are two ways you might employ critical evidence. You may introduce one critic's interpretation in order to argue with it. This may provide a way for you to explain how your project is necessary as a counterargument to this particular critic's stance. In this case, you might briefly summarize or quote from the critic you are referencing and then spend the most time on your own argument. The second way you can employ critical evidence is in direct support of your argument. You might cite a critic through direct quotation, paraphrase, or summary and then work to extend his or her argument. You might discuss how one critic uses a certain textual moment in a useful way. In some cases, it will be enough to simply mention a critic and his or her article in passing; however, you might find that the language used by a certain critic will be useful to include and discuss.

The following chart and sample paragraph illustrate how a body paragraph might be developed to include both textual evidence and critical evidence in a paper on Amanda from *The Glass Menagerie*.

Textual Moment of Focus (character, scene, passage, line, symbol)	Your Interpretation of Textual Moment of Focus	Name of Critic and Location of Source	Critic's Analysis or Interpretation of Textual Moment of Focus
Amanda as character	Amanda's obsession with the past disables her children and limits their futures.	Williams on Staging *TGM*	The whole play is a "memory play"
		Nichols from review of *TGM*	Describes Amanda as "amusing" and "pathetic" but trying to do best for her children
		Tischler from *Student Companion to TW*	Describes Amanda as a "devouring mother" and "monster woman"
		Bigsby from "Entering *TGM*"	The whole era was "nostalgic" and obsessed with memory and Amanda is an actress
		Thompson from *TW's Plays*	Amanda's "romantic expectations, momentary fulfillment, and ultimate loss" structures the movement of the whole play

After filling out the chart, Chris decided to begin by briefly mentioning those critics who only superficially addressed his topic so he could move onto those critics that firmly supported what he was saying. His argument was closely related to both Thompson's and Tischler's so he wanted to save his discussion of theirs for last. Williams, Nichols, and Bigsby provided more context and ideas he could react against so he decided to dismiss those first.

Sample Body Paragraph

Amanda's dangerous obsession with the past disables her children and limits their futures. From her repeated memories of the Sunday of seventeen gentleman callers to her outdated outfits, Amanda clearly lives in a bygone era. When Williams described the play as a "memory" play, he focused on the stage directions; however, the characterization of Amanda also illustrates the importance of this theme of memory. Critic C.W.E. Bigsby suggests the play reflects that the era itself was nostalgic, and Amanda is only one player in a drama where life is but a stage. Nichols's review of the play focuses almost exclusively on Amanda and, like Bigsby, he does not go far enough in indicting Amanda and describing her importance. He uses mild words like "amusing" or "pathetic" and concludes that she was "trying to do her best for her children" (519). In her chapter on the play, critic Judith Thompson proves that a certain pattern shaped Amanda's life: "a pattern of romantic expectations, momentary fulfillment, and ultimate loss" (527). She also maintains that this pattern structures Laura's and Tom's lives. Only Tischler emphasizes how dangerous Amanda's influence is when she describes Amanda as a "devouring mother" and "monster woman" (520). Throughout the play, Amanda influences Laura to make her believe she can have Jim court her as she was once courted. Because of Amanda, Laura's high expectations come crashing down by play's end.

Notice the verbs that Chris uses to describe the critic's responses: *suggests, focuses, concludes, proves, maintains, emphasizes.* Each verb suggests a different focus of interpretation. Check your own use of verbs to be sure they emphasize the meaning you intend. The following list may be helpful for introducing source material.

acknowledges	concedes	illustrates	responds
adds	concludes	implies	reports
admits	confirms	insists	reveals
agrees	contends	maintains	says
argues	declares	notes	shows
asserts	denies	observes	states
believes	disputes	points out	suggests
challenges	emphasizes	proves	thinks
claims	endorses	reasons	writes
comments	finds	refutes	
compares	grants	rejects	

Verb Tenses in Writing About Literature

Use the present tense to discuss literary or artistic works. They are assumed to exist in a kind of eternal present. Be sure to be consistent; both the action of the story as well as writers as they express themselves in their work stay in the literary present. Here are some examples:

- Amanda's dangerous obsession with the past **disables** her children and **limits** their futures.
- In Gilman's short story, the main character **finds** an outlet for her imagination in her furtive writing about the wallpaper.
- Many lessons **are** taught in Bambara's "The Lesson."
- Elizabeth Bishop **uses** irony in her villanelle, "One Art."

Historical events, such as the creation of a literary work, use the past tense:

- The African-American Civil Rights Movement **began** in the 1950s and its leaders, such as Martin Luther King Jr., **fought** to end racial discrimination in America.
- Kate Chopin **wrote** short stories and novels, among them *The Awakening*.
- For his work on *M. Butterfly*, David Hwang **won** four prestigious awards.

Integrating Sources

There are three main ways to cite primary and secondary sources in your essay. Each method of sharing source information is used to achieve a somewhat different purpose.

Summary

If you want to express the main idea of a text in a brief or streamlined way, **summary** is the appropriate strategy to use. To help make one of your main points clear, use your own words to summarize an action in the text you are analyzing or a point that a critic is making. For instance, if you need to quickly recount the plot of a story for readers who haven't read it so they can understand the analysis that follows, a summary allows you to take just a few sentences to give the outlines of the story. Or a critic may have discussed a story for ten pages, but if you are only concerned with the critic's main point because it offers a jumping-off point for your own ideas, you will likely summarize the idea. Similarly, you can use summary to suggest quickly the points of agreement or disagreement among critics by introducing a summary with a phrase like "Most feminist critics seem to agree that..." or "Although critic X and critic Y assume that Z, my own belief is that..."

When you summarize something, you distill your source material down to the main ideas, which you then state in your own words. Summaries are usually much shorter than the original source as they include only the most essential information. Supporting information or examples are often left out of summaries; instead, be sure to condense the ideas to only the most salient points.

Sample Summaries
Original Primary Source (from *Hamlet*)

To be or not to be, that is the question;
Whether 'tis nobler in the mind to suffer
The slings and arrows of outrageous fortune,
Or to take arms against a sea of troubles,
And by opposing, end them. To die, to sleep;
No more; and by a sleep to say we end
The heart-ache and the thousand natural shocks
That flesh is heir to—'tis a consummation
Devoutly to be wish'd. (III.i.58-65)

Summary of Original Primary Source

In the play's most famous soliloquy, Hamlet contemplates what to do with his life and wrestles with avenging his father's death by killing his uncle or escaping life by killing himself (III.i.58-90).

Original Secondary Source (from Tischler's chapter on *The Glass Menagerie* in *Student Companion to Tennessee Williams*)

> Amanda soon reveals herself as a symbol of the "devouring mother." Though apparently nurturing, she thwarts and hobbles her children, dominating not only their eating habits, but their entire lives, keeping them safely in the nest with her. Portraying herself as a martyr to their needs, she actually requires their submission to feel her own pride, crippling Laura by her outrageous expectations. If she could, she would emasculate Tom as well. As her own beauty fades, her appetite for adulation increases, making her a harpy rather than a saint. In a fit of anger, Tom calls his mother an ugly old "witch." Williams was to continue embellishing his archetypal monster-woman as he met more complex and powerful ogres throughout his career.

Summary of Original Secondary Source

In her chapter on *The Glass Menagerie*, Tischler looks at the damage Laura causes as a character representing the monstrous mother (520).

Paraphrase

To paraphrase a source, a writer restates the source's ideas in his or her own words, just as when summarizing. However, in contrast to a summary, a paraphrase includes all the details of the original. Paraphrase is useful when you need to share the particulars with readers, yet don't need to quote the source's language directly.

Because you are including the details, your paraphrase frequently will be longer than the original source material. You can use paraphrase to state ideas more clearly and simply and to better suit the language to your purpose. If you find a crucial phrase or keyword that doesn't yield easily to paraphrase, you can cite these few words inside a pair of quotation marks within your paraphrase. If the words used in the texts you are referencing can be reworded without losing any of the meaning, paraphrase will best serve your purpose. It is very important, though, to be sure you are indeed paraphrasing and not plagiarizing.

When paraphrasing, it is essential that you preserve the intent of the original author by reproducing the order and emphasis of the source.

Sample Paraphrases

Sample Paraphrase of Primary Source

Original Source (Charlotte Perkins Gilman's "The Yellow Wallpaper:")

> John is practical in the extreme. He has no patience with faith, an intense horror of superstition, and he scoffs openly at any talk of things not to be felt and seen and put down in figures (310).

Paraphrase

> In Gilman's short story "The Yellow Wallpaper," the main character and narrator Jane describes her husband as "practical." He is a doctor and a scientific person who believes in tangible and measurable things, not religion, superstition, or imagination (310).

Sample Paraphrase of Secondary Source

Original Source (Judith J. Thompson's *Tennessee Williams' Plays: Memory, Myth, and Symbol.* See Chapter 17.)

> From idealized beginning to realized end, Amanda's memories form a paradigm of experience that underlines the structure of the entire play—an ironic pattern of romantic expectations, momentary fulfillment, and ultimate loss.

Paraphrase with Some Quotation

> In her chapter on *The Glass Menagerie,* Thompson describes the rising and falling movement of the play in the recurring pattern of "romantic expectations, momentary fulfillment, and ultimate loss" (527).

Direct Quotation

Finally, if the language you are citing is essential to your discussion, quote it directly from the source text. In other words, if the passage, line, phrase, or word is worth specific examination and you want to discuss it in depth, be sure to include the language itself within quotation marks. When using quotations, be sure to:

- Explain the significance of the language as it relates to your thesis.
- Always introduce the quotation and then discuss its significance using your own words. Because you need to frame the quotation, you should never introduce a paragraph with a quotation or end it with a quotation.
- Maintain correct grammar and syntax when integrating quotations. If you integrate a quotation into your own sentence, be sure the quoted material fits this new context.

Sample Direct Quotation

In her article on Gilman's "The Yellow Wallpaper," Paula Treichler describes the patriarchal language of diagnosis in contrast to the feminized language of journal writing. This masculine language "imposes controls on the female narrator and dictates how she is to perceive and talk about the world" (66). By the end of the story, however, the language of diagnosis is overturned when Dr. John faints to the floor, leaving Jane's own story as supreme.

Quotations that Become Part of Your Sentence

The first time you quote from a work, provide the author's last name and the number of the page (or other location indicator) in which the words appeared. For fiction, cite the page number; for poetry, the line numbers; and for drama, the act, scene, and line numbers. When you quote more than one line of poetry, identify line breaks in the poem with a slash / surrounded by a space on either side.

Note that punctuation is important. Quotation marks always enclose a quotation. If you introduce a quotation with a complete sentence, you can follow your words with a colon and then open the quotation. If the quotation becomes a part of your own sentence structure, such as the verb or the object, do not use punctuation between your words and the quotation (aside from the quotation marks, of course). Study the following examples.

Quoting from a Short Story

O'Connor introduces Julian as self-righteous early in the story: "He walked along, saturated in depression, as if in the midst of his martyrdom he had lost his faith" (210).

Quoting from a Poem

The variations of the refrain in the last lines of Bishop's villanelle "One Art" challenge the poem's statement about the ease of losing: "the art of losing's not too hard to master / though it may look like (*Write* it!) like disaster" (17–18).

Quoting from a Play

Hamlet's examination of Yorick's skull inspires him to contemplate mortality and "[t]o what base uses we may return." (5.1.164).

(The bracketed *[t]* here shows a change from the original source that was made so the quotation would work grammatically within the writer's sentence.)

Quoting a Critic

When citing critics in MLA format, introduce the author's name as well as the text itself the first time you use it, and thereafter, refer to the text by the author's name with the page numbers referenced in parentheses.

> In her discussion of <u>The Tempest</u>, Meredith Anne Skura argues that our responsibility is to examine "how the colonial elements are rationalized or integrated into the play's vision of the world" (298).

> Skura describes the allusions to "colonialist discourse" in the play (299).

Quoting Larger Amounts of Text (Block Quotations)

Many block quotations are introduced by a complete sentence followed by a colon. When including long quotations, be sure to discuss them fully.

Rule for Citing Prose in a Block Quotation

When citing prose, if you are quoting text that takes four or more lines of your text, indent the quotation ten spaces from the left margin only, continue double spacing, use no quotation marks, and put end punctuation before the parenthetical citation of the page number at the passage's end.

Block quotation of prose from Ashley Walden's paper:

Chopin contrasts grief and joy:

> She knew that she would weep again when she saw the kind, tender hands folded in death; the face that has never looked save with love upon her, fixed gray and dead. But she saw beyond that bitter moment a long procession of years to come that would belong to her absolutely. And she opened and spread her arms out to them in welcome. (31)

Although Louise knows that she will grieve again over her husband, she also feels the lightness of a life without the burden of duty.

Rule for Citing Poetry in a Block Quotation

When citing poetry, if you are citing four or more lines of poetry, indent the quotation ten spaces from the left, continue double spacing, keep lines intact, use no quotations marks, and put end punctuation before parenthetical citation of line numbers at the passage's end.

Block quotation of poetry:

The refrains from earlier in "One Art" are different in the last stanza of the poem:

> —Even losing you (the joking voice, a gesture
> I love) I shan't have lied. It's evident

the art of losing's not too hard to master

though it may look like (*Write it!*) like disaster. (16–19)

The additions of "too" and "(*Write it!*)" suggest that the speaker is qualifying what she had been saying about the ease of losing.

Rule for Citing Drama in a Block Quotation

When citing drama, if you are citing four or more lines of a play, indent the quotation ten spaces from the left, continue double spacing, keep lines intact, use no quotation marks, maintain character names in all caps, followed by period. Subsequent lines of each entry should be indented three more spaces. Use no quotations marks and put the end punctuation before parenthetical citation of act, scene, and line at the passage's end.

Block quotation of drama:

In *A Raisin in the Sun*, Hansberry explores not only the differences between races but also between generations:

> MAMA. Oh—So now it's life. Money is life. Once upon a time freedom used to be life—now it's money. I guess the world really do change...
>
> WALTER. No—it was always money, Mama. We just didn't know about it.
>
> MAMA. No...something has changed. You something new, boy. In my time we was worried about not being lynched...You ain't satisfied or proud of nothing we done. I mean that you had a home; that we kept you out of trouble till you was grown; that you don't have to ride to work on the back of nobody's streetcar—You my children—but how different we done become. (I.ii)

Mama and her son Walter are at odds in their beliefs about what constitutes freedom and what really matters.

Common Knowledge

Common knowledge does not need to be documented. Common knowledge includes facts such as an author's birth or death date or any other information that appears in multiple public sources. Any common historical, cultural, or geographical information that an educated adult American person could reasonably be expected to know does not need to be cited. Only when an idea is attributable to a certain person's opinion or interpretation does it need to be documented.

Common knowledge:
- Freud coined the terms *libido* and *superego*.
- People are concerned about global warming.
- Most high school students read a play by Shakespeare.

Knowledge attributable to a person:
- In "Three Essays on Sexuality," Freud challenges the idea that sexuality is absent in children.
- In *An Inconvenient Truth*, Al Gore warns that global warming could drown out parts of Florida, Louisiana, and Manhattan.
- Stephen Greenblatt and Louis Adrian Montrose argue that Shakespeare's works not only reflect the Elizabethan culture of which they were a part, but also transformed that culture.

Avoiding Plagiarism

Plagiarism is the use of someone else's ideas or words without giving them the credit. As you are taking notes, you will have recorded many quotations and ideas from other critics. While you may incorporate some of these ideas into your own project, it is crucial that you indicate which ideas are yours and which ideas are those of others. Any ideas not referenced as from another source will be assumed to be yours. Therefore, leave no doubt in your reader's mind as to what is yours and what is someone else's.

By referencing a critic, you are acknowledging the research work you have done. Whenever possible, reference the author and summarize or paraphrase his or her ideas in your own words. In some cases, you will need to reference the author and then include a direct quotation for further discussion.

Be very careful when taking notes or cutting and pasting from online locations. Be certain to clarify for yourself where your information is coming from to avoid inadvertent plagiarism.

Paper mills and cheating websites have normalized plagiarism, and they may seem very tempting. However, these papers are not worth the price for many reasons. Not only can they jeopardize your career as a student—resulting in failure, suspension, or expulsion—but they are often not good quality. Instructors have been reading your work all term in Focused Free Writes and formal projects and will be disappointed to spot plagiarized passages and even more incensed in having to spend the time determining the online location of the stolen paper. Ultimately, the act of plagiarism cheats you from learning what it takes to be successful in writing a research paper.

A Checklist for Avoiding Plagiarism

When you take notes or download information:
- Write down the following information for every source you want to use.

Print Sources
- Author's, editor's, and/ or translator's complete names (sometimes there will be only an author; in other cases, there may be the author of the

individual work and the editor(s) of the collection in which the work appears; some works may even have author, editor, and translator)

■ Title of the individual literary work or critical essay and, if the work is collected in an anthology or journal, the title of that larger work; distinguish these in your notes by using quotation marks around individual titles and underlining or italicizing the collection title

■ Volume number if the work is part of a series of books

■ City of publication, publisher, publication date

■ Page numbers; and for poems, line numbers; and for plays, act, scene, and line numbers

Online Sources

■ Author's, editor's, and/or translator's name, as above

■ Title of the individual work or section of the work or subject line (for emails); and the title of the larger site or work (the first in quotation marks, the second underlined or italicized to distinguish them)

■ Date of publication or last revision or update

■ Date you accessed the material, or date of posting or email

■ Database used and library accessed

■ URL (electronic address)

■ Immediately put a pair of quotation marks around all quoted passages. Enlarge them to make sure you can't miss them.

■ Any time you take words out of the middle of a quotation in your notes or from a cut and paste, immediately put three spaced dots—ellipses—where you deleted text:...

■ After you read a passage from an article or finish reading a whole article, look away from the original source and put the ideas into your own words. If you cannot, reread the material to be certain you understood it. Often, it is tempting to use someone else's words when you don't understand exactly what was said.

When you are drafting your paper:

■ Immediately after every idea that you read somewhere else—whether you quote, paraphrase, or summarize it—place a note about where you read it. Be sure to include the page number. For example, you might write: (from Diehl, *Women Poets*, p. 12).

■ Double check every instance where you quote to make sure all of the source's words are enclosed in the quotation marks, and that you are quoting accurately.

When you are revising your paper:

■ Double-check every quotation, paraphrase, and summary against the original to make sure you haven't changed the original author's meaning or inadvertently plagiarized.

■ Double-check the exact page numbers that your use covers.

■ Double-check your in-text citations against your works cited page to make sure they match. (See Chapter 17.)

Sample Student Paper: A Research Paper

Erin Christian's biography can be found on page 567.

Erin Christian

Dr. Howells

English 102

5 May 2010

On Loss in Elizabeth Bishop's "One Art"

Elizabeth Bishop addresses the theme of loss in her villanelle "One Art" through the motif of a lesson to her readers. Encouraging her audience to practice the "art of losing," Bishop uses the two rhyming sounds of the villanelle form, evident in the repetition of "master" and "disaster," to promote the ideas that losing is a common human habit in which countries and keys can be lost with equal ease and that the loss of a person's companion is the closest thing to true disaster or tragedy that can be known. Initially, Bishop attempts to mute the pain of her loss with irreverence, but this stance gradually falls apart. Readers become aware of the shifts of mood through Bishop's manipulation of the sound scheme, enjambment, and syntax; the shift from third person to first person; and, in the final stanza, the disruption of the poem's rhythm and the introduction of parenthetical asides.

For anyone familiar with loss, the first line of "One Art" would seem to be an obvious assumption: "The art of losing isn't hard to master." Bishop allows her first tercet to set up a lesson on loss with an almost nursery-rhyme quality, focusing on the daily losses in life that pose no major threats of emotional harm. Writing loss off as commonplace, Bishop begins with a very general set of lines addressing the fact that "so many things seem filled with the intent / to be lost that their loss is no disaster" (2–3). This use of enjambment, the slippage of the sentence from one line to the next without any punctuation, foreshadows the slippage of the nature of the poem from trivial losses to larger and more intense instances of pain. This is the preface to the lesson to come, and Bishop is reminding us not to panic, that loss can be mastered and overcome with ease due to its frequency of occurrence and wide variety of instances. As Victoria Harrison notes in *Elizabeth Bishop's Poetics of Intimacy*, from the beginning Bishop delicately arranges the "taut structure" of the villanelle with a casual tone that will lead to further balancing of "defiance and pain, the daily and the extraordinary" as the poem progresses (194). Closing the tercet with the assertion that frequent losses are no "disaster," Bishop launches the race to the end of the poem between the two rhyming sounds of "master" and "disaster" and, in so doing, the two opposing ideas of victory over loss or destruction by loss.

The second tercet begins the more didactic tone of the poem. Moving on from the reassurance to her audience that losing things is no disaster, Bishop now begins her instructions. In the first line of the tercet, we are introduced to the manner in which Bishop thinks that loss can be overcome: "Lose something every day" (4). As the old cliché goes, practice makes perfect, and Bishop urges her audience to practice the "art of losing" in order to feel acceptance over the losses in our daily lives. Bishop continues using enjambment when she insists that we "Accept the fluster / of lost door keys, the hour badly spent," beginning the consistent slide from simply daily occurrences of loss to less tangible and more personal ideas and locations that one can lose in life (4–5). This slide leads to "losing farther, losing faster" and, far beyond door keys, Bishop moves on to less specific examples of "places, and names, and where it was you meant / to travel" that allow the reader to fill in the lesson with their own experiences of loss (7–9). As C. K. Doreski describes in *Elizabeth Bishop: The Restraints of Language*, "No longer does the homilist tally manageable, sympathetic incidents; the poem has moved beyond them to overwhelming concerns" (13). In "Writing Poetry like a 'Woman,'" Corrine Blackmer echoes Doreski's comments about the poem's development and argues it is no mistake that this final didactic tercet ends in "disaster" and, with the discreet and reticent tone of the third-person teacher, the narrator masters the "aesthetics of reserve" with the final sounding of "disaster" before allowing it to begin to break down as the items become more vast and the point of view shifts (150).

Just as Bishop begins to encompass larger items and ideas that can be lost, the point of view of the poem changes from that of a third-person lecturer on loss to that of a first-person narrator with personal experience. Continuing the pattern of pairing the tangible with the refrain that reminds us that "The art of losing isn't hard to master," Bishop abruptly shifts her point of view with the announcement of the loss of her mother's watch (12). The sudden introduction of "I" enhances the impression that "One Art" is truly, as Brett C. Miller observes, "a speech in a brave voice that cracks" (506). Shifting in the fourth tercet from the voice of a lecturer instructing others in something already mastered to a more auto-biographical stance, Bishop allows the seams to show in the argument for the aloof approach to loss that she spent the first three tercets developing. Diehl suggests that having cast "the illusion of authority over the inexorable series of losses she seeks to master" in the first three stanzas which are narrated from a third-person point of view, Bishop's further deconstruction of that seeming authority continues with the use of the interruptive "And look! my last, or / next-to-last, of three loved houses went" (10-11) (37). Even though Bishop begins with the personal admission of "I lost my mother's watch," according to Doreski, she is not yet comfortable facing the responsibility of losing "an artifact that links the living and the dead, recalling a time, expressing a generation—making tangible the feeling of irretrievable loss" (13). Bishop betrays this discomfort by drawing attention away from her own mistake of losing with the interjection "And look!" She places the responsibility of the next items to vanish, the houses, upon the objects themselves by simply saying that they "went."

Having faced for the first time in the poem her own personal losses, the narrator becomes brave enough to continue autobio-graphical exploration and begins the next to the last tercet once again with "I lost..." (13). Shifting again from the personal and tangible, Bishop approaches what Doreski describes as the "unspecified, the unembraceable, yet concrete type of loss" dealing with landmass and cities (14). Also, once again, the grander ideas of loss in this tercet are paired with the ending word "disaster," allowing for continued preparation for that which is to come in the final section.

Many critics have wrestled with the poem's final stanza. When we reach the final tercet of the villanelle, according to Susan McCabe in *Elizabeth Bishop: Her Poetics of Loss,* it becomes most evident that Bishop is conveying to her audience the truth that dictates that "the other side of will and choice must always be loss of control, abandon, renunciation" (202). This loss of control is exactly what Bishop imposes upon the final stanza when, after the initial dash, the first line breaks the pentameter that she had kept constant throughout the rest of the poem. Having stayed true to the poem's rigid structure up until the end, Bishop then adds a beat of rhythm to make six beats in the first line: the first crack in the control of the narrator. In this final quatrain, the loss is unlike any other previously mentioned; the narrator has lost a person.

Yet, even though she has transitioned into discussing human loss, Bishop's pain remains muted and, as Elizabeth Dodd notes, "Only parenthetically does Bishop reveal the importance of the you" (104). Tucked within the parenthesis, the second alteration of form that Bishop utilizes in this final section, is a brief description of the lost person: "(the joking voice, a gesture / I love)" (16-17). Bishop does not mean to hide these words by putting them in parentheses; indeed, as McCabe points out, the "most intimate words are not deemphasized by being parenthesized but blaze out as a temporary withholding, as her most prominent resistance to...losing" (203). Continuing with her trend of enjambment, Bishop leaves the parenthetical "I love" to stand alone as its own assertion beginning the next line and leaves any direct reference to the beloved lost for the parentheses. According to Brett Miller's biography, Bishop detested "confessional" poetry and attempted to distance and depersonalize the pain to avoid exemplifying what she saw as "tawdry self pity" (513). However, even though she limits direct mention of the person she has lost to a parenthetical aside, Bishop may have left another clue as to her identity.

At the time that she wrote this poem, Miller asserts that Bishop "seemed to have lost Alice, her dearest friend and lover, she of the blue eyes and fine hands" (513). Choosing the exact word "disaster" may have meant more than appears. Alice Methfessel and Bishop had become estranged by the time that Bishop wrote "One Art," and in earlier drafts of the poem, Victoria Harrison demonstrates that Bishop struggled to incorporate the detail of Methfessel's blue eyes within the final stanza: "'(eyes of the Azure Aster)' in draft 10 and '(eyes of the small wild aster)' in draft 11" (195). However, in his article, Mutlu Konuk Blasing makes the case that while Bishop had removed by draft 12 any direct reference to the color, her use of the "negative prefix 'dis-'" in the "dis-aster" that she employed as part of the main refrain can subversively signify the loss of the aster which she so adored (351).

Another alteration that differentiates the final quatrain of the villanelle from the rest of the poem occurs after the parenthetical aside regarding Methfessel. The refrain line is altered from the confidence of "The art of losing isn't hard to master" to "the art of losing's not too hard to master" (18). By the time Bishop faces the loss of human love at the end of the villanelle, she has lost the bravado exemplified earlier in the certainty of the instructive third-person narrator. Rather than firmly negating the difficulty of "the art of losing," by the end of the poem Bishop allows a fragment of doubt to creep into her assertions. Coupled with the addition of the qualitative "too hard to master," the future perfect tense that precedes that line solidifies the wave of doubt that rushes through the last section: "I shan't have lied" (17). By using the future perfect tense, Bishop insinuates that she will not have lied once she has mastered the loss of Methfessel, even though she has yet to overcome it at the time of writing the villanelle.

The anxiety over the loss of love is most strongly emphasized in the final line of the poem. According to McCabe, Bishop allows her most poignant "admission of strain [to appear] with the fiercely whispered '(*Write* it!)' between the stuttered double 'like'" when she has to practically force herself to finish the poem with "disaster" (203). Allowing her reticence to utterly break down by the end of the piece, Bishop adds another parenthetical aside, this time a command to herself, to implore her hand to finish the poem within the established rhyming pattern. McCabe concludes that the stutter of the repeated "like" that frames the parentheses illustrates the pain the narrator feels over the loss of love which she has endured, and the "(*Write it!*)" serves as a plea to herself to not "lose it" with emotion by the end (203).

In "One Art," Elizabeth Bishop attempts to convey the fragility of composure in the face of "disaster" by allowing her strict form to degenerate into revealed emotion by the end of the poem. Beginning in an instructive third-person tone of voice, Bishop confidently assures her audience that losing is common-place enough to be mastered with practice, and gives us directions to aid us in our own mastery of loss. When Bishop shifts into a first-person narrative she flippantly attempts to prove to her readers that she has mastered loss herself and fleshes out a laundry list of lost items to exemplify her mastery. However, as the items become more personal and evolve into discussion of the loss of love by the final paragraph, Bishop's composure falters. Not only does she break from traditional villanelle form by altering the poem's rhythm, but she also inserts parenthetical asides that both break from the precedent set by the earlier parts of the poem and further illustrate the emotional toll that the loss of her lover has wreaked.

Works Cited

Bishop, Elizabeth. "One Art." *Literature: Reading to Write.* Ed. Elizabeth Howells. New York: Pearson, 2010. 106. Print.

Blackmer, Corrine E. "Writing Poetry like a 'Woman.'" *American Literary History* 8.1 (1996): 130–153. *JSTOR*. Web. 26 May 2009.

Blasing, Mutlu Konuk. "'Mount d'Espoir' or 'Mount Despair' : The
    Re-Verses of Elizabeth Bishop." *Contemporary Literature*
    25.3 (1984): 341–353. *JSTOR*. Web. 26 May 2009.

Diehl, Joanne Feit. *Women Poets and the American Sublime.*
    Bloomington: Indiana UP, 1990. Print.

Dodd, Elizabeth. *The Veiled Mirror and the Woman Poet: H.D.,
    Louise Bogan, Elizabeth Bishop, and Louise Glück.* Columbia:
    U of Missouri P, 1992. Print.

Doreski, C. K. *Elizabeth Bishop: The Restraints of Language.*
    New York: Oxford UP, 1993. Print.

Harrison, Victoria. *Elizabeth Bishop's Poetics of Intimacy.*
    New York: Cambridge UP, 1993. Print.

McCabe, Susan. *Elizabeth Bishop: Her Poetics of Loss.* University
    Park: Pennsylvania State UP, 1994. Print.

Miller, Brett C. *Elizabeth Bishop: Life and the Memory of It.*
    Los Angeles: U of California P, 1993. Print.

17

USING THE MLA STYLE OF DOCUMENTATION

Long before you type up your research paper, you should be preparing to cite your sources properly.

Preparing to Cite Sources

As you conduct research, be certain to record complete publication information about the works you are considering using in your paper, most of which is available on the title page and the copyright page of books or the first page of the journal in which your article appears:

Print Sources
- Author's, editor's, and/or translator's complete name(s) (sometimes there will be only an author; in other cases, there may be the author of the individual work and the editor(s) of the collection in which the work appears; some works may even have author, editor, and translator)
- Title of the individual literary work or critical essay and, if the work is collected in an anthology or journal, the title of that larger work; distinguish these in your notes by using quotation marks around individual titles and underlining or italicizing the collection title
- Volume number if the work is part of a series of books
- Volume and issue numbers for journal articles
- City of publication, publisher, publication date
- Page numbers; and for poems, line numbers; and for plays, act, scene, and line numbers

For Internet sources, be sure to note as many of the following pieces of information as are relevant to your particular source.

Online Sources
- Author's, editor's, and/or translator's name(s), as above
- Title of the individual work or page of the work or subject line (for emails); and the title of the larger site or work (the first in quotation marks, the second underlined or italicized to distinguish them)

- Date of publication or last revision or update
- Date you accessed the material, or date of posting or email
- Database used and library accessed
- URL (electronic address)

If you focus on these details while you are doing research, all of the information you need will be at hand when you are ready to cite your sources in your paper.

Using The Modern Language Association (MLA) Style

The MLA style of documentation is used in the fields of literature, linguistics, English, and foreign languages. Other documentation styles are used in various other disciplines. For example, the American Psychological Association (APA) format is commonly used in the social sciences, such as psychology and sociology. *The Chicago Manual of Style* is standard for history, philosophy, religion, and the fine arts. Any time you are unsure which documentation style you should be using for a particular writing project, ask your instructor. This chapter offers selected examples of MLA citation forms. If you have questions about MLA style that this chapter doesn't cover, refer to a copy of the most recent *MLA Handbook for Writers of Research Papers,* which may be available in your college library or campus writing center. Your local library may also offer guides to citation either in handout form or through online links.

Citations in the Paper

How to integrate summary, paraphrase, and quotation from research sources is discussed in Chapter 16. You use the author's last name and page number to show where the source material was originally printed. The author's name acts as a key to the works cited page at the end of the paper, where each entry starts with the author's last name.

Example from Erin Christian's paper on "One Art"
Sentence in the paper:

> Shifting again from the personal and tangible, Bishop approaches what Doreski describes as the "unspecified, the unembraceable, yet concrete type of loss" dealing with landmass and cities (14).

Entry in the works cited list:

> Doreski, C. K. *Elizabeth Bishop: The Restraints of Language.*
> New York: Oxford UP, 1993. Print.

There are a few situations that differ slightly.

- If you are citing two authors who have the same last name, add the first initial to differentiate the two: (L. Smith 19).

- If you cite a work whose author is not named, you use a shortened version of the title in your in-text citation, like this: ("Mark My Words" 35).
- In cases where you use more than one work from a single author, include the author's last name, the shortened title, and the page number in the citation, like this: (Fish, *There's No Such Thing* 28).

In each of these cases, if you have mentioned some of the information in the sentence itself, you don't need to repeat it in the parenthetical citation:

As Lisa Smith observes, ... (19).

Works Cited at the End of the Paper

The works cited section is a comprehensive list of the sources you summarized, paraphrased, and quoted in your work. It appears on a separate page at the end of the paper. The works are listed alphabetically by the author's last name, or in the case of a work without a named author, the first major word of the title. (Skip the words *A, An,* or *The* at the beginning of the title.)

The format of a works cited entry varies somewhat, based on things like whether both authors and editors need to be included. Listed below are the most common variations.

For an example of a works cited list, see Chapter 16, pages 547–548.

Books and Material from Books
Book with one author

> Hansberry, Lorraine. *To Be Young, Gifted, and Black*. New York:
>
> Penguin Putnam, 1987. Print.

Notice that the author's name is given last name first. The book title is italicized. Most of the words of the book title are capitalized, but the following kinds of words are not (unless they are the first word of the title or the first word of the subtitle):

- *and, but, or, nor, yet, so, for*
- *a, an, the*
- prepositions such as *from* and *to*
- the word *to* used as part of a verb

Book with two or three authors

> Mason, David, and John Frederick Nims. *Western Wind: An*
>
> *Introduction to Poetry*. 5th ed. Boston: McGraw, 2006. Print.

Notice that only the first author's name is given in reverse order. Note, too, that publishers' names are shortened—for instance, McGraw-Hill has been shortened here to McGraw. Similarly, shorten Random House to Random; Holt, Rinehart, and Winston to Holt; HarperCollins to Harper; and Prentice Hall to Prentice.

Book with more than three authors

> Damrosch, David, et al. *The Longman Anthology of World Literature*.
>
>> Compact edition. New York: Pearson, 2008. Print.

While you may list the authors' names when there are one, two, or three authors, you can use *et al.* ("and all") to indicate more than three.

More than one work by a single author

> Brontë, Charlotte. *Jane Eyre*. Middlesex: Penguin, 1966. Print.
>
> ---. *Shirley*. Middlesex: Penguin, 1983. Print.

Give the author's name in the first entry only. Thereafter, in the place of the author's name, indicate that the same author is being repeated by three hyphens and a period. Works should appear in alphabetical order by title under the appropriate author.

Book with one or two editors

> Tracy, Steven C., ed. *A Historical Guide to Langston Hughes*.
>
>> Oxford: Oxford UP, 2004. Print.
>
> Gretland, Jan Nordby, and Karl Heinz Westarp, eds. *Flannery*
>
>> *O'Connor's Radical Reality*. Columbia: U of South Carolina P,
>>
>> 2006. Print.

Notice that the university publisher's name has been shortened: *U* is for *University* and *P* is for *Press*.

Work in an edited version

> Shakespeare, William. *The Tempest*. Ed. Gerald Graff and James
>
>> Phelan. Boston: Bedford, 2000. Print.

The citation begins with the author's name(s) and the editors are indicated with an "Ed." after the title.

Book with a translator

> Homer. *The Odyssey*. Trans. Robert Fagles. New York: Viking, 1996.
>
>> Print.

Sometimes, the editor is a translator as well and the citation would indicate as such with "Ed. and trans."

Reprint of an earlier work

> Dreiser, Theodore. *Sister Carrie*. Ed. Donald Pizer. 1900. New York:
>
>> Norton Critical Edition, 1970. Print.

The original publication date appears first and the subsequent publication date follows.

Revised edition

> *MLA Handbook for Writers of Research Papers*. 7th ed. New York:
>
> MLA, 2009. Print.

Your citation should indicate the current edition and publication date.

A reprinted work

> Welty, Eudora. "The Eye of the Story." *Yale Review* 55.2 (1966):
>
> 265–74. Rpt. in *Katherine Anne Porter: A Collection of Critical*
>
> *Essays*. Ed. Robert Penn Warren. Englewood Cliffs: Prentice,
>
> 1979, 72–80. Print.

"Rpt. in" stands for reprinted in.

A multivolume work

> McMichael, George, and James Leonard, eds. *Anthology of*
>
> *American Literature,* 9th ed. 2 vols. Upper Saddle River:
>
> Prentice, 2007. Print.

One work from an anthology
Citing a story

> Chopin, Kate. "The Story of an Hour." *Literature: Reading to Write*.
>
> Ed. Elizabeth Howells. New York: Pearson, 2010,
>
> 30–32. Print.

Citing a play

> Williams, Tennessee. *The Glass Menagerie. Literature: Reading to*
>
> *Write*. Ed. Elizabeth Howells. New York: Pearson, 2010,
>
> 117–168. Print.

Citing a poem

> Bishop, Elizabeth. "One Art." *Literature: Reading to*
>
> *Write*. Ed. Elizabeth Howells. New York: Pearson, 2010,
>
> 106. Print.

Notice that you begin with the author and title of the individual work before providing the title of the larger work and then its editor.

More than one work from a single anthology

> Booth, Alison, J. Paul Hunter, and Kelly J. Mays, eds. *The Norton
>
> Introduction to Literature*. 9th ed. New York: Norton, 2005.
>
> Print.

> Jonson, Ben. "On My First Son." Booth, Hunter, and Mays.
>
> 818–819.

> Wilbur, Richard. "The Beautiful Changes." Booth, Hunter, and
>
> Mays. 938–939.

Your reader should be able to find the complete citation information through the reference to the authors in your **cross-reference**.

Introduction, foreword, or afterword from a book

> Nemiroff, Robert. Introduction. *A Raisin in the Sun*. By Lorraine
>
> Hansberry. New York: Vintage, 1988. 5–14. Print.

Begin with the name of the author and then give the name of the part being cited, capitalized but neither italicized nor enclosed in quotation marks (Introduction, Preface, Foreword, Afterword). If the writer of the complete work is different, proceed with the author's name after the work's title.

Reference book

> "Irony." *The Oxford English Dictionary*. 2nd ed. 1989.

> Deutsch, Leonard J. "Ralph Ellison." *Dictionary of Literary Biography:*
>
> *Afro American Writers*. Vol. 76. Detroit: Gale, 1988. Print.

When citing familiar reference books, MLA does not require full publication information, simply edition and year of publication.

Articles from Print Periodicals

Articles from periodicals should include the name of the author, the title of the work, the title of the periodical, relevant publication information, and page numbers.

Article from a journal that paginates continuously from issue to issue

> Schneider, Elisabeth. "Prufrock and After: The Theme of Change."
>
> *PMLA* 87.3 (1972): 1103–18. Print.

In general, the issues of a journal published in a single year compose one volume and volumes are usually paginated continuously throughout each year or each annual volume.

Article from a journal that paginates each issue separately

> Wegley, Mark. "Stripping 'The Yellow Wallpaper': A Critical
>
> Remodeling of Gilman's Supernatural Subtext." *Philological*
>
> *Review* 30.1 (Spring 2004): 15–24. Print.

Sometimes the journal will indicate a volume number (30), which changes every year, and an issue number (1), with multiple issues published each year or in each volume. Each issue can be paginated separately. If such information is provided, include volume number, period, issue number in your citation.

Book review

> Schell, Orville. "Your Mother is in Your Bones." Rev. of *The Joy*
>
> *Luck Club*, by Amy Tan. *The New York Times Book Review*
>
> Mar. 19 1989: 3, 28. Print.

Review information should include the work reviewed and the publication information indicating the review location.

Article from a magazine published monthly or bimonthly

> Bethel, Tom, et al. "The Ghost of *Shakespeare*: Who, in Fact, Was
>
> the Bard: The Usual Suspect from Stratford, or Edward de
>
> Vere, 17th Earl of Oxford?" *Harper's* Apr. 1999: 35–62. Print.

Do not give the volume and issue numbers even if they are listed. If the article you are citing is not on consecutive pages, give only the first page number and a plus sign, e.g., 45+.

Article from a magazine published weekly or biweekly

> Als, Hilton. "The Show-Woman: Suzan-Lori Park's Idea for the
>
> Largest Theatre Collaboration Ever." *New Yorker* 30 Oct. 2006:
>
> 74–81. Print.

Give the complete date (day, month, year) for a magazine published every week or two weeks. Do not give the volume and issue numbers even if they are listed.

Article from a newspaper

> Rothstein, Mervyn. "Broadway Producers from Project to
>
> Commission Plays by Americans." *New York Times* 8 June
>
> 1988, late ed.: C17. Print.

When citing newspapers, give the day, month, and year, abbreviating all months except May, June, and July. If an edition is named on the masthead, add a comma after the date and specify the edition (for example, natl. ed., late ed.).

Electronic and Online Sources

Article found using an online subscription database

> Gruesser, John. "Walker's Everyday Use." *The Explicator* 61.3
>
> (2003): 183–85. *MLA Bibliography*. Web. 5 May 2010.

> Suess, Barbara A. "The Writing's on the Wall: Symbolic Orders in
>
> 'The Yellow Wallpaper.'" *Women's Studies* 32.1 (Jan./Feb.
>
> 2003): 79–97. *Academic Search Premier*. Web. 30 Jan 2010.

> Moses, Cat. "The Blues Aesthetic in Toni Morrison's *The Bluest*
>
> *Eye*." *African American Review* 33.4 (1999): 623–37. *JSTOR*.
>
> Web. 2 July 2010.

Subscription databases are databases that your library subscribes to like those illustrated above: MLA Bibliography and Academic Search Premier. You cannot use these databases for free; you must be affiliated with a subscriber such as your university or library; the library subscribes to services like EBSCO, Gale, or Lexis-Nexis. You must cite not only the publication information, therefore, but also the means by which you accessed the database. First, cite the article as it was originally published in print form. Then, provide the following information: the name of the database (italicized), the medium of the publication and the date you accessed the website.

Online scholarly project or website

> *Yeats Society Sligo Home Page*. Yeats Society Sligo, n. d. Web.
>
> 12 Nov. 2004.

Online journal article

> Lehmann, Courtney, and Lisa S. Starks. "Making Mother Matter:
>
> Repression, Revision, and the Stakes of 'Reading
>
> Psychoanalysis Into' Kenneth Branagh's *Hamlet*." *Early Modern*
>
> *Literary Studies* 6.1 (May, 2000): 2.1–24 Web. 7 Nov. 2009.

Some scholarly journals are available online independently. If the journal is included within a database, state the name of the database (italicized) after the print information, the medium of publication (Web), and the date of access.

Online magazine article

> MacIntyre, Jeffrey. "Don DeLillo." *Salon*. Salon Media Group, 2009.
>
> Web. 23 Oct. 2009.

Article in an online newspaper

> Dirda, Michael. Rev. of *The Book of Fables,* by W. S. Merwin.
>
> > *Washington Post,* Web. 1 July 2007. Washington Post, 2 July
> >
> > 2007.

Cite the author of the article, the title of the article, the title of the newspaper, the sponsor of the website, the original publication date, the medium of publication, and the date accessed. If citing a review like the above example, cite the author of the review, the title of the review if there is one (in this case there is not), "Rev. of" and the work reviewed, and the author of the work reviewed before citing the newspaper access information.

Periodical source on CD-ROM, disk, or magnetic tape

> Raines, Howell. "Scholars Doubt Poem Is Shakespeare." *New York*
>
> > *Times* 26 Apr. 1988, late ed.: C13. CD-ROM. *New York Times*
> >
> > *Ondisc.* UMI-ProQuest. Dec. 1988.

Begin with the publication data for the printed version of the information, then conclude with the medium of publication, title of the database (italicized), name of the vendor (if relevant), and electronic publication date.

Nonperiodical source on CD-ROM, disk, or magnetic tape

> "Irony." *The Oxford English Dictionary*. 2nd ed. Oxford: Oxford UP,
>
> > 1992. CD-ROM.

Cite these publications as you would a book but add information about the edition, release, or version; the place of publication, the name of publisher, and the date of publication; and the medium of publication.

Listserv (email list)

> Tucker, Herbert. "Re: Browning's Duchess." Online posting.
>
> > Victoria-L. 30 Mar. 1995. Web. 25 July 2008.

Cite the author's name, the subject heading for the discussion thread, the description (online posting), the name of the forum, the date posted, the medium of publication, and the date accessed.

Email communication

> Bachelder, Chris. "The Mulcher." Message to the author. 26 Mar.
>
> > 2007. Email.

Other Media
Film

Romeo and Juliet. Dir. Franco Zeffirelli. 1968. Paramount Home
Video, 1980. Videocassette.

Cite the film's title, director, original release date, distributor, edition release
date, and medium of publication (videocassette, laserdisc, or DVD). If you focus
on an individual's contributions, put that person's name first followed by their
title, abbreviated.

action The action of the narrative is made up of the moments in which the conflict must be overcome physically, intellectually, or emotionally by the characters.

aesthetic reading In this process, readers bring their own experiences and contexts to a text, and these individual histories mold their experiences of a given work of literature. Literature can have an "emotional effect" on the reader and the text then comes to light based on an individual reader's interaction with it.

allegory An allegory is a symbolic narrative in which the characters, the setting, and the events may have particular meanings. Abstract qualities are personified, or given human form, in a narrative that works as an extended metaphor, delivering a certain message or lesson.

alliteration Alliteration is the repetition of consonant sounds at the beginning of a series of words.

alternative literature Sometimes termed experimental literature, alternative literature challenges expectations in terms of a genre's content or form.

antagonist The antagonist is the character who opposes the protagonist in a play or story.

assonance Assonance is the repetition of vowel sounds in a series of words.

biographical context A reader might consider the background of the author when engaging in interpretation. For example, readers of Li Ho's poetry might use the facts of the author's early death and the theme of transience evident throughout his poetry as elements necessary in an interpretation.

caesura A pause or break in a line that may be represented by a double slash (//) when scanning a poem.

canon In the literary sense, the canon constitutes the group of works sanctioned or accepted as literature. Of course, the canon is an abstract and dynamic entity constructed subjectively by critics, anthologists, teachers, and readers, thus, informed by the values of a particular time period, culture, or person.

carpe diem poetry *Carpe diem* comes from the Latin "pluck, or seize the day." This theme of enjoying life in the moment because of the presence and inevitability of death has an ancient history in poetry. Poems like "To the Virgins Make Much of Time" by Robert Herrick and "To His Coy Mistress" by Andrew Marvell are examples of carpe diem poems.

character Characters people the story. They bring narratives to life and make them real to readers.

climax The climax is the point of highest tension in a narrative. Often the conflict rises to a kind of climax as the plot develops.

conflict Narratives center on a conflict or some problem that needs resolution.

connotation The connotation of a word is what it implies. Connotations take into account the range of associations of a word. While words may seem to have similar meanings, some may suggest something positive or negative in their connotations.

context The particular interrelated conditions in which the text occurs constitute its context.

critical context A reader might consider literary criticism or engage in research to make meaning of a text. For example, a reader could take a formalist or deconstructive approach to examine the use of metaphor or metonymy in Petrarch's "Sonnet 134."

denotation The denotation is the dictionary definition of the word or its primary meaning.

dialog The narration in a play is in the form of dialog in which the language, voice, and tone of the characters (and, when performed, the actors) create the action. Dialog involves two or more speakers, while a **monolog** refers to the speech of one. A **soliloquy** is a monolog that is spoken by a character as if alone, thereby expressing his or her state of mind. An **aside** is a much briefer comment made by a character directly to the audience.

diction Diction is the choice of words in a literary work. Authors choose their words carefully to express their meaning precisely. For example, they may use high diction, which means more formal language, or informal diction, which means more slang or colloquialisms. The words chosen have direct impact on readers' experiences of the narrative.

didactic literature Didactic literature is intended to teach a specific moral lesson, exemplify a doctrine, or provide a model for proper behavior. It can work to educate more than entertain, to teach more than to delight.

drama Drama is a major literary genre characterized by performed dialog. Conflicts and characters are meant to be developed in the presentation of dramatic literature on the stage.

dramatic irony Dramatic irony is the contrast between what the audience knows and what is actually taking place. The audience can foresee future action and implications of actions where certain characters cannot.

dramatic monolog Dramatic monologs are a form of poetry made famous by Robert Browning. These narrative poems have certain elements that make them read like a play or a dialog, though we only hear one side speak: an implied narrator, often a fictional or historical character; an implied setting and implied action; and an implied interlocutor or listener. The narrator will unwittingly reveal his or her character through the course of this "conversation."

efferent reading Efferent means "to take away." As opposed to an aesthetic reading, the reader must take away information from a text to use elsewhere.

elegy An elegy is an elaborately formal lyric poem on a serious subject, often lamenting the death of a friend or public figure.

enjambment Enjambment is when a sentence in a poem carries through a line break from one line to the next without a punctuated pause.

epigram An epigram is a short, witty poem.

exposition The exposition is the introduction of a narrative in which characters and conflicts are introduced.

fiction Fiction is a major literary genre defined as imaginative literature in which characters and conflicts are developed in prose form.

figures of speech Figures of speech are expressions or comparisons that do not rely on literal or denotative meanings but rather suggestive or connotative meanings. A few kinds of figurative language are **similes** and **metaphors**.

first person point of view If the narrator has a single, distinct voice, the point of view is **first person,** distinguished by the narrator's use of the pronoun "I." First person points of view are fairly common and the narrator may be involved either as a witness or participant.

flashbacks Some plots involve flashbacks and other shifts in time that serve to complicate a straightforward structure. A flashback introduces past events as background information for current and future actions in a narrative.

flat characters Characters who maintain their roles without changing may be flat characters.

foil A foil is a minor character who contrasts with a major character and, in so doing, highlights various facets of the main character's personality.

foreshadowing Moments of foreshadowing in narrative allude to future action and may give hints as to plot or character developments.

free verse form or open form Poems can be in free verse form or open form, characterized by freedom from consistency in such elements as rhyme, line length, metrical pattern, and overall structure. Open form poems can be equally as deliberate as closed form poems, yet not be able to be scanned for a predominant meter or rhyme. Free verse poetry can have other rhythmic qualities, however, achieved through repetition of words, images, phrases, or structures; arrangement of words on the page or spaces between the words or lines; or some other means.

Freytag's pyramid Conventional narrative structures can be imagined in the triangular form of Freytag's pyramid, adapted from Gustav Freytag's *Technik des Dramas* of 1863. This formula is made up of the introduction or exposition, the rising action of the conflict, the climax, and the denouement or resolution of the conflict.

genre A genre is a distinctive literary or artistic type or kind. Genres are characterized by certain contents, forms, conventions, or techniques. Works can be grouped more broadly into major literary genres such as poetry, fiction, or drama or may be grouped more narrowly based on particular audience expectations for subgenres such as horror, comedy, fantasy, or science fiction, to name just a few examples.

haikus From the Japanese tradition, a haiku is made up of three unrhymed lines of five, seven, and five syllables describing a highly specific image

hero's journey One example of a conventional narrative structure is the hero's journey, identified by comparative mythologist Joseph Campbell, who traced the basic pattern common in world mythologies and religions. He defined the hero's journey as consisting of the call to adventure (introduction), the rising action of the conflict made up of thresholds or trials, the climax, and the resolution of the conflict in the hero's return.

historical context A reader might consider the time period and location of a text when determining a work's meaning. For example, some readers might examine Robert Herrick's work in the style of the Cavalier poets, that is, poets who supported King Charles I during the English Civil War.

iambic pentameter Iambic pentameter is the most common pattern for poetry in English consisting of five feet of alternating unstressed then stressed syllables.

imagery Imagery is another tool writers use to make abstractions more concrete. Imagery refers to sensory experience: what we see, hear, smell, feel, and taste.

irony Irony is an implied meaning distinct from what is actually stated. An author uses irony to complicate his or her telling of a tale in offering further significance, often humorous, of a seemingly straightforward statement. There can be different kinds of irony. **Verbal irony** is the contrast between what is said and what is meant. **Dramatic** irony is the contrast between what the audience knows and what is actually taking place.

limited point of view A limited point of view confines our knowledge of a narrative to the observations of a single character or group of characters.

literary context A reader might consider the genre of a text, its literary allusions, or its relationship to similar works. In comparing works, we establish a literary context. For example, many readers of the poet Percy Shelley might consider his poetry in light of the Romantic Era and his fellow poets, such as Wordsworth and Coleridge, who were also at work writing dramatic lyrics.

literary nonfiction Nonfiction literature describes real events in artistic and imaginative ways.

literature As this textbook's subject of study, literature is understood to be artistic works that achieve meaning through the unity of content (subject matter) and form (style and technique).

metaphors Metaphors are comparisons that do not use *like* or *as*. This form of figurative language implies a comparison or identifies a common quality to offer a further description of a person, place, thing, or action. In her poem, "Metaphors," Sylvia Plath offers a number of metaphors describing pregnancy as a kind of riddle.

meter The pattern of stresses and pauses in a poem is the **rhythm**, and any fixed or recurring rhythm is the **meter**. The number of feet in a line determines a poem's meter:

> **monometer** one foot
> **dimeter** two feet
> **trimeter** three feet
> **tetrameter** four feet
> **pentameter** five feet
> **hexameter** six feet
> **heptameter** seven feet
> **octameter** eight feet

motifs Motifs are images, words, or ideas that are repeated to emphasize particular themes. Any recurring element that has symbolic significance can be considered a motif.

narration Stories are conveyed by narration, or through a recital of events. For example, the author might create a character to tell the story and our access to the story will be determined by this character. In plays, the narrative is delivered through dialog among characters though sometimes an explicit narrator is present to speak directly to the audience about the play's happenings.

narrator In some texts, particularly in novels, short stories, or narrative poems, an explicit **narrator** may tell the story. That is, the author creates a character to tell the story or provides the voice that conveys the story. The narrator should be considered as separate from the author and may participate in the action directly or just observe from a distance.

odes An elaborately formal lyric poem addressing a person or entity in an elevated and ceremonious way.

omniscient point of view An omniscient point of view has unrestricted knowledge of events in a narrative and may give access to characters' hidden thoughts as well as the actions and general knowledge.

persona The persona cannot be assumed to be the poet but should be considered as a kind of mask representing the poet's point of view.

personification Personification is a kind of figurative language endowing nonhuman things, animals, or abstractions with human characteristics.

plot Most simply, the plot is the arrangement of the action of the story. The narrative may have a conventional structure moving from an introduction through a climax to a conclusion, or an unconventional structure that develops characters and conflicts through flashbacks, episodes, or some other means.

poetic feet Often, lines of poetry develop a rhythmic pattern in which stressed and unstressed syllables recur. These units of repeated patterns are called **feet**. The basic unit of a **foot** has either two or three syllables in it. There are four basic feet:

    iambic unstressed syllable, then a stressed syllable
    trochaic stressed syllable, then an unstressed syllable
    anapestic two unstressed syllables, then a stressed syllable
    dactylic one stressed syllable, then two unstressed syllables

Two auxillary feet include:

    spondaic two stressed syllables
    pyrrhic two unstressed syllables

poetry Poetry is characterized as literature in metrical or verse form. It may be sung, spoken, or written in a fixed form such as a sonnet or villanelle or in an open verse or free verse form. Poetry is characterized by repetition of sounds and ideas as well as condensed language employed for emphasis and intensity.

point of view The narration is characterized by the **point of view**, which is the speaker, voice, narrator, or persona of a work or the position from which the narrative is conveyed.

propaganda Literature that is extreme to the point of upholding message over art may be categorized as propaganda, which is a shortened form of the Latin phrase *congregatio de propaganda fide*, "congregation for propagating the faith."

protagonist The protagonist is the chief character in a play or story.

reading transaction In her book, *The Reader, the Text, the Poem: The Transactional Theory of the Literary Work,* Louise Rosenblatt gives us terminology that can help us understand how to become actively engaged in texts. She describes the reading process in terms of a transaction. Our goal when reading is to engage with a text in a dynamic relationship involving a back-and-forth interaction, rather than a passive or static mode of mindlessly turning pages.

resolution The conclusion of the story is the resolution or denouement (literally, the unraveling) of all of the conflicts.

rhyme scheme Poems can be broken into segments based on particular repetitions of sound patterns. The rhyme scheme is the pattern in which rhymed line endings are arranged in a poem. Poetry can be open form, without a particular pattern of rhyme, or it can be in a **fixed form** (or **closed form**) that includes a specified pattern of repeated lines, rhymes, and rhythms. **Sonnets, villanelles, epigrams, haikus, elegies,** and **odes** are all fixed forms. A poem broken into a predictable, repeated pattern might contain the following forms:

    couplets pairs of lines that rhyme
    tercets three-line stanzas
    triplets three rhyming lines
    quatrain four-line stanzas with a rhyme scheme
    quintet five-line stanzas
    sestet six-line stanzas
    septet seven-line stanzas
    octave eight-line stanzas

rhythm The pattern of stress and pauses in a poem is the rhythm.

rising action The rising action is the portion of the narrative in which the conflict must be overcome. Narrative tension is developed as the conflict escalates to a climax.

round characters Characters who develop and change over the course of the story are **round** or **dynamic characters**.

scansion Scansion is the analysis of a line of poetry for **rhythm** and **meter**. To analyze the rhythm of a poem, we listen for the **stressed** (hard) and **unstressed** (soft) syllables in words. When you scan a line of poetry, you mark the stressed syllables or emphasized syllables with a **bold diacritical mark** (ˊ) above the hard syllables and a **soft diacritical mark** (˘) above the soft syllables.

second person point of view Second person points of view are rare. These narrators speak directly to "you," the reader, telling you what to notice or think or remember. On occasion, second person is used to connect with the reader in a particular way, such as convey the universal obsession with voyeurism in Don DeLillo's "Videotape" in Chapter 4 or even at moments throughout the narration of this textbook.

setting The location and time of a story is its setting. We must be aware of the setting to understand the context of a work.

similes Similes are comparisons using *like* or *as*. This form of figurative language can offer a more specific or vivid description of a person, place, thing, or action. In the first stanza of his poem, "Introduction to Poetry," Billy Collins compares a poem to a "color slide" held "up to the light" by students.

sonnet A sonnet is a fixed form of lyric poem made up of fourteen lines. It can be constructed based on the **Italian Petrarchan** model of an octave (an 8-line stanza with end rhymes such as abbaabba) and a sestet (a 6-line stanza with end rhymes such as cdecde). Or a sonnet can be constructed as an **English Shakespearean** sonnet consisting of three quatrains and a couplet with end rhymes such as abab, cdcd, efef, gg.

sound In poetry, listening for the sound is essential. A reader should listen for patterns and repetition in the sounds of words. Poems might repeat consonant sounds (**alliteration**), vowel sounds (**assonance**), or **rhymes** (two or more words containing an identical or similar sound).

stage directions The stage directions, sometimes stated by the playwright in the script of the play, can inform how the director stages the play, and in many cases, the stage directions can be found embedded in the dialog of the text itself. This is true of Shakespeare's plays; we must infer many of the stage directions from the dialog.

staging Another literary element important in plays is the aspect of the setting known as staging, to which the set, light, sound, backdrop, costumes, and scenery, as well as the movements and gestures of the actors, all contribute.

stanza Stanzas might be understood as the paragraphs that make up a poem. More precisely, they are the sets of verse lines that make up a poem, grouped into a section based on length of lines, meter, and rhyme scheme.

stock characters Characters who represent a certain stereotype or who are easily recognizable as a particular type are stock characters. Common examples might include the uptight librarian, the dumb jock, the damsel in distress, or the absent-minded professor.

stressed and unstressed syllables To analyze the rhythm of a poem, we listen for the stressed (hard) and unstressed (soft) syllables in words. When you scan a line of poetry, you mark the stressed syllables or emphasized syllables with a **bold diacritical mark** (ˊ) above the hard syllables and a **soft diacritical mark** (˘) above the soft syllables.

style The author's style is the individual and distinctive manner of expression evident in the work, or the way the writer chooses words (**diction**); arranges them in sentences, dialog, or verse (**syntax**); and conveys emotion (**tone**). By studying how a writer develops ideas and actions with description, imagery, and other literary techniques, readers can characterize the writer's style. While we might identify some aspects of an author's style through theme, plot, character, narration, and setting, we need to examine how these are created through language, that is, how the author precisely arranges the most basic elements of style: words.

subplots Stories can also have subplots, or conflicts which develop alongside the main plot or action of a story. These side stories can allow for additional parallels and complexities.

symbols Symbols are concrete objects that represent abstract ideas: people, objects, actions, situations, or images that come to characterize main ideas in the story or some larger idea or which are charged with meaning in some way.

syntax Syntax is sentence structure or verse structure of a work. It takes into account how phrases and clauses are structured, ordered, and connected into sentences.

theme The central meaning or dominant idea of a literary work is its theme. This meaning unifies the story and gives it purpose, though it may not be explicitly stated, but rather emphasized through repetition or recurrent motifs. All other elements are organized around a story's theme and should work in support of the central theme. However, one work might have multiple themes at work simultaneously.

third person A narrator speaking from the third person point of view reports what characters did or do, referring to them as "he," "she," or "it." The usage of this point of view is fairly common and establishes the narrator as a witness to the action. Just like the first person, the third person point of view can be **omniscient**, seeing into all the characters' perspectives or **limited** to just one perspective

tone Tone is the general mood or atmosphere of a work, and it can also be understood as the author's attitude toward the reader or subject matter. It can be conveyed through the narrator in the words he or she uses to deliver the narration and describe other characters and actions. Tone is also disseminated through the various elements of a narrative; thus, it is a vague term and is subject to the interpretation of the reader.

tragic hero Aristotle defined the figure of the tragic hero:

1. The tragic hero is better than ordinary people—but neither villainous nor exceptionally virtuous.
2. The tragic hero is a virtuous person brought from happiness to misery through some **harmartia** or tragic flaw, like **hubris** (arrogance and impiety). Because of this frailty, a **peripeteia,** or sudden reversal of circumstances or situation, occurs.
3. The tragic hero faces this fall with courage and nobility.
4. The tragic hero must take moral responsibility for what he or she has done through **anagnorisis**—a disclosure of the true circumstances or a recognition of the hero's true self or nature.

Through the audience's pity or fear for this hero, **catharsis,** a purifying release of emotions, occurs. For Aristotle, drama can serve a powerfully active and enlightening function.

verbal irony Verbal irony is the contrast between what is said and what is meant.

villanelle A villanelle, like the sonnet, is a closed form, also known as a **fixed form**. It consists of nineteen lines organized into six stanzas: five tercets (three line stanzas) and a concluding quatrain (four line stanza). The rhyme scheme is quite rigid with an aba rhyme repeated in each tercet and then repeated in the final two lines of the quatrain. Line one is repeated as lines 6, 12, and 18, while line 3 is repeated as lines 9, 15, and 19.

voice Voice is a general term for the distinctive features of a written work, the tone, style, or personality of the speaker.

STUDENT BIOGRAPHIES

Erin Christian was an English major with a minor in Writing at Armstrong Atlantic State University. She graduated with her BA in May of 2008 and went on to complete an MFA in Creative Writing at The University of Georgia in May of 2010. Because of her experience interning at *The Georgia Review* and the UGA Press, she hopes to build a career in editing. When she once again has some spare time, she plans to reteach herself how to play piano and video games.

James Lewis was an English major with a minor in Film Studies at Armstrong Atlantic State University in Savannah, GA. He graduated in May of 2009. Currently, James is weighing his options in regards to his academic future. In the meantime, he is watching as many low-budget horror and science fiction movies as he possibly can.

Stephanie Roberts graduated from Armstrong Atlantic State University in May 2007 with a Bachelor of Arts in English Literature and a minor in Gender and Women's Studies. In 2009, she earned a Master of Social Work from the University of South Carolina and relocated to Washington, DC. Stephanie works as a family counselor practicing multisystemic therapy with at-risk youth and their families. Between sitting in DC-Metro traffic and drinking too much coffee, Stephanie enjoys baking and learning to use her slow cooker.

Ashley Walden graduated from Armstrong Atlantic State University in 2007 with a Bachelor of Arts in English Literature and a minor in Gender and Women's Studies. She currently lives in Hinesville, GA, and teaches high school English at First Presbyterian Christian Academy. When she's not grading papers or cheering on the FPCA Highlanders, Ashley enjoys shopping for designer jeans and watching stock car races.

CREDITS

"Metaphors" from *The Collected Poems: Sylvia Plath*, 1981, Faber and Faber Ltd. Reprinted by permission.

"Diving into the Wreck". Copyright © 2002 by Adrienne Rich. Copyright © 1973 by W.W. Norton & Company, Inc, from *The Fact of a Doorframe: Selected Poems 1950–2001* by Adrienne Rich. Used by permission of the author and W.W. Norton & Company, Inc.

"My Papa's Waltz", copyright 1942 by Hearst Magazines, Inc., from *Collected Poems of Theodore Roethke* by Theodore Roethke. Used by permission of Doubleday, a division of Random House, Inc.

"The Drama Bug" from *Naked* by David Sedaris. Copyright © 1977 by David Sedaris. By permission of Little, Brown and Company.

"The Indian Girl's Song", from *Shelley's Poetry and Prose: Norton Critical Edition*, edited by Donald Reiman.

From *Maus I: A Survivor's Tale/My Father Bleeds History* by Art Spiegelman, copyright © 1973, 1980, 1981, 1982, 1984, 1985, 1986 by Art Spiegelman. Used by permission of Pantheon Books, a division of Random House, Inc.

"True Love" from *View with a Grain of Sand*, copyright © 1993 by Wislawa Szymborska, English translation by Stanislaw Baranczak and Clare Cavanagh copyright © 1995 by Houghton Mifflin Harcourt Publishing Company, reprinted by permission of the publisher.

"Two Kinds", from *The Joy Luck Club* by Amy Tan, copyright © 1989 by Amy Tan. Used by permission of G.P. Putnam's Sons, a division of Penguin Group (USA) Inc.

Excerpt from Judith Thompson, *Tennessee Williams' Plays: Memory, Myth, and Symbol*, pp. 13–15, Peter Lang Publishers. Reprinted by permission of the publisher.

Student Companion to Tennessee Williams by Nancy M. Tischler. Copyright © 2000 by Nancy M. Tischler. Reproduced with permission of ABC-CLIO, LLC.

"A & P" from *Pigeon Feathers and Other Stories* by John Updike, copyright © 1962 and renewed 1990 by John Updike. Used by permission of Alfred A. Knopf, a division of Random House, Inc.

"Shooting Dad". Reprinted with the permission of Simon & Schuster, Inc., from *Take the Cannoli: Stories from the New World* by Sarah Vowell. Copyright © 2000 by Sarah Vowell. All rights reserved.

"Everyday Use" from *In Love & Trouble: Stories of Black Women*, copyright © 1973 by Alice Walker, reprinted by permission of Houghton Mifflin Harcourt Publishing Company.

The Glass Menagerie by Tennessee Williams. Copyright © 1945, renewed 1973 The University of the South. Reprinted by permission of Georges Borchardt, Inc. for the Estate of Tennessee Williams.

"Production Notes" by Tennessee Williams, from *The Glass Menagerie*, copyright © 1945 by The University of the South and Edwin D. Williams. Reprinted by permission of New Directions Publishing Corp.

"I, Nightmare" by Scott Woods. From *Off the Mic: The 2004 Ann Arbor Poetry Slam Anthology*, The Wordsmith Press, Whitemore Lake, MI. Reprinted by permission of The Wordsmith Press.

Photo Credits

Page 2: 'The Briar Rose' Series, 4: The Sleeping Beauty, 1870–90 (oil on canvas), Burne-Jones, Sir Edward (1833–98)/Faringdon Collection, Buscot, Oxon, UK/The Bridgeman Art Library; 26: Ben Hider/Getty Images; 54: Image copyright © The Metropolitan Museum of Art/Art Resource, NY; 101: © Cineplex-Odeon Pictures/Courtesy Everett Collection; 212: © Harvard Art Museum/Art Resource, NY/Art Resource, NY; 252: AP/Wide World Photos; 307: Prudence Katze; 360: Joey Delvalle/NBCU Photo Bank; 410: © International Spectrafilm/Courtesy Everett Collection; 430: Michael Ochs Archives/Corbis.

INDEX